CLASSICS IN TRANSLATION

Volume I: Greek Literature

Classics in Translation

Volume I: Greek Literature

EDITED BY *Paul MacKendrick*

AND *Herbert M. Howe*

THE UNIVERSITY OF WISCONSIN PRESS

Published 1952

The University of Wisconsin Press
114 North Murray Street
Madison, Wisconsin 53715

The University of Wisconsin Press, Ltd.
1 Gower Street
London WC1E 6HA, England

Printings 1952, 1959, 1963, 1966, 1972, 1975, 1977, 1981

Printed in the United States of America

ISBN 0-299-80895-5; LC 52-10534

CLASSICS IN TRANSLATION

IN TWO VOLUMES

I Greek Literature

Complete translations of Aeschylus' *Agamemnon,* Sophocles' *Antigone,* Euripides' *Medea,* Aristophanes' *Frogs,* and "The Old Oligarch"; abridged translations of Homer's *Iliad* and *Odyssey, The Homeric Hymn to Hermes,* and Plutarch's *Life of Tiberius Gracchus;* selections from Hesiod's *Works and Days,* the Lyric Poets, Pre-Socratic Philosophers, Attic Orators, Herodotus, Thucydides, the Greek Scientists, Plato, Aristotle, Epicurus, Epictetus, and Lucian; introductory essays, explanatory notes.

II: Latin Literature

Complete translations of Plautus' *The Haunted House,* Terence's *Woman from Andros,* Seneca's *Medea,* and *The Deeds of the Deified Augustus;* an abridged translation of Vergil's *Aeneid;* selections from Lucretius' *On the Nature of Things,* Sallust, Cicero's speeches and philosophical works, Catullus, Vergil's *Georgics,* Horace's *Odes,* Ovid, Livy, Petronius, Quintilian, Pliny the Younger, Tacitus' *Annals* and *Germania,* Juvenal's *Sixth Satire,* and Suetonius' *The Deified Julius;* introductory essays, explanatory notes.

PREFACE

THIS is a book of new translations. Most of them have been made especially for this book; the few that are reprinted are in modern idiom. To professional scholars this will appear a mixed blessing, or perhaps not a blessing at all; to the two groups for whom the book is intended, university undergraduates and laymen, the modern idiom is indispensable. The book has been edited in the conviction that we must meet the student where he is; *maxima debetur puero reverentia*. If our Herodotus sends the student back to Rawlinson, or our Juvenal to Dryden, the student will profit; but he must meet the classical authors first on his own ground. We face the fact that classical civilization is *terra incognita* to the vast majority of Americans, and we argue that the student will never find his way through this strange new land, much less appreciate the marvels and the beauties which previous travelers have found there, if the very signposts are in a language he cannot understand. And it must be confessed that many of the translations now in print are not "classics," and that some of them are not worth reprinting. This is not to affirm supremacy for the translations here collected; they are uneven, and their authors would be the first to admit their imperfections. But they are the result of a canvassing of a cross section of American and Canadian classicists, and one Irishman, and for once the editors have the perfect retort for reviewers; if they dislike the choice or the style of the selections, they are hereby cordially invited to contribute different, better translations to the second edition. Scholar-poets—a rare breed—are especially welcome.

The book was planned to fit the needs of a course in Greek and Roman culture offered by the new department of Integrated Liberal Studies at the University of Wisconsin; much of the material has already been successfully used in mimeographed form. The course proceeds by contrasts of authors and ideas: Homer and Vergil, Herodotus and Livy, Euripides and Seneca, Thucydides and Tacitus, Aristophanes and Terence; the artistry of Greece, the efficiency of Rome. The course deals also with the political and social background of the literature; hence the selections from the "Old Oligarch" and the *Res Gestae*. The volumes are especially rich in examples of ancient rhetoric—eight Attic orators, eight orations of Cicero, Quintilian. There are seven plays. The selections from Cicero's philosophical works are unusually full, partly because of their profound influence on all subsequent thought, partly because they represent the Stoic point of view otherwise pretty much neglected. Of the authors omitted, the editors especially regret Menander, Theophrastus, and the Latin elegiac poets; but prospective translators have only to bring themselves forward to have this lamentable gap filled.

The editors have regarded the making of a glossary as an expense of spirit in a waste of shame. Instead, readers are referred to Sir Paul Harvey's *Oxford Companion to Classical Literature* (Oxford, 1937); an effort has been made to supply notes in explanation of proper names not found there. The Greek proper names in these two volumes have been transliterated in accordance with the rules given in Harvey's Introduction (pp. x–xi), but the editors have used *i* for the Greek *ei* more than is usual (*Pisistratus, Adimantus*). In pronouncing names, students should remember that final *e* is pronounced as a separate syllable (as in *Persephone, Eurydice*), and that *c* and *g* are "soft" before *ae, e, i,* and *y* (as in *Caesar, center, circle, cycle,gentle, giant, gypsum*). Rules for accent are complicated; but correct pronunciations may be found in Harvey also. The tendency to impress colleagues with bibliography has been resisted; colleagues will have their own, and most students will not feel the lack; those who do may be referred to the *Oxford Classical Dictionary.* The various introductions summarize current views. They were written by the translators without editorial censorship, and they deliberately present a number of different points of view in order to indicate to the student that *adhuc sub iudice lis est.*

Thanks are due to the following publishers for permission to reprint: Basil Blackwell, Ltd., for Mr. Havelock's Catullus; Harcourt, Brace, and Company for Mr. MacNeice's *Agamemnon;* and Little, Brown and Company for Messrs. Chase and Perry's *Iliad.* Other minor indebtednesses are acknowledged in the appropriate places. A number of individuals have graciously given permission to reprint, especially the Sargent Prize translators for the various versions of Horace done by them as Harvard undergraduates (here the kindness of Mr. Clifford K. Shipton, custodian of the Harvard University archives, must also be acknowledged); Mr. Robert Fitzgerald, for his *Georgic* from *A Wreath for the Sea,* and Mr. Maurice F. Neufeld, for the *Antigone* done by him as a Wisconsin undergraduate. Four Wisconsin graduate students have contributed to the volumes: Miss Violet Zielke (Hesiod), Mr. Warren Castle (Greek lyric poets), Mr. Carl Schuler (*The Deeds of the Deified Augustus*), and Mr. Charles Pinckney (introduction to Horace). Mrs. Gertrude Slaughter supplied Paul Shorey's *Eheu fugaces,* and Professor Jerome H. Buckley of the University of Wisconsin English department the Goldwin Smith versions of Horace.

Thanks are also due to the Department of Geography of the University of Wisconsin for contributing the end-sheet maps, and particularly to Mr. Andrew Burghardt, who designed and made them.

It remains to offer warm thanks to Mrs. Mary E. Bakken and Mrs. Margaret Hundt for able and expert secretarial assistance, and above all to Professor J. P. Heironimus and Miss Sina Spiker for their help in preparing the book for the press. Indeed, it is the pleasant part of the editorial task to acknowledge the unselfish help of a host of friends, the community of scholars scattered up and down the continent, some known to the editor only by correspondence, but all filled with an equal love for the ancient world which is for them—as we hope they have made it for the reader—so very much alive. Κοινὰ τὰ φίλων might well have stood as the title-page motto.

P. L. M.
H. M. H

Madison
March 1, 1951

CONTRIBUTORS

Walter R. Agard — *Reuben A. Brower*
Norman O. Brown — *Warren R. Castle*
Alston H. Chase — *H. Lamar Crosby*
Gerald F. Else — *William C. Greene*
John G. Hawthorne — *Herbert M. Howe*
Frank W. Jones — *L. R. Lind*
Paul MacKendrick — *Louis MacNeice*
Edwin L. Minar, Jr. — *Maurice F. Neufeld*
William G. Perry, Jr. — *Violet Zielke*

TABLE OF CONTENTS

GREEK CULTURE: AN ESSAY, by Walter R. Agard 3

THE *ILIAD* OF HOMER, translated by Alston H. Chase and William G. Perry, Jr. 13

THE WRATH OF ACHILLES—THERSITES—THE DEEDS OF DIOMEDES—THE FAREWELL OF HECTOR TO ANDROMACHE—THE EMBASSY TO ACHILLES—THE DEEDS OF PATROCLUS—THE SHIELD OF ACHILLES—THE KILLING OF HECTOR—PRIAM RANSOMS HECTOR'S BODY

THE *ODYSSEY* OF HOMER, translated by Reuben A. Brower 49

THE BARD TO THE MUSE—THE DIVINE PLAN FOR ODYSSEUS' RETURN—THE SUITORS HEAR THE STORY OF TROY—TELEMACHUS AT THE PALACE OF MENELAUS AND HELEN—CALYPSO PROMISES TO SEND ODYSSEUS ON HIS WAY—THE WRECK OF ODYSSEUS' RAFT—ODYSSEUS' WELCOME IN THE LAND OF THE PHAEACIANS—THE PALACE OF ALCINOUS—THE DINNER IN ALCINOUS' PALACE—THE CYCLOPS—CIRCE—ODYSSEUS' VISIT TO THE WORLD OF THE DEAD—THE SIRENS' SONG—ODYSSEUS' MEETING WITH THE SWINEHERD, EUMAEUS—ODYSSEUS IN HIS OWN HOUSE—THE NIGHT BEFORE THE KILLING OF THE SUITORS—THE BATTLE WITH THE SUITORS—PENELOPE RECOGNIZES ODYSSEUS

THE HOMERIC HYMN TO HERMES, translated by Norman O. Brown 81

SELECTIONS FROM HESIOD'S *WORKS AND DAYS*, translated by Violet Zielke 88

THE FIVE AGES OF MAN—THE HAWK AND THE NIGHTINGALE—JUSTICE—SUMMER—MAXIMS OF CONDUCT

LYRIC POETRY, translated by Warren R. Castle and L. R. Lind 92

ARCHILOCHUS *O Heart, Be Strong—The Better Part* 94
ALCMAN *Old Age—Sleep* 94
MIMNERMUS *The Sun* 95
SOLON *The Works of Mortal Pride Endure not Long* 95
ALCAEUS *To Sappho—Drinking Song* 95
SAPPHO *To a Philistine Woman—Passion—Letter to Atthis—Flower Song* 95
THEOGNIS *On Bad Company* 96
SIMONIDES *For the Greeks Who Died at Plataea* 96

HIPPONAX *On Marriage* 96

XENOPHANES *Pythagoras and the Dog—On Ease and Comfort* 97

PINDAR *The First Olympian—To Agesias of Syracuse—Music Hath Charms—What Is A Man?—The Fifth Nemean—Elysium* 97

AMPHIS *The Solace of Art* 100

ZENODOTUS (?) *On a Statue of Love* 101

CALLIMACHUS *I Loathe All Common Things* 101

ASCLEPIADES *To a Recalcitrant Virgin* 101

THEOCRITUS *The First Idyll* 101

ANTIPATER OF SIDON *On the Fall of Corinth* 102

ANONYMOUS *Nature and Man* 103

MELEAGER *To a Bee—Spring Song—To a Grasshopper—To Zenophile Asleep—To Heliodora, Dead* 103

PHILODEMUS *Moonlight* 104

EUENUS *The Vine to the Goat* 104

JULIUS POLYAENUS *On the Brevity of Hope* 104

MARCUS ARGENTARIUS *Reading Hesiod—I Live a Splendid Life* 104

PTOLEMAEUS *On Astronomy* 104

PALLADAS *On Life and Death* 105

DAMASCIUS *For a Slave Girl* 105

RUFINUS *To a Flirt* 105

ANONYMOUS *On a Child Untimely Dead* 105

THE PRE-SOCRATIC PHILOSOPHERS, translated by Herbert M. Howe 106

THE IONIAN MONISTS—THE PYTHAGOREANS—THE ELEATICS—THE PLURALISTS—THE ATOMISTS—THE SOPHISTS

SELECTIONS FROM HERODOTUS' *THE HISTORIES*, translated by Paul MacKendrick 111

HOW GYGES GAINED THE KINGDOM OF LYDIA—HOW ARION WAS SAVED BY A DOLPHIN—HOW SOLON PUT CROESUS IN HIS PLACE—HOW CYRUS CAPTURED CROESUS AND SET HIM FREE—HOW THE EGYPTIANS EMBALM THEIR DEAD—HOW RHAMPSINITUS REWARDED THE THIEF—HOW CHEOPS BUILT HIS PYRAMID—HOW THE PERSIANS DEBATED FORMS OF GOVERNMENT—HOW THE ATHENIANS WON THE BATTLE OF MARATHON—HOW HIPPOCLIDES DANCED AWAY HIS MARRIAGE—HOW XERXES BRIDGED THE HELLESPONT—HOW XERXES NUMBERED HIS HOST—HOW ATHENS BECAME THE SAVIOR OF GREECE—HOW LEONIDAS AND HIS SPARTANS FELL GLORIOUSLY AT THERMOPYLAE—HOW THE ATHENIANS WON THE BATTLE OF SALAMIS

THE *AGAMEMNON* OF AESCHYLUS, translated by Louis MacNeice 131

THE *ANTIGONE* OF SOPHOCLES, translated by Maurice F. Neufeld 155

THE *MEDEA* OF EURIPIDES, translated by Walter R. Agard 174

THE *FROGS* OF ARISTOPHANES, translated by John G. Hawthorne 192

THE CONSTITUTION OF ATHENS BY THE "OLD OLIGARCH," translated by Paul MacKendrick 223

SELECTIONS FROM THUCYDIDES' *HISTORY*, translated by Gerald F. Else 231

PREFACE: THE ANCIENT HISTORY OF GREECE—THE FUNERAL ORATION OF PERICLES AND THE PLAGUE—REVOLUTION IN THE GREEK CITIES—THE MELIAN DIALOGUE—THE END OF THE WAR IN SICILY

THE ATTIC ORATORS, translated by H. Lamar Crosby 264

ANTIPHON *On the Murder of Herodes* 265

ANDOCIDES *On the Mysteries* 269

LYSIAS *Against Eratosthenes* 274

ISOCRATES *The Areopagiticus* 278

AESCHINES *Against Ctesiphon* 282

DEMOSTHENES *The Third Philippic—On the Crown* 286

LYCURGUS *Against Leocrates* 296

HYPERIDES *The Epitaphius* 299

THE GREEK SCIENTISTS, translated by Herbert M. Howe 305

HIPPOCRATES *The "Sacred" Disease—The Methods and Origins of Medicine—A Public Health Report—The Physician's Observations—Reports on Two Cases* 307

ARCHIMEDES OF SYRACUSE *Pure and Applied Mathematics—The Principle of Archimedes—Archimedes' Own Statement of his Principle* 312

GALEN *The Purpose of the Human Hand* 314

SELECTIONS FROM PLATO, translated by William C. Greene 316

From the *Symposium* 319

From the *Phaedrus* 320

From the *Apology* 320

From the *Crito* 324

From the *Phaedo* 325

From the *Meno* 329

From the *Republic* 329

SELECTIONS FROM ARISTOTLE, translated by Edwin L. Minar, Jr. 351

Nicomachean Ethics 355

Politics 369
Parts of Animals 388

SELECTIONS FROM EPICURUS, translated by Herbert M. Howe 394
PHYSICS—PSYCHOLOGY—ANTHROPOLOGY—THE FEAR OF THE GODS AND OF DEATH—ETHICS—SELECTIONS FROM THE GOLDEN MAXIMS

PLUTARCH'S *LIFE OF TIBERIUS GRACCHUS*, translated by Herbert M. Howe 399

SELECTIONS FROM EPICTETUS, translated by Walter R. Agard 407
HUMAN FREEDOM—MAN AND GOD—MAN AND SOCIETY—MAN AND MISFORTUNE

SELECTIONS FROM LUCIAN, translated by Frank W. Jones 412
Charon, or the Observers 412
Ways of Life for Sale 419

GREEK LITERATURE

GREEK CULTURE: AN ESSAY

By Walter R. Agard

Many threads contribute to form the complex pattern of a culture—geographical, racial, economic, political, scientific, artistic, religious, and philosophical, and, certainly, temporal circumstances. Some acquaintance with this total Greek pattern is essential if we are to understand the values expressed in Greek literature.

A glance at the map of Europe will reveal the strategic position of Greece. "Europa Minor" it has been rightly called. This peninsula is the stepping stone from Asia to Europe; hundreds of little islands in the Aegean Sea led the way from the home of our earliest great cultures in Asia and Egypt to the mainland of Europe. Easy communication by sea was one of the chief geographical factors in the development of Greece. Everywhere were bays and estuaries, promontories and protecting headlands. And the sea was a friendly one, with no tides, no formidable distances between landing places. The Mediterranean is, in fact, a great lake, beautiful as well as useful; poets since Homer have sung of its exquisite color, its jeweled islands gleaming as the sunlight falls on their clean, limestone shores.

The country itself is composed of ridges of mountains, with small valleys lying between. These are not vast mountains; the highest one, Olympus, rises only about 10,000 feet. But they do effectively separate one plain from another, so that many settlements had no convenient outlet except to the coast.

The people who lived in these surroundings found the climate a favorable one for outdoor activity nearly all the year around. Except for a few weeks of heavy rainfall in the late autumn, Greece is a land of sunlight. Yet the sun is not often oppressively hot; even in summer the prevailing trade winds blow steadily and keep the atmosphere from becoming humid.

The soil, however, has never been favorable for easy living. Fertile plains are few, and even there the soil is thin and poor in comparison with our river valleys and Western plains. Greece has no rivers of importance; often irrigation had to be resorted to in an effort to make the earth yield enough to support the people. On the low slopes of the hills the chief products were raised: olives and grapes, and flocks of sheep and goats. Higher up there were forests of oak and chestnut, then beeches and evergreens, and finally alpine foliage nearer the summits of the mountains. The mountains contained scattered deposits of minerals—silver, lead, zinc, iron.

Insofar as surroundings influence human development we might expect to find in Greece a healthy, hard-working people. Sunlight and fresh breezes from the sea and conditions rugged enough to challenge men's energies are factors in making people healthy and enterprising. We would not expect them to be moody, introspective, romantic. An environment characterized by clear outlines, sharp, vivid colors, and well-defined forms does not usually produce either mysticism or morbidness. Directness, clarity, and common sense we might expect to find in the Greeks. As there is variety in the landscape, so in the people we might expect versatility. And the isolation of communities favored independence. Small local settlements could often flourish without danger from their neighbors across the mountains; with the communities there could easily develop a strong sense of local loyalty, of communal self-reliance. Finally, where could one expect to find a keener feeling for beauty? The land itself in design and color is a work of art. Lacking overpowering grandeur and mystery, it had nevertheless those qualities of symmetry, fine proportion, and intense color which stimulate discerning eyes and minds. Without laying too much stress on geographical factors, we may see in them a strong formative influence on the values cherished by the Greeks.

A rapid historical survey of Greek development may be roughly divided into the following four periods:

Heroic Age	2000–1100 B.C.
Transitional Age	1100–700 B.C.
Classical Age	700–323 B.C.
Pioneers	
Fifth Century	
Fourth Century	
Hellenistic Age	323–146 B.C.

Little is known about the inhabitants of Greece prior to 2000 B.C., although they were probably of Mediterranean stock. About that date there came into the peninsula wave after wave of nomad tribes from the north; a robust, youthful race of Alpine type, splendid fighters, with a language, religion, and social organization which were to form the basis of later Greek culture. It was from the amalgamation of the Mediterranean people and these northerners that the Greek people whom we shall study emerged. How the tribes of Ionians and Achaeans profited from the Mediterranean influences, especially those of the flourishing civilization centering in Crete, is obvious from the remains unearthed by excavators in such settlements as Mycenae and Pylos.

During such a restless age of migration and conquest, warfare was of course the leading activity. Military prowess was the characteristic which made men respected; kings like Achilles, Agamemnon, and Odysseus were their people's heroes. After the centuries of fighting subsided, stories of the great days of conquest were popular among the princes and nobles of the newly settled cities, especially on the coast of Asia Minor, and professional bards went from court to court singing the traditional accounts of battles. For a long time these songs were not written down because writing was as yet unknown; but ultimately certain selections were chosen by poets and fused into more or less unified poems. The *Iliad* remains as one of these works. The *Odyssey* was similarly composed, probably rather later, from legends, folklore, and fictional elements centering around the exploration of the Mediterranean and early commercial ventures.

The world described by Homer is one of adventure, of war and plunder, of the allegiance of fighting men to their leaders. The tribe, composed of many clans, is the basic institution; it is led by a king, but the leaders of the clans form a council of nobles whom he consults, and all the people meet in assembly to hear the policies explained and voice their opinion regarding them. Agriculture is the chief means of peaceful subsistence; land belongs to the tribe and is temporarily allotted to its members. Industry and commerce are in a primitive stage. The principal amusements are banquets, athletic meets, and listening to the recital of poets. The ethics of war are enlightened: men who fight part "reconciled in friendship"; there are truces for the burial of the dead; poisoned arrows are taboo; respect for themselves and for others saves these fighters from much of the cruelty associated with warfare. And they are not unreflective upon the mystery of life and the sorrows of mankind.

To the Heroic Age succeeded that more trying time when the warriors settled down and began to face the problems of peace. Less spectacular this, the adjustment to new conditions of community living by people who had previously been wanderers relying on plunder instead of agriculture, craftsmanship, and commerce to win them a living. The process was a slow and difficult one. During the period to about 700 B.C., little was produced from which we can see what was happening. But in hundreds of towns new conditions of life were being slowly but effectively forged, and cities were laying the foundations of a stable government and economic security. The rule of land-owning aristocrats supplanted that of kings; traders from Phoenicia brought imports from Egypt and the Orient which stimulated Greek craftsmen, and, most important of all, an alphabet which the Greeks appropriated. The life of the common people was hazardous; the stronger and more cunning nobles acquired most of the land and often reduced the workers to a state of serfdom. Life was not easy in this age of transition. An echo of the hardships comes to us in the writings of Hesiod, who advised his fellow-farmers how to live as tolerably as possible in a cruel world.

But finally from this period of ferment was born an orderly and progressive civilization. The period from 700 to 500 B.C. was one of rapid advance in many directions. The city-states were solving their economic and political problems, were profiting from growing commercial contacts, and were finding more leisure for the enjoyment of life. This is the time of Greek adolescence, when men relished a spirit of conscious growth, curiosity, and delight in the new, unfolding world.

Cities that had previously been self-sufficient agricultural towns now grew to be centers of trade. Coined money, invented by the Lydians, was quickly utilized by all the Greeks. The economic distress of the farmers was partly met by a colonization movement which relieved the over-population at home and opened new sources of supply and markets all over the Mediterranean. It was a period of the rise of the common man. Solon's reforms in Athens gave the people new economic security and political and judicial powers of such importance that he has justly been called "the father of democracy." The power of the nobles was undermined by unconstitutional rulers called tyrants, who relied upon popular support for their success. In those years of comparative peace, commerce and the arts flourished. Athletic games, local and international, were established, along with artistic and religious festivals; architects, sculptors, and vase-painters were active; poets wrote with the enthusiasm of freedom, and men began for the first time fearlessly to speculate on the nature of the physical world. This cultural flowering was most marked in the Ionian cities of Asia Minor, in the islands, and at Athens.

The final episode of the pioneer period was the repulse of Persia. The one serious menace to the further development of Greece lay in the extension of the great Persian Empire to the islands and continental Greece. Few chapters in history are more stirring than that of Herodotus which tells of the Greek refusal to submit to Persia's demands and of the almost incredible victories at Marathon and Salamis. The Greek cities emerged from the trial confident of their own powers, ready to build on the foundation laid by pioneers the splendid structure of maturity.

It was the Athenian navy which played the leading role in the defeat of Persia, and during the fifth century Athens became the dominant city of Greece in political and economic power and in cultural leadership. Profiting from the Spartan policy of isolation, Athens assumed the leadership of the Delian Confederacy, a league of over two hundred Greek cities formed to protect themselves from further Persian aggression. Gradually this league became virtually an Athenian Empire. Athens, at home devoted to freedom and individuality, refused to allow her subject states the same rights that she herself enjoyed. Sparta, autocratic and repressive of minorities at home, realized the danger to herself and her allies of such power in the hands of a democratic government, and proclaimed herself the champion of the rights of small states. Corinth, formerly the leading commercial city, saw her trade being strangled by Athens. In 431, war on a major scale broke out between Athens and a coalition of Sparta, Corinth, and Thebes. It lasted nearly thirty years, and it resulted in such draining of resources, human and material, that the cities engaged in it never fully recovered. Thucydides was the historian of this momentous conflict.

From that time until the conquest of Greece by Philip of Macedon there was a succession of wars, with the military supremacy passing from Athens to Sparta and then to Thebes. Philip, using all the military, political and propagandistic devices of dictators, began the invasion which was completed by Alexander the Great. Alexander was more than a military conqueror; he was also a missionary. Trained in his youth by Aristotle and devoted to the culture which Athens had created, he imposed on Asia Minor, Asia, and Egypt not only garrisons of soldiers but also colonies of Greeks. He began the process later continued by Rome, of making Greek culture international. Following his death, his empire was split into three parts—Europe, Asia, and Africa—and imperial unity was supplanted by the growth of local city kingdoms such as Antioch and Pergamon, Rhodes and Alexandria, which challenged both the commercial and cultural eminence of Athens. Alexandria in particular came to be the great university center of the world, with its famous library and its schools of science, literary criticism, and art. Oriental influences were sweeping in, bringing new luxury, new fashions, new religions.

The final act in this historical drama is the conquest of Greece by Rome. Macedon was defeated in 197 B.C.; in 146 B.C. the Achaean League was crushed; and in 86 B.C., after Athens had supported the campaign of Mithridates of

Pontus, Sulla sacked the city. Thereafter Greece became simply a part of the Roman Empire. But if Rome won the military victory, Greece was the cultural conqueror. Wealthy Romans sent their sons to Athens for their education; Greek teachers and artists were summoned to Italy; Greek architecture and sculpture, literature, religion, and philosophy were adopted by the Romans. Across Europe, Asia, and Africa, where Roman power extended, the culture of Greece spread. The seeds from the dying tree of Hellas were scattered to the four winds, to sprout into new life all over the world.

THE STAGE has been set, and we have reviewed the bare outlines of the plot of Greek development. It remains to do something much more important: to discover, if we can, the motives and aims of the characters, to understand the forces that shaped their evolution. What were the social conditions under which they lived? What enjoyment did they find in life? What were their views of the nature of the world and of man? These are the questions we must now ask about the Greeks, especially those who created the flower of Greek civilization in fifth- and fourth-century Athens.

In economic institutions we shall find probably the most striking difference between that ancient and our modern life. The Greeks were living in a world infinitely simpler and less complicated in this respect than our own. It was a world of handicraft rather than the machine, of limited resources, of small-scale production, modest competition and advertising, and the mere beginnings of a banking and credit system. The enormous creation and exploitation of wealth which have been developed since the Industrial Revolution were undreamed of. And the consequent standards, whereby we judge men's happiness in terms of material conveniences and men's prestige in terms of financial success, were also largely foreign to Greece. It may seem to us the strangest difference of all that in fifth-century Athens men were highly civilized without being what we would call comfortable, and that many, perhaps most, of the citizens regarded "business" as less important than politics.

The population of Athens in 430 B.C. has been estimated as around 425,000 including adult males as follows: citizens, 40,000; resident aliens, 25,000; slaves, 55,000. Now it is obvious that such a population could not be fed by the farmers of Attica. Most of the grain had to be imported. In order to provide goods for exchange, many industries had been developed during the sixth century—pottery, textiles, leather goods, jewelry—so that Athens became a thriving industrial and commercial center, importing workers from abroad and protecting with her navy the vital trade route to the Black Sea. But judged by modern standards the industry and commerce were of a very simple sort. Individual craftsmen had their little shops, seldom employing more than half a dozen assistants; contracts were made, but without much formality; there were no fixed prices, little credit, no system of competitive bargaining, no advertising campaigns. Among the experts and apprentices in each field there were organized guilds, which took pride in their standards of workmanship. The men engaged in commerce took a risk on every cargo, shipping what they hoped would bring good prices in a foreign market, from which they would bring back what was available for sale in Athens. Such ways of doing business encouraged caution and resulted in economic conservatism.

Much of this business was gladly entrusted to foreigners and slaves; the Athenian citizens insisted on as much time as they could afford for politics and sports, festivals and conversation, which they greatly preferred to being cramped over a bench or an office desk. Yet they must not be thought of as a leisure-class people. Only a small percentage of them did not have to work for a living, on farm or in factory, and fully half of the citizens were what we would call day laborers. Labor was so esteemed that there were laws against idleness, and fathers were expected to teach their sons trades. But it seems clear that in comparison with the attitude of our times the Athenians had modest economic ambition and a real distaste for too much devotion to mere business.

Two economic problems invite special consideration: the control of wealth by the government and the situation of those residents who were not citizens.

With the exception of a small tax levied on aliens, Athens had no system of personal taxation. People of unusual wealth in the city, whether citizens or foreigners, were expected regularly to make donations for public purposes, such as naval construction or musical and dramatic festivals. Commerce was carefully regulated. Duties were levied on exports and imports; a bureau of standards kept strict watch of weights and measures and the purity of goods; the coinage was never debased. For running expenses the city relied upon money from fines and revenues from state property, such as the silver mines. The obligation to workers and the families of soldiers was recognized; doles were paid to disabled workmen, grants were provided so that the poorer citizens could spare time from their work to participate in political activity and festivals, and the orphans of men killed in war received pensions.

Resident aliens were restricted in the ownership of land, but otherwise they were allowed to profit in every way from being in Athens. Many of the foremost artisans and professional and businessmen in the city were foreigners. The restrictions imposed on slaves (chiefly war captives) were, of course, much greater. The less gifted among them were consigned to the hardest of tasks, such as mining, or were sold to individuals for work in homes or factories. The abler ones were given state jobs as artisans on public work projects, clerks, or members of the police force. There they wore no distinguishing dress or brand, could become foremen directing citizens if their talents warranted, received the same pay as free workers, and could often save from it enough to buy their freedom. Obviously these are not the economic conditions usually associated with slavery. If, as is often said, the institution of slavery freed the Athenians for cultural activity, they acknowledged the debt by giving slaves an extraordinary amount of economic opportunity.

DEMOCRACY is a Greek word; and in Athens both the theory and the practice of democracy found their first expression. The practice was, of course, imperfect: aliens, slaves, and women were denied the right to vote. But among the Athenian citizens it was carried to a point which has rarely if ever been attained since.

How true this is appears when we study the life of the average Athenian. On any given day, one out of approximately every six citizens was engaged in some form of public service. The final decision on all matters of state policy was made by a majority decision of the citizens in public assembly. The agenda for these meetings were prepared and the laws administered by a council of five hundred citizens, chosen yearly by lot. Judicial cases were tried by jurors chosen from an annual panel of six thousand, also picked by lot. By constant rotation of office, any citizen of Athens might in the course of a few years expect to serve as a councilor, a juror, and an administrator in various civil offices, as well as constantly taking part in the passing of legislation in meetings of the assembly. Every Athenian might literally expect to be president, for the head of the government was chosen daily from the fifty members of the Council who were in active service during each month.

Here we have, not a representative democracy, but a direct one; instead of officials being elected or appointed for long terms they were, with a few exceptions, such as the generals, chosen by lot for annual terms; instead of laws being made by various groups checking and balancing one another, most of them could be immediately changed by a single vote of the assembly; instead of a professional judiciary to decide cases or instruct jurors, each legal case was decided by ordinary citizens on what they considered its merits.

Our first reaction to such a system of government is that it must necessarily have been clumsy and inefficient, relying upon inexperienced men, since a large majority of the citizens came from the working class. But upon reflection we must recognize that these men were not inexpert or inexperienced. Democracy provided a constant education in public affairs of the broadest scope, including the control of domestic and international policy in every conceivable area; the citizens learned their political science from actual experience. Graft and the building of political machines were discouraged by the device of selection by lot. Enforcement of law was rendered easier because the citizens were aware that they made their own laws and could change them readily. The system was, of course, far from perfect. Contemporary criticisms leveled against it of capricious judgment, intolerance, and even mob hysteria in times of emergency, were sometimes justified. But the chief evidence of its substantial success is the record of cultural achievement made by Athens under such a democratic government.

THE SAME restriction that applied to women in Athenian politics applied to girls in Athenian education. Up to the age of seven all children were told the time-honored stories of national heroes and played games together. After that the girls learned their lessons in their homes, a practical course in domestic art and science. The boys went daily to private schools, accompanied by a servant (pedagogue) whose duty it was to see that they minded their manners, did not play truant, and met with no trouble. They were taught reading, writing, and arithmetic, but the chief attention was given to the memorizing of poetry, playing the lyre, and gymnastics. The stories of heroes were supposed to inspire boys to copy their courage, ingenuity, and devotion to the public welfare; the rhythm and harmony of music were believed to "penetrate into the inward places of the soul and affect it powerfully"; the physical education aimed to develop endurance, skill, and sound coördination of body and mind. Boys who showed special ability to athletics received additional training to fit them for taking part in the city's athletic festivals and for representing Athens in the Panhellenic games held at Olympia, Delphi, Nemea, and the Isthmus of Corinth. The events included foot races, chariot and horse races, endurance races in full armor; field events in boxing, wrestling, and the pancratium, a fierce struggle for supremacy in strength permitting almost any kind of bodily attack; and the pentathlon, a comprehensive test including the broad jump, discus and javelin throwing, running, and wrestling.

At the age of fourteen the poorer Athenian boys went into various trades as apprentices, and except for their two years of military service, in which all Athenians from eighteen to twenty participated, had no further formal education. They had to rely on their own shrewd observation, their political experience, and the attendance at musical and dramatic festivals for their broader understanding of life. But the boys whose families had enough wealth to afford it enjoyed, in addition to more mathematics and rhetoric, the advanced instruction provided by two sorts of teachers, the scientists and the Sophists. Men like Anaxagoras and Democritus, physicists who were formulating theories about the nature of the world, spent much of their time in Athens, and while there were surrounded by eager young disciples. Other teachers, like Protagoras and Gorgias, did not claim to possess such scientific knowledge; they were, however, widely versed in information of a practical sort and taught men how to succeed in the competition of life by developing the ability to reason clearly about human problems, express themselves effectively, and understand better their fellows. Such education was far afield from the traditional sort; instead of making boys good citizens in the accepted way, obedient to their elders and the customs of the city, it encouraged them to criticize popular beliefs and to follow a philosophy of individual success. The more conservative people of Athens resented this attitude on the part of their sons; Aristophanes in the *Clouds* is speaking for them when he holds up to scorn and ridicule a caricatured Socrates, who is pictured as combining the worst characteristics of both physicists and Sophists.

The actual Socrates was neither a physicist nor a Sophist. He, too, was surrounded by young fellows, especially those of the aristocratic class, who relished his radical enquiry into the meaning of such facile generalizations as "justice" and "virtue," and the way in which his questions disconcerted the most supposedly successful men in Athens. But he never took money for his teaching, and he never pretended to answer questions for his followers. His mission was to start people thinking for themselves, even on such dangerous subjects as religion and government. It is not strange that he became highly unpopular during the later years of the Peloponnesian War and was eventually put to death as a subversive citizen. But because he taught not dogma but a sound and stimulating method of thinking, his influence on later intellectual leaders was incomparable. Plato and Aristotle founded schools of their own, the Academy and the Lyceum, where they taught not only the method of Socrates but some of the conclusions which men arrive at after such thinking. Plato's *Republic* is the first great analysis of human society; Aristotle's encyclopedic works covered many fields in science, politics, literature, and philosophy. The Cynics, Stoics, and Epicureans were also profoundly influenced by the ideas of Socrates.

In the arts—music, the dance, drama, literature, architecture, painting, and sculpture—the Greeks found joy in life and created forms which have been widely adopted in the later history of European culture. The analysis of a few of them will give us the clue to their greatness.

When we examine Greek buildings they seem rather simple. The plan is usually a rectangular mass, crowned with a gable roof and relying on rows of columns for its chief effect. Sometimes the form is circular; occasionally, as in the Erechtheum, it is irregular, but there is never any intricacy of essential design. Simplicity is its first characteristic. But as we study more in detail the architecture of the Greeks we find it is by no means as simple as we would at first suppose. Content with a plain essential form, the Greeks invested it with subtle refinement and variety which made it a living and glowing thing.

When we look at the Parthenon, for example, we are impressed first of all by its outward simplicity and dignity, its logical construction, planned with a mathematically exact relationship of the various parts. But it is not a cold and mechanical simplicity. The lines are not absolutely horizontal and vertical; they are delicately curved, so that the flexibility of life is in them. The base across the front rises in the center nearly three inches, and is slightly convex; the course over the columns has a slightly backward slope, and the cornice above bends gently outward; the side walls slope in toward the top. The columns diminish in diameter as they mount upward, with a slight swelling about a third of the way up. They are fluted, so that the shadows cast upon them repeat their curves and emphasize their mass as well as their grace. The capitals are also complex in their calculated proportions and curvatures. Furthermore there is decoration lavishly applied to the nonstructural parts of the building; the pediments and metopes are filled with a rich variety of sculptured figures, and the dividing lines between the various parts of the building are marked and the transitions softened by elaborate mouldings. This decoration was not merely in cold stone; glowing red and blue color was applied to the sculpture and the mouldings to relieve the eye from the glare of marble under a hot southern sky and to add to the vitality of the whole effect.

Of course temples were not the only buildings erected by the Greeks, although on them they expended most of their time and care. Their houses were of the simplest sort still popular in Mediterranean lands, boxlike affairs with an interior colonnade around a central court which was open to the sky. For the theater they designed semi-circular rows of seats on the slopes of a hill, the basic design of our modern theaters, and their form of athletic stadium has likewise come down to us.

In their sculpture the same general principles apply. Sculpture was a leading art to the Greeks. They were by nature people who liked to live in a world of clear-cut forms, practical and intellectual as well as aesthetic. So we find sculpture flourishing throughout Greek history as a popular community expression. On their buildings were scenes commemorating the founding of their cities and their ancient triumphs in battle; in their temples and shrines were statues representing their gods; after the festivals and athletic games monuments were erected to the victors. Sculptors were regarded as normal and necessary contributors to the national life; sculptural rivalry was often as keen as athletic or dramatic competition; and the masters of the art, like Phidias and Praxiteles, were held in the highest honor. Since sculpture was so closely related to the life of the people, its development naturally corresponds to the evolution of the Greek character. In the pioneer period there was pioneer sculpture, crude but vigorous, done with the sap and savor of youth. By the fifth century the same poise and harmony was attained in the Parthenon figures that characterized in other ways the Golden Age. Then, as individualism spread during the feverish period of the Greek wars, sculpture became less a community than a private affair; personal portraits and romantic groups succeeded the monumental and idealistic sculpture of the earlier day. During the Hellenistic period, genre scenes from ordinary life became popular, sentimentalism ran riot, and dramatic episodes were emphasized.

The greatness of Greek sculpture in its best period, from about 500 to 300 B.C., is to be understood in terms of its meeting four standards which apply to all great sculpture. First is sensitiveness to the beauty of material. The Greeks knew marble and bronze as few sculptors since have known them; they cut marble with such warmth and delicacy of surface that the play of light and shade across it gives it the glow of life, and under their hands bronze realized its native smooth, severe beauty. They were also masters of those crisp and flexible lines that appeal to people, physically and psychologically, as right and lovely. The third standard is that of design. Here the logical bent of the Greeks is clear in their creation of delightfully balanced forms. Finally, in their expression of figures in three dimensions, one contour merges into another, the design develops and changes, and a total impression of balance and harmony in depth is realized. The concentration of energy and power in Greek sculpture is nonetheless potent because it is expressed with a breadth of modeling which keeps it from becoming fussy and trivial.

To THE Greeks the drama was much more than an amusing spectacle; it was rooted in religious tradition. It dealt with urgent problems of individual and social experience and offered intellectual and moral as well as aesthetic interpretations of life. Everyone expected to see the plays during the great religious festivals; they were produced by the community, and the actors were respected as important contributors to the city's life.

The sheer spectacle appealed to the Greeks; their drama resembled our grand opera as well as our plays. Between the episodes of action a chorus in many-colored costumes danced to music the emotional interpretation of what had happened; the characters were dressed, and they spoke and moved, in a manner above that of ordinary life; often a god was introduced toward the end to heighten the spectacular effect. But essentially the tragedies had to do with themes involving the conflicts between individuals, between individuals and social forces, or between individuals and that universal force which was called Necessity or Destiny. Aeschylus was especially concerned with the operation of the moral law in its historical evolution, Sophocles with the conflict between men and social institutions, Euripides with the struggle of will and emotion between individuals.

Comedies were also part of the great city festivals. The greatest writer of these plays, Aristophanes, was first of all a robust and hearty comedian, using all the tricks of his trade: outlandish speech, caricature, impossible situations following one another at breakneck speed, and fantasy. But he was too typically Athenian to be content with provoking laughs; he was also a social critic, leveling his fire at the leaders of Athens with whose policies he disagreed. The Sophists he regarded as subversive, Pericles as a selfish imperialist, Euripides as a charlatan, war agitators and profiteers as beneath contempt, the Athenian democracy as a pampered and befuddled mob. He did not mince words in saying what he thought; and because he said it so cleverly and so courageously the crowd enjoyed listening, even though his point of view was usually far different from their own.

WE HAVE already seen how large a place religion had in Greek experience. The dramas and athletic games were connected with religious festivals; the chief buildings were temples to the gods; the most famous sculpture was dedicated to divinities. Yet it seems a strange religion, with its scores of great and lesser gods, corresponding to all sorts of natural phenomena and aspects of human experience, its lack of any sacred book or powerful priests, its richly imaginative and inconsistent mythology, its general disregard of dogma and ethical precepts. The gods, to most Greeks, were not distinguished by their moral greatness but by their superhuman power, beauty, and immortality. As administrators of Destiny they could control the affairs of men, so they were to be treated with deference and respect, worshipped with prayer and sacrifice. But it was ritual rather than dogma or ethics which was at the heart of Greek religion. Every citizen expected to offer sacrifices to the friendly gods of his farm and his home; to cunning Hermes if he engaged in trade; to Poseidon if he went on a sea voyage; to Hephaestus if he was an artisan. Before battle an Athenian prayed to Athena Promachos, the defender of the city, who was also, as Athena Parthenos, the virgin goddess of administrative sagacity. Artemis was the patron of hunters and the helper of women in childbirth. The god of health, patron of the arts and prophecy, was Apollo. Ares was the universal Greek god of warfare, Hera the domestic divinity,

Aphrodite the goddess of beauty, and Zeus, father of the gods, the court of last resort, to whose will both gods and men must bow. To these gods, in scores of festivals throughout the year, the Greek cities gave their tribute of praise and supplication; in their honor processions, songs, and games were held; temples were built to please them, and burnt offerings smoked on the altars.

One consolation of religion these gods did not provide: the assurance of a blessed immortality. This assurance many Greeks found in the worship of other divinities, notably Demeter and Dionysus. Demeter was worshipped in the sacraments of the Eleusinian Mysteries, which included the washing away of impurity and witnessing a symbolic representation of the resurrection of new life. In ecstatic dances the followers of Dionysus lost their consciousness of self and felt the divine madness of sharing in the experience of the god of the Spring rebirth of nature.

The general effect of Greek religion was healthy, picturing as it did a world governed by rational and lovely beings, who were worshipped in correspondingly beautiful rituals. It was also a religion of tolerance, which imposed few restrictions upon the human mind in the form of dogma and creed. For social ethics, however, the Greek relied on the institution which had religion in its keeping: the community itself.

There were, however, among poets and philosophers many who believed that religion and morality cannot be divorced, that the forces which control our world are one in character, and that character is goodness. Euripides and Plato agree in condemning stories about the gods which picture them as less moral than men. Socrates declared that God is responsible, not for the evil in the world, but only for the good. Aeschylus preached of a moral law which controls men's destiny. The Stoics believed that reason rules the universe, in accordance with which one must be a brother to all men.

Many other Greeks were not content with the religious interpretations of the world which were sufficient for the rank and file. As early as the sixth century B.C., scientists began to speculate regarding the nature of the world, enquiring of what substance it is composed, by what processes that substance takes the forms which we see, and what is the explanation of energy. Within the following two hundred years Greeks stated the atomic theory, the theory of evolution, many correct principles of astronomy and mathematics, and methods of scientific medicine.

We must, however, make two important distinctions between Greek science and our own. First, the Greek discoveries were largely brilliant guesswork, deductive rather than experimental, on the part of a few men; secondly, their discoveries were for the most part theoretical, and were seldom applied practically to make living conditions more convenient.

Even in these two respects, however, the Greeks had outstanding exceptions to the general rule. The biological researches of Aristotle and his followers remain as fine examples of scientific observation and description. In engineering and medicine the Greeks utilized their knowledge effectively as an agency in human progress. Hippocrates diagnosed and treated diseases objectively, and founded a school which continued his methods; sanatoriums were established for the sick, employing athletics and the theater to supplement the harsher therapy of surgery. Alexandria had a school of engineering in which many useful discoveries were made, such as the water screw, the principle of the lever, steam appliances, and measuring machines.

But neither the religious nor the scientific interpretations of life satisfied some Greeks. They were not content to say that the gods rule the world, or that we are atoms in a swirl of mechanically ordered motion. One school of philosophers, the Sophists, declared that the world is for us essentially one of human purposes and skills, and in order to live well we must first study how and why men act as they do in relation to their fellows. Socrates went further in his analysis of human thinking, declaring that "the uncritical life is not worth a man's living." From Plato we may learn to analyze the words we use so glibly, like "justice," "truth," and "freedom"; and he may persuade us that there are such qualities that exist in the nature of things, no matter how our opinions about them change in various times and places. From Aristotle we may learn some of the ways in which the human organism works and the institutions which it has created. We may not follow Epicurus in his frank refusal to concern himself about the gods, to hope for immortality, or to view the world as more than chance and convention, but we must respect his appreciation of the enduring values of life in the higher qualities of pleasure. And we must certainly render tribute to the rugged faith of the Stoics, who, regardless of the circumstances of a seemingly cruel world, believed that the law of the universe is reasonable and that men can rise superior to circumstance.

THESE are some of the values which the Greeks created. For the more detailed and richer picture of what they meant, we must go to Greek Literature.

THE *Iliad* OF HOMER

Translated by Alston H. Chase and William G. Perry, Jr.

INTRODUCTION

Of the two poems ascribed to Homer, the *Iliad* and the *Odyssey*, the *Iliad* was, to its first audiences and for generations after, their favorite poem. To a more recent, more romantic, and less classical age the *Odyssey*, which is easier to grasp on a quick reading, has proved more attractive. But to our own time, willing through bitter experience to face the facts of war, the *Iliad*, evoking as it does the pity and the terror, the splendor and the squalor, the nobility and the baseness, of men and women involved in the stress of conflict, is regaining its ancient and perennial appeal.

But for its understanding, the *Iliad* needs a translation which shall not lose Homer's rapidity through archaism, nor his dignity through a slick or crude colloquialism. This translation, therefore, uses the formal "thou" only in addresses to the gods, and relies for its archaic flavor upon the heroic epithets and the conventional formulae of the oral epic. The problem in a prose translation is of course to make the reader aware that Homer is poetry; where the translators have failed, the sense of poetry may still be supported by the vigor of Homer's stride. These requirements in a translation are met by George Herbert Palmer's *Odyssey*, but the *Odyssey* is full of feminine ease and grace, while the *Iliad* is bone and muscle; its sentences are passionate rather than romantic, active rather than adventuresome; their dignity is not in the leisure of fiction but in the facing of fact. Therefore a translation of the *Iliad* must be forceful; else it fails to do justice to the vast action of the battle setting and to the power of the central tragedy which Homer builds around Achilles' spurning of the supplication of his friends.

The forceful impress upon the reader of Homer's style in the *Iliad* is achieved, as always in the best Greek art, by extreme simplicity and economy of means. It is a mistake to confuse this simplicity with primitive naïveté. Homer, no more than Herodotus, is a childishly simple story teller. The very opening scene of supplication by a very minor character, the priest Chryses, is simplicity itself, but it strikes the major ethical key of the entire poem. The climactic decision in the *Iliad*, which in Book IX seals the fate of the tragedy, involves Achilles' refusal to accede to the request of his suppliant friends; the dramatic tensions of this terrible refusal are resolved in the final book through Achilles' acceptance of the request of his suppliant enemy. The effect of simplicity, then, is the art that conceals art.

The subtleties of Homer's art have always fascinated critics, even those absorbed in the unanswered scholarly question whether the *Iliad* was the work of a single poet, or the collective work of a long line of bards. To the more sensitive of these critics "Homer" is simply the genius that produced a masterpiece. The full appreciation of these subtleties by the modern reader may be impeded by the epic conventions Homer uses; by the assumption he makes that his reader is familiar with the background of the tale he has to tell; by the mass and bulk of the poem, which tends to obscure its dramatic structure.

The conventions Homer uses are imposed upon him in part by his meter, the dactylic hexameter, in part by his religious heritage, and in part by the exigencies of oral transmission. They include patronymics, genealogies, traditional epithets, exact repetition of messages, fixed narrative phrases, full-dress epic similes, detailed descriptions of sacrifices to the gods, and supernatural intervention in the action of the poem. This last, though especially irritating to the modern sense of fair play, has its artistic purpose, partly as metaphor, partly as reflecting the traditional idea that a hero shall not meet defeat even by a better man except through outside agency, partly as a harmonious part of a deadly destiny.

The tale Homer has to tell begins in the tenth year of the Trojan War with the insulting of Achilles by Agamemnon, and ends forty-seven days later with the funeral of the Trojan hero Hector. The poet, more dramatist than historian, follows throughout a single brief and tragic sequence, placing the immediate "now" of his action in sharp focus against a vast backdrop reaching out to the farthest limits of space, time, and number. This "epic breadth" may lose the reader if he is unfamiliar with the legendary setting of the story, which Homer takes for granted will be familiar to his audience.

Among the many women upon whom Zeus, the ruler of the gods, had once cast his wandering eye was Thetis, one of the fifty daughters of Nereus, a minor sea divinity. But Zeus' passion was quickly extinguished when he learned that it was fated that the son of Thetis should be greater than his father. She was, accordingly, married off to one Peleus, a respectable hero from Thessaly. To their magnificent wedding all the gods were bid, with the single and understandable exception of Eris, goddess of Discord. But Eris came nonetheless, and brought with her a golden apple inscribed "To the Fairest," which she cast upon the table at the wedding banquet. Immediately each goddess claimed it for herself, but all other claimants soon retired before the three great divinities, Hera, wife of Zeus and queen of the gods, Athena, goddess of wisdom, and Aphrodite, goddess of beauty. None of the gods was rash enough to judge between them, so they decided to submit their claims to a handsome, naïve prince, Paris, son of King Priam of Troy, who was tending sheep upon Mount Ida. Before him the goddesses appeared in their naked beauty, but each, not completely confident in her charms, offered Paris a further consideration. Hera promised him power and riches; Athena promised him glory; Aphrodite promised him the most beautiful woman in the world. Paris gave the apple to Aphrodite.

Unhappily, the acknowledged queen of beauty among women was Helen, who happened to be already married to Menelaus of Sparta. So furious had been the original rivalry for Helen's hand that her Achaean suitors had taken an oath to abide by her choice and to defend the rights of the man whom she married. So when, with Aphrodite's aid, Paris came to Sparta as guest of Menelaus and ran away with Helen and all her treasures, Menelaus immediately called upon his former rivals to fulfill their pledge. These, with some reluctance on the part of a few, assembled at Aulis under the leadership of Agamemnon, Menelaus' brother, and set sail for Troy. Besides Agamemnon and Menelaus, the army contained such notable heroes as Achilles, the son of Peleus and Thetis; the huge and valiant Ajax; Diomedes, Tydeus' son, a warrior second only to Achilles; Odysseus, the wiliest of men; and the aged and garrulous Nestor.

Troy, the object of their attack, was immensely rich from the tolls she levied on the Hellespont and was well fortified with beetling walls. Priam, her aged king, was the father of a numerous and valiant progeny. Chief among these was Hector, the leader of the Trojan forces, a man of character and fortitude. Other Trojan heroes were Hector's cousin Aeneas, son of Anchises and Aphrodite, and such warriors as Deiphobus, Glaucus, and Sarpedon. From all Asia Minor and Thrace allies poured in to help the Trojan cause.

For nine years the Greeks strove vainly to capture the city. They supported and amused themselves at times by raids upon near-by cities and islands, bringing back booty and women to divide among the various leaders. From one of these raids in the tenth year there fell to Agamemnon's share Chryseis, daughter of Chryses, priest of Apollo. It is at this point that the *Iliad* opens, with the attempt of Chryseis' father to ransom her from Agamemnon. The latter's angry refusal causes Apollo to send a plague upon the Greek army. Agamemnon is forced to yield, but in his anger he takes away from Achilles his prize, Briseis. This rouses the wrath of Achilles.

The wrath of Achilles is the unifying theme of the poem, the key to its dramatic structure. Running in a kind of counterpoint to this theme are two other themes, the war against Troy and the will of Zeus. These three themes are introduced in the first books and continue contrapuntally until they are welded together in the person of Achilles himself as he returns in passion to battle. In this return he works out the destiny to which his wrath led him, settles the fate of Troy, and brings to its close the plan of Zeus. Dramatically, the poem divides into three great acts or movements. The first movement ends with Achilles' refusal to accept either a reasonable apology from Agamemnon or the pleas of his friends (Book IX); the second ends in his grief over the death of his friend Patroclus (Book XVIII); and the last ends with his restitution of the body of Hector and its burial (Book XXIV).

The details of the plot are given in the headings to the selections below. Here it is important to note the artistic functions of the three movements. In the first, Homer presents dramatically all that we need to know: he introduces his themes, characterizes his dramatis personae, illustrates the ethics and the conventions by which they live, involves entire peoples in a tragedy which might otherwise have been a mere "triangle," paints his enormous setting of space and destiny, and allows his central character to become committed to a disastrous choice. The great artistic triumph of the second movement lies in the gradual acceleration of Achilles' involvement, beginning with his mild, speculative curiosity about the identity of a wounded fighter and ending with his eager sending of his friend Patroclus to battle in his stead, thereby bringing upon Achilles the calamity which Zeus has foretold. In the third movement, the *Iliad's* three themes, which have so far been contrapuntally arranged, join in a harmony as Achilles returns to war. The gods themselves join the battle, and the martial chords rise in a crescendo of slaughter and superhuman strife which ends abruptly in Hector's death. But the poem does not end until Achilles has found peace by accepting an old man's prayer and taking his hand "lest he be fearful in his heart."

The legend tells of the events which followed the *Iliad's* story. The war went on, and soon came the fatal day which Achilles had long foreseen. He was treacherously wounded in the heel with a poisoned arrow by Paris. The city eventually fell through Odysseus' clever devices, and was sacked, and burned among scenes of horror. Most of the Trojan men, including Priam, were slain, and the women and children were carried off into slavery. Few of the Greeks returned safely or happily home. Menelaus did take Helen back to Sparta, where she settled down to a blameless life. But Agamemnon was murdered on his return by his wife Clytemnestra and her lover Aegisthus. Ajax, Oileus' son, was slain by Athena. Odysseus returned to his Penelope only after those ten years of wandering which are the theme of the *Odyssey*.

This noble and tragic story, recited first by the bards in the halls of the nobles and kings of Asia Minor, made its way across the Aegean, where it won the hearts of the Athenians as it has won the hearts of men ever since. An Athenian tyrant is said to have established the text; the poem was recited in prize competitions at the great athletic festivals; schoolboys learned it by heart; Plato was for expurgating the uncomplimentary references to gods and heroes; the scholars of the Alexandrian Library, the "bird-coop of the Muses," revised the text and wrote commentaries upon it.

And so the *Iliad* came to Rome. There, too, it was a schoolbook, for to Roman boys of the upper class Greek was a second language. One schoolboy who read it was later to become Rome's greatest poet, Vergil. He has recorded in his literary epic, the *Aeneid*, the impress upon his sensitive mind and spirit of the greatest oral epic of ancient times. The last six books of the *Aeneid*, especially, recall the battle scenes of the *Iliad;* the hero, Aeneas, plays a minor role in Homer's poem (see selections from Book V, below). The description of the shield, the single combats, the epic similes of Homer recur in Vergil; most of the difference between the poems lies in the fact that Homer wrote for the ear, Vergil for the eye (which is not to deny to Vergil the magnificent sonorities which Mr. Humphries' translation brings out). Vergil, further, had to recreate in the atmosphere of the study the local color which to Homer was a part of his daily life; and his poem has an ulterior motive, the glorification of the Roman race and of Augustus, while Homer is free to unfold his tragedy for its own sake. But when all allowances are made for differences of temperament, milieu, and motive, the strongest artistic link that binds the Greek to the Roman is their common sense of the *lacrimae rerum*, "the tears of things." The same artistic sensitivity, the same overarching human sympathy, that described the farewell of Hector and Andromache tells the tale of the death of the warrior-maiden Camilla, and perhaps it is this overpowering sense of the nobility and the pathos of man's life that carries most clearly to us across the centuries.

THE SELECTIONS and abridged introduction have been made by the editors from the full text, by gracious permission of the publishers, Messrs. Little, Brown and Company. The Greek text followed is that of the third edition of D. B. Monro and T. W. Allen (Oxford, 1919); the summaries throughout the poem (in brackets) are paraphrased from A. R. Benner, *Selections from Homer's Iliad* (New York: D. Appleton–Century, 1903) and H. J. Rose, *A Handbook of Greek Literature* (London: Methuen, 1948).

Book I

THE WRATH OF ACHILLES

[Chryses, priest of Apollo, comes to the Greek camp to ransom his daughter, the captive and prize of the Greek commander Agamemnon. Rebuffed, he prays Apollo for vengeance, and the god sends into the Greek camp the deadly shafts of pestilence. Achilles, the greatest of the Greek warriors, calls an assembly in which the prophet Calchas declares that to appease the god, Chryseis must be restored to her father. With bad grace Agamemnon consents, demanding in recompense some other warrior's prize. He takes Achilles' prize, the maiden Briseis, and Achilles, in revenge, swears a mighty oath to hold aloof from battle. Chryseis starts on her homeward voyage, and the soldiers make themselves clean of the plague. Achilles prays to Thetis, his goddess mother, tells her of his wrongs, and begs her to persuade Zeus to bring disaster on Agamemnon and his soldiers. She visits Olympus and on Zeus's return from a festival of the Aethiopians, gets his assent to Achilles' prayer. Hera, wife of Zeus and partisan of the Greeks, complains at this and is rebuked; the lame blacksmith-god Hephaestus acts as peacemaker.]

SING, O GODDESS, of the wrath of Peleus' son Achilles, the deadly wrath that brought upon the Achaeans countless woes and sent many mighty souls of heroes down to the house of Death and made their bodies prey for dogs and all the birds, as the will of Zeus was done, from the day when first the son of Atreus, king of men, and godlike Achilles parted in strife.

Which one of the gods, then, set them to strive in anger? The son of Leto and Zeus. For in anger at the king he sent a grim plague throughout the army, and the men perished, because the son of Atreus scorned Chryses, the priest, who came to the swift ships of the Achaeans to free his daughter, bearing a boundless ransom and holding in his hands upon a golden staff the garlands of unerring Apollo. He entreated all the Achaeans, but especially the two sons of Atreus, the marshals of the people: "Sons of Atreus, and you other well-greaved Achaeans, may the gods, who have their homes upon Olympus, grant that you sack the city of Priam and go safely home. And may you release my dear child to me and accept these gifts of ransom, reverencing the son of Zeus, unerring Apollo."

Then all the rest of the Achaeans shouted their assent, to honor the priest and take the glorious ransom, but this did not please the heart of Agamemnon, Atreus' son; rather, he sent him rudely off and laid on him a harsh command: "Let me not find you, old man, beside the hollow ships, either lingering now or coming back hereafter, lest the staff and garland of the god avail you not. Her I will not set free. Sooner even shall old age come upon her in my home in Argos, far from her native land, as she paces before the loom and shares my bed. Now go, anger me not, that you may go the safer."

So he spoke, and the old man was afraid and obeyed his command and went in silence by the shore of the resounding sea. When he was far away, the aged man offered many a prayer to lord Apollo, whom fair-haired Leto bore: "Hear me, thou of the silver bow, who dost protect Chryse and hold Cilla and dost rule over Tenedos with might. Sminthian, if ever I roofed for thee a pleasant temple or if ever I burned for thee fat thighs of cattle and of goats, grant me this wish: may the Danaans pay for my tears beneath thy shafts."

So he spoke in prayer, and Phoebus Apollo heard him and came down from the peaks of Olympus angry at heart, his bow and covered quiver on his shoulders. The arrows rattled on the shoulders of the angry god as he sped, and he came like night. Then he sat down far from the ships and sent an arrow toward them; dreadful was the twang of his silver bow. First he shot the mules and the swift dogs, and then he shot a sharp arrow against the men and smote them. And the crowded pyres of the dead burned on, unceasing.

Nine days throughout the camp fell the missiles of the god, and on the tenth Achilles called the host to an assembly. For the white-armed goddess Hera had put the thought in his heart, since she pitied the Danaans as she saw them dying.

When they were gathered together, Achilles spoke to them: "Son of Atreus, now I think we shall be driven back and shall flee homeward, if, indeed, we escape from death, if war and plague alike are to destroy the Achaeans. Come, let us ask some prophet or priest or reader of dreams—for a dream, too, comes from Zeus—who might tell why Phoebus Apollo is so angered, whether he finds fault with some vow or offering, if possibly he may be willing to receive the fat of unblemished sheep or goats and ward off from us this plague."

So speaking, he sat down, and before them arose Calchas, Thestor's son, far best of readers of dreams, who knew things present, things to be, and things now past, and had guided the ships of the Achaeans to Ilium through his foresight which Phoebus Apollo gave him. With wise and kindly thought for them he spoke and said: "Achilles, dear to Zeus, you bid me explain the wrath of lord Apollo, the unerring. Therefore I shall speak; but for your part promise and swear to me loyally to protect me both by words and hands, for I expect to anger a man who rules mightily over all the Argives and whom the Achaeans obey. For a king is the mightier when he is angry with a lesser man. If he swallow his wrath on the day itself, still thereafter he nurses a grudge in his heart until he may satisfy it. Tell me if you will protect me."

Swift-footed Achilles answered him and said: "Be of good courage and declare the prophecy you know. For by Apollo, dear to Zeus, to whom you pray, Calchas, when you reveal to the Danaans the oracles of the gods, none of all the Danaans shall lay harsh hands upon you by the hollow ships as long as I live and look upon the earth, not even though you speak of Agamemnon, who now boasts to be by far the best of the Achaeans."

Then the blameless seer took courage and declared: "He finds no fault with us for vow or offering, but on his priest's account, whom Agamemnon scorned, neither did he free his daughter nor accept the ransom. Because of that the unerring one has sent suffering, and will yet send it until we give back the bright-eyed maiden to her father without price or ransom and take a sacred offering to Chryse. Then might we appease and win him."

So speaking, he sat down. Then before them arose the heroic son of Atreus, wide-ruling Agamemnon, furious; his dark heart was filled with rage and his eyes were like gleaming fire. First he addressed Calchas, with an evil glance: "Prophet of evil, never yet have you spoken a good omen to me. Always your heart loves evil prophecies and never have you spoken one good word, nor ever yet fulfilled one. Now, prophesying among the Danaans, you proclaim that for this cause the unerring one brings woe upon them, namely, because I refused to take the splendid ransom for Chryses' maiden daughter, since it is my great desire to keep her in my home. I prefer her, indeed, to Clytemnestra, my wedded wife, since she is inferior to her neither in form nor stature nor in mind nor skill at work. Yet even so I am willing to give her back, if that be better, after all. I had rather the men be safe than that they die. But do you at once prepare for me a prize, that I alone among the Argives be not prizeless, since that is not fitting. For you all see what a prize of mine goes elsewhere."

Then swift-footed, godlike Achilles answered him: "Most noble son of Atreus, greediest of men, how shall the great-hearted Achaeans give you a prize? For we know of no great store of common goods; those things which we took from the sack of cities have been divided, nor is it fitting that the men should gather them again. But do you now surrender her to the god; then we Achaeans shall repay you three and four times over, if ever Zeus grant that we sack the well-walled city of Troy."

Mighty Agamemnon answered him and said: "Seek not thus in your heart to deceive me, brave though you be, godlike Achilles, since you shall not trick nor persuade me. Is it your wish, so that you may keep your prize, that I meanwhile sit tamely lacking mine, and do you bid me give her back? Yet, if the great-hearted Achaeans will give a prize to suit my heart, one that will serve as well—but if they will not, then I myself will go and take your prize, or Ajax', or Odysseus', and bear it off. And angry will he be to whom I come. But we will think of this hereafter; now let us launch a black ship upon the shining sea, and let us quickly muster in it oarsmen and put in it an offering, and place on board the fair-cheeked Chryseis herself. Let one counsel-bearing warrior be its captain, Ajax or Idomeneus or godlike Odysseus or you, son of Peleus, most terrible of men, that you may offer sacrifice and appease for us the Warder."

Swift-footed Achilles looked at him scornfully and said, "Greedy one, clothed in shamelessness, how shall any of the Achaeans willingly obey your bidding, either to go a journey or stoutly to fight with men? For I did not come hither to do battle on account of the Trojan spearmen, since they are by no means guilty in my eyes. Never have they driven off my cattle or horses, never wasted the harvest in fertile Phthia, nurse of men, since in between lie many shadowy mountains and the resounding sea. No, it was you, utterly shameless, that we followed hither, to win revenge from the Trojans for Menelaus and for you, dog-face, that you might rejoice. But these things you neither care for nor consider. You even threaten to take away my prize yourself, the prize for which I labored much, and which the sons of the Achaeans gave me. Nor do I ever receive a prize equal to yours when the Achaeans sack some fair-lying city of the Trojans. The greater burden of furious war my hands sustain, yet whenever there comes division of the spoil, your prize is far the greater and I return to the ships with some small thing, but my own, when I am weary of war. Now I will go to Phthia, for it is far better to go home with the curved ships, nor do I intend unhonored to pile up wealth and riches here for you."

Then Agamemnon, king of men, replied to him: "Flee then, if your heart so bids you, nor will I beg you to remain for me. I have others who will honor me; above all, Zeus the counselor. You are the most hateful to me of Zeus-nurtured kings, for dear to you always are strife and wars and battles. If you are very strong, surely it is a god who made you so. Go home with your ships and your companions and rule over the Myrmidons; I do not care about you nor am I troubled by your anger. This warning I will give you: since Phoebus Apollo takes Chryseis from me, I will send her in my ship with my companions, but I will go myself and lead to my tent your prize, fair-cheeked Briseis, that you may know well how much I am your better, and that any other man may hate to speak as my equal and match himself against me face to face."

So he spoke, and anger arose in Peleus' son. His heart within his shaggy breast pondered two courses—whether, drawing his sharp sword from his thigh, he should disperse the others and slay the son of Atreus, or should quell his wrath and curb his spirit. While he was debating this in heart and mind and was drawing from the sheath his mighty sword, Athena came from heaven. The white-armed Hera sent her, she who loved and cherished in her heart both men alike. She stood behind the son of Peleus and grasped his yellow hair, appearing to him alone, and none of the others saw her. Achilles was amazed and turned about and at once knew Pallas Athena, for her eyes gleamed dreadfully. Addressing her, he spoke winged words: "Why hast thou come here, child of aegis-bearing Zeus? That thou mightest behold the insolence of Agamemnon, Atreus' son? This I will tell thee, and I think it will come to pass. By his overbearing pride he will soon destroy himself."

Then the bright-eyed goddess Athena addressed him: "I came from heaven to check your fury, if possibly you will obey. The white-armed goddess Hera sent me, she who loves and cherishes in her heart both men alike. Come, give up your wrath, draw not your sword in hand, but reproach him with words, even as it shall be hereafter, for thus I prophesy and thus shall it come to pass: some day you shall have thrice as many splendid gifts because of this piece of insolence; restrain yourself and obey us."

Swift-footed Achilles answered her and said: "I must respect your command, O goddess, though very angry at heart. For it is better thus. The gods give ear above all to him who obeys them."

So he spoke, and stayed his heavy hand upon the silver hilt and thrust the great sword back into its sheath, nor did he disobey the command of Athena. And she went toward Olympus to join the other gods in the house of aegis-bearing Zeus.

But the son of Peleus again with harsh words addressed the son of Atreus and still did not abate his wrath: "Sot, dog-eyed, deer-hearted, never has your spirit dared to arm for battle with the host to go forth to ambush with the best of the Achaeans. For this seems death to you. No doubt it is far better in the broad camp of the Achaeans to wrest away the prize of him who dares oppose you. A folk-devouring king you are, since you rule over men of no account; otherwise, son of Atreus, this would be your last insolence. But I shall speak out to you and swear a great oath upon it: By this scepter, which shall never put forth leaves and shoots once it has left its stump among the mountains nor shall it bloom again, for the bronze has stripped it of leaves and bark and now the sons of the Achaeans bear it in their hands, the judges, those who guard the laws that come from Zeus—and this shall be for you a mighty oath—truly a longing for Achilles shall some day come to all the sons of the Achaeans, and then, though you be frantic, you shall be able in no way to give aid when many fall in death before man-slaying Hector, and you shall rend your soul in rage within you that you paid no honor to the best of the Achaeans."

So spoke the son of Peleus and hurled the golden-studded scepter to the ground, and he himself sat down; and the son of Atreus faced him raging. Then among them arose Nestor, sweet of speech, the clear-voiced orator of the men of Pylos, from whose tongue the words flowed sweeter than honey. Already two generations of mortal men had passed before him, who were born and reared of old with him in sacred Pylos, and now he ruled among the third. With wise and kindly thought for them, he spoke and said: "Ah, a great sorrow has come upon the land of Achaea. Surely Priam and Priam's sons and the other Trojans would rejoice greatly in heart should they learn the full tale of this strife between you two, who are the leaders of the Danaans in council and in war. Come, listen to me, for you are both younger than I. Long ago I was the comrade of men far better than you and never did they scorn me. Never yet have I seen, nor shall I see, such warriors as Pirithous and Dryas, shepherd of the people, and Caeneus and Exadius and godlike Polyphemus and Theseus, Aegeus' son, like to the immortals. Mightiest of men reared on the earth were these, and with the mightiest they fought, the mountain-ranging centaurs, and fiercely they destroyed them. With these men was I companion when I came from Pylos, from a far distant land, for they summoned me themselves. I fought in single combat; with that foe no one of the mortals who are now upon the earth could fight. They listened to my counsels and heeded my word So do you two heed it, for it is better to heed. Brave though you are, do not deprive him of his maiden, but let her be, as the Achaeans first gave her to him as a prize. Nor do you desire, son of Peleus, to struggle with a king on equal terms, for a sceptered king, to whom Zeus has granted glory, holds no common honor. Even if you be mighty and a goddess mother bore you, still is he mightier, since he rules over more. You, too, son of Atreus, cease your anger. I beg you, check your rage against Achilles, who for all Achaeans is a mighty bulwark against evil war."

Then mighty Agamemnon answered him and said: "Indeed, old man, you have spoken all these things with justice. But this man would surpass all others; he would rule over all and lord it over all and give orders to all, which I think someone will not obey. Even if the gods who live forever have made him a spearman, do they therefore suffer him to speak reproach?"

Then godlike Achilles interrupted him and answered: "I should be called cowardly and worthless if I yielded to everything you say. Lay these commands on others, give them not to me, for I no longer intend to obey you. I will tell you something else, and do you turn this over in your heart: I will not for the maiden's sake lift a hand in strife with you or any other, since you are taking from me what you gave. But of all the rest that is mine beside my swift, black ship, naught could you seize and take away against my will. Or come and try, so that these men too may know; at once will your dark blood flow about my spear."

So having striven against one another with hostile words, they arose and dismissed the assembly by the ships of the Achaeans. Peleus' son went to his tents and his fair-lined ships with the son of Menoetius and his comrades. But the son of Atreus had a swift ship launched upon the sea and chose twenty oarsmen for it and sent on board an offering for the god and brought the fair-cheeked Chryseis and placed her on the ship. As captain, many-wiled Odysseus went aboard.

These, then, embarked and sailed the watery ways, and the son of Atreus ordered the men to purify themselves. So they purified themselves and cast the defilement into the sea, and they made to Apollo unblemished offerings of bulls and goats by the shore of the barren sea, and the savor, eddying amid the smoke, arose to heaven.

Thus they toiled throughout the camp. But Agamemnon did not cease from the wrath with which he first threatened Achilles. He spoke to Talthybius and Eurybates, who were his heralds and ready servants: "Go to the tent of Achilles, Peleus' son, and take the fair-cheeked Briseis by the hand and bring her here. If he will not give her, then will I myself go with more men and take her, and that shall be the worse for him."

So he spoke, and sent them forth, and he laid on them a harsh command. Unwillingly they went along the shore of the barren sea and came to the tents and ships of the Myrmidons. They found Achilles seated near his tent and his black ship; nor was he glad to see them. The two stood fearful and awe-struck before the king and neither spoke to him nor asked him anything. But he knew their errand in his heart and said: "Welcome, heralds, messengers of Zeus and men; draw near. For it is not you I blame, but rather Agamemnon, who sent you here for the maiden Briseis. Come, Zeus-born Patroclus, bring out the maid and give her to them to lead away. And do you two be witnesses before the blessed gods and mortal men and before that ruthless king, if ever hereafter there be need of me to ward off shameful ruin from the rest. For indeed he rages in his baneful heart and knows not how to look before and after, that his Achaeans may fight in safety by the ships."

So he spoke, and Patroclus obeyed his dear companion and brought the fair-cheeked Briseis from the tent and gave her to them to lead away. They went back past the ships of the Achaeans and the woman went with them, against her will. Then Achilles went apart from his companions and sat weeping upon the shore of the gray sea, looking out across the boundless deep. And stretching out his hands, he offered many a prayer to his dear mother: "Mother, since it was you who bore me, brief though my life may be, honor at least should high-thundering Zeus have granted me. But now he has not honored me in the least. For Atreus' son, wide-ruling Agamemnon, has insulted me. He has taken my prize and holds it, having wrested it away himself."

So he spoke, weeping, and his queenly mother heard him as she sat in the depths of the sea beside her aged father. Swiftly she rose from the gray sea like a mist and sat down beside him as he wept and caressed him with her hand and spoke and said to him: "My child, why do you weep? What grief has come upon your heart? Speak, hide nothing in your mind, so that we both may know."

Swift-footed Achilles sighed heavily and said to her: "You know; why should I tell all this to you when you know it already? We went to Thebe, the holy city of Eëtion, and we sacked it and brought all the booty here. The sons of the Achaeans divided the rest fairly among themselves and put aside for Atreus' son fair-cheeked Chryseis. Then Chryses, priest of unerring Apollo, came to the swift ships of the bronze-clad Achaeans to free his daughter, bearing a boundless ransom and holding in his hands upon a golden staff the garlands of unerring Apollo. He entreated all the Achaeans, but especially the two sons of Atreus, the marshals of the people. Then all the rest of the Achaeans shouted their assent, to honor the priest and take the glorious ransom, but this did not please the heart of Agamemnon, Atreus' son; rather, he sent him rudely off and laid on him a harsh command. The old man went away in anger, and Apollo heard him when he prayed, for he was very dear to him, and he sent an evil bolt upon the Argives. Now the people died in swift succession, for the shafts of the god fell everywhere throughout the broad camp of the Achaeans. Then a prophet, well informed, delivered to us the oracle of the unerring one. At once I was the first to urge that we appease the god. Then anger seized the son of Atreus, and straightway he arose and made a threat which has been fulfilled. For the bright-eyed Achaeans are sending the one maiden on a swift ship to Chryse and are bearing gifts to the god, but the heralds have just now departed from my tent taking the other maiden, the daughter of Brises, whom the sons of the Achaeans gave to me. But do you, if you can, protect your son. Go to Olympus and petition Zeus, if ever you have gladdened his heart by word or deed. For often in my father's halls have I heard you boasting, as you said that alone among the immortals you warded off shameful ruin from the black-clouded son of Cronus when the other Olympians wished to bind him—Hera and Poseidon and Pallas Athena. But you, goddess, went to him and loosed him from his bonds, quickly summoning to high Olympus him of a hundred hands, whom the gods call Briareus but all men Aegaeon—indeed, he was greater in strength than his own father. He sat beside the son of Cronus, exulting in his glory. And the blessed gods took fright and tried no more to fetter Zeus. Reminding him of this, sit by him and clasp his knees, in the hope that he may consent to aid the Trojans and hem the Achaeans about the sterns of their ships along the sea as they are slain, that they may all enjoy their king, and that Atreus' son, wide-ruling Agamemnon, may know his folly in paying no honor to the best of the Achaeans."

Then Thetis, weeping, answered him: "Ah, my child, why did I rear you, accursed in your birth? Would that you might sit tearless and free from sorrow by the ships, since your lot is brief and not for very long. Now you are both swift of doom and wretched beyond all. Therefore, to an evil fate did I bear you in our halls. To speak this word for you to Zeus, who delights in the thunder, I myself will go to snow-capped Olympus, in the hope that he may be persuaded. But do you sit beside the speedy ships and nurse your wrath against the Achaeans and withhold entirely from war. For Zeus went yesterday to the Ocean to feast with the blameless Aethiopians, and all the gods went with him. But on the twelfth day he will come again to Olympus and then I will go on your behalf to the bronze-floored house of Zeus, and I will clasp his knees, and I think that I shall persuade him."

So speaking, she departed, and left him there angered at heart because of the fair-girdled woman whom they had taken from him by force, against his will. [1–429]

[Lines 430–489, omitted here, tell of Odysseus' voyage to return Chryseis to her father, and of the propitiation of Apollo.]

Never did Achilles go to man-ennobling council nor to war, but he ate out his heart, abiding there, and longed for the battle cry and war.

When the twelfth dawn after this arose, the gods, who live forever, came all together to Olympus, led by Zeus. Nor did Thetis forget the bidding of her son; she arose from a wave of the sea and early in the morning went up into high heaven and Olympus. She found the far-thundering son of Cronus seated apart from the others on the highest peak of many-ridged Olympus. She sat down beside him and clasped his knees with her left hand, and, touching him beneath the chin with her right, she spoke in supplication to lord Zeus, Cronus' son: "Father, Zeus, if ever by word or deed I have helped you among the immortals, grant me this wish: honor my son, who is brief-fated beyond all others. Yet now Agamemnon, king of men, has insulted him, for he has taken his prize and holds it, having wrested it away himself. But do you avenge him, Olympian Zeus, the Counselor. Give might to the Trojans until the Achaeans reverence my son and pay him honor."

Thus she spoke, yet cloud-gathering Zeus did not address her but sat long in silence. Still Thetis clasped his knees, still clung to him, and once again implored him: "Promise me this in truth and confirm it with your nod, or else deny me, since there is no fear in you, that I may know well how much I am the least in honor among all the gods."

Then, greatly distressed, cloud-gathering Zeus addressed her: "This is a ruinous business, for you would bid me stir up strife with Hera, when she shall taunt me with reproachful words. Even as it is, she always nags at me among the immortal gods and says that in battle I support the Trojans. But do you now go back, lest Hera notice. It shall be my concern to carry out these things. Come now, I will nod to you, that you may trust me. For this is the greatest pledge from me even among the immortals. For I may not take back nor betray nor fail to carry out that pledge to which I nod my confirmation."

So speaking, the son of Cronus nodded with his black brows and the ambrosial locks flowed down from the lord's immortal head, and he made great Olympus tremble.

When they had plotted thus, they parted. She plunged to the deep sea from bright Olympus, and Zeus went to his home. All the gods arose from their seats before their father, nor did any dare abide his coming, but they all stood up to meet him. So he sat down there upon his throne; nor did Hera fail to realize, when she saw him, that silver-footed Thetis, daughter of the old man of the sea, had been taking counsel with him. At once she addressed Zeus, son of Cronus, with reproaches: "Which of the gods was taking counsel with you, deceitful one? Always it is your pleasure to sit apart from me and debate and pass judgment in secret. Never have you dared willingly to tell me what plan you are debating."

The father of gods and men replied to her: "Hera, do not expect to know all my words. For they will be hard for you, even though you be my wife. That which it is suitable for you to hear, no one of gods or men shall learn before you. But that which I wish to consider apart from the gods, of this do you not always ask or question."

Then ox-eyed, queenly Hera answered him: "Most dreadful son of Cronus, what sort of word is this which you have uttered? I have never before asked of you or sought to know too much, but you consider, quite unmolested, what you will. Yet now I fear dreadfully in my heart lest silver-footed Thetis, daughter of the old man of the sea, may have beguiled you. For, early this morning, she sat beside you and clasped your knees. I think you gave her solemn promise by a nod to honor Achilles and destroy many beside the ships of the Achaeans."

Then cloud-gathering Zeus answered her and said, "Mad one, you are always suspicious, nor do I escape you; yet you shall be unable to do anything; you will be but the further from my heart, and that shall be the worse for you. If it be as you say, such is my pleasure. Sit down in silence and obey my order, lest all the gods who dwell upon Olympus avail you not if I come closer, when once I lay my invincible hands upon you."

So he spoke, and ox-eyed, queenly Hera was afraid. She sat down in silence, curbing her heart. The heavenly gods in the house of Zeus were troubled, and Hephaestus, the famed artisan, began to address them, favoring his dear mother, white-armed Hera: "Truly this will be a ruinous business, no longer bearable, if these two strive thus because of mortals and bring wrangling among the gods. There will be no pleasure in our noble banquet, since the worse course prevails. But I advise my mother, who thinks the same herself, to humor my dear father, Zeus, that my father may not again be angry and trouble our feast. If the Olympian lord of lightning wishes to cast us from our seats, for he is mightiest by far—but soothe him yourself with soft words. Then straightway the Olympian will relent toward us."

So he spoke, and, springing up, he placed in his mother's hands the double-handled cup and said to her: "Take heart, Mother, and endure, though grieved, lest dear though you be, I see you struck before my eyes; then, however distressed, I shall be powerless to help you. For the Olympian is hard to counter. Already once before when I tried to save you, he caught me by the foot and hurled me from his awful threshold. All day I fell, and with the setting sun dropped upon Lemnos, and little was the life still in me. But the Sintians straightway cared for me after my fall."

So he spoke, and the white-armed goddess Hera smiled, and smiling received the cup in her hand from her son. Then going from left to right he poured sweet nectar for the other gods, drawing it from a bowl. And unquenchable laughter arose among the blessed gods as they watched Hephaestus bustling about the hall.

So all the day until the sun had set they feasted, and no heart lacked due portion of the feast, nor of the fair lyre which Apollo held, nor of the Muses, who sang in answer with their lovely voices.

But when the bright light of the sun had set, each of them went home to sleep where lame Hephaestus, the renowned, had by his skillful cunning made for each a house. And Zeus, the Olympian lord of lightning, went to his bed, where of old he used to rest when sweet sleep came upon him. There he went and slept, with Hera of the golden throne beside him.

[490–611]

Book II

Thersites

[Fulfilling his promise to Thetis, Zeus sends to Agamemnon a deceitful dream, promising the immediate capture of Troy. On awaking, Agamemnon summons the Greek elders to a council, repeats his dream, and proposes to arm the host for battle, first testing their spirit by suggesting that they throw up the siege. He then calls a mass meeting of the soldiers, and at this point our selection begins (lines 110–277). In it Agamemnon says nothing of his dream, but, to test them, proposes a return home. The soldiers take him at his word and rush for the ships. The goddesses Hera and Athena, intervening, send Odysseus to restrain the men. Thersites, a common soldier, disappointed in his hope to go home, abuses Agamemnon to his face, whereat Odysseus rebukes him and thrashes him soundly.]

"Friends, Danaan heroes, squires of Ares: great Zeus, Cronus' son, has snared me in ruinous folly, merciless god, for formerly he promised and assured me that I should sack well-walled Ilium and depart, but now he has devised a harsh deception and bids me go inglorious to Argos after losing many men. Such seems to be the pleasure of almighty Zeus, who has humbled the heads of many cities and shall humble more hereafter, for his power is mightiest. This is a shameful story for men to learn, even in times to come, that thus in vain so good and great a host of the Achaeans fought and strove in fruitless war with men less numerous, and the end is not in sight. For if we wished, Achaeans and Trojans both, to swear a solemn oath with sacrifice and both be counted, and the native Trojans were taken one by one and we Achaeans were grouped by tens and chose each squad a man of the Trojans to pour wine, many a squad of ten would lack a servant. So far, I say, do the sons of the Achaeans outnumber the Trojans who live within the city. But there are allies out of many cities, spear-wielding men, who greatly hinder me and will not suffer me to sack the fair-lying citadel of Ilium as I desire. Nine years of great Zeus have passed already, and now the timbers of the ships are rotten and the tackle loose, and our wives and little children sit in our halls and wait. Yet our task is quite unfinished, for the sake of which we came. Come, let us all do as I say: let us flee with our ships to our dear native land; for never shall we capture wide-wayed Troy."

So he spoke, and he stirred the spirit in the breasts of all of them throughout the throng, as many as had not heard his plan. The assembly stirred like the long waves of the deep, of the Icarian Sea, which the East Wind and the South have raised, roaring down upon them from the clouds of Father Zeus. Or as when the West Wind comes and stirs a field of tall grain, swiftly rushing down upon it, and the ears nod before the wind, so stirred their whole assembly. With a shout they rushed for the ships; and from beneath their feet the dust arose and hung above them. They called to each other to seize the ships and drag them to the shining sea, and they cleared the ways for launching. Their shouts went up to heaven as they yearned for home, and they took the props from underneath the ships.

Then to the Argives would have come a return

undestined, had not Hera spoken to Athena: "What, Atrytone, child of aegis-bearing Zeus, shall the Argives thus flee homeward across the broad back of the sea to their dear native land? They would leave a boast to Priam and the Trojans, even Argive Helen, for whose sake many of the Achaeans have died at Troy, far from their dear native land. But go now throughout the host of the bronze-clad Achaeans, with your gentle words hold back each man, and do not let them drag their curved ships to the sea."

So she spoke, and the bright-eyed goddess Athena did not disobey her; she went darting down from the peaks of Olympus and quickly came to the swift ships of the Achaeans. Then she found Odysseus, like to Zeus in wisdom, standing there. He had not touched his ship, well-benched and black, for grief had come upon his heart and soul. Standing close by, bright-eyed Athena said: "Zeus-born son of Laertes, Odysseus of many wiles, will you thus throw yourselves into your many-oared ships and take flight homeward to your dear native land? You would leave a boast to Priam and the Trojans, even Argive Helen, for whose sake many Achaeans have died at Troy, far from their dear native land. But go now throughout the host of the Achaeans; with your gentle words hold back each man, and do not let them drag their curved ships to the sea."

So she spoke, and he knew the voice of the goddess as she talked, and he started on the run, throwing aside his cloak (his herald picked it up, Eurybates the Ithacan, who served him). Odysseus went to Agamemnon, Atreus' son, and received from him the ancestral scepter, indestructible forever, and with it went among the ships of the bronze-clad Achaeans.

Any king or noted man he met he held back with soft words, confronting him: "Sir, it is not seemly you should fear like any coward. Come, sit down yourself and make the men as well sit down. For you still have no true knowledge of the mind of Atreus' son. Now he is trying the sons of the Achaeans, but soon he will chastise them. Did we not all hear what he said in council? May he not in anger harm the sons of the Achaeans? The spirit of Zeus-nurtured kings is proud, and their honor is of Zeus, and Zeus the counselor loves them."

But any man of the people whom he saw or found shouting, him he would beat with the scepter and call out to him: "Fellow, sit still and listen to the words of others who are your betters, whereas you are cowardly and weak and never count for anything in war or council. By no means shall we Achaeans all be kings here, nor is it good to have many rulers. Let there be one ruler, one king, to whom the son of crooked-counseled Cronus has given the scepter and the power to take counsel for his people."

So lording it he went throughout the army. And again they rushed to the assembly from their ships and tents, with such a noise as when a wave of the resounding sea roars on a wide beach and the ocean thunders.

The others sat them down and kept their seats, but Thersites still screamed on alone, the endless talker. His mind was filled with many unruly words with which to strive in rash disorder against kings—words which it seemed to him would raise a laugh among the Argives. He was the ugliest man who came to Ilium. Bandy-legged he was, and lame in one foot, with shoulders bent and rounded over his chest. His head rose to a peak and a sparse down grew upon it. Most hateful was he to Achilles above all, and to Odysseus, for he often nagged them. Now he was shrieking shrill reproaches against noble Agamemnon, so that the Achaeans were utterly disgusted with him, hating him in their hearts. Now, shouting loudly, he railed at Agamemnon: "Son of Atreus, why are you complaining? What do you lack? Your tents are full of bronze and in your tents are many chosen women whom we Achaeans give you first, whenever we take a city. Do you still want gold, which some one of the horse-taming Trojans shall bring from Ilium as ransom for his son, whom I or another of the Achaeans have bound and led off captive? Or are you seeking some young woman whom you may know in love and keep for yourself apart? It is not right that he who rules should bring the sons of the Achaeans to misfortune. Cowards, wretched fools, women of Achaea, not men, let us sail homeward with our ships and leave him to digest his prizes here in Troy, that he may know whether we are his defense or not. Even now he insulted Achilles, a far better man than he, for he has taken his prize and holds it, having wrested it away himself. But there can be no anger in Achilles' heart; no, he does not care at all.

Otherwise, son of Atreus, this would be your last insolence."

So, nagging Agamemnon, shepherd of the people, spoke Thersites; Odysseus was quickly at his side, and looking at him grimly, he rebuked him with harsh words: "Thersites, senseless babbler, clear-voiced orator though you be, restrain yourself and desire not alone to strive with kings. For I think no worse man than you exists among all who came to Ilium with the sons of Atreus. Therefore you should not speak with the names of kings upon your lips, nor should you heap reproaches on them nor work for your return. For we do not yet know clearly how these things shall be, whether we sons of the Achaeans shall go home for good or ill. You sit reproaching Agamemnon, Atreus' son, the shepherd of the people, because the Danaan heroes give him very many things, and you speak with railing. But this I tell you—and it shall surely come to pass: if again I find you playing the fool as now, may the head of Odysseus no longer be upon his shoulders, may I no longer be called the father of Telemachus, if I do not take you and strip your very garments off, your cloak and shirt, which hide your nakedness, and send you wailing back to the swift ships, after beating you from the assembly with shameful blows."

So he spoke, and with the scepter beat his back and shoulders. Thersites cringed, and a heavy tear fell from him, and a bloody welt arose upon his back beneath the golden scepter. So he sat down in terror, and in his pain looked foolishly about and wiped away a tear. The rest, though troubled, laughed at him gaily. And glancing at another close beside him, one would say: "Many a good deed has Odysseus done, offering wise counsel and preparing for war, but now this is by far the best thing he has done among the Argives when he checked this impudent slanderer in his talk. Surely not again will his arrogant spirit urge him to rail reproachfully at kings." [110–277]

[Odysseus finally persuades the host to arm and set out. Here follows a catalogue of the Greek and Trojan forces. In Book III the armies are advancing to meet one another, when Hector, the Trojan leader, and Paris, the paramour of Helen, propose that Paris and Menelaus, husband of Helen and brother of Agamemnon, fight a duel for Helen, winner take all. Priam, king of Troy and father of Hector, Paris, and many other Trojans, meets Helen on the wall; she points out to him the Greek leaders. He then goes to the armies to take the oath of armistice; Paris loses the duel, but the goddess Aphrodite saves him and takes him back to Troy. In Book IV, the gods decide to let the truce be broken, Menelaus is wounded, Agamemnon reviews his army, and a fierce fight begins.]

Book V

The deeds of Diomedes

[Here is introduced Aeneas, a Trojan, son of Anchises and Aphrodite, and the hero of the greatest Roman epic, Vergil's *Aeneid*. The Greek Diomedes, with the help of the goddess Athena, succeeds actually in scratching the wrist of the goddess Aphrodite as she tries to rescue her son Aeneas. Aeneas, abandoned by Aphrodite, is guarded by Apollo (lines 274–352, below). Diomedes tries in vain to kill Aeneas, even in Apollo's sheltering arms (lines 432–448, below), and even lays low Ares, the god of war, as he goes to the rescue of the Trojans.]

So Diomedes and his charioteer spoke to one another, and the other two, Aeneas and Pandarus, came quickly on, driving the swift horses. First Pandarus, the glorious son of Lycaon, addressed Diomedes: "Son of noble Tydeus, stout-hearted and wise, the swift bolt, the bitter arrow, did not slay you. But I will try now with my spear if I can hit you."

So speaking, he drew back the long-shadowed spear and hurled it and struck the shield of Tydeus' son. The speeding point of bronze drove right through to his breastplate. And over him Lycaon's glorious son cried loudly: "You are hit clean through the belly, and not for long, I think, will you survive; you have given me great glory."

But fearlessly the mighty Diomedes answered him: "You missed and did not hit me; I do not think you two will stop until the one has fallen and sated with his blood the warrior Ares with the bull-hide shield."

So he spoke, and hurled his spear, and Athena guided it to his nose beside the eye, and it passed his gleaming teeth. The stubborn bronze cut his tongue off at the root, and the point protruded from beneath his jawbone. He fell from the chariot and his splendid, gleaming armor clanged upon him and the swift horses shied away. Then his soul and strength were loosed.

Aeneas sprang down with his shield and lengthy spear, fearing lest the Achaeans drag the dead man from him. Over him he strode like a lion, trusting in his might, and before him held his spear and balanced shield, eager to slay whoever should come to face him, and shouting dreadfully. But the son of Tydeus grasped in his hand a stone, a weighty mass which two men, as men now are, could never carry; but even alone he handled it with ease. With it he smote Aeneas on the hip joint—the cup men call it—shattering the joint and crushing both sinews too, and the jagged stone tore through the skin. The hero fell to his knees and with his stout hand leaned upon the earth, and black night veiled his eyes.

Now would Aeneas, king of men, have perished, had not Aphrodite, daughter of Zeus, been quick to see, his mother, who bore him to Anchises as he tended cattle. She threw her white arms about her dear son and spread a fold of her bright robe before him, as a shelter against weapons, lest any of the Danaans with their swift steeds should thrust bronze into his breast and take away his life.

So she was bearing her dear son out of the battle. But Capaneus' son did not forget the orders given him by Diomedes of the mighty war cry. He halted his own single-hoofed horses apart from the conflict, binding the reins to the chariot rim, and then rushed upon the fair-maned horses of Aeneas and drove them away from the Trojans into the midst of the well-greaved Achaeans. He gave them to Deipylus to drive to the hollow ships—his dear companion whom he honored above all others of his age because he was like-minded. Then the warrior mounted his own chariot and took the gleaming reins and in haste drove his strong-hoofed horses hotly after Tydeus' son. The latter was pursuing Cypris with the pitiless bronze, knowing that she was a weakling goddess, not one of those who rule the wars of men, neither Athena nor Enyo, the sacker of cities. But when he had pursued her through a great throng and had come upon her, then great-hearted Tydeus' son reached out his spear and wounded the hollow of her hand, springing upon her with his sharp spear in her weakness. At once the spear passed through her ambrosial robe, which the Graces themselves had woven for her, and pierced her skin at the base of the fingers, above the palm. The ambrosial blood of the goddess poured out, ichor, which flows in the blessed gods, for they eat no bread and drink no gleaming wine; therefore they are bloodless and are called immortal. With a great shriek she cast her son from her and Phoebus Apollo rescued him in his arms, in a dark cloud, lest any of the Danaans with their swift steeds thrust bronze into his breast and take away his life. Over Aphrodite Diomedes of the mighty war cry shouted loudly: "Keep away, daughter of Zeus, from war and combat. Is it not enough that you seduce weak women? If you will enter battle, then truly I think you will come to shudder when you hear tell of war, even though from afar."

So he spoke, and she, beside herself, departed sore distressed. . . . [272–352]

Diomedes of the mighty war cry rushed upon Aeneas, though he knew that Apollo himself held forth his arms above him. But he had no reverence for the great god and still was eager to slay Aeneas and strip off his glorious armor. Thrice then he rushed upon him, eager for the kill, and thrice Apollo struck back his gleaming shield. But when for the fourth time he rushed upon him like a god, then with a dreadful cry Apollo the Warder said to him: "Beware, son of Tydeus, and give way, nor seek to match your spirit with the gods, for in no way alike are the race of immortal gods and that of men who walk the earth."

So he spoke and Tydeus' son drew back a little, avoiding the wrath of unerring Apollo. And Apollo laid down Aeneas far from the throng in holy Pergamus, where his temple had been built. Then Leto and Artemis the archeress healed him in the great shrine and gave him glory.

[432–448]

Book VI

The Farewell of Hector to Andromache

[While the battle is raging, Hector returns to Troy to ask his mother Hecuba to pray to Athena for her favor. After his interview with her, he has a short conversation with Helen, rebukes Paris and bids him arm forthwith, and finally sees and speaks to his wife Andromache and his little son Astyanax (lines 237–529, below).]

When Hector came to the Scaean gates and the oak tree, the wives and daughters of the Trojans ran about him, asking for their sons and brothers, for their kinsmen and their husbands. He bade them all in turn pray to the gods. But over many sorrow hung.

But when he came to the fair house of Priam, with its polished colonnade—in it there were fifty chambers of polished stone, built close beside each other, wherein the sons of Priam slept beside their wedded wives; and over against them on the other side within the court were twelve roofed chambers of polished stone, built close by one another, for his daughters, where slept the sons-in-law of Priam beside their wedded wives—there his bountiful mother came to meet him, bringing with her Laodice, fairest in face among her daughters. She put her hand upon him and spoke and said to him: "My child, why have you left the violent battle and come hither? I suppose the accursed sons of the Achaeans are pressing hard in their fight about the city, and your spirit bade you come hither and raise your hands to Zeus from the citadel. But wait while I bring you honey-sweet wine, that you may pour a libation to Father Zeus and the other immortals first, and then may be refreshed yourself, if you will drink. Wine greatly increases the strength of a man wearied even as you have grown weary bearing succor to your friends."

Then great Hector of the glancing helmet answered her: "Bring me no honey-hearted wine, queenly Mother, lest you deprive me of my might and I forget my valor. I fear to pour a libation of sparkling wine to Zeus with unwashed hands. Nor is it right to pray to the black-clouded son of Cronus when fouled with blood and gore. But do you go with burnt offerings to the temple of Athena, driver of spoil, gathering together the older women, and place upon the knees of fair-haired Athena the robe which is the fairest and largest in your chamber and which is far dearest to you yourself, and promise to sacrifice to her in her temple twelve yearling heifers which have never felt the goad, in hope that she may have mercy upon the city and the Trojans' wives and little children and that she may ward off from holy Ilium the son of Tydeus, the wild spearman, the mighty deviser of rout. Do you then go to the temple of Athena, the driver of spoil, and I will go after Paris, that I may summon him, if he will listen to what I say. Would that the earth would open beneath him on the spot, for the Olympian reared him to be a woe to the Trojans and to great-hearted Priam and his sons. If I should see him going down into the house of Death, then would I say that my heart had forgotten its sorrow."

So he spoke, and she went into the hall and gave orders to her handmaids, and they gathered the old women throughout the city. But she went into the fragrant, vaulted storeroom where were her richly embroidered robes, the work of Sidonian women whom godlike Alexander [Paris] himself brought from Sidon, sailing the broad deep, on the same voyage on which he carried away high-born Helen. Taking one of these robes, Hecuba bore it as a gift to Athena, that one which was the fairest with embroidery and the largest, and shone like a star, and lay beneath the others. Then she set out, and many aged women followed her.

When they came to the temple of Athena on the heights of the city, fair-cheeked Theano, Cisses' daughter, the wife of horse-taming Antenor, opened the doors for them, for the Trojans had made her priestess of Athena. Then all with lamentations lifted up their hands to Athena, and fair-cheeked Theano took the robe and laid it on fair-haired Athena's knees and prayed in supplication to the daughter of great Zeus: "Revered Athena, protectress of the city, goddess of goddesses, break now Diomedes' spear, and grant that he may fall headlong before the Scaean gates, so that we may now straightway sacrifice to thee in thy temple twelve yearling heifers which have never felt the goad, in the hope that thou mayest have mercy upon the city and upon the wives and little children of the Trojans."

So she spoke in prayer, but Pallas Athena refused her. Thus were they praying to the daughter of great Zeus, but Hector went to the fair palace of Alexander, which Paris himself had built, with the men who were then the best builders in fertile Troy. They had built him a chamber and hall and court close to Priam and Hector, on the heights of the city. There entered Hector, dear to Zeus, and in his hand he held a spear of eleven cubits; at the end of the shaft gleamed the brazen tip and around ran a golden ferrule. He found Paris in his chamber, busy with his beautiful armor, his shield and breastplate, and handling his curved bow. Argive Helen sat with the women of her household and appointed to her maids their glorious work. When Hector saw Paris, he reproached him with scornful words: "Accursed one, you have no right to nurse this anger in your heart. The people perish in battle about the city and the steep wall, and it is for your sake that the battle cry and war have flamed about this city. And you would rage against any other whom you might see shirking hateful war. Up then, lest soon the city burn with hostile fire."

Then the godlike Alexander answered him: "Hector, since you have reproached me after my deserts and not beyond, I will explain to you. Do you give heed and hear me. It was not so much because of anger and indignation at the Trojans that I remained sitting in my chamber, but I desired to give myself up to grief. And just now my wife, persuading me with soft words, urged me to war. And it seems to me also that it will be better thus. Victory visits various men in turn. Come now, remain; let me put on the arms of Ares; or go, and I will follow—I think that I shall overtake you."

So he spoke, but Hector of the glancing helmet did not answer him at all. And Helen addressed Hector with humble words: "Brother of mine, horrible, malicious vixen that I am, would that on the day when first my mother bore me, some evil blast of a storm had come to bear me away to the mountain or to the billow of the resounding sea where the waves would have swept me away before these things came to pass. But since the gods so decreed these things, would that I had been the wife of a better man, who knew the meaning of disgrace and men's numerous reproaches. But this man's heart is not firm now nor shall it ever be hereafter. Therefore I think that he shall reap its fruits. Come now, enter and sit down upon this chair, my brother, since weariness has fallen most upon your heart because of my shamelessness and Alexander's folly. Upon us both Zeus sent an evil fate, that we should make matter for song for men who shall be hereafter."

Then great Hector of the glancing helmet answered her: "Ask me not to sit down, Helen, though it be from love, for you shall not persuade me. For already my spirit is eager to help the Trojans, who greatly miss me in my absence. But do you arouse this man and let him make haste himself, so that he may overtake me while I am still within the city. I shall go home that I may see my household and my dear wife and infant son, for I do not know if I shall ever come back to them again, or whether the gods will now destroy me at the hands of the Achaeans."

So speaking, Hector of the glancing helmet departed and quickly came to his comfortable house, but he did not find white-armed Andromache within its walls, for she, with her child and fair-robed servant, had taken her stand upon the wall, with lamentation and tears. When, therefore, Hector did not find his blameless wife within, he went and stood upon the threshold and called to the serving women: "Come now, serving women, tell me truly, where went white-armed Andromache forth from the hall? Has she gone to the home of one of my sisters or of my brothers' fair-robed wives, or to Athena's temple, where the other fair-tressed Trojan women propitiate the dreadful goddess?"

Then the busy housekeeper addressed him: "Hector, since you bid us answer truly, she has gone neither to the house of one of your sisters nor of your brothers' fair-robed wives, nor to Athena's temple, where the other fair-tressed Trojan women propitiate the dreadful goddess, but she has gone to the great wall of Ilium because she heard that the Trojans were hard-pressed and the might of the Achaeans great. So she has gone to the wall in haste, like one distraught. And the nurse went with her, carrying the child."

So spoke the housekeeper, and Hector hastened from his home back the same way through the well-built streets. When in his passage through the great city he came to the Scaean gates, where he was about to pass through onto the plain, there his richly dowered wife came running to meet him, Andromache, the daughter of great-hearted Eëtion, Eëtion who dwelt under wooded Placus in Thebe-under-Placus, ruling over the men of Cilicia. His daughter was the wife of brazen-armored Hector. So then she met him, and the nurse came with her, holding in her arms the tender child, a mere infant, the beloved son of Hector, like to a fair star, whom Hector called Scamandrius, but the rest Astyanax, for Hector alone watched over Ilium. So Hector smiled and gazed upon his child in silence. But Andromache stood close beside him weeping, and she put her hand upon him and spoke and said to him: "What can possess you? Your own might will destroy you, nor have you any pity on your infant son or hapless me, who soon shall be your widow. For soon will the Achaeans all set upon you and slay you. When I am bereft of you, it would be better for me to pass beneath the earth. There will be no more warm comfort for me when you have met your doom, but only grief. No father have I nor queenly mother; godlike Achilles slew my father and utterly laid waste the comfortable city of the Cilicians, Thebe of the lofty gates. He slew Eëtion, but he did not despoil him of his arms, for he feared in his heart to do so. Rather, he burned him in his well-wrought armor and raised a mound above him. Around it the mountain nymphs, daughters of aegis-bearing Zeus, planted elms. And the seven brothers who were mine within those halls all in one day passed into the house of Death; for swift-footed, godlike Achilles slew them all among their shambling cattle and white sheep. And my mother, who ruled as queen under wooded Placus, he brought here with the rest of the spoil, but set her free when he had taken a boundless ransom; and Artemis, the archeress, slew her in her father's halls. Now, Hector, you to me are father and queenly mother and brother as well, and you are my stalwart husband. Come now, have pity; remain here upon the wall, lest you make your son an orphan and a widow of your wife. Station your army here by the wild fig tree, where the city may best be assaulted and the wall be scaled. For three times the best of them have come here to try the wall with the two Ajaxes and glorious Idomeneus and the sons of Atreus and Tydeus' valiant son; whether someone well skilled in soothsaying told them or now even their own spirit urges and drives them on."

Then great Hector of the glancing helmet said to her: "I, too, take thought of these things, dear wife. But I feel great shame before the Trojans and their long-robed wives if like a coward I skulk from war. Nor does my own heart permit it; for I have learned to be valiant always and to fight among the foremost Trojans, striving greatly for my father's glory and my own. For well I know this in my heart and soul: there will come a day when holy Ilium shall fall, and Priam and the people of Priam of the good ashen spear. But not so much does the anguish of the Trojans of aftertime move me, nor Hecuba's own nor King Priam's nor that of my brothers, many and brave, who may fall in the dust at the hands of their foemen, as your anguish, when some bronze-clad Achaean shall lead you forth weeping and rob you of your day of freedom. And then, perhaps, dwelling in Argos, you shall weave at another's loom or carry water from Messeïs or Hypereia, much against your will, and harsh necessity shall lie upon you. Then some man shall say as he sees you weeping, 'This was Hector's wife, he who was the best in battle of the horse-taming Trojans when they fought around Ilium.' So someone will say. And upon you then shall come fresh grief for want of such a man to ward off the day of bondage. But may the heaped earth cover me in death before I hear your cry or the sound of your captivity."

So spoke glorious Hector, and reached out for his son, but the child shrank back with a cry into the arms of his fair-girdled nurse, frightened at the sight of his dear father, afraid of the bronze and the horsehair crest as he saw it nodding dreadfully from the helmet's peak. His dear father and queenly mother laughed, and glorious Hector quickly took his helmet from his head and laid it all gleaming on the ground. Then, when he had kissed his dear son and dandled him in his arms, he spoke in prayer to Zeus and the other gods: "Zeus, and ye other gods, grant that this child of mine also may become, even as I am, pre-eminent among the Trojans, as great in strength, and that he may rule with might over Ilium. And may someone say of him one day, as he returns from war, 'This man is much better than his father.' May he slay his enemy and bear away the bloodstained spoils, and may his mother's heart rejoice."

So speaking, he put the child in the hands of his dear wife, and she took him in her fragrant arms, smiling through her tears. When her husband saw it, he pitied her, and he caressed her with his hand and spoke and said to her: "Foolish one, do not grieve too much at heart. For no man shall send me down to the house of Death contrary to my fate. No man, I say, has escaped his doom, be he cowardly or brave, when once he has been born. But do you go home and busy yourself with your own tasks, the loom and distaff, and bid your handmaids ply their work. And war shall be for all men, for all who live in Ilium, but especially for me."

So spoke glorious Hector, and took up his crested helmet. His dear wife went homeward, turning often to look back, and shedding great tears. Quickly then she came to man-slaying Hector's comfortable house. She found within her many handmaids, and she set them all to weeping. So they wept for Hector in his house while still he lived, for they thought he never would return again from war, escaped from the might and hands of the Achaeans.

Nor did Paris linger in his lofty house, but as soon as he had put on his glorious armor, all fairly wrought of bronze, he rushed out through the city, confident in his swift feet, like a horse from his stall, well fed at the manger, who breaks his tether and runs galloping over the plain, accustomed to bathe in a fair-flowing river. Proud he is; he holds his head high and the mane flows about his shoulders. His knees quickly bear him, trusting in his beauty, to the haunts and pastures of the mares. So Paris, Priam's son, strode down from the heights of Pergamus, gleaming in his armor like the shining sun, and laughing; and his swift feet bore him on. Quickly then he met his brother Hector, just as he was about to turn from the place where he had lingered with his wife. The godlike Alexander addressed him first: "Brother, surely I have delayed you in your haste by tarrying too long and I have not come quickly as you bade."

Then Hector of the glancing helmet answered him: "Fool, no man is just who would make light of your work in battle, when you are valiant. But you willingly grow slack and careless, and my heart is grieved within me when I hear reproaches against you from the Trojans, who suffer much hardship for your sake. But let us go; we shall make amends for this hereafter, if Zeus ever grant us to set for the heavenly gods, who live forever, a bowl to toast deliverance in our halls, when we have driven the well-greaved Achaeans out of Troy." [237–529]

[In Books VII and VIII, omitted here, Hector and Paris re-enter the battle, and Hector challenges any Greek to meet him in single combat. Ajax, son of Telamon, chosen by lot to face the Trojan champion, fights indecisively, though he has a slight edge. Then the two exchange presents, and a truce for the burial of the dead is agreed to. The Trojans propose that Paris be allowed to keep Helen, but give up her property. The Greeks indignantly refuse, and fortify their camp. Zeus forbids the other gods to take part in the fighting, but he encourages the Trojans, and the Greeks, after a day's indecisive battle, withdraw to their camp, while the Trojans camp on the plain.]

Book IX

The embassy to Achilles

[Agamemnon, discouraged, calls a council, which advises him to try to win Achilles' favor again by gifts and kind words. Agamemnon agrees, and as our next selection (lines 162–448) opens, Nestor, the wise old counsellor, king of Pylos, nominates as envoys Ajax and Odysseus, with Phoenix, Achilles' old tutor. Achilles welcomes them, and entertains them at dinner. Odysseus tells of the sad state of the Greeks, repeats Agamemnon's offer, and urges Achilles to lay aside his wrath. Achilles indignantly refuses. Then Phoenix speaks, reminding Achilles of his long devotion to him.]

Then Nestor, the Gerenian horseman, answered him: "Most glorious son of Atreus, Agamemnon, king of men, by no means contemptible are the gifts you offer lord Achilles. But come, let us send chosen men to go immediately to the tent of Peleus' son, Achilles. Let those whom I now fix with my eye obey. First, let Phoenix, dear to Zeus, be the leader, then great Ajax and godlike Odysseus. Of the heralds, let Odius and Eurybates follow, too. Bring water for our hands and call for pious silence, that we may pray to Zeus, the son of Cronus, in the hope that he may take pity on us."

So he spoke, and his words pleased all. Heralds at once poured water on their hands and young men filled brimming bowls with drink, and having performed the rites of dedication, they passed the wine in cups to all. When they had poured a libation and had drunk as their hearts desired, they started from the tent of Agamemnon, Atreus' son. And Nestor, the Gerenian horseman, glancing at each in turn, urged them all, but especially

Odysseus, to try to persuade Peleus' blameless son.

So they went along the shore of the deep-sounding sea, offering many prayers to him who encircles the earth and makes it tremble, that they might easily persuade the great heart of the son of Aeacus. And they came to the tents and ships of the Myrmidons and found him rejoicing his heart with a clear lyre, fair and well-wrought, upon which was a silver crossbar. He had taken it from the spoil when he destroyed the city of Eëtion, and with it he rejoiced his heart and sang the glorious deeds of heroes. Patroclus alone sat facing him in silence, waiting for the son of Aeacus to cease his singing. They stepped forward, led by godlike Odysseus, and stood before the hero. Amazed, Achilles started up, still with the lyre, leaving the seat in which he sat; and Patroclus too, when he saw the men, arose. Then swift-footed Achilles said to them in welcome: "Greetings; you come as friends. And so you should, for even in my wrath you are to me dearest of the Achaeans."

So speaking, the godlike Achilles led them in and seated them on chairs and purple rugs, and quickly said to Patroclus, who stood close by: "Set up a larger mixing bowl, son of Menoetius, and make the mixture stronger, for these men who are within my halls are very dear to me."

So he spoke, and Patroclus obeyed his dear comrade. He set a great meat tray in the light of the fire and placed on it the back of a sheep and of a fat goat and the chine of a fat hog, rich with fat. Automedon held them while the godlike Achilles cut them up. He skillfully cut them into bits and speared them on spits, and Menoetius' son, the godlike man, kindled a great fire. Then when the fire had burned down and the flames had died away, he raked the coals into a bed and stretched the spits above them and sprinkled on them excellent salt as he lifted the spits from the headstones. When he had roasted the meat and placed it on the dressers, Patroclus took bread and placed it on a table in fair baskets, but Achilles served the meat. He himself sat facing godlike Odysseus by the opposite wall, and bade Patroclus, his companion, make offering to the gods; and Patroclus cast the sacrificial parts into the fire. Then they stretched their hands out to the food that lay prepared before them. And when they had put aside the desire for food and drink, Ajax nodded to Phoenix, but godlike Odysseus noticed it, and filling a cup with wine he pledged Achilles:

"Your health, Achilles. We do not lack proper banquets either in the tent of Agamemnon, Atreus' son, or here and now, for many satisfying viands are at hand. But the affairs of a pleasing feast do not concern us; instead, O beloved of Zeus, we look on utter ruin and are afraid. We doubt whether we shall save or lose the well-benched ships, unless you clothe yourself in your valor, for the high-hearted Trojans and their far-famed allies have made camp near the ships and wall, kindling many fires throughout their army. And they say they will not halt again but will fall upon the black ships. Zeus, Cronus' son, sends them fair omens in his lightning, and Hector, exulting greatly in his strength, rages dreadfully, trusting in Zeus, and fears neither men nor gods. A mighty madness has possessed him. He prays for the shining dawn to come quickly, for he threatens to cut off the ships' high sterns and burn their hulls with devouring fire, and as for the Achaeans, to slay them as they wander frightened through the smoke beside the ships. I fear dreadfully in my heart lest the gods fulfill his threats and it be our doom to die in Troy, far from horse-raising Argos. Up then, if you wish even late to save the sons of the Achaeans, who are overwhelmed beneath the roaring press of Trojans. Your sorrow, too, it will be hereafter, nor is there any way to find a remedy for evil once it is done. Rather, long before that, think how you may ward off the evil day from the Danaans. Dear friend, surely your father Peleus thus advised you on that day when he sent you from Phthia to Agamemnon. 'My son, Athena and Hera will give you strength, if they so wish, but for yourself keep a great-hearted spirit in your breast, for it is better to be friendly. Refrain from anger and its evil schemings, that both young and old among the Argives may revere you more.' So the old man advised, but you forget. Cease even now, give up your anger with its heartache. Agamemnon offers you becoming gifts if you will put your wrath aside. And if you will hear me, I will tell you what gifts now in his tents Agamemnon promised you—seven tripods untouched by fire, ten talents' weight of gold, and twenty gleaming caldrons, twelve strong, prize-winning horses who take prizes with their swift feet. Not without wealth, not lacking in his share of precious gold would be the man who had all the prizes Agamemnon's horses won him with their feet. And he will give seven women skilled in faultless work, women of Lesbos, whom he chose as his share when you yourself took goodly Lesbos, for they then surpassed throngs of women in their beauty. Them will he give you, and with them will be she whom then he took away, the daughter of Brises. And he will swear a great oath that he has never entered her bed nor lain with her, as is the wont, my lord, of men and women. All this shall be yours at once, and if thereafter the gods grant that we sack the great city of Priam, you may fill your ship with abundant gold and bronze, after you have entered the town, when we Achaeans divide the booty. You yourself may choose twenty Trojan women who are the fairest after Argive Helen. And if we should return to Achaean Argos, the fat plowland, you might be his son-in-law, and he will honor you equally with Orestes, who, as his young son, is being reared in much abundance. Three daughters has he in his well-built halls, Chrysothemis, Laodice, and Iphianassa. You may take whom you will of these to the house of Peleus as your dear wife, yet give no wedding gifts. But he will give you very many soothing gifts—so many as no man yet has given with his daughters. Seven fair-lying cities will he give you—Cardamyle, Enope, and grassy Hire, most holy Pherae, deep-meadowed Antheia, fair Aepeia, and Pedasus rich in vines—all near the sea, neighbors to sandy Pylos. In them dwell men rich in sheep and cattle, who will honor you like a god with gifts and who will pay you splendid tribute under your scepter. This would he pay you if you would give up your wrath. But if the son of Atreus is too hated in your heart, he and his gifts, yet have pity on all the rest of the Achaeans, hard-pressed throughout the camp, who will revere you as a god. For you could surely win great glory in their eyes. For now you might take Hector, since he would come right up to you in his dire rage, for he thinks no Danaan his match, of all that the ships brought hither."

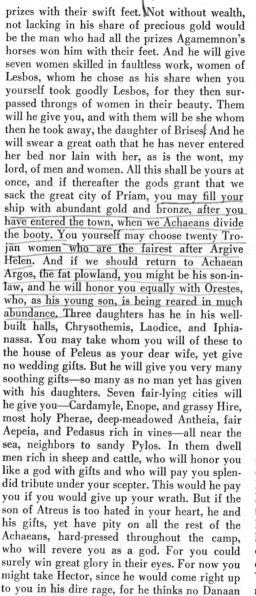

Swift-footed Achilles answered him and said: "Zeus-born son of Laertes, Odysseus of many wiles, I must refuse his offer without scruple, as I feel, and as it shall come to pass, so that you may not sit by me and din it in my ears from this side and from that. For hateful to me as the gates of Hades is the man who hides one thing in his heart and speaks another. So I will speak as seems best to me. I do not think that Atreus' son Agamemnon or the other Danaans shall persuade me, since there was never any thanks for always striving bitterly against the foe. The share was the same for him who stayed behind and for whoever battled hard. Coward and hero were honored equally; the idler and the man of many deeds alike must die. It is no gain for me when my heart must suffer woe by always staking life in battle. As a bird brings food in mouthfuls to her young, when she can find it, yet she herself fares ill, so I watched through many sleepless nights and fought through many bloody days, striving with heroes for their wives. Twelve cities of men I sacked from off my ships; on foot, eleven, I claim, in fertile Troyland. From all these I took much glorious treasure, and all I brought and gave to Agamemnon, Atreus' son. And he, staying behind by the swift ships, divided up a little, but kept much for himself. The other prizes that he gave to kings and nobles are theirs securely; from me alone of the Achaeans he snatched my pleasing mistress and retains her. Let him lie with her and rejoice. Why need the Argives war against the Trojans? Why did the son of Atreus gather the men and lead them hither? Was it not for fair-haired Helen's sake? Are the sons of Atreus the only mortal men who love their wives? Surely whatever man is good and prudent loves and cherishes his own, even as I loved her with all my heart, though I won her by my spear. Now, since he has seized her from my arms and deceived me, let him not try me out, for I know him well; nor shall he win me. Rather, Odysseus, let him with you and the other kings think how to ward the blazing fire from off the ships. He has done very much without me—indeed, he built a dike and ran a ditch beside it, wide and deep, and set a stockade there. Yet not even so can he check the might of man-slaying Hector. While I fought with the Achaeans, Hector dared not offer battle at any distance from the wall but came only to the Scaean gates and the oak tree. There he once awaited me alone and barely escaped from my attack. But now that I will not fight with godlike Hector, tomorrow, when I have made sacrifice to Zeus and all the gods, when I have loaded my ships well and when I put to sea, you shall, if you wish and care, see my ships very early sailing on the Hellespont, which teems with fish, and in the ships men eager to row. And if the famed earth-shaker would give fair sailing, on the third day I might come to fertile Phthia. I have many things I left when I came hither, and I shall take hence homeward other gold and ruddy bronze and fair-girdled women and gray iron, which have been my share. But the man who gave my prize has taken it away in insolence, the mighty Agamemnon, Atreus' son. Say to him all, just as I bid you, openly, so that the other Achaeans too may be indignant if he hopes still to deceive any of the Danaans, as he is ever clothed in impudence. Yet shameless as he is, he would not dare to look me in the face. I will not share in council or in deeds with him, for he deceived and sinned against me, nor could he again deceive me by his words. Enough for him; let him go his way for all of me, for Zeus the counselor has robbed him of his senses. His gifts are hateful to me and I set no value on them. Not even if he should give me ten or twenty times what he now has, and if he should get more from elsewhere, so much as comes into Orchomenus or Thebes in Egypt, where riches lie in greatest plenty in the houses—the city of a hundred gates; two hundred men can ride through each with chariots and horses—not even if he should give me gifts as many as the sand or dust, not even thus could Agamemnon persuade my heart before he has atoned to me for all this grievous outrage. I will not wed the daughter of Agamemnon, Atreus' son, not though she should rival golden Aphrodite in her beauty and should be the peer of bright-eyed Athena in her work; not even then will I marry her. Let him choose some other of the Achaeans, whoever befits him and is kinglier than I. For if the gods preserve me and I reach my home, Peleus himself will then seek out a wife for me. There are many daughters of Achaea in Greece and Phthia, daughters of nobles who guard their cities. Often there my noble heart urged me to wed a wife, a proper helpmate, to rejoice in the wealth that ancient Peleus had won. Not all they say that Ilium, that fair-lying town, possessed in former days of peace before the coming of the sons of the Achaeans, not all that the stone threshold of the archer, Phoebus Apollo, guards within in rocky Pytho, is worth my life to me. For plunder may win cattle and fat sheep, and purchase may gain tripods and the sacred heads of horses, but a man's soul cannot be seized or caught so that it will return once it has passed the barrier of his teeth. For my mother, the silver-footed goddess Thetis, says that two fates bear me to the goal of death. If I remain here and fight around the Trojans' city, then my homecoming is lost to me but my glory shall be undying; but if I come home to my dear native land, my glorious fame is lost to me but my life shall last long, nor will the end of death soon overtake me. The others too I would advise to sail for home, since never, now, will you attain the goal of lofty Ilium, for surely far-thundering Zeus holds his hand above it and its men have plucked up courage. Go then, and give this message to the chiefs of the Achaeans—this is the honorable task of elders—that they may devise a better counsel in their hearts that shall save their ships and the host of the Achaeans on the hollow ships, since this plan which they have now devised cannot be realized, because I shall continue in my wrath. But let Phoenix remain here and sleep with us, that he may go with me in the ships to our dear native land tomorrow, if he wish; for I will not take him by constraint."

So he spoke, and they were all hushed in silence, wondering at his speech, for vehemently did he refuse them. At length the aged horseman Phoenix spoke to him in tears, for he feared greatly for the ships of the Achaeans: "If you do indeed consider in your heart returning, glorious Achilles, and are quite unwilling to ward off devouring fire from the ships, since wrath has fallen into your heart, how then, dear child, could I be left here alone without you? The aged horseman Peleus sent me with you on the day when he sent you, a mere child, from Phthia to Agamemnon, when you as yet knew nothing of war, which deals with all alike, nor of councils, where men come to fame. Therefore he sent me to teach you all these things—to be both a speaker of words and a doer of deeds. Therefore I would not desire to be abandoned by you, dear child, not even though the god himself should promise to smooth away my age and make me young again, as when first I left Hellas with its fair women, fleeing the wrath of my father Amyntor, son of Ormenus. [162–448]

[Lines 449–478, giving details of Phoenix' father's anger and Phoenix' escape from it, are omitted. In the next passage (479–523) Phoenix continues his speech, pleading with Achilles to yield.]

I came to fertile Phthia, mother of flocks, to King Peleus. He received me with kindness and loved me as a father loves his cherished only son amid rich possessions, and he made me rich and gave me many men to rule. I dwelt in Phthia's borders, ruling the Dolopians. To your present greatness I have reared you, godlike Achilles, loving you from my heart, for with no other would you go to dine nor eat within the halls, until I set you on my knee and cut and fed to you your meat and held your wine cup to your lips. Many a time you wet the shirt upon my chest, spirting out wine in naughty childishness. Much have I toiled and suffered over you, thinking the gods would never give me child of my own; but I made you my child, godlike Achilles, that some day you might ward off unseemly ruin from me. Now, Achilles, master your great spirit, nor should you have a heart that knows no pity, for even the gods themselves are placable, although their excellence and honor and might are greater still. With sacrifice and gentle prayers, with libations and the smoke of offerings, men turn them by their supplications when someone has transgressed and erred. For there are Prayers, daughters of great Zeus, lame and wrinkled, with sideward-glancing eyes, who follow troubled behind blind Folly. Blind Folly is mighty and swift of foot, wherefore she runs far ahead of all and is first to reach all parts of the earth and do men harm, and the Prayers heal the hurt thereafter. Whoever reverences the daughters of Zeus as they draw near, him they help greatly and to his prayers they listen. But whoever repels them and harshly says them nay, they go to Zeus, the son of Cronus, and pray that Ruin may follow him so that he may atone in suffering. Come, Achilles, do you too grant that honor may follow Zeus' daughters, honor which bends the will of other noble creatures too. For if the son of Atreus were not bringing gifts and telling of more hereafter, but were persisting in furious anger, I would not bid you put aside your wrath and give protection to the Argives, however they might need it. But now he gives you much and has promised more hereafter and has chosen the best throughout the Achaean army and sent them to entreat you, even those who are dearest to you yourself among the Argives. Do not despise their words or their journey hither. Your earlier anger none can blame. [479–523]

[In lines 524–599, omitted here, Phoenix tells the cautionary tale of Meleager, who likewise sulked, but was finally forced to do without honor what he might have done before to great popular acclaim. Lines 600–713, below, contain Phoenix' closing plea, at which Achilles remains unmoved. Ajax adds his entreaties, and Achilles states the conditions upon which he will return to battle. The envoys return to camp, but Phoenix stays, since Achilles is toying with the idea of embarking for home the next day. The Greek council decides to go on fighting without Achilles.]

"But for my sake, hold no such plans in mind, and let not an evil spirit turn you toward that path, for it would be worse to protect the ships when they begin to burn. Come on terms of the gifts, for the Achaeans will honor you as a god, but if you enter man-destroying war without the gifts you will not have such honor even though you ward off war."

Swift-footed Achilles answered him and said: "Phoenix, aged father, Zeus-nurtured, I have no need of this honor. I think I am already honored by decree of Zeus, which will abide with me beside the curved ships as long as breath remains in my breast and my knees can move. Another thing I will tell you, and do you turn it over in your heart: do not trouble my soul with grief and lamentation for the sake of Atreus' heroic son; you must not love him, lest you win my hate, who love you. It is but fair that with me you should cherish him who cherishes me. Rule as my peer, share half my honor. These men shall bear my answer, but remain here yourself and lie down on a soft bed, and when the dawn appears we shall consider whether to return to our own or to remain."

He spoke, and to Patroclus he signaled with his brows in silence to make ready a thick bed for Phoenix, that the others might quickly consider their departure from his tent. And the godlike Ajax, Telamon's son, spoke out among them: "Zeus-born son of Laertes, Odysseus of many wiles, let us go. For it seems to me that the goal of our words cannot be reached by this road. We must with all speed report his reply to the Danaans, even though it be not good, for no doubt they now sit awaiting it. But Achilles has made his great-hearted spirit savage in his breast, unhappy man, nor does he care for the love with which his comrades honored him above others beside the ships, pitiless that he is. Men accept quit money from the slayer of their brother or dead son, and the slayer remains there among the people when he has paid a large forfeit, and the kinsman's heart and bold spirit are restrained when he has received the fine. But the gods have made the anger in your breast unceasing and bitter, for the maid's sake alone. Now we offer you seven of the best, and much else besides. Be gentle-hearted and revere your home; we from the Danaan host sit underneath your roof; we desire to be your closest, dearest friends, beyond all others among the Achaeans."

Swift-footed Achilles answered him and said: "Ajax, Zeus-born son of Telamon, leader of men, all you have said is spoken after my own heart, up to a point, but my heart is swollen with anger when I remember the insults heaped on me among the Argives by the son of Atreus, as if on some unregarded wanderer. Now go and tell your tidings. For I shall not think of bloody war until wise Priam's son, the godlike Hector, comes to the tents and ships of the Myrmidons, slaying Argives as he goes, and burns our ships with fire. At my own tent and black ships I expect to put a halt to Hector, eager though he be for battle."

So he spoke, and each of them took a double cup and poured a libation and then went back beside the ships, and Odysseus led the way. But Patroclus bade his comrades and handmaids make ready a thick bed for Phoenix, with all speed. They obeyed and made a bed as he commanded—a fleece, a blanket, and fine nap of linen. There the old man lay down and awaited bright Dawn. But Achilles slept in the inmost corner of his well-built tent. Beside him slept a woman whom he had brought from Lesbos, Phorbas' daughter, fair-cheeked Diomede. And Patroclus lay across from him, the fair-girdled Iphis at his side, whom godlike Achilles gave him when he took steep Scyros, Enyeus' city.

When the others entered the tent of Atreus' son, the sons of the Achaeans stood and pledged them from all sides out of golden cups, and asked their tidings. Agamemnon, king of men, was first to ask them: "Say now, much praised Odysseus, great glory of the Achaeans, is he willing to ward off blazing fire from the ships or did he refuse; does wrath still possess his great-hearted spirit?"

Then much-enduring, godlike Odysseus said to him: "Most glorious son of Atreus, Agamemnon, king of men, he will not quench his anger; he is filled but the more with wrath, and he rejects you and your gifts. He bids you contrive among the Argives how to save the ships and men of the Achaeans. He himself threatened at the light of dawn to drag his well-benched, curved ships to the sea. And he said he would advise the others to sail for home, since never, now, will they attain the goal of lofty Ilium, for surely far-thundering Zeus holds his hand above it and its folk have plucked up courage. So he spoke; these who went with me are also here to tell these things, Ajax and the two heralds, both wise men, but old Phoenix sleeps out there, as Achilles ordered, so that he may go with him in the ships to their dear native land, tomorrow, if he wish, for he will not take him by constraint."

So he spoke, and they all were hushed in silence, wondering at his words, for vehemently did he address them. Long sat the Achaeans in troubled silence, but at last Diomedes of the mighty war cry spoke: "Most glorious son of Atreus, Agamemnon, king of men, would that you had not begged the blameless son of Peleus, offering countless gifts, for he is proud enough without that. Now you have confirmed him in his pride the more. But let us forget him, whether he go or stay. He will fight whenever the spirit in his breast compels him and the god arouses him. But now let us all do as I say. So now to bed, when you have had your fill of food and wine, for thence come strength and valor. But when the fair, rosy-fingered Dawn appears, quickly rouse the host and horses and marshal them before the ships, and you yourself fight among the first."

So he spoke, and all the kings applauded, admiring the speech of Diomedes, tamer of horses. Then they poured libations and went each to his tent. There they lay down and took the gift of sleep. [600–713]

[We omit Books X–XV. Book X tells of a night attack by Diomedes and Odysseus upon the Thracian king Rhesus, a Trojan ally, who is killed and his horses stolen. In Book XI Agamemnon, Diomedes, and Odysseus are all wounded;

Achilles sends his closest friend, Patroclus, to Nestor's hut to inquire about casualties. Nestor begs Patroclus to put on Achilles' armor, in the hope of leading the Trojans to believe that Achilles is back in the battle. In Book XII Hector smashes in a gate of the Greek camp and captures its wall. Book XIII describes the fighting at the Greek ships, where Poseidon, god of the sea, encourages the Greeks, and Ajax keeps Hector in check. In Book XIV Hera charms Zeus into inattention, and while he sleeps the Greeks gain the upper hand, Ajax stunning Hector with a stone. In Book XV Zeus awakes, scolds Hera, orders his brother Poseidon out of the fight, and bids Apollo, god of healing, restore Hector. But the Trojans redouble the fury of their attack and once more drive the Greeks back to their ships. Patroclus, delaying on his return to Achilles, sees the danger and rushes to beg aid of his friend.]

Book XVI

The deeds of Patroclus

[In lines 1–95, below, Patroclus returns to Achilles in tears, and asks and receives permission to wear his armor.]

So they fought about the well-benched ship. But Patroclus stood beside Achilles, shepherd of the people, shedding warm tears, like a dark-watered spring which pours its dusky waters over some sheer cliff. Seeing him, swift-footed, godlike Achilles pitied him and spoke to him winged words: "Why do you weep, Patroclus, like some little girl, who runs beside her mother and bids her take her up, clinging to her robe and hindering her as she would hurry on, and looking tearfully up at her until she takes her up? Like her, Patroclus, do you shed soft tears. Are you trying to tell something to the Myrmidons, or to me myself, or have you alone had news from Phthia? They say Menoetius, Actor's son, is still alive and that Aeacus' son Peleus still lives among the Myrmidons. We should indeed mourn the death of both of them. Or do you pity the Argives, as they perish upon the hollow ships for their own transgression? Speak out, hide nothing in your mind, so that we both may know."

Then, horseman Patroclus, you sighed heavily and said to him: "Achilles, Peleus' son, by far the best of the Achaeans, be not angry, so great a woe has overwhelmed the Achaeans. All those who were once the bravest lie hit and wounded on the ships. Hurt is Tydeus' son, the mighty Diomedes, and Odysseus, famed with the spear, is wounded, and Agamemnon too, and hurt is Eurypylus by an arrow in the thigh. The physicians, with their many drugs, are tending them, dressing their wounds. But you are inflexible, Achilles. May no such anger seize on me as you with your dread bravery cherish. What profit shall any other have of you, though he be born hereafter, if you do not ward off disgraceful disaster from the Argives? Cruel one, the horseman Peleus was not your father, nor Thetis your mother. The gray sea and the steep rocks gave you birth, for your mind is harsh. But if you dread some prophecy in your heart, or if your queenly mother told you one from Zeus, yet send me at least quickly forth and arouse the rest of the host of the Myrmidons, in the hope that I may be a light to the Danaans. Give me your armor to wear upon my shoulders, in the hope that the Trojans, mistaking me for you, may hold back from battle, and the warlike sons of the Achaeans may catch their breath, worn as they are. For even a brief space is a breathing spell in war. Unwearied as we are, we might easily with a shout push back the wearied soldiers toward the city from the ships and tents."

So he spoke in supplication, the great fool, for it was to be his own evil death and doom for which he prayed. Greatly distressed, swift-footed Achilles said to him: "Ah, Zeus-born Patroclus, what sort of talk is this? I care for no oracle that I know of, nor has my queenly mother told me one from Zeus. But this dreadful anger strikes to my heart and soul, when a man desires to rob one who is his equal and to take away his prize, because he surpasses him in power. It is a dreadful source of wrath to me, since I have suffered grief at heart. The maid whom the sons of the Achaeans set aside as a prize for me, whom I won with my spear as I sacked her well-walled city, this woman the mighty Agamemnon, Atreus' son, tore from my arms as though I were some unhonored vagrant. But let us pass by what has happened. It is not really possible to rage unceasingly within my heart. I had not thought to cease my anger before the war cry and the battle reached my ships. But put my glorious armor on your shoulders and lead the war-loving Myrmidons to battle, if indeed a dark cloud of Trojans has victoriously engulfed the ships and the Argives have their backs to the sea beach, with but a little share of space remaining. The whole city of the Trojans has marched forth with courage, for they do not see the front of my shining helmet close at hand. They would quickly flee and fill the ditches with their dead if mighty Agamemnon should be reconciled with me. Now they are fighting around the camp. For no spear rages in the hands of Diomedes, Tydeus' son, to ward off destruction from the Danaans, nor have I yet heard the voice of Atreus' son speaking from his hateful head. But man-slaying Hector's voice rings out, calling orders to the Trojans, and they fill the whole plain with their war cry as they conquer the Achaeans in battle. So, Patroclus, fall on them mightily, and ward off destruction from the ships, lest they burn the ships with gleaming fire and take away our dear return. Now obey the purpose of the words I impress upon your mind, so that you may win me great honor and glory among all the Danaans and they may send back the lovely maiden and proffer generous gifts as well. When you have driven them from the ships, come back. And if Hera's loud-thundering husband grant that you win glory, seek not to fight far from me with the war-loving Trojans. You will dishonor me the more. Nor do you, exulting in war and strife as you slay the Trojans, lead on toward Ilium, lest some one of the eternal gods from Olympus enter the combat, for Apollo the Warder loves them much. But turn back, when you have set the light of victory among the ships, and let them struggle on the plain." [1–96]

[The omitted lines 97–125 describe the hard plight of Ajax as he tries to defend the ships from fire. Lines 126–154, below, present Achilles urging Patroclus forth, and describe the arming of the hero and the harnessing of Achilles' famous horses, now loaned to his friend.]

"Up, Zeus-born Patroclus, driver of horses, for I see the roar of devouring fire beside the ships. Up, lest they take the ships and there be no escape. Arm yourself quickly, and I will muster the men."

So he spoke, and Patroclus donned the flashing bronze. First he put on his shins fair greaves, fitted with silver ankle clasps. Next he strapped on his chest the intricately fashioned, starry breastplate of Aeacus' swift-footed son. About his shoulders he threw his silver-studded sword of bronze, and then his great, stout shield. On his mighty head he set his well-wrought helmet, with its horsehair crest, and the plume nodded dreadfully above it. He took two stout javelins, well fitted to his hand. Only the heavy, huge, and strong spear of the blameless son of Aeacus he did not take. No other of the Achaeans could wield it, for it was Peleus' ashen spear, which Chiron gave Achilles' dear father on Pelion's peak, to be the death of heroes. Then Patroclus bade Automedon to yoke the horses quickly, Automedon, whom he honored most after Achilles, breaker of men, for he was the most trustworthy to await his call in battle. For him Automedon yoked the swift horses, Xanthus and Balius, who flew like the winds. The whirlwind Podarge bore them to Zephyr as she pastured in a meadow by the stream of Ocean. In the side-traces he put blameless Pedasus, whom Achilles captured when he took Eëtion's city and who, though mortal, ran with the immortal horses. [126–154]

[In lines 155–220 Achilles' troops, the Myrmidons, are armed, and Achilles exhorts them to battle. In lines 220–256, below, he returns to his hut and prays to Zeus to protect Patroclus.]

But Achilles stepped into his tent and opened the cover of a fair and cunningly fashioned chest, which silver-footed Thetis put on his ship to take with him, filling it full of shirts and windproof cloaks and woolen rugs. There was his well-wrought cup. From it no other man drank the bright wine, nor did he pour libation from it to any of the gods save Father Zeus. Taking it from the chest, he cleansed it first with sulphur and then washed it in fair streams of water, and himself washed his hands and poured the shining wine. Then he stood in the center of the court and prayed, and looking up to heaven poured the wine, nor was he unseen by Zeus, who rejoices in the thunder: "Lord Zeus, Pelasgian, Dodonian, who dwellest afar and dost rule storm-swept Dodona; around thee dwell the Selli, thy spokesmen, who wash not their feet and make their bed upon the ground; thou hast heard my prayer before and hast honored me and greatly chastised the host of the Achaeans; fulfill now this wish of mine as well. For I myself shall remain in the space about the ships, but my comrade I am sending with many Myrmidons to battle. Grant him glory, far-thundering Zeus; make brave the heart within his breast, so that Hector too may know whether our comrade knows how to fight alone as well, or whether his arms rage only then invincible when I go into Ares' mill. But when he has repelled the battle and the shouting from the ships, may he come back to the swift ships unscathed, with all his armor and his close-fighting comrades."

So he spoke in prayer, and Zeus the counselor heard him. But the father granted him one thing and refused the other. He granted that Patroclus should drive the war and battle from the ships, but refused that he come back safe from battle. Achilles, when he had poured a libation and made prayer to Father Zeus, went back into his tent and put the cup back in the chest, and went and took his stand before the tent, still wishing in his heart to see the dreadful combat of the Trojans and Achaeans. [220–256]

[In the omitted lines (257–430), the Myrmidons march out under Patroclus, and the Trojans, as Nestor had hoped, are terror-stricken in the belief that Achilles has returned to the fray. Patroclus joins battle and drives the Trojans from the Greek ships, killing many. When we take up the text (lines 431–461), he has attacked Sarpedon, the Lycian ally of the Trojans, and Zeus and Hera in heaven are holding a conference over Sarpedon's fate.]

When the son of crooked-counseled Cronus saw them, he was filled with pity and said to Hera, his sister and his wife: "Alas, that it is fated for Sarpedon, dearest of men to me, to die beneath the hands of Menoetius' son Patroclus. My heart is torn at the choice as I debate in mind whether to snatch him living from tearful battle and set him down in the rich land of Lycia or now to let him fall beneath the hands of Menoetius' son."

Then ox-eyed, queenly Hera answered him: "Most dreadful son of Cronus, what is this that you propose? Do you wish to release from Death, the bringer of woe, a mortal man, long given over to fate? Do so, but by no means shall all we other gods approve. Another thing I will tell you, and do you turn it over in your heart. If you send Sarpedon to his home alive, beware lest some other of the gods also desire to send his dear son from the mighty conflict. For many sons of the immortals are fighting around Priam's great city; in them you will arouse a dreadful anger. But if he is dear to you and your heart pities him, let him be slain in the mighty conflict at the hands of Menoetius' son Patroclus. But when his soul and life depart from him, send Death and sweet Sleep to bear him until they reach the land of broad Lycia. There his brethren and friends will give him solemn burial with tomb and monument, for such is the portion of the dead."

So she spoke, and the father of gods and men failed not to heed her. But he sent a bloody rain upon the earth in honor of his dear son whom Patroclus was to slay in fertile Troy, far from his native land. [431–461]

[In the omitted lines (462–683) Sarpedon is slain and stripped of his arms, but Apollo, under orders from Zeus, rescues his body. In the final passage translated from this book (lines 684–867) Patroclus disobeys Achilles' order and pursues the Trojans to their walls. Apollo in person pushes him back, stuns and disarms him. Soon after, the Trojan Euphorbus wounds him, and Hector kills him.]

Patroclus, with an order to his horses and Automedon, went after the Trojans and Lycians, and greatly did he err, poor fool. If he had kept the command of Peleus' son he would have escaped black death's evil fate. But ever stronger than the mind of men is that of Zeus; sometimes he puts even a brave man to flight and easily takes away victory, yet sometimes of himself he urges a man to battle. He it was who then aroused the spirit in Patroclus' breast.

Whom then did you slay first, whom last, Patroclus, when the gods called you deathwards? First Adrastus and Autonous and Echeclus and Perimus, Meges' son, and Epistor and Melanippus; then Elasus and Melius and Pylartes—these he slew; each of the rest remembered flight.

Then the sons of the Achaeans would have taken high-gated Troy by the hands of Patroclus, for he raged forward and about him with his spear, had not Phoebus Apollo stood upon the well-built tower with evil purpose toward him, aiding the Trojans. Thrice Patroclus reached the corner of the lofty wall and thrice Apollo forced him back, striking his gleaming shield with immortal hands. But when a fourth time Patroclus reached forward, like a god, Apollo gave a dreadful shout and spoke to him winged words: "Draw back, Zeus-born Patroclus. It is not fated the brave Trojans' city should now be overthrown by your spear, nor even by Achilles, who is better far than you."

So he spoke, and Patroclus fell far back, avoiding the wrath of the unerring Apollo.

But Hector checked his single-hoofed horses in the Scaean gates; for he debated whether he should drive them back and fight again in the tumult or should call to the people to gather within the wall. As he pondered this, Phoebus Apollo stood beside him, in the likeness of a strong and mighty man, Asius, who was a maternal uncle of horse-taming Hector, own brother of Hecuba, and son of Dymas, who dwelt in Phrygia by Sangarius' streams. In this man's likeness Zeus's son Apollo addressed him: "Hector, why do you cease from battle? You ought not. Would I were as much your better as I am your inferior. Surely then you would withdraw from battle at your cost. Come, drive your strong-hoofed horses after Patroclus, in the hope that you may take him, and Apollo may give you glory."

So speaking, the god went back among the strife of heroes, and glorious Hector ordered prudent Cebriones to whip the horses into battle. But Apollo went and entered the fray and sent a disastrous tumult on the Argives and gave glory to the Trojans and to Hector. Hector let the other Danaans be and did not slay them, but drove his strong-hoofed horses after Patroclus. And Patroclus, on the other side, leaped from his chariot to the ground, holding his spear in his left hand; in the other he grasped a shining, jagged stone, which his hand covered. He braced himself and threw it; neither did he withdraw much from his foe, nor did he hurl the missile in vain, but hit Hector's charioteer Cebriones, the bastard son of far-famed Priam, as he held the reins of the horses. He hit him in the forehead with the sharp stone. The stone crushed both his brows, nor did the bone hold firm. His eyes fell to the ground in the dust before his feet. Like a diver he plunged from the well-made chariot and his spirit left his bones. In scorn you said to him, horseman Patroclus: "Well, well, the man is fast, he dives so easily. If he were on the fishy deep this fellow could feed many men, diving from his ship for oysters, even though it were stormy, so easily he now dives from his chariot on the plain. Even among the Trojans they have divers."

So speaking, he strode toward the hero Cebriones, with the spring of a lion which, ravaging the stall, is wounded in the chest, and his own valor destroys him. So you leaped eagerly upon Cebriones, Patroclus, and Hector on the other side leaped from his chariot to the ground. The two contended over Cebriones like two lions who battle on some mountain peak for a slain doe, both of them hungry and both high of heart. So the two raisers of the war cry, Menoetius' son Patroclus, and glorious Hector, rushed about Cebriones eager to cut one another's flesh with the pitiless bronze. Hector, when he had seized the corpse's head, would not let go, and Patroclus opposite him held to a foot. And then the rest of the Trojans and Danaans joined together in mighty battle.

As Eurus and Notus strive with one another to shake a deep wood in a mountain's glens—a wood of oaks and ash and slender cornel trees, which toss their tapering branches at each other with a fearful din and the noise of those that break—so the Trojans and Achaeans rushed on and slew each other, and neither thought of baneful flight. Many sharp spears were planted about Cebriones, many winged arrows leaping from the string, and many great stones smote the shields of those that fought about him. And in the whirls of dust the vast man vastly lay, his horsemanship forgotten.

As long as the sun was astride the heavens, the weapons struck both sides and soldiers fell, but when the sun passed on to ox-loosing time, then the Achaeans were superior beyond their fate. They dragged the hero Cebriones out of range of the missiles away from the tumult of the Trojans and stripped the armor from his shoulders and Patroclus rushed forward toward the Trojans with an evil purpose. Thrice then he darted forward, like swift Ares, with a dreadful shout, and thrice he slew nine men. But when a fourth time he rushed forward like a god, then, Patroclus, the end of life appeared to you. For dreadful Phoebus met you in the mighty conflict. But Patroclus did not see him as he passed through the tumult, for he was shrouded in thick mist as he came toward him. The god stood behind Patroclus and smote his back and broad shoulders with his palm, and Patroclus' eyes whirled round and round. Then Phoebus Apollo threw the helmet off Patroclus' head, and the plumed and crested helmet rattled as it rolled beneath the horses' feet, and its horsehair crest was fouled with blood and dust. Before that time no god had suffered the helmet with its horsehair crest to be fouled with dust, but it had guarded the head and handsome brow of the godlike warrior Achilles. Now Zeus gave it to Hector to wear upon his head, but his death was close upon him. In Patroclus' hands the long-shadowed spear was shattered—all of it, heavy, huge, strong, well-tipped. From his shoulders the fringed shield with its strap fell to the ground, and his breastplate was undone by lord Apollo, son of Zeus. Doom seized his mind, and his glorious limbs grew feeble and he stood astounded. From close behind a Dardanian struck him with a sharp spear in the back between the shoulders, Panthous' son Euphorbus, who surpassed all of his age with the spear and in horsemanship and swiftness of foot. Even on that day he had brought down twenty men from their chariots, though coming with a chariot for the first time himself, learning the art of war. He it was who first cast a missile against you, horseman Patroclus, but did not slay you; rather, he ran back and mingled with the throng, dragging his ashen spear from your flesh, nor did he abide Patroclus even when unarmed in conflict. And Patroclus, overwhelmed by the god's blow and the spear, shrank back into the throng of his companions, avoiding his fate.

When Hector saw great-hearted Patroclus drawing back, wounded by the sharp bronze, he drew close to him through the lines and wounded him with his spear in the lower flank and drove the bronze through. He fell with a crash, and brought great sorrow to the host of the Achaeans. As when a lion has worsted a tireless boar in conflict, when, with high hearts, they battle for some scant spring upon a mountain's peaks and both would drink, and the lion with his might overcomes the quickly panting boar, so Hector, Priam's son, deprived Menoetius' brave son of his life with the spear, from close at hand, after he had slain many. Boasting, Hector spoke to him winged words: "Patroclus, surely you thought to reach our city and take away the day of freedom from the Trojan women and lead them in your ships to your own dear native land, fool that you are. Before them, Hector's swift horses stretch their feet to battle. And I myself am outstanding with the spear among the Trojans, I that ward off from them the day of doom. The vultures shall eat you here, poor wretch, nor shall Achilles, for all his valor, help you, he who, though he remained behind, doubtless gave you many an order as you went: 'Horse-driving Patroclus, come not back to my hollow ships until you split upon the breast of Hector his tunic red with blood.' So he doubtless spoke to you and moved your foolish heart."

Then in your weakness you addressed him, horseman Patroclus: "Great are your boasts now, Hector. For Zeus, Cronus' son, and Apollo have given you victory, they who slew me easily. For they themselves have stripped the armor from my shoulders, but if twenty like you had met they would all have perished here, slain by my spear. But a baneful fate and the son of Leto slew me, and, among men, Euphorbus. You are third in my slaying. Another thing I will tell you, and do you turn it over in your heart. You shall not yourself live long; already Death stands close beside you, and mighty Fate, to be slain by the hands of Achilles, Aeacus' blameless son."

As he said this, the end of death enwrapped him, and his soul fled from his limbs and passed into the house of Death, bewailing its fate, forsaking manliness and youth. And glorious Hector spoke to him, even when dead: "Patroclus, why do you foretell sudden death for me? Who knows whether Achilles, son of fair-haired Thetis, will not be the first to lose his life, slain by my spear?"

So speaking, he set his heel upon him and drew the spear from the wound and pushed him from the spear upon his back. Immediately he set out with the spear after Automedon, the godlike squire of the swift-footed son of Aeacus, for he wished to smite him, but he was borne away by the swift, immortal horses that the gods gave as glorious gifts to Peleus. [684–867]

[In Book XVII, omitted here, Hector strips Achilles' armor from Patroclus' body, and puts it on. The Greeks, fighting desperately, retreat with Patroclus' body to the camp.]

Book XVIII

The shield of Achilles

[In lines 1–461, omitted here, Achilles, hearing of Patroclus' death, is half-crazed with grief. His mother Thetis comes from the sea to comfort him, and promises to get him new arms from Hephaestus. Achilles goes to the trench outside the camp, and scares away the Trojans with his battle cry. Hector, overbold, camps on the plain, against the advice of his kinsman Polydamas. In the lines translated below (462–617) Thetis fulfills her promise, and the poet describes the making of the arms, and especially of the shield. Compare and contrast the similar description in *Aeneid* VIII.]

Then the renowned lame god answered her: "Take courage. Let not these things disturb your mind. Would that I could as surely hide him away from death the bringer of woe when dread fate comes upon him, as he shall have fair arms of such a sort that any one of numerous mankind will marvel when he sees them."

So speaking, he left her there and went back to his bellows. He turned them on the fire and bade them fall to work. Twenty bellows all blow on the melting pits, sending out a strong blast for every need—now to help him when in haste and now to end the task according to his will and profit. He threw into the fire hard copper and tin and precious gold and silver. Then he placed a great anvil on the block and seized a mighty hammer in one hand and grasped the tongs in the other.

First he made a great, stout shield, adorning it on every side, and put a threefold glittering, shining rim about it, and fastened to it a silver strap. There were five layers in the shield itself, and on it he set many devices with his cunning skill.

On it he fashioned earth and sea, the unwearying sun and the full moon, and all the wondrous signs that wreathe the heavens—the Pleiades and Hyades, mighty Orion, and the Bear, that they also call the Wain, which turns in the same place watching Orion, and has alone no share in Ocean's baths.

On it he fashioned two towns of mortal men, most fair. In one there was a wedding feast, and they were escorting the brides from their chambers through the city by the light of shining torches, and the wedding hymn rose loudly. Dancing boys whirled round and round, and in their midst the flutes and lyres made music. The women, each in her doorway, watched with wonder. The people were gathered in the market place, where a dispute had arisen, and two men were quarreling about the blood-price of some murdered man. One said that he had given all, explaining it to the people; the other denied receiving it; and each was eager to win his case before the judge. The people applauded both, as both sides had supporters. Heralds held back the people, and the old men sat upon polished stones in a sacred circle and held the staves of loud-voiced heralds in their hands. Leaning on these, they rose and gave their verdict, each in turn. In the center lay two talents of gold, to give to him who spoke the straightest verdict.

About the other city sat two armies, gleaming in their armor. Their purpose lay between two choices, to destroy the town or each to take the half of all the wealth the lovely city held within it. But the citizens would not yet yield and were arming for an ambush. Their dear wives and tender children stood upon the wall to guard it, and with them those men upon whom age had come. The warriors were starting out, led by Ares and Pallas Athena, both wrought in gold and clad in golden garments, and both fair and tall, and splendid in their arms, as gods should be. The soldiers were of lesser stature. When they came to the place where it suited them to set their ambush, by the river, at the watering place of all the flocks, there they sat down, wrapped in gleaming bronze. Two lookouts lay apart from the soldiers, waiting to see the sheep and crooked-horned cattle. These soon appeared, and with them came two herdsmen, playing on panpipes, with no thought of treachery. When the men caught sight of them, they rushed upon them and quickly then cut off the herds of cattle and the fair flocks of shining sheep and slew the herdsmen by them. But when the besiegers, sitting before the assembly place, heard the great din about the cattle, they straightway leaped up behind high-stepping horses and drove toward it, arriving in a moment. Then they formed their lines and fought a battle by the river's bank and hurled their bronze-tipped spears at one another. Strife and Uproar moved among them, and baneful Fate as well, keeping one man alive though wounded, another free from wounds, while she dragged by the feet amid the din another who had perished, and she wore upon her shoulders a robe all reddened with men's blood. Like living men they joined and fought, and dragged dead bodies from each other.

On it he placed a soft fallow earth, a rich plowland, wide and thrice plowed. Many plowmen plowed thereon this way and that, turning their teams about. And when they had turned and reached the field's edge once again, a man stepped up and put into their hands a cup of honey-sweet wine; and they turned again along the furrows, eager to reach once more the edge of the deep fallow land. The earth was black behind them, and like earth freshly plowed, though wrought in gold. It was a very wondrous work.

On it he placed a royal field. Here reapers moved with sharp sickles in their hands. Some handfuls fell to earth along the swath, and others the sheave binders tied with bands of straw. Three binders followed, and behind came children gleaning, who never ceased to give them armfuls. The king stood in their midst in silence by the swaths, holding his staff and glad at heart. Heralds were preparing dinner underneath a distant oak, and were dressing a great bull which they had sacrificed. And the women were strewing much white barley on the meat as a dinner for the reapers.

On it he placed a fair golden vineyard, heavy-laden with fruit. There were dark clusters on it, and it was all held on silver vine props. Around it he made a ditch of blue enamel and a fence of tin. There was only one pathway through it, along which the vintagers would go when they harvested the vineyard. Light-hearted youths and maidens bore the honey-sweet fruit in woven baskets. In their midst a lad played on his lyre a tune to set one dreaming, and in a delicate voice sang a fair Linus song. Stamping in unison, they followed with shouts and dancing, beating the measure.

On it he placed a herd of straight-horned cattle. These were wrought in gold and tin, and pressed lowing from the barnyard to their pasture on a singing river by a bed of waving reeds. Four herdsmen in gold went with the cattle, followed by nine swift-footed dogs. Two grim lions had caught a bellowing bull among the foremost cattle, and he was bawling loudly as they dragged him off, and dogs and youths went after him. The lions, having broken the hide of the great bull, were gulping down the entrails and dark blood, and the herdsmen vainly set on the swift hounds with their urgings. The dogs shrank from biting the lions, but stood close by and barked and then fell back.

On it the renowned lame god placed a great pasture of sheep in a fair glen—folds and roofed huts and pens.

On it the renowned lame god placed a dancing floor like that which once in broad Cnossus Daedalus made for Ariadne of the lovely tresses. There youths and dearly courted maidens danced, holding each other's wrists. The maids wore robes of fine linen and the lads well-woven shirts, just touched with olive oil. The maidens wore fair garlands and the lads bore golden daggers, hanging from silver belts. Sometimes they ran most easily on skillful feet, as when a potter sits and fits his hand about his wheel and tries it, if it run; sometimes they ran in lines toward one another. A great throng stood in delight about the charming dance, and among them a divine bard played on his lyre, and two tumblers, beginning their sport, spun through their midst.

On it he placed the great might of Ocean around the outer rim of the well-wrought shield.

When he had made the great and mighty shield, he made for him a breastplate brighter than the gleam of fire, and he made for him a heavy helmet fitted to the temples, fair and subtly fashioned, and he set a golden crest upon it, and made him greaves of pliant tin.

When the renowned lame god had fashioned all the armor, he took it and laid it before Achilles' mother, and she swept like a hawk down from snow-clad Olympus, bearing the glittering armor from Hephaestus. [462–617]

[Books XIX–XXI are omitted. In XIX, Achilles is eager for battle, despite his mother's warning that he cannot live long after Hector. He is formally reconciled with Agamemnon. The women lament over the body of Patroclus. Achilles, who refuses to eat, is nourished by nectar and ambrosia supplied by his goddess mother. As he puts on the armor, his horse Xanthus foretells his death. In XX, Zeus withdraws the order given in Book VIII, and the gods come down to earth to take part in the fighting. Achilles forces the Trojans to give way; Aeneas faces him, and when in danger of death is rescued by Poseidon, who knows that Aeneas' descendants are fated to be lords of Troy. Hector is rescued from Achilles by Apollo, but many others are slain. In XXI, Achilles is nearly drowned by the river Xanthus (Scamander) which is angry with him for having choked its stream with dead bodies, but Hephaestus pits his fire against the water. The gods themselves do battle. Apollo, in the likeness of Hector, entices Achilles in pursuit away from the city; meanwhile the rest of the Trojans escape within their walls.]

Book XXII

The killing of Hector

[In the omitted lines (1–20), the Greeks approach the wall of Troy, and Apollo reveals his identity to the indignant Achilles. In lines 21–130, below, Achilles returns to the main battle. Priam, seeing him from the tower, begs Hector to withdraw within the city walls. His mother Hecuba adds her entreaties, but Hector, unpersuaded, decides to face Achilles on the plain.]

So speaking, he strode off toward the city in his pride, rushing like a prize-winning horse with its chariot, as it runs easily, stretching out across the plain. So Achilles plied swift feet and knees.

Old Priam was the first to see him, all shining as he rushed across the plain, like the star that rises with the autumn, and its rays shine bright to many men in the darkness of the night. Orion's Dog they call it, and it is the brightest, but an evil omen, and it brings much fever to unhappy mortals. So his bronze gleamed upon his breast as he ran on. The old man groaned and raised his hands aloft and beat his head and cried out with a mighty groan in supplication to his beloved son, who stood before the gates, insatiably eager to do battle with Achilles. The old man stretched his hands out to him and spoke piteous words: "Hector, dear child, please do not await this man alone, far from the others, lest you quickly meet your fate, overcome by Peleus' son, since he is much the stronger, the cruel man. Would the gods loved him as I do; then would the dogs and vultures soon devour him as he lay dead and a great grief would pass from my heart. For he has bereft me of many noble sons, slaying them or selling them to distant islands. Even now there are two sons, Lycaon and Polydorus, whom I cannot see among the Trojans gathered in the city. Laothoe bore them to me, that queen of women. If they are in his camp alive, we shall ransom them with bronze and gold; it lies within, for the famous old man Altes gave much to his daughter. But if they are already dead and in the house of Hades, it is a great grief to my heart and to their mother, to us who begot them. But the grief will be less lasting to the rest of the people unless you too perish, slain at Achilles' hands. Come, enter within the wall, my child, that you may save the Trojan men and women and not give great glory to the son of Peleus, and be yourself deprived of your dear life. Still more, have pity on me, wretched and ill-starred, yet still living. For Cronus' son, our father, will destroy me with a bitter doom upon the threshold of old age, when I have looked on many woes, my sons destroyed, my daughters dragged away, my chambers ravaged, the tender children dashed to the ground in dreadful conflict and my sons' wives dragged off by the harsh hands of the Achaeans. Me, last of all, the ravening dogs will drag away before the door, when someone by thrust or cast of the sharp bronze has taken the spirit from my limbs. The dogs I reared in my halls, fed from my table, and set to guard my door shall drink my blood, mad at heart, and lie in my courtyard. All things become a young man as he lies slain in war, cleft by the sharp bronze; dead though he be, all things are fair, whatever shows. But when dogs insult the gray head and private parts of an old man as he lies slain, that is indeed the most piteous sight for wretched mortals."

So spoke the old man, and he grasped his gray hairs with his hands and tore them from his head; yet he could not move the heart of Hector. The mother on the other side lamented and shed tears, loosening the fold of her robe, and with her other hand she held up her breast and weeping spoke winged words to him: "Hector, my child, revere this and have pity on me, if ever I gave you this breast that brought forgetfulness of care. Remember these things, dear child, and ward off our enemy from within the walls, nor stand as champion against him, stubborn one, for if he slays you I shall not weep for you as you lie upon your bed, dear child, even I who bore you, nor shall your richly dowered wife. Far away from us, beside the Argives' ships, the swift dogs will devour you."

So the two weeping spoke to their dear son with many a supplication, but they could not move the heart of Hector. He stood and awaited the approach of huge Achilles. As a mountain serpent by its hole awaits a man, when it has fed on noisome herbs and a dreadful rage has entered it and it gives a baleful glance as it coils about its hole, so Hector with unconquerable might would not withdraw, but propped his shield against the jutting tower and in his anguish said to his great-hearted soul: "If I enter the gates and walls, Polydamas will be the first to heap reproach upon me, he who bade me lead the Trojans to the city during the fatal night now past, when godlike Achilles arose. But I would not heed him, and far better would it be. Now, since I have destroyed the people by my blind folly, I am ashamed before the Trojans and the Trojan women with their trailing robes, lest some other, inferior to me, say: 'Hector brought ruin on the people by his trust in his own strength.' So they will say, and then it were far better for me to face Achilles and slay him and so return, or myself to perish gloriously before the city. Or what if I put down my bossed shield and heavy helmet and lean my spear against the wall and go myself and meet blameless Achilles and promise him to give Helen to the sons of Atreus to take away, and with her all the possessions Alexander brought in his hollow ships to Troy, which was the beginning of the quarrel, and furthermore to divide among the Achaeans all else this city hides and thereafter require from the Trojans an oath on the part of the elders to hide nothing but to divide in two parts all the wealth the lovely city holds—but why does my soul say this to me? Let me beware lest I go and reach him but he show me neither mercy nor honor, and slay me unarmed, helpless as a woman, when I have put off my armor. There is no way now to chat with him from oak or rock, like lass and lad, as lass and lad chat on together. Better will it be if I go forth to meet him in anger with all speed. Then let us see to which of us the Olympian will give the glory."

[21–130]

[In the omitted lines 131–305, Hector, in fear, is chased by Achilles three times around the walls of Troy. Athena enters the battle disguised as Hector's brother Deiphobus, and gives Hector false encouragement. Athena is helping Achilles, and Hector's spear cannot pierce the god-wrought shield of Achilles. Too late the Trojan discovers Athena's treachery. In lines 306–375, below, the final struggle is described; Achilles deals Hector his death-blow, and then makes an exulting speech, to which Hector feebly replies.]

So speaking, he drew the sharp sword that hung great and mighty at his side, and he crouched and darted like a high-soaring eagle that swoops earthward through dark clouds to seize a tender lamb or cowering hare. So Hector darted, brandishing his sharp sword. Achilles rushed forward, and his heart was filled with a wild fury. He held his fair and subtly fashioned shield before his breast and his helmet nodded with its shining, four-ridged crest, and around it waved the fair golden plumes which Hephaestus had set thick upon it. As the evening star moves among the other stars in the darkness of the night—it is the fairest star that stands in heaven—such was the radiance from the sharp spear point which Achilles brandished in his right hand with evil purpose against godlike Hector as he looked at his fair flesh, to see where it would be most yielding. All the rest of Hector's flesh was covered by the fair bronze armor he had taken when he slew mighty Patroclus, but it showed through where the collarbones separate the neck from the shoulder, the hollow of the throat, where life's destruction is swiftest. There godlike Achilles struck him with his spear as he rushed forward, and the point pierced straight through his soft neck. But the bronze-weighted ash did not sever his windpipe, so that he might speak to him and answer him with words. He fell in the dust, and godlike Achilles boasted: "Hector, you thought to be safe in despoiling Patroclus and took no heed of me, who was far away, fool that you were. I, his far mightier comrade, was left behind, far off by the hollow ships, I who have loosed your knees. You the dogs and birds shall rend shamefully, but him the Achaeans shall give burial."

Feebly Hector of the glancing helmet said to him: "I beg you by your life, by your knees and by your parents, do not let the dogs of the Achaeans devour me beside the ships, but accept ample bronze and gold, the gifts my father and my queenly mother will give to you, and give my body back home, that the Trojans and the Trojans' wives may give me in death the meed of fire."

Swift-footed Achilles looked at him scornfully and said: "Dog, beseech me neither by my knees nor by my parents. Would that my angry heart would let me cut off your raw flesh and eat it, for what you have done to me. There is none who could ward the dogs off from your head, not though they bring ten and twenty times your ransom and weigh it out here and promise yet more besides; not even though Dardanian Priam should bid them buy you for your weight in gold, not even so shall your queenly mother lay you in your bed and weep for you she bore herself, but the dogs and birds shall devour you entirely."

Then, as he died, Hector of the glancing helmet said to him: "Well do I know you as I look upon you; there was no hope that I could move you, for surely your heart is iron in your breast. Take care now lest I be cause of anger of the gods against you on that day when Paris and Phoebus Apollo shall slay you for all your valor at the Scaean gates."

As he said this, the end of death enwrapped him. His soul fled from his limbs and passed into the house of Death, bewailing his fate and forsaking manliness and youth. Even when he had died, godlike Achilles said to him: "Die, and my fate I will accept whenever Zeus and the other immortal gods desire to fulfill it."

He spoke, and dragged the bronze spear from the body and set it down apart. He stripped the bloody armor from Hector's shoulders, and the rest of the sons of the Achaeans ran about him and gazed at Hector's stature and surpassing beauty, nor did any stand beside him without giving him a wound. And thus would one speak, glancing at his neighbor: "Hector is much softer to touch than when he burned the ships with blazing fire."

So one would say, and deal him a wound as he stood beside him. [306–375]

[In the omitted lines (376–394), Achilles addresses the Greeks, saying that Hector deserved death, and that Patroclus is avenged. In lines 395–515, below, Achilles disfigures Hector's corpse, dragging it behind his chariot to the Greek camp and in full view of Hector's parents who are watching on the walls of Troy. The news of Hector's death is brought to his wife Andromache, who had not known that he had remained outside the walls to fight Achilles. With her lament the book comes to a close.]

He spoke, and devised foul treatment for godlike Hector. The tendons of both feet he pierced behind from heel to ankle and threaded them with ox-hide thongs and tied them to his chariot and allowed the head to drag. He mounted the chariot, held aloft the glorious armor, and lashed the horses to a gallop, and not unwillingly the pair flew off. A cloud of dust rose from the dragging Hector; his dark hair spread about, and all in the dust lay his head that was so fair before; but now Zeus gave him to his enemies to mutilate in his own native land.

So his head was all befouled with dust, and his mother tore her hair and cast her shining veil far from her and gave a great shriek when she saw her son. Then his dear father gave a piteous groan and the people around him were filled with cries and lamentations throughout the city. Most like this it was: as though all towering Ilium burned from top to bottom. For the people could scarcely hold the old man, who was beside himself with grief and wished to go out from the Dardanian gates. He rolled in the dust and begged them all, calling each man by name: "Stop, my friends, and despite your care for me let me pass out alone from the city and go to the ships of the Achaeans. I will beseech that wicked man of violent deeds, in the hope that perhaps he will respect my years and have pity on my old age. He has such a father, Peleus, who begot and reared him to be a trouble to the Trojans; he has caused me more woe than all the rest, so many stalwart sons of mine has he slain. Yet I weep not so much for all, though grieved for them, as for one, sharp grief for whom will bring me down into the house of Death, even Hector. Would he had died in my arms; then we should have had our fill of weeping and mourning, his mother who bore him, ill-starred woman, and I myself."

So he spoke, weeping, and the citizens wailed in answer. And Hecuba led the Trojan women in shrill lamentation: "My child, wretched am I. Why should I live, suffering dreadful grief now you are dead? Night and day you were my pride throughout the city, the protection of all Trojan men and women in the town. You were their greatest glory while you lived, but now death and fate have found you out."

So she spoke, weeping. Now Hector's wife had not yet heard the news, for no true messenger had gone to tell her that her husband remained outside the gates. She was weaving at the loom in the inmost corner of her lofty house, a double web of purple, and was working into its pattern many-colored flowers. She bade her fair-tressed handmaids in the house to set a great tripod on the fire, that a warm bath might be ready for Hector when he returned from battle, foolish that she was, nor did she realize that very far from baths bright-eyed Athena had slain him at Achilles' hands. She heard the wails and lamentations from the tower and her limbs shook and the shuttle fell from her hand to the floor. Again she spoke to her fair-tressed handmaids: "Come, two of you follow me; I will see what has happened. I heard the voice of my revered mother-in-law, and the heart in my breast leaps to my throat, and my knees are stiff beneath me. Some woe is near to Priam's children. But I am dreadfully afraid lest godlike Achilles has cut off my rash Hector alone from the city and is driving him toward the plain and will end his perilous courage, which possessed him, since he would never remain amid the press of warriors but ran far out in front, yielding in his might to none."

So speaking, she rushed through the hall like one beside herself, with throbbing heart, and the handmaidens went with her. When she reached the tower and the throng of men, she stood upon the wall with anxious gaze and saw him being dragged before the city. The swift horses were dragging him ruthlessly to the hollow ships of the Achaeans. Black night enwrapped her eyes and she fell back and breathed out her spirit. Far from her head she let the shining headdress fall, the fillet and the net, the braided headband and the veil which golden Aphrodite gave her on that day when Hector of the glancing helmet wed her from Eëtion's home, after he had given many gifts. Around her stood many of her husband's sisters and her brother's wives, who held her, in her deadly fright, among them. When she had caught her breath and the spirit had returned into her heart, she began to cry in lamentation to the Trojan women: "Hector, wretched am I. For we were born to a single fate, you in Troy in Priam's house and I at Thebe under wooded Placus in Eëtion's house, who reared me when I was a child, unhappy he, unhappy me. Would I had not been born! Now you have gone to Death's house beneath the depths of earth, but me you leave to a hateful grief, a widow in your halls. Your child is still a feeble infant whom you and I, unhappy ones, begot. You will be no protection for him, Hector, since you are dead, nor he to you. For if he escapes the lamentable war of the Achaeans, toil and woe will ever he his hereafter, for others will remove the boundaries of his fields. The day of orphanage robs a child of all his playmates; he is utterly bowed down and his cheeks are wet with tears. In his want the lad goes up to his father's comrades, pulling one by the cloak and another by the tunic, and when they have pity on him, one holds up his cup a moment to his mouth and wets his lips but does not wet his palate, and some child from the feast, with both his parents living, abuses him, striking him with his hands and upbraiding him with words: 'Get out, there; your father is not feasting with us.' And to his widowed mother the lad goes back in tears—Astyanax, who formerly upon his father's lap ate only marrow and the rich fat of sheep, and when sleep took him and he ceased his play, he slept in his bed within his nurse's arms, in a soft bed, his heart full of good cheer. Now he will suffer much for want of his dear father. Astyanax the Trojans call him, for you alone protected their gates and their long walls. Now as you lie naked beside the curved ships, far from your parents, writhing worms shall eat you when the dogs have had their fill. Fine, fair garments made by women's hands lie in your halls, but all these I will burn with blazing fire, not as any help to you, since you shall not lie in them, but as an honor from the Trojans and the Trojan women."

So she spoke, weeping, and the women wailed in answer. [395–515]

[In Book XXIII, omitted, the ghost of Patroclus, appearing to Achilles, begs for speedy burial, and the next day a sumptuous funeral is held. Twelve prisoners of war, horses, and dogs are killed on the pyre, and in the athletic sports that follow—chariot and foot-races, archery, boxing and wrestling—Achilles presides and gives the prizes. The funeral games in *Aeneid* V are inspired by this book.]

Book XXIV

PRIAM RANSOMS HECTOR'S BODY

[In the omitted lines (1–471) Hector's body has lain unburied and for eleven days in succession has been dragged round the tomb of Patroclus. The gods decide to intervene. Apollo has saved the corpse from corruption and mutilation; Thetis bids Achilles let it be ransomed, and Iris, the rainbow-messenger, tells Priam to go with gold by night into the Greek camp. The messenger-god Hermes guides him thither. In lines 471–691, below, Priam's appearance in Achilles' hut creates amazement. His pitiful plea for the body of his son moves Achilles to compassion, though he is annoyed with Priam's impatience to obtain his request and be gone. While the body is being made ready, Achilles persuades Priam to break bread with him; beds are then prepared, and all go to rest. While the Greeks sleep, Priam is guided by Hermes out of the camp.]

The old man went straight into the lodge where sat Achilles, dear to Zeus. He found him within, and his companions sat apart; two only, the heroic Automedon and Alcimus, scion of Ares, waited busily upon him. Achilles had just ceased from eating and drinking, and the table still stood beside him. Great Priam came in unnoticed, and, standing close by, seized in his hands Achilles' knees and kissed the hands, dreadful and murderous, that had slain many of his sons. As when a sore folly overtakes a man who slays some fellow in his native land and comes to the country of others, to a rich man's house, and wonder falls on those who see him, so Achilles wondered as he saw the godlike Priam, and the rest wondered and looked at one another. Priam addressed him then in supplication: "Remember your father, godlike Achilles, as old as I am, on the cruel threshold of old age. It may be that the dwellers round about mistreat him evilly and there is no one to ward off war and ruin. But he, hearing of you alive, rejoices in his heart and hopes all his days to see his dear son coming back from Troy. But I am utterly forlorn, since I begot the best sons in broad Troy, yet none of them, I think, is left. Fifty I had, when the sons of the Achaeans came. Nineteen were from one womb, and the rest the women in my halls bore to me. Impetuous Ares loosed the knees of many, but he who was my very own, who defended the city and its men, him you lately slew as he fought for his native land—Hector. For his sake I now come to the ships of the Achaeans, to ransom him from you, and I bring boundless gifts. Come, Achilles, revere the gods and have pity upon me, remembering your father. I am even more to be pitied, who have borne what no other mortal upon earth has borne, to lift my lips to the hand of the man who slew my son."

So Priam spoke, and he aroused in Achilles a longing to weep for his father. He took the old man by the hand and gently put him aside. The two of them, with their memories, wept—the one lay bent before Achilles' feet, mourning loudly for man-slaying Hector, while Achilles mourned for his father, and again for Patroclus, and the sound of their weeping rose throughout the house. But when godlike Achilles had had his fill of weeping, and the longing had passed from his heart and limbs, he arose at once from his chair and drew the old man up by his hand, pitying his gray head and gray beard, and he spoke and addressed to him winged words: "Unhappy man, you have indeed borne many sorrows in your heart. How did you dare to come alone to the ships of the Achaeans, before the eyes of the man who slew so many of your noble sons? Your heart is of iron. But come, sit down upon a chair and let us allow our woes to rest in our hearts, however grieved we are. There is no gain in chilling grief. For the gods so spun the fate of wretched mortals that they should live in sorrow, whereas the gods themselves are sorrowless. For two jars stand upon Zeus' threshold, full of the gifts he gives—one of evil, one of good. He to whom Zeus, that rejoices in the thunder, gives a mixture, meets sometimes evil, sometimes good; him to whom he gives hateful gifts he makes contemptible, and an evil, ravenous hunger pursues him upon the glorious earth, and he wanders about, honored by neither gods nor mortals. So the gods gave glorious gifts to Peleus from his birth, for he surpassed all men in wealth and plenty and ruled the Myrmidons, and the gods gave him, though a mortal, a goddess for his wife. But evil, too, God sent him, that no brood of mighty children was born to him in his halls, but he begot one short-lived son. Not even now do I protect him in his age, but very far from my native land I sit in Troy, vexing you and your children. You too, old man, were once blest, so we hear. All that Lesbos above, the seat of Macar, encloses, all that Phrygia inland and the boundless Hellespont—all these peoples you surpassed, old man, they say, in wealth and sons. But from the time that they who dwell in heaven brought this woe, ever about your city are battles and slayings of men. Bear up, nor weep unceasingly in your heart, for you will accomplish nothing by grieving for your son, nor shall you bring him back to life; sooner will you endure some other woe."

Then godlike, aged Priam answered him: "Sit me not yet upon the chair, Zeus-nurtured one, while Hector lies untended among the tents, but release him quickly, that I may see him with my eyes; and do you receive the abundant ransom which we bring you. May you have joy of it and reach your native land, when once you have let me live and see the sun's light."

Swift-footed Achilles looked at him askance and said: "Anger me no more, old man. I myself intend to release Hector to you; a messenger came to me from Zeus, my mother who bore me, the daughter of the old man of the sea. And I know you in my heart, Priam, nor does it escape me that some one of the gods led you to the swift ships of the Achaeans. For no mortal would dare come, not even though very young, into our camp, for he could not slip past the guards nor could he easily push back the fastening of our gates. Therefore, arouse my spirit in my grief no further, lest I spare not even you yourself, old man, in the tents, though you are a suppliant, and lest I transgress the commands of Zeus."

So he spoke, and the old man was afraid and obeyed his words. Peleus' son leaped from the door of the house like a lion; not alone, but two squires went with him, the hero Automedon and Alcimus, they whom Achilles honored most of his companions after the dead Patroclus. They then loosed the horses and mules from the yoke and brought in the herald, the old man's crier, and seated him in a chair, and from the well-polished wagon they took the boundless ransom for the head of Hector. But they left two cloaks and a well-woven shirt, so that Achilles might dress the body and give it to be carried home. He summoned the handmaids and bade them wash the body and anoint it, taking it away, so that Priam might not see his son, lest in his distress of heart he might not control his anger on seeing his son, and Achilles' heart be stirred to anger and he slay him and transgress the commands of Zeus. When, therefore, the handmaids had washed Hector and anointed him with oil, they threw a fair mantle and a shirt about him, and Achilles himself raised him and placed him on a bier, and his comrades with him lifted it to the well-polished cart. Then Achilles groaned and called his dear companion's name: "Be not angry with me, Patroclus, if even in Hades you learn that I have released Hector to his dear father, when he gave me no unseemly ransom. To you in turn I shall give a fitting share of these things too."

So spoke godlike Achilles, and went back into the lodge and sat down by the further wall in the richly fashioned chair from which he had arisen. He said to Priam: "Your son has been released to you, father, as you asked, and he lies on a bier. When dawn appears, you shall see and take him. Now let us remember food. For even fair-haired Niobe remembered food, she whose twelve children perished in her halls, six daughters and six youthful sons. The sons Apollo slew with shafts from his silver bow, in his anger at Niobe, and Artemis the archeress slew the daughters, because Niobe matched herself with fair-cheeked Leto. She said Leto had borne two, whereas she herself bore many. Therefore they, though only two, slew all. Nine days these lay in their blood, and there was none to bury them, for Cronus' son had turned her people into stone; then, on the tenth day, the gods who dwell in heaven buried them. But Niobe remembered food when she grew tired of shedding tears. Now somewhere among the rocks on the lonely mountains in Sipylus, where, they say, are the beds of the divine nymphs who dance beside Achelous, there she, though a stone, broods on the woes sent by the gods. Come then, let us too consider food, glorious father. Then you may mourn again for your dear son, taking him to Ilium, and he shall be much wept by you."

Swift Achilles spoke, and starting up he slew

a sheep of dazzling whiteness. His comrades flayed it and dressed it properly, cut it up skillfully, and spitted it and roasted it carefully and drew it all off the spits. Automedon took grain and set it on the table in fair baskets, while Achilles served the meat. Then they reached their hands out to the food which lay prepared before them. But when they had set aside desire for food and drink, Dardanian Priam wondered at Achilles, how great and fair he was, for he was like the gods to see. And Achilles wondered at Dardanian Priam, as he beheld his goodly appearance and heard his words. Then, when they had had their fill of gazing at one another, godlike, aged Priam was first to speak: "Show me now quickly to my bed, Zeus-born, that we may both take our fill of lying in soft slumber, for the lids have not closed upon my eyes since my son lost his life beneath your hands, but I have mourned continually and brooded upon my woes, rolling in the dust within my courtyard walls. Now I have tasted food and down my throat poured the shining wine; before this I had tasted nothing."

He spoke, and Achilles bade his comrades and the handmaids place bedding on the porch, and throw fair, purple blankets over it, and spread rugs over that, and pull woolly robes together over him. They left the hall with torches in their hands, and at once in haste made up two beds. Swift-footed Achilles said to him ironically: "Lie down outside, dear father, lest any of the Achaeans counselors come hither, they who ever sit by me holding council, as is right. If any one of them should see you in the swift, black night, he would at once report it to Agamemnon, shepherd of the people, and there would be postponement of the surrender of the body. Come, tell me this and report it truthfully—how many days you wish for Hector's funeral, that I may stay here and hold the soldiers back that long."

Then godlike, aged Priam answered him: "If you are willing for me to finish the funeral of godlike Hector, you would do me great favor, Achilles. For you know that we are penned up within the city and the wood is far away to bring from the mountains, and the Trojans are very fearful. Nine days we would mourn him in my halls, and on the tenth we would hold his funeral and the people would feast, and on the eleventh we would heap a barrow above him, and on the twelfth we will give battle, if we must."

Then swift-footed, godlike Achilles said to him: "This too shall be as you request, aged Priam. For I will stop the war as long as you command."

So speaking, he took the old man's right arm at the wrist, lest he be fearful in his heart. So the two of them slept there in the porch of the house—the herald and Priam—with clever counsels in their hearts, but Achilles slept in a corner of the well-built lodge, and beside him slept fair-cheeked Briseis.

The others, gods and warrior charioteers, slept all the night, overcome by soft slumber. But sleep did not seize upon Hermes the guide as he pondered in his mind how he might guide King Priam from the ships unnoticed by the mighty watchers at the gates. He stood at Priam's head and addressed him: "Old man, you have no thought of evil, that you sleep thus among the foe, since Achilles let you be. Now you have won your son's release and given much. But your sons you left behind would give three times that ransom for yourself alive, if Agamemnon, Atreus' son, shall recognize you and all the Achaeans see you."

So he spoke, and the old man was afraid and roused the herald. Hermes yoked the horses and mules for them and himself drove swiftly through the camp, and no one knew them.

[471–691]

[The last lines of the poem (692–804) give an account of the lamentations over Hector's body, ending with the words of the celebrated quiet close, "So they held the funeral for Hector, tamer of horses."]

THE *Odyssey* OF HOMER

Translated by Reuben A. Brower

INTRODUCTION

THE BEST cue to give a reader who wants to appreciate the special quality of the *Odyssey* is the obvious one: the *Odyssey* comes after the *Iliad.* It is the story of "a man who wandered far and wide after he had destroyed the sacred city of Troy." In the *Iliad* we are actively engaged in a cruel and destructive war; our eye is fixed on heroic action and its consequences. To be fully aware of death and destiny and yet to go forward and fight for one's people—that is the way of the hero in the *Iliad.* The constant motif of the poem is most clearly expressed in Sarpedon's cry to Glaucus: "Since now ten thousand forms of death stand around us, which no man can either flee from or escape, let us go forward, whether we are to give glory to someone else, or whether someone is to give it to us!"

The *Odyssey* tells what happens to one of the greatest heroes of the *Iliad* after the war is over. But though there are in the *Odyssey* no battles quite like those fought on the plains of Troy, there are many moments when we see Odysseus as a leader who is fully aware of the danger he is facing and who calls his men to join him in courageous action. We hear an echo of Sarpedon's cry in Odysseus' speech to his men as they approach Scylla and Charybdis and in his words urging them to help him blind the Cyclops.

But Odysseus is not a Sarpedon or an Achilles; he is not like Shakespeare's Coriolanus a man who

> rewards
> His deeds with doing them, and is content
> To spend the time to end it.

There is nothing paradoxical about Odysseus' heroic gestures; he is out to bring himself and his men back to Ithaca. The *Odyssey* is not a drama of fated violence but the story of a man who wants to get home, who longs to see his wife and son and "the smoke rising from his own land." It is a *Nostos,* a poem of "return," and this underlying theme is never wholly forgotten. (A much later poem, the *Nostoi,* tells how a number of the other heroes returned home after the fall of Troy.) Odysseus meets each adventure not as a welcome opportunity for a display of bravery but as one more obstacle to be overcome before reaching Ithaca. But while we feel that the difficulties are real ones, we are sure from the opening scene in Olympus that Odysseus will get home, and we are reminded here and at many other points in the poem of how different his welcome will be from that of Agamemnon. (See Aeschylus' *Agamemnon* in this anthology.)

This note of confidence is struck in the first line of the *Odyssey:* "Tell me the story of that clever man. . . ." The hero is "clever," a man of many resources, and his story represents a triumph of intelligence. Achilles and Odysseus symbolize two contrasting aspects of the Greek genius: the noble awareness of man's fate and the happy belief that by using their minds men can make a better life. In the mythological drama of the *Odyssey,* Athena, the goddess of intelligence, helps the hero escape from the anger of Poseidon, the god of the sea, a brute natural force.

But we shall miss altogether the quality of the poem if we think of it as a hero story symbolizing a struggle between human intelligence and nature. A bare outline of the narrative suggests something more novel and more complex. The story begins on Olympus, where Athena is telling the gods how Poseidon has kept Odysseus wandering for nine years since he sailed from Troy. She tells them too how the hero's wife, Penelope, and his son, Telemachus, are being victimized by a great crowd of suitors who are eager to marry Penelope and succeed Odysseus as the first lord of Ithaca (Book I). The gods at once make a plan to bring Odysseus home, and Athena carries out her part in it by sending Telemachus to Sparta, where he is to ask for news of his father (Books II–IV). Much later in the poem, Telemachus returns to Ithaca after barely escaping the suitors' plot to kill him.

Meanwhile Odysseus sets out on his voyage home. After being shipwrecked by Poseidon, he comes to Scheria, the land of the Phaeacians (Books V–VII). While staying there he tells the king and his courtiers of his strange and wonderful adventures since leaving Troy

(Books VII–XII). The Phaeacians now take Odysseus back by ship to Ithaca, where after meeting his swineherd, Eumaeus, he joins Telemachus and makes a plan to kill the suitors (Books XII–XVI). Odysseus, disguised as a beggar, goes to his house and is received very rudely by the suitors and their friends; but Penelope entertains him well and invites him to spend the night (Books XVII–XX). On the next day Penelope asks the suitors to enter a strange contest: the man who can string Odysseus' great bow and shoot it properly will have the privilege of marrying her. All of the rivals try and are unsuccessful, but "the beggar" Odysseus easily performs the feat (Book XXI). Plans for the final fight now being complete, Odysseus reveals who he is, and under Athena's direction and with the help of Telemachus, he kills the entire company of suitors (Book XXII). He is at last recognized by Penelope, and on the following day he is welcomed home by his father, Laertes. A battle is about to break out between the relatives of the suitors and Odysseus and his supporters, when Athena arrives and puts an end to the quarrel (Books XXIII–XXIV). The *Odyssey* comes to a close in a series of happy reunions and reconciliations.

A reader of the *Iliad* who hears only this brief outline of the later poem will see that the *Odyssey* brought something new into European literature. New, but extremely familiar to readers of the novel. The story of the *Odyssey* is full of "plot," in more than one sense of the term. For example, apparently separate narrative lines are followed and then connected at a crucial moment: Telemachus arrives just in time to help his father regain his rights. There is also a good deal of intrigue, of planning in heaven and on earth to bring Odysseus home and to prepare a trap for his enemies. Here is a complexity quite different from that of the *Iliad*, where the main narrative line is quite simple, though occasionally interrupted by episodes of Olympian comedy or heroic daring. The sense of richness in the *Iliad* arises in part from the mere accumulation of similar episodes. But it is created more especially through the leisurely and complete unfolding of the tragic irony of Achilles' action and through the evolution of his wrath from quarrelsomeness to violent hatred and a painful recognition of error and loss. We must use quite different terms to describe the organization of the *Odyssey:* we do not speak of accumulation or the unfolding of tragic irony, but of the connection of separate narratives, of intrigues and adventures, of happy reunions between father and son or husband and wife.

But external descriptions of this sort give a pale sense of the difference between the two epics. We can appreciate the novelty of the *Odyssey* only by getting into it, by turning to one or two points where the heroic quality of the *Iliad* seems almost forgotten. Consider, for example, the opening of the scene in which Odysseus meets the swineherd Eumaeus. A reader of the Greek will find that the heroic tone is not wholly lost: like Odysseus and Achilles, the swineherd is called *dios*, noble (or glorious), and *orchamos andron*, a leader of men. But in total effect and in detail the scene is quite unheroic; it is a Theocritean idyll written before its time. For however important the meeting is dramatically, as a step in Odysseus' plan to murder the suitors, the main effect of the scene is to present a particular place and a distinct person. We see Eumaeus' yard "lined with quarried stone and topped off with a layer of thorny brushwood" and "his four dogs, fierce as wild beasts," and the swineherd himself, "sitting in the doorway" of his cabin, "cutting some sandals out of a stout piece of cowhide and fitting them to his feet." When Eumaeus saw the dogs attacking his master, "letting the leather fall from his hand, he dashed through the gateway, and yelling at the dogs and flinging a shower of stones after them, he sent them all running in different directions." Through this emphasis on particular objects and gestures, we get a wonderful sense of a unique person; for the moment, at least, we are interested in character for its own sake. Readers of the whole poem will find many similar moments in the *Odyssey;* the kind of interest they arouse is as far removed as possible from what we feel in reading of Sarpedon's or Hector's or Achilles' deeds and death. The accent of those narratives is splendidly impersonal and larger than life: it is heroic rather than individual.

The scene between Odysseus and Eumaeus is striking in still another way: Eumaeus, the principal actor, is distinctly a servant; his occupation, his manner, the objects he uses belong to a social milieu that appears in the *Iliad* only in the similes, that is, in the background, never in the foreground, of the narrative. The *Odyssey* gives a surprising importance to the swineherd, to Melanthius the goatherd, to the village beggar Irus, and to Eurycleia, Odysseus' old nurse. We are again reminded of the novel. Though the Homer of the *Odyssey* was hardly a Balzacian realist, he was considerably interested in picturing humble persons and places and things. If much of the *Iliad* is heroic tragedy, the *Odyssey* often comes nearer to domestic comedy. In the swineherd scene the impression of comedy is underlined by the humor of this picture of a bustling, scolding, yet faithful servant. Eumaeus is like a New England farmer who puts a traveller up for the night while saying that he is overworked and half-starved and really not "up to much any more." Odysseus too is a figure of comedy: he stands in the background, the cunning master in disguise who smiles with delight as he sees the proof of loyalty in his servant's generous entertainment.

But the *Odyssey* has further surprises for readers fresh from the *Iliad*. In the seventh book, after a scene of delicious comedy in which a princess goes to wash her clothes and meets a shipwrecked traveller, we come with Odysseus to the palace of King Alcinous:

"Outside the courtyard of the palace, near the gates, there is a great square garden with a fence running all around it. Here the trees grow up tall and full, pear and pomegranate trees and apple trees bearing fine fruit, and sweet fig and flourishing olive trees. Their fruit never spoils or stops coming on, winter or summer, all the year through, but a west wind blows always, making some fruits grow and others fall. Pear after pear ripens and grows old, apple after apple, grape cluster after cluster, and fig after fig."

For a moment we may think we have been reading another Theocritean description. But half way through, something has happened. We have left any possible garden for a land out of Nature. The garden is magical, and no attempt is made to explain its wonders. If we think of romantic literature as reflecting the world of dream as opposed to normal waking experience, we have moved in Alcinous' garden from realism to romance. To borrow Henry James's definition of romance, we have entered the realm of "uncontrolled experience—uncontrolled by our general sense of 'the way things happen.' " The miraculous interventions of the gods in the *Iliad* are not romantic in the same sense, because for one thing the events that take place in the human drama are often the kind of thing that *does* "happen." The interventions of the gods offer a rationalization or symbolic enlargement of actions that are thoroughly explicable in human terms. But often in the *Odyssey*, as in the garden of Alcinous, the very human hero encounters creatures and events that are not normally explicable and not explained within the poem. A narrative poem composed only of the fabulous episodes from the *Odyssey* would read like a Greek *Faerie Queene* and would fit exactly a contemporary criticism of Spenser's dreamy epic: "Hobgoblin run away with a garland from Apollo."

Homer maintains a fine balance between heroic poetry and romance by setting his wondrous tales in a story whose dominant motif is the most normal imaginable: the desire to get back home. Odysseus is not a knight errant, not at all like Tennyson's Ulysses, who seeks "a newer world":

> for my purpose holds
> To sail beyond the sunset, and the baths
> Of all the western stars, until I die.

It is worth noting that Homer does not tell the most fantastic tales in his own person. He lets Odysseus tell them, and Odysseus was a man who could make up a good yarn when one was needed. The traditional epic language does not let us forget that these are tales told by a hero; and the constant stress on Odysseus' cool intelligence in all situations imparts a feeling of sanity to the most nightmarish adventures. We hear them through the voice of a man whose words "fell from his lips like snowflakes in winter." (*Iliad*, III, 222) We know that the story is a story and that the normal world goes along in its usual way. The narrative keeps coming around to scenes of everyday life that are cheerfully substantial and pleasantly comic.

The blend in the *Odyssey* of the fabulous and the comic with the heroic was nobly described by one of the greatest of ancient literary critics, Longinus, in his treatise *On the Sublime.* Longinus pictures the contrast between the *Iliad* and the *Odyssey* as the "sunset" of Homer, the ebbing of power that is a sign of old age. Without accepting Longinus' evaluation, we may agree that his chronology "is correct," that the *Odyssey* is the later of the two Homeric poems. It is worth noting in this connection, that the *Odyssey* as compared with the *Iliad* refers more often to conditions characteristic of the eighth and seventh centuries. Like the *Iliad* it also includes traditions that go back to the period of late Mycenaean civilization. But we may say that the "actual" world reflected in the *Odyssey* is more often that of a much later period, when the Phoenicians were the great traders in the Mediterranean, when the Greeks were newcomers to the seaways. Hence in a Greek poem, the atmosphere of "antres vast and desarts idle."

In the period following the composition of the two Homeric epics, a number of poems were composed, such as the *Nostoi* mentioned above, in which the whole tale of Troy was told, from the throwing of the apple of Discord to the death of Odysseus. But the greatest of all the continuations of Homer is Vergil's *Aeneid.* It is easy enough to see where Vergil followed the main narrative pattern of the earlier poems and where he borrowed whole episodes, but it is his omissions that are revealing. The first half of the *Aeneid* is an *Odyssey* minus most of the fabulous tales and with all the comedy of character and intrigue removed. What survives from the *Odyssey* is a heroic journey from Troy and a drama of divine thrusting on. Aeneas is not returning home; he is an exile driven by fate who has the high destiny of founding mighty Rome.

The difference between Vergilian and Homeric epic is well symbolized by the contrast between Iopas, the learned "Lucretian" singer at Dido's court, and Demodocus, the self-taught, divinely inspired bard who sings for Alcinous and his fellow-princes. Vergil is a poet of immense learning, a poet of ideas and reflective sentiments, a creator of ever varied expressions. He is as far removed as possible from the singer who practises an art of popular oral composition, who retells a familiar story in language that has been largely made for him by earlier singers. The Homeric bard is intent on his story, on the actions and sufferings of his heroes. In the *Odyssey* as in the *Iliad*, Homer's subject is his drama, the travels of Odysseus and the varied and developing relationships between the hero and other beings, both human and divine. There is nothing in the *Odyssey* quite like Vergil's comment near the beginning of the *Aeneid:*

> *tantae molis erat Romanam condere gentem.*

> such a struggle
> It was to found the race of Rome.

Vergil is stating a subject over and beyond the dramatic one announced in *arma virumque cano*. He is writing a new kind of poem, and he freely reshapes his borrowings to suit his new purpose. Aeneas is not clever, but pious; the *Aeneid* is a poem of noble Roman piety rather than Greek resourcefulness of mind. But Vergil was not crudely imitating; he was reading Homer imaginatively; and he saw, as have many writers since his time, that the story of Odysseus and of the wonderful persons and creatures he met was richly symbolic. Dante and Spenser, Tennyson and Joyce have found in the *Odyssey* symbols for very different voyages of the spirit. Homer, not merely by being first, but by creating a poem at once heroic, human, and fabulous may justly be said to be the master of them all.

THE TEXT translated is that of T. W. Allen, *Homeri Opera* (2nd ed., Oxford, 1916; 2 vols.). The summaries throughout the poem (in brackets) are paraphrased from W. W. Merry's *Odyssey* (Oxford, 1899–1901; 2 vols.) and from H. J. Rose, *A Handbook of Greek Literature* (London, 1948).

Book I

The Bard to the Muse

Tell me, O Muse, the story of that clever man who wandered far and wide after he had destroyed the sacred city of Troy. He went to see the cities of many different peoples and learned their ways and had many painful and bitter experiences at sea while trying to get his men and himself safe home. But still he did not save his men, however much he wanted to. They, poor fellows, lost their lives through their own madness, by feasting on the oxen of Hyperion, son of Helios, who took from them forever any chance of returning home. Tell us this story, goddess, daughter of Zeus, beginning wherever you will. [1–10]

The divine plan for Odysseus' return

At that time after the war in Troy all the other heroes who had escaped sudden death were at home, safe now from the dangers of war and the sea. Only Odysseus had not returned, though he longed so much to see his wife and home again. But a queenly nymph, the goddess Calypso, kept him in her hollow cave, hoping to make him marry her.

When the year came round that the gods had set for his return to Ithaca, he still was not at the end of his troubles, not even after he was back among his own people. All the gods except Poseidon felt some sympathy for him; the ruler of the sea never once dropped his violent anger against the hero until he had arrived in his own country.

Now Poseidon had gone to visit the Aethiopians, who live farther away than any other people, half of them in the east, the other half in the west. He had gone there to receive a hecatomb of bulls and goats, and he was thoroughly enjoying the feast.

The rest of the gods were gathered in the house of Olympian Zeus, where the father of men and gods was beginning to make a speech to them. He had just thought of the hero Aegisthus, whom Agamemnon's son, famous Orestes, had murdered, and he was still thinking of him as he spoke to the deathless gods: "Oh see how men blame the gods! They say that evil comes from us, while through their own madness they bring worse troubles on themselves than fate had ever planned for them. So Aegisthus went against the plan of fate and married the wife of Agamemnon, Atreus' son, whom he had murdered on the day he returned from Troy. Yet Aegisthus knew very well that sudden death would strike him, because we sent him word ahead of time by Hermes, the sharp-eyed killer of Argus, who told him not to kill Agamemnon and not to make love to his wife. 'Vengeance will come,' said Hermes, 'from Orestes, Agamemnon's son, when he grows up and begins to think longingly of his own country.' But these well-meant words did not make Aegisthus change his mind, and now he has paid for all his crimes at once."

Then the gleaming-eyed goddess Athena answered him: "My father, son of Cronus, lord of lords, it certainly was right for him to die! So let every one die who does such deeds! But my heart is torn by the thought of wise Odysseus and his undeserved bad luck. For a long time he has suffered all sorts of troubles, far away from his friends and family, off on a wave-washed island in the heart of the sea. That thickly wooded island is the home of Calypso, daughter of grim Atlas, the god who knows the depths of all the seas and who holds up the high pillars that keep heaven and earth apart. It is Calypso who keeps the poor man from going on, who always charms away his tears with soothing and clever speeches, in hope of making him forget Ithaca. But Odysseus, whose only wish is to see the smoke rising up from his own country, longs to die. And yet, O King of Olympus, your heart is not touched, you pay no attention to him. Were you not pleased with the sacrifices Odysseus made beside the Argive ships on the broad plain of Troy? Why, O Zeus, do you hate him so?"

Zeus the cloud-gatherer answered her and said: "My child, what a thing for you to say! How could I ever forget godlike Odysseus, who surpasses other men in intelligence and in gifts to the immortal gods who live in the broad heavens? But Poseidon, who holds the earth in his embrace, hates him unrelentingly because he blinded the Cyclops Polyphemus, who is the most powerful of all the godlike Cyclopes. (You must remember that his mother was the nymph Thoösa, daughter of Phorcys, lord of the barren waves, and that his father was Poseidon, who once slept with the nymph in a hollow cave by the sea.) Since that day Poseidon the earth-shaker, without exactly killing Odysseus, has kept him wandering far from the land of his fathers.

"So come now, let all of us here make some plan for him to return home. In time Poseidon will forget his anger, because he cannot fight against all the other gods, with no one on his side."

Then the gleaming-eyed goddess Athena said in reply: "My father, Cronus' son, lord of lords, if the blessed gods now really want wise Odysseus to return to his home, let us quickly send the messenger Hermes, killer of Argus, to the island of Ogygia. Let him tell the lovely nymph of our absolute and unchanging purpose to bring long-suffering Odysseus back home.

"In the meantime I shall go to Ithaca to rouse Odysseus' son and give him courage to call an assembly of the Achaeans and to speak out boldly to all the suitors for his mother's hand. For they keep feasting on sheep from his crowded flocks and on his horned oxen that walk with swinging gait. I shall send him to sandy Pylos and to Sparta to see if he can learn anything about his father's return, so that he too can earn a name for himself in the world." [11–95]

The suitors hear the story of Troy.

[Athena appears in disguise to Telemachus at Ithaca, complains of the presence of the suitors of his mother Penelope, and bids Telemachus dismiss them and set out in search of his father. The suitors are listening to the song of the bard Phemius.]

In the hall of Odysseus' palace the famous bard was singing to the suitors. While they sat listening in silence, he sang of the sad return from Troy which Pallas Athena had caused the Achaeans to suffer.

In her room above, thoughtful Penelope, the daughter of Icarius, heard his inspired song very clearly and came down the high stairway of her house—not alone, but with two attendants following her. When that noble woman had come to where the suitors were sitting, she stood still a moment holding her shining veil over her face while her faithful attendants stood with her, one at either side. As she spoke to the divinely taught bard, she burst into tears. "Phemius," she said, "you know many other songs that people enjoy, songs of the deeds of heroes and of gods that bards love to honor. Sit now and sing one of those to the suitors, and they will listen quietly as they drink their wine. But stop this terrible song at once! It always pains me deeply, because an unforgettable sorrow has come to me. Oh, I shall always remember and always long for that wonderful hero whose glory has spread through all the lands of Greece!"

Then her sensible son, Telemachus, said to her: "Mother, why won't you let our faithful bard entertain us in the way he wants to? The bards are not responsible for their songs, though Zeus, I suppose, is, since he gives each of us men whatever he wishes. But it is not right to be angry with Phemius for singing about the misfortunes of the Greeks, because people always give the most applause to the song that is newest. So tell your heart to hear him, and remember that Odysseus was not the only man at Troy who lost his chance of returning home, but that many others died there, too.

"Now go to your rooms, and look after your own work, your weaving and spinning, and tell your servants to tend to theirs. The talking and planning will be the business of the men, all of them, but it is mine especially, because I am master of this house."

Penelope, amazed at her son's new tone, walked back to her apartment, for she had taken his sensible words to heart. When she had come to her room, she lay weeping for her dear husband until gleaming-eyed Athena closed her eyes in pleasant sleep.

Meanwhile the suitors had raised an uproar in the great shadowy hall, everyone of them saying that what he wanted most was to share Penelope's bed. Then that sensible young man Telemachus began speaking to them and said: "Suitors for my mother's hand, insolent beyond all insolence, for tonight let us feast and enjoy ourselves. But no more shouting, please, because it's a pleasant thing to hear such a bard as Phemius, who has a voice like one of the gods.

"When morning comes, we shall all go and sit in formal assembly, where I intend to tell you quite frankly to leave my father's house. Go hold your feasts elsewhere, travel from one house to another, and eat up your own wealth! Or if you prefer to waste all of one man's property—naturally without paying the price for it—go ahead and do it! But I call the ever-living gods to hear my words, in hope that Zeus will give us a day of vengeance. Then you will die here in this house—and no one will pay the price for that, either!"

The suitors, biting their lips in fury, were astounded at the bold way Telemachus now talked to them. [325–382]

[In Books II and III, omitted here, Telemachus calls a council and asks the suitors to leave. Upon their refusal, he prays to the unknown god who had appeared to him the day before. Athena appears in a new disguise, borrows a ship and a crew for him, and together they leave Ithaca and arrive at Pylos, Nestor's city. Athena turns into a bird and disappears. Nestor, knowing nothing of Odysseus, sends Telemachus on to Lacedaemon, the kingdom of Menelaus and Helen, now reunited. Telemachus travels thither in a chariot of Nestor's, with Pisistratus, one of his sons, acting as his escort.]

Book IV

Telemachus at the Palace of Menelaus and Helen

[Arrived at Lacedaemon, Telemachus is welcomed by Menelaus, and admires the beauties of his palace. Menelaus, in replying, mentions the name of Odysseus, which makes Telemachus cry.]

From her high-ceilinged, sweet-scented chamber came Helen, looking like Artemis, the goddess who carries a golden distaff. When she had come to where Menelaus and Telemachus and Pisistratus were sitting, her servant Adraste drew up a finely made chair for her, and Alcippe brought a rug of soft wool, while Phylo carried in a silver basket that had been given Helen by Alcandra. She was the wife of Polybus, who lived in Egyptian Thebes in a house filled with great riches. He had given Menelaus two large silver bowls for bathing and two tripods and ten talents of gold. At the same time his wife had presented Helen with some beautiful gifts: a golden distaff and a silver basket on wheels that had its outer edges covered with gold. It was this basket, stuffed full of fine-spun wool, that Helen's servant Phylo had brought and placed beside her. Lying across it was the distaff holding the dark violet wool.

Helen sat down in the chair, resting her feet upon a stool, and at once began asking her husband many different questions: "Noble Menelaus, do we know who these men are who have come to our house? Tell me, shall I keep the truth back or speak it out? Yes, I shall say what I think. Though I am ashamed to say so to his face, I have never seen anyone, man or woman, except this young person, who looked so much like Telemachus, the son of great-hearted Odysseus. He was the newly born son Odysseus left behind at home when—I was the hateful cause of it—the Achaeans went to Troy full of bold thoughts of war."

In answering her, fair-haired Menelaus said: "My wife, I have been struck by the same idea; your guesses and mine agree. Certainly the boy had just such feet and hands, just such a head and hair, and just such a darting glance. A moment ago, when I was thinking about Odysseus and speaking of all the painful hardships he had endured for me, tears began to run down the boy's cheeks, and he raised his crimson cloak to cover his eyes."

Then Nestor's son, Pisistratus, said to him: "Noble Menelaus, son of Atreus, leader of armies, this really is Odysseus' son, as you say. But he is very reticent and feels that on his first visit to you he ought not to talk out of turn. You must realize that he and I enjoy hearing your voice as much as if it belonged to a god.

"I should explain to you that my father, Gerenian Nestor, sent me to come along with Telemachus on this trip. Telemachus was very eager to see you, thinking that you might give him some advice or help; for a son has many troubles in his household when his father is away and he has no other helpers. And that's Telemachus' situation now: his father is away, and there are no men in his country who might protect him from being badly treated."

In answering him fair-haired Menelaus said: "It is true then; he has come to my house, the son of the dear man who went through so many trials to help me! I used to say that if far-thundering Olympian Zeus would let us both cross the sea in our swift ships, I should welcome Odysseus more warmly than all the other Greeks. And I should have settled him in a city in Argos, and I should have built him a house, and brought him from Ithaca with his goods and his child and all his people. To make a place for him here, I should have emptied one of the near-by towns that is now under my own rule. Once we were both here we should have visited each other often; and nothing would have kept us from living in happy friendship until the black cloud of death came to cover us. But such happiness, I suppose, must be envied by the god who keeps poor Odysseus from coming back home."

Menelaus' words made every one of them feel that they must weep. Helen of Argos, daughter of Zeus, wept, and Telemachus and Menelaus, Atreus' son, wept; Nestor's son, too, could not keep the tears from his eyes because he was reminded of his brother Antilochus, who had been killed at Troy by Memnon, the glorious son of Eos, goddess of the shining dawn. [121–188]

[Menelaus tells Telemachus of the adventures of other heroes, as he heard them from Proteus, the old man of the sea. Odysseus is not dead, but prisoner on the island of the nymph Calypso, who wants to marry him. On Ithaca, meanwhile, the suitors plot to kill Telemachus on his homeward journey, but Athena comforts his mother in a dream.]

Book V

Calypso promises to send Odysseus on his way.

[Athena on Olympus complains of Odysseus' hard fate; Zeus sends Hermes to Calypso's island to tell her to release her prisoner. She reluctantly consents.]

The queenly nymph Calypso went to see great-hearted Odysseus as soon as she had heard the orders of Zeus. She found him sitting on the shore weeping bitterly. His cheeks were always wet with tears, and he was wearing his sweet life away with longing for his return, as he loved the nymph no longer. But at night they still slept together in her hollow cave, he unwillingly, she quite willingly. In the daytime as he sat on the rocks by the water, his heart breaking with sorrow, he looked across the barren sea and cried continually.

Standing near by, the goddess said to him: "Poor man, please do not weep here any longer, do not waste your life away in tears; very soon now I shall quite cheerfully send you on your way. Come, take your axe and cut some long timbers and build a broad raft with them. Next, set a half-deck on it so it will carry you over the misty sea. To keep you from starving, I shall put on board food, water, and red, heart-warming wine. I shall give you clothing, too, and send a good breeze after you, so that you may come safe to the land of your fathers—if, of course, the gods who live in the wide heavens are willing; for they can easily outdo me in their plans and their deeds." [149–170]

The wreck of Odysseus' raft

[Odysseus builds a raft and sets sail from the island, but Poseidon sees him and raises a storm.]

Then a great wave rose steeply up, and coming down with a dreadful rush it struck Odysseus and swiftly whirled his raft about. At the same moment the rudder slipped from his hands, and he fell from the raft into the sea. The winds now rushed together in a terrifying whirlwind that broke his mast in the middle, while the sail and its yard plunged far off into the water. For a long time the sea kept him under, and he could not make his way up quickly after being hit by the enormous wave, because he was so weighed down by the clothes that Calypso had given him. At last he rose to the surface and spat out the bitter salt water which poured down in streams from his head. Tired as he was, he did not forget his raft, but launching out in the waves he grabbed hold of it and managed to get up on it, and for the time being escaped death. The raft was being carried in the wash of the heavy seas, first one way, and then another. As in late summer the wind Boreas carries a great clinging mass of thistles over a field, so the winds were carrying the raft over the water, first one way, and then another. At one moment Notus would toss it to Boreas to carry; at the next Eurus would let Zephyrus chase it along.

But Cadmus' daughter, slender Ino Leucothea, caught sight of Odysseus. She had once been human and had a human voice, but now she was a divinity of the deep sea and had her place of honor given by the gods. She took pity on Odysseus, floating there in the waves and suffering terribly, and like a diving-bird she rose from the water and came to rest on his raft and spoke to him: "Poor man, why does earth-shaking Poseidon hate you so violently and send you all kinds of trouble? But never mind, he will not take your life, however much he may want to.

"Now do what I tell you—for you seem not unintelligent: take these clothes off, let the raft go with the winds, and swim off to the land of the Phaeacians. There you will find a way of getting home and there you are destined to escape from your troubles. Look! Bind this magical veil around your chest, and have no more fear of suffering pain or dying. When your hands touch the dry land, untie the veil and throw it from the shore back into the wine-colored sea. But as you do so, be sure to turn away and not look."

With those words the goddess gave him the veil, and like a diving-bird slipped again into the swelling sea, where the black waves covered her.

Then the long-suffering hero Odysseus said to himself in doubt and despair: "Oh, I fear that this god is weaving a snare for me by telling me to leave my raft. But I won't take her advice, because I had a glimpse of the land where she said I might find help, and it was a long way off. Here is what seems best to me and what I shall do. As long as the timbers hold together, I'll stay here and take what comes. But when a wave knocks the raft to pieces, I shall swim for it! That's as good a plan as I can think up now."

While he was worrying about this with all his mind and heart, Poseidon the earthshaker lifted up a great wave, a terrifying and mean one, that arched high over him and struck. As a violent wind tosses up a heap of dry chaff and scatters it in every direction, so the wave scattered the timbers of the raft. But Odysseus got up on one of them, and riding it as if it were a race horse, he took off the clothes Calypso had given him. He at once bound the veil around his chest and with hands outstretched dived into the waves, ready and eager to swim off. As he struck the water, the lord of the sea, the earthshaker, saw him and shaking his head, muttered to himself: "Go wander now over the sea, and suffer all kinds of trouble until you meet men who are dear to Zeus; but even then I hardly expect you will think your misery too slight." With these words he touched the whip to his fair-maned horses, and went to Aegae, where he has a famous palace.

But Zeus's daughter, Athena, had another plan. First she kept all the winds except the north from going on their way and told them they must stop and rest. Then she set swift Boreas blowing and broke a pathway in the waves ahead of high-born Odysseus, to help him escape death and destiny and reach the land of the Phaeacians, a people that love the sea.

For two days and nights after that he drifted in the heavy seas, and he thought he saw his end coming many times. But when Eos with her streaming locks had brought the third day, the wind fell and there was a breathless calm. As Odysseus rose on a great wave, he looked sharply ahead and caught a glimpse of land close by. That sight was as welcome to Odysseus as when children see life coming back to a father who has been wasting away from a long and painful illness. Some hateful power had sent him the disease; but now to their joy the gods have released him from pain. So welcome was the sight of land and woods to Odysseus, who now swam along, eager to set foot on solid ground again. But when he was within calling distance of the shore, he heard the thundering crash of the sea on the reefs, as a great wave went roaring and booming up on the dry land, covering everything in a veil of misty spray. There was not a sign anywhere of a harbor for ships, nor any roadsteads, nothing but jutting shores with reefs and cliffs.

Then Odysseus' legs grew weak, and his heart failed him. Feeling utterly miserable, he said to himself, "Oh, what is going to happen to me now? Zeus has let me see land—which I hardly had hoped for—and I have reached the end of my trip across these deep and terrible waters; but I can see no way of getting out of the grey sea. On the shore facing me there are only sharp cliffs with waves roaring and dashing around them and with smooth rock running straight up. The sea is deep close into shore, and there isn't a place where a man could set both feet and not get hurt. If I do step out, a big wave will probably pick me up and throw me against the cliff, and so my efforts to make the shore will be wasted. If I swim further along, on the chance of finding shores and coves where the waves come in sideways instead of head on, I'm afraid that a gust of wind will pick me up again and carry me groaning back over the sea. Or else some god may send a huge sea monster to attack me, one of the many creatures that glorious Amphitrite breeds. For I know that Odysseus is an odious name to the great earthshaker."

While he was turning these thoughts over in his mind, a great wave was carrying him toward the jagged shoreline. Then his skin would have been flayed from him and his bones crushed, if gleaming-eyed Athena had not put a good idea in his head. As he was rushing along towards shore, he took hold of a rock with both hands and clung to it groaning, until the wave had passed over him. In this way he escaped from being dashed against the cliff, but when the wave flowed back with a rush, it struck him and carried him far out to sea. As when an octopus is pulled from its hole and the pebbles cling to the suckers at the end of its tentacles, so Odysseus' skin stuck to the rocks and was stripped from his stout hands. At that same moment the wave completely covered him. Then unlucky Odysseus would have died before his time, if gleaming-eyed Athena had not blessed him with wisdom. Coming out from under the wave which was now roaring in to shore, he swam along with an eye on the land, trying to find shores and coves where the waves came in sideways. Finally he came to the mouth of a lovely river, where he saw an excellent landing place with smooth rocks that were sheltered from the wind.

As he caught sight of the stream flowing out to sea, he prayed most earnestly, "Lord of the river, whoever you are, you hear many prayers; now hear the prayer of a man who comes to you from the sea to escape Poseidon's anger. The immortal gods honor any wanderer who comes for help, as I come now to your stream after so many sufferings. Oh pity me, lord of the river, hear the prayer of a suppliant!"

At once the god stopped the flow of the waters, and checking the waves, he made a calm path in the sea for Odysseus and brought him safely to shore. Then Odysseus' legs gave way and his strong hands failed him, for he was heartsick and tired from the sea. His skin swelled up all over his body, and salt water gushed in a stream from his mouth and nostrils. He lay breathless and speechless, fainting with the terrible weariness that came over him. But when he had finally caught his breath and collected himself, he unbound the goddess's veil and let it drop into the river. A great wave began to carry it back down stream when suddenly Ino rose and received it in her hands. When Odysseus had walked back from the river, he lay down in the shelter of the reeds and kissed the life-giving earth. Feeling utterly miserable, he said to himself, "What is going to happen to me now? If I stay through the night down by the stream, the stinging hoar frost and heavy dew may be too much for me, because I'm so weak and exhausted. Besides, toward sunrise the breeze blows cold from the water. But if I walk up the slope into the deep woods and go to sleep in a thicket and sleep too well, I'm afraid of being eaten by wild beasts."

Still it seemed to him that the best idea was to go into the woods. He found some trees in an exposed place not far from the water and went into a dense thicket formed by two shrubs growing from the same spot, one of wild olive, the other of cultivated olive. They were so closely entangled that the strong misty winds from the sea had never blown through them, nor had a drop of rain come in, nor had the bright rays of the sun ever struck through their branches. When Odysseus came into the thicket he at once heaped up leaves to make himself a large bed. He made a good big pile of them, enough to cover two or three men on a winter's night even if the weather was really bad. Noble Odysseus looked at the leaves and felt very happy as he lay down and heaped them over his body. In much the same way a man living far off in the country with no near neighbors will bury a glowing coal in the black ashes of his hearth; by keeping a few sparks alive he saves himself the trouble of getting fire from someone else. As Odysseus lay there close covered with leaves, Athena poured sleep over his eyes and gently closed his lids, bringing him quick release from pain and weariness. [313–493]

Book VI

Odysseus' welcome in the land of the Phaeacians

While noble Odysseus, worn out with lack of sleep and fatigue, was sleeping there, Athena went to the country and city of the Phaeacians. Years ago this people lived in Hyperia, a land of broad open plains, where they were neighbors of the Cyclopes, a most arrogant race of men. But the Cyclopes, being more powerful than the Phaeacians, kept attacking them and plundering their land. So their godlike ruler Nausithous led them out of Hyperia and settled them far from other men in Scheria, where he made a walled town, built houses and temples, and divided the farm lands. But long before the coming of Odysseus Nausithous had died and gone to Hades' house, and Alcinous, a man who had been given good judgment by the gods, had become ruler of the country.

It was to his house that gleaming-eyed Athena had gone, to provide a way for brave Odysseus to return home. She went along to a room built with great art, where a young girl was sleeping who had the face and figure of a goddess. Her name was Nausicaa, and she was the daughter of brave Alcinous. Two waiting women whose beauty was a gift of the graces were watching over her, one at either side of the doorposts. The shining doors between them were closed.

Like a gust of wind Athena slipped through to where the girl was sleeping and stood bending over her. As the goddess spoke to Nausicaa, she took the form of the daughter of the famous mariner Dymas. She was just Nausicaa's age and a dear friend of hers. "Nausicaa," she said, "how did your mother ever come to have such a lazy daughter! Your beautiful clothes lie all soiled; and yet the time for your marriage is very near, when you must be beautifully dressed and provide clean clothes for your wedding attendants. That's how you can get a good name among people and please your father and mother. But let us do the washing this morning, as soon as it is light; I'll come along to help you so that you can finish as quickly as possible. For you will not be unmarried long, you know. You are already being asked for by the chief men of the Phaeacians, among whom you have some very good connections. Come, ask your father early in the morning to have the mules hitched to the cart. You can carry your sashes and dresses and gleaming shawls along with you; besides, you will find riding pleasanter than going on foot, as the washing place is very far from town."

With these words Athena went off to Olympus, where they say the gods live in a place that always remains unchanging. It is never shaken by winds or wet by rain or touched by snow, and cloudless ether enfolds it all, white light flows down in a dazzling flood. There the happy gods live delightfully forever, and that is where the gleaming-eyed goddess went after she had told Nausicaa what she was to do.

At once Eos came riding on her throne of brightness and awakened Nausicaa. When the princess awoke she was amazed at her dream and went through the house to tell it to her father and mother. She found both of them in. She came on her mother sitting by the hearth with her waiting women, spinning crimson wool; she met her father just as he was going out the door. He was on his way to join the famous princes at a council-meeting to which they had summoned him.

Nausicaa stopped beside her father and said to him: "Papa, won't you have our high cart hitched up for me, so I can carry my splendid clothes to the river and wash them? I find that they are all *very* dirty. Besides, you must have clean clothes to wear when you sit in council with the leaders of our people. And there are your five sons—two married ones, and three handsome young bachelors—who always want to wear freshly laundered clothes when they go to dance. All these matters are very much on my mind."

That is what she said, because she was ashamed

to say anything to her father about being married. But he understood everything and answered: "The team is yours to take, my child, and whatever else you need. Go along now; the servants will hitch up the cart for you." With these words he gave his orders to his men, and they did as they were told. They went out at once and got the light mule cart ready and yoked the team to it. While Nausicaa brought her gleaming clothes from her room and put them in the beautifully polished carriage, her mother packed a chest with all sorts of good hearty food and poured some wine into a goatskin bottle. When her daughter had stepped up on the cart, she gave her a gold flask of olive oil for her and her women to use after bathing. Nausicaa now took up the shining reins and with a touch of the whip started the mules off. With a loud clatter they went on their way; they stretched out eagerly, carrying the girl and the clothes. Of course she was not alone, for her waiting women went along with her.

Finally they reached the river's lovely stream and came to the washing pools, where there was always a strong current of fresh water pouring through, enough to wash the dirtiest clothes clean. When they had unhitched the mules from the carts, they drove them quickly down beside the eddying stream to graze on the luscious grass. Next they took the clothes from the cart and carried them to the deep water and trampled on them in the pits, each one eagerly trying to outdo the others. When they had washed all the clothes clean, they stretched them out along the seashore in a place where the most pebbles had been washed up by the tide.

After Nausicaa and her women had bathed and rubbed themselves with olive oil they had their lunch on the bank of the river, while they waited for the clothes to dry in the bright sun. When they were through eating, they threw off their scarves and began playing ball. Nausicaa (she had very beautiful white arms) led them in a song that went with the game. She looked like Artemis, the goddess who loves the arrow, when she goes eagerly hunting stags and swift does on high Mt. Taygetus or Mt. Erymanthus. Mountain nymphs, daughters of Zeus the aegis-bearer, go along with her and join in the sport, while her mother Leto happily looks on. Artemis holds her head and face high above all the others, and though all are beautiful, she is easily the first to be seen. In just the same way the young girl Nausicaa stood out among her companions.

When they had already hitched up the mules and folded the fine clothes and were about to go back home, gleaming-eyed Athena thought up quite a different plan for them, which was to have Odysseus awaken and see bright-eyed Nausicaa, who would then guide him to the city of the Phaeacians. Then the king's daughter tossed the ball to one of her women, but missed her, and as she threw it into the deep eddy at the river's mouth, they all cried out.

At the sound of their voices noble Odysseus awoke, and sitting up said wonderingly to himself: "And whose land have I come to now? Are the men here wild and savage and with no sense of right, or do they fear the gods and receive strangers kindly? Just now I heard around me the shrill cry of mountain nymphs who live on steeply sloping peaks and in the sources of streams and in grassy meadows. Or are those human voices I hear close by? Come, I'll go see what they are."

With those words noble Odysseus came from under the thicket. As he stepped out, he broke a leafy branch from the dense growth and held it in front of him to cover his male parts from being seen. Odysseus went along like a bold mountain lion when he goes with blazing eyes through wind and rain and makes his way among cattle or sheep on the range, or when he chases deer through the wilds, or when he is driven by his belly to come right into the fold and attack the flocks. In the same way Odysseus in his desperate need of help started to go in among those young girls. Naked as he was and all caked over with brine, he was a fearful sight for them to see, and they scattered in panic, running out on the jutting shores. Only Alcinous' daughter stayed behind; for Athena had filled her with courage and taken all feeling of fear from her body. The bright-eyed girl stood still and faced Odysseus, while he wondered whether he should clasp her knees as suppliants do and ask for help, or whether he should stand off and in a gentle voice ask her to give him clothes and show him the way to the city. It seemed wiser, he thought, for him to keep his distance and speak to her quite gently, for he was afraid that if he touched the girl, she would be angry with him.

He then began a clever and soothing speech: "I beg you to help me, noble lady—but tell me, are you a goddess or a mortal? If you are one of the divinities who live in the broad heavens, I think you are most like Artemis, daughter of mighty Zeus; yes, you are very nearly the same in looks and height and figure. But if you are one of the beings who live on this earth, your father and honored mother are supremely happy, and your brothers and sisters, too. Their hearts must glow with pleasure when they see so fair a flower entering the dance. But happiest of all men will be the one who wins you with his gifts and brings you home for his bride. For I have never seen such a person, either man or woman; when I look at you, I am filled with awe. Once in Delos I saw a young date palm growing up near the altar of Apollo. (I went there too, you know, with a huge company following me on the journey in which I was to suffer so cruelly.) When I saw that tree, I stood marvelling at it for a long time, because nothing like it had ever grown up from the earth. Looking at you, noble lady, I feel the same wonder and awe, and I am dreadfully afraid of touching you and asking for your help.

"But think of how bitterly I have suffered. Yesterday I escaped from the wine-dark sea after twenty days of being carried by waves and swift whirlwinds from the island of Ogygia. And now some deity has thrown me on this shore so that I may suffer some other misfortune here. For I hardly suppose my troubles will end now; no, I expect that before that day comes the gods will give me still more. Noble lady, do take pity on me! You are the first person I have come to after suffering so many blows, and I do not know a single other one of the people to whom this land and city belong. Do point out the way to the town and give me a rag to throw around me, if only some piece of cloth in which you wrapped up your linen when you came out here.

"In return, may the gods give you whatever your heart desires; may they bless you with a husband and a home and an understanding mind. For surely there is nothing better than when man and wife live together in perfect understanding; they are a great source of envy to their enemies, and a great joy to their friends; but they themselves feel their happiness most deeply."

Then Nausicaa answered: "Stranger, since you do not look like a bad or stupid person and since—it is Olympian Zeus that gives happiness to men, to high and low alike, just as he wishes; and he has given you these troubles, which you must nevertheless endure—since now you have come to our city and land, you will not lack clothing or anything else that a man in trouble ought to receive when he comes for help. And now, as you have asked me, I shall tell you the name of our people and point out the town to you. The Phaeacians own this city and country, and I am daughter of brave Alcinous, their king, who owes his power and might to them."

When she had finished speaking, she called to her women: "Wait! Where are you going, and why do you run off after merely catching sight of someone? You don't suppose he is an enemy, do you? There is not a man alive, nor will there be, who will come to the land of the Phaeacians to make war. For we are a people dear to the immortal gods, we live far off in the surging sea, at the end of the world, and no other people have anything to do with us.

"This man is only an unlucky traveller who has wandered our way and whom we must care for. Remember that all strangers and beggars are under the protection of Zeus, that even a small gift to them pleases him. Come now, my women, give the stranger food and drink, and wash him in the river in some place sheltered from the wind."

At her words they stopped running, and calling to one another they came and seated Odysseus in a sheltered place, just as Nausicaa, daughter of brave Alcinous, had ordered. They brought him a cloak and tunic to wear, gave him olive oil in a gold flask, and told him to bathe in the river.

Then noble Odysseus said to the women: "Ladies, stand over there while I wash the brine from my shoulders and rub myself with oil; my body has not had any care of this sort for a long time. But I certainly shall not bathe in front of you; I feel embarrassed to stand naked surrounded by lovely young girls." So they walked away and told their lady what he had said.

Standing in the stream Odysseus washed his body clean of the brine that covered his back and broad shoulders and wiped the sea foam from his head. When he had finished washing and had rubbed himself with oil and put on the clothes Nausicaa had given him, Athena, daughter of Zeus, made him look taller and stronger and covered his head with thick curly hair like the close-curling bloom of a hyacinth. As a craftsman, a maker of beautiful things who had been taught every sort of skill by Hephaestus and Pallas Athena, works silver in around gold, so Athena now shed beauty and grace around Odysseus' head and shoulders. Shining and handsome, he went and sat down on the shore of the sea.

The young princess looked at him for some time and then said to her attendants, "Listen, women, to what I say: this man has not come to visit the Phaeacians without the consent of the gods who live on Olympus. Earlier he seemed to be quite an ordinary person, but now he looks like one of the gods who make their home in the broad heavens. I wish that someone like him would settle here and become my husband and be willing to stay in this country always. Come, women, give our guest something to eat and drink."

They heard what she said, and following her orders, they served Odysseus with food and wine. Noble Odysseus drank and ate greedily, for he had not touched food for a long time.

In the meantime Nausicaa had turned her thoughts to other matters. After folding the clothes she put them in the high cart, and when she had hitched up the heavy-hoofed mules, she got in. Calling to Odysseus, she urged him to start along, "Up now, stranger! Let us go to the city so that I can bring you to my wise father's house, where I am sure you will make the acquaintance of all the noblest Phaeacians. You don't seem unintelligent, so please do what I say: as long as we are passing through open country and farms, walk along quickly with my women behind the mule-cart, and I shall lead the way.

"But when we come to the city with its high towered wall—well, first let me tell you about it. On either side of the town there is a fine harbor, which is crossed by the narrow roadway leading in. Along this road lie the curving ships, each one in its own slip. Next, you come to the Phaeacians' assembly place; it spreads around the temple of Poseidon and is smoothly paved with quarried blocks of stone. Near by you see where they work on the tackle for the ships—all the ropes and sails—and where they polish the oars. For the Phaeacians aren't interested in bows and arrows, but in sails and oars and finely balanced ships, in which they love to cross the grey sea.

"But some of these people are very high and mighty, and I want to avoid their unpleasant remarks now for fear of being blamed later. Some common fellow may meet us and say: 'Who is this tall and handsome stranger following Nausicaa? And where did she find him? I suppose he's to be her husband—she has probably picked up some shipwrecked sailor, a foreigner at that, because we have no neighbors around here. Or perhaps some god has heard her many prayers and has stepped down now from the sky and will keep her forever and ever. She might better have gone and found a husband somewhere else. As it is, she is openly insulting the men here at home, all the noble Phaeacians who want to marry her.' That is how they will talk, and I shall have to put up with their insults. I should be seriously angry with another girl who behaved in the same way, who without her parents' approval, and while they were still living, went around with men before her wedding had taken place.

"Now stranger, take in what I say quickly, so that you can soon get my father to help you make your way home. You will find near the roadway a splendid grove of poplars sacred to Athena, and inside the grove a spring of water bubbling up, and around it a meadow. There, within calling distance of the city, you will see the lands set aside for my father, and you will see his flourishing vineyard, too. Sit down there, and wait until we get to the town and reach my father's palace. When you think we have surely arrived at the palace, go into the city of the Phaeacians and ask for the house of my father, brave Alcinous. It is easily recognized; a mere child could show you the way because none of the houses of the Phaeacians are built anything like the wonderful palace of Alcinous.

"But when you get inside the building and are in the courtyard, pass on quickly through the great hall until you reach my mother. She always sits beside the hearth in the firelight, leaning against a column and spinning her crimson wool—a wonderful sight! Her serving-women are usually sitting somewhere in back of her. You will see my father's chair drawn up near hers, where like one of the immortal gods he sits drinking his wine. But pass by my father and clasp my mother's knees, if you want to see soon the happy day of your return, however far your land may be from ours. If she feels warmly toward you, then you may hope to see your friends and reach your handsome house and the land of your fathers."

With these words she touched the shining whip to the mules. They quickly left the river's stream and went swinging along at a fairly good pace. But Nausicaa drove carefully and used the whip with discretion so that her companions and Odysseus might follow on foot. As the sun was setting, she reached the famous grove sacred to Athena, where noble Odysseus sat down to wait.

At once he made a prayer to Athena, daughter of mighty Zeus. "O hear me, Atrytone, child of Zeus the aegis-bearer! This time do hear me, since you never heard my prayers when I was wrecked at sea by the glorious earthshaker. Grant that when I come to the Phaeacians they may love and pity me."

Pallas Athena heard his prayer, but she did not yet show herself to him, as she stood in awe of her brother Poseidon. Indeed he never once dropped his violent anger against Odysseus until the hero reached his own country.

Book VII

The palace of Alcinous

[Nausicaa reaches her home; Odysseus is met by Athena in the form of a young girl, who directs him to the king's palace.]

So Odysseus came to the famous palace of Alcinous, and his heart was filled with confusion and wonder as he stood there hesitating to cross the bronze threshold. A dazzling light like that of the sun or the moon shone throughout the high-ceilinged house of brave Alcinous, for walls of bronze with a cornice of blue enamel at the top ran along on each side from the threshold to the inner apartments. There were doors of gold to close the house tight, and silver doorposts set in the bronze threshold. The lintel was of silver; the door handle, of pure gold. At each side of the doorway stood gold and silver dogs, which Hephaestus had made with great art to guard the palace of brave Alcinous. They were immortal creatures, forever unaging.

Within, chairs were placed along each of the side walls, all the way from the threshold to the back of the house; and over them were thrown finely woven shawls that women had made by hand. Here the leaders of the Phaeacians sat drinking and feasting, enjoying the plentiful stores of the house. Beside the well-built altars stood golden figures of young men holding blazing torches in their hands to give light at night to the feasters in the palace.

Fifty women servants work in the king's household: some grind yellow grain in the hand-mills; and others weave at looms and sit turning their spindles with the swift motion of the leaves on a tall poplar, and while they work, the olive oil drips from the close-webbed cloth. As the Phaeacian men are more skillful than all others in guiding a swift ship over the sea, so the women of their country are most artful weavers. Athena has given them good sense and great skill in making beautiful things by hand.

Outside the courtyard of the palace, near the gates, there is a great square garden with a fence running all around it. Here the trees grow up tall and full, pear and pomegranate trees and apple trees bearing fine fruit, and sweet fig and flourishing olive trees. Their fruit never spoils or stops coming on, winter or summer, all the year through, but a west wind blows always, making some fruits grow and others fall. Pear after pear ripens and grows old, apple after apple, grape cluster after cluster, and fig after fig.

Near by is a vineyard that bears wonderfully. In one part of it there is a warm level spot where grapes are being dried in the sun; in another, they are gathering grapes; and in a third they are treading them for wine. In front, there are green grapes just shedding their flowers, and beyond, there are others that are turning dark. Here, along the outside row, are beautifully planned beds with all sorts of herbs growing in them, their leaves bright green throughout the year. Within the enclosure there are two springs, one that flows in various channels to water the whole garden; and another opposite, that runs under the gate of the courtyard to the high palace, and from which the people of the city get their water. Such were the glorious gifts of the gods in the royal home of Alcinous.

Noble Odysseus stood there at the entrance to the palace and admired its beauty. When he had looked at everything, he quickly stepped across the threshold and went in. [81–135]

[Odysseus, made invisible by Athena, reaches the palace unmolested and sits as a suppliant at the hearth. King Alcinous and Queen Arete receive him kindly, and grant his request to be sent home in one of the Phaeacian ships, the swiftest in the world.]

Book VIII

The dinner in Alcinous' palace

[Alcinous calls an assembly and proposes to send Odysseus home. A ship is manned, and meanwhile the elders meet for a banquet at the palace of the king.]

The herald Pontonous came in bringing the faithful singer, Demodocus. The Muse dearly loved him, though she had given him both good and evil; she had robbed him of his sight, but had given him in return the art of making sweet songs. The herald now placed a silver-nailed chair for him in the middle of the company at the feast, resting it against a high column. Then he hung the clear-sounding lyre from a nail above the bard's head and showed him how to reach it and take it down. Beside him he set a beautiful reed basket and a table and a cup of wine for him to drink from whenever he cared to.

The food was now set before them, and they eagerly began to eat. When they had had all they wanted to eat and drink, the Muse inspired the bard to sing of the glorious deeds of heroes. He began a song whose glory had at that time reached the broad heavens, the story of the quarrel between Odysseus and Achilles. The song told how they quarreled once at a rich feast in honor of the gods, how they shouted insults at each other, and how Agamemnon, king of heroes, was delighted that the bravest of the Achaeans were quarreling. For they were fulfilling the words spoken by Phoebus Apollo at holy Pytho when Agamemnon crossed the stone threshold of the shrine to consult the oracle. That was when the plans of mighty Zeus began to work and the wave of disaster first rolled over the Trojans and the Greeks.

As the bard sang this song Odysseus raised his great crimson cloak in his strong hands and drawing it down over his head, covered his face; for he was ashamed to have the Phaeacians see tears falling from his eyes. Whenever the divinely-taught bard stopped singing, he would wipe his tears away and pull the cloak from his head and, raising the two-handled cup, would pour an offering to the gods. But whenever the bard began to sing again—for the Phaeacian nobles loved hearing his words and were always urging him on—Odysseus covered his head and wept. He kept all of them but the king from noticing his tears; Alcinous alone knew what was happening, because he was sitting near Odysseus and heard the deep sighs that came from him. [62–95]

[Alcinous invites his nobles to games in Odysseus' honor, where Odysseus earns their respect by setting a record for the discus throw. A dance follows, and the bard Demodocus sings of the loves of Ares and Aphrodite. At the banquet that follows, Odysseus bursts into tears again when the minstrel sings of Troy, and Alcinous asks him his name.]

Book IX

The Cyclops

[Odysseus reveals his name and home, and tells the story of the departure from Troy, and how the north wind drove them upon the coast of the Lotus-Eaters.]

"We came next to the land of the Cyclopes, lawless and arrogant creatures who boldly put their trust in the immortal gods and neither plow nor plant any crops with their own hands. Everything they need grows without plowing and planting: wheat and barley and wine-grapes made rich and full by the rain Zeus sends from the sky. They have no governing assemblies nor any fixed laws, but they live on high mountain tops in smooth caves, where each one without regard for the rest lays down the law for his wives and children. [106–115]

[The Cyclopes' land is described, and the arrival of Odysseus and twelve companions at his cave.]

"When we finally reached the place where they live, we saw on the outermost shore close to the sea a cave, its high arch overhung with laurel. Here many flocks of sheep and goats were quartered at night. A yard ran around the front with a high stockade built of tall pines and oaks with leafy tops and rocks set deep in the ground. This cave was the home of a giant who pastured his flocks far away from his fellows. He never went to see others, but lived his lawless life alone; yes, he was a marvellous and monstrous creature, not at all like a human being, but like a wooded peak that you see rising above all the others in a range of mountains.

"Then I chose twelve of my best men to go along with me and ordered the rest of my good comrades to stay near the ship and guard it. I took along with us a goatskin of dark sweet wine which had been given me by Maron, the son of Euanthes, priest of Apollo, because once out of reverence for his calling we had protected him and his wife and child. (We had found him living in a grove sacred to Phoebus Apollo, the god who watches over Ismarus.) Now Maron had given me some splendid presents: seven talents of finely made gold, a wine bowl entirely of silver, and wine which he drew off in jars, twelve of them altogether. It was sweet and not mixed with water, a heavenly drink! None of the servants or attendants in the household knew about it, only Maron himself and his wife and one housekeeper. When he drank that ruddy wine, he poured one full cup of wine into twenty of water, and yet the fragrance that rose from the bowl was exquisite. Once poured, it was not a drink you would care to refuse!

"So I filled a great wineskin with it and carried it along and took other provisions in a leather sack. For brave as I was, the thought at once struck me that we were going to meet a man filled with immense strength, a savage who knew no rights or laws.

"We came quickly to his cave, but did not find him inside, as he was off tending his fat sheep. We went into the cave and looked everything over. There we found baskets loaded with cheeses and pens crowded full of sheep and goats. The sheep of different ages were shut up in separate places; in one there were spring lambs; in another, summer lambs, and in a third, the new born lambs. We saw there, too, the well-made crocks and bowls he used for milking, every one of them swimming with whey.

"My men were begging me to take some of the cheeses, then quickly to drive some sheep and goats from the pens and go back and sail over the salt sea. But I did not listen to them—it would have been much better if I had!—because I wanted to see the creature and find out whether he would offer me gifts. His coming, I discovered, was to be no joy for my comrades.

"After lighting a fire we made our offering to the gods; then helping ourselves to some cheeses, we ate them and sat waiting until the Cyclops came up with his flock. He was carrying a heavy load of dry wood to make a fire for his supper, and once inside he threw it down, letting it fall with such a loud rumble that we ran in terror to the farthest part of the cave. He now drove his fat sheep in, that is, all the ones he was milking; he left the rams and he-goats in the huge yard outside.

"After that he lifted up a huge door-stone and blocked the entrance. The boulder he used was so immense that twenty-two solid four-wheeled carts could not have dragged it from the doorway. He sat down and milked his sheep and bleating goats, all of them in their turn, and put each young one to its mother. When he was through, he curdled one half of the milk, collected it in baskets, and put it away; the other half he let stand in jars for his supper or for drinking at other times. As soon as he had finished his chores in his quick and energetic way, he lighted a fire and for the first time caught sight of us.

" 'You strangers, who are you?' he asked. 'From where did you sail here over the paths of the sea? Are you travelling on business or are you wandering about without any plan, as pirates do, who go here and there risking their lives and attacking people in other lands?' His deep voice and his monstrous size were so terrifying that our courage was completely shattered.

"But though I was really frightened, I answered him. 'We are Achaeans,' I said, 'on our way from Troy; we have been driven from our course by every wind that blows and sent here over the great gulf of the sea. Though we have been trying to reach our homes, we have actually gone in an altogether different direction, and by an altogether different route. But that seems to be the plan that pleases Zeus. We are proud to tell you that we are the soldiers of Agamemnon, son of Atreus, a king whose fame is now the greatest of any on earth; for he has wiped out many armies and destroyed a wonderfully great city.

" 'And now we are here at your knees, asking you to offer us a token of welcome or to make us a gift such as strangers have a right to receive. Remember, my good man, to honor the gods, and do not forget that we come as suppliants. For Zeus the Host protects strangers and suppliants and goes along with all strangers to see that they are respected.'

"He heard my words and immediately answered me in a cruel spirit, 'You are very simple, or else you have come from far off, if you tell me to fear the gods or avoid their anger. We Cyclopes, I tell you, feel no respect for Zeus the aegis-bearer or for any of the blessed gods, because we are much mightier than they. I wouldn't save you or your men merely to protect myself from the hatred of Zeus, not unless I happened to feel like it. Tell me now where you have left your well-built ship, whether it is very far off or close by, so that I can find it.'

"He said this to test me, but I was too wise to be fooled and answered him with some guile, 'My ship was wrecked by Poseidon the earth-shaker, who ran it up on a point and dashed it on the rocks at the very edge of your country. (A wind had already brought us in from the open sea.) But somehow or other I and these men escaped death.'

"This time he did not give me one of his cruel answers, but instead stretched out his hands towards my companions and grabbed two of them and dashed them on the ground as if they were a couple of puppies. Their brains flowed out and wet the ground. Then he cut their bodies in bits and prepared his meal. He ate like a mountain lion, swallowing down entrails, flesh, and bones filled with marrow, and leaving nothing. At the sight of his barbarous acts we wept and raised our hands in prayer to Zeus, feeling now that we were completely helpless. He went on eating human flesh and washing it down with plain milk until he had filled his great belly, and then lay down in the cave stretched out among his flocks. I at once hit on a bold plan of action: I would go up close to him with my sharp sword drawn and, feeling out the right spot with my hand, strike him in the breast exactly where the diaphragm covers the liver. But a second thought kept me back. If we killed him we should die a sure death there in the cave, because we could not push away the tremendous stone with which the Cyclops had blocked the entrance. So we stayed there, unhappily waiting for morning to come.

"When Eos, the early born, the rosy-fingered goddess, appeared, the Cyclops lighted a fire and in a very orderly way went through his flocks and did the milking and put each of the young ones to its mother. As soon as he had finished his chores in his quick and energetic way, he again grabbed two of my men and prepared his breakfast. When he had eaten, he drove his fat flock out of the cave. He had moved the huge gate-stone away with the greatest ease and had put it back again just as you might put the top on a quiver.

"With a loud whistle the Cyclops started his flocks towards the mountain. He left me thinking deep and ugly thoughts of revenge and hoping that Athena would answer my prayers. Here is what seemed to me to be the best plan. Near the sheepfold there was a big club lying that belonged to the Cyclops, a log of green olive wood that he had cut intending to dry it and carry it for a walking stick. We judged that it must be as large as the mast of a twenty-oared black ship, one of those broad freighters that cross the great gulf of the sea. To my eye it certainly looked that long and that thick. I cut off about a fathom's length from it and brought the piece to my men and told them to sharpen it. After they had made the piece smooth, I brought it to a point and hardened the end in a hot fire. Next I carefully put it out of sight under one of the many piles of dung which were heaped up everywhere in the cave.

"I now ordered the rest to draw lots and see who would join me in the dangerous business of raising the club and turning it in the monster's eye after he was sound asleep. The lot fell to exactly the four men whom I should have chosen, and I made myself the fifth in their party.

"At evening the Cyclops came driving his flocks with their fine coats of wool. This time he drove the fat flocks straight into the broad cave, and did not leave a single animal outside in the yard. Perhaps some god had suggested the idea to him, or perhaps he had some suspicions of his own. Then, raising the great door-stone, he put it in place and sat down and milked the sheep and bleating she-goats. As before, he took everyone in its turn and put each of the young to its mother. As soon as he had finished his chores in his quick and energetic way, he again grabbed two of my men and prepared his supper.

"I now stepped over beside the Cyclops and spoke to him, as I held out a wooden cup of dark wine, 'Here, Cyclops, now that you have fed on human flesh, drink some of this wine and you will see what a fine drink lies in the dark hold of our ship. I brought it to offer you a libation, in hope that you might pity us and send us on our way. But you should know that your madness is no longer to be endured. Cruel man, do you suppose that after such actions anyone will ever come to see you again? You must surely realize that you have done what you ought not to have done.'

"As I finished speaking, he took the wine and drank it off. He was hugely pleased with the sweet taste of the drink and asked me for a second cup. 'Be so kind as to give me more,' he said, 'and tell me your name at once, so I can offer you some agreeable token of hospitality. The Cyclopes too have wine from fine grapes which the life-giving earth bears and which are made fat by rain sent from Zeus; but this must be drawn from a cask of ambrosia and nectar!'

"When he had spoken I offered him another cup of the bright wine. Three times I brought it and gave it to him; and three times he madly drank it down. When the wine had clouded the Cyclops' thoughts, I spoke to him in a gentle and soothing tone. 'Cyclops, do you ask me my name? Well, I shall tell you, and you must give me a token of hospitality, just as you promised. Noman is my name. Noman I am called by my father and mother and all my friends.'

"He answered me in his cruel way, 'Noman, I shall eat you last of all; I shall eat all of your comrades first! And that will be your token of hospitality.'

"With these words he swayed and fell flat on his back, and as he lay there with his thick neck bending back, sleep that conquers all seized him. From his throat wine and bits of human flesh poured out, which he belched up in his drunken stupor. Then I shoved the club under a great heap of glowing coals to warm it up. At the same time I was urging my men to be brave, because I was afraid someone might be frightened and hold back.

"As soon as the olive-wood club was about to burst into flame, though it was quite green, and when it was giving off a fearful glow, I brought it from the fire and came up close to the giant, with my helpers standing around me. They lifted the sharp-pointed club and pressed it into his eye, while I pushed down on it and turned it around, just as a man bores through a ship's timber with a drill. (His helpers below whirl it around with a strap that they pull from either side, and so the drill keeps steadily turning all the while.) That's how we kept turning the fiery pointed club in the Cyclops' eye. The blood flowed out around the hot wood, and the blast from the burning eyeball singed his lids and eyebrows, and the roots of his eye burst in the heat. As when a smith with marvellous art dips a great ax or adze in cold water, and it send out a loud cry and a hiss—that is how iron gets its strength—so the giant's eye sizzled about the olive-wood club. He roared and bellowed in agony while the rocks about him resounded with his cries. We all ran from him in terror.

"Then he pulled the blood-soaked club from his eye, and mad with pain, flung it from him. In a tremendous voice he called to the Cyclopes who lived far above, in the caves on the windy heights. Hearing his cries, they came running from all sides, and standing outside around his cave, they asked him what was wrong. 'Polyphemus, why are you so desperate, and why do you shout so in the celestial nighttime and keep us all from sleep? Is any man driving your flocks off against your will? Is any man taking your life by trickery or violence?' From his cave mighty Polyphemus answered, 'My friends, Noman is killing me by trickery and not by violence.'

"Their words came flying in reply, 'If no man is mistreating you and you are alone and in pain—well, there is of course no way of escaping sickness sent by mighty Zeus. You can only pray for help from your father, Lord Poseidon.'

"With those words they went off, and my heart laughed because thanks to my cleverness the false name had fooled him. The Cyclops, groaning and suffering sharp pangs of pain, groped about with his hands and took the stone from the entrance. Then he sat down in the opening and stretched out his hands to see if he could catch anyone walking out among the sheep. That's how simple-minded he thought I was!

"All the while I was trying to find out the best way of saving my companions and myself. I was weaving all sorts of tricky schemes and plans, because I knew that this was a case of life or death and I felt that a real calamity was unpleasantly near. Here is the plan that struck me as best. The rams in the flock were well fed, big handsome fellows, with thick coats of dark-violet wool. Taking three at a time, I quietly tied them firmly together with some of the willow twigs on which the monster usually slept. The ram in the middle carried one of my men tied beneath him, while the two on the outside went along for protection. Thus there were three sheep carrying each one of my comrades. For myself, I chose a ram that was by far the best of the whole flock. Taking hold of him I doubled myself up under his shaggy belly; then with my face upwards I boldly clung tight to his marvellous wool. So we stayed there, unhappily waiting for morning to come.

"When Eos, the early born, the rosy-fingered goddess, appeared, the males ran out to pasture, but the females stood bleating about the pens, as they had not been milked, and their udders were almost bursting. Their master, though tortured by cruel pains, ran his hands over the back of every sheep as it came and stood beside him on its way out. Poor fool, he did not understand that my men were tied under the bellies of his thick-fleeced sheep! Last of all, the prize ram of the flock came walking toward the entrance. He had been slowed down by his thick fleece and by the weight of his tricky passenger.

"As he ran his hands over him, mighty Polyphemus said, 'Good old fellow, what does this mean? Why are you the last of the flock to leave the cave? You were never left behind before, but you always went striding ahead and were always the first to be grazing on the lush flowers of the grass, the first to reach the flowing streams, and the first to want to return to the fold at evening. But today you are the last of all! I think you feel the loss of your master's eye, which was put out by that bad man and his cruel comrades. Noman it was who drugged me with wine, but he is not safe yet, I swear! Oh, if you only could share my thoughts and had a voice to tell me where that man is hiding from me! Then I would scatter his brains through the cave in every direction, as I dashed him to the ground, and my heart would have some relief from the troubles that no-account Noman brought me.'

"With these words he let the ram go out the door. When we had gone a little way from the cave and the yard, I first let myself down and next untied my comrades. We quickly drove off the fat slender-legged flocks, often turning to look back until we finally reached the ship. Our good comrades were more than glad to see all of us that had escaped, and they began to sob and cry for the rest. But I would not let them weep and gave each man a stern look as I told him to stop.

"I ordered them to quickly throw plenty of the fleecy animals on the ship and then to sail the salt sea. Soon the men were going on board and taking their seats, and once in their places they struck the grey water with their oars and were off. When we were as far from shore as a loud cry can be heard, I began to shout insults at the Cyclops. 'Cyclops,' I said, 'you see I was not so helpless, and you see it was not meant for you to gulp down my men with all your might and main! But it was meant that your wicked deeds would find you out, because you were shameless enough to eat strangers who were staying in your own house. So Zeus and the other gods have punished you well.'

"When he heard me, his anger grew even more violent, and he broke off the top of a great mountain and flung it down ahead of our dark-prowed ship. When the rock struck, the sea was forced up in a great wave that swelled from the depths and carried the ship back to shore, driving it up on the dry land. But I grabbed a long pole and pushed her off, and called to my men and told them to start rowing if we were to avoid real trouble. My looks told them that I meant it; and they fell to their oars and rowed! When we were twice as far out as before, I began shouting to the Cyclops again, though my men stood around me, trying one after another to soothe me and hold me back. 'You poor fool,' they said, 'why do you want to bother this wild man? Just now he flung something into the sea that drove our ship straight back to shore again. We all thought we were done for then and there! If he had heard a shout or a word from anyone, he would have dashed our brains out and crushed our ship's timbers with a jagged mass of rock. That's how he can throw!'

"But their words did not move my brave

heart, and in my passion I called back to him, 'Cyclops, if any man asks you about the ugly blinding of your eye, say that it was put out by the great son of Laertes, Odysseus the destroyer-of-cities, who lives in Ithaca.'

"When he had heard me, he groaned and answered, 'Oh horrible! now I see that a prophecy made years ago has come true. We used to have a seer, a good man and true, Telemus, son of Eurymus, an excellent prophet who spent a long life in the service of the Cyclopes. He told me that all this would happen sometime, and that I should lose my sight at the hands of Odysseus. But I always expected that the person who came would be tall and well built, a man of immense strength. But now a little, lifeless, insignificant fellow has blinded me by drugging me with wine. Come here, Odysseus, let me offer you some token of hospitality, and let me ask the glorious earth-shaker to help you make your way home. For I am his son, and he says he is my father. He will heal my eye, and no one else, either blessed god or mortal man.'

"I answered him and said, 'If I only could be as sure of taking your life and sending you to Hades' kingdom, as I am that the earthshaker will never heal your eye!'

"When I had finished, he raised his hands to the sky and prayed to Lord Poseidon. 'Dark-haired Poseidon,' he said, 'you who hold the earth in your embrace, hear me now, if I really am your child and you are my father: never give a safe return to the son of Laertes, Odysseus the destroyer of cities, who lives in Ithaca. But if it is part of the divine plan for him to reach the land of his fathers and to see his well-built house and his dear ones, may he have a long and hard time getting there, and may he lose all his comrades and come home in a strange ship; and may he find sorrow and trouble in his home.' So he spoke, and the dark-haired god heard his prayer." [181–536]

Book X

Circe

[The wanderers are involved in adventures at the floating isle of the wind god Aeolus; they fall among the cannibal Laestrygonians; and they then reach the island of the enchantress Circe, where Odysseus slays a huge stag for his crew.]

Eurylochus and a number of Odysseus' men visit Circe.

"In a deep and secluded valley they came on Circe's house; it was built of highly polished stone and stood in a place that could be seen from far and wide. In the fields around there were mountain wolves and lions, men that Circe had charmed by giving them evil drugs. They did not attack my comrades, but wagged their long tails and stood up on their hind legs and fawned on them. Sharp-clawed wolves and lions played about them as dogs play about their master when he comes away from a feast because they know that he usually brings them a few choice bits. But when my men saw such fearful animals coming up to them, they were thoroughly frightened.

"When they reached the doorway of the beautiful goddess' house, they stopped and waited for a moment. Inside, they could hear Circe singing in her lovely voice as she went back and forth, weaving on her marvellous loom the exquisite and lovely and splendid things that only a goddess can make. The first of them to speak was Polites, a brave leader, who was one of my closest and truest friends. 'There is a woman inside working at a great loom and singing beautifully. Listen. The whole place is full of the sound! Is she human or divine? Let's call to her at once and see.'

"When he had finished speaking, they raised their voices and called. Circe came quickly and opening the shining doors, invited them in, and in their madness and ignorance, they followed her. But Eurylochus, suspecting some trickery, held back. She took the others in and seated them on chairs and couches and made them a drink by stirring cheese, barley, and amber honey in Pramnian wine. She also mixed in some harmful drugs which soon were to make them forget their homeland. When she had passed the drink and they had drunk it down, she suddenly struck them with her wand and shut them up in pigsties. At once they had the heads and bodies, the voices and bristles even, of swine; but their minds remained exactly as before. So they wept when Circe shut them in the sties. For food she threw them chestnuts and acorns and seeds of the cornel tree, all the things that pigs eat as they lie wallowing in the mud.

"Right after this happened, Eurylochus came back to the black ship to tell us about our comrades' gruesome experiences." [210–245]

Odysseus goes to rescue his men.

" 'Eurylochus,' I said, 'you may stay here by the hollow black ship and have something to eat and drink; but I shall go, because something stronger than I am forces me on.'

"With those words I went up from the sea and the ship, and passed through that magical valley on my way to the great house of the enchantress Circe. As I was turning in to the house, Hermes, the god who always carries a golden staff, came up to me. He appeared in the form of a boy who is beginning to show the first signs of a beard, who is at the time of life when youth is most charming.

"He clasped my hand and said to me: 'Unlucky man, where are you going now alone in these mountains, in a country you cannot know well? Your comrades are here in Circe's house, shut up like pigs and well hidden in their pens. Are you coming to set them free? I think you won't ever get back yourself, but stay here along with the others. Listen to me, and I shall get you out of trouble and save you. Take this magical drug that grows here and carry it with you when you enter Circe's house, and it will protect you from all harm.'

" 'But first I must describe to you all of Circe's dangerous arts. When you arrive, she will prepare you a drink, and as she stirs it, she will throw in potent drugs. But she will not be able to cast a spell over you, because the magical drug I shall give you will not let her, and also because I shall tell you exactly what to do. When Circe strikes you with her great long wand, draw your sharp sword from your side and rush toward her as if you really meant to kill her. In her fright she will beg you to come and sleep with her, and when she does, do not refuse to share her bed, at least if you want her to treat you well and set your companions free. But tell her to swear the great oath of the gods not to think up some worse trouble for you, or when you are stripped she may unman you and make you a coward.'

"With these words the Argus-slayer pulled the magical herb from the ground and gave it to me and showed me what it looked like. The root of the plant is black; the flower, milk-white. The gods call it 'moly.' Mortal men find it very hard to pull up, but of course gods can do anything.

"Hermes went off through the wooded island toward high Olympus, while I went on my way to Circe's house, feeling badly stirred up and uneasy. When I came to the home of the beautiful goddess, I stopped at the door and called. The goddess heard my voice and coming out quickly, opened the shining doors and invited me in. I followed her, but with a heavy heart. She took me in and seated me in a finely made silver-nailed chair with a stool for my feet; she prepared me a drink in a golden cup and with evil intentions dropped a magical herb in it. When she had passed it to me, and I had drunk it down (though without being cast under a spell), she struck me with her wand and said, 'Come to the sty now, and lie down with the rest of your comrades!'

"As she was speaking I drew my sharp sword and rushed toward her as if I really was going to kill her. With a loud cry she fell at my feet and threw her arms about my knees and bursting into tears, said to me, 'Who are you, and from where have you come? Where is your home city and where do your mother and father live? I am amazed that you could drink this magical potion without being cast under a spell; no one else has ever resisted the power of these drugs, not a single man who has once swallowed them or even let them pass his lips. But you have a mind that cannot be charmed by magic. You must be Odysseus, the master of many tricks. The Argus-slayer, the god who carries a golden staff, always said that Odysseus would come to me when he was going home from Troy in his swift black ship. O please, Odysseus, put your sword in its sheath, and follow me to my bed, so that we can become lovers and learn to trust each other.'

"I answered her and said, 'O Circe, how can you ask me to be kind to you, when you have changed my men into swine! And now you treacherously urge me to come to your room and lie with you, perhaps only to unman me and make a coward of me once I am stripped! I shall never be willing to lie in your bed unless you swear a great oath that you will not invent some worse trouble for me.'

"When I had finished, Circe at once promised to do what I had asked, and after she had solemnly repeated the words of the oath, I went to her lovely bed.

"There were four women servants who worked in Circe's house, nymphs, children of springs and groves and holy streams that flow to the sea. One of them was now spreading crimson throws over the linen covering of the chairs. The second was setting silver tables in front of the chairs and placing golden baskets on them, while the third was mixing honey-sweet wine in a silver bowl and setting golden cups at each place. The fourth was bringing water and lighting a fire under a very large tripod. When the water had boiled in the flashing bronze bowl, she led me to my bath. After mixing the water to suit me she poured it from the bowl over my head and shoulders and bathed me until the killing weariness had left my body. After she rubbed me with olive oil and had dressed me in a fine cloak and tunic, she made me sit down in a silver-nailed chair of exquisite workmanship. . . .

"The nymph now urged me to eat, but I had no heart for it and sat thinking of other things, fully expecting trouble. When Circe saw me sitting there not touching the food and looking sorrowful, she came over to me and said: 'Odysseus, why do you sit like a man without a voice, eating your heart out and not tasting any food or drink? You are looking for some new piece of trickery, I suppose; but you must not be afraid. Remember that I have sworn to you a mighty oath.'

"I answered her and said: 'O Circe, what man with a sense of decency would touch food until he had seen his comrades freed and able to join him? If you are really being kind in asking me to eat and drink, free my comrades so that I can see them with my own eyes.'

"When I had finished, Circe walked out of the house with her wand in her hand, opened the gates of the sty and drove my men out, who now looked exactly like full-grown pigs. As they stood facing her, she walked among them rubbing each one with some magical drug. The bristles that had grown because of the harmful drug Circe had given them earlier completely disappeared. They became men again, but younger than before, and much handsomer and taller. When they recognized me, each of them grasped my hand, and every one of us felt we must weep. The whole house echoed strangely with the sound, and even the goddess shared our sorrow."

[271–364, 373–399]

[Odysseus brings the rest of his companions to Circe's palace. He is eager to leave; Circe tells him of his fated voyage to Hades.]

Book XI

Odysseus' visit to the World of the Dead

[The fair wind brings them to the Cimmerians' land. The ghosts come up from Hades to drink the blood of sacrificial victims. After Elpenor, one of Circe's victims, comes the blind seer Tiresias, who reveals to Odysseus his further trials and how he is to die.]

He meets his mother.

"I waited there without moving until my mother came near and drank the black blood of the offering. [Odysseus has been told by Tiresias that the souls of the dead must drink the blood of the offering before they will recognize him and speak to him.] She immediately recognized me and, bursting into tears, said: 'My child, how did you ever come alive into the land of darkness and mist? It is a difficult thing for the living to visit this world, for between us and you there are great rivers and terrible streams, first of all the Ocean, which no one can cross unless he has a well-built ship. Or have you come here now on your way from Troy? Have you been wandering so long and not yet reached Ithaca or seen your wife and home?'

"When she had finished speaking, I answered: 'Dear Mother, I came down to Hades' realm to consult the soul of Theban Tiresias. I have not yet come near Achaea nor yet set foot in our country, but I have been wandering and suffering terribly ever since I followed Agamemnon to fight the Trojans in Ilium, the city of fine horses. But do tell me this, and explain it to me: What blow struck you and brought death's unending sorrow? Was it a long illness, or did Artemis, goddess of the bow, attack you and kill you with her painless arrows? And tell me about my father and my son whom I left behind. Is my royal power still in their hands? Or does it now belong to someone else, and do they think that I will not return? Tell me too what are my wife's plans and thoughts? Is she staying with our child, and is she keeping all our property as it was, or has she already married one of the noblest of the Achaeans?'

"When I had finished, my lady mother answered: 'Of course Penelope is staying in your house! Her spirit never wavers; but as the sad days and nights drag by her tears are always falling. No one has as yet taken over your royal powers, but Telemachus still holds your lands without any trouble and has his place at all the feasts that a judge of the people ought to attend. Everyone, you can be sure, invites him.'

" 'Your father stays out in the country and never comes to town at all. He has no bed with a mattress and covers and gleaming rugs, but during the winter he sleeps in the house where the servants do, in the ashes near the fire, his back covered only with the poorest kind of clothes; and when summer comes and rich autumn, he lies down somewhere on a sloping place in his vineyard and makes his bed in a pile of fallen leaves.'

" 'And now I shall tell you how I died. The sharp-eyed goddess did not attack me and kill me in my home with her painless arrows, nor was I struck by one of the diseases that so often cruelly waste the body and destroy life; but it was longing for you, glorious Odysseus, and for your wise advice and gentleness that took my sweet life from me.'

"As I heard my dear mother's words, I longed to take her into my arms. Three times I reached out for her and three times she flew from my hands like a shadow or a dream. Now a keener sorrow struck my heart, and I called to her and said: 'Dear Mother, why don't you stay when I so want to touch you? Why can't we throw our arms about each other and at least enjoy the cold comfort of weeping? Or has noble Persephone sent your ghost to me only to make me cry more bitterly?'

"When I had finished, my lady mother answered, 'My child, most unlucky man, you must realize that Persephone is not trying to deceive you; you are merely discovering what happens to all men when they die. Flesh and bone no longer hold together, but after the breath of life has left the white bones, the strong blast of blazing fire destroys the fleshly parts, while the soul flies off on wings like a dream. Make your way now as fast as you can to the world of light, but keep in mind all I have said, and tell it to your wife at some later time.' " [152–224]

[Odysseus meets the ghosts of famous women, wives and daughters of heroes; and the ghost of Agamemnon, who tells how he was murdered by the adulterer Aegisthus and his wife Clytemnestra; Aeschylus used a different version of the story.]

He meets Achilles.

"The ghost of Achilles came up next, along with the ghosts of Patroclus and noble Antilochus and Ajax, the hero who was handsomest and bravest of all the Greeks excepting the noble son of Peleus. Swift-footed Achilles recognized me, and bursting into tears, said: 'Princely son of Laertes, clever Odysseus, why do you go on planning still greater exploits? Poor man, how could you think of coming down to Hades' realm, where the only inhabitants are ghosts, the mere images of men worn out by life?'

"When he had finished, I answered him and said: 'Achilles, Peleus' son, mightiest of the Achaeans, I came to talk with the seer Tiresias, to see if he could tell me some way of getting to rocky Ithaca. For you must know that I have not yet come near Achaea or set foot in my own country, but have run into one disaster after another. But, Achilles, no man has been or ever will be more fortunate than you. Before, when you were alive, we honored you as if you were a god, and now here in the world below you are the great chieftain of the dead. So don't feel sad about your death, Achilles.'

"When I had finished, he answered me and said: 'Don't talk to me of death, glorious Odysseus! I had rather work in the fields as a hired hand for a man who has little land and less means than be king of all the dead in the world below.' " [467–491]

[The ghost of Ajax turns away in angry silence. Next are seen to approach the ghosts of others among the departed—Minos, Orion, Tantalus, Sisyphus, and Heracles. Odysseus retires for fear he may see the Gorgon's head and be turned to stone.]

Book XII

The Sirens' song

[Odysseus returns to Circe's island to bury Elpenor. Circe tells him of dangers to come: the Sirens, the Wandering Rocks, the monster Scylla and the whirlpool Charybdis, and the cattle of the Sun, which it is sacrilege to kill. Odysseus and his men set sail and reach the Sirens' coast.]

" 'Friends,' I said to my comrades, 'it is not right for only one or two of us to know the prophecies that the goddess Circe made to me, so I shall tell them to all of you, and you will at any rate have heard them—whatever happens to us, whether we die or whether we come through safely without meeting death and doom.

" 'She warned us first of all to beware of the voices and flowery meadows of the wonderful Sirens. I am the only one, she said, who is to hear them sing, and I am to stand on the mast block while you bind me with ropes tight to the mast so that I must surely stay there without moving. If I beg you or even order you to let me go, you are to tie me with even more ropes than before.' So I told my men all the prophecies and explained every single detail of them.

"In the meantime our well-built ship had reached the island of the Sirens, for a good breeze had been carrying her quickly along. But suddenly the wind fell, and there was a breathless calm. Some deity, it seemed, had put the waves to sleep. My men jumped up, lowered the sails and threw them in the hold, and then taking their places they struck the water with the smooth blades and made it white with foam.

"When I had cut a large ball of wax into small pieces with my sharp knife, I pressed it firmly in my hands, and the wax quickly grew warm both from the pressure and from the bright rays of the sun. Going down the boat from one man to another, I smeared some of the wax over each one's ears. Next I stepped up on the mast-block, and they bound me hand and foot with ropes drawn tight about the mast. Again they took their places and struck the grey sea with their oars.

"We were about as far from shore as a loud shout will carry and speeding rapidly along, when the Sirens saw our swift ship coming near and began to sing in their piercingly clear voices: 'Come here, come here, famous Odysseus, glory of the Achaeans, anchor your ship and stay to hear our song. Never yet has anyone passed this way in his black ship without hearing the thrilling and sweet sounds that come from our lips, and once he has known the joy of our song, he goes on his way with a great treasure of wisdom. For we know everything the Argives and Trojans suffered on the broad plain of Troy; yes, we know everything that happens on the earth, from which all things grow.'

"So they sang in their high lovely voices; and I longed to hear more, and shaking my head at my men, I signalled to them to set me free. But they bent over their oars and rowed on. Perimedes and Eurylochus jumped up at once and bound me with more ropes even tighter to the mast. When we had finally passed the Sirens and I could no longer hear their voices or their song, my comrades took off the wax with which I had sealed their ears and released me from the ropes that bound me to the mast." [154–200]

[Odysseus and his men undergo the other trials foretold by Circe. Zeus promises the Sun vengeance for the slaughter of his cattle, and sends a storm which shipwrecks the hero. He is cast up on Calypso's island, and the long flashback is over.

In Book XIII, omitted here, the Phaeacians give Odysseus rich gifts and send him home to Ithaca in one of their ships, which Poseidon turns into a rock on the voyage back to Scheria. Odysseus is landed in a deep sleep, and does not know where he is until Athena, disguised as a young man, tells him. Revealing herself to him, she tells him he must overcome the suitors by trickery, and changes his appearance into that of an old beggar. She then goes to Lacedaemon after Telemachus, while Odysseus goes to the hut of Eumaeus, his old swineherd.]

Book XIV

Odysseus' meeting with the swineherd, Eumaeus

Odysseus left the harbor and went along a rough trail through wooded hills until he came to the place where Athena had shown him the house of the swineherd. Of all the servants of Odysseus, he was the most faithful in caring for his master's property.

Odysseus found him sitting now in the doorway of a cabin that faced a fine big yard which was surrounded with a high fence and which lay in an open spot that could be seen from far and near. The swineherd had built this yard while his master was away, without any help from his mistress or old Laertes. On the inside he had lined it with quarried stones and topped them off with a layer of thorny brushwood. On the outside, he had driven in stakes of split black oak, setting them close together all the way around. Within the yard, he had built twelve pens close together as shelters for his pigs. At night fifty big sprawling sows were shut up in each one, while the boars slept outside. There were many fewer boars than sows, only 360 in all; and the wicked suitors were making their numbers smaller and smaller because they were always having the swineherd send up the very fattest ones for their daily feasts. Near by every night slept four dogs, fierce as wild beasts, which the princely herdsman had bred.

As he sat there, he was cutting some sandals out of a stout piece of cowhide and fitting them to his feet. Three of his helpers had gone off in various directions to herd their swine; the fourth he had been obliged to send to town with a pig for the arrogant suitors so they could kill it and have their fill of meat.

Suddenly the dogs saw Odysseus and ran down on him howling and barking, but when they came close Odysseus cleverly crouched down and let his walking stick fall from his hand. But in spite of his cunning he might very well have been cruelly hurt then and there, near his own stockyard, if the swineherd had not come running to help him. Letting the leather fall from his hand, he dashed through the gateway, and yelling at the dogs and flinging a shower of stones after them, he sent them all running in different directions.

Then he turned to his master and said, "Old man, my dogs came within a little of doing you in just now, and if they had, you would have put the blame on me. The gods have already given me troubles and sorrows enough: here I sit weeping and grieving for my noble master, while I fatten his swine for other men to eat! And he goes hungry and wanders like a beggar in strange countries and cities—at least if he's alive and still sees the light of the sun. Well, come along, old fellow, let's go to my cabin so you can have your fill of food and wine and tell me where you have been and what troubles you have been through, too."

With these words the worthy swineherd led Odysseus toward his cabin, took him in, and made a place for him to sit down. First he heaped up a thick pile of twigs and then spread over them the great thick wild-goat skin on which he slept at night. Odysseus was pleased because the man received him so well and turned to him and said: "My host, may Zeus and the other immortal gods give you whatever you most desire, since you have welcomed me with such kindness."

Eumaeus the swineherd answered him and said: "Friend, even if a poorer man than you came along, it would not be right for me to treat a stranger with disrespect. All strangers and beggars, you know, are under the protection of Zeus, and our smallest gift to them is pleasing to him. But servants can do only a little when they live in fear of their new masters. My own master, you see, cannot get home; the gods have kept the one man away who would have used me kindly and given me property of my own, a house and a piece of land and a wife—in short, everything that a good-hearted master gives to his faithful servant. A good servant works hard for his master and the gods bless what he does, as they bless me for sticking to my work here. That's how my master would have helped me, if he had lived on and grown old in his own home. But he's dead. I wish all of Helen's family were dead and gone, too! She has been the death of many brave men, and it was only because of Agamemnon that my master went to Ilium to fight the Trojans."

With these words he drew the belt tight around his tunic and went out to the pens where his pigs were kept. He brought in two and killed them; then he singed them, cut them up, and ran spits through the various pieces. When he had roasted all the meat, he brought it piping hot on the spits and served it. After he had scattered white barleymeal over the meat and mixed some honey-sweet wine in a cup, he sat down across from Odysseus and urged him to begin.

"Come, stranger, eat what the servants get, the young pigs. The suitors of course feed on full grown ones, without a thought in their heads of the gods' wrath and with no feeling of shame whatever. Still the blessed gods do not love wicked deeds; they honor only men who do what is right and fair. Even pirates who make a raid on some foreign country, who seem to take what they want with Zeus' blessing, when they have filled their ships and sailed back home—even men like that are struck with an awful fear of the gods' wrath.

"But the suitors know something about my master, I'm quite sure. Perhaps they have heard the voice of some god telling of his death, and that is why they are unwilling to make their suit in a decent way or go back to their own places. So they go on wasting my master's goods in a high-handed way, with no thought of saving anything. Every night and every day Zeus sends us they kill more victims for their feasts, and not merely one or two, at that. And in the same high and mighty way they keep drawing off our wine and wasting it.

"Yet my master's wealth is immense; no other nobleman, on the dark mainland or here in Ithaca, has as much. There aren't twenty men together who are as rich as he is. But let me tell you what he owns. On the mainland he has twelve herds of cattle, as many flocks of sheep, as many herds of swine, and as many herds of goats scattered far and wide. All of these are tended by foreigners or by his own herdsman. On the island he has, all told, eleven herds of goats grazing on the shorelands, and good men to watch over them, too. But every day each herdsman takes the finest of his fat goats and drives it up for the suitors. And here I am looking after his pigs and trying to protect them, and yet every day I must pick out the best one and send it up to those fellows."

While he talked, Odysseus was ravenously eating the meat and eagerly drinking the wine. He did not say a word, but he was thinking up plenty of troubles for the suitors. When he had eaten all he wanted, the swineherd took the cup from which he usually drank and filling it to the brim gave it to his master. Odysseus received it with real delight and said: "My friend, what is the name of the man who bought and paid for you—this rich and powerful nobleman you have been telling me about? You say he died defending the honor of Agamemnon. Tell me his name, just on the chance that I may know someone like him. Only Zeus and the immortal gods can know whether I actually have seen him and might bring you news of him, but certainly I have travelled far and wide in my wanderings."

The princely swineherd answered: "Old man, no adventurer who comes with news of Odysseus would ever convince his wife and his dear son, because beggars who are looking for food and a bed make up all sorts of tales and don't have much concern for telling the truth. All the wanderers who reach the land of Ithaca come to my mistress and tell her lies, and yet she always receives them kindly and entertains them well. As she asks about everything, the tears fall from her eyes and she cries bitterly, which is always the way with wives when their husbands die in some strange country.

"You, too, old man, would be quick to make up a good story if someone would give you a cloak and tunic. But it's too late. By now dogs and swift birds have torn the flesh from Odysseus' bones, and his soul has left his body. Or perhaps fish have fed on him in the sea, and his bones lie on some shore wrapped deep in sand. Yes, he has died away off there; but he has left sorrow for all who love him, for me more than anyone else.

"I shall never find so kind a master wherever I go, not even if I go back to my father's and mother's house where I was born and brought up. I don't grieve so much for them any more, though I should like to see them with my own eyes and be in my own country again. But I am filled with longing for Odysseus dead and gone. Believe me, stranger, I hardly dare speak of him by name even when he is not here: he loved me so dearly and cared for me so genuinely. However far away he is, I still call him my master."

[1–147]

[In the remainder of Book XIV, the pretended beggar professes to know something of Odysseus, who, he says, will return shortly, and he parries Eumaeus' questions about himself with a string of lies. In Book XV Athena appears in a dream to Telemachus, advises him to go home at once, and warns him to return by a different way, to avoid the suitors' ambush. He arrives safely, picking up on the way a seer, Theoclymenus of Argos, who has had to leave home on account of a blood-feud and asks him for shelter. In Book XVI Telemachus reaches the house of Eumaeus and there sees the supposed beggar. When father and son are alone together, Athena restores

Odysseus to his true shape, and the two plot vengeance on the suitors. Odysseus is to go to the palace as a beggar and learn the lay of the land for himself. In Book XVII Telemachus returns to the palace, where Theoclymenus prophesies to Penelope that her husband will come back very soon, if he is not already in the country. Odysseus, on his way to the palace, meets the goatherd Melanthius, who strikes and insults him. He is recognized by his old dog Argus, who dies after feebly trying to greet him. He begs from the suitors; their leader Antinous strikes him. In Book XVIII the suitors match Odysseus against another beggar; the hero wins, and becomes a tolerated hanger-on. One of the suitors speaks kindly to him but does not understand his veiled warning. Penelope, who has been made marvelously beautiful by Athena, appears in the hall; the suitors give her rich presents. After she leaves, one of them throws a stool at Odysseus, for which Telemachus rebukes him.]

Book XIX

Odysseus in his own house

[After the suitors are gone, father and son remove the armor which hangs in the hall. Then Odysseus has an interview with Penelope, in which he warns her that her husband will certainly return before long. She is much moved by his speech and by a lying yarn he tells her about himself, and bids her old nurse Eurycleia wash his feet.]

Then thoughtful Penelope said to Odysseus: "Dear sir, of all the travellers who have come to my house not one has ever been so intelligent as you. Everything you say is wisely and discreetly said. I have an old woman here, full of good sense, who was my poor husband's nurse and who cared for him from when she took him in her arms on the day he was born. Though she is failing and quite weak, she will wash your feet for you.

"Come now, thoughtful Eurycleia, get up and bathe the stranger. He must be very nearly your master's age; yes, by now Odysseus' hands and feet must look like his; for when men suffer a great deal they quickly grow old and ugly."

The old woman covered her face with her hands, and warm tears fell from her eyes as she said sadly: "Look at me, Odysseus! How little I can do for you now, my child! Though you had the fear of the gods in your heart, Zeus must have hated you more than most men. Certainly no one ever gave the God of Thunder so many burnt offerings, so many fat thighs and fine hecatombs, as you did. And you always prayed that you might live to a bright and happy old age and bring up your noble son to manhood. But still Zeus keeps you from coming back home.

"I suppose, stranger, that at this moment the women of some foreign lord are making fun of my master when he comes to their fine house, just as all these bitches here are laughing at you.* And you shake off all their insults and nasty remarks and won't let them wash you!

"But I, though I don't want to, I am ordered to bathe you by the daughter of Icarius, thoughtful Penelope. And I shall, for Penelope's sake, and for your own, too, because my heart is so stirred up and troubled. But look here. Listen to what I say. Many long-suffering strangers have come to us, but not a single one of them has looked so much like Odysseus. Your build, your voice, your very feet, are like his."

Resourceful Odysseus answered her and said: "Old woman, that's what everyone says who has seen us both, that we are very like one another, as you have said yourself, and very shrewdly, too."

When he had spoken, the old woman took a brightly gleaming bowl and got ready to wash his feet. First she poured in plenty of cold water and then added some hot. Odysseus—he was sitting by the hearth—quickly turned away toward the shadow, for he suddenly thought that when she touched him she might recognize an old wound of his and that then the true state of things might be clear to everyone.

She came over now and began to wash her master's feet, and at once she recognized the wound. It was where a boar had bitten him when he had gone to Parnassus on a visit to his grandfather Autolycus. . . . [349–394]

[The omitted lines give the details of the boar-hunt that occurred many years before, in which Odysseus was wounded.]

Once Eurycleia had put her hands on the wound and felt it, she let Odysseus' foot slip from

* The women servants were the mistresses of the suitors.

her grasp. His leg fell against the edge of the bowl, and the bronze rang out like a gong. The bowl tipped to one side, and the water poured out on the ground. The old woman was at once overcome with joy and sorrow; her eyes filled with tears, and her rich voice choked. Laying her hand on Odysseus' face she said to him, "You are really Odysseus, dear child! And to think that I did not know you before! No, not until I touched my master with my hands, not until then, was I sure!"

As she spoke, her eyes glanced towards Penelope, for she wanted to show her that her dear husband was there in his own house. But Penelope could not look toward her or take any notice because Athena had turned her thoughts elsewhere.

Before Eurycleia could speak, Odysseus grabbed her by the throat with his right hand, and with the other drew her closer to him and said, "Dear woman, do you want to ruin me! You know that you nursed me at your breast; know too that after enduring many sufferings for over nineteen years I have at last come to the land of my fathers. But since some god has put the thought in your heart and you have seen who I am, keep still, for fear someone else may find out, too. Otherwise, let me tell you what will happen: if some god lets me kill the suitors, I won't spare you, even though you are my nurse, when I kill the rest of the serving women in this house."

Then thoughtful Eurycleia said to him: "My child, what a thing for you to say! You know how firm and unyielding my spirit is: I will stand fast like a solid block of stone or iron. But one thing I shall tell you, and don't forget it, either. If some god lets you kill the suitors, I shall go over the names of all the women in the house and tell you which ones are a disgrace to you and which are innocent."

Resourceful Odysseus answered her and said: "Why speak of them? You hardly need to. I shall watch them closely myself and know what each one of them is like. But keep from talking, and leave everything to the gods."

When he had finished, the old woman went through the hall to fetch some more water to wash his feet, because all the other had spilled out. When she had washed him and rubbed him with oil, Odysseus drew his chair closer to the fire and carefully covered his scar with his ragged clothes. [465–507]

[Penelope confides to the supposed stranger her misgivings and recounts to him a strange dream she had the night before. Odysseus interprets it favorably, but she still doubts, and wishes to put an end to the suitors' wooing by a decisive test.]

Book XX

THE NIGHT BEFORE THE KILLING OF THE SUITORS

So noble Odysseus made his bed on the porch of his house. He spread out an untanned ox hide and over that many fleeces from sheep that the Achaeans had killed for their feasts. When he had lain down, the maid Eurynome threw a cloak over him.

Odysseus lay there wide awake, his mind full of plans for punishing the suitors. The women of the house, who had long been the suitors' mistresses, came out of the hall laughing and joking with each other. When Odysseus heard them he grew violently angry, and he wondered whether he should jump up and strike them dead now or whether he should let them sleep with the arrogant suitors for one last time. His heart was fairly howling with fury. As a dog, seeing a stranger, walks around her helpless puppies and barks and gets ready to fight, so his heart howled with anger at their wicked acts.

He struck his breast and scolded himself in these words: "Bear up, my heart! You once endured something still more vile than this on the day when the Cyclops with irresistible fury ate my strong comrades. But you bore up until my cleverness brought you out of the cave, though you thought you were doomed to die."

So he talked to himself, and his heart obeyed and remained brave and unshaken. But still he kept tossing this way and that on his bed. As a man holds a sausage stuffed with fat and blood over a great blazing fire and turns it now this way and now that in his eagerness to get it roasted quickly, so Odysseus tossed and turned. He kept wondering how he alone, one against many, could get his hands on the shameless suitors.

At once Athena came down from the sky and appeared beside him in the form of a woman. As she stood looking down at him, she said,

"Most unhappy man, why are you lying awake now? This is your house, and here in the house is your wife; and you have seen your boy, who is everything that anyone could want a son to be."

Resourceful Odysseus answered her and said, "All you say is quite true, but I keep wondering how I can get my hands on the shameless suitors. I am alone and have no help, while they are always together. But besides that, I have even a greater worry. If I should kill them with your and Zeus's help, where should I run for safety and hide? I want you to think about all these things."

Then the gleaming-eyed goddess Athena said to him: "Poor fellow, many a man takes the advice of some friend who is only a mortal and not so strong or so wise as I; but I am a god who will protect you in your troubles straight to the end. Let me speak right out to you: even if fifty bands of men stood around us ready and eager to kill, you could drive off their cows and fat flocks of sheep. So let sleep come now, for it is miserable to lie awake all night long. Soon you will be safe and out of trouble." When she had finished speaking, the glorious goddess shed sleep over Odysseus' eyes and at once went back to Olympus.

As soon as sleep came over him, sleep that dissolves the cares of the heart and relaxes the body, his loving wife awoke and sat up in her soft bed and wept. But when she had cried her fill, her first thought was to pray to Artemis. "Artemis, august goddess, daughter of Zeus, if only you would shoot an arrow into my breast and take my life from me this instant, or if only a whirlwind would lift me up and carry me off over dark misty ways and drop me in the streams of the world-encircling Ocean!

"So once storm winds lifted up the daughters of Pandareus and carried them away. Their father and mother had been killed by the gods and they were left living alone in their home, but glorious Aphrodite fed them with cheese and sweet honey and fragrant wine, Hera gave them intelligence and beauty above that of all other women, pure Artemis made them divinely tall, and Athena taught them to make wonderful things with their hands. But when at last glorious Aphrodite went up to high Olympus to ask the blessing of a happy marriage for them—she had gone to Zeus because he knows both what is fated and what not fated for mortals—at that moment the Harpies snatched them up in a whirlwind and gave them to the hateful Erinyes to be their servants. I wish that the dwellers in Olympus would carry me off in the same way, or that lovely Artemis would strike me dead so that I could go under the grim earth with Odysseus' image in my eye and never have to give pleasure to any man less noble than he!

"Misery is at least endurable, though our hearts are deeply hurt and though we weep all day, if sleep comes at night; for sleep makes us forget everything, both good and bad, when once it closes our eyes. But some god keeps sending me bad dreams, and tonight again a man seemed to lie beside me who looked exactly like Odysseus when he went off with Agamemnon. For the moment I was happy, because I thought it was not a dream but the truth."

As she finished speaking, Eos appeared, throned in golden light. At that moment Odysseus heard her crying and awoke. As he lay there thinking, it seemed to him that Penelope stood near his head and that she already knew who he was.

He gathered up the cloak and fleeces that had covered him while he slept and put them down on a chair in the hall. Then he carried the cowhide outdoors, and raising his hands, prayed to Zeus: "Father Zeus, if you gods in heaven wished me well in bringing me over land and sea to my own country, though you did treat me rather badly, let some of the people now awaking speak a word of omen in the house, and let some other sign appear outside."

Zeus the counsellor heard his prayer and at once sent a thunderbolt from shining Olympus, high up in the clouds; and noble Odysseus was mightily pleased. The omen from the house came through one of the grinding women who was working near her master in the place where his handmills stood. Twelve women usually worked at them, making barley meal and wheat flour, the staff of life. The others had ground their wheat and were sleeping; and only this one, a very feeble old woman, had still not finished her work. She stopped grinding a moment and spoke the words which her master was waiting to hear. "Father Zeus, ruler of gods and men, that was a loud thunderbolt you sent from the sky! Still there isn't a cloud anywhere! I think you must have meant it for a sign to someone in this house.

Now hear my words, and answer the prayer of a poor old woman: let this be the very last day on which the suitors have one of their fine feasts in the house of Odysseus! I have worn out life and limb grinding corn for them; let them have their last feast today!"

Noble Odysseus was pleased with her words of good omen and with Zeus's thunderbolt. He at last felt sure of punishing the suitors.

And now the servants in Odysseus' beautiful house had come to work and had lighted the flaming fire on the hearth. [1–123]

[Odysseus meets his cattleman Philetius, who also proves faithful. At a feast yet another suitor insults the supposed beggar by throwing a bone at him. Soon after, the seer Theoclymenus foretells destruction for the suitors, but they laugh at him, and he leaves the hall. In Book XXI Penelope brings out the great bow of Odysseus; the suitor who can best string and shoot it is to have Penelope to wife. One after another the suitors try and fail; Telemachus tries, but he purposely fails on a nod from his father. Finally Odysseus, who has meanwhile revealed himself to Eumaeus and Philetius, obtains, after difficulties, permission to try. He strings it easily and performs the required feat, shooting an arrow through a row of axes. Telemachus quietly slips on his sword and takes a spear.]

Book XXII

The battle with the suitors

[Odysseus throws off his rags and springs upon the threshold of the hall. Promising to try his skill at a mark never shot at before, he hits Antinous and kills him. He reveals himself to the rest, and rejecting offers of truce, proceeds to shoot them down. They resist as best they can with their swords, using the tables as shields. Telemachus brings from the storeroom arms for his father, himself, and the two herdsmen. The traitor Melanthius, trying to steal into the storeroom to get arms for the suitors, is caught there and left fast bound. Athena, in the form of a swallow, sits on a rafter and uses her arts to frighten the suitors and divert their spears, while she eggs Odysseus on. They beg in vain for mercy.]

The bard Phemius, who sang for the suitors only because he was forced to, had so far escaped death. With his clear sounding lyre still in his hands, he stood near the door at the back of the hall, trying to decide what he should do. Should he leave the hall and go to the altar of mighty Zeus, God of the Courtyard, where Laertes and Odysseus had burned many oxen? Or should he run to Odysseus and throw his arms about his knees and ask for mercy? The best thing, he decided, was to go to Odysseus. So he laid the hollow lyre on the ground between a bowl and a silver-nailed chair, and rushing up to his lord, clasped his knees and eagerly begged him for mercy.

"I come to you as a suppliant, Odysseus; respect my prayer and take pity on me. In time to come you will suffer bitterly if you kill a bard, for like all singers I honor both gods and men. No one else taught me, a god made all kinds of songs grow and flower in my mind; and if I live you will hear me singing to you as if you were a god.

"So do not kill me! Your dear son Telemachus can tell you that I did not come here of my own free will to sing for the suitors at their feasts, and I did not come for money either. They got me here only because there were so many of them and they were so much stronger than I."

Good Telemachus heard his words with respect and quickly spoke to his father, who was standing near by, "Stop! Don't strike this innocent man! And save Medon the herald, too, because when I was a boy he was always my protector here. But Philetius or the swineherd may have already killed him, or perhaps you ran into him when you went storming through the hall."

Medon, a very shrewd fellow, had heard these words from where he lay safely hidden. He had escaped harm by crouching under a chair and wrapping himself in a freshly-flayed ox hide. He now quickly threw off the hide and suddenly darted out from under the chair. Running up to Telemachus, he clasped his knees and asked him for mercy, "My friend, here I am! Stop fighting now and save me! Your father's strength is tremendous; tell him not to strike me simply because he is angry at the suitors! They were the ones, and not I, who wasted his wealth and who were foolish enough to have no respect for you."

Resourceful Odysseus smiled at him and said, "Cheer up, my son has protected you and saved you. Now you will be able to understand and tell others that well-doing is much better than evil-doing. You and the singer of many songs, both of you, go out of the hall into the courtyard, and stay far away from all this gore so I can do here the work that I must do."

When he had finished, they walked out of the hall and sat down near the altar of mighty Zeus, both of them still looking around in all directions and expecting death at every moment.

Meanwhile Odysseus was searching his house to see if any of the suitors were alive and safely hidden out of sight. But he found every one of them—and there were a great many, too—lying there in the blood and the dust, like fish that fishermen have drawn up from the grey sea in a fine-meshed net and tossed in a pile on the curving beach. They all lie on the sand, gasping for water, while the bright sun takes the life out of them. That is how the suitors lay piled up on top of one another in the great hall of Odysseus' house. [330–389]

[The maids who had been the suitors' mistresses are forced to carry out the bodies and cleanse the hall; they are then hanged by Telemachus, and Melanthius is horribly mutilated.]

Book XXIII

Penelope recognizes Odysseus

[Penelope, who has been cast into a deep sleep by Athena, is told the news but at first will not believe that the stranger is really Odysseus. She enters the hall, where a pretence of dancing and feasting is kept up to deceive casual passers-by. Odysseus, dressed like a king, enters and chides her coldness. Convinced at last, by his knowledge of their own secret bedroom, that it is really Odysseus, she throws herself into his arms.]

Suddenly Penelope felt weak and faint, when she realized that Odysseus had given her sure proof of knowing their secret room. Bursting into tears she ran straight to Odysseus and threw her arms around his neck and kissed him and said: "Don't be angry with me, Odysseus! You have always been a most sensible man; remember now that all our troubles have come from the gods. They would not give us the happiness of going through life side by side and of reaching the threshold of old age together.

"So do not be angry and find fault with me because I did not welcome you like this the first time I saw you. I was always dogged with the fear of being tricked by some lying traveller's tale. You know that many men think up such schemes only to fill their own pockets. . . .

"But now you have given me clear proof that you know about our bed, which no other living person had ever seen except you and me and one servant, Actoris. My father gave her to me at the time I came here, and she used to watch at the door of our bedroom. Yes, you have really overcome my feelings, though they were so hard to change." As he heard her words, Odysseus felt that he could no longer keep back his tears.

So he cried, holding his wife in his arms and thinking how dear and how loyal she was. This was a moment as happy for her as when swimmers from a shipwreck first catch sight of land. The wind and heavy seas have struck their well-built boat, and Poseidon has dashed it to pieces, but a few of them escape from the grey sea by swimming to the shore. At last, with their bodies covered by a thick crust of brine, they step out on the land, more than happy at their escape. That was how Penelope felt when she saw her husband and held him in her arms. She clung to him and could not let him go.

And Eos, the rosy-fingered goddess of morning, would surely have found them still weeping if gleaming-eyed Athena had not planned things differently. First she held Night back for a long time in his journey over the earth; next, she made Eos stay by Ocean's stream and would not let her hitch up swift Lampus and Phaethon, the colts that carry the goddess and bring the morning light to men.

Then resourceful Odysseus said to Penelope: "My wife, we have not yet come to the end of all our troubles, but there will be one more trial, an immeasurably great and difficult one, that I must go through. That is what the shade of Tiresias prophesied on the day I went down to Hades' house, when I was trying to discover a safe way home for my men and myself. Come, let us go to bed, wife, and enjoy the pleasure of sweet sleep."

Then thoughtful Penelope said to him: "Your bed will be ready whenever you wish, now that the gods have brought you back to your handsome house and to the land of your fathers. But since some god has put the thought into your head, please tell me about this trial you spoke of. I suppose I shall hear it later, but it's no worse for me to learn the truth now."

Resourceful Odysseus answered her and said, "Dear woman, why are you so eager to have me tell you?—Very well, I'll tell you the whole story and cover up nothing. But it will not make you feel any happier; certainly I am not very happy about it.

"Tiresias told me I must travel to very many cities and that I must carry a well-shaped oar in my hand and keep going until I come to men who do not know the sea and who eat their food unsalted. These people, he said, know nothing about red-prowed ships or well-shaped oars that are the wings of ships. He gave me a very clear sign by which I might recognize them and which I shall not keep from you, either: when another traveller meets me on the road and says that I am carrying a winnowing fan on my shoulder, then, said Tiresias, I am to set the oar firmly in the ground. After making a fine sacrifice to lord Poseidon of a goat, a bull, and a boar, I am to return home and offer holy hecatombs to the immortal gods who live in the broad heavens, to every one of them in their proper order. Death will come to me from the sea at the end of a serene old age and very gently take me from the company of a happy and prosperous people. All this, Tiresias said, would certainly come to pass."

Then wise Penelope said to him, "If the gods intend to make your old age a happier time, there is hope that then you will find a rest from all your troubles."

So they talked on together while Eurynome and the nurse, by the light of flaming torches, were making up their bed with soft covers. When they had quickly spread it with good thick bedclothes, the old nurse came down and went to her room. Holding a torch in her hands to light the way, Eurynome then escorted Penelope and Odysseus to bed. Once she had brought them to their room, she went below too. They were both more than happy to have come again to where their old bed stood.

At the same time Telemachus and the cowherd and the swineherd stopped dancing, and they made the women stop, too. Then all three of them went to bed in the great shadowy hall.

When Odysseus and Penelope had loved one another, they began talking happily together. First Penelope told what she had endured from seeing the wastefulness of the crowd of suitors, how they had killed so many cows and sheep and drawn off so many jars of wine merely because they all wanted to marry her. Then Odysseus told his story, all the cruel things he had done to his enemies and all the bitter sufferings he had himself lived through. It was a joy for her to hear him, and she did not fall asleep until he had told her everything. [205–217, 225–309]

[Next morning Odysseus gives the house into Penelope's keeping, while he goes to visit his father Laertes. In Book XXIV he reveals himself to his father, and they muster men to resist the vengeance of the suitors' kinsfolk; Hermes has meanwhile taken the ghosts of the dead to Hades. The father of the suitor Antinous heads the avengers, but Laertes, his youth restored by the gods, kills him. Zeus hurls a thunderbolt between the opposing forces, and peace is made through the agency of Athena, first and last the champion of Odysseus.]

The Homeric Hymn to Hermes

Translated by Norman O. Brown

INTRODUCTION

THE SEVENTH and sixth centuries B.C. saw the composition of the Homeric Hymns—poems in the meter and language of Homer dealing with episodes in the careers of the Olympian gods. *The Homeric Hymn to Hermes* (written in the sixth century) is a fine example of this mythological poetry in the archaic Greek style. It tells how the impudent upstart Hermes obtains equality with his august and noble brother Apollo. The humor of the story, judged by Hebraic-Christian notions of the divine, is blasphemous; but in Greek religion of the archaic age, gods are anthropomorphic—and therefore often comical—without ceasing to be gods. The sympathies of the author are on Hermes' side: Apollo is the aristocrat, rich in cattle; Hermes, the god of merchants, by a combination of technical ingenuity, shrewdness, and unscrupulousness "makes good" on the very day of his birth and cheats the elder god.

FOR A further discussion of the hymn, see Norman O. Brown, *Hermes the Thief* (Madison, Wis., 1947), Chapters V and VI. The text translated is that of T. W. Allen, *Homeri Opera* (Oxford, 1911), Vol. V.

A HYMN to Hermes, Muse, to Hermes the son of Zeus and Maia, the lord of Mount Cyllene and of Arcadia and its flocks of sheep, the messenger of the gods. Maia, the good nymph with the beautiful hair, gave birth to him after her union in love with Zeus. She lived in the shady depths of a cave, to avoid the company of the blessed gods; there Zeus, the son of Cronus, used to lie with her in the dead of night, for as long as the sweet chains of slumber held Hera, his wife with the white limbs; and he kept it secret from the immortal gods and from mortal men. When the time had come to fulfill the purpose of great Zeus, and her tenth month had risen in the sky, she brought the infant forth into the light, and deeds of signal note ensued. Then it was she gave birth to that ingenious child, that cunning schemer, that raider and rustler of cattle, the shepherd of dreams, that denizen of night who loiters in doorways. It did not take him long to prove his prowess to the immortal gods. Born in the morning, in the noonday he performed upon the lyre, in the evening he stole the cattle of the archer-god Apollo—all on that first fourth day of the month that the lady Maia gave birth to him.

As soon as he leaped from the immortal thighs of his mother, he did not lie long in the sacred winnowing basket that was his cradle; instead he jumped up, and was off in search of the cattle of Apollo. As he stepped across the threshold of the high-overarched cave, he discovered a tortoise, from which he made an immense fortune: it was Hermes who first made the tortoise into a singer. This tortoise faced him in the dooryard, as she grazed the luxuriant grass in front of the house, moving with deliberate steps; when the lucky son of Zeus saw her he laughed and right away spoke to her and said: "I accept you as a sign of good fortune coming to me. Welcome, dancing girl with the lovely figure. How pleasing you are to my eyes! Where did you get that pretty toy, that dappled shell, tortoise whose home is in the hills? I am going to take you and carry you into the house, you will bring me profit, and I will not disdain it; you will be my first lucky venture. You must come into my parlor, for the outside world is full of danger. While you live you will be a magic charm against the evil eye; and if you die, you will learn to sing pretty songs."

This was what he said, and at the same time

lifting it with both his hands he carried the lovely toy back inside the house. Then, tossing her over, he scooped out the marrow of the mountain tortoise with a chisel of gray steel. As fast as a lightning thought crosses the mind of a man worried with many troubles, or as fast as twinklings flash from eyes, even so noble Hermes' plan was no sooner said than done. He cut measured lengths of reed, and fixed them in position, boring through the shell of the tortoise's back. Over it he stretched an ox-hide with thoughtful skill; he added arms, and placed a bridge to join them, and strung it with seven strings of sheepgut, harmoniously attuned. When it was all made, he took the lovely toy and struck up a melody; in his hands the tortoise raised a stirring din. The god sang a pretty song in accompaniment, trying his skill at improvising, as young men revelling in their cups improvise impudent sallies of wit; his subject was Zeus, the son of Cronus, and Maia of the beautiful sandal, how they used to dally in companionate love, and his own birth; he even cited his own name. He celebrated the splendid mansion of the nymph his mother, her attendants, and the tripods and bowls that stood constantly in the house. But while he was still on this song, his mind was busy with other plans. He took the hollow lyre and set it down in the sacred winnowing basket that was his cradle. Ravenous for meat, he sprang out of the fragrant hall to spy the land, his mind bent on a stroke of trickery such as men whose business is stealing prepare in the pitch-black season of night.

The Sun was setting under the earth in the ocean, and his horses and chariot with him, when Hermes came running to the shady mountains of Pieria, where the immortal cattle of the blessed gods were penned, and where they grazed on lovely virgin meadows. From this herd the son of Maia, the keen-eyed killer of Argus, cut off fifty cows. He drove them over the sandy ground in labyrinthine ways, turning their tracks around; using his skill at trickery, he reversed their hooves so that the front ones went behind, the hind ones were in front, while he himself faced forward. Then on the sandy shore he made a pair of wicker sandals, a piece of work marvellous past telling, past belief. Combining tamarisk and myrtle twigs, he gathered an armful of them in their verdant prime and tied them safely under his feet, leaves and all—skidding sandals which the noble killer of Argus plucked. He improvised a unique invention to avoid having to walk the road, since he was in a hurry and his way was long.

As he was speeding toward the plain through Onchestus with its deep beds of grass, an old man who was tending the budding vineyards spied him. The son of noble Maia spoke to him first, and said: "Old man digging the planted rows with bent shoulders, you will have plenty of wine when all these vines bear fruit, if you follow my advice and are blind to what you have seen and deaf to what you have heard and hold your tongue, if you know what is good for you."

That was all he said; then he drove the sturdy herd of cattle onwards. On his way noble Hermes passed many shady mountains and noisy ravines and flowery plains. The divine night of darkness, which was his accomplice, was now mostly spent, and dawn, who summons the world to work, was about to begin soon; also mistress Moon, daughter of Lord Pallas, the son of Megamedes, had just scaled her mountain lookout; that was the hour at which the stout son of Zeus brought Phoebus Apollo's cattle, so broad in the brow, to the river Alpheus. Unforced they went towards the cave with its lofty roof and towards the troughs facing the shining meadow.

When he had fed the lowing cattle well with fodder and driven them towards the cave all together in a herd, grazing on clover and rush grass wet with dew, he began to gather a pile of wood, and turned his mind to the invention of fire. He took a good stick of laurel and trimmed it with his steel blade; and then he drilled with a piece of wood grasped tight in his palm, and the hot glow sprang into life. It was Hermes who first gave the world firesticks and fire. Then in a pit dug in the ground he placed an ample number of dry logs which he lifted whole; the streaming flame shone far as the fire burned big. While the fire, potent instrument of famous Hephaestus, was kindling, he dragged two bellowing cows through the door towards the fire; great was the strength he showed. He threw them both panting on their backs on the ground, and bearing down upon them he rolled them over and pierced their spines. Work piled on work: he cut slices of meat rich in fat, ran wooden spits through them and roasted them; the flesh, choice cuts from the back, together with black blood stuffed in gut, was all left lying in the place. The skins he stretched on a hard rock, where from that day to this they have gathered age, and still exist in spite of the untold lapse of time. Then Hermes in cheerful spirits spread the rich harvest on a smooth slab, and divided it into twelve portions which he assigned by lot; each portion had a choice cut of honor added to it. Noble Hermes felt a desire for the sacred offerings of meat: immortal though he was, the good smell tempted him; nevertheless his manly soul did not yield, in spite of his great longing to stuff his holy throat. Instead he carried it all—the meat and fat—into the cave with its lofty roof and placed it away up high, as a monument to his recent theft. Then, adding dry wood to the fire, he destroyed the rest—the feet and heads—in the blaze. When all his business had been finished, the god threw his sandals into the deep current of the Alpheus, extinguished the embers and sprinkled the spot with black dirt; all night he worked, and the beautiful light of the lady Moon shone down on him.

He arrived back at the sacred peak of Cyllene at dawn; on the long way he encountered no one, neither of the blessed gods nor of mortal men; nor did the dogs bark. Hermes the lucky son of Zeus entered the house by slipping sideways through the keyhole, in the shape of a breath of air in autumn, like a mist. He made straight for the cave and went to the inner sanctuary, stepping softly with his feet: he made no sound on the hard floor. Noble Hermes hastened to occupy his cradle: he wrapped the baby blankets round his shoulders and lay like an infant child wriggling the covers round his legs with his fingers, and clutching the lovely tortoise shell in his left hand.

Nevertheless he did not escape his mother's watchful eye; she was a goddess no less than he was a god. She spoke to him and said: "Where have you been, you devious schemer? What have you been up to, coming here in the nighttime and showing your shameless face? I see now that either you are going to go right out of the front door in Apollo's hands, with adamantine chains around your sides, or else you will make a career of prowling through the hills. Go back where you came from; when your father made you, he made a deal of troubles for mortal men and for the immortal gods."

Hermes answered his mother with a speech which revealed his shrewdness: "Mother mine, why do you throw all this at me, as if I were an infant child who does not know any bad words, who is timid, and afraid of his mother's scoldings? I intend to take up whatever career is best, working all the time for myself and for you. We belong to the immortal gods: we will not put up with staying here, denied the gifts and prayers that are our due, as you advise. It is better to spend our days in the pleasant company of the immortals, in wealth, prosperity, and abundance, than to sit at home in a dreary cave. In rank I intend to get the same divine honor as Apollo. If my father does not give it to me, then I will attempt—and this is within my power—to be the prince of thieves. And if the son of noble Leto tracks me down, I think he will find something he had not expected, something too big for him: I will go to Pytho and break into his great house; there I will find plenty of beautiful tripods and bowls and gold to carry away. Just you wait and see."

These were the words exchanged by the son of aegis-bearing Zeus and the lady Maia. Meanwhile dawn leapt from the deep waters of Ocean, its early birth bringing light to mortal men, and Apollo arrived on his journey at Onchestus, the lovely grove sacred to the rumbling earthshaker. There beside the road he found the old man grazing the brute that was a tower of strength to him in the vineyard. The son of noble Leto spoke to him first, and said: "Old man working this briar patch in grassy Onchestus, I come here from Pieria looking for some cattle, all female, all with twisted horns, from my herd. The bull, a black one, was grazing apart from the others; the dogs with their flashing eyes were following behind him, four dogs with a single purpose, just like humans. They—the dogs and the bull—were left behind, which is, indeed, passing strange. As for the cows, they went away from the soft meadow and their sweet pasture a little after the setting of the sun. So tell me, good old man, if you have caught any glimpse of a man on the road after these cattle."

The old man answered him, saying: "My friend, it is hard for a man to tell the whole story of what has passed before his eyes. Many travelers take the road, and of them some travel with many evil plans in their hearts, and some with good; it is difficult to read the mind of each one. Now all day till the setting of the sun I was digging the ground of my vineyard. And, sir, I thought I saw a child—but I have no certain knowledge who the child might be—following behind the cows with their fine horns. A mere infant he was, and he had a wand; he kept going from side to side, forcing the cattle to go backwards and keeping their heads facing him."

These were the old man's words. The other went faster on his road after he had heard the story. He saw a bird spreading his wings in flight: at once he knew that Hermes the son of Zeus the son of Cronus had been the thief. Lord Apollo, son of Zeus, sped direct to holy Pylos in search of his shambling cows, his ample shoulders curtained in a purple cloud. There the archer-god found the tracks, and exclaimed: "Heavens, here is a very strange thing that I see with my own eyes. These are the tracks of straight-horned cows, but they face backwards towards the asphodel meadow. And here are footprints that belong neither to man nor woman nor tawny wolves nor bears nor lions. Nor do I think they are the prints of a shaggy-maned centaur. Who can it be who steps in such monstrous fashion with his quick feet? This side the tracks are strange, that side they are stranger still."

Thus the lord Apollo, son of Zeus, spoke, and then he hurried on till he came to Cyllene's forest-clad mountain and to the cave deep in the shadows of the rocks where the immortal nymph gave birth to the son of Zeus the son of Cronus. A lovely fragrance pervaded the holy mountain, and many sheep grazed and stretched their legs. Then he hurried on and went across the stone threshold, down into the dreary cave, the archer-god Apollo in person.

When the son of Zeus and Maia saw that the archer-god Apollo was furious about his cattle, he dived down inside his fragrant baby blankets. As dust buries a pile of embers of logs, so Hermes covered himself up when he saw the master archer. He huddled his head and hands and feet together in a little space, just like a baby fresh from the bath and ready for sweet sleep, although he was really awake; he held the tortoise-shell lyre under his arm. But the son of Zeus and Leto knew and did not fail to know the beautiful mountain nymph and her son, the little baby who had plunged himself so deep in tricky schemes. He scanned every nook in the great house, and opened three secret chambers with a shining key. They were full of nectar and lovely ambrosia, and there was also much gold and silver and many robes belonging to the nymph, purple and silver-white—indeed everything that the sacred houses of the blessed gods contain. When he had searched the recesses of the great house, the son of Leto turned to noble Hermes and said: "Child lying in the cradle, inform me where the cattle are, and be quick about it, else you and I may find ourselves in an ugly fight. For I shall hurl you to the murky depths of Tartarus, to the world of darkness where all men have their sad inevitable end. Neither your mother nor your father will restore you to the light of day; you will drag out your life underground with only pigmy men to serve as guide."

Hermes answered him with words which revealed his shrewdness: "Son of Leto, what is the meaning of this rough language? Why do you come here looking for cattle, which should be grazing in the fields? I have seen nothing; I have heard nothing; no one has told me anything. I cannot inform you, I could not even accept a reward for information given. I don't look like a cattle raider, a strong-armed fellow; that is not my line of work. My business has been quite different: my business has been sleep, and my mother's milk, and keeping my baby blankets round my shoulders, and hot baths. It would be best if no one heard about this quarrel; the gods would be incredulous at the idea that a new-born infant should take a herd of cattle which should be grazing in the fields and bring them into the grounds of his house. There is no sense in what you say: I was born yesterday, my feet are tender and the ground is rough. But if you wish, I will swear a mighty oath by my father's head; I solemnly declare that I am not guilty myself, nor have I seen anyone else who might be the thief of your cattle—whatever these cattle may be; all I know is just a rumor."

This was what Hermes said. With his eyes twinkling all the time, he shook his head, looking from side to side and giving a long whistle to show how lightly he regarded the story. The archer-god Apollo laughed softly and replied: "My lad, you are a deceiver and your heart is tricky. I fancy that there will be many occasions when you will break into well-to-do homes by night and go round the house bagging stuff without making a sound; you will turn more than one person out into the street, to judge from the way you have just spoken. Many a country shepherd also will suffer injury at your hands in mountain valleys, whenever you are ravenous for meat and you run onto cattle herds or woolly flocks of sheep. But enough. Unless you wish to fall into the final endless sleep, get down out of your cradle, you denizen of night. One title at least the gods will recognize as yours from now on: you will be called forevermore the Prince of Thieves."

This was what Phoebus Apollo said; then he lifted up the infant and began to carry him off. The stout killer of Argus thought quickly and as he was being lifted up in Apollo's hands, he let out an omen—an outrageous kind of messenger, in vile service to his belly; and immediately after that he gave a sinister sneeze. Apollo heard, and dropped noble Hermes to the ground. He sat down in front of him, in spite of his eagerness to to be on his way, and began to scold Hermes, saying: "Never fear, child in baby blankets, son of Zeus and Maia; in the end I will find my sturdy head of cattle; these omens will guide me, and you yourself will lead the way."

When Apollo said this, Hermes the god born on Mount Cyllene jumped up with a quick gesture. Rubbing both his ears back with his hands and wrapping his baby blanket round his shoulders, he said: "Where do you want to take me, archer-god? You are the cruelest of all gods. Is it all on account of some cattle that you assault me so angrily? Oh, I wish the whole breed of cattle would die. I did not steal your cattle, I did not see anyone else steal them—whatever these cattle may be; all I know is just a rumor. Let us appear as plaintiff and defendant before Zeus the son of Cronus."

Hermes the shepherd and the glorious son of Leto cross-examined each other on every particular, but their minds went opposite ways: Apollo, with words of truth on his lips, and justice on his side, wanted to arrest noble Hermes on account of the cattle. The other, the god born on Mount Cyllene, tried with cunning tricks and false words to deceive the god with the silver bow. But when he found that all his ingenuity was matched by the ingenious maneuvers of the other, he quickly turned and walked along the sand: he went in front and the son of Zeus and Leto followed behind. Soon they came to the edge of the incense-fragrant Olympus—two beautiful sons of Zeus going to appear before their father the son of Cronus. There the scales of justice were laid out ready for both of them. Festivity reigned throughout snow-clad Olympus; the gods who cannot die had gathered together as soon as dawn had set her golden throne in the east. Hermes and Apollo, the god with the silver bow, took their stand in front of the knees of Zeus. Zeus, the god who sends the thunder from on high, questioned his illustrious son, saying: "Phoebus, where did you pick up this likely booty that you have there—this newborn baby with the appearance of a herald? Here is solemn business to come before the assembly of the gods."

Lord Apollo the archer-god replied: "Father, you scold me as if I were the only one who had a liking for booty; you are going to hear a story which cannot be shaken. After covering much ground I found this infant in the mountains of Cyllene—he is a robber who can penetrate any defense, a brazen rascal such as I have never seen the like of among the gods or among those men on earth who practise fraud upon their fellows. He stole my cattle from the meadow; he was away towards evening, driving them along the shore where the tumbling ocean roars, straight towards Pylos. There were two kinds of tracks, both monstrous strange, the work of some mighty spirit. The black dust which held the footprints of the cattle showed them pointing towards the asphodel meadow. And as for this fellow here, he was an uncanny kind of traveler: he did not use either his feet or his hands to walk along the sandy ground; he had some other device, and left such monstrous tracks as if walking on saplings of trees. As long as his road took him over sandy ground, the tracks were all evident and easy to see; but when he had left the long path through the sand, his tracks and those of the cattle became invisible in the hard ground. Nevertheless he was seen by a mortal man driving the herd of broad-browed cattle straight towards Pylos. After he had quickly penned the cattle and had juggled his tracks around and about, he lay down in his cradle looking like the darkness of night, in a gloomy cave below the ground, where not even the piercing eye of an eagle could have seen him. He kept on rubbing his eyes with his hands as he turned over plans of trickery in his mind. With his own lips he immediately said lightly, 'I have seen nothing, I have heard nothing, no one has told me anything, I cannot inform you, I could not even accept a reward for information given.' "

After he had spoken, Apollo sat down and Hermes told his version of the story before the immortal gods. Directing him to the son of Cronus, who has commanding power over all the gods, he said: "Father Zeus, I will tell you the truth; there is no falsehood in me, and I cannot tell a lie. He came to our house today just after sunrise searching for some shambling cattle; he brought none of the blessed gods with him as witnesses or observers. He demanded information from me, with much use of force and violence; he threatened to hurl me into the broad pit of Tartarus. He, of course, is in the tender flower and glory of young manhood, while I was born only yesterday, as he knows very well himself. I do not look like a cattle raider, a strong-armed fellow. Believe me—remember you call yourself my father, too—I did not drive the cattle to our house, I did not even step over the threshold; so may I one day be rich, I am telling you the truth. I respect the Sun and all other spirits; you I love; and this fellow here I dread. You know yourself how guiltless I am. I now add this solemn oath: by the splendid porticos of heaven, not guilty. The day will come when I will make this fellow pay for his atrocious trespassing, even if might is on his side. But you, uphold the cause of the weak and helpless!"

The killer of Argus, the god born on Mount Cyllene, had a crooked look in his eyes as he spoke; he kept his baby blanket on his arm and did not throw it aside. Zeus gave a great laugh after he had watched his naughty son show such skill and expertness in his denial about the cattle. He ordered the two of them to make a search in a spirit of reconciliation: Hermes, the god of guidance, was to lead the way and, without any mischievous intent, to disclose the place where he had hidden the sturdy head of cattle. The son of Cronus sealed his order with a nod, and glorious Hermes hastened to obey; the will of Zeus who wears the aegis was sufficient to persuade him. The two beautiful sons of Zeus hurried on their way till they came to sandy Pylos and the ford across the Alpheus. They reached the fields and the cave with its lofty roof where the loot had been stored in the nighttime. Then Hermes went into the cave in the rocks and drove the sturdy head of cattle out into the light of day. Meanwhile the son of Leto looked around and noticed the ox-hides on the bare rock. "How was it possible, you trickster," he asked noble Hermes, "for you to skin two oxen, when you are just a tiny infant? Nor is this the first time that I am amazed at your power. You do not need to grow up to great size, son of Maia born on Mount Cyllene."

This was what he said; then he took some twigs of willow in his hands and began to twist them into a stout rope. But the twigs immediately began to take root in the ground under their feet, twining and grafting on each other and easily covering all the grazing cattle; such was the will of Hermes, the cunning god of Magic. Apollo was amazed when he saw it. Then the stout killer of Argus looked sideways over the ground with fire twinkling in his eyes; he had made up his mind to cheat the son of noble Leto. He had no difficulty in pacifying the archer-god as he wanted to do, in spite of the latter's strength: he lifted up the lyre on his left arm and struck a melody. In his hands the lyre raised a stirring din, and Phoebus Apollo broke into happy laughter; the lovely notes of divine song pierced his heart, and as he listened sweet passion gripped his soul. The son of Maia stood confidently on Phoebus Apollo's left, playing lovely music on the lyre. With the clear notes of the lyre as accompaniment, he raised his beautiful voice and started to sing a prelude in honor of the immortal gods and the dark earth, telling of how they first came into being and how their destined share was assigned to each. Foremost among the gods his song celebrated Mnemosyne, the mother of the Muses, since her destined partner was the son of Maia himself. Next the glorious son of Zeus honored the rest of the immortal gods, each in due order according to his birth; he observed propriety in every word, and kept playing the lyre on his arm. Apollo felt an irresistible passion invading his heart and soul, and addressed the other with these excited words: "You butcher of cattle, cunning schemer, hard worker, good entertainer, what you have invented there is worth the fifty cattle. From this moment I think we can settle our dispute peacefully. But tell me now, ingenious son of Maia, was this miracle yours from the time of your birth, or did some mortal or immortal present you with a wonderful gift and teach you this inspired music? This miracle of song is new to my ears; I have never heard it from any man nor yet from any of the gods who live on Mount Olympus—only from you, you cunning son of Zeus and Maia. What art, what muse, what skill is this that governs ungovernable sorrows? Truly here are three in one to be had for the asking—gaiety, love, and sweet sleep. I, too, belong to the fellowship of the Olympian Muses, whose life is spent in dances, and the glorious paths of music, in the beauty of song with the lovely accompaniment of flutes; but never has my heart been so touched by any talent displayed by young men at their banquet entertainments. I am amazed, son of Maia, at this lovely music you make upon the lyre. Since you show that you possess precious skills, in spite of your small size, sit down, my friend, and listen to the words of your elders. Surely an honored rank among the immortal gods shall be yours and your mother's. This I solemnly declare: upon this dogwood spear I swear that I will make you the noble and wealthy messenger of the gods; I will give you fine gifts and to the very end I will never deceive you."

Hermes replied with a speech which revealed his shrewdness: "You ask me a question, clever archer. I do not grudge you the privilege of engaging in my art. You shall master it today. I want to be generous with you in the proposal I am about to state. You in your wisdom know everything. You have the first seat among the gods, son of Zeus; you are big and strong. Wise Zeus loves you, as in all conscience he should, and has presented you with fine gifts; it is said that you, archer-god, have received from Zeus the privilege of knowing all the oracles and prophecies that proceed from his mouth. But as for that art the knowledge of which I have just now acquired, you are free to learn as much as you wish. Since your mind is turned toward playing the lyre, play and sing and make merry. You will have received it from me; let the glory be mine. Take this wench with the musical voice in your arms and lead the dance. But be sure that your expressions observe the rules of art and beauty: then with cheerful heart you may take her to a festive banquet, to a lovely dance or to a noble feast; she will be a comfort to you both by night and by day. If someone who has mastered the art and the skill speaks to her, she speaks to him and gives him all sorts of knowledge that adorns the mind; her playful nature responds easily to the gentle touch and shrinks from the unpleasantness of heavy work. But if some novice accosts her brutally, her answer is wild and empty. You are free to learn as much as you wish; see, I will give you this lyre, glorious son of Zeus. In return, archer-god, you and I will both herd the grazing cattle in their pastures on the mountains and in the plains where the horses feed. Then the cows will couple with the bulls and bear plenty of calves both male and female. Though you always love a shrewd bargain, there is nothing here that should stir your furious anger."

After he had finished his speech he held out the lyre and Phoebus Apollo accepted it. In return he entrusted Hermes with the splendid whip which he had in his hand and placed him in charge of cattle tending. The son of Maia was delighted to receive the gift. The glorious son of Leto, the archer-god Apollo, grasped the lyre in his left hand and struck up a melody; in his hands the lyre raised a stirring din, while the god sang a pretty song in accompaniment.

Afterwards the two gods drove the cattle toward the celestial meadow. The two beautiful sons of Zeus quickly made the journey back to snow-clad Olympus, amusing themselves with the lyre as they went. Wise Zeus was happy at the outcome, and established a relation of friendship between the two. Hermes has never to this day ceased to be friendly towards the son of Leto; the proof of this is that Hermes entrusted the archer-god with the enviable gift of the lyre which the latter has learned to hold and play skillfully. Hermes also invented another clever art; he made reed pipes into the musical instruments which can be heard from afar. [1–512]

hetaerae

SELECTIONS FROM HESIOD'S *Works and Days*

Translated by Violet Zielke

INTRODUCTION

THE WRITINGS of the didactic poet Hesiod offer the best record of the social and economic changes which were taking place during the archaic period. The father of Hesiod had migrated from Aeolia to the small town of Ascra in Boeotia, and had acquired a farm. The poet was born in Ascra, and, according to his own account, should have inherited a fair share of the estate; but of this he was cheated by his brother Perses, who bribed the corrupt judges who decided the distribution. The incident forced Hesiod to work even harder on what was left, and as a result he writes practically and realistically of the life of the small farmers who were suffering oppression at the hands of the "nobles"—the landholders into whose hands power had passed.

Several mythological poems were attributed to Hesiod, among them the *Theogony*, an account of the origin of the gods and the creation of the world. But the best known of his writings is the *Works and Days*, a didactic poem which serves as a practical handbook for the farmer, instructing him in the works he must do to make a living and the days which are favorable for doing them. The poem is filled with reflections on society and offers maxims and precepts for living in a world where might makes right. Hesiod protests against the arbitrary judgments of the nobles and enjoins them to practise justice, and he exhorts his brother Perses to forsake his evil ways and engage in hard and honest toil. The *Works and Days* was one of the first expressions of a social conscience. It was later to have a great influence on the *Georgics* of Vergil.

THE TEXT translated is that of T. A. Sinclair (London, 1932).

I. THE FIVE AGES OF MAN

First of all the immortal gods who dwell upon Olympus made a golden race of speaking men; these lived in the time when Cronus ruled in heaven. Like gods they dwelt, lighthearted and free from care, far removed from toil and hardship. For them was no bitter old age, but strong throughout life they took delight in merrymaking, free from harm, and they died as though overcome by sleep. All good things were theirs; for then the fertile cornland of its own accord bore its rich and abundant fruit. Freely and peacefully they cultivated their lands, surrounded by blessings. But since earth covered over this race, they have been spirits, by the will of mighty Zeus—kindly spirits who dwell upon the land; clothed in mist they wander everywhere over the earth, guardians of mortal men, keeping watch over just acts and evil. They are givers of riches; this royal privilege too they have.

Next the dwellers upon Olympus made a second and far poorer race—a race of silver, like the golden race in neither body nor spirit. For a hundred years a boy was reared by the side of his watchful mother and played in his home, an overgrown child. But when men came of age and reached the full measure of manhood, they lived only a short time, suffering the penalty of their folly. They could not refrain from insult and outrage upon one another; they would not pay service to the immortal gods, nor sacrifice upon the holy altars of the blessed, as men should, wherever they dwell. Whereupon Zeus buried them in his anger, because they did not give honors to the blessed gods who dwell upon Olympus. But since earth covered over this generation, they, though dwelling beneath the earth, have been called blessed by mortals, and though they are second in order, yet to them also honor is given.

Father Zeus created a third generation of speaking men, a race of bronze, a race sprung from ash trees, strong and terrible, not at all like the silver race. Violence and the cruel deeds of Ares were their joy. They ate no grain; unapproachable men were they with dauntless heart of adamant. Great was their strength; invincible hands grew from their shoulders upon brawny arms. Bronze were their weapons, bronze their houses, and with bronze they tilled the fields, for black iron had not yet been discovered. Slain by their own hands, they went down inglorious into the clammy realms of chill Hades. Black Death seized these men, formidable as they were, and they left the gleaming light of the sun.

After earth buried this generation, Zeus the son of Cronus brought forth a fourth race, more righteous and better, upon the bounteous land, a godlike race of hero-men who are called demigods, the race before this present one upon the boundless earth. These cruel war and the dread battle cry destroyed, some at seven-gated Thebes, in the land of Cadmus, as they fought for the flocks of Oedipus; others perished when war led them in ships over the great gulf of the sea into Troy, for the sake of the fair-haired Helen. There the finality of death encompassed them, but Zeus, son of Cronus, gave them a life and a dwelling place apart from men, and made them to dwell at the ends of the earth. They abide with heart free of care in the Islands of the Blest, near deep-eddying Ocean—blessed heroes, for whom the fertile earth yields honeyed fruit three times a year.

Would that I had not been born in the fifth race of men, but either had died before or been born afterwards! For now indeed the race is one of iron. Never will men cease from toil and misery by day and by night as they plunge to their ruin; the gods will give them endless suffering. Yet some blessings are still mingled with sorrows for them. But Zeus will destroy also this race of men whose tongues have speech, when the time comes that they are grey-haired as soon as they have been born. Father will not resemble his children nor children their father; guest will not be dear to his host, nor friend to friend, nor brother to brother, as they once were. This race of men will not honor their feeble and aging parents, but hard hearted, they will rebuke them with angry words, not considering the vengeance of the gods. No restitution will they make to their old parents for the expense of their rearing. There will be no reverence for the man who keeps his oath, nor for a just or good man, but the insolent, the evildoer, will they honor. Right shall rest in the power of the hand; there will be no sense of honor. The worse will harm the better man, addressing him with guile and swearing falsely on oath. Malice and scolding envy with angry face will pursue all mortals in their wretched state. Then shall shame and retribution, covering their fair heads with white mantles, abandon mortal men and depart for the realms of the immortals. Misery alone will be left for men, and they will have no defense against their sorrows.

[109–201]

II. The Hawk and the Nightingale

Now I shall tell a tale for princes, however wise they be. A hawk clutched with his talons a gaily-colored nightingale and bore her aloft into the clouds. When she wailed piteously, pierced by the crooked claws, the hawk said arrogantly to her: "Wretch! Why do you shriek? One much stronger now holds you and you must go wherever I take you, singer though you are. I shall make a dinner of you, if I so wish, or I shall let you go! But foolish is he, who sets himself against the stronger, for not only can he not win, but suffering is added to his shame." So spoke the fleet, long-winged hawk. [202–212]

III. Justice

O Perses, hearken to justice. Do not foster insolence, for insolence is bad for a poor man, and not even a noble man is able to bear it easily; weighed down under it, he falls into ruin. It is better to take the road on the other side, in the direction of justice. Justice triumphs over arrogance in the end, and the fool comes to know this after much suffering. For Horcus, god of oaths, catches up with twisted judgments. There is an uproar when Justice is dragged off by bribe-devouring men, who decide the law by crooked judgments. And she follows, clothed in mist, weeping for the city and its homes, and bringing woe to the men who have driven her out and who have not rendered fair judgments. But those who deliver straight judgments to stranger and fellow-townsmen, who swerve not a bit from what is just—their city flourishes and the people prosper in it. Peace is the nurse of children up and down their land, and upon them far-seeing Zeus never sends savage war. Never does famine or failure attend those who deal out simple justice, but with feasting and merry-making they tend their appointed tasks. For them the earth yields a rich livelihood, and the lofty mountain oak bears acorns at its top, bees in its middle. Their woolly sheep are weighed down by fleeces; their wives bear children who resemble their father; at all times they prosper with good things. They do not go to sea in ships, for the bounteous earth yields fruit for them.

But as for those who resort to rank insolence and cruel deeds, for them the far-seeing son of Cronus ordains punishment. Many times, indeed, a whole city reaps the fruits of the villainous man who sins and plots brazen deeds of folly. From heaven the son of Cronus lets loose upon them great suffering, famine together with pestilence. The people perish; women do not give birth to children; houses fall in decay at the will of Olympian Zeus. But sometimes the Father of Men destroys their great army or their great city walls, or he plunges their ships to the depths of the sea.

O Princes, you too reflect upon this vengeance. For the immortal gods are near to men, and they make note of those who oppress one another with crooked judgments, not heeding the wrath of the gods. For thrice ten thousand immortals walk upon the fruitful land, the guardians of mortal men. They keep watch over cruel deeds and judgments; wrapped in mist, they wander everywhere over the earth. And the maiden Justice, daughter of Zeus, also watches over men—Justice, who is glorious and honored among the gods of Olympus. Whenever anyone harms her with vile slanders, at once she sits down beside her father Zeus and tells of the unjust purposes of men, until the people atone for the bold crimes of princes, who with cunning design turn aside righteous verdicts and judge perversely. Pay heed to these things, O Princes, and despite tempting bribes, make straight verdicts and forget crooked judgments entirely.

The man who prepares evil for another prepares evil for himself, and the villainous plan injures the plotter most. The all-seeing eye of Zeus even now looks down, at his will, upon these acts of men; he is not unaware what kind of justice this city holds within it. Now neither I nor my son would be just among men, since it is a bad thing for a man to be righteous, if the more unjust man will have the greater justice.

[213–272]

IV. Summer

When Zeus has completed sixty days of winter after the solstice, the star Arcturus ascends from the holy stream of Ocean and rises radiant at twilight. Then is the best time to prune the vines, before the shrill voiced daughter of Pandion, the swallow, returns to herald the arrival of the spring.

But when the snail, the house-bearer, leaves the ground and creeps into the foliage to avoid the summer's heat, then spade the vines no longer, but sharpen the sickles and rouse the workers. Spend no time in shady retreats; do not be asleep after dawn in harvest time, when the sun parches the body. Then hurry to bring home your harvest, rising at dawn that your livelihood may be sure. For dawn takes over a third part of the work, dawn helps a man on his way and enriches his labors, dawn causes men to start on journeys, and dawn places many oxen under the yoke.

But when the thistle is in flower, and the chirping cicada sits in a near-by tree, pouring forth his shrill song from under his wings in the languorous summer days, then she-goats are fattest and wine is ruddiest, then are women most wanton but men most weak, for the Dog Star slackens their knees and dulls their brain, and flesh withers under the blazing sun. Then would I choose a rock-shaded nook and Biblian wine, with the richest of barley cakes and milk from goats drained dry; the flesh of a heifer, fed on fresh leaves, that has not yet borne young, and the flesh of firstborn kids. When my soul is satisfied with food, I would sit in the shade while the gentle zephyr plays about my face and I would drink of the sparkling wine, mixing three parts of water from an unmuddied, ever flowing spring, with one part of wine. [564–596]

v. Maxims of conduct

The immortal gods have placed sweat ahead of virtue; long and steep is the road into virtue, and at first the going is rough. [289–290]

That man is best of all who ponders and decides all things for himself, and this is the best way in the end. But he also is good who heeds wise counsel. The man who neither weighs matters for himself nor listens to another is foolish. [292–297]

Hunger is everywhere a meet companion for an idle man. [302]

Work is no disgrace, but idleness is indeed a matter of reproach. [311]

He has a share in honor who shares a good neighbor. [347]

It is well to receive measure from a neighbor, but it is well to repay him in the same measure or even more, if you are able, so that if at some later time you are in need, you may depend upon him for help. [349–351]

Love him who loves you and attack him who attacks you. Give to the one who gives to you, but do not give to one who does not. [353–354]

Smile and get a witness even for your brother. Trust and distrust both ruin men. [371–372]

Do not put off your work until tomorrow or the next day, for the man who works sluggishly does not fill his granary, nor the man who puts off his tasks. [410–412]

Keep to the mean; moderation is best in all things. [694]

Do not treat a friend like a brother. But if you do, be not the first to provoke a quarrel and do not lie merely for the sake of lying. If he injures you first, insulting you in word or deed, remember to repay him twice as much. If he desires friendship with you once again and is willing to make satisfaction to you, accept him. For worthless is the man who makes one friend here, another there.

Let not your outward appearance belie your true feelings.

Do not get a name for lavish entertaining, nor yet for inhospitality; do not become known as a boon companion of worthless men nor as the wrangling foe of good men.

Reproach not a man for deadly poverty—always the gift of the blessed immortals.

A sparing tongue is the finest treasure among men; the well-ordered tongue has infinite charm.

If you speak ill, you will soon hear greater ill spoken of yourself.

Do not be rude at a feast where many guests are present, for the fun is greater and the expense is less where a dinner is shared in common.

Never pour out a libation of sparkling wine to Zeus in the morning with unwashed hands, nor to any other of the immortal gods. For they will not hearken to you, but will spit out your prayers. [707–726]

LYRIC POETRY

Translated by Warren R. Castle and L. R. Lind

INTRODUCTION

To the Greeks the word *lyric* designated only that poetry which was sung to the accompaniment of the lyre; they had no general term to designate that vast body of poetry which was neither epic nor dramatic. We use the word *lyric* to fill this deficiency, meaning by it to describe all personal utterance which, by and large, expresses the emotional response of the individual to his own world. Such poetry assumed two forms, monodic and choral. In the former, the poet spoke of and for himself; in the latter he spoke for the group with which he identified himself.

The roots of lyric poetry go deep into the remotest past. Homer mentions hymns and chants connected with religious ceremonies. There were wedding chants, funeral dirges, and paeans of thanksgiving, as well as rustic chants of various kinds, all of which were wholly popular in nature. True poets were interested only in the epic which sang the glories of an ideal heroic past. Sometime in the eighth century, however, when epic poetry more or less died out, poets turned to the contemporary world as a subject for art, and lyric poetry began to come to full splendor.

This shift from the epic to the lyric was a reflection of the transformation which was taking place in the social structure of the time. Patriarchal kingdoms in which the individual was submerged gave way to tyrannies, revolutions, and the first experiments in democracy. Civic patriotism and interest in politics deepened. Further, it was an age of exploration, colonization, and commercial exploitation. In the midst of this widening experience and political upheaval, the individual sought to find himself and define his relation to the rapidly shifting social organization. So for the next few centuries the great names in poetry were those of the lyricists, such as Archilochus, Mimnermus, Sappho, Alcaeus, Solon, Simonides, and Pindar, until finally lyric poetry gave way to the drama which largely absorbed both it and the epic. Though it later regained briefly some of its former splendor in the idylls of Theocritus, in subsequent centuries it ceased to be national and popular and became the property of cosmopolitan intellectuals and professional scholars.

These men, though not great poets themselves, continued to cultivate poetry as an art, usually pedantically, but often with fine taste. In addition to writing poetry themselves, they sometimes made anthologies of the works of former poets, in which they included their own poems. The result of their labors was that unique phenomenon, the Greek Anthology, a collection of poems covering more than a thousand years. Most of these are short poems, which the Greeks called epigrams, written in elegiac couplets, the ancient equivalent of our heroic couplets. Many of them are like carved gems. There are love poems, epitaphs, prayers, dedications, satires, and many other kinds. Some of the later poems in the collection, like the epigrams of Meleager and Philodemus, are notable for their cosmopolitan outlook and luxuriant fancy. The writers of the Greek Anthology are included here in one convenient unit, though in date some of them are a thousand years later than the first lyric poets.

Greek lyric poetry differs from modern poetry in several important respects and, without going into disputed matters, I should like to give some idea of what these are. There was, first, always some connection with instrumental music. The importance of the musical accompaniment varied with the different types. Sometimes, as in the case of iambic poetry, which was originally satirical, it consisted of merely a few notes intended to provide a background for the voice of the reciter. Again, the elegy, originally chanted with a flute accompaniment, soon lost the musical element; if used at all, this served as a prelude to the poem. Other forms, like the light odes of Sappho and Terpander, were sung to the accompaniment of an instrumental melody. These types were real songs in the modern sense. Of course, the music was all very simple and would sound pretty thin to the modern ear. The instruments were few, various types of flutes and stringed devices, always plucked, never bowed. Harmony was practically unknown. The aesthetic effect of such music on the modern ear would be something like that of Greek vase painting on the eye. The essential qualities were simplicity and exquisite clarity. It should be remembered, however, that of the two elements, poetry and music, the poetry was the predominant one. In still other forms, like the choral lyric, there was a third element, the dance. The chorus moved in a fixed pattern designed by the poet, who also composed the music; the dance movement determined and was determined by the structure of the poem. So in the most elaborate lyrics these three elements—words, music, and dance—combined to produce an effect which must have been most powerful. Left to us today are only the words and the rhythm; of the music and dance we know next to nothing, and even the precise nature of the rhythm is still disputed.

In the inner nature of Greek poetry there are further differences from the modern, though here the line is harder to draw. Characteristic of nearly all Greek poetry is a kind of simplicity, sometimes almost naïveté, resulting partly from a tendency to treat subjects of universal interest only, and partly from a tendency to treat all subjects in general rather than in particular terms. Since the Greeks lacked any real sense of antiquity or of remote ages of culture, such as pervades the works of a modern poet like T. S. Eliot, they were able to impart to their poetry a quality of immediacy which lends it an atmosphere of youngness, what nineteenth-century critics called an early-morning freshness. Closely allied to these qualities is directness of utterance. Through its entire range of effects, from the most delicate loveliness to the most sublimely tragic, Greek poetry is almost wholly direct statement, not the poetry of suggestion. Further, it does not attempt to communicate private or unique experiences. Hence, you will look in vain for the rich and subtle symbols which give modern works like *The Waste Land* or *Lord Weary's Castle* their dense texture and evocative overtones. The directness of Greek poetry is achieved through a severe economy of means which makes it seem bare and colorless compared to English poetry, which is usually richly colored and expansive. The Greeks had a proverb, "Sow from the hand, not from the whole sack," which admirably sums up the qualities of restraint and moderation that they pursued in art, if not in their lives. Finally, they emphasized form in poetry more than any other people. Their poetic forms represent the most consummate art and the highest technical perfection of any literature. Modern poetry reminds one of painting, Greek poetry of sculpture.

I said above that Greek lyric poetry is either monodic or choral. Choral poetry, which is usually associated with the Dorian Greeks, expresses public or collective attitudes through the poet who considers himself the organ of the group. In form it tends to be very elaborate and ornate; the meter is varied and complex; the effect is grandiose. The monody, on the other hand, closely associated with the Ionians, is nearer to popular folk poetry. The poems are short, the meters are simple, and the strophes, or stanzas, are always the same in any one poem. The monody also includes the types known as iambic and elegiac poetry, both of which originated in Ionia and were used in expressing personal sentiments.

Probably the two most celebrated lyric poets of antiquity were Sappho in monody and Pindar in choral lyric.

It is difficult to separate the facts of Sappho's life from the legends and conjectures that have gathered around her. Known for certain, however, is that she lived toward the end of the seventh and the beginning of the sixth centuries B.C. at Mitylene on the island of Lesbos where she conducted a kind of school for girls devoted to instruction in music, poetry, and the dance. This school was also a *thiasos*, or religious association, dedicated to the worship of Aphrodite, goddess of love and beauty. Sappho wrote nine books of poetry including elegies, hymns, and epithalamia, as well as her personal odes. Extant are two complete odes and numerous fragments. The Greeks called her "the tenth muse" and ranked her equal to Homer.

Love was the subject of all her poems, and she sang of it in its varying aspects with a poignancy and sensuous simplicity unequalled in European literature until Goethe. Her method is direct and piercing; her art is an exquisite combination of simplicity, grace, and passion. Though she treats only one theme, she avoids monotony through a continual renewal of unforgettable images: she sings of "the new wine of the spring wind," of "golden-sandaled dawn," of love "that sways her soul like the mountain wind that falls upon the oaks." She compares a young bride to a sweet red apple on the topmost bough of a tree "which the fruit-pickers somehow forgot. Forgot? No, for none could reach so high." Swinburne says, rather rhapsodically, "Her verses strike and sting the memory in lonely places, or at sea, among all loftier sights and sounds . . . seem akin to fire and air, being themselves all air and fire." The opening of one of her poems sums up perfectly her philosophy: "Some say the fairest thing on earth is a troop of horsemen, others a band of foot soldiers, others a squadron of ships. But I say the fairest thing is the beloved." No other Greek poet so powerfully asserted the unique significance of the inner life.

Pindar (518–438 B.C.) too sings of the "I," but beyond that the resemblance is slight. Born near Thebes of a noble family (possibly Dorian), he travelled widely and was intimately associated with the great Dorian families of Sicily and Aegina. He wrote seventeen books of poetry, of which three and fragments of a fourth are extant.

Pindar is the most remote and difficult of all ancient poets. This is due not only to the difficulties of his language and to the strangeness of his subject matter—the poems are mostly about horse races and wrestling matches—but also to the peculiar nature of his thought. He was the supreme voice of aristocracy, a thoroughgoing blue blood. He believed that the quality of *areté*, which we loosely translate as *virtue*, or more exactly as *excellence*, was the exclusive property of the nobility. It was inherited through the blood and went back to the gods, from which aristocrats, at least a good many of them, traced their descent. It was in victory at one of the great athletic festivals like the Olympic games that this *areté* found its highest spiritual and physical manifestation. Pindar's poems are glorifications of the victors and their families. Further, Pindar was a devout follower of the traditional, that is to say, the aristocratic, religion of Greece, which was centered at Delphi. Hence the profound religious tone of his odes. All in all, he was politically conservative, sympathetic with the ideal of stable government exemplified by the Spartans, believing that only the best and wisest should rule. And by the best he meant the landed nobility, who alone possessed "virtue." He had nothing of what we call "social consciousness."

But he wrote poetry of such transcendent grandeur and magnificence that the Greek and Roman critics placed him at the head of all lyric poets. He is lofty and sublime however you view him. His moral tone is high; though he follows the traditional religion, he tries to purify it. Though severely limited by his subject, he is never monotonous. His images are the boldest and most luminous that ever appeared in ancient poetry.

A typical ode speaks of the victor and the occasion, then tells—usually impressionistically—a myth connected with the victor's family, and finally returns to the victor with moral exhortations to higher endeavor. The ode is interspersed with philosophic reflections and many little bypaths of beauty and sentiment. The metrical structure of the odes is symphonic in effect and complex in a way that is not possible in English. There is a synthesis of opposites: the meter is incredibly elaborate, and yet the impression of the whole is one of freedom and swiftness. At one time the poem moves slowly like a dreamy ode of Keats, then it runs and soars like a free rhapsody of Whitman, or like the eagle to which Pindar is fond of comparing himself. He speaks at once of mules and stars and blood and mincemeat, yet all fuses together in light and splendor. Though he has many memorable sentiments on the lot of man and the transience of life, Pindar is primarily the poet of its beauties and its happiness. There are many passages in his poems that have about them, as one critic has put it, "the light of setting suns." The following passage may be said to epitomize his message—if there is any other than his insistence on the beauty of gold, water, and fire, and the other things of earth: "Creatures of a day, what is man? What is he not? The dream of a shadow is man. But when a ray from heaven comes, there is a shining light upon men, and their life is sweet."

—W.R.C.

TRANSLATIONS by Mr. Castle in the following pages are those of poems by Alcaeus, Alcman, Antipater of Sidon, Archilochus, Callimachus, Mimnermus, Philodemus (version No. 1), Pindar, Sappho, and Theocritus; "To a Bee," "Spring Song," "To a Grasshopper," and "To Zenophile Asleep" by Meleager; and the anonymous "Nature and Man" from the *Lament for Bion.* Translations by Mr. Lind are those of poems by Amphis, Asclepiades, Damascius, Euenus, Hipponax, Julius Polyaenus, Marcus Argentarius, Palladas, Philodemus (version No. 2), Ptolemaeus, Rufinus, Simonides, Theognis, Xenophanes, and Zenodotus; "To Heliodora Dead" by Meleager; and the anonymous poem "On a Child Untimely Dead."

The Greek texts translated are as follows: J. M. Edmonds, *Lyra Graeca* (rev. ed., London, 1927–1931), for the poems of Archilochus, Alcman, Alcaeus, and Sappho; Hiller-Crusius, *Anthologia Lyrica* (Leipzig, 1890) for those of Solon and Xenophanes; Bowra, *Pindari Carmina* (Oxford, 1935); J. W. Mackail, *Select Epigrams from the Greek Anthology* (London, 1930) for Meleager's "To a Bee" and "To Zenophile Asleep"; *The Oxford Book of Greek Verse* (Oxford, 1931) for all others.

ARCHILOCHUS

(About 711 B.C.)

O Heart, Be Strong

O heart, my heart, by hopeless woes oppressed,
Rise up, take guard, offer the foe your breast!
Stand firmly where the spears of battle fly;
But, if you conquer, never glorify
Yourself, nor, overcome, lie down and wail
At home. In joys take joy, and if you fail,
Grieve not too much, but know what fortunes
men assail.

The Better Part

My goodly shield some Thracian proudly wears;
Unwillingly I tossed it in a bush.
At least, I saved my neck—so let it go,
For I can get another just as good.

ALCMAN

(About 630 B.C.)

Old Age

No more, ye honey-tongued maidens
With voices ravishing-fair,

My limbs no longer sustain me—
Give over your yearning air.

Ah, that I were a ceryl-bird
With the halcyons a-wing,
On the flowering foam with glad heart—
Sea-purple bird of spring!

Sleep

Now sleep the mountain peaks, the chasms,
The crags, the promontories;
Now sleep all creeping things that dark earth breeds,
The mountain-roaming beasts, the swarming tribes of bees,
The monsters in the depths of the murky sea;
Asleep too are the flocks
Of long-winged birds. . . .

MIMNERMUS

(About 630 B.C.)

The Sun

The sun has been allotted labor all his days,
And never any pause or respite stays
Horses and god as soon as rosy-fingered Dawn
Has left the sea and heavenward is gone;
At night a hollow, winged bed of precious gold,
Forged by Hephaestus, lovely to behold,
Gently conveys the sleeping god across the seas
From the dark shore of the Hesperides
To the Aethiopian strand where steeds and charioteer
Wait until Dawn, the early-born, appear.

SOLON

(About 640–560 B.C.)

The Works of Mortal Pride Endure not Long

(Frg. 12, ll. 1–8, 13, 16–25)

Pierian Muses, shining offspring of
Olympian Zeus and Memory, hear my prayer:
Grant that I always have prosperity
From the blessed gods and good repute from men;
Let me be sweet to friends, bitter to foes,
Both terrible and reverend to behold.
I long for wealth, but not unrighteous wealth,
For Dike always follows afterwards,
And Ruin quickly mingles with injustice.
The works of mortal pride endure not long,
Since Zeus surveys the ends of everything.
For suddenly, even as a wind of spring
Scatters the clouds and moves the barren seas
And, laying waste the fair works of the fields,
Mounts even to high heaven where sit the gods
And brings the blue once more to sight, until
The lovely sunlight shines upon the earth
And no more clouds are anywhere to see——
So moves the punishment of Zeus.

ALCAEUS

(Born about 620 B.C.)

To Sappho

Pure sweetly-smiling Sappho of the violet hair,
I want to tell you something, but do not dare.

Drinking Song

Come soak your lungs in wine;
The dog-star's returning,
The summer is a hard one,
And the thirsty world is burning.

The cricket from the tree-top
Sweetly sings his air,
And in field and wood the thistles
Are blowing everywhere.

Now the girls are most romantic,
But the men faint from the heat,
For the fire of Sirius
Parches from head to feet.

SAPPHO

(Born about 612 B.C.)

To a Philistine Woman

Because thou hast no portion
Of the roses of the Graces,
And the fair Pierides
Avert and hide their faces,

When thou shalt die hereafter,
No one will long for thee,
But thou shalt lie lost and unknown
To fame and memory—

Yes, even in Hades' dim realm,
Flitting among the glades,
Obscurely shalt thou wander,
Unheeded by the shades.

Passion

That man seemeth like to the gods in fortune,
He who sits before thee in absent rapture
And oblivious, witched by thy nearness, hears thee
Murmuring sweetly,

Laughing lovely laughter: ah, this it is which
Shakes my heart and sets it a-flutter wildly;
For when I but glance at thee sitting near him,
Then is my voice gone—

Yes, my tongue is frozen, and on a sudden
Thin and subtle flame underneath my skin runs—
Vision leaves my eyes and my trembling ears are
Filled with a ringing—

Sweat runs down me—tremor attacks me wholly—
And, becoming greener than grass in spring, I
Faint away distracted, and death itself seems
Almost upon me.

Letter to Atthis

Atthis, our Anactoria, dear to thee
And me, in distant Sardis dwells,
But often sends across the severing sea

Her longing thoughts to us, remembering
How once we lived our life, we three,
When she delighted most to hear thee sing,

And thou didst seem to her a goddess fair;
But now among the Lydian maids
She shines as, in the sun-abandoned air,

The rosy-fingered moon shines splendidly
Among the ambient stars and lights
The flowering meadows and the briny sea,

When sweet the dew lies, and the roses live
Again, the delicate anthrysc blooms,
And all the honeyed melilots revive.

And though she wanders far from us, I know,
Recalling gentle Atthis' love,
Her tender breast is laden deep with woe;

And loud she cries for us to come, and we
Know what she cries full well, for night,
The many-eared, speaks over the severing sea.

Flower Song

With delicate fingers, Dika,
Gather the shoots of dill,
And weave a lovely garland,
And wear it in your hair;

For the brow uncrowned with garlands
The goddesses take ill,
And only the flower-wreathed
Shall win the Graces' care.

THEOGNIS

(About 540 B.C.)

On Bad Company

Know this, my lad; don't mix with evil men.
Keep to the good, and with them drink and dine;
Sit down with them in pleasure, I say again,
They have a corner on everything that's fine.
You'll learn good habits from them; with the bad
You'll only lose the good sense that you had.

SIMONIDES

(About 556–468 B.C.)

For the Greeks Who Died at Plataea

If to die nobly is the greatest share of valor,
Then Fortune has given us this beyond all who were bold;
For we who hastened to keep the freedom of Hellas
Lie here and enjoy a name that will never grow old.

HIPPONAX

(About 540 B.C.)

On Marriage

Marriage is best for any prudent man;
No better gift than woman's aid is found.
Her very marriage-portion often can
Save house and home; and when she is around,
He has a helper, not a mistress, who

With her good sense stands firm his whole life
through.

XENOPHANES

(About 530 B.C.)

Pythagoras and the Dog

Once when he saw a beaten pup go by
Pythagoras said in pity with a sigh:
"Don't beat him; it's the soul of some dear
man
I knew in life that utters such a cry."

On Ease and Comfort

So might we say, by the fire lying
On a soft couch in the winter chill,
Sated, drinking the sweet wine, plying
The stomach with roasted chick-pease still:
"Whence do you come, O gallant stranger,
And what, pray tell us, may be your name?
How many are yours of the years that change, sir?
How old were you when the Persian came?"

PINDAR

(518–438 B.C.)

The First Olympian

STROPHE I

Even as water is best, while gold, like burning fire
By night, outgleams all other princely wealth,
Even so, my heart,
Would you sing of games,
Seek never a brighter star
Than the sun shining by day through the desert
air,
Nor any contest better to chant than Olympia's;
Whence the minds of poets put on
The hymn of praise to sing
The son of Cronus. They come
To the wealthy hearth of Hieron

ANTISTROPHE I

Who wields the lawful scepter in fruitful Sicily,
And culls the flower of every excellence,
Delighting himself
In the light of the music
We play at his friendly table.
Then take from the peg the Dorian lyre,
If the glory of Pisa and the steed Pherenicus
Ever stirred your heart with sweetest thoughts,
When along the river Alpheus
He sped his ungoaded limbs
And brought his warlike master victory,

EPODE I

The lord of Syracuse. His fame shines far
In the manly land of Lydian Pelops
Whom once Poseidon, mighty earth-surrounder,
Loved, when Clotho lifted him out of the stainless
cauldron,
His shoulder radiant ivory.
Aye, marvels are many, but tales embroidered
with glittering lies
Beyond the truth delude the speech of men.

STROPHE II

Grace, that renders all things soothing for hu-
mankind,
Bringing her charm, full often makes believable
Even what is past belief;
But the days to come
Are the wisest witnesses.
It is fitting for man to speak fair of the gods; his
blame is less.
O son of Tantalus, I shall say, whatever the old
bards say,
When your father invited the gods to his stately
board
At beloved and lovely Sipylus,
And gave them a feast, giving like for like,
The god of the shining trident, his heart

ANTISTROPHE II

Enthralled with desire, carried you off on his
golden steeds
To the glorious high-placed home of Zeus,
Where, in later days,
Came Ganymede too
For the same need in Zeus.
And when, after many a search, you were seen no
more by your mother,
An envious neighbor secretly told the story
That they minced your limbs with a knife
And put them in boiling water,
And in the last course at the table
Divided your flesh and feasted.

EPODE II

I will call no god a cannibal. I revolt.
Often has little good befallen the speakers of evil.
But if ever the Olympian guardians honored a mortal man,
That was Tantalus. But he could not digest
His surpassing fortune and for insolence
Got from the father the awful doom of the mighty stone hung over his head,
And ever awaiting its fall, he wanders far from delight.

STROPHE III

He has a helpless life of everlasting pain,
His toil the fourth among three others, for he stole from the gods
And gave to his fellow-feasters
The nectar and ambrosia
Wherewith they had made him immortal.
That man errs who hopes, in aught he does, to cheat the gods.
Wherefore the immortals sent forth his son again
Into the midst of the short-lived tribes of men.
And when, toward the time of the flower of youth,
The down brought a dusky growth to his cheek,
He turned his thoughts to winning a bride, ready at hand,

ANTISTROPHE III

Glorious Hippodamia, the lord of Pisa's daughter.
Drawing near to the gray sea, walking alone in the darkness,
He called on the loud-thundering
God of the goodly trident,
Who came to him, close at his feet,
And he said to the god, 'If love's sweet gifts ever brought you joy,
Poseidon, then fetter the spear of Oenomaus,
And speed me to Elis in the fleetest chariot,
And bring me to victory;
For thirteen suitors has he slain,
Deferring his daughter's wedding-day.

EPODE III

Great peril never comes to the faint of heart.
But if all are fated to die, why should a man,
Sitting idly in darkness, grow old without renown
And unacquainted with beauty? Let mine be the hazard,
And yours to grant the desirable end.'
He hit on no idle words, and honoring him the god
Gave him a golden chariot and horses with tireless wings.

STROPHE IV

Breaking the might of Oenomaus, he won the maid as his bride;
Six sons she bore him, princes eager for deeds of valor.
And now, lying by the ford of Alpheus,
He shares in the splendid
Blood-offerings to the dead,
His busy tomb by the altar where many strangers pass.
And the glory of Olympia shines from afar in the courses
Of Pelops, where swiftness of foot is tried
And the bold heights of strength;
And the winner has for the rest of his life
Honey-sweet fair weather,

ANTISTROPHE IV

So far as the games can give it. Yet the highest good
That comes to man is the good that comes to him day by day.
I must crown the victor
In Aeolian strains with the rider's hymn,
And I believe of all men living
I shall never deck in the beauteous folds of song
A friend more wise in beauty, more sovereign in power.
Hieron, some watching god,
Who cares for you, broods
Over all your thoughts; if he leave not soon,
I hope one day to celebrate

EPODE IV

The sweeter thought of the swift chariot, when, having found
A helpful path of words, I come to the sunny hill of Cronus.
For me the Muse is keeping the mightiest shaft of song.
The great are great in various ways; the summit is for kings.

Look no further. Be it yours
To walk this life on the heights, and mine to consort with victors,
Foremost in the poet's lore among all the Hellenes everywhere.

To Agesias of Syracuse

(Olympian 6, *ll.* 1–7)

Even as architects, who build some wondrous palace,
Set golden pillars under the fair-walled porch,
So on our work's beginning must we set a front
That gleams from afar. Now, if a man were Olympian victor
And steward at Zeus' prophetic altar in Pisa,
And co-founder of glorious Syracuse, what hymn would he escape,
Finding his fellow-citizens ungrudging in lovely songs?

Music Hath Charms

(Pythian 1, *ll.* 1–12)

O golden lyre, common treasure of Apollo
And the violet-haired Muses, the footstep hears you and the gladness begins;
The singers obey your measures
When, trembling with music, you strike up the choir-leading prelude.
You quench the speared thunderbolt
Of ever-flowing fire; and the eagle sleeps on the sceptre of Zeus,
Drooping his two swift wings,

The lord of birds, and over his bending head
A dark mist you pour, sweet seal of the eyelids, and sleeping
He ripples his soft back, caught
In the tides of music. Even stern Ares, putting aside
His rude spears, melts his heart in drowsiness.
Your shafts enchant even the minds of the gods by grace of the skill
Of Leto's son and the deep-bosomed Muses.

What Is A Man?

(Pythian 8, *ll.* 88–100)

Whoever, in the days of his youth,
Wins some fair new thing,
Flies on the wings of manhood
With the highest hopes,
And his thoughts are greater than wealth. But short is the time
The pleasure of mortals grows, and soon it falls to the ground
When shaken by an adverse will.

We are things of a day. What is a man? What is he not? A dream
Of a shadow is man; but whenever the gleam from heaven comes,
A shining light is on men and their life is gentle.
Aegina, dear mother, speed on this city
In her voyage of freedom with the aid of Zeus and king Aeacus,
Of Peleus, and good Telemon, and Achilles.

The Fifth Nemean

STROPHE I

I am no sculptor who shapes images
That idly stand on the same base forever:
No—go, sweet song of mine, forth from Aegina
On every skiff and merchantman
To bear the news abroad
That Lampon's son, the mighty Pytheas, his cheeks
Not showing yet the downy flower of life's young summer,
Has won the crown of the Nemean pancratium

ANTISTROPHE I

And given splendor to the Aeacidae,
Heroic spearmen sprung from Zeus and Cronus
And from the golden daughters of the sea,
And glorified his mother-state,
The land that strangers love,
Which they, by the altar of their sire, Hellenic Zeus,
With hands outspread to heaven, once prayed might be renowned
For men and ships, Endais' famous sons and Phocus,

EPODE I

The lordly son of Psamathia whom
His goddess-mother bore beside the sea.
I shame to say what thing was ventured on,

Great but not righteous, how they left the far-famed isle,
What god it was that drove the heroes from Oenona—
I stop—it is not always gain
When truth unveils her face,
And often silence is man's highest wisdom.

STROPHE II

But if it is decreed that I should praise
Wealth or the strength of hands or iron war,
From here let someone dig long leaping places;
My knees now have a nimble spring,
The eagles leap the sea.
Yea, graciously the Muses' fairest chorus sang
Even to them on Pelion, and in their midst
Apollo stroked the seven-tongued lyre with golden quill

ANTISTROPHE II

And led the varied air; and they, beginning
With Zeus, hymned holy Thetis first and Peleus,
How Cretheus' daughter, soft Hippolyta,
Was fain to shackle him by craft,
With subtle purposes
Persuading the Magnesian guardian, her lord
And partner, and she framed a false invented tale
That Peleus had sought Acastus' bridal bed.

EPODE II

The truth was otherwise; for she herself
Had wooed, with much entreaty tempting him,
But with her wanton words she scratched his anger,
And straightway he repelled the girl, fearing the wrath
Of Zeus, Guest-guardian, Cloud-raiser, King of Gods,
Who, seeing, willed that he should win
One of the ocean-nymphs,
Who weave with golden spindle, as his bride,

STROPHE III

Thereto prevailing on Poseidon who
From Aegae often journeys to the splendid
Dorian Isthmus where glad companies
Welcome the god with shout of flutes
And vie in strength of limbs.
Blood-destiny decides all deeds. And at Aegina,
Euthymenes, you fell into the arms of Nike
And won the many-sounding hymns of victory.

ANTISTROPHE III

And, Pytheas, even yet your kinsman sheds
Glory on Peleus' seed. To him are joined
Nemea and his country's festal month
Which great Apollo loves. You beat
All comers of your age
At home and on the lovely-gladed hill of Nisus.
And I rejoice that every city strives for honors.
Know that your fortune is sweet recompense for all

EPODE III

Menander's labors (for from Athens must
The athlete have his builder). Shiver not,
My song, if you come to Themistion
To sing, but raise your voice, and run the sails aloft
That, boxer and pancratiast at Epidaurus,
He won twofold success and wears
At Aeacus' gates
The grassy garlands of the fair-haired Graces

ELYSIUM

(Frg. 114)

For those below the sun's might ever shines, while here the earth is dark;
And, in meadows crimson with roses, the space before their city
Is shaded with incense-bearing trees, laden with golden fruits.
There some delight themselves with horses and exercise,
Others with draughts and the lyre, while beside them blooms
The fair flower of all felicity.
Fragrance is ever spread throughout that lovely region,
And there they mix all kinds of frankincense
With the far-shining fire on the altars of the gods.

AMPHIS

(About 322 B.C.)

THE SOLACE OF ART

There is no sweeter thing in life than Art
To soothe the ills of earth and all their smart;

The mind, bent on improvement, soon lets go
Each sorrow; like a boat, sails past all woe.

ZENODOTUS (?)

(About 285 B.C.)

On a Statue of Love

Who carved this Eros, set him standing near
The fountain, and thought to quench that fire here?

CALLIMACHUS

(About 305–240 B.C.)

I Loathe All Common Things

I hate the cyclic epics. I take no
Delight in ways where mobs hither and thither go.
I hate a wandering lover. From public springs
I never drink. I loathe all common things.

ASCLEPIADES

(About 270 B.C.)

To a Recalcitrant Virgin

You guard your maidenhood, my girl; but why?
In Hell you'll find no lover when you die.
Love's pleasure only living souls can know;
We'll lie but dust and ashes there below.

THEOCRITUS

(About 310–250 B.C.)

The First Idyll

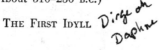

THYRSIS

Sweet is the whispering of yonder pine
That sings beside the spring, and, goatherd, sweet
Your piping; after Pan, the prize is yours.
If he receives the horned ram, you win
The goat; if he the goat, to you will fall
The kid, whose unmilked flesh is best to eat.

GOATHERD

Your song is sweeter than the echoing water,
Shepherd, that tumbles from the rocks above.
If as their prize the Muses take the sheep,
Yours is the stall-fed lamb; but if they choose
The lamb, the sheep as second prize is yours.

THYRSIS

Come, Goatherd, by the nymphs, sit here upon
This sloping hill beneath the tamarisk
And pipe a song, and let me tend your goats.

GOATHERD

I dare not, Shepherd, dare not pipe at noon
For fear of Pan who, weary of the hunt,
Rests at this hour. He is morose and stern,
And at his nose sits ever-biting anger.
But, Thyrsis, since you sing the woes of Daphnis,
And have high place among the woodland Muses,
Come sit beneath the elm, facing Priapus
And the spring-nymphs, there by the shepherd's seat
And the oak trees. And if you sing as when
Of old you sang against the Libyan Chromis,
I'll give you, first, a goat to milk three times
That, though she has twin kids, can fill two pails;
Then a deep beaker, coated with sweet wax,
Two-handled, newly made, and smelling of
The chisel. Ivy, dusted with helichrys,
Is wreathed about his lips; the curling tendrils
Wander, rejoicing in the saffron fruit.
Inside appears a godlike work of art,
A carven maiden wearing robe and snood;
Two long-haired suitors stand on either side
Fighting with words that never touch her heart;
But, laughing, now at one she throws a glance,
And now the other. Meanwhile they, with eyes
Long swollen with love, but labor all in vain.
Beyond them stands an ancient fisherman
On a rough rock toward which the old man drags
Painfully his great fishing net, like one
That labors mightily. You'd say he fishes
With all his strength, so swell the veins about
His neck; though gray, he has a young man's might.
A short space from the sea-worn old man stands
A vineyard laden fair with fire-red grapes.
A boy sits on the stone fence guarding them.
Two foxes skulk about: one ranges up
And down the rows devouring the ripe grapes;
The other plots against his dinner-basket,
Vowing to leave him stranded dinnerless.
But he, weaving a pretty locust-cage
With stalks of asphodel and fitting it
With rushes, all enamoured of his weaving,

Has little care for vines or dinner-basket.
Around the cup is spread the soft acanthus,
Aeolic art for you to marvel at.

. . . .

With this I'll very gladly please your heart,
My friend, if you'll but sing that lovely lay.
I do not jest. Sing, friend! for you'll forget
Your song in Hades, where all things are forgotten.

THYRSIS

Begin, dear Muses, begin the pastoral song.
This is the voice of Thyrsis, him of Aetna.
Where were you, O where were you, Nymphs, when Daphnis
Was pining? By Peneus' beautiful dells,
Or dells of Pindus? You surely haunted not
The great stream of Anapus, nor the peaks
Of Aetna, neither Acis' sacred waters.
Begin, dear Muses, begin the pastoral song.
For him the wolves, for him the jackals howled;
The lion of the forest mourned his death;
And many kine and bulls about his feet,
And many calves and heifers wailed for him.
Begin, dear Muses, begin the pastoral song.
First from the mountains Hermes came and said,
"Who wastes thee, Daphnis? lad, whom lovest thou so?"
Begin, dear Muses, begin the pastoral song.
The cowherds came, the shepherds and the goatherds,
And asked what ailed him. Then Priapus came
And said, "Poor Daphnis, wherefore pinest thou?
The maid, wandering up all the glades and springs,
Seeks thee: how love-sick art thou and how helpless!"

. . . .

No answer did the herdsman make to these,
But bore his bitter love-fate to the end.
Begin, dear Muses, begin the pastoral song.
Now even sweetly smiling Cypris came,
Craftily smiling, holding back her wrath,
And said, "Thou boasted Love to overthrow;
But, Daphnis, hath not Love thrown thee instead?"
Begin, dear Muses, begin the pastoral song.
And Daphnis answered her, "Oppressive Cypris,
Terrible Cypris, foe to human kind,
Think'st thou that all my suns are set? A bane
Will Daphnis prove to Love, even in Hades,
Begin, dear Muses, begin the pastoral song.
Where it is said a herdsman once with Cypris—
Go thou to Ida, go thou to Anchises;
Tall oaks are there, here only marsh-grass grows,
Here sweetly hum the bees about the hives.
Begin, dear Muses, begin the pastoral song.
And thine Adonis blooms who herds the flocks
And slays the hares and chases all the beasts.
Or go to Diomed again and say,
"I conquered Daphnis; now fight thou with me."
Begin, dear Muses, begin the pastoral song.
You wolves and jackals, you cave-haunting bears,
Farewell! The herdsman Daphnis shall be seen
No more in forest, glade, or coppice; and farewell,
O Arethusa, and farewell, you streams
That pour down Thymbris' side your lovely waters.
Begin, dear Muses, begin the pastoral song.
I am that Daphnis who here herd my cattle,
Daphnis who water here the bulls and calves.
Begin, dear Muses, begin the pastoral song.
O Pan, Pan, whether high Lycaeus' peaks
Thou rangest or great Maenalus, come hither
To this Sicilian isle! Forsake the tomb
Of Helice and that steep cairn—adored
Even by the immortals—of Lycaon's son.
O cease your pastoral song, you Muses, cease.
Approach, my king, and take this fair-made pipe,
Fitting the lip, sweet-breathing from the wax;
For Love it is that drags me off to Hades.
O cease your pastoral song, you Muses, cease.
Now let the thorns and brambles violets bear,
And fair narcissus deck the juniper,
And pines grow pears, and nature be reversed;
For Daphnis dies. Let deer drag off the hounds,
And mountain-owls fight with the nightingales.
O cease your pastoral song, you Muses, cease."
And having spoken thus, he spoke no more.
Cypris would have restored him, but the threads
Of fate were spun; so down the stream he went:
The whirling flood destroyed the lad who was
Dear to the Muses, unhated by the nymphs.

ANTIPATER OF SIDON

(About 130 B.C.)

ON THE FALL OF CORINTH

Where, Corinth, is your far-sung beauty flown,
Your ancient wealth and sky-crowned colonnades?

Where are your temples and your castles gone,
Your vanished thousands and your queenly
maids?

Of your lost splendor, hapless, not a stone
Is left, for war has seized and eaten all;
And we unravaged halcyons alone
Are left, old ocean's brood, to wail your fall.

ANONYMOUS

(Late second or early first century B.C.)

Nature and Man

(*Lament for Bion,* ll. 98–104)

Ay me, when mallow in the meadow dies,
When parsley green and crinkled anise fade,
They live again, they rise another spring.

But we, the great, the mighty, and the wise,
Once dead, dumb in the hollow earth are laid
To sleep a sleep endless and unawakening.

MELEAGER

(About 140–70 B.C.)

To a Bee

Flower-pastured bee,
Why dost thou cease to seek
The buds of May and kissest
My Heliodora's cheek?

Dost thou wish to signify
With thy caressing wing
That there lurketh in her skin
Love's sweet and bitter sting?

O friend of lovers, go,
If this be all thy lore,
Back to the buds of May;
I knew it long before.

Spring Song

Now blooms the mountain lily,
The snow-drop stirs again,
The daffodil awakens,
Lover of the rain

Now blooms amid the flowers
Persuasion's sweetest rose,
My love's delight, Zenophile,
Loveliest that grows.

You meadows, why do you laugh
For the splendor in your hair?
You laugh in vain—my girl
Bedims your garlands fair.

To a Grasshopper

O chattering cicada,
Drunken with the dew,
Do you chirp your woodland ditty
Only for me and you?

Perched on the petal-tips
You make a lyric din
With your saw-jagged legs
And sun-burnt skin.

But now, my friend, to the wood nymphs
Sing new delight again,
Or wake the ear of Pan
With an echoing refrain,

That having fled from love
I may not seek in vain
My noontide sleep, reclining
Beneath this shady plane.

To Zenophile Asleep

Sleepest thou, Zenophile,
Delicate flower? Ah that I might creep
Beneath thine eyelids in the guise
Of wingless sleep

That even he who charms
The eyes of Zeus should never visit thee,
And thou be inaccessible
To all but me.

To Heliodora, Dead

Tears tnrough the earth I send you, Heliodora,
Last token of my love, among the dead.

I pour them and remember you with longing,
Upon your grave—they are so hard to shed.

Dearer are you in grief to Meleager,
Empty the grace he pays to Acheron;
He weeps in pity for his heart's desire;
Death ravished her; now Death and she are
gone.

Dust fell upon the flower in full blossom.
But mother Earth, who bore us, hear my call:
I pray you, hold her softly in your bosom,
She who is dead brought sorrow to us all.

PHILODEMUS

(About 110–40 B.C.)

Moonlight

(*Two Versions*)

I

Shine down, O twin-horned moon of night,
Lover of night-long festival,
Shine down and let thy quivering light
Full through the latticed casement fall.

Illume the sleeping form of gold
Callistion from thy heights above,
For thou, O deathless, mayst behold
Ungrudgingly the works of love.

And well I know, my lady moon,
That thou dost bless my love and me,
For did not once Endymion
Enkindle even the soul of thee?

II

O moon of evening, two-horned one, shine
down,
Lover of routs, through windows from
above;
Shine upon bright Callistion, nor frown
In spying envy on the deeds of love.
You make me happy with Callistion:
For one has seared your heart—Endymion.

EUENUS

(First century B.C.)

The Vine to the Goat

Though to the root you eat me, goat, I swear,
Fruit for a cup of wine I yet shall bear
To pour on you and make you sweet and nice
When you are slaughtered for the sacrifice.

JULIUS POLYAENUS

(About A.D. 60)

On the Brevity of Hope

Hope ever steals the time for life away,
But one last dawn outstrips the empty day.

MARCUS ARGENTARIUS

(About A.D. 60)

Reading Hesiod

Once, turning in my hands old Hesiod's book,
I saw my Pyrrha coming, so I took
The volume, cast it down, and thus began:
"Why do you give me work, Hesiod, old man?"

I Live a Splendid Life

The golden chorus of the evening stars
I gaze upon, and revel, nor depress
The sport of others with a tread that mars
All joy. While garlands on my head I dress,
With hands that serve the Muses fair, I touch
My harp, and thus aspiring no higher,
I live a splendid life; the world's not much
Without the garland and the sounding lyre.

PTOLEMAEUS

(About A.D. 180)

On Astronomy

I know I am mortal, living for a day:
But when the stars gleam down their winding
way,
I taste no drink of earth, no longer pine,
But with immortal Zeus immortal shine.

PALLADAS

(About A.D. 395)

On Life and Death

Naked I came upon the earth and naked I go underneath it:
Why do I labor in vain, seeing, naked, the end?

DAMASCIUS

(About A.D. 529)

For a Slave Girl

Zosima, a slave girl bound
To serve till her last breath,
Who found no liberty in life
Finds freedom now in death.

RUFINUS

(About A.D. 550)

To a Flirt

I love all of you but your wandering eye
That flirts with all my rivals on the sly.

ANONYMOUS

(? A.D. sixth century)

On a Child Untimely Dead

Hades, inflexible and stern,
Why have you taken him from me,
Callaeschron, who had still to learn
His babbling words beside my knee?
Through Hell a small delight he'll roam—
But he left only grief at home.

THE PRE-SOCRATIC PHILOSOPHERS

Translated by Herbert M. Howe

INTRODUCTION

THE WRITINGS of the philosophers who lived before the end of the fifth century B.C. have almost all perished, so that we are faced with the problem of reconstructing the origins of Greek philosophy from such fragments as have been preserved and from references by later writers. From them we can see that the Pre-Socratics laid the foundations for later thought; they formulated the problems and indicated some ways of approach. The selection given here will serve as an outline of their work, but an incomplete one; it is largely limited to their speculations about physics and omits important parts of their other teachings, especially those in theology.

The first group to arise appeared in the Greek cities of western Asia Minor; it is called, after that region, the Ionian school. These cities had become very prosperous by trading during the seventh and sixth centuries; politically and economically they were far in advance of the mainland of Greece, where farming was still the main means of livelihood and where the cities had not yet grown to their later importance. Moreover, the Ionians were in close contact with the Near East, and its ideas exerted great influence on the Greek world.

The first concern of the Ionians was with the material substance of the universe. The world was commonly regarded as being composed of four "elements"—earth, water, air, and fire. (The word "element" corresponds fairly closely to the modern "physical state"; the four are the equivalents of solid, liquid, gas, and heat. Modern chemistry has given a different meaning to the term "element.") Thales of Miletus, who flourished about 575, tried to reduce the four elements to one; he suggested that ultimately everything is derived from water, but he gave no explanation of how or why it assumes so many forms. His younger contemporary, Anaximander of Miletus, held the view that visible matter arises from an undefined and unlimited substance, from which each of the elements separates out. About 550 Anaximenes of Miletus returned to one of the elements, air, as his primal matter; but he made the advance of giving condensation and rarefaction as its method of change into the others. The last of the great Ionians, Heraclitus of Ephesus (about 500) took fire as his elemental substance, which he viewed as something which is always altering; his emphasis was on the process of change, where that of his predecessors had been on the matter itself. The Ionians gave no satisfactory explanation of the government of the universe, but they seem to have assumed some sort of natural law and justice, not unlike those of human society.

Whereas the Ionians were concerned chiefly with the material of things, Pythagoras of Samos, who moved to southern Italy about 530, was interested primarily in their form, and especially in the quantitative expression of it. His mathematical work led him to an examination of proportion and harmony; his name is still attached to a famous geometrical theorem. He (or his followers) made the important musical discovery that the harmonious intervals correspond to simple ratios of lengths of strings having the same weight and tension. Thus, if a tight string sounds the note C, it will sound an octave higher if it be stopped at its mid-point; if it be stopped at a point two-thirds of its length, it will sound a fifth higher, and so forth. Pythagoras finally reached the conclusion that the universe and everything in it is the representation of proportion and harmony. His followers even went so far as to regard number as the actual material of things.

The Eleatic school, named for Elea in south Italy, was foreshadowed by Xenophanes of Colophon, who lived at about the same time as Pythagoras. His chief concern was theological; the gods of popular belief, he taught, are only enlarged copies of the men who imagine them. The true god is not many but one; he is, in fact, the universe itself. This notion of the unity of all things was taken up by Parmenides of Elea, who flourished at the beginning of the fifth century. Being, he said, is one, without parts, without motion, without time; there can be nothing else, no "not-being." Being, moreover, can only be apprehended by reason; the senses, through which we perceive the world around us, are subject to error and illusion—especially that time and change exist. A pupil of Parmenides, Zeno, produced a series of paradoxes to demonstrate the illusory nature of change and motion.

The Eleatic criticism made the Ionian theories untenable, for in a universe of one substance and nothing else there can be no change. Accordingly, we find various sorts of *pluralism* making their appearance, in contrast to the earlier *monisms;* the belief that there are several primary causes of things replaces the attempts to reduce everything to one elemental material. Empedocles of Agrigentum, who lived in the middle of the fifth century, accepted the four elements; but he also introduced the opposing forces of attraction and repulsion ("love" and "strife"). By their interaction these bring things together and tear them apart.

Anaxagoras of Clazomenae, a contemporary of Empedocles and a teacher of Pericles, tried to solve two problems: the rise of so vast a number of things from only four elements, and the nature of the force which could have set them in motion. He assumed that there is an immense number of substances, and that every object contains some particles ("seeds" is the word he uses) of each of them. Originally the seeds were all mixed in one chaotic mass, but Mind, which stood outside, imparted a whirling motion to it and caused the seeds to join together to form separate objects. As Anaxagoras wanted his universe to be as mechanical as possible, he limited the work of the Mind to starting the rotation.

Leucippus, who lived at about the same time as Anaxagoras, and his follower Democritus of Abdera developed the atomic theory. Democritus is properly not a Pre-Socratic, since he lived for thirty years after the death of Socrates; but he is best treated with the early thinkers. The atomic theory involves a universe of empty space, through which move a vast number of indivisible particles, differing from each other in size and shape. Their collisions make them bounce off in different directions; when enough of them meet and join, objects are formed, and even the worlds themselves. This philosophy was later adopted and modified by Epicurus.

Toward the end of the fifth century the chief efforts of philosophers were turned from the study of physical nature to the study of man. Despairing of finding unquestionable truth, thinkers began to investigate human conduct and to use their reasoning powers in the study of the arts, especially that of persuasion—rhetoric. The Sophistic movement arose in suspicion of the speculations of the earlier philosophers. Thus Protagoras of Abdera (about 445) maintained that the reality of anything is not something independent of an observer, but exists only as a man asserts it; Gorgias of Leontini, who visited Athens in 427, went so far as to deny the existence of the truth and the possibility of man's reaching it or communicating it to others. Thus the enquiries of the Sophists reached a dead end; the next advances in philosophy were made by Socrates and his followers, who will be considered elsewhere.

THE TEXT translated is that of Hermann Diels, *Die Fragmente der Vorsokratiker* (second edition, Berlin, 1906–7).

THE IONIAN MONISTS

Thales of Miletus

(Aristotle, *Metaphysics* A 3. 983 b 7) Most of the earliest philosophers supposed that the origin of things was to be sought only in some kind of matter. From this, they thought, all things have their origin, and into it they finally dissolve; its existence underlies theirs, although it alters its form as they change. This, they said, is the elemental stuff and the origin of things; and it follows that nothing new is ever created, nor can anything be utterly destroyed, since the elemental matter always maintains its nature. . . . (Diels 1 a 12) Thales, the first proponent of such a philosophy, declared that this elemental matter was water. (D. 1 a 1, paragraph 23) According to some, he was the first to study the heavens and to predict eclipses and the changes in the course of the sun.

Anaximander of Miletus

(D. 2, 9) Anaximander of Miletus, the pupil and follower of Thales, was one of those who maintain that there is one first principle of things, infinite in quantity and extent and capable of motion and change; he was the first to use the term "the infinite" [or "the undefined"] for this elemental matter. It is, according to him, neither water nor any of the so-called elements, but something quite different in its nature; from it arise the heavens and the worlds in them, and to it all things inevitably return. For they must—in the poetical terms he uses—make reparation to each other for the injustices they have committed, at the time ordained for them. Anaximander had evidently considered the changes of the four elements into each other, and did not feel that any one of them should be regarded as the elemental matter; this, he felt, must be something quite different.

Anaximenes of Miletus

(D. 3 a 5) Anaximenes of Miletus, a companion of Anaximander, agreed with him that the elemental stuff underlying things is one and unlimited, but unlike him he maintained that its nature is not undefined, but that it is, in fact, air. It varies in density and thinness as it becomes one object or another. If it is rarefied, it becomes fire; if it is condensed, it first becomes cloud, then water, earth, and finally stone; other things are formed from these. Motion, he asserts, is eternal, and through it all these changes come about.

Heraclitus of Ephesus

(D. 12 b 30) This world . . . was created by no god or man; it was, it is, and it always will be an undying fire which kindles and extinguishes itself in a regular pattern. (D. 12 b 90) All things change place with fire and fire with all things, as money does with goods and goods with money.

(D. 12 a 6) Heraclitus says that everything is in motion, nothing stands fast. Comparing things to the flow of a river, he says that you cannot step twice into the same stream . . . (D. 12 b 91) for new water is always flowing down. By the violence and swiftness of its change, it tears itself away, yet renews itself again. It has no past and no future; it is in advance and in retreat at the same time. . . . (D. 12 b 60) The way up and the way down are the same. [Both have the same beginning and end.]

(D. 12 b 80) Know that conflict is universal, that justice is strife; through strife all things arise and disappear. (D. 12 b 51) Men do not realize that a thing which thrusts out in opposite directions is at unity with itself; harmony is a matter of opposing tensions, like those in a bow or a lyre. . . . (D. 12 b 53) Conflict is the father and ruler of all.

THE PYTHAGOREANS

(D. 45 b 4) At this time [the middle of the fifth century] and a little earlier the men called Pythagoreans worked at the deductive sciences and were the first to develop them. From their constant training in the nature of mathematics they came to the conclusion that it lies beneath all things. Now numbers are the natural bases of mathematics, and in number (rather than in fire or earth or water) they thought that they could see many similarities to the things which are and to those which come into being. Thus they thought that justice is a certain arrangement of number, life and intelligence another, and the pattern of circumstances which we call "the right time" a third, and so with other things. Moreover, they discerned in number the conditions and workings of harmony. Since, then, other things show similarity to number throughout their whole being, they concluded that the elements of number are the bases of all things; the heavens themselves are a harmony and a ratio.

These men, then, seem to have thought of number as the root of things, as their matter, their relations, and their state. The elements of number are the even and the odd [the Greek words originally meant "complete" and "excessive"], the first of which is limited and the second infinite. If these are combined we have a unity, which is both even and odd. The numbers we use are developed from unity; and the whole heaven, as I mentioned above, is a "number."

THE ELEATICS

Xenophanes of Colophon

(D. 11 b 23) God is the One and the All-embracing; he is the greatest among gods and men, and resembles mortals neither in body nor in mind. (D. 11 b 24) He is the whole, which sees, which feels, which hears. (D. 11 b 25) By his thought he sets all things in motion, without difficulty or effort. (D. 11 b 26) He remains eternally fixed and immovable, for it is unthinkable that he should come and go hither and yon.

(D. 11 b 11) Homer and Hesiod attributed to the gods all the practices which among men are disgraceful and bring shame, theft, adultery, and deceit. (D. 11 b 14) Men seem to think that the gods are born, that they wear clothes, that they have human voices and faces. (D. 11 b 15) Now if cattle or horses or lions had hands, so that they could carve and make statues as men do, the horses would carve gods like horses and the cows gods like cows, and they would give them such bodies as they themselves have. (D. 11 b

16) The Ethiopians say that their gods have black skins and snub noses, while the Thracians say that theirs are blue-eyed and red-headed.

Parmenides of Elea

(D. 18 b 4) Now I shall show you—do you listen well and mark my words—the only roads of inquiry which lead to knowledge. The first is that of him who says, "That which exists is real; that it should not exist is impossible." This is the reasonable road, for Truth herself makes it straight. The other road is his who says, "There are, of necessity, things which do not exist," and this, I tell you, is a fantastic and impossible path. For how could you know about something which does not exist?—a sheer impossibility. You could not even talk about it, (D. 18 b 5) for thought and existence are the same.

(D. 18 b 8) There remains only to tell of the way of him who maintains that Being does exist; and on this road there are many signs that Being is without beginning or end. It is the only thing that is; it is all-inclusive and immoveable, without an end. It has no past and no future; its only time is *now*, for it is one continuous whole. What sort of creation could you find for it? From what could it have grown, and how? I cannot let you say or think that it came from nothing, for we cannot say or think that something which does not exist actually does so [i.e., if we say that Being comes from Not-being, we imply that Not-being exists, which is self-contradictory]. What necessity could have roused up existence from nothingness? And, if it had done so, why at one time rather than at another? No; we must either admit that Being exists completely, or that it does not exist at all. Moreover, the force of my argument makes us grant that nothing can arise from Being except Being. Thus iron Law does not relax to allow creation and destruction, but holds all things firm in her grasp.

Zeno of Elea

(D. 19 a 25) There are four problems of Zeno about motion whose solution presents serious difficulty. The first is that which claims that motion is impossible, because a moving body must pass the halfway mark before it reaches its goal, [then the three-quarters mark, then the seven-eighths, and so on *ad infinitum*, never reaching the end].

(D. 19 a 26) The second is the problem called "Achilles." It claims that the slowest runner can never be caught by the fastest. For the pursuer must first reach the point from which the other started, but the slower will then have moved on a little. This argument is the same as the first, except that the distance is not repeatedly halved.

(D. 19 a 27) The third . . . holds that an arrow in flight stands still; it assumes that time is made up of a succession of instants, and if this is not granted the train of reasoning fails. He says that everything is either in motion or at rest. Nothing is in motion which occupies a space equal to itself. But at every instant everything occupies a space equal to itself. Therefore the flying arrow does not move.

(D. 19 a 28) The fourth problem is that of objects of equal size moving at equal speeds but in opposite directions in a stadium, some starting at the ends and some in the middle, and passing fixed objects of the same size, as well as each other. From this problem he thinks he can show that half of any period of time is equal to double the same period. [The statement of the problem is omitted here; it may be summed up as a demonstration that it will take one of the moving objects only half as long to pass the other as it will take it to pass a fixed one.]

The Pluralists

Empedocles of Agrigentum

(D. 21 b 6) Hear, now, that there are four roots to all things—shining Zeus [the heavens, thought of as fire], life-giving Hera [the air], Hades [the earth], and Nestis [a Sicilian water goddess], who with her tears gives water to the springs for men. (D. 21 b 8) Another thing I shall tell you: there is no beginning for the things that are mortal, nor is there an end for them in dreadful death; there is only mixture and separation of things which are mixed. This is the process which men call creation.

(D. 21 b 17) Now shall I speak a double truth. Sometimes a unity grows up out of many things, and sometimes it separates into many parts formed from the one. Thus the creation of mortal things is twofold, and their destruction likewise. For the combining of things puts an end to their separation, yet it also engenders it; their creation, which feeds on the parts that were separated, is scattered apart in its turn. And this continual change never ceases; sometimes all things are brought together by Love, sometimes they are borne asunder by the hatred arising from Strife, until once more they come together in the unity of the whole. Thus One keeps arising from Many, and Many flourish from the wreckage of One; thus things arise, but do not remain fixed forever. Unending change never stops, but all things are bound to its unalterable cycle.

Anaxagoras of Clazomenae

(D. 46 b 12) All other things include portions of every kind of matter, but Mind alone is infinite, controlled only by itself, and mixed with nothing else; it exists alone, subject only to its own rule. If it were not composed only of itself, but were mixed with something else, it would include parts of everything; for in all matter are parts of everything else. Such a mixture would prevent Mind from ruling the rest, but, being self-controlled, it is able to do this. It is the thinnest and purest of all things; it understands all, it has power over all. Mind rules everything that has life, both great and small.

It was Mind which controlled the whirling universe, so that it first started its rotation. In the beginning it was only a small eddy; a greater and yet greater part of the mass entered in, and more is destined to join it yet. Mind, moreover, determined the mixing and separation and distinction of things; Mind ordained the number and nature of all that was and is and is to be; it established the course of the sun, moon, and stars, and the motion of the air and the heavens. These the rotation of things separated each from the other; thus dense is parted from thin, warm from cold, light from darkness, and dry from wet.

The Atomists

Leucippus of Miletus

(D. 54 a 8) Leucippus assumed the atoms ["indivisible particles"] and their unnumbered combinations as the elements of things; these atoms are unlimited in number and are eternally in motion. This he did because the atoms cannot be said to be one material rather than another, and because their creation and change cannot be perceived by examining visible objects. Being, he asserted, is no more real than Not-being, for both alike are the causes of the generation of things. The nature of the atoms he described as solid and compact; this he defined as "Being." The atoms are in motion through empty space, which he called "Not-being"; but he asserted that it is just as real as "Being."

Democritus of Abdera

(D. 55 a 38) In like manner his friend Democritus of Abdera assumed solidity and void as the roots of things; these he too called "Being" and "Not-being." These men postulated the atoms as the material source of things, and derived visible objects from their different arrangements. There are three sorts of arrangements: form, context, and position; (D. 54 a 6) thus the letter A differs from N in form, AN differs from NA in context, and N from Z in position [Z is the same as N turned on its side]. (D. 55 a 38) Like is naturally moved by like; so related atoms are attracted to each other, and each group, joining itself to another combination, forms an object of new pattern. Thus reasonably do these men profess to account for the changes and nature of all things on the grounds that their original atoms are innumerable, and thus do they explain how and by what force things come into being.

The Sophists

Protagoras of Abdera

(D. 74 b 1) Man is the measure of all things, of the existence of those that exist, and of the nonexistence of those that do not.

Gorgias of Leontini

(D. 76 b 3) One of the same group, Gorgias of Leontini, took the part of those who deny any standard of judgment, though his attack was different from that of the followers of Protagoras. He sums his position up . . . in three successive propositions: the first, that nothing exists; the second, that even if anything did exist, man could not comprehend it; and the third, that even if he could comprehend it, he could not communicate and explain it to his neighbors.

SELECTIONS FROM HERODOTUS' *The Histories*

Translated by Paul MacKendrick

INTRODUCTION

HERODOTUS, the "Father of History" and chronicler of the first great conflict between East and West, was born in the Dorian city of Halicarnassus, in southwest Asia Minor, about 484, and died either in Athens or in south Italy about 428 B.C. His busy and adventurous life embraced the period in which Athens, having proved herself the savior of Greece in the Persian War, embarked upon a course of empire which brought her material prosperity, an intellectual Renaissance, and great unpopularity among her subject allies. From the Athenians he is said to have received a prize of ten talents: Athens owed him much more for the picture of her greatness drawn in his pages.

Herodotus' major intellectual trait, curiosity, must early have been stimulated by conversations on the docks of his native Halicarnassus with the tanned and bearded sailors fresh back from voyages beyond the Pillars of Hercules. In fact, his whole book is a conversation of a master story-teller, far-travelled, who had seen the cities of men, and knew their minds. Like Solon, he had travelled to see the world, and perhaps also for trade; he knew Byzantium and the Black Sea, Egypt and Babylon, Greece, Italy, and Sicily. When Pericles founded a colony in Thurii, in South Italy, in 443 B.C., Herodotus was one of the pioneers. He was a friend of the dramatic poet Sophocles, an admirer of Pericles; he was in touch with the movement of intellectual enlightenment which was stirring in Athens in the middle years of the fifth century. Born in a Doric-speaking community, trained in the Ionic dialect, a resident in Athens, a citizen in South Italy, he was in the best sense a "Sophist": *deraciné*, in touch with all cultures, owing allegiance to none, preserving a quality of skepticism which his critics have not always credited him with: "I must tell what I have been told," he says (7.152), "but I am under no obligation whatever to believe it."

The main characteristics of Herodotus' history are unity in diversity, masterly character-drawing, comedy and pathos, a power of vivid description, a delight in a good story, and above all a simplicity in his character and his art, which has won most hearts for 2500 years. The selections presented here have been chosen to bring out these qualities.

The unity of his work consists, first, in his relating of every episode, however remotely, to his main theme of the conflict of East and West out of which Athens emerges as the savior of Greece; and, second, in the recurring theme of the pride that goeth before destruction, and the haughty spirit before a fall. If the stories told to bring out these points are good stories, so much the better. For example, the curious tale of Gyges, the unwilling onlooker at the nakedness of his queen, with which our selections open, is both a good story, well told, with full use of devices of suspense, indirect character-drawing, and concision, and an evidence of the unsavory bases upon which rest the claims to sovereignty of Lydia, the first Eastern kingdom to commit an act of aggression against the Greek West. The later king of Lydia, Croesus, who sets his money so far above the mere intelligence of his visitor, Solon of Athens, is a fine example of the pride (Hybris) that leads, Herodotus believes, inevitably to destruction (Atē). Another such example, the greatest in the book, is Xerxes, the scourger of the Hellespont, the scorner of the brave little band of Spartans at Thermopylae, the capricious beheader of his trembling subjects, who is destined finally to escape barely with his life from the disaster of Salamis, and to appear in rags, as Aeschylus shows him in his *Persians*, at his once proud court of Susa, to be his own messenger of the humbling of his pride. Even Arion, that master rider upon dolphins, earns his place in the history not only because of his wonderful adventures, but because his patron Periander, tyrant of Corinth, opposed the designs of the Lydians upon the Ionian Greek city of Miletus.

Of the five great historians of antiquity, Herodotus

probably excels in the subtlety of his character-drawing. We have already mentioned his sketches of Croesus and Xerxes; the selections also present his portraits of Rameses III (Rhampsinitus), Pharaoh of Egypt, who was able to recognize a foeman worthy of his steel when he saw one; of the three Persians, Otanes, Megabyzus, and Darius, each arguing as his own character dictates for the form of government which would best serve his own interests; of Leonidas the brave leader of the doomed Spartan three hundred at Thermopylae, as he sends his allies away to safety while facing certain death himself; of the canny queen of Herodotus' own city, Artemisia, who knows how to turn an ally's misfortune to her own profit; of Alcmaeon of Athens, whose low mercantile cunning founds the fortunes of an aristocratic house.

Few authors, and no historians, rival Herodotus in his power of bringing out the pathos or the comedy of a scene. The pathos is masterfully handled in the story of the life of Croesus, from Solon's visit to the scene on the pyre; the comedy—always with a sardonic twist, which makes it hard to understand where Herodotus got his reputation for credulity—in the picture of Alcmaeon staggering from Croesus' treasure-chamber, his cheeks puffed out like a chipmunk with gold, his clothes bulging every which way, his feet dragging, so that he looks like anything in the world but a man; in the fixation of Candaules, insisting on displaying to the reluctant Gyges the charms of his wife; in the proof of Arion's adventure—the dolphin, "but not a very big one," dedicated at Taenarum; in the portraying of both the thief who beheaded his brother and the princess who turned prostitute as dutiful children who did as their parents told them.

Herodotus' power of vivid description comes out as clearly in his exposition of technical details like embalming or building a pyramid as in his narrative. Arion, resplendent in his embroidered robes, singing his tenor aria as the sailors, avid but aesthetically aware, wait amidships for his money; the rustling of the oak leaves of the mountain pass, foretelling doom to the Spartans who know their fate, and dare face it like men—these are vignettes worthy of a Hemingway.

As for Herodotus as a story teller, I am tempted to say that the story of Rhampsinitus and the thief is the finest short story in western literature. At any rate for conciseness, economy of plot, and fine pretended primness in the recounting of gory detail it would be hard to equal, from the Arabian Nights to the latest horror story. A brother beheaded, a corpse cut down, a dead man's severed hand left in a princess' fingers—the story has every quality to make the flesh creep, and it is only one of dozens with which Herodotus' rich pages are crammed.

Yet with all his richness and variety, Herodotus is instinct with that simplicity which is the hallmark of the best Greek art: the use of minimum means to attain maximum effect. The style is straightforward and easy, devoid both of jargon, and, to tell the truth, of that profundity which loads the pages of Thucydides, and, to a lesser degree, of Sallust, with almost more meaning than language can bear. He has been called the most Homeric of historians, and he is Homeric in his epic breadth and in his simple appreciation of the virtues which made the epic heroes noble and of the gods which the Greeks of a simpler time had made in their own image. The simplicity of a child, a certain romantic wonder at the obvious, he combines with the gift of a man, the ability to *select*—a combination which makes great art. With none of the merits of Thucydides—keen critical sense, ability to isolate in a situation the generic without falsifying the unique—he has yet virtues of his own which have always endeared him to readers: his relish of anecdote, his breadth of view, his simple piety, his ability to compress a mighty theme into synoptic proportions, his power to make the writing of history a great art. Only Livy among classical historians can rival him as a story teller. He represents the transition which the Athenians of his generation went through, from an age of traditional faith to the self-critical questionings of the Periclean Renaissance. As long as men are interested in other men or in marvels, or in the struggle of freedom with despotism, Herodotus will hold his place as the favorite historian of western man. He deserves the sonnet that T. R. Glover wrote for him,* and with which I end:

You come and tell us of so many things—
Satraps and oracles, Nile and Italy,
And fairy-tales as splendid as there be,
The Phoenix with his father on his wings,
Great marvels of Greek art, strange fates of Kings,
Soils, climates, customs, and the Southern Sea,
And how Greek citizens battled to be free,
And all the breadth of soul that freedom brings.
You loved your story, and the things it shows,
Dear critic, who part doubt and part believe,
Lean, like the Greek you are, to what man knows,
Yet hold that in long time and other lands
God may do stranger things than Greeks conceive—
You that have met such wonders on all hands.

THE TEXT translated is that of H. Kallenberg (Leipzig, 1929), except for the accounts of Marathon, Thermopylae, and Salamis, which are taken from the abridged Greek text of Amy L. Barbour (Boston, 1929).

---

* Reprinted from Glover's Sather Classical Lectures, *Herodotus* (Berkeley, 1924), p. xv, by gracious permission of the publishers, The University of California Press.

HERODOTUS OF HALICARNASSUS

THE PUBLICATION OF HIS RESEARCHES

TO THE END THAT

NEITHER MEN'S DEEDS MAY FADE WITH TIME

NOR THE GREAT AND MARVELOUS WORKS

SHOWN FORTH BY BOTH THE GREEKS AND THE BARBARIANS

REMAIN UNSUNG,

BOTH OTHER MATTERS AND

THE CAUSE

OF THEIR WARRING WITH ONE ANOTHER

[In his pursuit of the causes of the Persian War, Herodotus first dismisses the myths, then deals with history, beginning with Croesus of Lydia, "the first who wronged the Greeks." One of his predecessors, Gyges, obtained the throne about 685 B.C. by intrigue with the wife of King Candaules; Herodotus' account of the incident reveals both his art as a story-teller and the skeptical quality of his mind, for which moderns give him too little credit. Contrast the use by Plato of the story of Gyges' ring of invisibility (*Republic*, II, 359–360) to reinforce the argument that anyone will commit injustice if he thinks he can get away with it.]

From Book I

How Gyges gained the kingdom of Lydia

8 Now this Candaules actually fell in love with his own wife, and since he was in love with her, he thought he had by far the most beautiful wife in the world. This opinion had fatal results. He was especially fond of one of his bodyguard, Gyges the son of Dascylus, upon whom he used to place the responsibility for his most serious business, particularly the job of listening to the praises of the queen's beauty. After a short while the ill-fated Candaules said to Gyges, "Gyges, I don't think you believe me when I talk about my wife's beauty. Since men's eyes are more dependable witnesses than their ears, do arrange to see her naked." But Gyges cried out in great astonishment, saying, "Sire, what unhealthy proposal is this, that I should look upon my queen naked? When a woman takes off her clothes, her modesty goes with them. Men of old discovered the proprieties, and it is our duty to learn from them. One of their sayings is 'Let each man look on his own.' I do believe she is the most beautiful of all women, and I beg of you to ask of me nothing improper." *9* He made this speech to ward off such proposals, for he was in deadly fear that they would bring him some harm. But the king replied, "Cheer up, Gyges, and don't be afraid either that I am testing you by this suggestion, or that my wife will cause you any harm. For to begin with I will arrange it so that she will not even know that you are looking at her. For I will put you behind the open door in our bedroom. My wife will come in after me to go to bed. There is a chair near the doorway, on which my wife will put her clothes one by one as she takes them off, and give you plenty of opportunity to see her. When she walks from the chair to the bed and turns her back on you, it is up to you to get away without her seeing you going out the door." *10* Since Gyges could not get out of it, he declared himself ready. When Candaules thought it was time for bed, he escorted Gyges to the bedroom, and immediately afterward the queen came in also, and after she had come in and while she was putting her clothes on the chair Gyges got a good look at her. And when the queen turned her back to go to bed, Gyges slipped out from behind the door and got away. And the queen saw him making his getaway. But, since she knew that her husband was responsible for what had happened, she neither cried out in alarm, nor appeared to notice anything, intending to take vengeance on this Candaules. For among the Lydians, and almost without exception among all other barbarians, it is considered the depth of disgrace for even a man to be seen naked. *11* For the time being, then, she made no sign, but kept quiet. With the dawn, however, she mustered those of her household whom she knew to be most faithful to her, and then sent for Gyges. And he, all unsuspecting that she knew what had happened, came when he was sent for; for he had often before come running at the queen's summons. When Gyges arrived, the queen said, "Look here, Gyges: of the two courses that are open to you I give you your choice of which way you want to turn: for either you must murder Candaules and take me and the kingdom of Lydia, or you must die yourself right on the spot, so that you may not hereafter, in your unquestioning obedience to Candaules, see what you shouldn't. But rest assured that one of you two must die, either the man who planned this, or you who in seeing me naked violated our conventions." Gyges at first was speechless with surprise at her words, but afterwards found speech to implore her not to force him to make such a choice. However, he could not persuade her, but saw that he was indeed under compulsion either to kill his master or himself to suffer death at others' hands: he chose survival, and asked her, "Since you force me to kill my master against my will, let me hear how we are to attack him." She replied, "The attack will take place on the very spot where he showed me to you in my nakedness, and we shall lay hands on him as he sleeps." *12* After they had hatched their plot, and night had fallen, Gyges followed the queen into the bedroom, since she would not let him off, and he could not get out of it, but had to destroy either himself or Candaules. She gave him a dagger and hid him behind the same door. Then when Candaules was asleep Gyges slipped out from behind the door, killed him, and got the queen and the kingdom.

[Herodotus is the master of the digression within the digression. The expansion of Lydia brought her into collision with Miletus; Corinth helped Miletus; Periander, tyrant of Corinth (about 625–585 B.C.) had a favorite musician, and the following is his miraculous story.]

How Arion was saved by a dolphin

24 About this Arion the story goes that he had spent the greater part of his time at Periander's court, but had taken it into his head to make a voyage to Italy and Sicily, and after making a great deal of money wanted to take ship back to Corinth. He set sail from Tarentum, but since he trusted no one more than Corinthians, he hired a ship with a Corinthian crew. And they, when they were well out at sea, plotted to throw Arion overboard and keep his money. He, discovering their plan, begged them to take his money and spare his life. His words did not convince them, however; they gave him orders either to make an end of himself, if he wanted a grave on dry land, or to jump into the sea forthwith. Thus threatened, Arion, in a quandary, begged them, since they felt that way about it, to let him stand on the stern thwarts in full costume and sing; he promised that after he had sung he would do away with himself. Pleasure came over the crew at the prospect of hearing the world's best singer, and they withdrew from the stern into the waist of the ship. He put on his full costume, took his lyre, stood in the stern sheets and sang a tenor aria all the way through, and when he had finished it he pitched himself into the sea just as he was, in full costume. The crew sailed off to Corinth, but as for Arion, the story goes that a dolphin picked him up and gave him a ride to Taenarum [the central peninsula of the southern Peloponnese]. Arion got off and made his way to Corinth in his costume. On arrival, he told the whole story. Periander was suspicious and kept Arion under house arrest while he anxiously awaited the arrival of the crew. On their coming he sent for them and inquired whether they had any news of Arion. When they said that he was safe in Italy, and that they had left him doing well in Tarentum, Arion appeared before them just as he had been when he jumped overboard; terror stricken, the men could not stick to their denials under cross-questioning. This is the story the Corinthians and the Lesbians tell, and there is a bronze dedication of Arion's, not a very big one, on Taenarum, the statue of a man riding on a dolphin.

[A generation after Periander in Corinth, Croesus (about 560–546 B.C.), a byword for his wealth, became king of Lydia; he pursued a policy of overlordship over the Greek squatters in Asia, though he was on friendly terms with mainland Greeks. Herodotus by stretching his chronology brings together the wisest man of the time, Solon of Athens (about 640–560 B.C.) with the richest, in order to show that Croesus' prosperity is riding for a fall.]

How Solon put Croesus in his place

30 When Solon arrived in Sardis, Croesus entertained him in the palace. After three or four days, servants at Croesus' bidding took Solon on a conducted tour of the treasuries, and showed him how mighty and prosperous everything was. When Solon had admired and examined it all at his leisure, Croesus asked him, "Athenian stranger, many a tale has reached us about your wisdom and your travels, about how in your search for knowledge you have covered much ground in order to see the world, so now the desire has come over me to put the question, who, in your opinion, is the happiest man in the world." He asked the question in the expectation of turning out to be himself the happiest of mortals; however, Solon refused to fawn upon him, but instead told the truth and said, "Tellus the Athenian, Sire." In amazement, Croesus rounded on him and asked, "What are your grounds for judging Tellus happiest?" Solon replied, "In the first place, in the midst of his city's prosperity Tellus had handsome and dutiful sons, and they in turn all had children who all grew up; in the second place, in the midst of material prosperity, as we judge such matters, his life came to a glorious end; for in a battle at Eleusis between the Athenians and their neighbors he came to the rescue, routed the enemy, and died a hero's death; and the Athenians gave him a state funeral with full military honors on the spot where he fell." *31* So Solon told Croesus his cautionary tale about Tellus, with many details about his happiness. Then Croesus asked whom he had seen who was second happiest after this man, thinking that at any rate he would surely carry off the second prize. But Solon said, "Cleobis and Biton. They were from Argos, had an adequate income, and were besides so strong that they had both been equal prize winners at the Games. The following is an instance of their strength: The Argives were holding festival in honor of Hera, and their mother absolutely had to ride in a wagon to the temple, but her oxen were not brought from the farm in time. Since time was short, the young men put the yoke on their own necks and drew the wagon, with their mother riding on it, for over five miles until they reached the temple. After they had performed this feat and been seen by the whole company of the faithful, their life came to the finest possible end, wherein the goddess [Hera] plainly showed that it is better for a man to die than to live. For the Argive men who were standing about congratulated the young men on their strength, and the Argive women congratulated their mother for having borne such sons. The mother, overjoyed at both the deed and the comments, stood before the cult-statue and prayed that to her sons Cleobis and Biton, who had done her great honor, the goddess would give whatever it is best for a man to have. After this prayer they sacrificed and feasted, and then the young men lay down to sleep in the temple itself, and never got up again, but were held fast in their life's end. And the Argives, on the ground that the young men had proved themselves heroes, had statues made of them which they dedicated at Delphi." *32* Croesus said angrily, "Athenian stranger, do you rate my happiness so low that you not even put me on a level with private citizens?" Solon replied: "Croesus, you are asking a question about human life of me, a man who understands that God is entirely jealous and apt to cause confusion. For in a long life one may see and suffer much against one's will. I set the limit of mortal life at seventy years . . . not one day of which brings a single event that is in any way like another. Man, then, Croesus, is entirely accident. To me you seem to be very rich and king over many men, but as for your question, I cannot yet answer it, until I hear that you have finished your life happily. For the very rich man is in no way happier than the man who has a day's livelihood, unless he has the luck to end his life happily in all prosperity. For many very rich men are unhappy, while many of moderate means have been lucky. A man who is very rich but unhappy has the best of the lucky man in two ways only, while the latter has the best of the former in many. The former is better able to satisfy his desires and endure great tragedy when it falls upon him, but the latter has the best of him thus: it is not as easy for him to endure tragedy and desire, but his luck keeps him free of them; however, he is sound of limb, healthy, unacquainted with grief, blessed with children, and good to look upon. If besides this he also ends his life happily, he is worthy to be called the happy man you are looking for, but until he dies, keep from ever calling him happy; simply call him lucky. For a single mortal to have all this good fortune at once is impossible. Just as no one country suffices to supply all its own needs, but has one thing and lacks another, and the best is the one that has the most, even so no one human body is in any way self-sufficient, for it has one thing and lacks another. Whoever keeps on having most, and then dies happily, ought in my judgment to bear the name of 'happy.' But in every case one must look at how the end turns out; for to many men God gives a glimpse of happiness and then overturns them root and branch." For this speech, I suppose Solon received no reward from Croesus, who dismissed him as a man of no account, thinking a man to be a complete fool who would let the present good go, but bid men in every case to look to the end.

[Croesus' present good did not last long, for Cyrus the Great of Persia (559–529 B.C.) invaded his kingdom, besieged his capital, and took him prisoner. According to Herodotus, Croesus became Cyrus' friend and counsellor; according to the poet Bacchylides (505–450 B.C., frg. 3.15–62; *Oxford Book of Greek Verse in Translation,* No. 306) he was miraculously saved by Apollo and carried to the land back of the North Wind.]

How Cyrus captured Croesus and set him free

86 The Persians took Sardis and made a prisoner of Croesus himself, in the fourteenth year of his reign and on the fourteenth day of the siege, according to the oracle that he would destroy a mighty empire—his own. When the Persians had seized him they brought him before Cyrus, who had had a great pyre built, and set Croesus upon it fettered, and twice seven sons of the Lydians with him, either having in mind to sacrifice him to some god, or wishing to fulfill a vow, or setting him upon the pyre because he had heard that Croesus was a god-fearing man, and wanted to know if one of the powers above would save him from being burned alive. At any rate this is what Cyrus did, and as Croesus was standing upon the pyre it occurred to him, though he was in such straits, that the saying of Solon, "No man is happy while he lives," had been spoken with divine inspiration. When the thought struck him, he heaved a heavy sigh and groaned aloud after a deep silence, crying, "Solon! Solon! Solon!" When Cyrus heard this, he bade his interpreters ask Croesus whom he was invoking, and they went up and asked him. Croesus for a while kept silent under their questioning, but then under pressure he said, "One whom I would give much money if all tyrants might talk to." Since what he said was incomprehensible to the interpreters, they asked him the same question again. Since they were pestering him and making nuisances of themselves, he told them how once upon a time Solon, an Athenian, had come, and seeing all his wealth, had called it rubbish, etc., and how everything had happened to him just as Solon had said, though Solon's remarks applied no more to him than to any other man, and especially to those who think themselves happy. Croesus gave this explanation while the pyre, already kindled, was burning on its outer edges. When Cyrus heard from the interpreters what Croesus had said, he changed his mind and fell to thinking that he, a mortal, was burning alive another mortal who had in his time been no less happy than he; besides this, Cyrus feared retribution, and, pondering the fact that nothing mortal is secure, he bade the kindled pyre to be put out as quickly as possible, and Croesus and his companions to be brought down from it. His men tried, but were still not able to get the fire under control. *87* Then, as the Lydians tell the tale, Croesus, discovering Cyrus' change of heart from the sight of all the Persians trying to put out the fire, cried out with a great voice and invoked Apollo, praying that if the god had ever received from him any gift with which he was well pleased, he should stand by and save him from his present plight. As Croesus with tears was invoking the god, out of a clear and windless sky clouds suddenly gathered, a storm broke, and it rained with a violent rain, so that the pyre was put out. Thus Cyrus learned that Croesus was a good man and beloved of the gods, so he had him brought down from the pyre and said to him, "Croesus, who in the world persuaded you to make an expedition against my country, and become my enemy instead of my friend?" Croesus answered, "Sire, it was lucky for you and unlucky for me that I did it; it was the god of the Hellenes who was responsible; he gave me the delusions of grandeur to make the expedition. For no one is so witless as to prefer war to peace; for in peace the children bury the fathers, but in war the fathers bury the children. But I suppose a power above willed it so." *88* This is what Croesus said, and Cyrus unbound him, seated him at his side, and showed him every consideration, both he and all his courtiers marveling at the sight of him.

[The rest of Book I deals with Greece in the time of Croesus, the rise of Persia, and the Persian conquest of Ionia. The second king of the Persian empire was the mad Cambyses (529–521 B.C.), whose chief claim to fame is the conquest of Egypt. Herodotus therefore devotes his second book to the geography, anthropology, and history of Egypt.]

From Book II

How the Egyptians embalm their dead

86 There are men in Egypt who work at embalming and make it their profession. When a body is brought to them, they show the bearers painted wooden models of corpses, and the best of the likenesses is said to be of him [Osiris] whom I do not think it holy to mention in such a context; they show a second which is inferior to the first and less costly, and a third which is the cheapest of all. When the embalmers have explained this, they ask the bearers according to which model they want the corpse prepared. As soon as the bearers have agreed upon the fee, they scurry away; the others, left to their own devices in the embalming rooms, thus prepare the mummies of the best grade. First with a crooked piece of iron they draw out the brain through the nostrils, cleaning out part of it in this way, and the rest by an infusion of chemicals. Then with a sharp flint embalming knife they make an incision along the flank, out of which they draw the whole of the entrails, next cleaning and rinsing the abdominal cavity with palm oil, and then swabbing it with spices pounded fine. Then they fill it with pure chopped myrrh, cinnamon, and other spices, all but frankincense, and sew it up again. After they have done this, they pickle the body for seventy days in nitre, keeping it entirely covered. The embalming should not take longer. When the seventy days are up, they wash the body and wrap it all up in strips of fine linen, and smear it with gum, which the Egyptians generally use instead of glue. Then the relatives take it back from the embalmers and make a wooden case shaped like a man, in which they insert the body, after which they fasten the case and treasure it up in a burial chamber, standing it upright against a wall. *87* This is their top-grade embalming method; for those who want the middle grade, avoiding great expense they prepare the body as follows: they fill syringes with cedar oil, which they inject rectally into the abdominal cavity, without either making an incision or drawing out the guts, and then prevent the liquid from flowing out again. Then they steep the body for the prescribed number of days, and on the last day let out of the cavity the oil which they have previously injected. This oil has the property of dissolving and drawing out with it the stomach and entrails. The nitre dissolves the flesh, and nothing is left of the corpse but skin and bones. When the embalmers have done this, they return the body to the family without taking any further trouble over it. *88* This is the third method of embalming, which takes care of those who are not so well off financially: they clean out the intestines with purge-plant [radish], steep it for seventy days, and then it is carried away by those who brought it.

[Turning from anthropology to history, Herodotus gives a somewhat garbled account of some early Egyptian kings, including a Rameses whom he calls Rhampsinitus.]

How Rhampsinitus rewarded the thief

121A Rhampsinitus acquired great wealth in silver, such that none of the kings who succeeded him could surpass or even equal it. Wanting to keep his money safe, he had a stone building erected, one wall of which was next to the outer wall of his palace. The builder, with an eye on the treasure, contrived the following device: he made one of the stones easily removable from the wall, either by two men or by one. When the building was finished, the king kept his treasure in it; as time passed, the builder, on his death bed, sent for his two sons and explained to them how with a view to their having an adequate income he had included his contrivance in the treasure house he had built for the king. After he had clearly explained to them how to remove the stone, he gave them its measurements, telling them that if they kept the secret they would be controllers of the king's treasury. Then the father died, and his sons did not long refrain from their work, but went to the palace by night, found the stone in the building, extracted it with ease, and made off with a great deal of money. *121B* The next time the king happened to unlock his treasure house, he was surprised to see the low level of the money in his coffers, but did not know whom to accuse, since the seals had been unbroken and the treasure-house locked. Since the next two or three times he unlocked it the money seemed less every time (for the thieves kept plugging away at their plundering) this is what the king did: he ordered some traps made, and set around the coffers in which the money lay. When the thieves made their regular visit, and one of them had crawled into the treasure house and approached the coffers, he was immediately caught in the trap. As soon as he saw the pickle he was in, he called to his brother, explained his predicament, and told his brother to crawl in as fast as he could and cut off his head, since otherwise his being seen and identified would involve his brother in his own ruin. The brother thought this was a good idea, and, yielding to persuasion, did the job. Then he replaced the stone and went off home, carrying his brother's head. *121C* At daybreak, the king, entering the treasure house, was amazed to see the body of the thief headless in the trap, though the seals of the building were still intact and it had no other entrance or exit. Having no other recourse, this is what he did: he hung the body of the thief over the palace wall, and stationed guards over it with strict orders to arrest and bring before him anyone they might see weeping or wailing near by. At the news that the body had been hung up to public view, the mother was vexed, and had words with her surviving son, telling him he was to find a way, she didn't care how, to cut down his brother's body and carry it home. If he failed to attend to this, she said, she would go to the king and expose him as the thief. *121D* Since the mother was giving the surviving son some rough handling, and, try as he would, he could not convince her to leave him alone, this is the device he hit upon: he got hold of some donkeys, and, loading some wineskins on their backs, drove them past the place where the guards were stationed over the hanging body, where he jerked on two or three of the skins and untied the fastenings of the necks of them. As the wine was flowing out, he began to beat his head, and bellow, as though he could not make up his mind which one of the donkeys to turn to first. When the guards saw the wine flowing so free, they all ran into the road with pans in their hands, caught up the spilled wine, and carried it away, turning the "accident" to their profit. He distributed curses liberally among them, acting angry, but they calmed him down in time, and he pretended to relent and simmer down, finally driving the donkeys out of the road to rearrange their burdens. A long conversation got started, and one of the guards began to crack jokes and make him laugh, so he gave him one of the skins of wine. The guards decided then and there to relax and have a drinking party, including him; they invited him to stay and drink with them. He was talked into it, of course, and stayed. They got very friendly over their wine, and he gave them a second wineskin. The guards drank deep, got drunk, and lay down and fell asleep on the very spot where they had been drinking. The thief, as soon as the night was dark enough, cut down his brother's body, shaved the right cheeks of the guards out of mockery, loaded the body on his donkeys and drove them off home, thus doing what his mother had told him. *121E* But when the king was told that the thief's body had been stolen, it was his turn to be vexed, and, being especially eager to find out who in the world had managed it, this is what he did (though for my part I do not believe it): he put his own daughter in a house of ill-fame, and told her to take on all comers, but, before she went to bed with them, to make them tell her what was the cleverest and wickedest thing they had ever done in their lives; whoever told the story of the thief's body, she was to grab him and not let him get away. The daughter did as her father told her. The thief learned the true motive, and, wishing to show himself a man of more devices than the king, this is what he did: cutting off at the shoulder the arm of a freshly-murdered corpse, he went off with it under his tunic, to pay a call on the king's daughter. When he was asked the same question as the others, he explained that his wickedest act had been the cutting off his brother's head as he lay caught in the trap in the king's treasure house, and his cleverest one, getting the guards drunk and cutting down his brother's hanging body. When she heard this, she made a grab at him; but the thief in the darkness held out to her the corpse's arm, which she seized and held on to, thinking that the arm she held was that of the thief himself. He, letting her keep her prize, ran outdoors. *121F* When news of this further exploit was brought to the king, he was astonished at the cleverness and daring of the fellow, and sent into all the cities a dispatch proclaiming pardon and a large cash prize to the thief if he would identify himself. The thief trusted the king and appeared before him, and Rhampsinitus was lost in admiration of him, and gave him that same daughter in marriage, on the ground that he was the wisest man in the world. "The Egyptians," said the king, "are smarter than anyone else, and this fellow is smarter than the Egyptians."

How Cheops built his pyramid

124 Through the reign of Rhampsinitus, according to the priests, there was excellent, responsible government in Egypt, but his successor Cheops plunged the kingdom into all kinds of trouble. First he closed all the temples and kept his subjects from worship; next he ordered them all to slave for him. Some he forced to quarry stone in the Arabian Mountains and drag it down to the Nile; others he made to receive the stone after it had been ferried across the river and drag it to the so-called Libyan Hills. They worked in gangs of 100,000 each, relieved every three months. It took ten years for this oppressed people to make the causeway on which the stone was dragged, a job they dreaded as being not much easier, in my judgment, than the building of the pyramid itself, for it is five-eighths of a mile long, sixty feet wide, and forty-eight feet high at its highest point, and is built of polished stone with animals carved on it. It took ten years to build this, plus the construction on the hill where the pyramids stand and the underground vaults which he built for his own use on an artificial island, with the Nile as a moat around it. The Pyramid itself took twenty years in the making. Its ground is square, eight hundred feet on a side, and its height is the same [actually 756 × 480]; it is built of polished and carefully mortised stone, no block being less than thirty feet square. *125* This is how the pyramid itself was built: in a series of what some call steps, others battlements, and still others altars. When they had built the first level, they raised the stones for the next up onto it from the ground with specially built wooden cranes. Then the stone was hooked to a second crane on the first level, which transferred it to a third crane on the second level. Either there were as many cranes as there were levels, or they had just one portable crane which they transferred from level to level as the structure rose: I report the alternative versions as I heard them. They finished the pyramid from the top down. A hieroglyphic inscription on the pyramid records how much radish, onion, and garlic was eaten by the workmen, and, if memory serves, the interpreter who translated the inscription for me said that the expense was 1,600 talents of silver. If this is true, what is a reasonable estimate of other expense, for iron tools to work with, and food and clothing for the workmen? The construction work lasted the length of time I have already mentioned, and no small stretch, I think, must be allowed for cutting and dragging the blocks and building the underground vault.

[This is the country which the mad Cambyses conquered. He was succeeded, after a revolt, by Darius I (521–486). Herodotus, possibly because he knew the fondness of Athenians for political debate, inserts into his narrative of the accession of Darius the following series of speeches—typical of ancient historiography—on rival forms of government.]

From Book III

How the Persians debated forms of government

80 Otanes urged them to put the power into the hands of the Persian community in the following speech: "I think no one of us should ever become sole ruler, for that would neither be a good thing nor a pleasant one. You saw the extent to which Cambyses' insolence went, and you know from experience that of the Magus. How could monarchy be a properly disciplined thing, when a monarch can do what he pleases, and render an account to no one? Why, even the most upright man in the world, if he were king, would stand quite outside the customary conventions of conduct. The good things that surround him breed insolence in him, and envy is a rooted human instinct. Having insolence and envy he has the sum of vice, for in a state of surfeit he is prompted to wickedness sometimes by the one, sometimes by the other. And yet a tyrant, of all people, ought to be free of envy, because every good thing is in his possession; yet his natural attitude to his subjects is the opposite of this: he grudges the survival and existence of the nobles, but takes delight in the basest of the townsfolk; and he is a first-rate listener to malicious gossip. And he has absolutely no sense of proportion: if you are moderate in your admiration, he is angry because he is not flattered to the top of his bent; if you flatter him, he calls you a toady. What follows is the keynote of my speech: he upsets tradition, rapes women, and kills men without trial. The rule of the many, on the other hand, has first of all the fairest of names, Equality; and secondly, it commits none of the monarch's crimes: office is held by lot, and subject to audit, and all matters of policy are referred to the common people. I move therefore that we abolish monarchy and exalt the common people; for all strength depends on numbers."

81 Otanes expressed this opinion, but Megabyzus urged them to turn the government over to an oligarchy. This was his speech: "As for what Otanes said about putting a stop to tyranny, those are my sentiments also; but when he tells you to hand the power over to the majority, he is very wide of the mark, for there is nothing stupider nor more insolent than a useless mob. And yet for men trying to escape a tyrant's insolence to fall prey to that of an undisciplined mob is absolutely unbearable. When a tyrant does something, he at least knows what he is doing, but the mob is not even capable of knowledge. For how would it know, when it has neither been taught anything noble or fitting, nor knows it for itself, but barges in and falls upon politics witlessly, like a spring freshet? Let the enemies of Persia, then, be democrats, but let *us* choose a group of our best men and vest them with power. In that way we ourselves shall be among the number, and it is likely that the best men will make the best policy."

82 Such was Megabyzus' opinion. The third speaker was Darius, who said: "I thought Megabyzus was sound in his attack upon democracy but not in advocating oligarchy. For if we have a choice of three constitutions, each at its best—democracy, oligarchy, and monarchy—I say the last is head and shoulders above the rest. For there would appear to be nothing better than the rule of one man, if he be the best. Since his judgment would match his character, he would be a blameless trustee of his people, while in a monarchy the policy toward malcontents would be most easily kept secret. But in an oligarchy, where many practise public virtue, strong private animosities invariably arise, for each man wants to lead the chorus and have his opinion prevail, so that the result is enmity all round, which breeds revolution, and revolution murder, and murder culminates in the rule of one man, which is proof how much the best it is. Whereas if the people rule, there is bound to be corruption, but the corruption in the body politic does not lead to the corrupt persons' hating one another, but to strong friendships, for the corrupters of the commonwealth put their heads together. These goings on continue until someone becomes champion of the people and puts a stop to the crooked politicians. The result is that the people admire their champion, and in the midst of the admiration he stands revealed as a monarch, and provides another proof of the potency of one-man rule. To sum it all up in a word, where did we get our freedom, and who gave it to us? Was it democracy, oligarchy, or monarchy? Very well, then; I move that since we were freed by one man [Cyrus] we maintain one-man rule, and that apart from this we do not abolish ancestral customs when we are doing well under them; for that is not the better course."

[Darius prevailed, reformed the administration of the empire, and took Samos, the last free Ionian town. Persian aggression next turned toward Europe and Africa ("Today Persia, tomorrow the whole world!"), and Book IV does for Scythia and Libya what Book II had done for Egypt. Book V deals with the organization of Darius' European conquests, the abortive revolt of the Ionian Greeks, the expansion of Athens, and the rivalry of Athens and Sparta: finally East and West meet (490 B.C.) upon the fateful plain of Marathon.]

From Book VI

How the Athenians won the Battle of Marathon

109 The Athenian generals were divided in their opinions, some opposing an attack on the ground that they were few to attack the Persian host, while others, including Miltiades, favored it. They were evenly divided and it looked as though the more cowardly counsel would prevail, but there was an eleventh vote: the Athenian chosen by lot as polemarch (for in the old days the Athenians used to give the polemarch an equal vote with the generals). On this occasion the polemarch was Callimachus of the deme Aphidna, whom Miltiades approached and said: "It is up to you, Callimachus, either to enslave Athens or to make her free and leave behind for yourself a reputation forever, better even than that of Harmodius and Aristogiton. The present danger is the greatest since there have been Athenians, and if they knuckle under to the Medes, it has been resolved what they shall suffer, being handed over to Hippias; whereas if this city should win, it can become the first city of the sons of Hellas. Now how this can happen, and how it devolves upon you of all people to hold the key to the situation, I shall now explain. There are ten of us generals, and our votes are evenly divided, half of us favoring attack, the other half opposing. Now if we do not attack, I expect that some great spirit of faction will descend upon the minds of the Athenians and so shake their confidence that they will go over to the Persians, but if we attack before any unsound thought occurs to any of the Athenians, and if the gods grant us an even chance, we can win the battle. All this applies to *you*, and depends on *you*, for if you side with me, yours is a fatherland that is free and a city first of those in Hellas; but if you should choose the side of those who are discouraging the attack, then of the good things I listed the opposite will befall you." *110* By this speech Miltiades won Callimachus over, and with the addition of the polemarch's vote the attack had been officially approved. Afterward, the generals who were in favor of the attack, as each one's day of command came up, turned it over to Miltiades, who accepted it, but did not attack until his own day of command came up. *111* When his turn came, this is the way the Athenians were drawn up for the attack: The polemarch Callimachus led the right wing, as was in those days the Athenian custom. Under his leadership, the tribes were drawn up in numerical order, next to one another. And last of all were drawn up on the left wing the Plataeans. (From the time of this battle on, when the Athenians offer sacrifices at the quadrennial festivals, the herald invokes blessings "on the Athenians and the Plataeans both.") This was roughly the method of drawing up the Athenians at Marathon: their line was stretched out equal to the Persian line, but its center was only a few ranks deep, and here the line was weakest, whereas each wing was strong in numbers. *112* When the troops had been deployed and the sacrifices had turned out propitious, the Athenians were given the command to charge, and they made for the barbarians on the dead run. The distance between the armies, from spear point to spear point, was not less than a mile. The Persians, seeing them attacking at the double, prepared to receive them, thinking them the victims of a madness that would destroy them utterly, seeing that they were few, and yet coming on at a run without either cavalry or archers for cover. That is what the barbarians thought; but when the Athenians in a body came to grips with the barbarians, they fought a battle worthy of the name. For they were the first of all the Greeks we know of to use the charge against the enemy; they were the first to bear up against the sight of the Persian uniform and the men wearing it; up to then the very name of Mede had been a terror for the Greeks to hear. *113* While they fought at Marathon, a long time passed. And in the center of the line the barbarians were winning, where the Persians themselves and the Sacae had been drawn up. Victorious in this quarter, the barbarians had broken through and were chasing their foes into the interior, but on each wing the Athenians and the Plataeans were winning. In their victory they let the repulsed barbarians go, but linked their two wings and fought those of the enemy who had broken through, and the Athenians won. They followed the fleeing Persians, cutting them down, until they came to the sea; then they called for fire and seized hold of the ships. *114* And in this struggle the polemarch lost his life, having proved his mettle (and of the generals, Stesilaus the son of Thrasylaus). Also Cynegirus the son of Euphorion [brother of Aeschylus the tragic poet] fell there, his hand cut off with an axe as he was laying hold of a ship's stern, and many other famous Athenians were killed. *115* The Athenians overpowered seven of the ships in this way, but with the rest the barbarians backed off, and picking up the Eretrian slaves from the island where they had left them, they sailed round Cape Sunium, wanting to beat the Athenians to Athens. *116* So the barbarians sailed round Sunium, but the Athenians went to the relief of the city as fast as their legs would carry them, and they beat the barbarians to the city. They arrived from the precinct of Heracles in Marathon and encamped in another Heracleum in Athens, the one in Cynosarges. The barbarians with their fleet lay off Phalerum (which in those days was the port of Athens) a while at anchor, and then sailed back to Asia. *117* In this battle at Marathon there died of the barbarians about 6,400 men, and of the Athenians 192. . . . *120* Of the Spartans there came to Athens 200 after the full moon, so eager to be on time that they were in Attica on the third day after leaving Sparta. Though they came too late for the battle they were nevertheless eager to see the dead Medes, so they went to Marathon and looked at them. Afterwards they congratulated the Athenians on their work and went off home.

[Prominent—some said traitors—in the battle of Marathon were members of the Athenian noble clan of Alcmaeonidae, whose most famous members were the reformer Clisthenes and—on his mother's side—Pericles. Herodotus tells the story of a dynastic marriage which consolidated the clan's strength; but the hero of the story is an unsuccessful suitor.]

How Hippoclides danced away his marriage

125 Even before this the Alcmaeonids had been famous in Athens, but from the time of Alcmaeon and Megacles they became especially famous. For Alcmaeon the son of Megacles had been helpful to the Lydians who came from Croesus at Sardis in the matter of the oracle at Delphi, and had gone out of his way to give them a hand; Croesus therefore, having heard from the Lydians who visited the oracle that this man had served him well, summoned him to Sardis, and on his arrival granted him as much gold as he could carry away on his own person all at one time. Alcmaeon with an eye on the size of the gift turned up in the following costume: he put on a shirt that was too big for him, and very full in front, and the widest shoes he could find, and went to the treasury to which they escorted him. Falling upon a pile of gold dust he first stuffed into the space between his shanks and his shoes as much gold as they would hold, then he filled his shirt front, sprinkled the dust in his hair, and taking some more in his mouth emerged from the treasury, dragging his feet behind him and looking like anything in the world but a man, for his mouth was stuffed full, and he stuck out all over. Laughter overcame Croesus at the sight of him, and he let him keep all he already had and besides gave him as much again. The clan thus became very rich, and thus this Alcmaeon became a breeder of chariot horses and won with them at Olympia. *126* And in the second generation after, Clisthenes the tyrant of Sicyon exalted it, so that it became much better known among the Greeks than it formerly had been. Clisthenes . . . had a daughter whose name was Agariste. He wanted to search for the best man in Greece, and give her to him as wife. So when the Olympic games were held, and he won in them with his four-horse chariot, he had a proclamation made that any Greek who thought himself worthy to become Clisthenes' son-in-law should report to Sicyon on or before the sixtieth day from that date; that Clisthenes was going to solemnize the marriage in a year's time, counting from the sixtieth day. So as many of the Greeks as were puffed up about their own merits or those of their ancestors came flocking as suitors, and for them Clisthenes had a running-track and a wrestling-ground made and reserved for their special use. *127* [There were among a number of suitors from all parts of the Greek world] two Athenians, Megacles the son of Alcmaeon who visited Croesus, and another, Hippoclides the son of Tisander, well above average among the Athenians in wealth and good looks . . . . *128* When all the suitors had come, on the appointed day Clisthenes first inquired their family and each man's clan, and after that kept them for a year and made trial of their courage, temper, upbringing, and disposition, by associating with them singly and as a group. And he both pressed those who were young enough to compete in sports, and most important of all, made trial of them at the banquet-table. As long as he kept them, he did all these things and at the same time entertained them magnificently. Somehow the wooers that pleased him most were the ones who came from Athens, and of these he preferred Hippoclides the son of Tisander, both because of manly virtue and because his ancestors were related to the [ruling house of the] Cypselids in Corinth. *129* When the day came which was appointed for the wedding banquet and Clisthenes' announcement of his choice from the whole group, he sacrified a hundred oxen and feasted the suitors themselves and all the people of Sicyon. When the banquet was over, the suitors had a contest in music and telling stories for all to hear. As the drinking continued, Hippoclides, who was holding the others quite entranced, told the flute player to play a tune to dance to. The flute player did his bidding, and he danced. And he danced somehow very much to his own satisfaction, but Clisthenes looked on the whole business with a fishy eye. After a while Hippoclides told someone to bring in a table, and when it was brought, first he danced some Spartan measures on it, then some others, Attic ones, and as a third act he rested his head on the table and waggled with his feet. Clisthenes during the first and second dances, though he loathed the thought that Hippoclides should still become his son-in-law, because of his dancing and his effrontery, nevertheless restrained himself, not wanting to lash out at him. But when he saw him waggling with his feet, he was no longer able to contain himself and said, "Son of Tisander, though you dance well, you have danced away your marriage." And Hippoclides, interrupting, said, "Hippoclides should worry."

[So Megacles the Alcmeonid got the girl, and their son was Clisthenes the political reformer. The rest of Book VI follows the adventures of Miltiades, his failure, unpopularity, trial, and death. In Book VII Darius dies (486 B.C.) but his son Xerxes vows vengeance against the Greeks and prepares a mighty expedition.]

From Book VII

How Xerxes bridged the Hellespont

34 . . . Those who were assigned the job built the double bridge starting from Abydus. The Phoenicians built one with ropes of white linen, the Egyptians with papyrus fibre. It is seven-eighths of a mile from Abydus to the opposite shore. When the channel had been bridged, a great storm came up and cut to pieces and destroyed all the work that had been done. *35* When Xerxes heard this news, he was vexed with the Hellespont and ordered it scourged with 300 lashes, and a pair of fetters let down into the sea. I have even heard it said that on this same occasion he sent branders out to brand the Hellespont. He ordered his whippers to utter these barbarous and wicked words: "Bitter water, our master lays this punishment upon you because you have done him an injustice, though you have suffered none at his hands. But King Xerxes will cross you, whether you will or no. It serves you right that no man sacrifices to you, for you are a treacherous and brackish river." This is the way he ordered the sea punished; as for those in charge of bridging the Hellespont, he ordered their heads cut off. *36* Those assigned to this job did their unpleasant duty, and other master builders were appointed, who proceeded as follows: they lashed together fifty-oared vessels and triremes, 360 for the Black Sea bridge, and 314 for the other, at right angles to the Black Sea, but with the current of the Hellespont, so as to slacken the tension of the hawsers. When they had lashed together the vessels, they made them fast with outsize anchors, on the Black Sea side, against the winds that blow from the Sea of Marmora; toward the west and the Aegean, against the winds from the southeast and south. And in three places they left a narrow gap for the passage of triremes and fifty-oared ships so that anyone who wanted to could sail into or out of the Black Sea in small vessels. When they had done this, they tightened the cables from the shore by winding them on wooden capstans, this time not using the two kinds of rope separately, but for each bridge using two strands of linen rope, and four of papyrus. Both kinds were of the same thickness and fine appearance, but the linen ones were proportionately heavier, weighing about fifty-five pounds to the foot. When the strait was bridged, logs were sawn to a length equal to the width of the bridge, and laid in a row above the taut hawsers, and when they had them in order they fastened them again on top. Next they brought brushwood and arranged it neatly; then they put earth on top of the brushwood and packed it down. Finally they built a fence on each side so that the animals would not be frightened at looking out over the sea.

[It took the army seven days and seven nights to cross, under the lash of their officers. When they had crossed Xerxes counted his men.]

How Xerxes numbered his host

60 How many men each nation supplied to the host I cannot say for certain, for none of the sources reports it, but the total number of infantry appears to have been 1,700,000. This is the way they were counted: 10,000 men were marched as a unit to one spot, and made to stand together as closely as possible, after which a circle was drawn around them and they were dismissed. Then they built a fence on the circle, as high as a man's navel, after which they marched successive units into the enclosed space until in this way they had counted them all, and then they mustered them by nations.

[The news of the approaching host filled the Greeks with panic, but the Athenians remained cool, and proved the saviors of Greece.]

How Athens became the savior of Greece

139 At this point necessity prompts me to state an opinion unpopular to many, but, since to me at any rate it seems a true one, I shall not withhold it. If the Athenians in terror at the oncoming danger had left their land, or even not left it but stayed and given themselves up to Xerxes, no one would have tried to stand against the king by sea, and then this is what would have happened on land: though the Peloponnesians had built ever so many walls across the Isthmus, yet the Spartans would have been betrayed by their allies, not of their own free will, but under compulsion, as city by city fell to the barbarian navy. Then the Spartans would have stood alone, performed heroic deeds, and died nobly; either that, or, having previously seen other Greeks also go over to the Persians, they would have reached an agreement with Xerxes. For I cannot make out what the use of the walls built across the Isthmus would have been if the king controlled the sea. But as it is, if anyone should say that the Athenians proved themselves the saviors of Greece, he would not go far wrong. For whichever side they inclined to, the balance was bound to tip in their favor; and, choosing that Greece should remain free, it was they who roused up all the rest of Greece, as many as had not gone over to the Persians, and, with the gods' help, repulsed the king.

[The Greeks resolved to make a stand at the pass of Thermopylae (August, 480 B.C.) where Leonidas and his three hundred Spartans earned immortality.]

How Leonidas and his Spartans fell gloriously at Thermopylae

207 The Greeks at Thermopylae, when the Persians had come near the pass, were in terror and took counsel about retreat. The rest of the Peloponnesians favored going to the Peloponnese and mounting guard over the Isthmus, but Leonidas voted to stay where they were (since the Phocians and Locrians were highly incensed at the other proposal), and to send dispatch riders to the various cities asking for reinforcements, on the ground that they were too few to stand off the Persian host. *208* While they were holding this conference, Xerxes sent a spy on horseback to see how many they were and what they were doing. He had heard that only a small force held the place, and that their leaders were Spartans under Leonidas, of the Heraclid clan [the royal house of Sparta]. When the horseman had ridden up to the camp, he looked around but did not see all the detachment. For those assigned to duty inside the wall which they had rebuilt and were guarding, he could not see, but he took note of those who were outside and had grounded arms in front of the wall. At the time the Spartans happened to have this duty. And he saw some of the men at athletic practice, and others combing their long hair. He was surprised at this sight, but he took note of their number. When he had taken all his notes accurately, he rode back unmolested, for no one chased him or paid him the slightest attention. When he got back he told Xerxes all he had seen. *209* When Xerxes heard the report, he was not able to put two and two together and guess that the Spartans were getting ready for an all-out last-ditch struggle. He simply thought they were acting silly, but he sent for Demaratus the son of Ariston [a deposed Spartan king], who was on his staff. When he arrived, Xerxes asked him detailed questions about the spy's report, since he wanted to know what the Spartans were doing. Demaratus said, "You heard my story about these men long ago, when we were first setting out to attack Greece, and you made me a laughing stock, though I told you exactly the way I foresaw things would happen. For to tell you the truth always, Sire, is my aim. Listen now also. These men have come here to fight you for the pass and they are preparing for battle. For this is their standard practice: whenever they are about to risk their lives, they do their hair. Understand this: if you overthrow these men and those who are left in Sparta, there is no other race of men who will have the courage to raise a hand against you, Sire; for the kingdom you are now attacking is the finest in Greece, and its men the bravest." To Xerxes, of course, what he said seemed quite unbelievable, and he asked a second time how the Spartans, being so few, would fight against his host. Demaratus said, "Sire, treat me like a liar, if this business does not turn out in exactly the way I say." *210* His speech did not convince Xerxes. He actually let four days slip by, in the constant hope that they would run away. On the fifth day, since they were not retreating but as it seemed to him standing their ground out of sheer effrontery and lack of common sense, in his anger he sent against them his Medes and his Cissians, with orders to take them alive and bring them before him. The Medes charged and fell upon the Greeks, and many fell, but others filled the gaps in the ranks, and though the Medes smote them with all their force, they could not dislodge them, thus making it clear to everyone and not least to the king himself that he had plenty of men but few heroes. The battle lasted all day. *211* Since the Medes were taking a beating, they withdrew, and the Persians relieved them in the assault, whom the king called his "Immortals," with Hydarnes at their head, since the king thought that they, at any rate, would finish off the business in short order. These too, when they tangled with the Greeks, fared no better than the Medes had done, but exactly the same, since they were fighting in a narrow pass, using shorter spears than the Greeks, and unable to bring to bear the weight of their numbers. The Spartans put up a fight that was a fight, in many ways proving themselves expert warriors among novices, and especially in the way in which they would turn their backs as though to run away, whereat the barbarians would make after them with a hue and cry, and the Spartans would turn on them and catch them flat-footed, killing countless numbers of Persians; a few of the Spartiates themselves also fell there. Since they were not able to gain the pass, though they tried by divisions and every other way, the Persians fell back. *212* In these assaults of the battle it is said that the king, as he watched, three times started up from his throne, fearing for his army. So they struggled on that day, and on the next the barbarians fared no better. Since the Greeks were so few, the barbarians hoped to cripple them completely so that they would not be able to come to grips, and so they made their assault. But the Greeks were drawn up in divisions city by city, and each division fought in rotation, except the Phocians, who had been posted on the mountain to guard the path. Since the Persians found nothing different from what they had seen the day before, they withdrew. *213* While the king was at his wit's end what to do in the present difficulty, Epialtes the son of Eurydemus, a Malian, asked for an audience, hoping to get a rich reward from the king; he told him about the path that leads over the mountain to Thermopylae and thereby destroyed the Greeks who had taken their stand there. . . . *215* Xerxes was delighted with what Epialtes promised to do, and in his delight dispatched Hydarnes and his "Immortals," who left the camp about lamplighting time. . . . *216* This is the route of the path: it starts from the Asopus river where it flows through a gorge, and the name of the mountain and the name of the path are the same: Anopaea; and the path Anopaea stretches along the back of the ridge, and ends at the town of Alpenus, the first Locrian town you hit as you come from Malis, by the stone called Blackbottom and the seats of the Cercopes [dwarfs who stole Heracles' weapons], which is its narrowest part. *217* Along this path in this direction the Persians crossed the Asopus and marched all night, keeping Mt. Oeta on their right and the mountains of Trachis on their left. Day dawned, and they were on the summit of the mountain. This part of the range was guarded, as I have already explained, by a thousand heavy-armed Phocians, guarding their country and keeping an eye on the path. The pass below was guarded by those I have mentioned, but the path over the mountains the Phocians guarded as volunteers, according to their promise to Leonidas. *218* This is the way the Phocians discovered the Persians had climbed up: the Persians were able to climb up unnoticed, because the whole mountain is covered with oak trees. But it was windless, and there was naturally a great rustling of leaves kicked up by the Persians' feet, so the Phocians started up and buckled on their armor, and at the same moment the barbarians were upon them. They were surprised to find men arming, for they had expected to find no opposition and here they fell in with an army. At this point Hydarnes was afraid the Phocians were Spartans; he asked Epialtes from what country the army came, and when he had a clear answer drew up the Persians for battle. The Phocians were a target of a thick rain of arrows, and ran away to the top of the mountain, thinking it was they the Persians had been out to get in the first place, and ready to die. This is what they thought: however, the Persians with Epialtes and Hydarnes paid no attention to them, but went down the other side of the mountain on the double.

219 To the Greeks at Thermopylae the first to tell of the death that awaited them at dawn was the seer Megistias as he inspected the sacrifices, and then on top of that there were deserters who brought them word that the Persians were taking them from behind. These men brought the news while it was still night, and thirdly the daywatchers ran down from the hills and told them just as day was dawning. The Greeks then held a council of war, and opinion was divided: some did not want to desert their posts, others thought the opposite. Afterward they split up, and some withdrew and scattered, each returning to his own city, but Leonidas' band made ready to stand their ground. *220* It is said that Leonidas himself sent the others away, holding their safety close to his heart, but he and the Spartiates with him did not think it seemly to desert the post which they had come to guard in the first place. . . . *222* So the allies who were dismissed stood not upon the order of their going, but went at once, convinced by Leonidas. Only the Thespians and the Thebans stayed with the Spartans. And of these the Thebans stayed much against their will, for Leonidas kept them as hostages, but the Thespians quite willingly, saying they would not go away and desert Leonidas and his men, but would stand by and die with them. Their general was Demophilos the son of Diadromes.

223 Xerxes poured libations at sunrise, and then waited till the time when the market place is generally full, and then made his attack. He did this on instructions from Epialtes, since coming down the mountain is quicker and shorter by far than the circuit and the climb up. So Xerxes' barbarians advanced, and so did Leonidas' Greeks, who, since they were marching out to die, went much farther forward than they ever had before, to the wider part of the pass. For they had formerly defended the stone wall, and on former days had fought withdrawing gradually into the narrower part of the pass. Now they clashed with the barbarians outside the narrows, and the barbarians fell in droves. For behind them their division leaders with whips lashed on each man, urging him ever forward. Many of them fell into the sea and were drowned, far more were trampled to death by their own side; no one paid any attention to the dying. Since the Spartans knew the death that awaited them from those who were coming round the mountain, they exerted every last ounce of strength against the barbarians, with reckless disregard of life and blind fury. *224* By this time most of their spears were broken, so they dispatched the Persians with their swords. And Leonidas fell in this fray, having proved himself a hero, and other famous Spartiates with him, whose names I have learned, all three hundred of them, for they were men of merit. Of course many famous Persians fell, too, including two sons of Darius. . . . *225* Two of Xerxes' brothers fell there fighting, and over the body of Leonidas there arose between the Persians and the Spartans a great jousting, until the Greeks by heroism carried it off, after driving the enemy back four times. This lasted till the detachment with Epialtes appeared on the scene. When the Greeks knew they were coming, they changed their way of fighting. They drew back into the narrow part of the pass, and crossing the wall, they went and took up a position on a knoll, all in a unit together except the Thebans. This hill is in the entrance to the pass, where now the stone lion stands to commemorate Leonidas. On this spot they defended themselves with daggers—those that still had them—with their bare hands, and with their teeth, until the barbarians snowed them under with weapons, some of them having pulled down the wall and attacked them head on, others having gone round and fenced them in on every side.

226 This was the kind of men that the Spartans and the Thespians proved themselves to be, yet the man said to have proved himself most valiant was the Spartiate Dieneces, who, they say, made this remark before they joined battle with the Medes: when he heard from one of the men of Trachis that whenever the barbarians let fly their arrows, the sun was hidden by the number of the shafts, so great was their number, he was not in the least dismayed by this, but paid no attention to the size of the Medes' host, saying that what the stranger from Trachis told them was all to the good; if the Medes hid the sun, the Spartans could fight in the shade instead. This and other similar sayings they say that Dieneces the Spartan left behind as his memorial. . . .

228 They were buried where they fell, and in their memory, and in memory of those who died there before those dismissed by Leonidas went home, the following epitaph was engraved:

HERE ONCE ON A DAY AGAINST THREE MILLION MEN
FOUR THOUSAND MEN OF PELOP'S ISLE DID BATTLE.

This was the epitaph for all of them, but there was a separate one for the Spartiates:

STRANGER, TIDINGS TO THE SPARTANS BRING
THAT HERE WE LIE, THEIR WORDS REMEMBERING.

This was for the Spartans, and this for the seer:

THIS IS THE TOMB OF FAMED MEGISTIAS
WHOM ONCE THE MEDE SLEW, BY SPERCHEIUS RIVER.
A SEER, HE SAW FULL WELL HIS FATE LOOM UP,
BUT HAD NOT HEART TO LEAVE THE SPARTAN LEADERS.

It was the Amphictyons who did them honor with epitaphs and gravestones, except for the epitaph of the seer Megistias, which Simonides the son of Leoprepes [the famous poet] had engraved for their friendship's sake.

[Xerxes had Leonidas' body beheaded and the trunk crucified. He then pushed on unopposed into mainland Greece, where he seized and burned the buildings on the Acropolis of Athens; the Athenians under Themistocles had taken to the sea, in two hundred vessels, and made ready to engage the Persian fleet in the narrows between the island of Salamis and the mainland of Attica (Sept., 480 B.C.).]

From Book VIII

How the Athenians won the Battle of Salamis

83 The Greeks prepared for a naval battle. Dawn came, and they held a briefing of the marines, at which Themistocles made by far the best speech. All his remarks contrasted what was better with what was worse in all that involves man's nature and conditions; he urged them to choose the better part, wound up his speech, and gave the order to embark, which they did. At that point the trireme which had gone off to fetch the statues of the sons of Ajax came back from Aegina, and then the Greeks put to sea with their full fleet. *84* As they were putting to sea the barbarians immediately attacked them. The rest of the Greeks backed water and were beaching their ships, but Ameinias, an Athenian of Pallene, broke formation and charged an enemy ship. The ship became involved and his men could not get away, so the rest came to Ameinias' rescue and joined battle. The Athenians say that this was how the battle started, but the men of Aegina say that the ship that started the battle was the one which had gone to Aegina after the statues. This story is also told, that the apparition of a woman appeared to them and egged them on so that the whole Greek force could hear, first reproaching them thus: "Strange men, how long are you going to back water?" *85* Opposite the Athenians were drawn up the Phoenicians, who held the wing toward Eleusis and the west; and opposite the Spartans were the Ionians, who held the wing toward the east and the Piraeus. Of these a few hung back deliberately, as Themistocles had advised, but the majority did not. . . . *86* Most of the Persian ships were disabled at Salamis, some destroyed by the Athenians, others by the men of Aegina. For the Greeks fought in orderly fashion and kept station while the barbarians had no battle plan and did nothing intelligently, so that the business was bound to turn out just as it did. Yet they were and proved themselves to be on this day far better than they had been in the battle by Euboea, for every man had the will to distinguish himself, and all were afraid of Xerxes, each man thinking that the king's eye was on him alone. *87* In most cases I cannot tell accurately how each crew, barbarian or Greek, fought, but in the case of Artemisia [queen of Halicarnassus] this is what happened, and it made her reputation even higher in the eyes of the king. When the king's cause was falling into complete confusion, at this critical moment Artemisia's ship was being chased by an Attic vessel. And she was not able to get clean away, for in front of her were other ships of her own side, and her own ship was, as it happened, farthest forward toward the enemy, so she decided to do something that was to her advantage when she had done it: as she was being pursued by the Attic ship she bore down on and rammed a friendly vessel, one of the Calyndians, with their king himself, Damasithymus, aboard. Whether she had quarrelled somehow with him while the fleet was still in the Hellespont, I am of course not in a position to say, nor whether she did it on purpose, or whether the Calyndian ship just happened to fall foul of hers. When she had rammed and sunk it, she was lucky and gained for herself a double advantage; for when the Attic skipper saw her ram a barbarian ship, he thought that Artemisia's vessel was either Greek or had deserted from the barbarians, and was fighting for the Greeks, so he slacked off and changed course after other quarry. *88* So in the first place she was lucky enough to escape destruction, and besides it turned out that though she had done wrong, the result was that she reached the peak of her reputation with Xerxes. For it is said that as the king watched the battle he noticed her ship ramming the other, and of course one of his aides said, "Master, do you see how well Artemisia is fighting? She has sunk an enemy ship!" The king asked if it was really Artemisia who had done the job, and they said that it was, for they recognized clearly the insignia of her flagship, while they were convinced that the sunken ship had been an enemy vessel. It was not only, as I have said, that things in general conspired to her good fortune; she was especially lucky in that not one of the crew of the Calyndian ship survived to become her accuser. Xerxes is said to have replied to what they said to him, "My men have turned into women, and my women into men!" *89* In this fray there fell the admiral, Ariabignes the son of Darius, and Xerxes' brother, and also many other famous Persians, Medes, and other allies, but very few Greeks. For since the Greeks knew how to swim, those whose ships were lost and who did not die in the hand-to-hand fighting swam across to the Island of Salamis. But many of the barbarians died in the water because they did not know how to swim. The height of the carnage took place at the moment when the first ships turned to make their getaway. For the ships that were stationed at the rear tried to push forward to the front so as to display their prowess also to the king, and so fell foul of their own retreating vessels.

90 This also happened in the confusion: Some of the Phoenicians, whose ships had been destroyed, came to the king and accused the Ionians of treason, saying that it was their fault that the ships had been lost. But it turned out that the Ionian admirals did not die, while their Phoenician accusers were thus rewarded: while they were still speaking, a ship of Samothrace rammed an Attic ship and sank it, and then a ship of Aegina bore down and sank the Samothracian vessel. But the men of Samothrace, who were good with the javelin, fired at the marines aboard the attacking vessel, cleared its decks, boarded it and took it as a prize. This incident rescued the Ionians: for when Xerxes saw them do their heroic deed he turned to the Phoenicians—being extremely out of sorts and ready to find fault with anyone—and ordered their heads cut off, to keep them from turning coward and then blaming better men. So that he might see any one of his men doing deeds of valor in the sea fight, Xerxes sat under the lee of the hill called Aegaleus, opposite Salamis, and asked the name of the doer, and then the scribe wrote it down, with the name of his father, his captain, and his city. Besides this Ariamnes, a Persian friend of the Ionians, who was present at the time, contributed somewhat to the fate of the Phoenicians.

91 So they turned their attention to the Phoenicians. But when the barbarians turned to run away and were sailing out toward Phalerum, the men of Aegina lay in wait for them in the channel and did deeds worthy of record. In the confusion the Athenians disposed of the ships that offered resistance or tried to run away, while the men of Aegina took care of those that tried to sail out; and whenever any escaped the Athenians, they ran full tilt into the ships of Aegina. . . . *93* In this sea battle the men of Aegina set up the finest record, and the Athenians next; of individuals, from Aegina Polycritus and from Athens Eumenes of Anagyra and Ameinias of Pallene, the man who had chased Artemisia. . . . *95* Aristides the son of Lysimachus, an Athenian, whom I mentioned a little while ago as a man of superlative justice, did this deed in the confusion round Salamis. He picked up many of the Athenian heavy-armed troops who had been stationed along the beach at Salamis, took them and set them ashore on the island of Psyttalia, and of the Persians on that islet the Athenians butchered every one.

The battle of Salamis is also described in the *Persians* of Aeschylus, produced in 472. Two passages from this play (lines 350–432, 447–471) follow in a verse translation made from the text of A. Sidgwick (Oxford, 1902).

ATOSSA. Tell what the start was of the clash of ships.
Which began the battle? Was it the Greeks,
Or my son, proud of his almighty fleet?
MESSENGER. All our ills started, Lady, when a spirit
Or foul fiend from somewhere came, an apparition.
For a man, a Greek, from the Athenian fleet,
Came and said to your son Xerxes this:
That when the clouds of blackest night should come
The Greeks would not remain, but on the thwarts
Of their ships, leaping, each on his own course
In hidden flight would try to save their lives.
When Xerxes heard, he failed to grasp the guile
Of this Greek fellow, or God's jealousy;
Proclaimed the word to all his admirals
That when the rays of the blazing sun should leave
The earth, and night hold sway in heaven's precinct,
They range their ranks of ships in triple row
To guard the channels and salt-flowing straits,
While others circled Ajax' island round,
And if the Greeks escaped their destined doom,
And found some secret pathway for their ships,
The captains one and all should lose their heads.
He made this speech in confidence of heart,
Not knowing what was yet to come from God.
Not without order, but with obedient heart
They took each man his dinner, and the crews
Looped their oars round the neatly-fitted thole-pin.
And when the light of the sun had died in the west
And night came on, each man, lord of his oar,
And every expert marksman went aboard.
Rank to rank of warships passed the word;
They sailed, and each kept well his station,
And all night long they kept up their patrol,
The captains and the crews of all the ships.
The night crept on, and no ship of the Greeks
Made any trial anywhere of flight;
But when the gleaming horses of the day
Held all the land, most fair to look upon,
First there rang out a shout from all the Greeks,
A good-omened battle hymn. At the same moment
There sounded forth from all the island rocks
An echo; fear in barbarian hearts
Dashed all their hopes, for not as if for flight
Did the Greeks then raise their holy battle-hymn,
But setting out for battle with high hearts:
The trumpet's blast set all their side afire.
At once, with even stroke of churning oar,
They beat the salt water to the coxswain's call
And swiftly all were crystal clear to see.
The right wing first in all good order led,
And next the whole fleet fared forth: all could hear
The mighty shout, "O sons of Hellas, go,
Set free your fatherland, set free your sons,
Your women, and the shrines of your fathers' gods,
Your forebears' tombs; now is your all in hazard."
And then from us the surge of Persian speech
Made answer; there was no more time for waiting.
At once the brazen beak of ship on ship
Dashed; a Greek ship began the shock of battle,

Splint'ring the stern-post of a Phoenician galley.
Then one kept steering straight upon another.
At first the flood of Persian men stood firm,
But when the press of ships in the narrow strait
Was packed, then friend could bring no aid to friend,
But they by their own brazen-studded beaks
Were rammed, and all the oar-blades shorn clean off.
The Grecian ships, with clever strategy
Ranged round in a ring; our hulls turned upside down,
No more could the sea be seen, so choked it was
With wrecks of ships and dead men's floating corpses.
The capes, the reefs were piled with human bodies,
And every ship rowed off, confused, in flight,
Yes, every ship of all the invading host.
As though at tuna, or some haul of fish,
With bits of oar, and splinterings of wreckage
They hacked and hewed; at the same time a cry,
An anguished shrieking filled the salt sea-wave,
Until the eye of black night stayed its sound.
The tale of woes, not if I had ten days
All ranged in order, could time serve to tell.
For know this well, that never on one day
Were ever done to death so many men. [432

. . . .

There is an island facing Salamis, [447
Small, rough anchorage for ships, where Pan,
Who loves the dance, treads on the beach a measure.
There Xerxes sent men, that when a Grecian ship
Was lost, and the crew might swim to the island,
Our men might slay them there, an easy prey,
And save our sailors from the salty straits.
But he misjudged the issue. For when God
Gave to the Greeks the victory in the battle,
On that same day they donned their brazen armor,
And leaped from their ships, encircling all the island,
So that the Persian host was at a loss
Which way to turn. For many were beat down
With stones from Greek hands, and from Grecian bowstrings
The arrows of destruction fell upon them;
Making at last a charge all in one surge,
They hacked and butchered the ill-fated limbs,
Until they took the life of every one.
Xerxes groaned deep to see that depth of woe;
He had a throne in full view of the host,
On a high hill close to the salt sea wave;
He tore his garments, wailing loud and shrill,
And sent his orders to his infantry
To fall into disorderly retreat.
Such double tragedy is yours to mourn.

[After Salamis Xerxes retired to Asia with the remnant of his fleet, but the war did not end formally until over thirty years later, when by the Peace of Callias the independence of Asiatic Greeks was recognized and the Aegean Sea was closed to Persian warships. But meanwhile the Athenians had assumed command of the liberated Greeks in the Aegean islands and Asia Minor. The Delian League thus formed became, when its treasury was transferred to Athens in 454 B.C., the cornerstone of the Athenian Empire, which under Pericles was to reach new heights of commercial prosperity and intellectual splendor.]

THE *Agamemnon* OF AESCHYLUS

Translated by Louis MacNeice

INTRODUCTION

AESCHYLUS (b. 525 B.C.), the first great writer of tragedy in our western world, was criticized in his own time for the limited action in his plays and the violence and obscurity of the language. The criticism, as far as it went, was just. It is not in neatly contrived plots or fluid poetic expression that his greatness lies, but rather in the magnitude of the problems which he presented and the verbal imagery with which he made their significance penetrate beyond the mind, into the most profound emotions of his audience. As in much of the best contemporary poetry, the complete emotional reaction is realized only after patient effort, perhaps after surrender to the urgency of the tempestuous rhythms, the metaphorical allusions, the philosophical ideas. But the effort is well rewarded.

Only a large canvas satisfied Aeschylus, and he required a trilogy of plays for his sturdy designs. The universal conflict between selfish power and kindness is the theme of the Prometheus trilogy; in the *House of Atreus,* of which the *Agamemnon* is the opening play, it is the evolution of justice. On such a canvas, once the chief characters were strongly sketched, complicated and contrasted colors were applied, chiefly by means of the lengthy choral odes. If those odes are not understood—and felt—a large part of the significance of the plays will be lost.

In the *House of Atreus* (produced in 458 B.C.), the first play tells of the homecoming of Agememnon, victorious leader of the expeditionary force against Troy, and of his murder by his wife, Clytemnestra. According to early notions of justice, such a murder must be avenged by the son; so in the next play, the *Choephoroe* (Libation-Bearers), Orestes, aided by his sister Electra, kills Clytemnestra. But a better way to deal with murder had to be found, and was found, in the institution of a legal trial for the crime; and the third play, the *Eumenides* (Furies) portrays the first such trial, held in Athens with the goddess Athena herself as judge, a jury of Athenian citizens, the Furies prosecuting the murderer, and Apollo pleading Orestes' defense. For the verdict the reader is referred to the play.

Why was Agamemnon killed by his wife? One reason, eagerly advanced by her, is that he comes of an accursed family and must atone for his father's sin. But she has reasons enough of her own for wanting him out of the way: before setting sail for Troy he had sacrificed their daughter, Iphigenia, in order to get favorable winds for his fleet; * during the ten years of the siege he had enjoyed the favors of various girls captured in raids on the near-by villages ("darling of each courtesan at Troy"); and with him on his return he was bringing a captive prize, the princess Cassandra, as his "oracle-delivering concubine." During his absence Clytemnestra had consoled herself by taking as her lover-consort Agamemnon's cousin and most bitter enemy, Aegisthus, not, obviously, because of any passionate love for him, but because of her hatred for her husband.

In view of these circumstances Clytemnestra has no alternative—she must kill Agamemnon at the earliest possible moment after his return, before he learns of her attitude toward him and her infidelity. She must therefore have a signal to warn her when his ship rounds the last promontory (hence the watchman and the fictitious account of the signal beacons from Troy); she must make the herald believe she is lovingly impatient for Agamemnon to come, and not allow him to linger long enough to be warned by the people before he returns to the harbor; when Agamemnon arrives she must pretend that she welcomes him as a dutiful wife should; she must persuade him to walk from his chariot to the palace on a purple carpet, thus identifying him with Oriental *hybris* in the eyes of the onlookers and conditioning them to accept her later with more willingness than they otherwise would as their ruler. It is a situation requiring careful planning, the most exacting self-control, and precise timing, on the part of a woman who can rely only on a craven consort and a few among the helpless old men in the Chorus who are sympathetic to her. But Clytemnestra asks—and needs—no odds. Intellectually abler than her husband, and more decisive and daring, she carries her plan to completion.

If the plot is simple, the psychological overtones and

---

* Cf. Lucretius, *On Nature,* I, 84–101.

undertones are extremely complex: the ominous reflections of the Chorus, even after the old men realize that the war is over, their feeling that the fighting was unnecessary, their attempt to explain the reason for human suffering, their description of sin and its punishment. The herald, too, in the hour of triumph cannot forget the earlier anguish of all the soldiers and the sorry place won by those who rest under the hostile earth of Troy. Cassandra weaves a tangled skein of the horrors of the past and the future before she goes in to meet her own death. The earlier coldly dissimulating Clytemnestra, once her aim is accomplished, becomes hotly sincere as she justifies the deed to the horrified Chorus, then scornful of them, then tolerantly amused as she watches Aegisthus and the old men in a taunting scene that approaches comedy. These are only a few of the many emotional complexities that are woven into this play. And the situations are not merely stated; they are strengthened by allusions, innuendoes, metaphors, until the effect is almost one of music, encompassing the full richness of emotional reactions to the action. In achieving such an effect no later tragedian has surpassed or even equalled the pioneer Aeschylus.

—WALTER R. AGARD

THE TEXT is that of A. Sidgwick (Oxford, 1902).

THE CHARACTERS

WATCHMAN
CHORUS OF OLD MEN OF THE CITY
CLYTEMNESTRA
HERALD
AGAMEMNON
CASSANDRA
AEGISTHUS

The scene is the palace of AGAMEMNON *at Mycenae.*

A space in front of the palace of AGAMEMNON *in Argos. Night. A* WATCHMAN *on the roof of the palace.*

WATCHMAN. The gods it is I ask to release me from this watch
A year's length now, spending my nights like a dog,
Watching on my elbow on the roof of the sons of Atreus
So that I have come to know the assembly of the nightly stars
Those which bring storm and those which bring summer to men,
The shining Masters riveted in the sky—
I know the decline and rising of those stars.
And now I am waiting for the sign of the beacon,
The flame of fire that will carry the report from Troy,
News of her taking. Which task has been assigned to me
By a woman of sanguine heart but a man's mind.
Yet when I take my restless rest in the soaking dew,
My night not visited with dreams—
For fear stands by me in the place of sleep
That I cannot firmly close my eyes in sleep—
Whenever I think to sing or hum to myself
As an antidote to sleep, then every time I groan
And fall to weeping for the fortunes of this house
Where not as before are things well ordered now.
But now may a good chance fall, escape from pain,
The good news visible in the midnight fire.

Pause. A light appears, gradually increasing, the light of the beacon.

Ha! I salute you, torch of the night whose light
Is like the day, an earnest of many dances
In the city of Argos, celebration of Peace.
I call to Agamemnon's wife; quickly to rise
Out of her bed and in the house to raise
Clamor of joy in answer to this torch
For the city of Troy is taken—
Such is the evident message of the beckoning flame.
And I myself will dance my solo first
For I shall count my master's fortune mine
Now that this beacon has thrown me a lucky throw.
And may it be when he comes, the master of this house,
That I grasp his hand in my hand.
As to the rest, I am silent. A great ox, as they say,
Stands on my tongue. The house itself, if it took voice,
Could tell the case most clearly. But I will only speak
To those who know. For the others I remember nothing.

Enter Chorus of Old Men. *During the following chorus the day begins to dawn.*

Chorus

The tenth year it is since Priam's high
Adversary, Menelaus the king
And Agamemnon, the double-throned and sceptered
Yoke of the sons of Atreus
Ruling in fee from God,
From this land gathered an Argive army
On a mission of war a thousand ships,
Their hearts howling in boundless bloodlust
In eagles' fashion who in lonely
Grief for nestlings above their homes hang
Turning in cycles
Beating the air with the oars of their wings,
Now to no purpose
Their love and task of attention.

But above there is One,
Maybe Pan, maybe Zeus or Apollo,
Who hears the harsh cries of the birds
Guests in his kingdom,
Wherefore, though late, in requital
He sends the Avenger.
Thus Zeus our master
Guardian of guest and of host
Sent against Paris the sons of Atreus
For a woman of many men.
Many the dog-tired wrestlings
Limbs and knees in the dust pressed—
For both the Greeks and Trojans
An overture of breaking spears.

Things are where they are, will finish
In the manner fated and neither
Fire beneath nor oil above can soothe
The stubborn anger of the unburnt offering.
As for us, our bodies are bankrupt,
The expedition left us behind
And we wait supporting on sticks
Our strength—the strength of a child;
For the marrow that leaps in a boy's body
Is no better than that of the old,
For the War God is not in his body;
While the man who is very old
And his leaf withering away
Goes on the three-foot way
No better than a boy, and wanders
A dream in the middle of the day.

But you, daughter of Tyndareus,
Queen Clytemnestra,
What is the news, what is the truth, what have you learnt,
On the strength of whose word have you thus
Sent orders for sacrifice round?
All the gods, the gods of the town,
Of the worlds of Below and Above,
By the door, in the square,
Have their altars ablaze with your gifts,
From here, from there, all sides, all corners,
Sky-high leap the flame-jets fed
By gentle and undeceiving
Persuasion of sacred unguent,
Oil from the royal stores.
Of these things tell
That which you can, that which you may,
Be healer of this our trouble
Which at times torments with evil,
Though at times by propitiations
A shining hope repels
The insatiable thought upon grief
Which is eating away our hearts.
Of the omen which powerfully speeded
That voyage of strong men, by God's grace even I
Can tell, my age can still
Be galvanized to breathe the strength of song,
To tell how the kings of all the youth of Greece
Two-throned but one in mind
Were launched with pike and punitive hand
Against the Trojan shore by angry birds.
Kings of the birds to our kings came,
One with a white rump, the other black,
Appearing near the palace on the spear-arm side
Where all could see them,
Tearing a pregnant hare with the unborn young
Foiled of their courses.
Cry, cry upon Death; but may the good prevail.

But the diligent prophet of the army seeing the sons
Of Atreus twin in temper knew
That the hare-killing birds were the two
Generals, explained it thus—
"In time this expedition sacks the town
Of Troy before whose towers
By Fate's force the public
Wealth will be wasted.
Only let not some spite from the gods benight the bulky battalions,

The bridle of Troy, nor strike them untimely;
For the goddess feels pity, is angry
With the winged dogs of her father
Who killed the cowering hare with her unborn young;
Artemis hates the eagles' feast."
Cry, cry upon Death; but may the good prevail.

"But though you are so kind, goddess,
To the little cubs of lions
And to all the sucking young of roving beasts
In whom your heart delights,
Fulfill us the signs of these things,
The signs which are good but open to blame,
And I call on Apollo the Healer
That his sister raise not against the Greeks
Unremitting gales to baulk their ships,
Hurrying on another kind of sacrifice, with no feasting,
Barbarous building of hates and disloyalties
Grown on the family. For anger grimly returns
Cunningly haunting the house, avenging the death of a child, never forgetting its due."
So cried the prophet—evil and good together,
Fate that the birds foretold to the king's house.
In tune with this
Cry, cry upon Death; but may the good prevail.

Zeus, whoever He is, if this
Be a name acceptable,
By this name I will call him.
There is no one comparable
When I reckon all of the case
Excepting Zeus, if ever I am to jettison
The barren care which clogs my heart.

Not He who formerly was great *
With brawling pride and mad for broils
Will even be said to have been.
And He who was next has met †
His match and is seen no more,
But Zeus is the name to cry in your triumph-song
And win the prize for wisdom.

Who setting us on the road
Made this a valid law—
"That men must learn by suffering."
Drop by drop in sleep upon the heart
Falls the laborious memory of pain,
Against one's will comes wisdom;
The grace of the gods is forced on us
Throned inviolably.

So that time the elder
Chief of the Greek ships
Would not blame any prophet
Nor face the flail of fortune;
For unable to sail, the people
Of Greece were heavy with famine,
Waiting in Aulis where the tides
Flow back, opposite Chalcis.

But the winds that blew from the Strymon,
Bringing delay, hunger, evil harborage,
Crazing men, rotting ships and cables,
By drawing out the time
Were shredding into nothing the flower of Argos,
When the prophet screamed a new
Cure for that bitter tempest
And heavier still for the chiefs,
Pleading the anger of Artemis so that the sons of Atreus
Beat the ground with their scepters and shed tears.
Then the elder king found voice and answered:
"Heavy is my fate, not obeying,
And heavy it is if I kill my child, the delight of my house,
And with a virgin's blood upon the altar
Make foul her father's hands.
Either alternative is evil.
How can I betray the fleet
And fail the allied army?
It is right they should passionately cry for the winds to be lulled
By the blood of a girl. So be it. May it be well."

But when he had put on the halter of Necessity
Breathing in his heart a veering wind of evil
Unsanctioned, unholy, from that moment forward
He changed his counsel, would stop at nothing.
For the heart of man is hardened by infatuation,
A faulty adviser, the first link of sorrow.
Whatever the cause, he brought himself to slay
His daughter, an offering to promote the voyage
To a war for a runaway wife.

Her prayers and her cries of father,
Her life of a maiden,
Counted for nothing with those militarists;

* Uranus. † Cronus.

But her father, having duly prayed, told the attendants
To lift her, like a goat, above the altar
With her robes falling about her,
To lift her boldly, her spirit fainting,
And hold back with a gag upon her lovely mouth
By the dumb force of a bridle
The cry which would curse the house.
Then dropping on the ground her saffron dress,
Glancing at each of her appointed
Sacrificers a shaft of pity,
Plain as in a picture she wished
To speak to them by name, for often
At her father's table where men feasted
She had sung in celebration for her father
With a pure voice, affectionately, virginally,
The hymn for happiness at the third libation.
The sequel to this I saw not and tell not
But the crafts of Calchas gained their object.
To learn by suffering is the equation of Justice; the Future
Is known when it comes, let it go till then.
To know in advance is to sorrow in advance.
The facts will appear with the shining of the dawn.

Enter CLYTEMNESTRA.

But may good, at the least, follow after
As the queen here wishes, who stands
Nearest the throne, the only
Defense of the land of Argos.

LEADER OF THE CHORUS. I have come, Clytemnestra, reverencing your authority.
For it is right to honor our master's wife
When the man's own throne is empty.
But you, if you have heard good news for certain, or if
You sacrifice on the strength of flattering hopes,
I would gladly hear. Though I cannot cavil at silence.

CLYTEMNESTRA. Bearing good news, as the proverb says, may Dawn
Spring from her mother Night.
You will hear something now that was beyond your hopes.
The men of Argos have taken Priam's city.

LEADER. What! I cannot believe it. It escapes me.

CLYTEMNESTRA. Troy in the hands of the Greeks. Do I speak plain?

LEADER. Joy creeps over me, calling out my tears.

CLYTEMNESTRA. Yes. Your eyes proclaim your loyalty.

LEADER. But what are your grounds? Have you a proof of it?

CLYTEMNESTRA. There is proof indeed—unless God has cheated us.

LEADER. Perhaps you believe the inveigling shapes of dreams?

CLYTEMNESTRA. I would not be credited with a dozing brain!

LEADER. Or are you puffed up by Rumor, the wingless flyer?

CLYTEMNESTRA. You mock my common sense as if I were a child.

LEADER. But at what time was the city given to sack?

CLYTEMNESTRA. In this very night that gave birth to this day.

LEADER. What messenger could come so fast?

CLYTEMNESTRA. Hephaestus, launching a fine flame from Ida,
Beacon forwarding beacon, despatch-riders of fire,
Ida relayed to Hermes' cliff in Lemnos
And the great glow from the island was taken over third
By the height of Athos that belongs to Zeus,
And towering then to straddle over the sea
The might of the running torch joyfully tossed
The gold gleam forward like another sun,
Herald of light to the heights of Mount Macistus,
And he without delay, nor carelessly by sleep
Encumbered, did not shirk his intermediary role,
His farflung ray reached the Euripus' tides
And told Messapion's watchers, who in turn
Sent on the message further
Setting a stack of dried-up heather on fire.
And the strapping flame, not yet enfeebled, leapt
Over the plain of Asopus like a blazing moon
And woke on the crags of Cithaeron
Another relay in the chain of fire.
The light that was sent from far was not declined
By the look-out men, who raised a fiercer yet,
A light which jumped the water of Gorgopis
And to Mount Aegiplanctus duly come
Urged the reveille of the punctual fire.
So then they kindle it squanderingly and launch

A beard of flame big enough to pass
The headland that looks down upon the Saronic gulf,
Blazing and bounding till it reached at length
The Arachnaean steep, our neighboring heights;
And leaps in the latter end on the roof of the sons of Atreus
Issue and image of the fire on Ida.
Such was the assignment of my torch-racers,
The task of each fulfilled by his successor.
And victor is he who ran both first and last.
Such is the proof I offer you, the sign
My husband sent me out of Troy.

LEADER. To the gods, queen, I shall give thanks presently.
But I would like to hear this story again,
To wonder at it in detail from your lips.

CLYTEMNESTRA. The Greeks hold Troy upon this day.
The cries in the town I fancy do not mingle.
Pour oil and vinegar into the same jar,
You would say they stand apart unlovingly;
Of those who are captured and those who have conquered
Distinct are the sounds of their diverse fortunes,
For *these* having flung themselves about the bodies
Of husbands and brothers, or sons upon the bodies
Of aged fathers from a throat no longer
Free, lament the fate of their most loved.
But *those* a night's marauding after battle
Sets hungry to what breakfast the town offers
Not billeted duly in any barracks order
But as each man has drawn his lot of luck.
So in the captive homes of Troy already
They take their lodging, free of the frosts
And dews of the open. Like happy men
They will sleep all night without sentry.
But if they respect duly the city's gods,
Those of the captured land and the sanctuaries of the gods,
They need not, having conquered, fear reconquest.
But let no lust fall first upon the troops
To plunder what is not right, subdued by gain,
For they must still, in order to come home safe,
Get round the second lap of the doubled course.
So if they return without offence to the gods
The grievance of the slain may learn at last
A friendly talk—unless some fresh wrong falls.
Such are the thoughts you hear from me, a woman.
But may the good prevail for all to see.
We have much good. I only ask to enjoy it.

LEADER. Woman, you speak with sense like a prudent man.
I, who have heard your valid proofs, prepare
To give the glory to God.
Fair recompense is brought us for our troubles.

CLYTEMNESTRA *goes back into the palace.*

CHORUS

O Zeus our king and Night our friend
Donor of glories,
Night who cast on the towers of Troy
A close-clinging net so that neither the grown
Nor any of the children can pass
The enslaving and huge
Trap of all-taking destruction.
Great Zeus, guardian of host and guest,
I honor who has done his work and taken
A leisured aim at Paris so that neither
Too short nor yet over the stars
He might shoot to no purpose.

From Zeus is the blow they can tell of,
This at least can be established,
They have fared according to his ruling. For some
Deny that the gods deign to consider those among men
Who trample on the grace of inviolate things;
It is the impious man says this,
For Ruin is revealed the child
Of not to be attempted actions
When men are puffed up unduly
And their houses are stuffed with riches.
Measure is the best. Let danger be distant,
This should suffice a man
With a proper part of wisdom.
For a man has no protection
Against the drunkenness of riches
Once he has spurned from his sight
The high altar of Justice.

Somber Persuasion compels him,
Intolerable child of calculating Doom;
All cure is vain, there is no glozing it over

But the mischief shines forth with a deadly light
And like bad coinage
By rubbings and frictions
He stands discolored and black
Under the test—like a boy
Who chases a winged bird.
He has branded his city for ever.
His prayers are heard by no god.
Who makes such things his practice
The gods destroy him.
  This way came Paris
  To the house of the sons of Atreus
  And outraged the table of friendship
  Stealing the wife of his host.

Leaving to her countrymen clanging of
Shields and of spears and
Launching of warships
And bringing instead of a dowry destruction to
    Troy
Lightly she was gone through the gates daring
Things undared. Many the groans
Of the palace spokesmen on this theme—
"O the house, the house, and its princes,
O the bed and the imprint of her limbs;
One can see him crouching in silence
Dishonored and unreviling."
Through desire for her who is overseas, a ghost
Will seem to rule the household.
  And now her husband hates
  The grace of shapely statues;
  In the emptiness of their eyes
  All their appeal is departed.

But appearing in dreams persuasive
Images come bringing a joy that is vain,
Vain for when in fancy he looks to touch her—
Slipping through his hands the vision
Rapidly is gone
Following on wings the walks of sleep.
Such are his griefs in his house on his hearth,
Such as these and worse than these,
But everywhere through the land of Greece which
    men have left
Are mourning women with enduring hearts
To be seen in all houses; many
Are the thoughts which stab their hearts;
  For those they sent to war
  They know, but in place of men
  That which comes home to them
  Is merely an urn and ashes.

But the money-changer War, changer of bodies,
Holding his balance in the battle
Home from Troy refined by fire
Sends back to friends the dust
That is heavy with tears, stowing
A man's worth of ashes
In an easily handled jar.
And they wail speaking well of the men how that
    one
Was expert in battle, and one fell well in the car-
    nage—
But for another man's wife.
Muffled and muttered words;
And resentful grief creeps up against the sons
Of Atreus and their cause.
  But others there by the wall
  Entombed in Trojan ground
  Lie, handsome of limb,
  Holding, and hidden in, enemy soil.

Heavy is the murmur of an angry people
Performing the purpose of a public curse;
There is something cowled in the night
That I anxiously wait to hear.
For the gods are not blind to the
Murderers of many and the black
Furies in time
When a man prospers in sin
By erosion of life reduce him to darkness,
Who, once among the lost, can no more
Be helped. Over-great glory
Is a sore burden. The high peak
Is blasted by the eyes of Zeus.
  I prefer an unenvied fortune,
  Not to be a sacker of cities
  Nor to find myself living at another's
  Ruling, myself a captive.

AN OLD MAN. From the good news' beacon a
    swift
  Rumor is gone through the town.
  Who knows if it be true
  Or some deceit of the gods?
ANOTHER O. M. Who is so childish or broken in
    wit
  To kindle his heart at a new-fangled message of
    flame
  And then be downcast
  At a change of report?
ANOTHER O. M. The over-credulous passion of
    women expands

In swift conflagration but swiftly declining is gone
The news that a woman announced.

LEADER OF THE CHORUS. Soon we shall know about the illuminant torches,
The beacons and the fiery relays,
Whether they were true or whether like dreams
That pleasant light came here and hoaxed our wits.
Look: I see, coming from the beach, a herald
Shadowed with olive shoots; the dust upon him,
Mud's thirsty sister and colleague, is my witness
That he will not give dumb news nor news by lighting
A flame of fire with the smoke of mountain timber;
In words he will either corroborate our joy—
But the opposite version I reject with horror.
To the good appeared so far may good be added.

ANOTHER SPEAKER. Whoever makes other prayers for this our city,
May he reap himself the fruits of his wicked heart.

Enter the HERALD, *who kisses the ground before speaking.*

HERALD. Earth of my fathers, O the earth of Argos,
In the light of the tenth year I reach you thus
After many shattered hopes achieving one,
For never did I dare to think that here in Argive land
I should win a grave in the dearest soil of home;
But now hail, land, and hail, light of the sun,
And Zeus high above the country and the Pythian king—
May he no longer shoot his arrows at us
(Implacable long enough beside Scamander)
But now be savior to us and be healer,
King Apollo. And all the Assembly's gods
I call upon, and him my patron, Hermes,
The dear herald whom all heralds adore,
And the Heroes who sped our voyage, again with favor
Take back the army that has escaped the spear.
O cherished dwelling, palace of royalty,
O august thrones and gods facing the sun,
If ever before, now with your bright eyes
Gladly receive your king after much time,
Who comes bringing light to you in the night time,
And to all these as well—King Agamemnon.
Give him a good welcome as he deserves,
Who with the axe of judgment-awarding God
Has smashed Troy and levelled the Trojan land;
The altars are destroyed, the seats of the gods,
And the seed of all the land is perished from it.
Having cast this halter round the neck of Troy
The King, the elder son of Atreus, a blessed man
Comes, the most worthy to have honor of all
Men that are now. Paris nor his guilty city
Can boast that the crime was greater than the atonement.
Convicted in a suit of rape and robbery
He has lost his stolen goods and with consummate ruin
Mowed down the whole country and his father's house.
The sons of Priam have paid their account with interest.

LEADER OF THE CHORUS. Hail and be glad, herald of the Greek army.

HERALD. Yes. Glad indeed! So glad that at the gods' demand
I should no longer hesitate to die.

LEADER. Were you so harrowed by desire for home?

HERALD. Yes. The tears come to my eyes for joy.

LEADER. Sweet then is the fever which afflicts you.

HERALD. What do you mean? Let me learn your drift.

LEADER. Longing for those whose love came back in echo.

HERALD. Meaning the land was homesick for the army?

LEADER. Yes. I would often groan from a darkened heart.

HERALD. This sullen hatred—how did it fasten on you?

LEADER. I cannot say. Silence is my stock prescription.

HERALD. What? In your masters' absence were there some you feared?

LEADER. Yes. In your phrase, death would now be a gratification.

HERALD. Yes, for success is ours. These things have taken time.
Some of them we could say have fallen well,
While some we blame. Yet who except the gods
Is free from pain the whole duration of life?
If I were to tell of our labors, our hard lodging,
The sleeping on crowded decks, the scanty blankets,
Tossing and groaning, rations that never reached us—
And the land too gave matter for more disgust,
For our beds lay under the enemy's walls.
Continuous drizzle from the sky, dews from the marshes,
Rotting our clothes, filling our hair with lice.
And if one were to tell of the bird-destroying winter
Intolerable from the snows of Ida
Or of the heat when the sea slackens at noon
Waveless and dozing in a depressed calm—
But why make these complaints? The weariness is over;
Over indeed for some who never again
Need ever trouble to rise.
Why make a computation of the lost?
Why need the living sorrow for the spites of fortune?
I wish to say a long goodbye to disasters.
For us, the remnant of the troops of Argos,
The advantage remains, the pain cannot outweigh it;
So we can make our boast to this sun's light,
Flying on words above the land and sea;
"Having taken Troy the Argive expedition
Has nailed up throughout Greece in every temple
These spoils, these ancient trophies."
Those who hear such things must praise the city
And the generals. And the grace of God be honored
Which brought these things about. You have the whole story.

LEADER. I confess myself convinced by your report.
Old men are always young enough to learn.

Enter CLYTEMNESTRA *from the palace.*

This news belongs by right first to the house
And Clytemnestra—though I am enriched also.

CLYTEMNESTRA. Long before this I shouted at joy's command
At the coming of the first night-messenger of fire
Announcing the taking and capsizing of Troy.
And people reproached me saying, "Do mere beacons
Persuade you to think that Troy is already down?
Indeed a woman's heart is easily exalted."
Such comments made me seem to be wandering but yet
I began my sacrifices and in the women's fashion
Throughout the town they raised triumphant cries
And in the gods' enclosures
Lulling the fragrant, incense-eating flame.
And now what need is there for you to tell me more?
From the King himself I shall learn the whole story.
But how the best to welcome my honored lord
I shall take pains when he comes back—For what
Is a kinder light for a woman to see than this,
To open the gates to her man come back from war
When God has saved him? Tell this to my husband,
To come with all speed, the city's darling;
May he returning find a wife as loyal
As when he left her, watchdog of the house,
Good to *him* but fierce to the ill-intentioned,
And in all other things as ever, having destroyed
No seal or pledge at all in the length of time.
I know no pleasure with another man, no scandal,
More than I know how to dye metal red.
Such is my boast, bearing a load of truth,
A boast that need not disgrace a noble wife.
[*Exit.*]

LEADER. Thus has she spoken; if you take her meaning.
Only a specious tale to shrewd interpreters.
But do you, herald, tell me; I ask after Menelaus
Whether he will, returning safe preserved,
Come back with you, our land's loved master.

HERALD. I am not able to speak the lovely falsehood
To profit you, my friends, for any stretch of time.
LEADER. But if only the true tidings could be also good!
It is hard to hide a division of good and true.
HERALD. The prince is vanished out of the Greek fleet,
Himself and ship. I speak no lie.
LEADER. Did he put forth first in the sight of all from Troy,
Or a storm that troubled all sweep him apart?
HERALD. You have hit the target like a master archer,
Told succinctly a long tale of sorrow.
LEADER. Did the rumors current among the remaining ships
Represent him as alive or dead?
HERALD. No one knows so as to tell for sure
Except the sun who nurses the breeds of earth.
LEADER. Tell me how the storm came on the host of ships
Through the divine anger, and how it ended.
HERALD. Day of good news should not be fouled by tongue
That tells ill news. To each god his season.
When, despair in his face, a messenger brings to a town
The hated news of a fallen army—
One general wound to the city and many men
Outcast, outcursed, from many homes
By the double whip which War is fond of,
Doom with a bloody spear in either hand,
One carrying such a pack of grief could well
Recite this hymn of the Furies at your asking.
But when our cause is saved and a messenger of good
Comes to a city glad with festivity,
How am I to mix good news with bad, recounting
The storm that meant God's anger on the Greeks?
For they swore together, those inveterate enemies,
Fire and sea, and proved their alliance, destroying
The unhappy troops of Argos.
In night arose ill-waved evil,
Ships on each other the blasts from Thrace
Crashed colliding, which butting with horns in the violence
Of big wind and rattle of rain were gone
To nothing, whirled all ways by a wicked shepherd.
But when there came up the shining light of the sun
We saw the Aegean sea flowering with corpses
Of Greek men and their ships' wreckage.
But for us, our ship was not damaged,
Whether someone snatched it away or begged it off
Some god, not a man, handling the tiller;
And Saving Fortune was willing to sit upon our ship
So that neither at anchor we took the tilt of waves
Nor ran to splinters on the crag-bound coast.
But then having thus escaped death on the sea,
In the white day, not trusting our fortune,
We pastured this new trouble upon our thoughts,
The fleet being battered, the sailors weary,
And now if any of *them* still draw breath,
They are thinking no doubt of us as being lost
And we are thinking of them as being lost.
May the best happen. As for Menelaus
The first guess and most likely is a disaster.
But still—if any ray of sun detects him
Alive, with living eyes, by the plan of Zeus
Not yet resolved to annul the race completely,
There is some hope then that he will return home.
So much you have heard. Know that it is the truth. [*Exit.*]

CHORUS

Who was it named her thus
In all ways appositely
Unless it was Someone whom we do not see,
Fore-knowing fate
And plying an accurate tongue?
Helen, bride of spears and conflict's
Focus, who as was befitting
Proved a hell to ships and men,
Hell to her country, sailing
Away from delicately-sumptuous curtains,
Away on the wind of a giant Zephyr,
And shielded hunters mustered many
On the vanished track of the oars,

Oars beached on the leafy
Banks of a Trojan river
For the sake of bloody war.
But on Troy was thrust a marring marriage
By the Wrath that working to an end exacts
In time a price from guests
Who dishonored their host
And dishonored Zeus of the Hearth,
From those noisy celebrants
Of the wedding hymn which fell
To the brothers of Paris
To sing upon that day.
But learning this, unlearning that,
Priam's ancestral city now
Continually mourns, reviling
Paris the fatal bridegroom.
The city has had much sorrow,
Much desolation in life,
From the pitiful loss of her people.
So in his house a man might rear
A lion's cub caught from the dam
In need of suckling,
In the prelude of its life
Mild, gentle with the children,
For old men a playmate,
Often held in the arms
Like a new-born child,
Wheedling the hand,
Fawning at belly's bidding.

But matured by time he showed
The temper of his stock and paid
Thanks for his fostering
With disaster of slaughter of sheep
Making an unbidden banquet
And now the house is a shambles,
Irremediable grief to its people,
Calamitous carnage;
For the pet they had fostered was sent
By God as a priest of Ruin.

So I would say there came
To the city of Troy
A notion of windless calm,
Delicate adornment of riches,
Soft shooting of the eyes and flower
Of desire that stings the fancy.
But swerving aside she achieved
A bitter end to her marriage,
Ill guest and ill companion,
Hurled upon Priam's sons, convoyed
By Zeus, patron of guest and host,
Dark angel dowered with tears.

Long current among men an old saying
Runs that a man's prosperity
When grown to greatness
Comes to the birth, does not die childless—
His good luck breeds for his house
Distress that shall not be appeased.
I only, apart from the others,
Hold that the unrighteous action
Breeds true to its kind,
Leaves its own children behind it.
But the lot of a righteous house
Is a fair offspring always.

Ancient self-glory is accustomed
To bear to light in the evil sort of men
A new self-glory and madness,
Which sometime or sometime finds
The appointed hour for its birth,
And born therewith is the Spirit, intractable, unholy, irresistible,
The reckless lust that brings black Doom upon the house,
A child that is like its parents.
But Honest Dealing is clear
Shining in smoky homes,
Honors the god-fearing life.
Mansions gilded by filth of hands she leaves,
Turns her eyes elsewhere, visits the innocent house,
Not respecting the power
Of wealth mis-stamped with approval,
But guides all to the goal.

Enter AGAMEMNON *and* CASSANDRA *on chariots.*

Come then, my King, stormer of Troy,
Offspring of Atreus,
How shall I hail you, how give you honor
Neither overshooting nor falling short
  Of the measure of homage?
There are many who honor appearance too much
Passing the bounds that are right.
To condole with the unfortunate man
Each one is ready but the bite of the grief
  Never goes through to the heart.
And they join in rejoicing, affecting to share it,

Forcing their face to a smile.
But he who is shrewd to shepherd his sheep
Will fail not to notice the eyes of a man
Which seem to be loyal but lie,
  Fawning with watery friendship.
Even you, in my thought, when you marshalled the troops
For Helen's sake, I will not hide it,
Made a harsh and ugly picture,
Holding badly the tiller of reason,
Paying with the death of men
  Ransom for a willing whore.
But now, not unfriendly, not superficially,
I offer my service, well-doers' welcome.
In time you will learn by inquiry
Who has done rightly, who transgressed
  In the work of watching the city.

AGAMEMNON. First to Argos and the country's gods
  My fitting salutations, who have aided me
  To return and in the justice which I exacted
  From Priam's city. Hearing the unspoken case
  The gods unanimously had cast their vote
  Into the bloody urn for the massacre of Troy;
  But to the opposite urn
  Hope came, dangled her hand, but did no more.
  Smoke marks even now the city's capture.
  Whirlwinds of doom are alive, the dying ashes
  Spread on the air the fat savor of wealth.
  For these things we must pay some memorable return
  To Heaven, having exacted enormous vengeance
  For wife-rape; for a woman
  The Argive monster ground a city to powder,
  Sprung from a wooden horse, shield-wielding folk,
  Launching a leap at the setting of the Pleiads,
  Jumping the ramparts, a ravening lion,
  Lapped its fill of the kingly blood.
  To the gods I have drawn out this overture
  But as for your concerns, I bear them in my mind
  And say the same, you have me in agreement.
  To few of men does it belong by nature
  To congratulate their friends unenviously,
  For a sullen poison fastens on the heart,
  Doubling the pain of a man with this disease;
  He feels the weight of his own griefs and when
  He sees another's prosperity he groans.
  I speak with knowledge, being well acquainted
  With the mirror of comradeship—ghost of a shadow
  Were those who seemed to be so loyal to me.
  Only Odysseus, who sailed against his will,
  Proved, when yoked with me, a ready trace-horse;
  I speak of him not knowing if he is alive.
  But for what concerns the city and the gods
  Appointing public debates in full assembly
  We shall consult. That which is well already
  We shall take steps to ensure it remain well.
  But where there is need of medical remedies,
  By applying benevolent cautery or surgery
  We shall try to deflect the dangers of disease.
  But now, entering the halls where stands my hearth,
  First I shall make salutation to the gods
  Who sent me a far journey and have brought me back.
  And may my victory not leave my side.

Enter CLYTEMNESTRA, *followed by women slaves carrying purple tapestries.*

CLYTEMNESTRA. Men of the city, you the aged of Argos,
  I shall feel no shame to describe to you my love
  Towards my husband. Shyness in all of us
  Wears thin with time. Here are the facts first hand.
  I will tell you of my own unbearable life
  I led so long as this man was at Troy.
  For first that the woman separate from her man
  Should sit alone at home in extreme cruelty,
  Hearing so many malignant rumors—First
  Comes one, and another comes after, bad news to worse,
  Clamor of grief to the house. If Agamemnon
  Had had so many wounds as those reported
  Which poured home through the pipes of hearsay, then—
  Then he would be gashed fuller than a net has holes!
  And if only he had died . . . as often as rumor told us,
  He would be like the giant in the legend,
  Three-bodied. Dying once for every body,

He should have by now three blankets of earth above him—
All that above him; I care not how deep the mattress under!
Such are the malignant rumors thanks to which
They have often seized me against my will and undone
The loop of a rope from my neck.
And this is why our son is not standing here,
The guarantee of your pledges and mine,
As he should be, Orestes. Do not wonder;
He is being brought up by a friendly ally and host,
Strophius the Phocian, who warned me in advance
Of dubious troubles, both your risks at Troy
And the anarchy of shouting mobs that might
Overturn policy, for it is born in men
To kick the man who is down.
This is not a disingenuous excuse.
For me the outrushing wells of weeping are dried up,
There is no drop left in them.
My eyes are sore from sitting late at nights
Weeping for you and for the baffled beacons,
Never lit up. And, when I slept, in dreams
I have been waked by the thin whiz of a buzzing
Gnat, seeing more horrors fasten on you
Than could take place in the mere time of my dream.
Having endured all this, now, with unsorrowed heart
I would hail this man as the watchdog of the farm,
Forestay that saves the ship, pillar that props
The lofty roof, appearance of an only son
To a father or of land to sailors past their hope,
The loveliest day to see after the storm,
Gush of well-water for the thirsty traveller.
Such are the metaphors I think befit him,
But envy be absent. Many misfortunes already
We have endured. But now, dear head, come down
Out of that car, not placing upon the ground
Your foot, O King, the foot that trampled Troy.
Why are you waiting, slaves, to whom the task is assigned
To spread the pavement of his path with tapestries?
At once, at once let his way be strewn with purple
That Justice lead him toward his unexpected home.
The rest a mind, not overcome by sleep
Will arrange rightly, with God's help, as destined.

AGAMEMNON. Daughter of Leda, guardian of my house,
You have spoken in proportion to my absence.
You have drawn your speech out long. Duly to praise me,
That is a duty to be performed by others.
And further—do not by women's methods make me
Effeminate nor in barbarian fashion
Gape ground-grovelling acclamations at me
Nor strewing my path with cloths make it invidious.
It is the gods should be honored in this way.
But being mortal to tread embroidered beauty
For me is no way without fear.
I tell you to honor me as a man, not god.
Footcloths are very well—Embroidered stuffs
Are stuff for gossip. And not to think unwisely
Is the greatest gift of God. Call happy only him
Who has ended his life in sweet prosperity.
I have spoken. This thing I could not do with confidence.

CLYTEMNESTRA. Tell me now, according to your judgment.

AGAMEMNON. I tell you you shall not override my judgment.

CLYTEMNESTRA. Supposing you had feared something . . .
Could you have vowed to God to do this thing?

AGAMEMNON. Yes. If an expert had prescribed that vow.

CLYTEMNESTRA. And how would Priam have acted in your place?

AGAMEMNON. He would have trod the cloths, I think, for certain.

CLYTEMNESTRA. Then do not flinch before the blame of men.

AGAMEMNON. The voice of the multitude is very strong.

CLYTEMNESTRA. But the man none envy is not enviable.

AGAMEMNON. It is not a woman's part to love disputing.

CLYTEMNESTRA. But it is a conqueror's part to yield upon occasion.
AGAMEMNON. You think such victory worth fighting for?
CLYTEMNESTRA. Give way. Consent to let me have the mastery.
AGAMEMNON. Well, if such is your wish, let someone quickly loose
My vassal sandals, underlings of my feet,
And stepping on these sea-purples may no god
Shoot me from far with the envy of his eye.
Great shame it is to ruin my house and spoil
The wealth of costly weavings with my feet.
But of this matter enough. This stranger woman here
Take in with kindness. The man who is a gentle master
God looks on from far off complacently.
For no one of his will bears the slave's yoke.
This woman, of many riches being the chosen
Flower, gift of the soldiers, has come with me.
But since I have been prevailed on by your words
I will go to my palace home, treading on purples.

He dismounts from the chariot and begins to walk up the tapestried path. During the following speech he enters the palace.

CLYTEMNESTRA. There is the sea and who shall drain it dry? It breeds
Its wealth in silver of plenty of purple gushing
And ever-renewed, the dyeings of our garments.
The house has its store of these by God's grace, King.
This house is ignorant of poverty
And I would have vowed a pavement of many garments
Had the palace oracle enjoined that vow
Thereby to contrive a ransom for his life.
For while there is root, foliage comes to the house
Spreading a tent of shade against the Dog Star.
So now that you have reached your hearth and home
You prove a miracle—advent of warmth in winter;
And further this—even in the time of heat
When God is fermenting wine from the bitter grape,
Even then it is cool in the house if only
Its master walk at home, a grown man, ripe.
O Zeus the Ripener, ripen these my prayers;
Your part is to make the ripe fruit fall.

She enters the palace.

CHORUS

Why, why at the doors
Of my fore-seeing heart
Does this terror keep beating its wings?
And my song play the prophet
Unbidden, unhired—
Which I cannot spit out
Like the enigmas of dreams
Nor plausible confidence
Sit on the throne of my mind?
It is long time since
The cables let down from the stern
Were chafed by the sand when the seafaring army started for Troy.
And I learn with my eyes
And witness myself their return;
But the hymn without lyre goes up,
The dirge of the Avenging Fiend,
In the depths of my self-taught heart
Which has lost its dear
Possession of the strength of hope.
But my guts and my heart
Are not idle which seethe with the waves
Of trouble nearing its hour.
But I pray that these thoughts
May fall out not as I think
And not be fulfilled in the end.

Truly when health grows much
It respects not limit; for disease,
Its neighbor in the next door room,
Presses upon it.
A man's life, crowding sail,
Strikes on the blind reef:
But if caution in advance
Jettison part of the cargo
With the derrick of due proportion,
The whole house does not sink,
Though crammed with a weight of woe
The hull does not go under.
The abundant bounty of God

And his gifts from the year's furrows
Drive the famine back.

But when upon the ground there has fallen once
The black blood of a man's death,
Who shall summon it back by incantations?
Even Asclepius who had the art
To fetch the dead to life, even to him
Zeus put a provident end.
But, if of the heaven-sent fates
One did not check the other,
Cancel the other's advantage,
My heart would outrun my tongue
In pouring out these fears.
But now it mutters in the dark,
Embittered, no way hoping
To unravel a scheme in time
From a burning mind.

CLYTEMNESTRA *appears in the door of the palace.*

CLYTEMNESTRA. Go in too, you; I speak to you, Cassandra,
Since God in his clemency has put you in this house
To share our holy water, standing with many slaves
Beside the altar that protects the house,
Step down from the car there, do not be overproud.
Heracles himself they say was once
Sold, and endured to eat the bread of slavery.
But should such a chance inexorably fall,
There is much advantage in masters who have long been rich.
Those who have reaped a crop they never expected
Are in all things hard on their slaves and overstep the line.
From us you will have the treatment of tradition.

LEADER OF CHORUS. You, it is you she has addressed, and clearly.
Caught as you are in these predestined toils
Obey her if you can. But should you disobey . . .

CLYTEMNESTRA. If she has more than the gibberish of the swallow,
An unintelligible barbaric speech,
I hope to read her mind, persuade her reason.

LEADER. As things now stand for you, she says the best.
Obey her; leave that car and follow her.

CLYTEMNESTRA. I have no leisure to waste out here, outside the door.
Before the hearth in the middle of my house
The victims stand already, wait the knife.
You, if you will obey me, waste no time.
But if you cannot understand my language—

(*To* CHORUS LEADER)

You make it plain to her with the brute and voiceless hand.

LEADER. The stranger seems to need a clear interpreter.
She bears herself like a wild beast newly captured.

CLYTEMNESTRA. The fact is she is mad, she listens to evil thoughts,
Who has come here leaving a city newly captured
Without experience how to bear the bridle
So as not to waste her strength in foam and blood.
I will not spend more words to be ignored.

She re-enters the palace.

CHORUS. But I, for I pity her, will not be angry.
Obey, unhappy woman. Leave this car.
Yield to your fate. Put on the untried yoke.

CASSANDRA. Apollo! Apollo!

CHORUS. Why do you cry like this upon Apollo?
He is not the kind of god that calls for dirges.

CASSANDRA. Apollo! Apollo!

CHORUS. Once more her funereal cries invoke the god
Who has no place at the scene of lamentation.

CASSANDRA. Apollo! Apollo!
God of the Ways! My destroyer!
Destroyed again—and this time utterly!

CHORUS. She seems about to predict her own misfortunes.
The gift of the god endures, even in a slave's mind.

CASSANDRA. Apollo! Apollo!
God of the Ways! My destroyer!
Where? To what house? Where, where have you brought me?

CHORUS. To the house of the sons of Atreus. If you do not know it,

I will tell you so. You will not find it false.
CASSANDRA. No, no, but to a god-hated, but to an accomplice
In much kin-killing, murdering nooses,
Man-shambles, a floor asperged with blood.
CHORUS. The stranger seems like a hound with a keen scent,
Is picking up a trail that leads to murder.
CASSANDRA. Clues! I have clues! Look! They are these.
These wailing, these children, butchery of children;
Roasted flesh, a father sitting to dinner.
CHORUS. Of your prophetic fame we have heard before
But in this matter prophets are not required.
CASSANDRA. What is she doing? What is she planning?
What is this new great sorrow?
Great crime . . . within here . . . planning
Unendurable to his folk, impossible
Ever to be cured. For help
Stands far distant.
CHORUS. This reference I cannot catch. But the children
I recognized; that refrain is hackneyed.
CASSANDRA. Damned, damned, bringing this work to completion—
Your husband who shared your bed
To bathe him, to cleanse him, and then—
How shall I tell of the end?
Soon, very soon, it will fall.
The end comes hand over hand
Grasping in greed.
CHORUS. Not yet do I understand. After her former riddles
Now I am baffled by these dim pronouncements.
CASSANDRA. Ah God, the vision! God, God, the vision!
A net, is it? Net of Hell!
But herself is the net; shared bed; shares murder.
O let the pack ever-hungering after the family
Howl for the unholy ritual, howl for the victim.
CHORUS. What black Spirit is this you call upon the house—
To raise aloft her cries? Your speech does not lighten me.
Into my heart runs back the blood
Yellow as when for men by the spear fallen
The blood ebbs out with the rays of the setting life
And death strides quickly.
CASSANDRA. Quick! Be on your guard! The bull—
Keep him clear of the cow.
Caught with a trick, the black horn's point,
She strikes. He falls; lies in the water.
Murder; a trick in a bath. I tell what I see.
CHORUS. I would not claim to be expert in oracles
But these, as I deduce, portend disaster.
Do men ever get a good answer from oracles?
No. It is only through disaster
That their garrulous craft brings home
The meaning of the prophet's panic.
CASSANDRA. And for me also, for me, chance ill-destined!
My own now I lament, pour into the cup my own
Where is this you have brought me in my misery?
Unless to die as well. What else is meant?
CHORUS. You are mad, mad, carried away by the god,
Raising the dirge, the tuneless
Tune, for yourself. Like the tawny
Unsatisfied singer from her luckless heart
Lamenting "Itys, Itys," the nightingale
Lamenting a life luxuriant with grief.
CASSANDRA. Oh the lot of the songful nightingale!
The gods enclosed her in a winged body,
Gave her a sweet and tearless passing.
But for me remains the two-edged cutting blade.
CHORUS. From whence these rushing and God-inflicted
Profitless pains?
Why shape with your sinister crying
The piercing hymn—fear-piercing?
How can you know the evil-worded landmarks
On the prophetic path?
CASSANDRA. Oh the wedding, the wedding of Paris—death to his people!
O river Scamander, water drunk by my fathers!
I was brought up and cared for.
But now it is the river of Wailing and the banks of Hell
That shall hear my prophecy soon.
CHORUS. What is this clear speech, too clear?
A child could understand it.

I am bitten with fangs that draw blood
By the misery of your cries,
Cries harrowing the heart.

CASSANDRA. Oh trouble on trouble of a city lost, lost utterly!
My father's sacrifices before the towers,
Much killing of cattle and sheep,
No cure—availed not at all
To prevent the coming of what came to Troy,
And I, my brain on fire, shall soon enter the trap.

CHORUS. This speech accords with the former.
What god, malicious, over-heavy, persistently pressing,
Drives you to chant of these lamentable
Griefs with death their burden?
But I cannot see the end.

CASSANDRA *now steps down from the car.*

CASSANDRA. The oracle now no longer from behind veils
Will be peeping forth like a newly-wedded bride;
But I can feel it like a fresh wind swoop
And rush in the face of the dawn and, wave-like, wash
Against the sun a vastly greater grief
Than this one. I shall speak no more conundrums.
And bear me witness, pacing me, that I
Am trailing on the scent of ancient wrongs.
For this house here a choir never deserts,
Chanting together ill. For they mean ill,
And to puff up their arrogance they have drunk
Men's blood, this band of revellers that haunts the house,
Hard to be rid of, fiends that attend the family.
Established in its rooms they hymn their hymn
Of that original sin, abhor in turn
The adultery that proved a brother's ruin.
A miss? Or do my arrows hit the mark?
Or am I a quack prophet who knocks at doors, a babbler?
Give me your oath, confess I have the facts,
The ancient history of this house's crimes.

LEADER. And how could an oath's assurance, however finely assured,
Turn out a remedy? I wonder, though that you
Being brought up overseas, of another tongue,
Should hit on the whole tale as if you had been standing by.

CASSANDRA. Apollo the prophet set me to prophesy.

LEADER. Was he, although a god, struck by desire?

CASSANDRA. Till now I was ashamed to tell that story.

LEADER. Yes. Good fortune keeps us all fastidious.

CASSANDRA. He wrestled hard upon me, panting love.

LEADER. And did you come, as they do, to child-getting?

CASSANDRA. No. I agreed to him. And I cheated him.

LEADER. Were you already possessed by the mystic art?

CASSANDRA. Already I was telling the townsmen all their future suffering.

LEADER. Then how did you escape the doom of Apollo's anger?

CASSANDRA. I did not escape. No one ever believed me.

LEADER. Yet to us your words seem worthy of belief.

CASSANDRA. Oh misery, misery!
Again comes on me the terrible labor of true
Prophecy, dizzying prelude; distracts . . .
Do you see these who sit before the house,
Children, like the shapes of dreams?
Children who seem to have been killed by their kinsfolk,
Filling their hands with meat, flesh of themselves,
Guts and entrails, handfuls of lament—
Clear what they hold—the same their father tasted.
For this I declare someone is plotting vengeance—
A lion? Lion but coward, that lurks in bed,
Good watchdog truly against the lord's return—
My lord, for I must bear the yoke of serfdom.
Leader of the ships, overturner of Troy,
He does not know what plots the accursed hound
With the licking tongue and the pricked-up ear will plan
In the manner of a lurking doom, in an evil hour.
A daring criminal! Female murders male.
What monster could provide her with a title?
An amphisbaena or hag of the sea who dwells
In rocks to ruin sailors—

A raving mother of death who breathes against her folk
War to the finish. Listen to her shout of triumph,
Who shirks no horrors, like men in a rout of battle.
And yet she poses as glad at their return.
If you distrust my words, what does it matter?
That which will come will come. You too will soon stand here
And admit with pity that I spoke too truly.

LEADER. Thyestes' dinner of his children's meat
I understood and shuddered, and fear grips me
To hear the truth, not framed in parables.
But hearing the rest I am thrown out of my course.

CASSANDRA. It is Agamemnon's death I tell you you shall witness.

LEADER. Stop! Provoke no evil. Quiet your mouth!

CASSANDRA. The god who gives me words is here no healer.

LEADER. Not if this shall be so. But may some chance avert it.

CASSANDRA. *You* are praying. But others are busy with murder.

LEADER. What man is he promotes this terrible thing?

CASSANDRA. Indeed you have missed my drift by a wide margin!

LEADER. But I do not understand the assassin's method.

CASSANDRA. And yet too well I know the speech of Greece!

LEADER. So does Delphi but the replies are hard.

CASSANDRA. Ah what a fire it is! It comes upon me.
Apollo, Wolf-Destroyer, pity, pity . . .
It is the two-foot lioness who beds
Beside a wolf, the noble lion away,
It is she will kill me. Brewing a poisoned cup
She will mix my punishment too in the angry draught
And boasts, sharpening the dagger for her husband,
To pay back murder for my bringing here.
Why then do I wear these mockeries of myself,
The wand and the prophet's garland round my neck?
My hour is coming—but you shall perish first.
Destruction! Scattered thus you give me my revenge;
Go and enrich some other woman with ruin.
See: Apollo himself is stripping me
Of my prophetic gear, who has looked on
When in this dress I have been a laughing-stock
To friends and foes alike, and to no purpose;
They called me crazy, like a fortune-teller,
A poor starved beggar-woman—and I bore it.
And now the prophet undoing his prophetess
Has brought me to this final darkness.
Instead of my father's altar the executioner's block
Waits me the victim, red with my hot blood.
But the gods will not ignore me as I die.
One will come after to avenge my death,
A matricide, a murdered father's champion.
Exile and tramp and outlaw he will come back
To gable the family house of fatal crime;
His father's outstretched corpse shall lead him home.
Why need I then lament so pitifully?
For now that I have seen the town of Troy
Treated as she was treated, while her captors
Come to their reckoning thus by the gods' verdict,
I will go in and have the courage to die.
Look, these gates are the gates of Death. I greet them.
And I pray that I may meet a deft and mortal stroke
So that without a struggle I may close
My eyes and my blood ebb in easy death.

LEADER. Oh woman very unhappy and very wise,
Your speech was long. But if in sober truth
You know your fate, why like an ox that the gods
Drive, do you walk so bravely to the altar?

CASSANDRA. There is no escape, strangers. No; not by postponement.

LEADER. But the last moment has the privilege of hope.

CASSANDRA. The day is here. Little should I gain by flight.

LEADER. This patience of yours comes from a brave soul.

CASSANDRA. A happy man is never paid that compliment.

LEADER. But to die with credit graces a mortal man.

CASSANDRA. Oh my father! You and your noble sons!

She approaches the door, then suddenly recoils.

LEADER. What is it? What is the fear that drives you back?
CASSANDRA. Faugh.
LEADER. Why faugh? Or is this some hallucination?
CASSANDRA. These walls breathe out a death that drips with blood.
LEADER. Not so. It is only the smell of the sacrifice.
CASSANDRA. It is like the breath out of a charnel-house.
LEADER. You think our palace burns odd incense then!
CASSANDRA. But I will go to lament among the dead
My lot and Agamemnon's. Enough of life!
Strangers,
I am not afraid like a bird afraid of a bush
But witness you my words after my death
When a woman dies in return for me a woman
And a man falls for a man with a wicked wife.
I ask this service, being about to die.
LEADER. Alas, I pity you for the death you have foretold.
CASSANDRA. One more speech I have; I do not wish to raise
The dirge for my own self. But to the sun I pray
In face of his last light that my avengers
May make my murderers pay for this my death,
Death of a woman slave, an easy victim.

She enters the palace.

LEADER. Ah the fortunes of men! When they go well
A shadow sketch would match them, and in ill-fortune
The dab of a wet sponge destroys the drawing.
It is not myself but the life of man I pity.
CHORUS. Prosperity in all men cries
For more prosperity. Even the owner
Of the finger-pointed-at palace never shuts
His door against her, saying "Come no more."
So to our king the blessed gods had granted
To take the town of Priam, and heaven-favored
He reaches home. But now if for former blood-shed
He must pay blood
And dying for the dead shall cause
Other deaths in atonement
What man could boast he was born
Secure, who heard this story?
AGAMEMNON (*within*). Oh! I am struck a mortal blow—within!
LEADER. Silence! Listen. Who calls out, wounded with a mortal stroke?
AGAMEMNON. Again—the second blow—I am struck again.
LEADER. You heard the king cry out. I think the deed is done.
Let us see if we can concert some sound proposal.
SECOND OLD MAN. Well, I will tell you my opinion—
Raise an alarm, summon the folk to the palace.
THIRD OLD MAN. I say burst in with all speed possible,
Convict them of the deed while still the sword is wet.
FOURTH OLD MAN. And I am partner to some such suggestion,
I am for taking some course. No time to dawdle.
FIFTH OLD MAN. The case is plain. This is but the beginning.
They are going to set up dictatorship in the state.
SIXTH OLD MAN. We are wasting time. The assassins tread to earth
The decencies of delay and give their hands no sleep.
SEVENTH OLD MAN. I do not know what plan I could hit on to propose.
The man who acts is in the position to plan.
EIGHTH OLD MAN. So I think, too, for I am at a loss
To raise the dead man up again with words.
NINTH OLD MAN. Then to stretch out our life shall we yield thus
To the rule of these profaners of the house?
TENTH OLD MAN. It is not to be endured. To die is better.
Death is more comfortable than tyranny.
ELEVENTH OLD MAN. And are we on the evidence of groans
Going to give oracle that the prince is dead?

TWELFTH OLD MAN. We must know the facts for sure and *then* be angry.
Guesswork is not the same as certain knowledge.
LEADER. Then all of you back me and approve this plan—
To ascertain how it is with Agamemnon.

The doors of the palace open, revealing the bodies of AGAMEMNON *and* CASSANDRA. CLYTEMNESTRA *stands above them.*

CLYTEMNESTRA. Much having been said before to fit the moment,
To say the opposite now will not outface me.
How else could one serving hate upon the hated,
Thought to be friends, hang high the nets of doom
To preclude all leaping out?
For me I have long been training for this match,
I tried a fall and won—a victory overdue.
I stand here where I struck, above my victims;
So I contrived it—this I will not deny—
That he could neither fly nor ward off death;
Inextricable like a net for fishes
I cast about him a vicious wealth of raiment
And struck him twice and with two groans he loosed
His limbs beneath him, and upon him fallen
I deal him the third blow to the God beneath the earth,
To the safe keeper of the dead a votive gift,
And with that he spits his life out where he lies
And smartly spouting blood he sprays me with
The somber drizzle of bloody dew and I
Rejoice no less than in God's gift of rain
The crops are glad when the ear of corn gives birth.
These things being so, you, elders of Argos,
Rejoice if rejoice you will. Mine is the glory.
And if I could pay this corpse his due libation
I should be right to pour it and more than right;
With so many horrors this man mixed and filled
The bowl—and, coming home, has drained the draught himself.
LEADER. Your speech astonishes us. This brazen boast
Above the man who was your king and husband!
CLYTEMNESTRA. You challenge me as a woman without foresight
But I with unflinching heart to you who know
Speak. And you, whether you will praise or blame,
It makes no matter. Here lies Agamemnon,
My husband, dead, the work of this right hand,
An honest workman. There you have the facts.
CHORUS. Woman, what poisoned
Herb of the earth have you tasted
Or potion of the flowing sea
To undertake this killing and the people's curses?
You threw down, you cut off—the people will cast you out,
Black abomination to the town.
CLYTEMNESTRA. Now your verdict—in my case—is exile
And to have the people's hatred, the public curses,
Though then in no way you opposed this man
Who carelessly, as if it were a head of sheep
Out of the abundance of his fleecy flocks,
Sacrificed his own daughter, to me the dearest
Fruit of travail, charm for the Thracian winds.
He was the one to have banished from this land,
Pay off the pollution. But when you hear what I
Have done, you judge severely. But I warn you—
Threaten me on the understanding that I am ready
For two alternatives—Win by force the right
To rule me, but, if God brings about the contrary,
Late in time you will have to learn self-discipline.
CHORUS. You are high in the thoughts,
You speak extravagant things,
After the soiling murder your crazy heart
Fancies your forehead with a smear of blood.
Unhonored, unfriended, you must
Pay for a blow with a blow.
CLYTEMNESTRA. Listen then to this—the sanction of my oaths;
By the Justice totting up my child's atonement,
By the Avenging Doom and Fiend to whom I killed this man,
For me hope walks not in the rooms of fear
So long as my fire is lit upon my hearth

By Aegisthus. Loyal to me as he was before.
The man who outraged me lies here,
The darling of each courtesan at Troy,
And here with him is the prisoner clairvoyante,
The fortune-teller that he took to bed,
Who shares his bed as once his bench on shipboard,
A loyal mistress. Both have their deserts.
He lies so; and she who like a swan
Sang her last dying lament
Lies his lover, and the sight contributes
An appetizer to my own bed's pleasure.

CHORUS. Ah would some quick death come not overpainful,
Not overlong on the sickbed,
Establishing in us the ever-
Lasting unending sleep now that our guardian
Has fallen, the kindest of men,
Who suffering much for a woman
By a woman has lost his life.
O Helen, insane, being one
One to have destroyed so many
And many souls under Troy,
Now is your work complete, blossomed not for oblivion,
Unfading stain of blood. Here now, if in any home,
Is Discord, here is a man's deep-rooted ruin.

CLYTEMNESTRA. Do not pray for the portion of death
Weighed down by these things, do not turn
Your anger on Helen as destroyer of men,
One woman destroyer of many
Lives of Greek men,
A hurt that cannot be healed.

CHORUS. O Evil Spirit, falling on the family,
On the two sons of Atreus and using
Two sisters in heart as your tools,
A power that bites to the heart—
See on the body
Perched like a raven he gloats
Harshly croaking his hymn.

CLYTEMNESTRA. Ah, now you have amended your lips' opinion,
Calling upon this family's three times gorged
Genius—demon who breeds
Blood-hankering lust in the belly:
Before the old sore heals, new pus collects.

CHORUS. It is a great spirit—great—
You tell of, harsh in anger,
A ghastly tale, alas,
Of unsatisfied disaster
Brought by Zeus, by Zeus,
Cause and worker of all.
For without Zeus what comes to pass among us?
Which of these things is outside Providence?
O my king, my king,
How shall I pay you in tears,
Speak my affection in words?
You lie in that spider's web,
In a desecrating death breathe out your life,
Lie ignominiously
Defeated by a crooked death
And the two-edged cleaver's stroke.

CLYTEMNESTRA. You say this is *my* work—mine?
Do not cozen yourself that I am Agamemnon's wife.
Masquerading as the wife
Of the corpse there the old sharp-witted Genius
Of Atreus who gave the cruel banquet
Has paid with a grown man's life
The due for children dead.

CHORUS. That you are not guilty of
This murder who will attest?
No, but you may have been abetted
By some ancestral Spirit of Revenge.
Wading a millrace of the family's blood
The black Manslayer forces a forward path
To make the requital at last
For the eaten children, the blood clot cold with time.
O my king, my king,
How shall I pay you in tears,
Speak my affection in words?
You lie in that spider's web,
In a desecrating death breathe out your life,
Lie ignominiously
Defeated by a crooked death
And the two-edged cleaver's stroke.

CLYTEMNESTRA. Did he not, too, contrive a crooked
Horror for the house? My child by him,
Shoot that I raised, much-wept-for Iphigeneia,
He treated her like this;
So suffering like this he need not make
Any great brag in Hell having paid with death
Dealt by the sword for work of his own beginning.

CHORUS. I am at a loss for thought, I lack
All nimble counsel as to where
To turn when the house is falling.

I fear the house-collapsing crashing
Blizzard of blood—of which these drops are earnest.
Now is Destiny sharpening her justice
On other whetstones for a new infliction.
O earth, earth, if only you had received me
Before I saw this man lie here as if in bed
In a bath lined with silver.
Who will bury him? Who will keen him?
Will you, having killed your own husband,
Dare now to lament him
And after great wickedness make
Unamending amends to his ghost?
And who above this godlike hero's grave
Pouring praises and tears
Will grieve with a genuine heart?

CLYTEMNESTRA. It is not your business to attend to that.
By my hand he fell low, lies low and dead,
And his household need not weep him.
For Iphigeneia his daughter
Tenderly, as is right,
Will meet her father at the rapid ferry of sorrows,
Put her arms round him and kiss him!

CHORUS. Reproach answers reproach,
It is hard to decide,
The catcher is caught, the killer pays for his kill,
But the law abides while Zeus abides enthroned
That the wrongdoer suffers. That is established.
Who could expel from the house the seed of the Curse?
The race is soldered in sockets of Doom and Vengeance.

CLYTEMNESTRA. In this you say what is right and the will of God.
But for my part I am ready to make a contract
With the Evil Genius of the House of Atreus
To accept what has been till now, hard though it is,
But that for the future he shall leave this house
And wear away some other stock with deaths
Imposed among themselves. Of my possessions
A small part will suffice if only I
Can rid these walls of the mad exchange of murder.

Enter AEGISTHUS, *followed by soldiers.*

AEGISTHUS. O welcome light of a justice-dealing day!
From now on I will say that the gods, avenging men,
Look down from above on the crimes of earth,
Seeing as I do in woven robes of the Furies,
This man lying here—a sight to warm my heart—
Paying for the crooked violence of his father.
For his father Atreus, when he ruled the country,
Because his power was challenged, hounded out
From state and home his own brother Thyestes.
My father—let me be plain—was this Thyestes,
Who later came back home a suppliant,
There, miserable, found so much asylum
As not to die on the spot, stain the ancestral floor.
But to show his hospitality godless Atreus
Gave him an eager if not a loving welcome,
Pretending a day of feasting and rich meats
Served my father with his children's flesh.
The hands and feet, fingers and toes, he hid
At the bottom of the dish. My father sitting apart
Took unknowing the unrecognizable portion
And ate of a dish that has proved, as you see, expensive.
But when he knew he had eaten worse than poison
He fell back groaning, vomiting their flesh,
And invoking a hopeless doom on the sons of Pelops
Kicked over the table to confirm his curse—
So may the whole race perish!
Result of this—you see this man lie here.
I stitched this murder together; it was my title.
Me the third son he left, an unweaned infant,
To share the bitterness of my father's exile.
But I grew up and Justice brought me back,
I grappled this man while still beyond his door,
Having pieced together the programme of his ruin.
So now would even death be beautiful to me
Having seen Agamemnon in the nets of Justice.

LEADER. Aegisthus. I cannot respect brutality in distress.
You claim that you deliberately killed this prince

And that you alone planned this pitiful murder.
Be sure that in your turn your head shall not escape
The people's volleyed curses mixed with stones.

AEGISTHUS. Do you speak so who sit at the lower oar
While those on the upper bench control the ship?
Old as you are, you will find it is a heavy load
To go to school when old to learn the lesson of tact.
For old age, too, jail and hunger are fine
Instructors in wisdom, second-sighted doctors.
You have eyes. Cannot you see?
Do not kick against the pricks. The blow will hurt you.

LEADER. You woman waiting in the house for those who return from battle
While you seduce their wives! Was it you devised
The death of a master of armies?

AEGISTHUS. And these words, too, prepare the way for tears.
Contrast your voice with the voice of Orpheus: he
Led all things after him bewitched with joy, but you
Having stung me with your silly yelps shall be
Led off yourself, to prove more mild when mastered.

LEADER. Indeed! So you are now to be king of Argos,
You who, when you had plotted the king's death,
Did not even dare to do that thing yourself!

AEGISTHUS. No. For the trick of it was clearly woman's work.
I was suspect, an enemy of old.
But now I shall try with Agamemnon's wealth
To rule the people. Any who is disobedient
I will harness in a heavy yoke, no tracehorse work for him
Like barley-fed colt, but hateful hunger lodging
Beside him in the dark will see his temper soften.

LEADER. Why with your cowardly soul did you yourself
Not strike this man but left that work to a woman
Whose presence pollutes our country and its gods?
But Orestes—does he somewhere see the light
That he may come back here by favor of fortune
And kill this pair and prove the final victor?

AEGISTHUS (*Summoning his guards*). Well, if such is your design in deeds and words, you will quickly learn—
Here my friends, here my guards, there is work for you at hand.

LEADER. Come then, hands on hilts, be each and all of us prepared.

The old men and the guards threaten each other.

AEGISTHUS. Very well! I too am ready to meet death with sword in hand.

LEADER. We are glad you speak of dying. We accept your words for luck.

CLYTEMNESTRA. No, my dearest, do not so. Add no more to the train of wrong.
To reap these many present wrongs is harvest enough of misery.
Enough of misery. Start no more. Our hands are red.
But do you, and you old men, go home and yield to fate in time,
In time before you suffer. We have acted as we had to act.
If only our afflictions now could prove enough, we should agree—
We who have been so hardly mauled in the heavy claws of the evil god.
So stands my word, a woman's, if any man thinks fit to hear.

AEGISTHUS. But to think that these should thus pluck the blooms of an idle tongue.
And should throw out words like these, giving the evil god his chance,
And should miss the path of prudence and insult their master so!

LEADER. It is not the Argive way to fawn upon a cowardly man.

AEGISTHUS. Perhaps. But I in later days will take further steps with you.

LEADER. Not if the god who rules the family guides Orestes to his home.

AEGISTHUS. Yes. I know that men in exile feed themselves on barren hopes.

LEADER. Go on, grow fat defiling justice . . . while you have your hour.

AEGISTHUS. Do not think you will not pay me a price for your stupidity.

LEADER. Boast on in your self-assurance, like a cock beside his hen.

CLYTEMNESTRA. Pay no heed, Aegisthus, to these futile barkings.

You and I,
Masters of this house, from now shall order all things well.

They enter the palace.

THE *Antigone* OF SOPHOCLES

Translated by Maurice F. Neufeld

INTRODUCTION

IN BOTH personality and achievement Sophocles (*ca.* 496–406 B.C.) was a true son of the Golden Age in Athens. Born in a prosperous family, possessed of physical beauty, liberally educated, an accomplished musician, actor, and conversationalist, and a consistent winner of dramatic prizes, he was also successful in public life, serving twice as a general and being chosen a member of the treasury board of the Delian Confederacy. His contributions to the technique of the theater included increasing the number of actors from two to three, inventing scene-painting, and breaking the traditional tetralogy into plays with different subjects.

Sophocles' dramatic art, distinguished for closely woven plots, penetrating analysis of character, and poetic fluency and poise, is revealed admirably in the *Antigone*. In the following translation much of the poetic quality is inevitably lost, but an attempt has been made in both dialogue and choruses to approximate the meters of the original.

The main theme is the conflict between an individual and absolute authority, a theme which concerns us because it has assumed special importance in our own time. Antigone, sensitive to the obligations of religious duty and family devotion, insists that those obligations are superior to any imposed by a dictator, regardless of the price she must pay for her disobedience. King Creon, on the other hand, is equally convinced that law and order, enforced by his authority, are of primary importance. The clash of these unswerving convictions results in tragedy. But along with the central theme there are several others interwoven. One is the psychological conflict between the sexes. Another is the conflict between two theories of government, the dictatorial one pronounced by Creon, the democratic one urged by his son, Haemon. And implied by the outcome of the play is the final theme, also of democratic significance: that the clash of dogmatic and emotional wills can only be resolved successfully by an attitude of give-and-take on both sides and the exercise of reasoned judgment.

Similarly complicated are the characters in this play. Creon and Antigone are neither of them drawn in black and white; their motives are exceedingly complex. Antigone is courageous in defying Creon on what she believes are compelling grounds of religious conscience and love for her persecuted brother. But she is also swayed by less idealistic motives: she hates Creon intensely and taunts him without mercy; she is resentful of his assumption of masculine superiority; she scorns Ismene beyond the deserts of that well-meaning but ineffective sister; and she glories overmuch in martyrdom. And, in perhaps the psychologically most interesting scene in the play, when she is being led out to her death she becomes a prey to agonizing self-pity and tries to convince herself and the Chorus by sorry logic that in this one instance she was justified in breaking the law. (That scene disturbed Goethe so much that he wanted it removed from the play; but actually it is quite in keeping with Antigone's high-strung nature and makes her a much more interesting character.) Her refusal to call on Haemon for help or even think of him is a further indication of her intense self-will. She consistently refuses to admit that there is anything to be said on the other side, or any possibility of reasonable compromise.

Creon's motives are likewise complex. He is genuinely patriotic, seeking his city's welfare. But his concept of a ruler's responsibility is a narrow one, he despises women, he resents his son's devotion to Antigone. His basic feeling of insecurity is shown by his suspicion of everyone and by his speedy reversal of policy once the priest adds the sanction of religion to the objections already raised against his ruling by less formidable adversaries, including the Chorus. To his credit is his eagerness to assume full responsibility for the ultimate disaster.

Other elements in the play which should be noted are the intellectual and emotional reaction of the Chorus to the action, the irony of the opening ode on victory and peace, the final foreboding in the famous choral song, "Many things are wonderful, but none more wonderful than Man," and the decisive characterization in the minor roles. If the question be raised as to whose is the tragic error, the answer must be that it is shared by both Antigone and Creon: the error of arbitrary self-will. As such Sophocles' play has as much relevance for our times as when it was first written and produced, about the year 441 B.C.

Mr. Neufeld's translation was made when he was a student at the Experimental College of the University of Wisconsin, was dedicated to Alexander Meiklejohn, director of the college, and was produced by the Experimental College Players on February 28 and March 1, 1930.

—WALTER R. AGARD

THE TEXT is that of Sir R. C. Jebb (3rd edition, Cambridge, 1900).

THE CHARACTERS

ANTIGONE, ISMENE } Daughters of Oedipus
CREON, King of Thebes
EURYDICE, his wife
HAEMON, his son
TIRESIAS, the blind prophet
WATCHMAN
MESSENGER
CHORUS OF OLD MEN

Before the palace of CREON *in Thebes. Dawn.*

Enter ANTIGONE *and* ISMENE.

ANTIGONE. My sister, dear Ismene, my own sister,
Of all those griefs we owe to Oedipus,
Do you know any Zeus has not fulfilled
For both of us while we are still alive?
For nothing painful, nothing ruinous,
And no dishonor and no shame exist
I have not seen, in your grief or in mine.
And now, what is this edict they are saying
That Creon has proclaimed to all the city?
You know of it? And have you learned the news?
Or are you unaware that evils suited
For enemies are coming to our friends?

ISMENE. No word of friends, Antigone, for good
Or bad, has come to me since we were robbed
Of our two brothers, murdered in one day
By the double blow. And since the night just past,
When the Argive army left, I know no more,
If fate is brighter or more sorrowful.

ANTIGONE. But I knew everything, and sent for you
To come outside so you could hear alone.

ISMENE. What is the trouble? For your restlessness
Shows that your mind is seething with dark thoughts.

ANTIGONE. What? Has not Creon judged of our two brothers,
One worthy of a grave, the other not?
They say that he has buried Eteocles
With due respect, regarding right and custom,
To be esteemed among the dead below.
But the corpse of Polynices, so they say,
Our ruler has commanded none shall mourn
Or bury him, but leave unwept, unburied,
Sweet treasure for the birds that will appraise
His corpse as lovely food. And such decrees
They say good Creon sets for you and me,
Even for me, and will come here to make
His order plain to those who do not know;
Nor takes the matter lightly, but whoever
Should disobey in anything, will find
His death by public stoning in the city.
So now you know, and you shall soon reveal
If you are really nobly born, or just
The coward daughter of a noble line.

ISMENE. If Creon has commanded this, poor sister,
How could I help? How could I be of use?

ANTIGONE. Decide if you will share the work with me—

ISMENE. What venture now? What are you thinking of?

ANTIGONE. If you will help my hand to lift the dead.

ISMENE. You plan to bury him against the law?

ANTIGONE. My brother and yours, I will, if you will not.
I never will be caught deserting him.

ISMENE. Reckless still, when Creon has forbidden?

ANTIGONE. He has no right to keep me from my own.

ISMENE. Think, sister, how our father died, despised
And scorned, when sins discovered by himself
Forced him to strike both eyes with his own hand.
His mother and his wife, the double name,
Outraged her life with rope, twisted for hanging.

And lastly our two brothers, in one day,
Each murdering the other, wretched ones,
Worked out their death with one another's hands.
Now we in turn, we two left all alone,
Think, how we shall die more miserably,
If in defiance of the strength of law,
We should resist the order of the king.
We must remember, first, that we were born
Women, who should not strive with men; and next,
As we are ruled by the stronger, so we must
Yield to men in this, and even things more painful.
I, therefore, asking all the dead forgiveness,
Since I am forced, will yield to those in office.
Only a fool does more than he is able.

ANTIGONE. I would not urge you. No. Nor if you wished
To do so, would I welcome you to help me.
Follow your own nature. I will bury him.
To die in doing that is beautiful.
For I shall rest, beloved, with him I loved,
Performing righteous deeds in ways unsanctioned.
For I must please the dead below much longer
Than people here. For I shall be there always.
You, if you will, insult the laws of gods.

ISMENE. I do them no dishonor, but to work
Against the state, my strength is weak for that.

ANTIGONE. Make these excuses. I will go to heap
The earth above the brother whom I love.

ISMENE. Unhappy sister, how I fear for you!

ANTIGONE. You fear for me? Look after your own fate.

ISMENE. At least, reveal this plan to none, but keep
It closely hidden, as I, too, intend.

ANTIGONE. Go. Tell. You shall be hated more for silence,
If you do not proclaim my plan to all.

ISMENE. You have a boiling heart for chilling deeds.

ANTIGONE. I know I please those I need most to please.

ISMENE. Yes, if you can. You seek the impossible.

ANTIGONE. When I can do no more, I shall have finished.

ISMENE. But to begin with, there is little sense
In hunting things that never can be caught.

ANTIGONE. If you will talk like that, you shall be hated
By me, and justly hated by the dead.
Leave me alone, together with my folly,
To suffer this that seems to you so dreadful.
For I shall never suffer anything
So dreadful as to die unbeautifully.

ISMENE. If it seems wise, go, remembering,
Although you start upon a foolish venture,
That you are really dear to those you love.

ANTIGONE *leaves.* ISMENE *goes into the palace.*

CHORUS

Beam of the sun, fairest light of beautiful lights that have ever dawned
Here on Thebes of the seven gates,
You shine now, appearing at last,
Sun, the eyelid of golden day, coming over the streams of Dirce.
You have stirred the man, the white-shielded, fully-armored, coming from Argos,
As he ran forward, headlong in flight, urging him into swifter motion.

The armed men of Polynices marched to our land
Because of the quarrels and wrangling disputes,
Shrilly, with screams,
Shrieked like the eagle and flew over our land,
Covered with wings that are white as the snow,
Armed with many swords,
With horse-hair that waved in the plumed helms.

Standing over our houses he yawned for blood with the killing spears,
Circling the mouths of the seven gates.
He left, before filling his jaws
With our blood, before the Hephaestus torch, the torch of the fire-god, pine-fed,
Seized the crown of towers. Such was the battle-clatter that stretched behind him,
A struggle hard to conquer in, while wrestling the Dragon, unconquered Thebes.

For Zeus exceedingly hates high boasts
Of a loud tongue, and when he sighted them
Advance, coming like the flood of the river stream,
And clanging with boldness of bright gold,
Threw hurled fire on Capaneus rushing there now

To the last of the goals,
All ready to shout in victory.

Struck back, he fell with a crash and was hurled to the hard ground,
The fire-bearer who, at that time, when he raged with eagerness,
Frenzied, blew against Thebes with blasts of the most hostile of winds.
But events turned in other ways,
While to the rest, Ares, the right-handed trace-horse, had now scattered doom, the mighty helper.

For the seven captains against seven gates,
Equals who were placed facing equals, had left
Tribute of brass to the god turning all, Zeus.
Except those two, abhorrent, the two
Men, born of one mother, of one father,
Having fought against each other with doubly
Powerful spears, sharing the same death.

But since now victory giving all glory has come,
Joyous in the gladness of Thebes-of-the-many-chariots,
Let us, after the battles, surrender to forgetfulness,
Visiting all the temples of the gods
All through the night, bringing the chorus, and then let Bacchius lead us, shaking all Thebes.

But now, the new king of the land comes here,
Creon, the new leader, son of Menoeceus,
And advanced by the latest events of the gods.
What plan is he now urging in his mind
That he has asked for this group of the old men,
Specially summoned,
Called out by the general mandate?

Enter Creon *from the palace.*

Creon. Old men, the gods have once again restored
The safety of our city, tossed about
Upon the heavy sea. So I have brought
You here, apart from all the rest, by order,
Because I know you always have respected
The power of the throne in the time of Laius;
Again, when Oedipus upheld the state.
And even when he died, with faithful hearts
You stood around the children of his house.
And since these two have fallen in one day
By double doom, each murdered by the other,
And stained by blood from one another's hand,
I now possess the power and the throne
By closeness of relation to the dead.
It is impossible to learn completely
The heart and mind and judgment of a man
Until he has been seen to be accomplished
In ruling and in giving of the law.
For, to me, whoever guides the state
And fails to advocate the wisest plans,
But fearing something, holds his lips shut,
He seems to me, and always seemed, most worthless.
Whoever should regard or make his friend
More than his land, I count no man at all.
For I, I swear by Zeus, who knows all things,
Would not be silent if I saw distress
Instead of safety coming to the people.
Nor would I ever make that man my friend
Who is an enemy against my land,
Remembering this, she is the one who saves us,
And sailing with her secure, we gain true friends.
Such are the principles by which I make
This city prosper. In accord with them
I have announced to all the citizens
The law about the sons of Oedipus.
Eteocles, who fell defending this city,
While winning all distinction with his spear,
Let him be laid within the grave, and crowned
With honors worthy of the noblest dead.
However, for his brother Polynices,
Who came from exile and then tried to burn
His native land and all his father's gods
With fire, and tried to taste his people's blood,
And lead the rest in slavery, this man,
(And I have published this throughout the city)
No one shall honor with a grave, and none
Lament, but let his corpse be left unburied
For birds and dogs to eat, a shameful sight.
This is my wish. Evil men shall never stand
Before the just in honor because of me.
But he who is well-minded toward the state
Will be esteemed by me in life and death.

Chorus. Son of Menoeceus, Creon, this is your will,
Toward both the city's enemy and friend.
And you have power to take what course you wish

In dealing with the dead, or us, the living.
CREON. Then be observant keepers of these orders.
CHORUS. Please lay this burden on some younger man.
CREON. But watchers for the body have been found.
CHORUS. If so, what further task have you for us?
CREON. You must not side with those who disobey.
CHORUS. Who is such a fool? What man is in love with death?
CREON. Death is what he will earn. Yet greediness
Has often ruined men through futile hopes.

Enter WATCHMAN.

WATCHMAN. Sir, I will not say that I stand here
All out of breath from speed, or that I ran.
For many times I hesitated, stopped
By thoughts, upon the road, and turned around.
My mind was talking hard to me, and said,
"Where are you going, you fool? You'll answer for it
When you get there." "Fool, wasting time again?
If someone tells this news to Creon first,
How can you help but suffer in the end?"
Debating so, I hurried slowly on,
And travelling in this way, short roads grow long.
At last, to come to you here won the day.
And even if I haven't much to tell,
Yet I shall speak. I'm here and trust to luck
I won't get any more than I deserve.
CREON. Why is it you are so discouraged then?
WATCHMAN. I want to tell you first about myself.
That thing, I didn't do, nor saw who did.
It wouldn't be right for you to punish me.
CREON. Your aim is careful and you fence your story
On every side. You bring some news, that is plain.
WATCHMAN. It's true. And bad news makes me hesitate.
CREON. Will you not speak, and when you finish, go?
WATCHMAN. I'm speaking now. The corpse, someone has buried,
And gone away, and sprinkled thirsty dust
Upon the flesh, and done the fitting rites.
CREON. What do you say? What man has dared to do this?
WATCHMAN. I do not know. No pickaxe mark, or dirt
Thrown up by mattock was there at the place.
The ground was hard and dry and bare, unbroken,
Without the track of wheels, no sign of the doer.
And when the first day-watch reported it,
Annoying wonder fell upon us all,
For he had disappeared, not in a grave,
But only dust was lightly scattered over,
As though somebody shunned a dreadful curse.
No signs appeared that any beast of prey
Or any dog had come to him, or torn him.
Then angry words came clashing among us,
Guard cursing guard, and would have turned to blows,
With none to stop us. For each man was guilty;
No one convicted; all denied all knowledge.
We were prepared to handle red-hot iron,
To walk through fire, and swear by all the gods
We had not done, nor knew who planned or did it.
At last, when no more questions came, one spoke
And made us turn our faces to the ground
In fear. We did not know how we could answer,
Nor if we did the thing that he advised,
How we could prosper. His advice was this:
The matter should be brought to you, not hidden.
And this seemed best. The lot selected me,
Unlucky as I am, to win the prize.
So here I am, unwilling as unwelcome.
For no one likes the bringer of bad news.
CHORUS. My thoughts, Sir, have been hinting for some time,
Perhaps this may have been the work of gods?
CREON. Stop, before you anger me by talking,
And you are proved at once both old and foolish.
You speak intolerably, saying gods
Have any thought for such a corpse as this.
Rewarding service, did they cover him,
Who came to burn their pillar-circled shrines,
And votive treasures, and to burn their land,
And scatter all their laws upon the winds?
Or do you see gods honoring the wicked?
That cannot be. But from the first, some men
In town have been dissatisfied with me,

Shaking their heads in secret, and have not kept
Their necks within the harness as they should,
Like men who are contented with my rule.
I have no doubt that by such men as these
The watchmen have been bribed, and led to do this.
For nothing evil as money ever grew
In use among mankind. This ruins cities,
This drives so many men from home, instructs
And leads the honest minds of men astray
To deal in treachery, and teaches men
To know all wickedness and godless deeds.
Those who buried him for money can be sure
That they will pay the price, sooner or later.
As Zeus has still my reverence, know this,
I tell it to you and I swear to it,
If you fail to find the man who buried him,
And bring him here to me, before my eyes,
Mere death will not suffice for you, until
Hung up alive, you have revealed this outrage.
And learn from this time on where gain is won,
And steal there in the future. Learn this, too,
Gain should not be desired from every source.
For you will find from such disgraceful earnings
More people cursed than rendered safe, or bettered.

WATCHMAN. Then can I answer, or just turn and go?

CREON. Do you not see how what you say annoys me?

WATCHMAN. It stings your ears, or does it sting your soul?

CREON. Why should you wonder where my sorrow is?

WATCHMAN. The doer grieves your mind, but I, your ears.

CREON. It is very plain that you were born a babbler.

WATCHMAN. At any rate, I never buried him.

CREON. But even more, you sold your soul for silver.

WATCHMAN. It's sad when he who judges, judges falsely.

CREON. Now quibble all you want of judgment, but,
If you do not find the man who did this crime,
You will admit that guilty gain brings sorrow.

WATCHMAN. I hope he's found. But if he's caught or not—
Good fortune settles that—you won't see me
Again, for now, saved way beyond my hope
And thought, I ought to give the gods great thanks.

WATCHMAN *leaves.*

CHORUS

Many things are wonderful, but none more wonderful than man.
Over the white of the sea he goes, driven by the stormy southwind of winter;
He wanders under the surges,
Engulfed by the waves around him.
And the most ancient of the gods, the Earth,
The everlasting, the unwearied, he wears away,
Rolling the plowshares, as years follow on years,
Turning the furrows with mules, the offspring of horses.

Flocks of the nimble-hearted birds he snares, and all the herds of wild
Beasts that wander in the fields, and the ocean brood of the sea he catches
In the woven coils of the meshy net,
This man forever thoughtful.
And creatures roaming in the fields,
And all the herds that roam on the mountains,
He masters artfully, yoking the shaggy-necked
Horse, and the never-tiring mountain bull.

And language, and wind-rapid thought,
And feelings of social life, he has taught himself; and how to run from the arrows
Of uncomfortable frost when the weather is clear or stormy;
Ever resourceful. Without resource he never meets
The future. From death alone he shall not invent escape,
But from baffling diseases he has found release.

The subtle designs of his skill,
Ingenious beyond thought, now bring him to evil and now to good.
While honoring his country's laws and the justice he swore to uphold,
He is honored in his city. Cityless is he,
Who thanks to his rashness, lives in dishonor. May he never

Share my hearth or think my thoughts, who lives in sin.

I linger in doubt at this portentous sight.
But how can I see and then deny
That this is the girl, unfortunate
Antigone,
Child of unfortunate father, Oedipus.
But what? They are not bringing you here
Disloyal to the ordered commands of the king;
Surely you are not taken in folly?

Enter WATCHMAN, *leading* ANTIGONE.

WATCHMAN. Now here she is, the one who buried him.
We caught her in the act. But where is Creon?
CHORUS. He comes out of the palace just in time.

Enter CREON.

CREON. But what is this I am coming just in time for?
WATCHMAN. Sir, men should swear nothing impossible.
For after-thoughts show up your first opinion.
I could have sworn I would not soon be here
Again, right after I was stormed by threats.
But since the joy that passes every hope
Is like no other joy in open fullness,
I come, although I break my oath in coming,
And bring this girl, caught honoring the dead.
No casting lots this time. This luck was mine,
And no one else's. Sir, you take her now,
And question as you wish. But I am free,
By right, for good and all, from all this trouble.
CREON. You bring her here, and found her where, and how?
WATCHMAN. Burying the man. Now you know everything.
CREON. You understand and mean the things you say?
WATCHMAN. I saw her burying the corpse you had forbidden.
There, do I speak more clearly, plainly now?
CREON. Where did you see her? Was she caught in the act?
WATCHMAN. This is the way it was. When we came there
With all those awful threats of yours on us,
We swept off all the dust that hid the body,
And laid the wet corpse altogether bare;
We sat upon the hill, against the wind
So that the stink from his body would not hit us.
Each kept the other man awake with threats,
If any should be careless of his task.
For some time this went on, until the sun's
Bright circle stood within the arch of heaven;
The heat burned. Suddenly a whirlwind lifted
A cloud of dust from earth that blurred the sky,
And filled the plain, and tattered all the leaves
Within the wood, and all the air was choked.
We closed our eyes and faced the plague of gods.
And when the storm had passed, after some time,
The girl was seen. She cried a piercing cry,
The bitter cry of a mother bird, as when
Within the empty nest, she sees the bed
Stripped of her young. She, when she saw the corpse
Was bare, began to weep, and cursed the doers.
At once, she brought dry, thirsty dust in her hands,
And raising up a jar of hammered bronze,
She crowned the dead with offerings poured three times.
On seeing this, at once we hurried forward
And quickly caught her. She was not confused.
We charged her with her past and present doings;
She denied nothing, to my joy and pain.
For getting clear of trouble brings great joy,
But bringing friends to grief is very painful.
However, to consider all such things
Less weighty than my safety, that's my way.
CREON. You there, you, with head bent toward the ground,
Do you acknowledge or deny this crime?
ANTIGONE. I say I did it; I will not deny.
CREON. (*To* WATCHMAN) Go where you will, clear of a serious charge.

WATCHMAN *leaves.*

(*To* ANTIGONE) You tell me now, and not at length, but briefly,
You knew the edict had forbidden this?
ANTIGONE. I knew. How could I help it? It was plain.

CREON. And you presumed to disobey these laws?
ANTIGONE. Yes. For it was not Zeus who made this edict,
And Justice, dwelling with the gods below,
Had never set such laws as these among men.
Nor did I think your edicts of such force,
That you, being just a man, could override
Unwritten and unchanging laws of gods.
Their life is not of now or yesterday,
But always. No man knows when they appeared.
In view of them, I would not, through the fear
Of human will, meet judgment from the gods.
That I must die I knew. Why should I not?
Though you had never even made an edict.
And if I die before my time, I shall gain.
For when one lives, as I, in many troubles,
How can he help but find a gain in death?
Meeting my death this way does not pain me.
But when my mother's son had died, if I
Had left his corpse unburied, I would have grieved.
For this, I am not grieved. And if I seem
To do some foolish things at present, perhaps
The man who charges folly is the fool.
CHORUS. The headstrong, savage temper of this child
Comes from her headstrong father. She does not know
The way to bend before her griefs and troubles.
CREON. Yet I would have you know most stubborn spirits
Fall hardest, and the strongest iron, baked
Within a furnace to excessive hardness,
You see most often snap, most often shatter.
And horses, showing temper, I have found
Are managed by a little leather bridle.
There is no room for pride in those who are
Their neighbors' slaves. This girl was skilled in pride
When she transgressed the laws that had been published.
And then, that done, the further insolence,
To boast of it and laugh at having done it.
I am no longer man, she is the man,
If this success remains with her unchallenged.
No, she can be my sister's child, or closer
Than all who bend before our household Zeus.
She and her sister never will escape
The worst punishment. I also count Ismene
An equal plotter of this burial.
But summon her. I saw her even now,
Within the house, raving, uncontrolled.
It happens often that the stealthy heart
Will be convicted long before the act
When men will fashion mischief in the dark.
But I hate that, when one is caught in crime,
And seeks to glorify his wickedness.
ANTIGONE. You want what more than, having caught, to kill me?
CREON. I? Nothing. Having that, then I have all.
ANTIGONE. So why delay? For nothing in your words
Can give me pleasure. May they never please.
And what I say, I am sure, displeases you.
Yet how could I have gained more glorious glory,
Than placing my own brother in a grave?
All here would say that they approve of this
If fear of speaking did not seal their lips.
For rulers, fortunate in much besides,
Have power to do and say what they desire.
CREON. Of all the Thebans you alone think so.
ANTIGONE. They also do, but shut their mouths to you.
CREON. And are you not ashamed to act unlike them?
ANTIGONE. No, there is no disgrace in honoring a brother.
CREON. Then was it not a brother, who died, his rival?
ANTIGONE. Mine, by one mother and one father too.
CREON. Then why pay honors that dishonor him?
ANTIGONE. The dead man would not testify to that.
CREON. Yes, if you honor him just like the wicked.
ANTIGONE. It was no slave, who died, it was his brother.
CREON. Wasting this land, and he, defending it.
ANTIGONE. Yet all the same, these rites are claimed by death.
CREON. The good should not share with the bad alike.
ANTIGONE. Who knows but this is blameless there below?
CREON. A hated man, though dead, is not a friend.
ANTIGONE. My nature joins in love and not in hate.
CREON. Then go down there; if you must love, love them.
But while I live, no woman masters me.
CHORUS. Ismene is coming from the gate,

And is weeping the tears that sisters weep. The cloud
Upon her brow has marred her darkly-flushing face,
And it falls in rain
Upon her beautiful cheek.

Enter ISMENE *from the palace.*

CREON. You, lurking like a viper in my house,
While I was unaware of nurturing
Two pests to rise against my throne, come, tell me,
Will you confess your sharing in this burial,
Or will you swear that you knew nothing of it?
ISMENE. I did the deed if she allows this claim.
I take my share and burden of the charge.
ANTIGONE. No, justice will not let you. You did not wish,
Nor I allow you to take part in it.
ISMENE. But in your time of grief, I am not ashamed
To make myself a sharer of your sorrow.
ANTIGONE. Whose deed, the dead and Hades are the witness.
A friend in words is not the friend I love.
ISMENE. I beg you, sister, not to scorn my dying
With you and paying honor to the dead.
ANTIGONE. No, do not share my death and claim for yours
What was not yours. My dying is enough.
ISMENE. What good is life to me, deprived of you?
ANTIGONE. Ask Creon, for you care about him most.
ISMENE. Why pain me so when nothing like this helps?
ANTIGONE. And if I really mock, in grief I mock you.
ISMENE. But even now, what can I do to help?
ANTIGONE. Save yourself. I do not grudge your freedom.
ISMENE. So I, unhappy, shall not share your fate?
ANTIGONE. No, for you chose to live, and I to die—
ISMENE. But not through any words I left unsaid.
ANTIGONE. And I seemed wise to some, and you to others.
ISMENE. But now the error is the same for us.
ANTIGONE. Take heart. You live. But long ago I gave
My life to death so I could serve the dead.
CREON. One girl has just now shown herself a fool,
The other since the first day she was born.
ISMENE. No, King, however reason starts, it never
Lingers long with the unfortunate, but leaves.
CREON. Yours did in doing evil with this criminal.
ISMENE. How could I live alone, away from her?
CREON. No, do not speak of her. She lives no more.
ISMENE. What, you will kill the bride of your own son?
CREON. The fields of others are left for him to plow.
ISMENE. But not such harmony as grew between them.
CREON. I do not like evil women for my sons.
ANTIGONE. Dear Haemon, how your father dishonors you.
CREON. You and your marriage trouble me enough.
CHORUS. And you will really rob your son of her?
CREON. No, death will stop this wedding for me now.
CHORUS. So it is clear, it seems, that she must die.
CREON. To you and me. No more delaying. Servants,
Take them inside. They must be women now,
And not allowed to roam around. For even
The brave will run when they see death approach.

Attendants lead ISMENE *and* ANTIGONE *into the palace.*

CHORUS

Fortunate are they whose years have never tasted sorrow.
For when once a house has been shaken by the gods, the curse
Never fails, but spreads throughout multitudes of generations,
Even as the swelling sea spreads over the lower waters
Under the wild Thracian sea-winds, and rolls from the bottom
The black sand of the storm, and as the headlands sullenly
Resound with roaring while they are beaten by the onrushing waves.

I see from of old the sorrows of the house of Labdacus,

Heaped upon the sorrows of men already gone;
Generation is not freed by generation, but some god
Strikes, and there is no release. Even now the hope that has spread
Upon the last root of the house of Oedipus,
Now, even now, the bloody knife of the gods below,
And folly of speech, and craziness of mind have cut off that hope.

For Zeus, what trespasses of men can strip you of your power?
That power that sleep, all-snaring sleep, or the untiring
Months of the gods cannot master, but you, not growing old with time,
Possess the power in the dazzling splendor of high Olympus.
And through the future, and through the past,
And the time that shall come, this law
Shall always hold, for nothing vast
Enters into the life of men without great suffering.

For wide-wandering hope is comforting gain to many men,
But to many the treachery of empty longings.
Hope comes unawares to man, until he has burned his feet
In hot fire. For in wisdom was the famous saying uttered,
That evil always seems good
To him whose judgment the god
Entices toward mischief.
And he spends but short time entirely free from suffering.

But here is Haemon, the youngest
Of your sons. Does he come grieving
For the fate of his promised
Bride, Antigone, and is he bitter
At the vanished hope of his marriage?

Enter HAEMON.

CREON. We shall soon know, and more than seers could say.
My son, because you learned the sentenced fate
Of your bride, do you come raging at your father?
Or are we dear to you, do what we may?

HAEMON. My father, I am yours. And you devise
The wisest rules for me that I shall follow.
No marriage ever will be thought more gain
To me than the wisdom of your management.

CREON. Yes, so it should be settled in your heart,
My son, to stand behind your father's judgments.
For this men pray to have obedient children
Grow up about them in their homes, to pay
The father's enemy with evil things,
And honor, as their father does, his friend.
But he who has unprofitable children,
What shall we say but that he has produced
Pain for himself, loud laughter for his foes?
My son, do not give up your better judgment
For any girl because of pleasure's bidding,
While knowing that embraces soon grow cold
When she who shares your house with you is false.
What ulcer can be worse than the faithless friend?
With loathing, leave this girl, as if she were
Your enemy, to find a man in Hades.
For since I caught her, the only one in the city
In open disobedience, I will
Not make myself a liar to the city,
But I shall kill her. Let her pray to Zeus,
The god of kindred. If I train my own
To be disorderly, then I must bear
Surely, with those who are outside my own.
For he who is a faithful man at home
Will prove himself upright in public too.
But he who forces law with violence,
And thinks that he can dictate to the rulers,
That man will never win applause from me.
Whoever is established by the state
Should be obeyed in matters large and small,
In matters just, and things unjust as well.
And I am sure this man would govern wisely,
And easily be ruled, and in the storm
Of spears would hold his ground where he was placed,
A true and loyal comrade to his friend.
There is no greater fault than lawlessness.
This ruins cities, overturns the homes,
And when this joins the spear, the ranks are broken.
Obedience saves most lives whose course is steady.
And so, we must defend the public order,

And we must not be subject to a woman.
Better defeat, if need be, from a man,
Than to be known as weaker than a woman.
CHORUS. Unless we are deceived by our old age,
You seem to say with wisdom what you say.
HAEMON. Father, the gods plant reasoning in men,
The highest of all things that we possess.
I could not say, nor would know how to say,
In what respects you have not spoken rightly.
But surely someone else can be right too.
I naturally watch for you all things
That men will do, or say, or find to blame.
For your eye terrifies the common man
And checks the words you would not wish to hear.
But I can hear these murmurs in the dark.
I know just how the city mourns this girl,
"She, of all women, least deserving it,
Is suffering worst death for noblest deeds.
And when her brother fell in bloody fight,
And lay unburied, she would not leave him
To be devoured by savage dogs and birds.
Is she not worthy of some golden honor?"
Such guarded talk spreads secretly around.
To me, my father, nothing that I own
Is dearer than your welfare and success.
For what can be of more delight to children
Than a successful father's honored name?
Or to a father than his son's renown?
So do not wear one mood within yourself,
That what you say, and nothing else, is right.
When any man thinks he alone is wise,
And that in speech and thought there is none like him,
When he will be revealed, will be found empty.
No, though a man is wise, there is no shame
To learn, learn much, and not to be too firm.
You see along the winter streams how trees
Bend down and save their branches, while all those
Remaining stiff go trunk and root to ruin.
So, he who tightly draws the vessel's sail,
And never slackens, soon upsets the boat,
And ends it all with benches upside down.
Lay down your temper and give way to change.
If an opinion is allowed from me,
Though younger, I still think a man should be
By nature, very thoughtful. And if not,
For usually the scale does not incline so,
Then it is good to learn from good advisers.
CHORUS. You ought to learn of him, if he speaks well,
Sir; and you, Haemon, you should learn of him.
For both of you have spoken very well.
CREON. Men of my age, are we to learn to think
From men who are his age, from men so young?
HAEMON. Yes. Nothing but the truth. If I am young,
You should regard my merit, not my years.
CREON. Then is it merit to respect the evil?
HAEMON. I would not ever wish to honor evil.
CREON. Is she not tainted with that same disease?
HAEMON. With one accord, the men of Thebes say no.
CREON. And shall the city tell me how to rule?
HAEMON. You see, there, you have spoken like a child.
CREON. And so I am to govern in this land
By reasoning that is other than my own?
HAEMON. There is no city belonging to one man.
CREON. Is not the city thought to be the ruler's?
HAEMON. That is fine! To rule alone, the land deserted.
CREON. This boy, it seems, is championing the woman.
HAEMON. If you are a woman. All my care is for you.
CREON. Shameful, to press a case against your father.
HAEMON. No. For I see you offending justice.
CREON. Do I offend when I respect my office?
HAEMON. You do not respect it, trampling on gods' rights.
CREON. Disgusting nature, that bends before a woman.
HAEMON. But you will never find me yield to evil.
CREON. But all your words, at least, are for that girl.
HAEMON. For you, for me, and for the gods below.
CREON. But you will never marry her alive.
HAEMON. So then she dies, and dying, kills another.
CREON. Will your boldness lead to open threats?
HAEMON. Is it a threat to battle empty schemes?
CREON. You shall mourn your teaching, void yourself of wisdom.
HAEMON. Were you not my father, I would call you foolish.

CREON. You woman's slave, do not talk like that to me.

HAEMON. You wish to speak and when you speak, hear nothing.

CREON. Really? But no, by Zeus, be sure of this:
You shall not heap affronts on me so lightly.
Bring me that hated thing at once, so she
Can die before his eyes, beside her bridegroom.

HAEMON. Not at my side. So never think of that.
For she shall never die while I am near.
And you shall never see my face again.
Rave on with friends who wish to yield to you.

HAEMON *leaves.*

CHORUS. The man is gone in angry hurry, Sir.
The spirit at his age bears sorrow hard.

CREON. Well, let him do and reason more than is human.
But he shall never save these girls from sentence.

CHORUS. And so you really plan to kill them both?

CREON. Not her whose hands are clean. You speak with sense.

CHORUS. And by what means do you plan to kill the other?

CREON. I shall lead her where the way is clear of people,
And shut her in a rocky cave alive,
Allowing only food for expiation
That this whole city may escape the stain.
And if she calls on Hades, the only god
She bows before, she may obtain release
From death; or else will learn at last, though late,
That honor done to Hades is lost labor.

CREON *leaves.*

CHORUS

Love, unconquered in the fight, Love who falls even on riches,
Who couches all through the night on the delicate cheeks of the young girl,
You roam beyond all the seas, among dwellers in wild places.
No immortal can escape you, and no man
Whose life is for a day, and whoever holds you becomes maddened,
The minds of the just men you turn toward injustice, for their ruin.
And you have stirred up this household struggle between these men.
Resistless is the marriage-bringing love that comes
From the eyes of the bride; and in power is equal
To the greatest laws. For Aphrodite is resistless in her mockery.

But already, while seeing this sight,
I am now carried beyond all laws.
I am no longer able to hold back
The flowing tears as I see Antigone
Pass to the bridal chamber where all sleep.

Enter ANTIGONE, *led by guards.*

ANTIGONE. Citizens of my native land, see me going on my last way,
Looking for the last time on the light of the sun that is for me no more.
No, but Hades, where all must sleep, is leading me alive
To Acheron's shore,
Without having my share in the wedding songs, for never has any song
That crowns the wedding sung out for me; no, I shall marry Acheron.

CHORUS. Famous, and glorious, and with praise,
You depart for that deep place of the dead,
Not wasted by blows of slow disease,
And not sharing in the wages of the sword,
But self-possessed, alone among men,
You go alive to Hades.

ANTIGONE. And I have heard what a pitiful end came to the stranger, the woman
From Phrygia, daughter of Tantalus, on Mount Sipylus, long ago.
How the rocky growth subdued her, like clinging ivy. And as men say,
Snow and showers
Are never absent from her wasting body, but drop from her weeping lids
Upon her bosom. And very much like hers is the fate that brings me to rest.

CHORUS. But she was a god and born of the gods,
While we are men and of human birth.
But it is a great honor for a woman
To speak of her as sharing the same
Fate as the gods, whether alive or dead.

ANTIGONE. So, I am mocked. In the name of the gods of my fathers,
Why insult me when I am not yet gone, but before you,
My own city, and the wealthy men of my city?
You fountain springs of Dirce,
And the grove of the beautifully-charioted Thebes, I call you to bear me witness,
How all unwept of friends, and also by what laws,
I go to the rock-heaped prison mound of my unheard-of tomb.
I am unhappy. I have found a home neither
With men nor with corpses, with the living nor the dead.

CHORUS. You rushed to the utmost edge of daring,
And fell on the deepest foundation stone
Of right, but you fell grievously,
And you are paying your father's penalty.

ANTIGONE. Now you have touched on my bitterest feelings,
The continuous lament for my father, repeated three times,
And all the unmeasured doom of the famed house of Labdacus.
The horrors of my mother's bed,
The sleep of my unfortunate mother with her own son, my father.
And from such parents I was born, wretched.
So I am going to share their home with them, unmarried and cursed.
My brother, by making an unfortunate marriage,
In your death you have now stripped me, while living.

CHORUS. In reverent action is some reverence.
Yet power, when in the care of someone
Should in no manner be overthrown.
But your self-willed temper destroyed you.

ANTIGONE. Unwept, unfriended, without marriage-song, I am led in sorrow
On this appointed way.
I shall be able to see the sacred
Eye of the sunlight no more, unhappy
As I am. Yet none of my friends
Weep for my tearless destiny.

Enter CREON.

CREON. You know, of course, that songs and wails, before death
Would never stop, if thought to be of use.
So take that girl away immediately.
When you have closed her in a vaulted grave,
As I have said, leave her alone and helpless,
To die, if so she wishes, or to stay
Alive within her grave, in such a home.
For we are clean in reference to this girl.
But she shall be deprived of life on earth.

ANTIGONE. My tomb, and bridal chamber, hollow home,
Forever holding me, where I am going
To join my own because Persephone
Has now received by far the greatest number,
Entirely gone, among the dead below.
I, last of all, and far unhappiest,
Shall pass below, before life's term is ended.
But going, I cherish still among my hopes
To have my coming welcome to my father,
Welcome to you, my mother, to you, dear brother.
When you all died, with my own hands I washed
And honored you, poured offerings at your grave.
And now, for tending to your corpse, I win
Such recompense as this one, Polynices.
I honored you, the wise will say, well.
Never, if I had been a mother of children,
Or if my husband moldered in the grave,
Would I have done this task, despite the townsmen.
I say these things according to what law?
Well, if my husband died, I might have had
Another. And I might have had a child
By any other man, if I lost my own.
But with my father and mother closed in Hades,
There is no brother ever to be born.
And, when upon such law I held you first
In honor, I seemed to Creon very sinful
And terribly over-bold, my brother dear.
And now he leads me, captive in his hands;
No marriage-bed, no marriage-song, no joy
Of marriage, and no nurturing of children
Have been my share. Cut off from friends, I go
Alive, unhappy, to the cave of death.
And what decree of heaven have I transgressed?
Why should I ask the gods for help? I am
Unhappy, but what aid shall I invoke,
When I received this name of impious
Through piety? If such things please the gods,

When I have suffered, I may know my faults.
But if these sin, may they not suffer harm
Greater than what they wrongly do to me.

CHORUS. The same rush of the same winds is still
Swaying the soul of this girl.

CREON. Let her guards hurry up. They have delayed too long.
They will be sorry for this and pay for it yet.

ANTIGONE. He has spoken this word,
Meaning my death.

CREON. No, I cannot speak a comforting word.
You are sentenced to die. You must die.

ANTIGONE. City of my fathers in the land of Thebes,
Gods, the first to be born,
I am led and I cannot stay longer.
Look at me, you commanders of Thebes,
The last daughter remaining in the house of your kings,
See what I suffer, and from what men,
For I honored what should be honored.

ANTIGONE *is led away by the guards.*

CHORUS

Even so was the beauty of Danaë forced
To change the light of the day for the brass-bound walls;
Hidden and imprisoned in that chamber, secret as the grave.
And yet she was of noble family, daughter, daughter,
She was the keeper of the golden-showering seed of Zeus.
But the mysteriously-powered fate is dreadful.
Neither wealth, nor war, nor cities surrounded with walls, nor storm-black ships
That groan through the surges can escape fate.

And the fiercely-tempered son of Dryas,
King of the Edonians, was also imprisoned,
When, for his angering taunts, he was shut in a rocky hold
By the will of Dionysus. The dreadful force
Of madness ebbed away when at its surging. He came to know
The god whom in madness he had touched with his taunting tongue.
For he had tried to stop the god-inspired women and the Bacchic fire,
And had angered the Muses that love the flute.

By the waters of the Dark Rocks, by the waters of the double sea,
Rise the headlands of Bosporus and the Thracian
Salmydessus, where Ares, neighbor of the city,
Saw the cursed and the blinding wound
Dealt to the two sons of Phineus
By his savage wife: the wound that blinded
Those vengeance-receiving circles of the eyes
So furiously dashed out by her bloody hands
And the edge of the shuttle that she used for a dagger.

As they wasted away in sorrow, they bitterly wept
Their bitter destiny, those sons of a mother, unblessed in marriage.
But she traced her descent from the far line
Of the Erechtheidæ,
And she grew in the far caves,
Among her father's furious hurricanes,
That child of Boreas, swift as horse on the steep hilltop,
This daughter of the gods. And still, upon her
The everlasting Fates came down hard, my child.

Enter TIRESIAS, *led by a boy.*

TIRESIAS. You lords of Thebes, we come with linking steps,
Two served by one. The blind man's way of walking
Is just like this, dependent on a guide.

CREON. What is the news now, old Tiresias?

TIRESIAS. I shall explain. You listen to the seer.

CREON. I never yet withdrew from your advice.

TIRESIAS. And that is the way you steered the city right.

CREON. I felt and have confessed your benefits.

TIRESIAS. Take care again. You walk on fortune's edge.

CREON. What is it? How I shiver at your words.

TIRESIAS. You shall learn, so hear the warnings of my art.
While sitting at my old, prophetic seat
That is the haven for all kinds of birds,
I heard an unaccustomed noise of birds,
They screamed in rage that made their language jargon.
I learned they tore each other with fierce claws.
The whirring of their wings was not obscure.
Right there, in fear, I burned an offering
Upon the blazing altar, but from this,

Hephaestus showed no flame. Upon the coals
A dankish moisture trickled from the thighs,
And smoked, and sputtered, and the gall was scattered
Into the air. The streaming thighs protruded
From underneath their covering of fat.
I learned such failing signs of doubtful rites
From this boy here who serves me as a guide,
As I am guide and serve the other people.
And so, the state is suffering from your counsel.
For all our altars and our hearths are foul
With carrion eaten by the birds and dogs
From the poor and fallen son of Oedipus.
The gods no longer take our prayers and offerings,
And they no longer take the flame of thighs,
No bird shrieks out with any open signs,
For they ate the blood-fat of a murdered man.
Then think of this, my son. All men can make
Mistakes, but when an error has been made,
That man who heals the wrong in which he falls,
And is not hard to move, or very stubborn,
No longer is unwise, or yet, unblessed.
Self-will soon charges heavy-handedness.
Give way before the dead, and do not stab
The fallen. What strength is it to kill the dead?
I wish you well, and tell you what is good.
For nothing gives more pleasure than to learn
From someone who can give you good advice,
And if he speaks for your own benefit.

CREON. Old man, all of you, like archers at the mark,
Bend bows at me. I am not left untried
Even by your prophetic art. For some time
I have been bought and sold by men like you.
Well, gain your profits, barter me for the metal
Of Sardis and the gold of India,
If you wish. But you shall never hide that man
Inside a grave. Not even if the eagles
Of Zeus should snatch away the rotting flesh,
And take it to the very throne of Zeus.
No, not in fear of that pollution, would I
Allow this funeral. I know too well
No man can bring pollution to the gods.
But, old Tiresias, the wisest men
Fall with a shameful fall whenever they speak
Evil thoughts in pleasant words for love of money.

TIRESIAS. Does any man know, does any man consider—

CREON. What is this? What commonplace do you announce?

TIRESIAS. How good advice is far the best of treasures.

CREON. As far, I think, as mischief is the worst.

TIRESIAS. Yet you yourself are filled with that same sickness.

CREON. I do not wish to speak against the seer.

TIRESIAS. But still you do; you say I speak in lies.

CREON. The prophet tribe was always fond of money.

TIRESIAS. And that of tyrants loves all shameful gain.

CREON. You know that you are speaking to your king?

TIRESIAS. I do. For with my help you saved this city.

CREON. Yes, you are wise, but you love evil things.

TIRESIAS. You will make me tell the secret in my heart.

CREON. Out with it, only do not speak for gain.

TIRESIAS. I think it will not be to your gain now.

CREON. Then know, you cannot bargain with my purpose.

TIRESIAS. You understand me now. Not many courses
Of the chariot of the sun will be completed
When you shall give in payment, one conceived
Of your own loins, one corpse for many corpses;
You sent below those who should walk in sunlight,
You shut a living soul within the grave,
But keep a corpse cut off from gods below,
Without the rites of burial, unhallowed.
Neither you nor the gods above can do this.
These bodies are now profaned by you alone.
For this, the late-destroying avengers, the Furies
Of the gods of Hades, lie in wait for you,
To take you in the very same offense.
So now consider if I talk for money.
For but a little while will pass, and shrieks
Will rise within your house from men and women.
In hatred, all the cities are in tumult,
Where dogs, or savage beasts, or some winged birds
Had honored the mangled corpses with burial,

And took the unholy stink to the city's hearths.
Such arrows, for you pain me, like an archer,
Have I set loose against your heart in anger,
And steady arrows, whose sting you cannot avoid.
Boy, take me home, so he can spend his anger
On younger men, and learn to keep his tongue
More silent, more at ease, and learn to bear
A better heart within his breast than now.

TIRESIAS *is led away by the boy.*

CHORUS. The man has gone, foretelling evil, King.
And since this hair that once was dark, and now
Is white, has clothed my head, I know that he
Has never spoken falsely to the city.
CREON. I know it too, and I am troubled in mind.
To yield is hard, but to resist and strike
My pride with ruin, that is just as hard.
CHORUS. Son of Menoeceus, take good counsel now.
CREON. What shall I do? Tell me. I shall obey.
CHORUS. Then go and free the girl from her rocky chamber,
And make a tomb for the unburied dead.
CREON. And this is your advice. You would have me yield?
CHORUS. Quickly as possible, King. The harms from gods,
Quick-footed as they are, cut short the evil.
CREON. It's hard, but from my heart I yield, to do
The thing you want. We must not fight with fate.
CHORUS. Go, do it now. Do not leave it to others.
CREON. I go just as I am. So come, come,
My servants, each and every one of you.
Take axes in your hands and hurry on
To the place before you. Since my thoughts have taken
This turn, I shall be present to unloose her,
As I myself was present when I bound her.
And yet, I fear that it is best to spend
Our lives in keeping the established laws.

CREON *leaves.*

CHORUS

God of many names, the glory of the Cadmeian bride,
And child of Zeus, the thunderer,
You watch over famous Italy,
You rule in the dales of Eleusinian
Deo, where all guests are welcome,
Bacchus, you live in Thebes, the Bacchic
Mother-city, by the soft-gliding
Stream of Ismenus,
In the country where the teeth of the savage dragon were sown.

Above the double-crested rock, the smoking torch flames
Have seen you, where the Corycian nymphs
Are moving as Bacchantes; the spring
Of Castalia has seen you. The ivied
Slopes of the Nysaean hillside,
And that shore, green with many-clustered vines, send you,
And your name is lifted up,
Cries of Bacchus are raised,
With more than mortal words, as you keep watch over the streets of Thebes.

You have honored Thebes most, above all other cities,
You, and your mother, killed by lightning.
And now, when our whole town is plagued
With violent disease and sickness,
Come with healing footsteps over the heights of Parnassus,
Or over the moaning strait.

Iö, lead the fire-breathing stars, Master
Of the voices of evening,
King, son born of Zeus, appear,
With your attending Thyiads,
Who dance before you in their maddened revels, lasting through the night,
Giver of gifts, Iacchus.

Enter MESSENGER.

MESSENGER. You dwellers by the house of Amphion
And Cadmus, there is no human life that I
Would ever praise or blame, however placed.
For fortune raises, fortune overthrows
The lucky and unlucky from day to day.
No prophet can reveal fixed things to men.
Creon once I thought was enviable,
For he had saved this Cadmeian land from foes,
And having full possession of the land,

He ruled, was blessed as well with noble children.
All is gone. When man parts with his happiness,
I do not place him longer with the living,
But I consider him a breathing corpse.
If you wish, heap up money in your house,
And live in kingly fashion, yet, if gladness
Is far away from this, I would not pay
A puff of smoke for the rest, compared with joy.

CHORUS. What new disaster have you to tell our kings?

MESSENGER. They are dead. The living guilty for the dead.

CHORUS. Who is the killer? Who the victim? Speak.

MESSENGER. Haemon is dead, and murdered by no stranger.

CHORUS. What? By his father's hand or by his own?

MESSENGER. His own, incensed at his father for the murder.

CHORUS. Prophet, how truly you fulfill your word.

MESSENGER. As this is so, consider now the rest.

CHORUS. I see unhappy Eurydice near by,
The wife of Creon, coming from the palace,
By chance, or because she knows about her son?

Enter EURYDICE.

EURYDICE. You people of the town, I caught your words
As I was going out to offer prayers
To goddess Pallas. Just as I released
The bolts of the door to open it, the sound
Of my own sorrow fell upon my ears.
I sank into the arms of my maids, and lost
My senses. Tell me what the message was.
I shall not hear as someone strange to sorrow.

MESSENGER. Dear lady, I was there, and I shall tell you,
And shall not miss a single word of truth.
Why should I soothe you, when I should be found
A liar soon? The truth is always best.
I followed with your husband as his guide
To that high plain, where still unpitied, torn
By dogs, the corpse of Polynices lay.
We asked the goddess of the roads and Pluto
To check their wrath in mercy. So we washed
What parts of him remained in holy washing,
And burned them all on branches newly cut.
We raised a lofty mound of native earth,
And hurried to the hollow, floored-with-stone,
Sad bridal room of Hades and the girl.
Someone, still far off, heard the voice of loud
Lament at the bride's unconsecrated room,
And then he came and told his master, Creon.
As the king came nearer, the uncertain sounds
Of bitter cries came floating all around him.
He groaned and uttered these despairing words,
"Unhappy as I am, am I a prophet too?
And do I travel down the saddest road
Of all the roads that I have ever passed?
My son's voice greets me. Go, and hurry nearer,
My servants. When you reach the burial place,
Pass through the entrance of the vault where stones
Are loose up to the very mouth of the cell,
And learn if it is really Haemon's voice,
Or if I have been fooled by all the gods."
We made this search at our despairing master's
Command, and in the far corner of the tomb
We found her hanging by the neck, and held
By a noose of woven cloth. He was embracing
Her waist; had fallen forward, and bewailed
The ruin of his bride, now lost in death,
His father's work, his own unhappy marriage.
And when his father saw him, he went in
With bitter cries, and called to him wailing,
"Unhappy boy, what have you done? What thought
Possessed you? By what trouble were you crazed?
Come out, my son, I ask you, and I beg you."
The boy just glared at him with savage eyes,
And spat into his face, and answering nothing, drew
His two-edged sword. He missed his father, who sprang
Aside and rushed away. And then the poor boy,
In anger with himself, bent over where
He stood, and pressed his sword half-way in his side.
And while his senses remained, he clasped the girl
Within his feeble arms, and as he gasped,
Sent out on her pale cheeks the rapid streams
Of flowing blood. He lies now, corpse with corpse,
Receiving his nuptial rites, unhappy boy,

In the halls of Hades. All this teaches men
That bad advice or lack of wisdom is
The greatest evil that can fall on man.

EURYDICE *goes into the palace.*

CHORUS. What does this mean? The woman has gone back
And has not said a word of good or bad.
MESSENGER. I am surprised. And yet I cherish hopes
That hearing this disaster of her son,
She does not think it right to weep in public,
But underneath her roof will set her maids
To mourn the awful sorrow of the house.
Her mind is not untried that she should err.
CHORUS. I am not sure. To me, strained silence seems
As perilous as loud and useless cries.
MESSENGER. I shall go within the house and learn for certain
If she is hiding in her labored heart
Some secret purpose. Yes, for you are right.
Too much of silence is a thing to fear.

MESSENGER *leaves.*

CHORUS. But now, the king is coming near,
Bearing in his arms a clear memorial,
If I can say so: no stranger's madness,
But work done by his own mistakes.

Enter CREON. *Attendants are carrying the body of* HAEMON *on a bier.*

CREON. The sins,
The sins of a troubled, sorrowful soul,
So stubborn and deadly.
You see the murderer now,
And the son, killed by his own father.
I am so filled with sorrow for my luckless advice.
My son, so young in life and young in sorrow,
My son, my son,
Now you are dead and gone,
Not by your folly, but by mine alone.
CHORUS. But you appear to see the right too late.
CREON. Unhappy,
I have now learned the bitter lesson, but then, some god
Had struck my head from above with a great blow,
And had hurled me to the ways of cruelty,
Overthrew and then trampled my joy.
I pity the wearisome toil of men.

Enter MESSENGER.

MESSENGER. Sir, you have, and are still getting sorrow.
You bear one sorrow in your hands. But there
Within the house you soon shall see another.
CREON. But what worse grief can follow on these griefs?
MESSENGER. The queen is dead, true mother of that corpse.
Unhappy woman, killed by wounds just made.
CREON. The gulf
Of Hades never satisfied, why do you
Destroy me as you do?
Unfeeling messenger,
Announcing this bitter news, what are you
Saying? And though I was already as dead,
You kill me again. What do you say,
My son, and what
Other news do you bring me?
And must the slaughter of my wife follow on death?
CHORUS. Now you can see. It is concealed no longer.
CREON. I see
A new, a second grief, over there, unhappy.
What has destiny still in store for me?
Just now, now, I held my son in my arms,
And there, face to face, I see a corpse again.
Unhappy mother, unhappy child.
MESSENGER. There, at the altar, killed with her own knife,
She closed her darkened eyes, but first she mourned
The glorious grave of Megareus, who died first,
And then, with her last breath, she cursed you,
She cursed you, the killer of her sons.
CREON. I tremble with dread.
Is there no one here, no one here at all,
Who will kill me with the double-edged sword?
I am so miserable,
And I am filled with double sorrow.
MESSENGER. This dying woman found you guilty, both

For this son's death, and for the other one's.
CREON. And by what sort of death did she pass away?
MESSENGER. She struck beneath her heart with her own hand,
As soon as she had learned her son's sad death.
CREON. This guilt never can be shifted from me
To any other man, for I, I killed
You, I, unhappy as I am. And now
I tell the truth. Take me away, my servants.
Take me out of the way as quickly as possible,
To be, from now on, less than nothing.
CHORUS. Your wish is good, if good can mix with bad.
Most brief is best when evils clog our feet.
CREON. Let it come. Let it come.
Let it appear, that very best fate,
That brings me, that leads to me, my last day.
Let it come, let it come,
So I may never see tomorrow again.
CHORUS. These things will come. The present needs our care.
So let the future rest with those it should.
CREON. All I desire was summed up in that prayer.
CHORUS. Now pray no more, since there is no release
For any man from his appointed fate.
CREON. Then lead me away, a useless man.
I killed you, my son, not purposely,
And you too, my wife. I am unhappy.
I do not know where to look or where
To turn. Everything that was in my hand
Was tangled, and crushing fate fell on my head.

CREON *is led into the palace.*

CHORUS. Wisdom, first above all, brings the greatest
Portion of happiness. And the gods must be
Treated with reverence. For the great words of men
That are boastful are always punished
With great suffering;
They at last, in old age, teach wisdom.

THE *Medea* OF EURIPIDES

Translated by Walter R. Agard

INTRODUCTION

EURIPIDES (*ca.* 480–406 B.C.) during his long life witnessed the pioneer development of democratic Athens, the triumphs of the established empire, and the disastrous effects of the war, which led to growing disillusionment in Athens and ultimate defeat two years after his death. His plays, to some extent, mirror these circumstances. But he was chiefly influenced by his association with the materialistic philosopher Anaxagoras, the skeptical Sophists (according to tradition it was in Euripides' home that Protagoras first read the agnostic declaration which led to his expulsion from Athens), and the impact of war on the people who waged it and suffered from it; and he became primarily interested in analyzing the emotional and intellectual conflicts within and between maladjusted individuals. Like the Sophists, he enjoyed especially the way in which such characters reasoned in an attempt to justify their decisions. As Hippocrates made case studies of his patients, so Euripides diagnosed the mental and emotional aberrations of his characters.

A nonconformist (like Ibsen or Bernard Shaw in modern times), he applied his radical analysis chiefly to three fields: the questioning of conventional religion, an attack on the Athenian attitude toward women, and a bitter denunciation of the brutality unleashed by war.

Do the gods exist? Can they be as lacking in plain human decency as they are represented in the traditional stories about them? Such questions are raised in the *Ion, Hippolytus,* and the *Bacchae.* In the *Alcestis* and *Medea* Euripides pleaded the cause of women, consigned by Athenian prejudice to an inferior economic and political position. And the *Trojan Women,* written during a period of ruthless Athenian imperial policy, obviously projects the brutality of the conquerors at Troy into a contemporary situation.

As Euripides dealt realistically with personal problems, so in his manner of writing he used familiar language and a conversational idiom. Although he was a lyric poet of great skill, and many of his choral odes, notably in the *Bacchae* and *Hippolytus,* are masterpieces of poetic art, he usually relegated the chorus to a subordinate position; if dramatic convention required the choral songs, they were best dismissed as quickly as possible, so that the action and argument could proceed. But to theatrical devices of plot and character which heightened the emotional effect of the scenes he devoted the most careful attention, introducing pitiful beggars, young children in helpless distress, hypnosis, magic, and insanity, and, to cap the climax, a *deus ex machina* in its spectacular appearance.

The *Medea* is perhaps the least "dated" of his plays, representing as it does, even in exaggerated terms, the perennial conflict between the sexes. Produced in 431, before Athens became involved in the turmoil of war, it deals with domestic conflict—the injustice done to women in general and to one woman (a foreigner at that) in particular. Medea is pictured, magnificent in emotional depth and intellectual acumen, defeating the purposes of those who would insult her and her children. Her intuitive probing for the weaknesses of various men—Jason, Creon, Aegeus, in order to use them to serve her ends, her intense psychological conflict between hatred for Jason and love of her children, her superb duplicity cloaking a fierce sincerity, her ultimate triumph—all are revealed in the most direct and poignant way, through action and soul-searching soliloquy. Secondary are the smugly stupid Jason, the seemingly invincible Creon, the courteous old Aegeus, the servants and children, and the kindly women of Corinth; but all are drawn with undeviating discernment. Especially telling is the irony involving the noble-born, "civilized" Jason and Medea, a "barbarian." The language is for the most part that of ordinary conversation, heightened at times by fiery feeling; Jason, in his arguments aimed at self-justification, shows the effect of Sophistic training. The plot is firmer in structure than many of Euripides' plots. The despair of Medea, the supremacy of Creon, and the arrogance of Jason are balanced in reverse (after the interlude scene of Medea and Aegeus) by the deceiving of Jason, the death of Creon, and the exultation of Medea.

As was usually the case, Euripides was voted only

third prize for the trilogy of which this play was a part. During his entire career he won only four first prizes. If the people of Athens enjoyed seeing his plays, apparently most of them refused to approve of his ideas. But that doubtless caused him no great concern; unlike Jason, Euripides paid slight service to counsels of expediency.

THE TEXT is that of Gilbert Murray (Oxford, 1901), with eclectic readings from Page and others.

THE CHARACTERS

MEDEA, Princess from Colchis (on the Black Sea), wife of JASON
JASON, Prince of Iolcus (Thessaly), former leader of the Argonauts
CREON, King of Corinth
AEGEUS, King of Athens
NURSE OF MEDEA
TWO CHILDREN OF JASON AND MEDEA
ATTENDANT OF THE CHILDREN
MESSENGER
CHORUS OF WOMEN OF CORINTH
SOLDIERS, ATTENDANTS

The scene is Corinth, *in front of* MEDEA'S *house.*

Enter aged NURSE, *who accompanied* MEDEA *from Colchis and now serves as nurse of* MEDEA'S *children.*

NURSE. How I wish that the ship Argo had never flown between the blue Clashing Rocks to Colchis, that the pine had never been cut down to make oars for the hands of those princes who sought the Golden Fleece for Pelias! For then my mistress would never have fallen in love with Jason and sailed with him to the towers of Iolcus; she would never have persuaded the daughters of Pelias to kill their father; she would never have come to live in this land of Corinth with her husband and children.

To be sure, the people here were pleased when she came. She helped Jason in every way. They never had arguments, and it's a happy home when husband and wife agree. But now love has sickened, and everything is hatred between them. Jason has betrayed his children and my mistress. He is taking to his bed the royal princess, and wretched Medea, outraged, cries aloud the promises he gave her, their right hands clasped in loyalty to each other, the greatest pledge there is, and summons the gods to witness how Jason repays all she did for him. She lies without food, her body smitten with grief, wasting away all the time in tears, brooding over the wrong done her by her husband. She doesn't lift her face from the floor, she's like a rock or a wave of the sea, deaf to her friends' advice, turning away from them as she moans for her father, her native land, and the home she deserted to follow a man who has now dishonored her.

Yes, poor woman, she has learned from disaster what it is to lose one's country. She even hates her children, they give her no joy when she looks at them. I'm afraid she has something terrible in mind, for in her sullen fury she won't put up with being insulted. I know her! What will she do? Will she go silently into a bedroom and drive a dagger through someone's heart? Or will she kill the King and the bridegroom and then pay for it with even greater suffering? A terrible woman she is, and no one will easily harm her and sing a song of triumph.

But here come the children, through with their morning sport. How little they know of their mother's troubles, for the mind of the young does not take to grief.

Enter CHILDREN *and* ATTENDANT.

ATTENDANT. Aged retainer of my mistress, why have you come out here by yourself to mourn over your sorrow? Why are you willing to leave Medea alone?

NURSE. You know, old guardian of Jason's children, how faithful servants feel the troubles of their masters. I had such pain I longed to come out and tell earth and sky the agony of my mistress.

ATTENDANT. Isn't the poor woman over her wailing yet?

NURSE. I envy you the thought. It's only beginning.

ATTENDANT. What a fool!—if we can speak of masters that way. How little she knows of newer troubles.

NURSE. Newer ones? What are they, old man? Don't be afraid to tell me.

ATTENDANT. It's nothing. I'm sorry I ever mentioned it.

NURSE. Don't, I beg of you, don't hide it from

your fellow servant. If I have to I'll keep it to myself.

ATTENDANT. Well, I heard someone saying (he didn't know I was listening), after I came where the old men were playing checkers around the sacred spring of Pirene, that Creon plans to exile these children and their mother from Corinth. Whether the report is true or not I don't know. I hope it isn't.

NURSE. Surely Jason won't allow his children to suffer, even if he is at odds with their mother?

ATTENDANT. Old loves yield to new, and he has no more care for this house.

NURSE. We are done for if a new wave swamps us before the last one is bailed out.

ATTENDANT. Mind that you keep quiet about this. It isn't the right time for your mistress to know it.

NURSE. O children, do you hear what sort of a father you have? May he perish! No, not that, for he is my master. But he has certainly proved heartless toward his dear ones.

ATTENDANT. What man isn't? Have you just now realized that everybody loves himself more than his neighbor? It isn't strange that the father has no regard for these children when he gets married again.

NURSE. Go inside the house, children. I think that will be safe. But you keep them to themselves, and don't let them go near their maddened mother. For just now I saw her glaring like a bull, as if she would do something awful to them. She'll never stop her fury, I know it well, until she blasts someone. May it be her enemies, not her friends, that she attacks!

MEDEA (*within the house*). O God!
Wretched am I and full of woe,
How I wish I were dead!

NURSE. Do you hear that, dearest children? Your mother's
Heart is racked, her fury full.
Hasten quickly inside the house,
And don't approach within her sight,
Don't go near her, but guard against
The savage nature and raging hate
Of her self-willed heart.
Come now, go in as fast as you can.
For a cloud has arisen above the earth,
A cloud which will quickly burst into flame
With rising fury. What will she do,
That heart, proud and hard to control,
That spirit stung by injustice?

MEDEA (*within*). How I have suffered, suffered things
Full of agony! O cursed children
Of a hated mother, I wish you were dead!
May your father and our home perish!

NURSE. O God, O God, you pitiful woman!
What part have the children in their father's sin?
Why do you hate them? O my dears,
How I fear lest you will suffer!
For terrible are the moods of princes,
Ruled in few things, controlling many,
They find it hard to govern their wrath.
To learn to live as an equal with equals
Is better. In modest and quiet ways
May I come to life's end securely.
Best is the middle road. To use it
Is good for mortals, but any excess
Brings no advantage whatever to people.
Greater ruin, when he becomes outraged,
A god brings on prosperous homes.

As she finishes speaking, the CHORUS *of women of Corinth, with their* LEADER, *enter.*

LEADER. I heard the voice, I heard the cry
Of the wretched
Woman of Colchis, savage still.
Tell me, old woman, why is she wailing
Within her home? I am unhappy
At the pain she suffers, for this home
I have come to regard with devotion.

NURSE. It's a home no more, all that is gone.
He has a bed in the royal palace,
She wastes her life away in her room.
My mistress allows herself no comfort
In words that her friends would offer.

MEDEA (*within*). O God,
Through my brain let a lightning bolt from heaven
Smite. What's the gain of living longer?
If only death would give me release
And I could leave hated life behind!

CHORUS. Do you hear, Zeus, Earth, and Light,
What a cry the unfortunate wife
Utters of woe?
Why, wretched one, long for the last
Bed on which all of us once must lie?
Death will hasten all too soon,
Do not beg for it.

If your husband
Rejoices in a new marriage
That is common. Do not be agonized,
Zeus will befriend you. Do not so bitterly
Waste away grieving over your husband.

MEDEA (*within*). O great Themis and Lady Artemis,
You see what I suffer, after I bound
That cursed husband to me with great oaths.
Now may I see him and his bride
Crumble to dust in their new home,
They who dared wrong me without cause.
O father, O city, which I fled from
After I shamelessly slew my brother!

NURSE. Do you hear what she says, and how she calls
On Themis and Zeus with her entreaties,
Zeus the trusted steward of promises?
Certainly no mild revenge
Will satisfy my lady's anger.

CHORUS. If only she would let us see her,
Let us soothe her with comforting words,
Then she might lessen her fierce rage
And her frenzy of spirit.
I would never be alien to my friends.
So go to her,
Bring her forth from the house,
Tell her friends are here.
Hurry before she harms those within,
For great grief journeys fast.

NURSE. I will do it, but I am afraid
I can never persuade my mistress.
Yet I will do this labor of love.
Like a lioness with her brood
She glares at us servants, whenever one
Approaches her with soothing words.
Stupid I call them, and no way wise,
Those men of old,
Who discovered songs for festivals
And for banquet feasts, to accompany joy,
But in music and many-chorded song
They found no cure for hellish griefs
From which there strike the homes of men
Death and terrible doom.
Yet these it would be gain to cure
With song, but when the feast is spread,
Why do they vainly add their voice?
The full-heaped table brings delight
Enough of its own to please one's belly.

Exit NURSE *into the house.*

CHORUS

I heard the cry weighted with woe
Of the woman grieving over betrayal
By the husband who forsook her bed,
And she calls on the gods to avenge the injustice,
On Themis, keeper of oaths for Zeus,
Who led her to Hellas over the sea,
The sea to the north, through the endless gate
Of the Hellespont.

MEDEA *enters.*

MEDEA. Women of Corinth, I have come out of the house so that you will not blame me for keeping to myself. For I know that many people are too reserved toward others; they stay at home too much or are not friendly in company, and some by sheer laziness get the reputation of not caring for their neighbors. But it isn't fair to judge and dislike at first sight people who have done no wrong, without understanding them. A foreigner must be especially careful to conform to the customs of the city, but even a Greek who lives entirely to himself is criticized for it and becomes unpopular, because people do not know him.

As for me, you must be tolerant, because a totally unexpected blow has fallen on me and ruined my life. I go about with all joy in life gone, friends, wishing only to die. The man in whom all my happiness rested has turned out to be the basest of all men—my husband.

Of all things that live upon the earth and have intelligence we women are certainly the most wretched. First we must get a great amount of money to buy a husband, and then it's a master of our bodies that we take. Not to succeed in getting one brings even greater unhappiness. Then comes the greatest gamble of all—will he be kind or cruel to us? You know how hard it is for women to get a divorce, and it's impossible to reject a husband. So then, entering among new ways of life and customs, a bride must be a seer—she never learned those things at home—to get on well with this man who sleeps beside her. If by working our hardest we bring it about that our husbands stay with us without fretting, life is enviable, but if we fail we were better dead. When a man finds life unbearable at home he goes out to visit some friend, or to his club, and gets relief, but we have no one to look to but him. Then they say we lead a sheltered life at home, avoiding danger, while they go out to fight, but I say that's absurd. I'd sooner go three times into battle than bear one child.

But beyond these things we share in common, my situation is different from yours. You have this city and your father's homes, security, and the company of your friends. I am alone, without a city, and now I am outraged by the man who dragged me from a foreign country. I have no mother, no brother, no kin to take refuge with from this disaster.

There is only one thing I shall ask of you. If I find some way of repaying my husband for the way he has treated me, keep quiet about it. For you know that a woman is timid in other things, and is a coward in looking on cold steel, but whenever she is wronged in her marriage there is no heart so murderous as hers.

LEADER. I will do that for you, for it's right that you should pay back your husband, Medea, and I don't wonder that you are suffering. But look, here comes Creon, our King, to announce his latest decree.

Enter CREON, *with bodyguard.*

CREON. You there, sullen-eyed and angry at your husband, Medea, I say you are to go forth from this land in exile, taking your two children with you. There shall be no delay, either, since I am here to execute the decree, and I shall not go home until I have you thrown outside the boundaries of the country.

MEDEA. Utterly ruined I am, utterly ruined! My enemies pursue me with full sail, and there is no harbor for me from their deadly attack. Yet I will ask you, even though you persecute me so, why are you exiling me from this country, Creon?

CREON. I am afraid of you. There's no need to pretend otherwise. I am afraid you will do harm beyond curing to me and my daughter. Many things justify the fear. You are a clever woman, well versed in making trouble, and the loss of your husband pains you. I hear you are threatening to do something to me and the new bride and groom. So I shall guard against it before anything happens. Better for me to incur your hatred, woman, than to be soft with you now and regret it later.

MEDEA. This is not the first time, Creon, that my reputation for cleverness has hurt me greatly. Really, a man who is sensible should never teach his children to seem to be too intellectual. Apart from the reputation they get of being impractical, they are disliked by their neighbors; to stupid people a person who offers knowledge of new things will seem useless and not sensible, and those who pride themselves on their own sophistication will be jealous. This is my misfortune; as a clever woman I am envied by some, despised by others. But I am not actually so very clever.

You are afraid of me? Why? Afraid that I will disturb the harmony of your household? Have no fear, Creon. I am not the sort of woman to oppose the authority of kings. Besides, what harm have you done me? Marry your daughter to whomever you choose. It isn't you, it's my husband that I hate. You have acted sensibly, as far as I can see, and I don't begrudge you your happiness. Marry her off, and may all go well with you. But let me keep on living here. I shall be quiet, even though I have been wronged by those who are stronger than I.

CREON. You sound meek enough, but I suspect you are planning some revenge and I trust you even less than before. A woman who is quick to anger (the same, of course, is true of a man) is easier to guard against than one who puts a curb on her tongue. So get away from here as fast as you can. Don't waste your time arguing. Everything is arranged, and no matter how clever you are you won't succeed in staying here as a menace to me.

MEDEA (*throwing herself at* CREON'S *feet and clinging to him*). Don't, I beg you by your knees and your new-wedded daughter—

CREON. You waste your words. You could never persuade me.

MEDEA. So you will drive me out? You will not listen to my prayers?

CREON. Exactly. I consider my home more important than you.

MEDEA. O fatherland, how I remember you now!

CREON. Naturally. Except for my children I, too, love my country most.

MEDEA. What disaster love brings!

CREON. Disaster or blessing—that is, I imagine, a matter of chance.

MEDEA. Zeus, I hope you will never forget who did this crime.

CREON. Away with you, wretched woman, and rid me of my trouble.

MEDEA. Trouble, you say! Is it not I who know what trouble is?

CREON. Shall I have to order my soldiers to drag you away?

MEDEA. Not that! I only beg of you, Creon—

CREON. It seems that you are determined to make more of a scene.

MEDEA. I accept *exile.* I am not asking to escape *that.*

CREON. No? Why do you force yourself on me, then, and cling to my hand?

MEDEA. Just let me stay here this one day. To make up my mind where to go, and provide some refuge for my children, since their father gives them no thought. Pity them! You, too, have children, it is right you should show mercy to mine. It isn't myself that I am thinking of if I have to be an exile, it's those unfortunate little ones I am weeping for.

CREON. Well, I am far from being a tyrant. In fact, I have often harmed myself by being too kind. I realize that I am making a mistake, woman, yet you shall have this request granted. Stay, if you must, this one day—you can hardly do what I fear in that short time. But I warn you, if tomorrow's sun sees you still within my kingdom with your children, you shall die. Accept that as final.

Exit CREON *and bodyguard.*

CHORUS. Wretched, wretched woman of sorrow,
Where will you go? In what strange land
Will you find home and place to save you?
On a pathless sea of troubles
God has mapped your course, Medea.

MEDEA. Everything has gone wrong. Who will deny it? But do not think it will turn out the way he plans. There are still struggles for those just wed, and for the bride's father no mean suffering. For do you think I would ever have groveled to him except to get what I wanted? I would never have spoken to him, never have touched him with my hands! But he has shown himself such a fool that when he could have checked all my plans by driving me right out of the country he has granted me this day, in which I shall lay out my three enemies as corpses—the father, the girl, and my husband.

With many means of death to choose from, I do not know which one to use, friends. Shall I burn down their house? Shall I steal into their bridal chamber and thrust a dagger through their hearts? One thing stands in the way: if I shall be captured entering their house I will pay for it with my death and be laughed at by my foes. So I think the sure road is best, to kill them by the means in which we women are most skillful—poison.

Very well, then, they are dead. But what city will receive me then? What host will offer me refuge and security? There is none. So I must wait yet a little longer, until I arrange for some safe refuge. Then, in trickery and silence I shall commit this murder.

If fate allows me no way of saving myself, even though I die for it I will take the sword and kill them, for I shall stop at nothing in my desperation. By Hecate, the goddess whom I revere most of all and have chosen for my fellow-sorceress living in the secret recesses of my hearth, no one shall break my heart and then be merry. A bitter and painful marriage I shall make for them, a bitter alliance, and bitter my exile from this land.

Come now, spare nothing of your cleverness, Medea, in planning and contriving! Go to the extremity of horror, now it is a contest of daring! You see what you suffer! Is it right that you, of the noble race of the Sun-god Helios, should be laughed at by those descendants of Sisyphus? You know what to do. And, besides, you are a woman—and although women can do little good, perhaps, they are the most devilish contrivers of pain!

MEDEA *goes into the house.*

CHORUS

Backward are flowing the springs of the sacred
rivers,
Justice and all things again are overturned,
Men are deceitful, their pledges
To the gods unfulfilled.
Our good name in the future
Shall be spoken of with respect,
Glory shall come to the race of women,
No longer will an evil repute be theirs.
The themes of the ancient bards will cease,
Singing our lack of loyalty.
And this is right. If into our keeping

God had entrusted poetry,
Phoebus, the Lord of music,
There would have been a song challenging
The song of men. Long years could tell
The wrongs forced upon us by men.

You have sailed from your father's home
In your frenzy of heart, passing the double
Rocks of the Hellespont,
And you live in a foreign land,
Widowed while your husband lives,
Wretched woman, and as an exile
You are driven out in dishonor.

The grace of loyalty has fled, nor does honor
Live in great Hellas, it has flown heavenward.
You have no father's home,
Poor woman, for harbor
In your suffering.
Another princess, with greater power,
Holds sway in your husband's home.

Enter JASON *and* MEDEA.

JASON. This is by no means the first time that I have seen what trouble beyond mending is caused by a violent temper. Now you, when it was perfectly possible for you to keep on living in Corinth if you would only submit quietly to the orders of your superiors, have been sentenced to exile because of your foolish talk. It won't bother me if you never stop saying that Jason is the most cruel of husbands. But when you talk about the royal family as you have done, consider yourself fortunate to be punished merely by banishment. I have tried to soften the anger of the King, I wanted you to stay here, but you kept on with your folly, always threatening royalty. So you are going to be driven out of the country.

In spite of all that I have not deserted you, but I've come here to look after you, my dear, so that you and the children won't have to wander forth without resources and in need of anything. We all know what a bitter time refugees have. I am doing this because, even if you hate me, I could never think of you except with kindness.

MEDEA. You cowardly scoundrel! That's the only way I can describe your lack of manliness. So you have had the insolence to come to me, come to me when you are my most bitter enemy? Perhaps you think it is brave and daring to come and look at your wife and children when you have wronged us so, but I say it's the worst disease there is—shamelessness. However, you did well in coming, for now I can relieve my pain by telling you how base you are, and you'll suffer when you hear it.

I shall begin the story from the very start. I saved your life, as all the Greeks know who made the voyage with you in the Argo, when you were sent to yoke and master the fire-breathing bulls and sow the earth with death-bringing seed. As for the dragon who guarded the Golden Fleece, that sleepless dragon with weaving coils, I killed him for you and saved you from death. Then I betrayed my father and family and came with you to Iolcus—more devoted than wise, I was—and for your sake I killed Pelias by the most painful death, at the hands of his own daughters. Oh, you had nothing to fear while I was with you! And after profiting from all this, you vilest of men, you have forsaken me, you have made a new marriage, after you had children by me. If you had been childless I would have forgiven you for wanting a new wife, but I bore you children. You have no sense of loyalty, and I'm at a loss to know whether you think those gods you swore by no longer hold sway, or that right and wrong have lost their old meaning, since you know that you have broken all your promises to me. Oh right hand of mine, which so often you grasped, and these knees which you, no true husband, so lightly held! I have no hope left.

But come, I will share my troubles with you as if you were still friendly. Expecting to get any help from you? Oh no, but I'll do it, to make you show yourself even baser when I ask you, where am I to go now? To my father's home and those whom I betrayed when I left them for your sake? Or to the wretched daughters of Pelias? They would give me a splendid welcome after I had slain their father. That's how it is. I have made myself detested by those who loved me at home, and the ones whom I should have harmed last of all I have made my enemies by helping you.

What a fortunate woman you have made me throughout Greece, in the eyes of many women! What a wonderful, what a faithful husband I have in you! If I am thrown out of this country and become a refugee, wandering alone with my lonely children, what a fine reproach that will be to you, happy bridegroom, your children roaming as beggars with their mother who saved your life! O Zeus, why have you stamped on gold its clear value, but on men's bodies when one needs to recognize who is base, there is no natural sign?

LEADER. Terrible is anger and hard to heal
When loved ones quarrel.

JASON. It seems that I must present my case clearly, and, like a shrewd helmsman, ride out this storm with sails close-hauled, the storm of your noisy abuse, my dear. To begin with, since you make a towering exaggeration of your help to me, it was Aphrodite, not you, whom I consider the only one who steered my way to safety. Your subtle mind will surely realize that it was Eros who forced you with his inescapable arrows to save my life. But I dislike making too much of that point, for you did well in helping me, regardless of who forced you to do it. But you must admit that you got more from my being saved than you gave. Listen, and I will tell you why.

First, you have the privilege of living in Greece instead of a foreign country, and you live under a regime of law and order instead of one of brute force. Next, all the Greeks know that you are a clever woman and admire you for it. If you had kept on living far from civilization you would never have had such prestige. Prestige! I'd never choose wealth or musical skill surpassing Orpheus' unless the right people appreciated it. So much I can claim I have done for you, and I had to say it in answer to the charges you flung at me.

But now about this royal marriage which you throw in my face. I'll show you first that I was clever and sensible in making it, and finally that I did it in loving thought for you and the children—but keep quiet and hear me out.

After I left the land of Iolcus, in the midst of difficulties that seemed insurmountable, what luckier fortune could I have had than to marry the king's daughter, I, a refugee? It's not true, the suspicion that devours you, that I was bored with you and fell passionately in love with a younger woman, or that I was eager to have more children by another wife. No, those I have were enough, and I have no criticism of you on that score. My only aim was to establish all of us prosperously and save us from want, realizing that everyone shuns a poor man. In that way I could rear my children in a manner befitting my princely rank, and beget sons to be brothers to ours, and by uniting the families we would all prosper. You have no need of more children, and I would be glad to help those we have by getting more. That wasn't such bad planning, was it? You wouldn't say so if you weren't jealous because I am marrying again. But like all women, you think you have everything if your marriage goes smoothly, but if your husband doesn't share your bed any more you call what is really best most hateful. Why can't men have children in some other way, and the race of women perish? Then men could really be happy.

LEADER. Jason, you have worked up a very clever speech, but even if I offend you I must say that you seem to be doing wrong in forsaking your wife.

MEDEA. I am different from many people in many ways, I suppose, for I consider that a blackguard who has it in him to defend himself cleverly is all the more guilty. To do wrong and then try to swagger it out with boasting words is the courage of a scoundrel, it's not really so very clever. Yes, that applies to you, my fine husband. Don't think you have made out such a brilliant case for helping me and have been so persuasive, for one answer will lay you low. If you were not base, you would have been open about this marriage and would have talked it over with me first.

JASON. That would have been a great help in arranging the marriage, I am sure, if I had told you about it! Even now you can't control your fury.

MEDEA. That wasn't what kept you from it. You didn't think going to bed with me, a foreigner, would give you enough prestige as the two of us grew older.

JASON. Understand this once for all, it wasn't for the sake of the girl that I made this new alliance. As I have kept telling you, it was because I wanted to save you and beget brothers for our children to be our safeguard in old age.

MEDEA. I want no such bitter prosperity, no such wealth that eats out one's heart.

JASON. Don't you realize how you can change that wish, and appear more sensible? Don't mistake prosperity for bitterness and good fortune for bad.

MEDEA. Insult me with your platitudes, since you have a place to lay your head, but I shall be a helpless refugee.

JASON. Well, you chose it for yourself. Don't blame anyone else.

MEDEA. Chose it? By doing what? By marrying again and deserting you?

JASON. By wickedly cursing the royal family.

MEDEA. I seem indeed to be a curse to your home.

JASON. I'm not going to argue this with you further. But if you want to take anything of mine to help yourself and your children in exile, tell me. I am ready to give it lavishly, and I'll communicate with friends of mine abroad who will do well by you. If you don't accept this offer, my dear, you are very foolish. You'll fare much better, I assure you, if you get over your anger.

MEDEA. I'd never make use of friends of yours. I'd never take a thing, don't offer it. The gifts of a scoundrel bring no good to any one.

JASON. The gods witness that I want to do everything to help you and the children. But advantages don't satisfy you; you arrogantly thrust your friends away. By behaving like that you'll suffer the more. [*Exit.*]

MEDEA. Go! You are mad with desire for your newly trapped bride, you cannot bear to be away from her. Enjoy your marriage. But perhaps—if God wills—one of these days you will want to renounce it.

CHORUS

When love over-passionate comes,
It brings neither glory nor good
To mankind. But if Aphrodite
Comes in fair measure, then
No divinity is so gracious.
Never, goddess, aim at me
Your arrows poisoned with desire,
Inescapable, winged from your golden bow.

May I cherish moderation,
The fairest gift of the gods.
Never by angry quarrels
And strife that knows no end
May a hostile Aphrodite
Drive me to vagrant love.
But, quick in understanding,
May she bless us with peaceful wedlock.

O my country, my home,
Always be mine, securely,
And may I live out my years
Free from hopeless wandering.
Sooner than exile I would submit to death
And end life's day. For loss
Of one's native country
Is a loss beyond all reckoning.

We see what it means, not
From report do we know it.
For you have no city, no friends
To pity you in your trouble.
Cursed may he perish who refuses
To respect his dear ones, and open
Frankly his heart. To me
Such a man shall never be a friend.

While MEDEA *sits brooding,* AEGEUS, *King of Athens, comes in from the left accompanied by Attendants. He stops when he sees* MEDEA.

AEGEUS. Joy to you, Medea, for this is the most honored of friendly greetings.

MEDEA. Joy to you, Aegeus, son of wise Pandion. Where have you come from?

AEGEUS. I have recently left the ancient oracle of Phoebus.

MEDEA. And what advice did you seek at that divine center of the earth?

AEGEUS. I asked how I might succeed in begetting children.

MEDEA. By the gods, are you childless until now?

AEGEUS. Childless, by some god's hard will.

MEDEA. Are you married, or does no one share your bed?

AEGEUS. I bear the yoke of marriage.

MEDEA. What did Phoebus say to you about having children?

AEGEUS. A reply too profound for me, a man, to understand.

MEDEA. Could I hear the oracular response?

AEGEUS. Of course. It needs a shrewd mind for its interpretation.

MEDEA. What was the response? Tell me, if it is proper for me to hear it.

AEGEUS. I was not to release the jutting foot of the wineskin—

MEDEA. Before you should do what, or arrive where?

AEGEUS. Until I came again to my ancestral hearth.

MEDEA. And why are you voyaging to Athens by this route?

AEGEUS. There is a certain Pittheus, King of Troezen—

MEDEA. I have heard of him—the son of Pelops, a very pious man.

AEGEUS. With him I want to share the divine utterance of the god.

MEDEA. I am not surprised. He is a wise man and knows about such things.

AEGEUS. And, besides, he is the dearest to me of all my friends in foreign lands.

MEDEA. May you succeed and get everything you want.

AEGEUS. But you don't look well, Medea. Why are you so pale? Haven't you been crying?

MEDEA. Aegeus, no husband in all the world has been so cruel as mine.

AEGEUS. What's that you say? Let me know clearly what your trouble is.

MEDEA. Jason has wronged me, although I never harmed him.

AEGEUS. Just what has he done? Tell me more about it.

MEDEA. He has deserted me and taken a new wife.

AEGEUS. Surely he never dared do such a disgraceful thing!

MEDEA. Indeed he did. He used to love me, but now he has flung me away.

AEGEUS. Did he fall in love with her, or merely want to get rid of you?

MEDEA. Can you expect love from a man who honors no pledge he gave?

AEGEUS. Come now, if he is as you say, he is dishonorable.

MEDEA. His only love was for a royal alliance.

AEGEUS. Who gives him the bride? Tell me the rest.

MEDEA. Creon, the ruler of this land of Corinth.

AEGEUS. I can understand how you suffer, poor woman.

MEDEA. My life is ruined. And besides that I am being exiled.

AEGEUS. By whom? That's another new misfortune you are telling me.

MEDEA. Creon is driving me out of Corinth.

AEGEUS. And Jason approves it? I cannot commend him for that.

MEDEA. He says he doesn't, but he is willing to be patient under the affliction! O Aegeus, I beg you, I throw myself at your knees as a suppliant—pity me, pity me in my suffering, and don't see me cast out without refuge. Receive me in your country and at your hearth. If you should, your desire for children would be fulfilled and you would die a happy man. You don't know how lucky you are in having met me. I will stop your being childless, I will make you able to beget many children. Believe me, I know the drugs for that.

AEGEUS. For many reasons I am eager to grant you the favor you ask, my dear, first because the gods bid men to be hospitable, and next because of the assurance you give me about having children—for I am completely at a loss in that respect. But here is my situation. If you come to my country by yourself I shall try to give you hospitality, since I am a fair-minded man. But I must tell you this frankly, my dear, I shall not consent to bring you personally out of Corinth. You must by yourself reach my palace. Then you shall find a permanent refuge, and I will not yield you up to any man. So plan your journey. For I wish to be free from blame in the eyes of my friends.

MEDEA. That is the way it shall be, then. But could I have a pledge of this? Then you would have done nobly by me.

AEGEUS. Don't you trust my word, or what is it that worries you?

MEDEA. I trust you now. But the royal house of Pelias hates me, and Creon does too. If you were bound by a pledge you wouldn't hand me over to anyone who demanded me from you. But if it was just a promise you gave me without swearing to it before the gods, you might, in friendship, yield to their demands. You see my power is slight, but they have royal resources.

AEGEUS. This is great foresight, my dear. Well then, if it seems best to you I shall not refuse. It would be a safer course for me to have some excuse to offer your foes. Besides, it fits your plans better. Name the gods for me to swear by.

MEDEA. Swear by Earth, Helios, father of my father, and the whole race of gods.

AEGEUS. To do or not to do what? Be plain.

MEDEA. Not to drive me out of your country, nor, if any of my enemies wish to lead me forth, to hand me over to them willingly as long as you live.

AEGEUS. I swear by Earth, the holy Light of the Sun, and all the gods that I will abide by what you ask.

MEDEA. That is enough. But what would you expect to suffer if you broke your oath?

AEGEUS. Whatever suffering comes to impious men.

MEDEA. Go on your way rejoicing, for everything is as it should be. I shall come to your city as fast as I can, once I have finished what I have in mind and accomplish what I want to do.

Exit AEGEUS *and his* ATTENDANTS.

CHORUS

May Hermes, the Escort Lord,
Bring you safe to your home.
And may you speedily get
All that your heart desires,
Since to us, King Aegeus,
You seem a noble man.

MEDEA. O Zeus, Justice, and Light of the Sun, now, my friends, I shall have a song of victory to sing over my enemies, and I have already set my feet on the path that leads to triumph. I have good reason to expect them to pay the penalty. For this man fitted into my plans just when I was most in need of a harbor. Now I can go to the city and fortress of Athens and find there a haven to moor my craft securely. So the time has come, friends, to tell you all my plans. Listen to them, even if they cause you pain.

I shall send one of my servants to Jason and tell him to come to me, and when he comes I shall tell him a soothing story, how I see things his way, and it's sensibly planned for our advantage for him to make the royal marriage and betray me. But then I shall beg him to let my children stay here—not really meaning to leave them in a hostile land to be insulted, but in order to kill the King's daughter. For I will send them to her bearing gifts in their hands, a fine dress and a diadem riveted with gold, to save them from banishment. If she takes the precious things and puts them on her body she shall die in agony, and so shall any one who touches her, with such deadly poison shall the gifts be smeared.

So much for settling that account. But afterwards there is a further step for me to take, and my heart is torn by the deed I must do. I shall kill my children. No one shall take them from me. And then, after I have wrecked his home for Jason, I shall leave this country, escaping from the scene of the murder of my most beloved children after I have dared to commit that unholiest of crimes. I must do it, women, for it is unendurable that I should be insulted by my foes. Very well. But what will be the use of my living any longer? I shall be a woman without a country, without a refuge from disaster. I lost all that when I left my father's palace, captivated by the smooth words of a Greek who shall now, with God's help, pay me back in full. He shall never again see the children I bore him alive, never get more children from his new bride, since that loathsome girl must die a loathsome death by my poisons. Let no one think I am a common and weak woman, or mild of mood. No, I am of a different sort, cruel to my enemies, kind to my friends, and thus find life surpassingly glorious.

LEADER. Since you have shared your plan with us and we want to help you, upholding the moral law I advise you not to do what you threaten.

MEDEA. It must be so. I forgive you for talking as you do, for you have not suffered as I have.

LEADER. My dear, however desperate you are you won't kill your own children!

MEDEA. Indeed I shall, for that will torture my husband most.

LEADER. And you would be the unhappiest of women.

MEDEA. No more talk about it! Words are useless now!

She claps her hands. The NURSE *comes out.*

Nurse, go and summon Jason. I rely on you, for you are always faithful. Don't tell him a word about my plans, if you love me and if you are a woman.

Exit NURSE.

CHORUS

Fortunate forever the sons of Athens,
Sons of the blessed gods, enjoying
A land holy, unravaged by war,
Feasting on famous wisdom, and always
Walking buoyantly through shining air,
Where they say once golden-haired Harmony
Gave birth to the nine Pierian Muses.

And Aphrodite draws the fair flowing
Streams of Cephisus to water the earth,

And blows on it gentle, sweet-breathed
breezes.
Crowning her head with a fragrant wreath
Of roses, she sends loves to be
Comrades of wisdom, and blithe helpers
In every kind of noble service.

But how shall that fair country
Of sacred streams receive you,
Medea, murderess of children
Unholy among the blessed?
Think what the blow will mean!
Think of the slaughter you plan!
Do not, we implore you,
Do not kill your children!

Where will you get the daring
Of heart and hand to do it?
Such unspeakable daring!
How can you look at your children
And tearlessly plot their death?
You will never be able
When they kneel, imploring,
To wet reckless hands with their blood.

Enter JASON.

JASON. I have come at your bidding. And I'm glad to do it, for even though you hate me I would never deprive you of help. I shall listen to whatever new thing you wish to ask of me, my dear.

MEDEA. Jason, I beg of you, pardon me for everything I said before. It is right you should bear with my moods, isn't it, for the sake of the happy times we once had together? Now I have thought things over and come to my senses at last. I have been reviling myself for my folly. "Silly woman," I said, "why am I crazy, why so angry with those who plan for my good? Why do I make myself hated by the rulers of the land and especially my husband, who is doing what is most to my advantage in marrying a princess and getting sons by her to be brothers of my own boys? Shall I not change my mood? Why be so foolish? The gods are providing well for me. Have I not children left me? And I realize that we are fugitives and have no friends." Yes, I thought it out that way and saw how senseless I had been, how foolish my anger was. So now I commend you. I think you are sensible in making this alliance for our sakes, and I was a fool not to share in your plans and help them succeed, even escorting your bride to her bed, since that would make you happy. But you know how it is. We women are what we are. Not wholly lacking in sense, but mere women. You, a man, oughtn't to repay me in kind and return folly for folly. I give in, I admit that I was wrong. Now I have changed my ways for the better. (*She claps her hands.*) Children, children, come here!

The CHILDREN *come from the house.*

Kiss your father, and tell him, with me, that you and your mother are going to be friends with him now, for we have come to understand one another, we are not angry any longer. Shake hands with him and prove it!—Oh, how I fear some future calamity! Children, how long will you be able to hold out those sweet arms? Now I'm wretched again, crying and fearful. Right after mending the strife between your father and us I have wet your soft faces with my tears.

LEADER. I, too, cannot keep back my tears, and I fear a greater woe.

JASON. My dear, I commend you for this change of mind, and I don't blame you for your earlier folly. It is natural for women to give way to anger when husbands contract new marriages. But you have reasoned well and come to realize how weak you are—although it took you a long time. Now you are acting as a sensible woman should.

As for you, my sons, I have been a not inconsiderate father to you, if I may say so. I imagine you will be in the top rank in Corinth some day, along with your brothers yet to be born. All you need do is to grow big and strong. Your father will look after everything else for you, I and whoever of the gods is kind to us. I want to see you reach manhood as sturdy fellows, able to defend me against my foes.

Medea, why are you crying over them and turning away your head? Why aren't you glad when you hear what I say?

MEDEA. It's nothing. I was only worrying about the children.

JASON. Don't worry about them now. I shall look after them well.

MEDEA. I won't worry, I have confidence in you. But you know how women can't help crying.

JASON. Why, wretched woman, do you keep on grieving over these children?

MEDEA. Because I love them, and when you were praying for their future I was anxious about it.

Well, I have told you some of the things I wanted to talk over with you, and now I shall mention a few more. Since it seems best to the king to exile me—and I agree it is best, I realize it perfectly, I shouldn't live here to embarrass you and the royal family, for I'm a burden to all of you—I shall leave this country. But the children! Ask Creon to let you bring them up, and not to banish them.

JASON. I don't know whether I could persuade him, but I must try.

MEDEA. Ask your bride to plead with her father not to banish the children.

JASON. Very well. I am sure that I shall persuade *her.*

MEDEA. You will if she is like other women. And I will help you do it. I will send her some gifts, the most beautiful ones on earth, I know they are, borne by the children. A fine dress and a gold-riveted diadem. One of you servants, go inside quickly and bring out the gifts for the princess.

A SERVANT *goes into the house.*

She will be a happy woman in a thousand ways—she has you as the noblest husband a woman could find, and she will possess the beautiful things that Helios, father of my father, once bequeathed to his descendants.

The SERVANT *comes out, bearing a metal box.*

Take these precious things, children, and give them to the princess, fortunate bride. They are gifts that no one would scorn.

JASON. Why, foolish woman, do you empty your hands of them? Do you think the princess has no royal robes, no golden diadem? Keep them, don't give them away. If my new wife thinks me of any account she will certainly value my advice more than any such bribe.

MEDEA. Please don't forbid my doing it. As the saying goes, gifts persuade even the gods, and gold is worth more than countless arguments. The lucky woman, young, a princess, and soon to have increased fortune! To save my children from exile I'd give her more than gold, I'd give my life. Come, children, go to the palace, the home of father's new wife, my mistress, and beg her, implore her not to exile you. Then give her this gift. You must be very sure that she herself takes it. Go, as fast as you can. May you be successful in your errand, and return bringing good news to mother, the news she longs to hear.

JASON, *the* CHILDREN, and their ATTENDANT *depart toward the palace.*

CHORUS

Now hope has gone for the children's life,
Gone. They are on the road to death.
The bride will take the gold clinging thing,
Will take it, poor girl, for her doom,
On her golden hair she shall place her doom,
Fitting it there with her hands.

The heavenly grace and gleam of the dress
Will entrance her, and the gold-wrought diadem
Placed on her head will wed her to Death.
Such is her pitfall, such her fate.
Joy will be followed by agony,
She shall never escape it.

You, Jason, pitiful bridegroom,
Pitiful in your royal marriage,
Little know you are leading your sons
And your bride to utter ruin,
Leading them to a horrible death,
Yourself to a wretched fall.

Medea, how I suffer with you,
Mother of misery, you who will slay
Your children because of your deserted bed.
Deserted when your husband lawlessly
Left you to take into his bed
A bride of royal honor.

Enter ATTENDANT *and* CHILDREN.

ATTENDANT. Mistress, the children have won release from exile! And the royal bride was delighted with your gifts! Now all's fair sailing for the children!

But what's this? Why do you stand there as if all were lost when you have succeeded so well?

Why aren't you glad when you hear the news I bring?

MEDEA. O God!

ATTENDANT. This isn't the way to hear good news.

MEDEA. God!

ATTENDANT. Can it be that I've brought bad fortune without knowing it? Shall I get no credit for bringing good news?

MEDEA. You have reported what you reported. I don't blame you.

ATTENDANT. Then why is your face downcast? Why weep?

MEDEA. I have great reason, old man. For the gods and I have planned and done a terrible thing.

ATTENDANT. Courage! Your children shall one day bring you back home.

MEDEA. I shall bring them home before that.

ATTENDANT. You're not the only woman who has lost her children. Mortals must learn to be reconciled to misfortune.

MEDEA. I shall learn it. But go inside now and arrange things for the boys.

The ATTENDANT *goes in.*

O children, children, for you there is a city and a home in which, without your wretched mother, you will live forever. But I am going to another country for refuge before I am of any further help to you, before I see you happily grown up, before I make arrangements for your weddings—the marriage bath, the bed, the torches, the bride. What agony my ambition has brought me! It was not for this, children, that I labored and was racked with pain when you were born, it was not for this I brought you up. Oh no, once I had great hopes in you, that you would comfort me in my old age and when I died would lay me out tenderly with your own hands. What woman doesn't yearn for that? But now I have no such lovely dream. Without you I shall lead a bitter life and a hopeless one. And you shall never again look on your mother with those dear eyes, but will be living in an alien land.

O God, why do you look at me so, children? Why do you laugh that last laughter?

What am I about? My courage has left me, women, when I see my children's shining faces. I can never do it. I abandon the plan I had. I shall take my children with me. To make their father suffer why must I suffer twice as much as he? No, I won't do it. Farewell to my whole plan.

And yet, what am I dreaming of? Do I want to become a laughing stock to my enemies by letting them go unpunished? This must be dared! Away with my cowardice and the tender thoughts that undermine my resolution. Go into the house, children.

The CHILDREN *slowly go in.*

Whoever is forbidden to attend my sacrifice, let him beware. I shall not let my hand swerve.

O my soul, do not do it! Let them live, wretched Medea, spare your sons! If they live with you in Athens they will give you joy.

No, by the avenging spirits of Hades, I shall never let my sons be handed to my foes to gloat over. There is no way out of it, they must die. And since they must die, I, who gave them birth, shall kill them. There is no way to evade it. Already the diadem is on the princess' head, the bride is being eaten by that robe of poison, I know it well. But before I walk the path of utter misery, I must speak again to my sons.

A SERVANT *brings them out to her.*

Give mother your hands, children. O dearest hands, dearest lips and bodies, princely faces! May you be happy! But there, not here! Your father took away any happiness you could have here. O lovely look, O soft flesh and sweetest breath of my children—— Go in the house! Go!

The SERVANT *takes them in.*

I can no longer look at them; I am overcome by my woe. Now I realize what a terrible thing I am going to do. But I have more passion than reason, even though I know what disaster passion brings.

CHORUS

Often have I debated keenly about life
And struggled to resolve its many mysteries
More than women are credited with doing.
For there is the gift of speculation
Even among women, the craving to understand,
Not among all, only a few of them,

You might find one in a great number,
But women, too, are lovers of wisdom.

And I conclude that those among mortals
Who are childless have the best fortune.
For being childless and unaware
Whether their loss is woe or joy,
They live free from many a pain.
But those who have within their homes
The fragrant flower of tender youth
Are burdened all their days with care.

First to rear them properly,
And then to leave them means to live.
Never sure if all their toil
Is for good or worthless sons.
And then there comes a final fear—
They have found wealth to rear the young,
The bodies have grown to manhood, the mind
Noble—but if a god decrees,

Death comes. Down to the dark of Hades
He takes the bodies of your sons.
How then profits a man, having suffered
All else, to have this pain the more,
The sharpest pang given by the gods,
The bitterest grief imposed on men?

MEDEA. Friends, I have waited a long time for this to happen, and I am expecting now the report of it. I see one of Jason's servants approaching. From his labored breathing he shows what sort of news he brings.

Enter MESSENGER.

MESSENGER. You who have done this criminal thing, Medea, escape, escape, by any means you can, ship on the sea or wagon rolling over the earth!

MEDEA. What has happened that should force me to escape?

MESSENGER. The Royal Princess is dead, and Creon her father, slain by your poison.

MEDEA. That's wonderful news. Hereafter you shall be counted among my benefactors and friends.

MESSENGER. What? Are you sane and in your right mind, to do such injury to royalty and then rejoice when you hear about it? Aren't you afraid?

MEDEA. I shall have something to say to that later. But now take your time, my friend, and tell me how they died. You will make me twice as happy if they died horribly.

MESSENGER. When your two children came with their father to the bride's apartment we were delighted, we servants who shared your troubles. The rumor spread through the palace that you and your husband had become reconciled, and one of us would kiss the hand, another the golden hair of your children, and as for me, in my happiness I followed them even to the women's quarters.

The mistress whom we now pay homage to instead of you did not see the children at first, but was all eagerness when she saw Jason coming in. Then when she caught sight of the children, she was disgusted and half closed her eyes and turned her head away, but your husband soothed her and calmed her by saying, "Don't be unkind to those who love you. Stop being angry; just look at them and treat those who are dear to your husband as dear to you, too. Take these gifts they bring you, and persuade your father to let them stay here for my sake, won't you?" And she, when she saw the box of finery, did not hold back any longer, but granted her husband all he asked.

When the children and their father had just left the room she took out the embroidered dress and tried it on, and fastened the golden diadem about her head, fixed her hair before a gleaming mirror, and laughed gaily at the image—already as good as dead—that she saw there. Then she got up from her seat and walked to and fro, treading delicately across the room with white feet flashing. How happy she was over those presents! Often she would look over her shoulder to see how the train fell. . . .

But all of a sudden a sickening change took place. She became deathly pale, she staggered sideways, her legs started to tremble, and she just managed to sink into a chair to avoid falling on the floor. One of the old servants thought she fainted through emotion sent by Pan or some other God, and gave a cry of holy rejoicing—until she saw the white foam oozing on the princess' lips, and her eyeballs twisted upward, and her face drained of its color. Then she raised a cry of another sort, a piercing cry of pity. One servant ran to the King's apartment, another to the bridegroom's, to let them know of the bride's illness, and the whole palace resounded with people running.

It was about as long a time as a swift walker would cover the stadium course before she recovered her speech and opened her eyes and began to moan terribly. Then she wrenched herself up, poor woman, and entered the field against two merciless foes. The golden diadem which encircled her head sent forth a terrifying stream of devouring fire, and the delicate dress—those gifts your children brought her—began to eat away her white flesh. She leaped to her feet and ran all ablaze, shaking her hair and head, trying to throw off the diadem, but the golden clasp held firm, and the fire, as she shook her head, blazed twice as fiercely. She fell on the threshold, no match for her doom, hardly recognizable by anyone except her father. For her eyes were nearly gone, her face eaten away, blood dripped from the top of her head, clotted with fire, and the flesh was oozing from her bones like resin from a pine tree. Such jaws your secret poison had. She was a horrible sight. Everyone was afraid to touch her dead body, for we had seen enough to teach us better.

But her father, poor man, not knowing what had happened, suddenly appeared in the room and fell on the corpse, moaning and folding his arms around her and kissing her. "My poor child," he kept saying, "What god has ruined you so cruelly? Who has brought me to death by robbing me of you? I wish I could die with you, my daughter." At last he stopped his moaning and tried to raise his old body, but he was held as ivy clings to laurel branches. The delicate dress clung to him, and gave him a fiendish wrestling match. When he wanted to lift a knee, the cloth gripped it, and if he wrenched it away the aged flesh was stripped from his bones. Finally he gave up, the ill-fated King, and breathed his last, for he was no longer able to struggle with his doom. There they lie together, a sight for tears, the bodies of the girl and the old father.

As far as I am concerned—what will happen to you is your own affair; you will perhaps know how to find a refuge from punishment—I have always thought that mortal life is only a shadow and that men who seem wise and subtle of speech pay the greatest penalty. No man, in fact, is truly happy. In prosperity one man might be luckier than another; that's all you can say.

LEADER. It seems as if some divinity has heaped up woe for Jason on this day, and rightly so. O poor princess, how we pity you, who go to Hades because of having married Jason.

MEDEA. Friends, my mind is made up to kill my children at once, and then escape from this land. I must not by any delay let my sons be seized and murdered by a crueler hand than mine. This must be; there is no escape. And since it must be, I who bore them shall kill them. Come my heart, steel yourself. Why do I delay doing the terrible thing that must be done? Come wretched hand, take the dagger, take it, run the tragic race of pain, never flinch, never remember they are your children, how unspeakably dear they are, how you bore them—forget for this one short day that they are your children. Then for the rest of your life you can grieve for them. And grieving will be easy, for even if you kill them they were dear to you, and no woman is so miserable as I.

MEDEA *goes into the house.*

CHORUS

O Earth and all-seeing Light
Of the sun, look, oh look
On this accurst woman
Before she murders her children.
For from your golden race
She was born. Blood of the gods
Should not be spilt by men.
Keep her from doing it, Light
Immortal. Stop her, drive her
Away, the murderess, the Fury
Spurred by evil spirits.

In vain the mother's pains,
In vain you bore your children,
After leaving the Clashing Rocks
And the inhospitable strait.
Why did such fury seize you,
Such raging hunger for blood?
A terrible scourge on mortals
Are stains from blood of kinsfolk,
Murderous feuds in families
Wrought on homes by gods
In tune with bitter music.

A cry is heard from within.

ONE OF THE CHORUS. Do you hear the cry, do you hear the children?

ANOTHER. O poor, poor, unhappy woman!

A CHILD FROM WITHIN. What can I do? How can I get away from mother?

THE OTHER CHILD. There's no way, brother. She means to kill us.

ONE OF THE CHORUS. Shall I go in? Can I save
The children from death?

A CHILD. For God's sake, help!
Take the dagger away from her!

CHORUS

Like a rock or a piece of iron
You have no heart, you who kill
The children born of your body.
I have heard of another woman
Who cast murderous hands on her children,
Ino, driven mad by jealous Hera
And sent wandering across the sea.
She threw herself from a towering cliff
Into the waves, holding her babies
Close in her arms.
There is no agony worse than this.
Bridal bed, what woes you inflict!

Enter JASON *with* ATTENDANTS.

JASON. You women, tell me, is that infamous Medea inside her house, or has she taken flight? If she has, it's beneath the earth she would have to hide herself, or take wings into the sky above to escape paying the price for what she has done to the royal family. Does she think she can kill the King and get away unpunished? But it's not her I am thinking of, but the children—she'll get her just deserts from the kin of those she slew—it's the children I have come to save before Creon's family kill them in revenge for the mother's crime.

LEADER. Unhappy man, you little know what you have come to. If you did, Jason, you would not have spoken so.

JASON. What is it? Do you mean she intends to kill me, too?

LEADER. The children are dead by their mother's hand.

JASON. My God, what are you saying? That does destroy me, women.

LEADER. You must think of your children as no longer living.

JASON. Where did she kill them? Out here? Inside the house?

LEADER. Open the door and you will see their bodies.

JASON. Smash open the door as fast as you can, servants, tear off the hinges, let me see the two pitiful bodies. If they are dead she shall pay for it with her life.

MEDEA *appears on top of the house, in a chariot drawn by winged dragons. Beside her are the children's bodies.*

MEDEA. Why all this disturbance about tearing the house down? Why do you seek the corpses and me who did the deed? Labor no more. If you have need of me, say what you want. But you shall never lay hold of me again. This chariot is my present from Helios, father of my father, to protect me from every foe.

JASON. You hateful thing, loathesome to the gods and to me and to all mankind! You who had the reckless daring to destroy your children by the sword, and made me a childless, ruined man, and then can look on the sun and the earth after such a monstrous deed! The curse of death on you! Now I know what you are. If only I had known before I brought you from a savage country to a Greek home! It was a curse that I brought, betrayer of the fatherland that reared you, a blast of lightning that the gods launched against me. By killing your own brother you made your escape on the beautiful-prowed Argo. But that was only your beginning in murder. After you married me and had children by me you slew them because I left your bed. No Greek woman would have done such an outrageous thing, but I had to marry you instead of a decent Greek, you who have ruined me. It's a lioness you are, not a woman, and your heart is more brutal than the monster Scylla's. But I realize I couldn't sting you with any amount of reviling, such is your innate lack of shame. Go, abhorred thing, murderess of your children! I can only mourn my fate, I who shall never find joy in my new bride, nor in the children whom I begot and raised. I shall never have them to speak to again. Everything is lost.

MEDEA. I might answer you at length, if Father Zeus did not know what treatment you have had from me and I from you. You couldn't scorn my bed and then spend a joyous life laughing at me, nor could Creon, who gave you your royal bride, exile me from his land and escape punishment for it. Call me a lioness if you want to, call me Scylla. It's enough for me that I have broken your heart as it deserved to be broken.

JASON. You will suffer over the loss of the children as much as I.

MEDEA. Why not? The pain will be worth enduring if you weep.

JASON. My children, what a savage mother you had.

MEDEA. My children, how your lustful father wronged you.

JASON. It wasn't my hand that killed them.

MEDEA. Your arrogance and new marriage did.

JASON. You justify killing them because I made a new marriage?

MEDEA. Do you think a wife is willing to forgive that?

JASON. A sensible wife, yes. But you make everything vile.

MEDEA. They are dead, and you shall never get over the pain of it.

JASON. They live, as avenging spirits for me against you.

MEDEA. The gods know who began the wrong.

JASON. They know, indeed. It was you, you detestable woman.

MEDEA. Loathe me. I hate you, hate the sound of your voice.

JASON. And I yours. But we can be rid of each other easily if you are willing.

MEDEA. How? I am as eager for that as you are.

JASON. Let me have their bodies to bury and mourn over.

MEDEA. Never! I shall bury them with my own hands, after I have carried them to the shrine of Hera of the Heights, so that none of my enemies may open their grave and defile their bodies. And in this land of Sisyphus I shall establish a holy festival and rites for the dead, as propitiation for all time to come of this crime against heaven. Then I shall go to the land of Erechtheus, where King Aegeus, son of Pandion, will give me refuge. As for you, you shall die the death a low villain deserves—after long, lonely years, deprived of that lovely bride of yours, you shall be felled by a rotten plank of your ship Argo.

The chariot starts to move.

JASON. May the Furies and Justice destroy you, Medea,
Murderess of your children!
MEDEA. Who of the gods or spirits will listen
To you, perjurer, faithless guest!
JASON. Detestable destroyer of children!
MEDEA. Go to your home and bury your bride.
JASON. I am going, bereft of my children.
MEDEA. You don't know yet what mourning means,
Just wait and grow old.
JASON. Beloved children!
MEDEA. To their mother, not to you!
JASON. You who slew them?
MEDEA. To cause you pain.
JASON. Oh, just let me kiss their lips,
The dear lips of my children.
MEDEA. Now speak to them, now caress them,
You who thrust them away?
JASON. Let me
Stroke again their tender faces.
MEDEA. No. All you ask is asked in vain.

The chariot disappears.

JASON. Zeus, do you hear me, how I am spurned,
What I have suffered from this lioness,
This monstrous murderess of her children?
Yet in whatever way I am able
I shall mourn my sons, and call
All the gods to be my witness
How you slew them and then forbade me
Even to touch and bury their bodies.
Would I had never begotten the children,
To see them now slain by you.

He throws himself on the earth.

CHORUS

Zeus in Olympus guides our fate,
And sends us many things undreamed of.
What is expected does not happen,
The unexpected comes to pass.
So has it happened here.

THE *Frogs* OF ARISTOPHANES

Translated by John G. Hawthorne

INTRODUCTION

THE COMEDIES of Aristophanes are not the least of the great cultural monuments which Athens in the fifth century B.C. created and bequeathed to posterity. On the one hand they exhibit a creative originality, a technical excellence and a universal humor that have scarcely been equaled in the realm of comic drama; on the other, they present a vivid picture of life in Athens during and after the great war which overwhelmed her, and of the gradual but never quite complete disillusionment of a literary genius.

The audience for which Aristophanes composed consisted of the male citizens of Athens and of any foreigners or visitors to her festivals. It was a compact and intimate group in which the author lived and worked, and where he recognized his friends, neighbors, and enemies. From the beginning of the century, they and their fathers before them had been educated and trained in the appreciation of drama at the regularly recurring religious festivals. It is therefore not entirely with his tongue in his cheek that Aristophanes in the *Frogs* compliments his audience on its high level of understanding and erudition.

The major honor at the festivals went to tragedy, as the earlier and more serious art form. Therefore, although the origins of tragedy and comedy were different, it is not surprising that comedy modeled itself to some extent on its weightier rival. Thus the structure of comedy is closely parallel to that of tragedy, alternating between the spoken dialogue, the sung or danced dialogue, and the choral song and dance. The early importance of the chorus in tragedy is reflected in the title roles of the earlier comedies; the later tragic dissociation of the choral song from the plot, especially under Euripides, is paralleled by the unimportance of the chorus in the last extant play of Aristophanes. One innovation, which is peculiar to the earlier comedies and may have been a survival from original comic representations, is the "parabasis," a patter song in which the leader of the chorus voices the author's personal opinions directly to the audience. Such an interlude in the play did in time prove to be out of tune and has indeed scarcely been revived to this day, with the notable exception of T. S. Eliot's *Murder in the Cathedral*. Another important though often overlooked parallelism to tragedy is the diction. Today, a distinction is often drawn, and even considered desirable, between a colloquial style for comedy and a grand or elevated style for tragedy. But Aristophanes used the same meters, words, and tone as tragedy and derived from this use a very great deal of his humor; it gave him an extensive field for parody, paronomasia, and bathos. Owing to the fact that the majority of fifth-century tragedies and comedies have been lost, it is impossible to judge the extent of this playing upon tragedy, but from the parallels already adduced by scholars, it can be conjectured that the range was greater than will ever be proved.

However, despite these impressive connections between tragedy and comedy, criticism must not be led astray into establishing the same principles of judgment for these two art forms, contenting itself merely with the distinction of serious and comic. In the first place, Greek tragedy took a well-known myth and wove it into a tightly-knit plot; in comedy, on the other hand, the plot is of little importance; what counts is the idea and the series of situations. The genius of Aristophanes is revealed first in his invention of original and funny ideas: the private armistice of the *Acharnians*, the thinking-shop of the *Clouds*, the cloud–cuckoo-land of the *Birds*, the monstrous regiment of *Lysistrata*, to name a few. Nor is there any lack of comic situations, great and small; for example, Philocleon trying to escape from his house in the *Wasps*, Trygaeus on his beetle in the *Peace* or Dionysus rowing across the Styx in the *Frogs*. Secondly, the treatment of characters is entirely different in tragedy and comedy. In the former the author sets up a bond of sympathy, touched with admiration and pity, between the audience and his heroic characters; in the latter, such a bond is absent, for the author's intention is not to make the audience feel with the characters, but laugh at them. This Aristophanes achieves in various ways; sometimes, as in the *Acharnians*, he presents a composite character drawn from society to typify the average Athenian, attributing to him everyman's faults and failings; again, he takes an almost heroic champion, like Lysistrata, and setting her in an intricate situation endows her with a farcical inventiveness for the solution of a problem that has not been entirely solved even today; again he will take a god and turn him into a buffoon. But the most striking, because almost unique, characterizations of Aristophanes are those of men of real flesh and blood: Cleon, Socrates, Aeschylus, Euripides, and so forth. It is here that Aristophanes has been most severely criticized, for instance, for using comedy as an instrument for political propaganda against Cleon or for misrepresenting Socrates and his earnest mission or for scandalously defaming the character of Euripides. The separation of art and politics, the gravity of educators, the laws of libel make our consciences tender today and appeal is sought to decency and good taste. But Aristophanes was too good a comedian not to realize that an accurate representation of any character, real or imaginary, does not charm the comic muse. Just as a tragic character must be ennobled, so a comic one must be made ridiculous. Nor is such criticism informed. There are today hundreds of private skits or "smokers" being produced every year, in which real, living people are lampooned. The circumstances and audience of Aristophanes enabled him to publicize the licence of our private showings. Thirdly, a comedy differs from a tragedy, in that, before all other considerations, a comedy must be funny. This is an obvious observation, but it is in need of emphasis, particularly with reference to comedies from an older and different civilization. Too many critics have explained the greatness or weakness of Aristophanes on other grounds; too many translators have lessened his humor by expurgation. The failure of the *Clouds* to win first prize has been explained by a variety of technical and other reasons; the fact remains that, though the idea is good and the portrayal of Socrates unforgettable, the play is not very funny. Again the expurgators of Aristophanes do both him and their readers a great injustice by leaving a blank or a mistranslation, so that the critical faculty cannot operate. Some bawdy jokes are funny and some are merely vulgar and Aristophanes has his full share of both sorts. In short, while there are undoubted failures on one score or another, there are few readers or audiences who would deny that Aristophanes was a masterly creator and executor of humor.

Yet beneath this humor lies the tragedy of a society; the loss by death or exile of many of the great figures of the fifth century and the conquest and destruction of Athens. It is natural that Aristophanes should be concerned in his plays with literature and with his rivals in tragedy and comedy, and this topic forms the basis of several of his plays and appears in them all. His other great themes are education, law and the rights of men and women. But overshadowing them all is his intense interest in politics and the welfare of Athenian society. From the *Acharnians* of 425 through the exultation of the *Peace* in 421 to the last pathetic chorus of the *Frogs* in 405 and even beyond, his constant preoccupation is with peace and a restoration of the rich and noble days of the Athenian past. This accounts for the recurrent Utopia theme of so many of his plays and his virulent opposition to demagogues and new-fangled ideas; and the portraits and references to contemporary Athenians, which form so valuable an addition to the impersonal history of Thucydides, reflect also the aspirations of a gifted and noble Athenian who was constrained to watch the gradual suicide of his own country. Nonetheless Aristophanes, like Athens, recovered. He wrote extensively after the fall of the city, although only two complete plays have survived from this period, both of them Utopian and, apart from certain changes, both in idea and incident true to the genius of his younger and more intense days.

The *Frogs* was produced at the Lenaean Festival in 405 B.C., a dark and gloomy period for Athens. The death of Euripides in the preceding year may well have been the motivation of the play. On the whole the tone of the play is unusually elevated and erudite, leaning rather to wit than to farce; its relative lack of bawdiness is introduced by the criticism of former comedians in the prologue. The idea of a parody on a descent to Hades is a happy one and has been not infrequently imitated. The scene on the Styx with the Frogs from whom the play gets its name is lively and animated and greatly effective when set to music. The parody of the Mystery Chorus, brave in conception, is, however, restrained and not without beauty. With the entrance of Aeschylus and Euripides a violent change of tempo occurs, for up to this point the action has been moving, but from now on it is static. This abrupt change and lack of movement in the latter half of the play is the reason why many critics feel that the play drags. But it is more than a change of tempo; it is also a change from the farcical to the witty. In shorter passages Aristophanes is very fond of such abrupt changes, which do not as a rule suit the taste of audiences who prefer their tones to be kept more level and distinct. They do, however, seem to have pleased the quickness of the Athenian temper. But an abrupt change on such a large scale is unique even for Aristophanes. The ensuing literary duel between Aeschylus and Euripides is famous and is the finest example of Aristophanes' capacity for wit and parody. The change of mind which Dionysus undergoes in the final scene, when he chooses Aeschylus rather than Euripides, has also bothered some critics, who like comic plots to be consistent, but it is part of the humor and is certainly realistic. Might it be called Aristophanes' private joke?

The translation is as literal as taste allows. A colloquial rather than a grand style has been adopted, where called for, as being more suited to modern taste. The

Greek meters have been transposed into appropriate English verse.

THE TEXT translated here is that of F. W. Hall and W. M. Geldart (Oxford, 1907). For help in preparing the notes, the translator is indebted to the edition of W. W. Merry (Oxford at the Clarendon Press, 5th ed., 1905).

THE CHARACTERS

XANTHIAS, a slave of DIONYSUS
DIONYSUS, a god
HERACLES, a retired hero
DEAD MAN
CHARON, a ferryman
AEACUS, a porter
MAID
LANDLADY
PLATANE, a servant of the LANDLADY
EURIPIDES, a poet
AESCHYLUS, a poet
PLUTO, a king
CHORUS OF FROGS
CHORUS OF MYSTIC DANCERS

Enter DIONYSUS *disguised as* HERACLES, *and his slave* XANTHIAS. *The latter carries the baggage, but he rides on a donkey.*

XANTHIAS. Master, shall I raise the curtain with a crack
That always gets the audience laughing back?
DIONYSUS. For God's sake, anything you wish, but not that stuff
About the squeeze play; we have biliousness enough.
XANTHIAS. Nor that smart pun?
DIONYSUS. No, no. No itches i' the crutch.
XANTHIAS. What then? The very funny one?
DIONYSUS. Why not? You're much
Too shy. But see you don't repeat your old——
XANTHIAS. What's it?
DIONYSUS. Switch of your baggage-crutch to let you have a sit.
XANTHIAS. Nor that this bag's so heavy on my shoulder there
That, if I'm not relieved, I'll simply let out air.
DIONYSUS. Oh please, not yet awhile; just wait till I throw up.
XANTHIAS. Then tell me why I had to bring this cargo up,
When I can't do the things that Phrynichus has done
Or take the risks that Lycis and Amipsias run? [1]
DIONYSUS. Don't take them; for when I am looking at their plays
And see some of their tricks and clever, clever ways,
I swear I leave my seat a whole year older.
XANTHIAS. Three curses on this poor old suffering shoulder!
It itches like a—No; that joke is not allowed.
DIONYSUS. Is this not insult and effeminacy proud
When I, great Dionysus, of the Liquor Clan,
Walk on my feet and labor, while I set this man
Astride an ass to bear his efforts and his weight?
XANTHIAS. I bear a weight as well.
DIONYSUS. How come, when you're the freight?
XANTHIAS. By freighting this.
DIONYSUS. And how?
XANTHIAS. Too weightily for me.
DIONYSUS. No, no; the weight you freight the ass freights for you, see?
XANTHIAS. Indeed it doesn't. This is what I have to bear.
DIONYSUS. How can you bear it, when you're borne yourself up there?
XANTHIAS. I don't know how; my shoulder's being squashed again.
DIONYSUS. Well, since you say the donkey does not help you, then
Change places, curse you, carry it yourself instead.
XANTHIAS. Damnation! If I'd fought the war, I would be freed [2]
And then I could have made you scream as loud as hell.
DIONYSUS. Get off the ass, you blackguard. You can walk as well
As I. But, wait a minute, here's the door quite near
Where we must first turn in. Hey, porter, hey, I'm here.
HERACLES (*opening the door*). Who's knocking the door? Who's beating it down, whoever it is, like a bull?
Heaven on earth! What is this?

DIONYSUS. Sst, sst!
XANTHIAS. What's up?
DIONYSUS. Don't you notice, my man?
XANTHIAS. Notice what?
DIONYSUS. He's scared stiff of me.
XANTHIAS. God, so he is! (But it's you who's the fool!)
HERACLES. I can't help myself laughing, Demeter above, but I'll do what I can
By biting my lips. It's no good. I must laugh, I must laugh or I'll burst.
DIONYSUS. Come here, please, sir. I wish to ask a question first.
HERACLES. But I can't smear the smile off my face when I see
My lion-skin laid on a yellow silk gown.
What's the plan? How do buskin and my club agree?
And where in the world have you come from, you clown?
DIONYSUS. I embarked on Clisthenes'—— [3]
HERACLES. And fought a battle on the seas?
DIONYSUS. Sank the enemies' ships, no less
Than twelve or thirteen, at a guess.
HERACLES. Just you two did that alone?
DIONYSUS. As Apollo's on his throne!
XANTHIAS. Then I woke and found him out.
Nothing but a dream, that rout!
DIONYSUS. As I sat on deck I read
Euripides' *Andromeda,*
And a sudden longing sped
And burst my heart asunder.
HERACLES. How strong a longing did you feel?
DIONYSUS. As big as Molon's tiny heel.[4]
HERACLES. Longing for a woman?
DIONYSUS. No.
HERACLES. For a boy, then?
DIONYSUS. No, no, no.
HERACLES. For a man?
DIONYSUS. Oh, oh, oh, oh!
HERACLES. Did you lie with Clisthenes?
DIONYSUS. Brother, do not mock me, please.
I am not well, and this desire
Burns me through and through like fire.
HERACLES. Little brother, tell me why.
DIONYSUS. I cannot say. Yet I will try
A riddling analogy:
Did you ever suddenly
Get a craving for—pea-soup?
HERACLES. A thousand times I have—— Pea-soup!
DIONYSUS. You know it then, or shall I tell
Some other way—— ?
HERACLES. I know it well.
DIONYSUS. So I'm being eaten by degrees
With hunger for Euripides.
HERACLES. For him? A corpse?
DIONYSUS. None shall prevent
My visiting his tenement.
HERACLES. Down there, in Hell?
DIONYSUS. And lower yet,
If Hell has any cellaret.
HERACLES. Why, what d'you want?
DIONYSUS. A clever man
To write a poem. All who can
Are dead; the living are no good.
HERACLES. Not Iophon? [5]
DIONYSUS. Perhaps he would
Be one, the only one, but still
I doubt if he would fit the bill.
HERACLES. If you have to resurrect,
Wouldn't you rather first select
Sophocles?
DIONYSUS. Not till I've had
Iophon without his dad
And played a tune or two on him.
Besides, Euripides would skim
Through Hell and Heaven to come back
With me; he's such an artful quack;
While Sophocles, in life serene,
Serenely waits on Proserpine.
HERACLES. And what's become of Agathon? [6]
DIONYSUS. Good poet, he is up and gone
And all his friends commiserate.
HERACLES. Where is the wretch?
DIONYSUS. He dines in state.[7]
HERACLES. And Xenocles? [8]
DIONYSUS. God damn his hide!
HERACLES. Pythangelus then? [9]
XANTHIAS. Oh! My poor side
Aches terribly, but not a word
Of comfort from them have I heard.
HERACLES. Are there not other effete little youths
Scribbling their thousands of tragical truths,
Who outchatter by miles your Euripides?
DIONYSUS. They're just barren foliage, a quavering breeze

Symphonic swallows, who dirty their art.
Why, a chorus of theirs could not even start
Making up to Queen Tragedy, such is their funk!
You can't find a poet who has enough spunk
To bark out a glorious phrase!

HERACLES. What's this spunk?

DIONYSUS. Spunk is when a man says
Something risky and dangerous. Thus:
"God's Shack, the Air" or "Time the Macropus"
Or "Hearts swear not upon the Holy Writ,
While tongues will perjure both themselves and it!"

HERACLES. This can't please you!

DIONYSUS. I'm mad about it, though.

HERACLES. I swear it's tricky, if you think it so.

DIONYSUS. Don't use my mind to think in. You've a house.

HERACLES. Well then, I think it's simply blasphemous!

DIONYSUS. Teach me to eat my supper!

XANTHIAS. Not a word of me!

DIONYSUS. Well, let me tell you why I've come here, as you see,
Disguised like you. I thought you'd tell me, should I ask,
The names of all your friends you stayed with on your task
Of fetching Cerberus, the harbors, restaurants,
Inns, brothels, fountains, roads, retreats, and haunts
Of citizens and soldiers, and the landladies who see
Their beds are free of bugs.

XANTHIAS. And not a word of me!

HERACLES. You brazen fool, will you too brave the road to Hell?

DIONYSUS. No more of that. Tell me the quickest way we well
May take, and see it isn't far too hot or cold.

HERACLES. Now, let me see, the first—— well, which?—— that should be told——
There's one, by rope and rowing. It's the hanging road.[10]

DIONYSUS. Stop, stop. That chokes too much!

HERACLES. Then try the traitor's mode.
A quick and well-worn path, well pounded down.

DIONYSUS. You speak
Of Hemlock Lane?[11]

HERACLES. I do.

DIONYSUS. It's awfully cold and bleak.
Your ankles start to freeze up stiff immediately.

HERACLES. D'you want me to suggest a short, steep, uphill way?

DIONYSUS. By God, that suits me fine. I'm no pedestrian.

HERACLES. Just wander down to the Ceramicus——[12]

DIONYSUS. And then?

HERACLES. Climb up the big, tall tower.

DIONYSUS. And what do I do there?

HERACLES. You watch the torch race starting, from high up in the air,
And when the people shout "They're off!" Why, off you go.

DIONYSUS. Off where?

HERACLES. Below.

DIONYSUS. Oh no. I do not wish to show
My brains are filled with sausage-meat. I'll skip that way.

HERACLES. Well, which way do you want?

DIONYSUS. The same as you, I say.

HERACLES. That is a trying trip; for, first you'll meet a lake
Quite bottomless and vast.

DIONYSUS. What ferry can I take?

HERACLES. You'll come across a sailor, a man with greying hair,
Who will take you in his dinghy; two obols is the fare.[13]

DIONYSUS. Those tyrannizing obols! They're everywhere in town.
How come they went to Hell?

HERACLES. King Theseus took them down.
Next you'll see the serpents and a terrible array

Of awe-inspiring monsters . . .
DIONYSUS. Don't frighten me away
Or scare me from my wits. For I shall not relent.
HERACLES. And an ever-flowing sea of mud and excrement,
In which the wicked wallow, who cheated their best friend,
Or stole a lad's virginity with his dividend,
Or broke their father's jaw or shook their mother loose,
Swore falsely or repeated a phrase of Morsimus.[14]
DIONYSUS. You surely ought to add in those who've learnt the score
Of Cinesias' latest number, the Pantomime of War.[15]
HERACLES. From there a breath as of soft pipes will strike your ear
And you will see a light as beautiful as here
Shining on myrtle groves, and happy throngs of men
And women, and a clapping loud of hands again.
DIONYSUS. And who will these folk be?
HERACLES. Those blessed by Mystery.
XANTHIAS. I'm blessed if I'm the ass to carry them on, see?
Nor will I hold this bag a minute more, d'you hear?
HERACLES. And they will tell you everything. They live quite near,
Just up that very road where Pluto's lodgings end.
So good-bye, brother.

HERACLES *retires into his house.*

DIONYSUS. Thanks. God bless you, too, my friend.
Hey, pick up those bags again.
XANTHIAS. Before I've even put them down?
DIONYSUS. Jump to it too, you scatterbrain.
XANTHIAS. No, please; not me. Spare half a crown
To hire a porter; they're all set
To carry out this deadly task.
DIONYSUS. And if there isn't one to get?
XANTHIAS. Try me again.
DIONYSUS. All right. I'll ask.

He catches sight of a funeral procession.

Say you; yes, you; dead man, awake.
You're being carried out, I see.
Would you be kind enough to take
Some things of mine to Hell for me?
CORPSE. How much?
DIONYSUS. Just this.
CORPSE. Two drachmas, please.
DIONYSUS. You won't accept a lower fee?
CORPSE. No. Porters, clear the road of these.
DIONYSUS. Hold on, please, sir; could we agree?
CORPSE. Two drachmas down or say no more.
DIONYSUS. Nine obols, here.
CORPSE. I'd sooner live!

The funeral procession moves on.

XANTHIAS. He's a damned old pompous bore
And due for a sticky alternative.
I'll take the things myself.
DIONYSUS. Good man.
On to the boat, my trusty Xan.

They arrive at CHARON'S *wharf.*

CHARON. Stand off, stand off.
XANTHIAS. What's that? D'you hear?
DIONYSUS. That? God, that must be the mere
He told us of. Look; here's a boat.
XANTHIAS. And Charon too, the old sea-goat.
DIONYSUS. Charon, come on; come on, Charon;
Come on, Charon; Charon, come on.
CHARON. Who's for a rest from ills and woes?
Who's for the plain of Lethe? Who's
For the fleecing ground, the dead, the Crows?
Who's for Sparta and all our foes?[16]
DIONYSUS. I am.
CHARON. Board quickly.
DIONYSUS. Where d'you stop?
The Crows, you say?
CHARON. For you. So hop
Aboard.

DIONYSUS. Come, boy.
CHARON. I don't take slaves
Unless they've fought upon the waves
And won their liberty and—— spam!
XANTHIAS. I wasn't drafted, for I am
Weak-eyed.
CHARON. Your legs at any rate
Can run you round.
XANTHIAS. And where'll I wait?
CHARON. The hotel by the Blasted Stone.
DIONYSUS. D'you understand?
XANTHIAS. I do, and groan
To think I met you passing out.
CHARON. Sit to the oar. Come, all about
To sail, get in at once. Hey, you!
What's up?
DIONYSUS. What's up? I stuck onto
The oar, just as you ordered me.
CHARON. Fat guts, not there. Sit here, d'you see?
DIONYSUS. I see.
CHARON. And put your hands just so
And stretch.
DIONYSUS. I see.
CHARON. No nonsense, though.
Brace both your feet and row with zest.
DIONYSUS. How can I row without a test,
Untried, unsea'd, un-Salamized?
CHARON. Quite easily, once you've set your fist
To oar. You'll hear a soft swan song,
Most siren-like.
DIONYSUS. From where?
CHARON. A throng
Of wondrous frogs will sing to you.
DIONYSUS. Let's go; give me the beat.
CHARON. One-two, one-two.

The boat ride begins.

FROGS

Brekekekex Koax Koax,
Brekekekex Koax Koax.
Children of the lake and spring,
Lovers of the choral ring,
Raise our ancient voices high,
Hymn our sacred melody:
Brekekekex Koax Koax.
Nisaean Bacchus, son of Zeus,
At Limnae's shrine you came to loose
Your drunken throng of hierophants;
Vouchsafe a pitcher for our chants:
Brekekekex Koax Koax.

DIONYSUS. Vouchsafe to heal my bottom too;
It hurts, Koax! Koax to you!
FROGS. Brekekekex Koax Koax.
DIONYSUS. Koax be damned! Or don't you care?
Koax, Koax. It packs the air.
FROGS. Of course, you busy-body, since
The lovely Muses and the Prince
Of song and sport, horn-hoofèd Pan,
Delight in me, and Bacchus can
Rejoice to think that he will get
Reeds for his pipes, for damp and wet
I nurture them beneath the lake
To play his tunes without a break:
Brekekekex Koax Koax.
DIONYSUS. My hands are blistered; when I bend
A sweaty noise bursts from my end:
FROGS. Brekekekex Koax Koax.
DIONYSUS. Please stop your tuneful melody.
FROGS. No, no. We'll sing as merrily
As when we hop from sedge to reeds
And chase the sunshine through the weeds,
Rejoicing in our swooping song;
Or when the rain beats hard and strong,
Fleeing to the depths we flop,
Burbling, gurgling, plip and plop:
DIONYSUS. Brekekekex Koax Koax.
There's the tune I've learnt, d'you see?
FROGS. Bad for us——
DIONYSUS. But worse for me!
Rowing splits me right in two.
FROGS. Brekekekex Koax Koax.
DIONYSUS. Croak away! I don't mind you.
FROGS. Listen. We shall croak away,
Gaping wide our throats all day——
DIONYSUS. Brekekekex Koax Koax.
No. You won't outcroak me now.
FROGS. Nor you won't us, not anyhow!

DIONYSUS. Nor you me either! I shall shout
Brekekekex Koax Koax
If I must, till day is out,
And I beat you at one stroke——
Brekekekex Koax Koax.
There, you see. I've stopped your croak.

The boat has now reached the other side of the Styx.

CHARON. Stop, stop. Lay off the oars. Get out and pay the fare.
DIONYSUS. Two obols, here you are. Where's Xanthias? Oh, where
Is Xanthias? My Xan!
XANTHIAS. Hullo!
DIONYSUS. Come here at once.
XANTHIAS. Well met, my master!
DIONYSUS. Sst! What's that? Look there, you dunce.
XANTHIAS. Darkness and dung.
DIONYSUS. And do you see the men he said
Who swear to lies and beat their fathers on the head?
XANTHIAS. Why, yes. Don't you?
DIONYSUS [*looking at the audience*]. God's little fishes! Now I do.
Oh! What's for us?
XANTHIAS. We'd better move a step or two,
Since here's the place he said the awful monsters were.
DIONYSUS. To Hell with his tall stories! He won't make me stir.
He knows I'm full of fight, the jealous Pekinese.
There's nothing quite so proud as Mister Heracles!
I wish I could meet someone who'd make this trip worth while!
I'd take him on at once and throw him half a mile.
XANTHIAS. Oh God! What's that I hear? A sort of rustling sound——
DIONYSUS. Where is it?
XANTHIAS. Just back there.
DIONYSUS. Get back and stand your ground.
XANTHIAS. But now it's up in front.
DIONYSUS. Go forward; guard the van.
XANTHIAS. God help me! Now I see a great big monster.
DIONYSUS. Xan,
Be careful. What's it like?
XANTHIAS. It's awful every way;
At first a bull, and then a mule, and then a—say!—
Most seasonable maid!
DIONYSUS. Where? Let me go. Where? Which?
XANTHIAS. She was a maid, but now she's changed into a bitch.
DIONYSUS. Oh! That must be Empusa.[17]
XANTHIAS. And all her head's aglow!
DIONYSUS. She got a brazen leg as well?
XANTHIAS. By God, you know,
The other's just a cowpat.
DIONYSUS. Oh! Where can I recline?
XANTHIAS. Or I?
DIONYSUS (*to the Priest of Dionysus, prominent in audience*). High Priest, preserve me! I'll pay you back in wine.
XANTHIAS. Lord Heracles! We're lost.
DIONYSUS. Don't call me that, my man,
Or say that name, I ask you.
XANTHIAS. Then Bacchus! Help your Xan!
DIONYSUS. That's worse. Just keep on where you're going.
XANTHIAS. Master, here.
DIONYSUS. What is it?
XANTHIAS. Cheer up now. All's well; we're in the clear.
Hegelochus and we can say, "The storm is past;
The cats and dogs it rained have gone to rest at last!" [18]
Empusa's disappeared.
DIONYSUS. Swear it.
XANTHIAS. By God, she has.
DIONYSUS. And swear again.
XANTHIAS. By God!

DIONYSUS. Again.
XANTHIAS. By God!
DIONYSUS. Alas!
She made me go all green. Where has my courage fled?
XANTHIAS. The High Priest trembled too and all his face went red!
DIONYSUS. Alas! What doom is this that overwhelms my cries?
What God shall I accuse of plotting my demise?
XANTHIAS. Why not "God's Shack, the Air" or "Time the Macropus?"
DIONYSUS. Xan!
XANTHIAS. What's it now?
DIONYSUS. Just listen! D'you hear that noise and fuss?
XANTHIAS. What noise?
DIONYSUS. A breath as of soft pipes.
XANTHIAS. I do.
They smell
Like mystic torches.
DIONYSUS. Hush! Crouch down and mark them well.

Enter chorus of mystic celebrants in torch-light procession.

CHORUS

Iacchus O Iacchus!
Iacchus O Iacchus!

XANTHIAS. That's them, sir. They're the people blessed by Mystery,
Of whom he told us; and they're playing here close by
And chanting the Iacchus, Diagoras's song.[19]
DIONYSUS. I think so too. Be quiet; we'll hear it before long.

CHORUS

Thou that dwellest full of honor
In this sacred choral grove,
Come, Iacchus, through the meadow,
Lead the dances that we love.

Here thy holy band of Mystics
Worships thee with waving bough;
Shake the brimming myrtle cluster
Of the garland on thy brow.
Iacchus, O Iacchus, come.

Step forth boldly to the music;
Start the wild ungoverned dance;
Lead us in the sportive measure
With the honor of thy glance.

See, the Graces bow before thee;
See, thy Mystics gather round.
Bless us with thy sacred presence;
Purify this hallowed ground.

XANTHIAS. Come, Lady full of honor, my Persephone,
And purify this pig; it smells very good to me![20]
DIONYSUS. Be quiet. You'll be blessed with a bit of gut, maybe.

CHORUS

Raise aloft the flaming torches;
Boldly brandish them on high.
Come, Iacchus, star of splendor,
Bless this night of mystery.

See, the meadow gleams and flashes
Underneath thy sacred light,
And the knees of old men quiver
With the frenzy of our rite.
Iacchus, O Iacchus, come.

Soon the grief and pain of ages
Which the long years set in place
Will be shaken off and conquered
By the magic of thy grace.

Come, Iacchus, join our dances;
Spread the flame of holiness.
In the flow'rs of this thy meadow
Grant us youth and happiness.

Stand off and keep quiet. Depart from this riot of dancing and chanting and bright revelry,
Every stranger whose breast carries sins unconfessed and who knows not the secrets of our mystery,
And never before us has danced in our chorus nor seen the wild orgies of our noble Muse,
Nor tasted the rites of the Bacchic delights, which

the tongue of Cratinus, the bull-eater, spews, [21]
Nor burgles the altar with joy, but will falter and think that such thieving is quite out of place,
Or who does not help out at an enemy's rout and is mean to his citizen's friendly embrace,
And stirs up a treason without any reason except for his private, particular gain,
And takes every bribe, if he's head of the tribe, when the city is under a dangerous strain,
Or sells to blackmailers our soldiers and sailors or secretly starts an "Aegina" affair
That he's learnt how to do from Thorycion's cue—may he cook his accounts till he dies of despair—
By sending a cargo against the embargo to fill Epidaurus with hides, cloth, and pitch,[22]
Or who tries to persuade some millionaire's aide into making our enemy's arsenal rich,
Or defecates at you near Hecate's statue, while learning his part in the ritual play,
Or obtains a high rank from the orator's plank and then nibbles the wages of poets away
Because we've marooned him, decried and lampooned him, in rites Dionysus enjoined on our sires;
To all these I proclaim, and again I proclaim, and a third time proclaim in the name of our choirs:
Stand off and keep quiet. The Mysteries riot. So raise up your voices and all the night long,
As befits our sublime, holy festival time, let the meadow resound with the echo of the song!

Onward, Mystic dancers,
Bravely beat the ground,
Where the flowering meadows
Girdle you around.
Now's the time for jesting,
Now for sport and play;
Our repast should easily last
For the livelong day!

Onward, greet your Savior,
With uplifted arms;
Nobly raise your voices,
Praising all her charms.
She has saved our country
Till the winter's gone
In despite of all the might
Of Thorycion.

Now let your voices swell again; with sacred song adorn
Our gracious Goddess, Demeter, the Queen of harvest corn!

Queen Demeter, star of night,
Hither, stand before us.
Celebrate your sacred rite;
And protect your chorus.
Grant that safely all night long
We may sing your praises,
Sporting in a happy throng,
Dancing in the daisies.

We have jests and we have jokes
Worthy of your fêting
And some really serious strokes
Long in need of stating.
So we'll banter while we may,
Joyful, glad and clowning;
Pray, our jests may win the day
And give us the crowning!

Now sing a hymn to summon here our God of joy and youth
To dance with us in revelry and jest with us at truth!

Great Iacchus, full of honor,
Founder of the sweet feast-song,
In the Goddess' steps come hither,
Show the way is not too long.
Praise him, praise him,
O Iacchus,
Go before and guide our song.

Thou didst rend thy cloak and sandal
For thy poor and simple throng,
That in laughter, without scandal,
They might join thy dance and song.
Praise him, praise him,
O Iacchus,
Go before and guide our song.

Look! I see a maiden dancing
Fair of face and full of song,
And she's tripped and torn her lacing
Where her bosom slants along.
Praise him, praise him,
O Iacchus,
Go before and guide our song.

DIONYSUS. I always like going before it's too late
And I want to go dancing with her as my date.
XANTHIAS. I agree she looks sporting. For what do we wait?

CHORUS

Shall we together lampoon
The seven-year-old poltroon,
Archedemus, whose bribes
Have lost him the tribes
Of the generals he tried to maroon? [23]

The course of his present ambition
Will make him the worst politician
Up there, above ground,
And the dead and the drowned
Will elect him their finest mortician.

I hear next the tearing and gnashing
Of Clisthenes' jaws, and the clashing
Of buttocks that squat
In the graveyards and spot
The poor wretch with the spray of their splashing.

He sits and he shouts and he screams
And he strikes and he spumes and he steams,
For Sebinus, he's told,
Has tossed him off cold
And returned to his trusted triremes.[24]

Then Callias, too, they declare,
Who was born of a man and a mare,
Has been fighting at sea
In the brave panoply
Of a lion skin, draped from his hair.[25]

DIONYSUS

Would you mind telling us, please,
If we don't interrupt, which of these
Is Pluto's abode,
For we're new to this road
And have only just come, if you please?

CHORUS

You don't have to go a step more,
For here you are right at the door,
And now may I say,
Get out of the way
And don't interrupt any more.

DIONYSUS. Here we are, Xanthias, then.
Pick up the baggage again.
XANTHIAS. Oh! What have I done?
This thing weighs a ton!
Damn all Corinth! I say, what a strain! [26]

CHORUS

Come, circle through the sacred grove
And dance amid the flowers,
You who share the Goddess' love
And banquet in her bowers;
While I, with maidens old and young,
Shall bear the sacred light
And lead them to the Goddess' throne
To celebrate the night.

Let us dance our sacred way
Through the rosy meadow flowers,
Sporting in our chorus gay
With the happy, happy Powers;
We who keep thy Mystery
Safe from friend and stranger's eye,
We alone are blest by thee,
Giver of the light on high.

DIONYSUS *stands before the door of Hades.*

DIONYSUS. I'd better knock the door, and yet, I fear . . .
How do the natives knock on doors down here?
XANTHIAS. Don't beat about the bush; try this way in.
Be Heracles in heart as well as skin.
DIONYSUS. Ho, porter!
AEACUS (*flinging open door*). Who is there?
DIONYSUS. Stout Heracles!
AEACUS. Thou noisome, unashamed, presumptuous fool!
Vile, viler and of all the vilest yet,
Who fought, beat, throttled, stole and drove to earth
Our watchdog Cerberus, my faithful ward,
And then thyself wert gone. I have thee now,
So nearly yon black-hearted Stygian crag
And these blood-oozing cliffs of Acheron
Do lock thee in; the circling hounds of Hell
And serpent with the hundred heads will tear
Thy entrails, and Tartessus' lamprey-leech
Will fasten on thy lungs, what time thy ribs,
All blooded with their very inward parts,

Will feast the Gorgons of Tithrasia—
To whom I point forthwith my speedy foot!

He rushes off inside.

XANTHIAS. What have you done?
DIONYSUS. I've crapped. Invoke the god.
XANTHIAS. Get up before you're seen, you silly clod.
At once. D'you hear me?
DIONYSUS. No. I'm going to faint.
Please bring a sponge. My heart feels very quaint.
XANTHIAS. Here. Hold it close.
DIONYSUS. Where is it?
XANTHIAS. Gods of gold!
D'you keep your heart down there?
DIONYSUS. It got so cold
With fear, it sank right to the bottom, see?
XANTHIAS. Of gods and men most craven-hearted . . .
DIONYSUS. Me?
What's craven in my asking you for one?
None other would have done it. They'd have done . . .
XANTHIAS. What?
DIONYSUS. Grovelled there and snivelled like a skunk,
While I stood up and cleared off all my funk.
XANTHIAS. God! That was brave!
DIONYSUS. Yes, I think so, I do.
Weren't you afraid of all his big words too.
And those vile threats?
XANTHIAS. I didn't mind at all.
DIONYSUS. Come, then, since you're so fond of gain and gall,
You take my club and skin and play my part
And I'll be porter now, Sir Brave-in-Heart!
XANTHIAS. Give me them quick. No need of urging me.
Now watch Heracloxanthias and see
If I have donned your craven heart as well!
DIONYSUS. You jail bird from a Melitean cell! [27]
Come, let me have the baggage, then.

MAID (*appearing at the door of Hades*). My love, my Heracles! It's really you
Returned again? Come in. Persephone
No sooner heard you'd come, immediately
She baked some bread, boiled two or three pots full
Of pea-soup, roasted whole a juicy bull
And toasted jumbo buns. Do come in, please.
XANTHIAS. Sounds wonderful. but——
MAID. By Apollo, she's
Just braised some partridges and jugged a hare,
And brought the sweetest wine up, I declare.
So, please come in with me. I'll see you won't
Escape this time.
XANTHIAS. Thanks very much, but don't . . .
MAID. Don't babble. I won't let you go and, mind,
We have a lovely flute girl, just your kind,
And two or three the chorus lent us, so . . .
XANTHIAS. The chorus, did you say?
MAID. Yes, and, you know,
They've learnt some facts of life just recently;
They're quite abreast. So come in. Look, you see,
The carver's just about to serve the fish
And set the table. Come on, if you wish.
XANTHIAS. First, go and fetch those chorus girls, suggest
That Heracles in person is their guest.
My boy will fetch the bags and bring them here.

The MAID *retires.*

DIONYSUS. No, wait. You can't believe I was sincere,
Because I dressed you up like that in fun?
None of your nonsense, Xanthias, just run
And take these bags again, confound your game!
XANTHIAS. What's that? You surely don't propose to claim
The gifts you gave yourself?
DIONYSUS. I don't propose.
I'm doing it right now. Take off those clothes.
XANTHIAS. God be my witness! I will trust in Him.
DIONYSUS. You vain and foolish mortal! Trust in Him!

D'you think you'll be Alcmena's son, you slave?
XANTHIAS. Oh! All right. Take them then. Perhaps you'll have
Some need of me sometime, if so He wills.

CHORUS

If by chance you are a student
Of the man who's wise and prudent
And has travelled many seas,
You will find he always ranges
To the winning side and changes
Every sail to catch the breeze;
He won't be a graven image
And alone resist the scrimmage,
But will cultivate his ease.
Keep on twisting, keep on turning;
That's the clever way of earning;
That's what made Theramenes.[28]

DIONYSUS

I should laugh, if my own porter
Kept on turning to a daughter
Of the chorus for a kiss,
Twisting on the soft and frilly
Cushions from Miletus, till he
Found his ardor went amiss;
Then I'd let the scoundrel watch me,
Though, I fear, if he could scotch me,
While I played about with this,
He might feel it was his duty
To knock out a toothsome beauty
And undo my dentifrice!

LANDLADY (*at door*). Platane, Platane, hurry; that scoundrel is once again here,
Who came to the inn and devoured sixteen loaves of bread at a go.
PLATANE. Ow, Ma'am! That's the fellow right there.
XANTHIAS. Someone will catch it, I fear!
LANDLADY. Yes, and twenty full plates of roast beef, at a whole half-obol a throw!
XANTHIAS. And now is the time for the bill.
LANDLADY. And all that garlic, you know.
DIONYSUS. Nonsense, my good woman, you know not what you say.
LANDLADY. You thought I wouldn't recognize you in those buskins, eh?
And what about that salted fish I haven't mentioned yet?
PLATANE. And those wretched greening cheeses that the devil went and ate,
And made away as well with the very baskets too!
LANDLADY. And when I brought the bill, he glared me through and through
And bellowed something awful.
XANTHIAS. Exactly like his ways!
He does it all the time.
LANDLADY. Then his eyes began to glaze;
He drew his sword and threatened like a madman.
PLATANE. Deary me!
LANDLADY. We scampered to the loft in fear, immediately.
He darted on the mat, took and tore it, then he went.
XANTHIAS. That's just like him too!
PLATANE. But shouldn't we prevent . . . ?
LANDLADY. By all means. Go and call our champion Cleon here.
PLATANE. And if *you* see Hyperbolus, we'll grind him, never fear.[29]
LANDLADY. Vile maw! How gladly would I beat your teeth in with a bit
Of stone, for chewing all my stores!
PLATANE. I'd throw you in the pit!
LANDLADY. I'd take a scythe and slit the throat that swallowed all my food!
PLATANE. I'll go fetch Cleon. He'll unwind this fellow's guts for good.

The LANDLADY *and* PLATANE *retire.*

DIONYSUS. It looks as though I'm due for Hell! But, Xanthias, my friend . . .
XANTHIAS. Stop, stop right there. I do not understand a bit what you intend.
I won't be Heracles again.
DIONYSUS. You won't? Dear, little Xan!

XANTHIAS. How could I be Alcmena's son, a slave and mortal man?
DIONYSUS. You're angry now, and, I must say, it's properly incurred;
And even if you beat me blue, I won't return a word.
But if I take these clothes from you at any time to come,
May I, my wife and children all be struck completely dumb
With blear-eyed Archedemus too!
XANTHIAS. Accepted on those terms!

CHORUS

Now it is your earnest duty,
Since you have the club and suit he
Wanted to exchange before,
To remember that you image
Heracles the God, and scrimmage
Toughly, roughly with a roar.
But if you're caught cultivating
Just one word of ease, or prating
Silly nonsense like a bore,
You will have to change your station,
Tote the bags to your damnation
And become a slave once more.

XANTHIAS

Thank you all for your kind warning.
Such a thought was just adorning
My suspicious, slavish brain.
For I know quite well the bounder
Will demand my skin and pounder,
If they promise any gain.
Still, I'll tackle every bustard
With a heart as bold as mustard
And a pepper pot of pain.
No more time for funk or cringing,
For I think I hear the hinging
Of the door begin to strain.

AEACUS *appears at the door with two grim male servants.*

AEACUS. Quickly bind this dog-thief here.
Hurry him to jail.
DIONYSUS. I fear
Someone will catch it!
XANTHIAS. Go to Hell!
Don't move.
AEACUS. You want to fight? Well, well.

He calls additional attendants.

Ditylas, Sceblyas, Pardocas; quick,
Come here and teach this man a trick.[30]
DIONYSUS. Surely it's a double fault
To thieve and then commit assault?
AEACUS. Far worse. It's plumb unnatural.
DIONYSUS. You dirty, dangerous criminal!
XANTHIAS. Strike me dead, if ever I
Was here before, or tried to pry
A single hair loose from your head!
But I'll propose a test instead,
That is quite generous and kind.
Take this boy; refresh his mind
With torture. If I'm proved to be
A criminal, you may kill me.
AEACUS. What refreshment do you like?
XANTHIAS. Every kind; rack, rope, hang, strike,
Use the cat, the screw, the whip,
Put weights upon his chest and drip
Strong vinegar up his nose, but not
The scourge with leeks or new shallot![31]
AEACUS. That's fair; and if I cripple him,
I'll credit you for every limb.
XANTHIAS. Don't bother. Take him off and start.
AEACUS. We'll do it here. Then every part
Of his confession will be seen.
Put down your baggage. You, I mean;
And see you don't tell any lies.
DIONYSUS. I denounce this enterprise,
Being immortal. Any blame
Attaches only to your name.
AEACUS. What's that you say?
DIONYSUS. I say again:
I am immortal, known to men
As Dionysus, son of Zeus,
And this man here's my slave.
AEACUS. The deuce!
Do you hear that?
XANTHIAS. I do, and say
The more you ought to flay away.
If he's a god, he will not feel.
DIONYSUS. Why then, if you claim to be real,
Don't you match equal blows with me?
XANTHIAS. That's fair. Whichever one you see

First notices the blows or cries,
You may consider in disguise.
AEACUS. You are a noble man, to tax
Yourself so fairly! Bare your backs.
XANTHIAS. How will you torture us alike?
AEACUS. Quite easily. Strike one, then strike
The other in his turn.
XANTHIAS. That's fine.
AEACUS (*with a blow*). There!
XANTHIAS. Watch and see me cringe or whine.
AEACUS. I've struck you once.
XANTHIAS. You don't say so!
AEACUS. It doesn't look it. But I'll go
And strike the other fellow.

He strikes.

DIONYSUS. When?
AEACUS. I've struck you too.
DIONYSUS. How was it then
I didn't even start to sneeze?
AEACUS. I really do not know. Now, please,
I'll try the first man once again.
XANTHIAS. Well. Hurry up; I won't complain.

Aeacus strikes.

Oh! Attati!
AEACUS. What's that attati?
D'you feel it?
XANTHIAS. God, no! I'm just spry;
My Diomean feast is due.[32]
AEACUS. The man's a priest! Now one for you!

He strikes.

DIONYSUS. Gee-gee!
AEACUS. What is it?
DIONYSUS. I can spy
The cavalry.
AEACUS. That make you cry?
DIONYSUS. No; onions.
AEACUS. Sure you didn't sniff
At something else?
DIONYSUS. No; not a whiff.
AEACUS. Now back we go to this one. (*To one of his slaves*) Strike!
XANTHIAS. Ow!
AEACUS. What?
XANTHIAS. I've trodden on a spike.
AEACUS. A likely story! Him again (*to slave*).
DIONYSUS. O Lord!——"Apollo, thou that dwellst around
On Delos' isle or Pytho's rugged ground!"
XANTHIAS. That hurt, see?
DIONYSUS. No. I had you hexed
By quoting from Hipponax' text.[33]
XANTHIAS. That's no good. Give his guts a go.
AEACUS. You're right. Just bare your belly; so!

The slave strikes.

DIONYSUS. O Lord Poseidon!——
XANTHIAS. Someone's hurt!
DIONYSUS. "Thou dost bide on
Cliffs Aegean, calm and free,
Or in shiny
Depths and briny
Caverns of the murky sea!"
AEACUS. By Demeter, I can't spot
Which of you is god or not!
Come inside. Persephone
And my master soon will see
Which is which, for they're gods too.
DIONYSUS. Thank you. But I wish that you
Had said so sooner and foregone
The trial that's been going on!

All retire into Hades.

CHORUS

Muse of the sacred dances, fleet
Come to the pleasure of my song;
Here thou shalt see a mighty throng,
Where all the Graces have their seat:
Here is the wisdom infinite
Which thou hast given to thine own;
Come to the place where thy sages sit
Greater in honor than Cleophon.[34]

See how the Thracian swallow drips
Terrible thunder on his head,
Perching himself on a foreign bed,
Singing his song from treacherous lips!
Hark, 'tis the nightingale's refrain
Presaging tears and deathly gloom!

What if the voting is split in twain?
He will certainly meet his doom! [35]

This sacred chorus should advise and teach [36]
The city well. First, then, it seems to us
Democracy and freedom from all fear
Should be the people's right, and, have men failed
And slipped beneath the grasp of Phrynichus,[37]
I say we should give opportunity
To those who then did wrong to clear themselves
And mend the error of their former ways.
All citizens, I say, must freely vote;
For it is shameful that a single fight
Should make some masters, who were slaves before,
And give them forthwith sacrosanctity,
(Though it was noble, I admit thus far,
And praise you for 't—your only prudent act),
While others, fellow-kinsmen, who have fought
And seen their fathers fight a hundred times
In line with you, should find their loyalty
Impugned, unheeded, for a single sin.
Let us, my friends, forget our angry mood,
As God has given us wisdom beyond most,
And join in willing kinship, rights and honor
All men who fight in our united cause.
But if we boast and puff ourselves with pride,
Guarding our city in the hidden sea
Of isolation, then posterity
Will mock our wisdom and refute our power.

If I am right in seeing clear
Habits and ways that indicate
Someone is due for a sticky fate,
Foremost of all is this ape here,
Troublesome, tiny Cligenes,[38]
Guttersnipe giant, Lord of lies,
Slinger of mud and privily wise,
Pliant as putty and eager to please.
But, guessing his fate,—and it's nearly come!—
He mongers war and thumps the tub,
Lest he be stopped when walking home,
Drunk and alone without his club!

Too often we have thought the state observes
The same distinction to its noblest men
As to its old and recent currency.
That ancient coin, of gold uncounterfeit,
The fairest yet, it seems, of all in Greece
Or foreign lands, alone well struck and true,
Stamped in the die of purest ringing worth,
We never use, but tinkle with these baubs,
Base metal, struck awry, and scarcely yet
In circulation upwards of a day.
So our own citizens, well born and wise,
True men of justice and nobility,
Bred in the schools of gentleness and strength
Where grace and art are master, these
We scorn, for brassy, strange, red-headed thugs,
The spawning of foul sires, of whom we use
The last to be dredged up, for everything.
Why! Formerly the city would not dare
To pick on such so lightly, random-like,
And turn them out for scapegoats! So, I say
'Tis time to change your foolish, feckless ways
And entertain nobility again
As fits an upright state. And, if you fail
And suffer aught, the wise at least will know
You suffered on a cross of worthy wood!

AEACUS *and* XANTHIAS *return to the scene.*

AEACUS. Lord save us, there's a perfect gentleman,
Your master.
XANTHIAS. Sure; that's why he only can
Tipple and tumble. That's nobility today.
AEACUS. To think he didn't beat you, caught at bay,
A slave, pretending to be master then!
XANTHIAS. He'd better try!
AEACUS. And was I happy when
You did as slaves do; that's a thing I love!
XANTHIAS. You love it?
AEACUS. Yes, and seem to see above
Ecstatic visions, when I curse and swear
Behind my master's back.
XANTHIAS. And when you tear
Outside, with blows about your back, d'you do
The mumbo-jumbo curse?
AEACUS. I like that too.
XANTHIAS. And nosey-parkering?
AEACUS. God help me, yes.
XANTHIAS. God sent you, brother. Tell me, when you press

Your ear to keyholes for your master's chatter——

AEACUS. Yes, yes; that drives me madder than a hatter.

XANTHIAS. D'you like to chatter it to strangers?

AEACUS. Sure.
I splatter it all round just like manure.

XANTHIAS. Phoebus Apollo! Let me shake your hand
And give you kiss for kiss, and by the brand
The devil stamped on every fellow-bum,
Tell me what is that pandemonium
Inside? What's all that din and cursing, please?

AEACUS. It must be Aeschylus and Euripides.

XANTHIAS. Oh?

AEACUS. There's a helluva, helluva how-d'ye-do
Among the dead; revolt and bloodshed too.

XANTHIAS. What's up?

AEACUS. It's been a law about these parts,
Whoever wins the prize in liberal arts,
Shall have his meals provided by the state
And sit on Pluto's right.

XANTHIAS. I get it.

AEACUS Wait—
Until another better in his field
Arrives down here, and then the first must yield.

XANTHIAS. But why should Aeschylus be disturbed by that?

AEACUS. He used to hold the tragic prize and sat
As master of that field.

XANTHIAS. Who else instead?

AEACUS. Euripides came down, exhibited
To all our sneak thieves, footpads, murderers,
Our father-beaters and adulterers,
(There's quite a number here in Pluto's courts),
Who heard his dialectical retorts,
His fancy fencing and his twist-and-hit
And went quite mad and thought him King of Wit.
So up he got, all proud, and seized the chair
Of Aeschylus.

XANTHIAS. And wasn't thrown from there?

AEACUS. Good God, no; but the people yelled to see
A trial of their verbal subtlety.

XANTHIAS. That gang of jail birds?

AEACUS. All the blessed lot.

XANTHIAS. There were some friends of Aeschylus, were there not?

AEACUS. Virtue's just as scarce in there as here!

XANTHIAS. Well then, does Pluto mean to interfere?

AEACUS. Immediately. He's setting up a trial
To test and judge their artistry.

XANTHIAS. Meanwhile
The chair has gone to Sophocles to claim?

AEACUS. He wouldn't take it. Why, when first he came,
He just kissed Aeschylus and shook his hand;
And he gave way a bit, but made him stand
And lean against the chair. So Sophocles
Intends—I quote Clidemides— [39]
"To hold his reservation in reserve."
Should Aeschylus win, he's quite content to serve;
If not, he says he'll battle for his skill
Against Euripides.

XANTHIAS. Then tell me, will
It really happen?

AEACUS. Yes, and on this spot
The blows will soon be falling thick and hot.
They're going to measure music by the pound . . .

XANTHIAS. What? Short-sell tragedy, like beef that's ground?

AEACUS. They'll bring straight rules, syllabic measurers,
Clause-clamping frames . . .

XANTHIAS. What clever plasterers!

AEACUS. And diametric squares and compasses
To torture every line of tragedies.
That's what Euripides says he will do.

XANTHIAS. I guess that Aeschylus was angry too!

AEACUS. He put his head down, glowering like a bull.

XANTHIAS. And who's the judge?

AEACUS. Well, that was hard to rule.
Both found a lack of wise men, good and true,
And Aeschylus refused Athenians too.

XANTHIAS. Perhaps he thought there were too many thugs!

AEACUS. And all the rest he reckoned utter mugs
At judging an artistic soul. At length

They chose your master, for his poetic strength.
Still, we must go; when masters are severe,
It's time for us to look for trouble here.

The scene shifts to the place of the contest, where EURIPIDES *and* AESCHYLUS *stand before* DIONYSUS *with* PLUTO *in the background.*

FIRST HALF-CHORUS

wrathful the thunderer's heart within black anger filled
watches tooth-whetting of rival scream-scraping skilled
wrathful his madness-shrilled
eyes shall roll

SECOND HALF-CHORUS

word-wrestlings flash to respond gleamings of horse-hair crest
splintering axles yes crashing of arms to test
structures of wit and best
charge their goal

FIRST HALF-CHORUS

shaking his shaggy-maned neck beetling wrathful brow
he bellows fury and belches clamped clauses now
tearing by root and bough
blasts from earth

SECOND HALF-CHORUS

tugging at envious bit in turn the mounting tongue
twists to attack word-mincing ardent among
laborings long of lung
to kill worth.

EURIPIDES. No more advice. I will not yield the chair.
I beat him to it. That's what I declare.
DIONYSUS. Why are you silent, Aeschylus, for you
Must surely understand the fellow's words?
EURIPIDES. He builds a silence, mystic and sublime,
Just like his prologues every single time.
DIONYSUS. Euripides, my dear friend, please restrain
Your tongue, and do not talk so loud and big.
EURIPIDES. I know the man and long have watched him dress
Uncivilized, inhuman stubbornness
In words unbridled, uncontrolled, unbarred:
Unmeaningfulness packaged-by-the-yard!
AESCHYLUS. How now, thou Goddess-nurtured—tilthy sprout! [40]
Thou callst me thus, thou phraseologist!
Unsightly bumbard, ragamuffin sewer,
Thou'lt weep for it, I trow!
DIONYSUS. Stop, Aeschylus,
And do not overheat yourself with angriness.
AESCHYLUS. Stop! Nay; not ere I show this brazen up
Such as he is, a cripple-poetaster!
DIONYSUS. Quick, boys, fetch a lamb to sacrifice,
Black as the storm wind that's about to break.
AESCHYLUS. Thou who dost cull the Cretan monodies [41]
And set incestuous loves upon the stage!
DIONYSUS. Aeschylus, full of honor, please be still.
And you, young scoundrel, dear Euripides,
Escape from all these hailstones, if you're wise,
Lest you should find your forehead is struck by
A heady word and anger makes you spew
The *Telephus;* [42] and you in turn calm down
And hold the trial, Aeschylus, in peace.
Poets should not curse like harridans;
But you are roaring like an oak on fire.
EURIPIDES. I am quite ready and shrink not a whit
To bite first, if he wills, or first be bit.
My words, my songs, the sinews of my art,
The *Peleus, Aeolus* in whole or part,
Are ready to be tried and, Aeschylus,
The *Meleager* and the *Telephus.*
DIONYSUS. What are your wishes, Aeschylus? Speak up!
AESCHYLUS. I had not willed to hold the jousting here;
The lists are not matched fairly for us twain.
DIONYSUS. How so?
AESCHYLUS. My poetry died not with me:
His died with him; he has it there to read.
Yet, since thou judgest so, needs must I try.
DIONYSUS. Bring frankincense and fire for sacrifice
That I may pray, before these tricky wiles,
To judge this contest musically well!
And to the Muses let your voices swell.

CHORUS

Sacred maidens, nine in number,
Virgin Muses, born of Zeus,
Guardians of poetic wisdom,
Homely saw and wit abstruse;
You rejoice in sharp debaters,
Wrestling, wriggling, battling haters,
Dialectic consummators;

Come, then, Muses, watch the power
Of this grim and awful pair;
Grant them sawdust separators
To dissect words to a hair!
Now the great examination
For the top poetic station
Comes to actualization!

DIONYSUS. Both should pray before you test your lines.

AESCHYLUS. Demeter, thou who foster'dest my heart,
Grant I be worthy of thy Mysteries!

DIONYSUS. Do you too take and sprinkle frankincense.

EURIPIDES. Thanks! I have other gods to watch and ward.

DIONYSUS. Some of your own, of recent circulation?

EURIPIDES. Correct.

DIONYSUS. Then pray to your divinities.

EURIPIDES. Our Fodder Air! Our Tongue's Vibrating Cord!
O Understanding! Nostrils Osmotic!
Grant I test rightly every verbal trick!

CHORUS

Here we stand, our hearts all yearning
For the test of poetry.
We shall hear what path, what turning
You will blaze in rivalry.

See, their tongues are twisting wildly;
See, their tempers flare and burn,
And their wits unreconciledly
Stir with anger for their turn.

One, we think, will use a pretty,
Witty dagger from the city,
Smoothly glancing down his nose.
While the other by the roots
Tears up, lunges, scatters, shoots
Circusfuls of vocal blows.

DIONYSUS. Come quickly to the contest. Speak and see you argue thusly:
Both full of wit; no images; unplatitudinously!

EURIPIDES. If I am first, I'll handle last the test of my own verses
And first refute this boasting cheat and show how he rehearses
His tricks before an audience he takes for foolish persons
Because they were accustomed to old Phrynichus's versions.[43]
Well, first of all, he introduced a figure, veiled and lonely,
Achilles, say, or Niobe, who showed no face, but only
Stood stock still like a stage prop and didn't even rumble . . .

DIONYSUS. By God, it didn't either.

EURIPIDES. No. The chorus sang a jumble
Of four continuous stanzas then, each standing on the other,
While the actors stood in silence . . .

DIONYSUS. But I liked that silence, brother.
It made me far more happy than these modern, mouthing mummies.

EURIPIDES. You were too small!

DIONYSUS. Maybe. But what's the purpose of those dummies?

EURIPIDES. To show off to the audience and keep their minds suspended
To see if Niobe would speak before the play was ended.

DIONYSUS. The wicked fellow! I admit I fell for it completely.
What makes you belly-ache and scowl?

EURIPIDES. Because I have him neatly.
For after all the song-and-dance of these mad chorus-fellows,
The play half over, Niobe emits twelve bully bellows,
Bushy browed, crestiferous, all gremlin-eyed and growling,
Which no one understands at all . . .

AESCHYLUS. Alas! Alack!

DIONYSUS. Stop howling!

EURIPIDES. In fact, there's not a word of sense——

DIONYSUS And keep those teeth ungrated!

EURIPIDES. In streams Scamandrous, moats-a-moss or shield-borne brazen-plated
Paratrooping gryphon-eagles, bare-faced hoarse-expressions,
All very badly-hyphenated . . .

DIONYSUS. God! How many sessions,
Sleepless through the long, long night, I've spent in wondering whether
His ruddy "hippalectryon" is fish, flesh, fowl or feather!

AESCHYLUS. Thou fool. 'Tis only one of those engraved ship's-prow's prefixes.

DIONYSUS. I thought it was Philoxenus's latest friend Eryxis!

EURIPIDES. Is tragedy the place, d'you think, for cocks to be erected?

AESCHYLUS. Blasphemer; and what monstrous things has thy foul mind selected?

EURIPIDES. No hippalectryons at least or tragelaphs tremendous
Like those on Persian tapestries, as you did, Lord defend us!
I found that you bequeathed to me an art of boils and boasting
And heavy-handed vocables, to which I gave a roasting,
And eased its weight with many a little ditty and tricky turning,
With candid cabbage, savory sips and literary learning;
Then fed it up on monodies——

DIONYSUS. And mixed Cephisophon in! [44]

EURIPIDES. And didn't charge on randomlike, with bedlam madly thrown in,
But my first actor gave at once the drama's genealogy . . .

DIONYSUS. And that was better done, God knows, than giving your own ancestry!

EURIPIDES. And from the very first remarks, I made them all work faster;
The mistress spoke, the slave no less, the nurse and maid and master.

AESCHYLUS. What communism!!! I would say, thou shouldst be hanged emphatically!

EURIPIDES. Good Heavens! No. That proves I only acted democratically.

DIONYSUS. Hush! Comrade. Not a word of that. You just keep right of center.

EURIPIDES. So then I taught them all to chatter——

AESCHYLUS. There I'm no dissenter!
But wish that thou hadst burst thy guts instead of training actors!

EURIPIDES. . . . By arming them with fine-edged rules and versicule-contractors
To mark, see, understand and twist, make love and try inventions,
Suspect and question everything . . .

AESCHYLUS. I still have no contentions!

EURIPIDES. And introducing homely things, which we all share and handle,
By which I could be easily tripped; for they would make a scandal
At any errors in my skill in things they knew so fully.
No lightning-quiver was my mind; I didn't bark and bully
Or scare their wits with thunder-claps or turn them into jellies
With Swans and Memnons riding high on brazen-bellèd bellies.
Our pupils you can tell apart (and needn't be too brainy!):
Phormisius is his, yes, and Megaenetus the Zany,[45]
Both sword-and-trump, club-thump-and-glare, mustachio'd banditti,
While mine is Clitophon, yes, and Theramenes the Witty.[46]

DIONYSUS. Theramenes? A clever man, but dangerous to rely on.
For though he's thrown from bad to worse, he'll never die a Chian!
For he turns as the tables turn and playing them from both ends
He throws the winning die himself and ruins all his friends!

EURIPIDES. This was the learning I produced
To fill their minds with questions;
For into art I introduced
My skeptical suggestions.

So now they think of everything
With nice discrimination
And have improved their home-living
By sharp investigation.
They ask: How does this come about?
Where am I orientated?
What is the circumstantial doubt?
Who understands what's stated?

DIONYSUS. At any rate, all Athens now
Has got a wider jaw-span,
For going home, they start a row
By asking: Where's the saucepan?
Who's eaten up my pilchard's head?
The pot I bought last year is dead!
Where is the leek of yesterday?
Who has nibbled my olive away?
But formerly they sat around
Like mummy's darlings, fawning,
Without a curse, without a sound,
Just yawning, yawning, yawning!

CHORUS

Great Achilles, mark this clearly.
Come, what wilt thou in recourse?
Only let thy heart not seize thee,
Carry thee beyond the course.
Grim has been his accusation!
Terrible his demonstration!

Noble sir, speak not in anger.
Furl thy sails and bare thy mast.
Thou shalt guide and guard his clangor
Better when the gale is past.
Let the storm subside and settle
Ere thou com'st to prove thy mettle.

DIONYSUS. Thou who first of all the Hellenes built the towers of lofty song,
Robed the Muse in tragic numbers, boldly loose thy lightning prong.

AESCHYLUS. I rejoice at this occasion, though my bile is sorely spent,
To refute this foolish mortal, lest he deem me impotent.
Answer, churl, what skill in poets should the world admire the most?

EURIPIDES. Wit and wisdom and the power to educate a city's host.

AESCHYLUS. So if thou hast not done this, but made the best and noblest men
Into criminals most wicked, what should be thy sentence then?

DIONYSUS. Death. No need to ask him that one.

AESCHYLUS. Then, sir, please deliberate
On the kind of men I left him when he entered my estate,
Loyal, noble, six-foot giants, who would not betray their friends,
Not these modern idle sissies, loitering to gain their ends,
But the breath of spear and halberd, tossing plume and white-hair crest,
Axe and armor, greave and heart of seven-fold oxhide in their breast.

DIONYSUS. Here is that damn list again! He'll squash me flat with armor plate!

EURIPIDES. What did you do to produce the fine nobility you state?

DIONYSUS. Speak up, Aeschylus; don't get the huffy, puffy heebie-jeebies.

AESCHYLUS. I wrote a drama full of Ares.

DIONYSUS. What?

AESCHYLUS. The *Seven against Thebes*.
Everyone who saw it lusted to become a man of war.

DIONYSUS. That was badly done, you know. You made the Thebans dread no more.
So they battled far too bravely, beat you, too, by your own play!

AESCHYLUS. Ye too might have practised bravely, but ye always turned away.
Then I wrote the *Persians* later, and aroused a strong desire
Aye to conquer rival armies, painting it with vivid fire.

DIONYSUS. How I loved to watch Darius' ghost appear and have his say,
While the chorus clapped their hands and chanted loudly, "Blaze away!"

AESCHYLUS. This is what the poets ought to practise, for perpend again
How the noblest poets have been useful to all kinds of men.
Orpheus gave us revelation and restraint from blood and crime,
While Musaeus gave us medicine and the oracle sublime;

Agriculture, fruits in season, ploughs and ploughshares Hesiod
Handed down to us, while Homer won his glory like a god
Just because he taught manoeuvres, prowess and a soldier's trade—

DIONYSUS. Not to Pantocles, he didn't, clumsy oaf, who on parade
Donned his helmet first, then later tried to fix the crest inside!

AESCHYLUS. There are many other brave ones, like old Lamachus who died,
Whence I drew my inspiration and portrayed the good and true,
Lion-hearted Teucers and Patrocluses, to rouse a few
Citizens to lay themselves out, when they heard the trumpets loud,
But, 'fore God, no whores like Phaedra, Stheneboea or their crowd!
Not a single woman falls in love in any play I penned!

EURIPIDES. Aphrodite never troubled you, 'fore God!

AESCHYLUS. May God forfend!
But she rode on thee and thine many times and many ways
And she threw thee for a fall.

DIONYSUS. True, by God. For in your plays
You did things to wives of others, which bounced back and caught you flat!

EURIPIDES. Tell me how my Stheneboeas hurt the city, wretch, at that.

AESCHYLUS. Thou it was who harried noble wives of noble men with shame,
Forced them into drinking hemlock with Bellerophon to blame!

EURIPIDES. Well then, was the drama I composed of Phaedra not all true?

AESCHYLUS. True enough, 'fore God, but poets should hide evil from the view
And not dramatize or teach it; for as little children learn
From their elders, so their elders learn from poets in their turn.
We must therefore speak good only.

EURIPIDES. And your Lycabettan brood
And Parnassan monster-words, is that what you call teaching good?
You should use more human phrases.

AESCHYLUS. Curses on thee! There must be
Words engendered that are equal to their high philosophy.
Godborn heroes rightly utter words of greater emphasis,
Just as they are clothed in raiment far more dignified than this!
I established this good practice till thou cam'st to spoil it.

EURIPIDES. How?

AESCHYLUS. First by clothing kings in tatters, so that men might watch them bow
Underneath a yoke of pity.

EURIPIDES. Well, what harm did I do there?

AESCHYLUS. That's the reason why the rich no longer want to pay their share
By contributing a trireme, but they dress in rags and cry
Tears of lying protestation, falsely pleading poverty.

DIONYSUS. While below they wear a tunic of the finest wool they wish
And if they're believed, they hurry off to buy the fattest fish!

AESCHYLUS. Then thou taughtest the art of chatter and the practice of hot air,
Which has emptied every gym and softened every buttock there,
While the lads are hot in chatter. Then he tried to agitate;
Made the sailors disobedient to their rulers! Let me state,
When I lived, they knew no more than call for "chow" and "ship ahoy!"

DIONYSUS. Yes, by God, and how to blow a bubble at the cabin boy,
Drop upon their fellow-crewmen, go ashore and slit a throat.
Now they argue, row no longer, sail about and simply float!

AESCHYLUS. He's to blame for all our troubles!
He brought on the female pimps,
Bearing children in the temples,
Marrying their brother simps,
Swearing life was death, the frimps!

He's the man who filled our city
With a swarm of sorry scribes,
Fat baboons and church banditti,
Cheating all our honest tribes
With their never-ending bribes!
Everyone has too much fat on
For the torch race or the baton!

DIONYSUS. Gods above! I wept with laughter
At the Panathenian race,
When a slow one staggered after,
Fat and fainting, white of face,
Acting like a damn disgrace!

Meanwhile at the half-way station
All the plotters in their ranks
Struck him with determination,
Beating with flat, stinging planks
Belly, buttocks, ribs and shanks,
Till the poor man loudly started,
Blew his torch out and departed.

CHORUS

Great the question, strong the struggle, fierce the warfare comes and goes!
Hard to discriminate!
One lunges in a spate,
One has power, feinting backwards, cleanly to return his blows!
But do not sit and wait.
There are also many other sophistries that pack a punch!
As you have learnt to strive,
So speak, charge, flay alive,
Tricks old and new contrive,
Risking all to land a witty, jesting knockout with a crunch.

If by chance you have a fear that ignorance may overcome
These our spectators, lest
They miss a single jest,
Shudder not at all for that; no longer are they quite so dumb:
They're veterans at rest!
Each has fought his bookish battle! Each has learnt correct syntax!
Talent superlative!
Sharp beyond normative!
Fear not at all, but give
Tongue to every thrust and parry. They will understand your cracks!

EURIPIDES. Well then, I shall turn to prologues first
And in that part of tragedy I'll burst
The bubble of this bumble-headed wit.
His telling of the tale was never fit.

DIONYSUS. Which will you prick?

EURIPIDES. He wrote a lot of plays,
But . . . Quote the *Oresteia's* opening phrase.

DIONYSUS. Silence, I say, silence! Speak, Aeschylus.

AESCHYLUS. "Lord of the Dead, guarding a father's sway,
Protect, befriend me, Hermes, as I pray.
For I come home, returning to this land!"

DIONYSUS. Any of these to blame?

EURIPIDES. Yes, twelve or so.

DIONYSUS. He's only spoken three lines, don't you know?

EURIPIDES. And each has twenty errors at a guess!

DIONYSUS. Oh! Please be silent, Aeschylus, unless
You want to seem to chalk up more than three.

AESCHYLUS. I silent at that!

DIONYSUS. If you're advised by me.

EURIPIDES. Right at the start he made a heavenly bloomer.

AESCHYLUS. Stuff! Fiddlesticks!

DIONYSUS. And yet I have a humor . . .

AESCHYLUS. What did I do?

EURIPIDES. Begin at first again.

AESCHYLUS. "Lord of the Dead, guarding a father's sway,"

EURIPIDES. Orestes says this at the sepulchre
Of his dead father?

AESCHYLUS. Do I not concur?

EURIPIDES. Did he not say that, when his father died
Beneath a woman's sudden, secret pride,
Hermes yet guarded thus his father's sway?

AESCHYLUS. Not his! 'Twas Hermes Eriounius,[47]
Lord of the Dead, he thus addressed and showed
His father's guerdon fell to his estate.

EURIPIDES. Still greater is your fault than I desired,
If 'twas his father's deadly guerdon he acquired!
DIONYSUS. A god, despoiling his dead father's tomb!
AESCHYLUS. Dionysus, charnel-scented is thy wine!
DIONYSUS. The next two lines. You watch for faults to come.
AESCHYLUS. "Protect, defend me, Hermes, as I pray.
For I come home, returning to this land."
EURIPIDES. Ragged redundancy, wise Aeschylus!
DIONYSUS. How so?
EURIPIDES. I'll tell you. Watch his phrasing—thus:
"Come home" he says and then "returning" too!
"Come home" "return"—two words where one would do!
DIONYSUS. By God! As if you bid a neighbor "Hail.
Lend me a bucket or, if you will, a pail!"
AESCHYLUS. Thou addle-pated fool! They're not the same.
The verse is truly unimpeachable!
EURIPIDES. How so? Instruct me in your meaning, please.
AESCHYLUS. He only comes home, whom a home awaits;
No ceremony else. An exile though
Must first return and then he may come home.[48]
DIONYSUS. Good, by Apollo! Now, Euripides.
EURIPIDES. Orestes never did return, because
A secret entry is against the laws!
DIONYSUS. Good, by Hermes!——What was that you said?
EURIPIDES. Another line.
DIONYSUS. Yes, quite. Go right ahead,
Aeschylus. You spot another one.
AESCHYLUS. "Upon this heaping tomb I bid my sire
Listen, lend ear . . ."
EURIPIDES. Redundancy redone!
"Listen, lend ear" is trite tautology!
DIONYSUS. He's talking to the dead, you prodigy!
Three times we call on them, but all in vain.
AESCHYLUS. How didst thou then write prologues?
EURIPIDES. I'll explain.
And if I say the same thing twice or add
An extraordinary word to pad
The argument, then spit it back at me.
DIONYSUS. Do speak. I long to hear the nicety
Of your poetic terminology.
EURIPIDES. "At first was Oedipus a happy man . . ."
AESCHYLUS. God's wounds! Unhappiness was Nature's gift!
Foretold by Apollo, ere his birth, to slay
His father, ere he saw the light of earth!
A happy man at first! How could this be?
EURIPIDES. "And then became the saddest of our clan."
AESCHYLUS. God's death! Such had he ever been! For why?
No sooner born, harsh winter at its height,
He was exposed, an infant in a crib,
To stay his growth and spare his father's blood!
Thence dragged his swelling feet to Polybus,
Waxed to young manhood, mated with a dame
Of greying years, his own too natural mother!
Which found, he stabbed his bloody, blinded eyes!
DIONYSUS. Why, had he fought with Erasinides,[49]
He'd still be happy—for Euripides!
EURIPIDES. Nonsense! The prologues that I write are fine.
AESCHYLUS. God's life! I shall not nibble word for word
At each particular phrase, but with God's help
Annihilate thy prologues with a bottle! [50]
EURIPIDES. My prologues with a bottle?
AESCHYLUS. One; no more.
For everything will grace a line of thine,
A blanket, bottle or a laundry bag;
Such is thy tragic diction, as I'll prove!
EURIPIDES. You mean, you'll prove it?
AESCHYLUS. Yea, I do.
DIONYSUS. Then quote.
EURIPIDES. "Great king, Aegyptus, as the tale is spread
Far among men, in sea-borne vessel fled
With all his fifty sons and drawing near
To Argos' country"
AESCHYLUS. lost his bottle here!

DIONYSUS. Bottle? What bottle? He'll be sorry now.
Quote him another prologue. Teach me how.
EURIPIDES. "Lord Dionysus, who with Bacchic wands,
In fawn skin clad and garlanded with fronds,
On Mount Parnassus 'neath the torches clear
Leapt 'mid his dancers"
AESCHYLUS. lost his bottle here!
DIONYSUS. Again that bottle strikes a sober note.
EURIPIDES. No matter. For a third time let me quote
A prologue where his bottle will not fit:
"There is no mortal man on earth below
Whom fortune favors fully without woe.
For he whose birth is brave, lacks wealth and cheer,
While the ignoble born"
AESCHYLUS. hath lost his bottle here!
DIONYSUS. Euripides . . .
EURIPIDES. What is it?
DIONYSUS. Draw in sail;
The bottle's apt to raise a howling gale!
EURIPIDES. Demeter's curse! I won't bemuse my wits,
For now I'll knock it from him all in bits!
DIONYSUS. Well, quote another and stay off the bottle.
EURIPIDES. "Cadmus once, Agenor's son and peer,
In leaving Sidon"
AESCHYLUS. lost his bottle here!
DIONYSUS. You'd better buy the bottle, funny top,
Before he grinds our prologues to a stop.
EURIPIDES. What! Buy from him?
DIONYSUS. On my advice you will.
EURIPIDES. No, never. I have lots of prologues still
Where he can't fit his bottle anywhere!
"Pelops, of Tantalus born, in swift career
Fleeing to Pisa"
AESCHYLUS. lost his bottle here!
DIONYSUS. You see, he's put the bottle right in there!
Give him a new one, though, with all your skill.
You get a good one for an obol still!
EURIPIDES. By heavens, no! There's plenty more of mine.
"Oeneus Demeter"
AESCHYLUS. lost his bottle here!
EURIPIDES. Let me at least first finish out the line.
"Oeneus Demeter's riches to revere
While sacrificing"
AESCHYLUS. lost his bottle here!
DIONYSUS. At sacrifice! Who was the silent thief?
EURIPIDES. Forget him, friend. Here's one to bring him grief!
"Zeus, Lord of Heaven, as the truth speaks clear,"
DIONYSUS. Will kill you, for "he's lost his bottle here!"
Figs in your eyes! Your prologues find a place
For bottles, like the warts upon a face!
In Heaven's name, turn to his choral songs.
EURIPIDES. There, too, I have a battery of wrongs
To show in him; for, first, he's very tame,
And then his songs are always all the same!

CHORUS

Oh dear, what will the matter be?
I think it will be hard to see
What blame he can expect to be
Bringing to one so fair!
The man is the author of songs beyond measure,
The finest and noblest of all that bring pleasure,
The king of the Bacchants, the Mysteries' treasure,
The best of the poets that were!
Oh dear, I am amazed to see
How he ever will muster the
Blasts of critical rivalry,
Fearful lest he despair.

EURIPIDES. His songs are quite remarkable, you'll see,
For I'll reduce them all to one degree!
DIONYSUS. I'll take some pebbles then and count the score.

Music of flutes is heard.

EURIPIDES. "Phthian Achilles, why dost close thine ears to man's fierce battling"
Disaster and no help at need?
"Our Father Hermes, we lake-dwellers honor thee with rattling"
Disaster and no help at need?

DIONYSUS. Disasters double, Aeschylus, for you!

EURIPIDES. "Achaea's noblest, son of Atreus, learn from me, proud majesty"
Disaster and no help at need?

DIONYSUS. Disasters triple, Aeschylus, for you!

EURIPIDES. "Hush! Bee-fed virgins celebrate by Artemis's sacristy"
Disaster and no help at need?
"I tell of the way of fate to man, I, Lord of their true destiny"
Disaster and no help at need?

DIONYSUS. Disasters everywhere! O Lord of Heaven,
Vouchsafe to me a healing bath be given!
Disasters gnaw my kidneys without end.
EURIPIDES. Not ere you hear the other song, my friend,
That he composes to the sweet lyre's ease.
DIONYSUS. On with it, then, but no disasters, please.

EURIPIDES. "How does Achaea's twin-throned might, the youth and prime of Greece"
Tophlattothrat Tophlattothrat,
"The Lady of the Storms, the bitch, th' ill-tempered Sphinx release"
Tophlattothrat Tophlattothrat,
"With spear and hand of deadly deed, impetuous on the wing"
Tophlattothrat Tophlattothrat,
"To meet and greet the snapping hounds, aëroscampering"
Tophlattothrat Tophlattothrat,
"In full descent on Ajax' tent"
Tophlattothrat Tophlattothrat.

DIONYSUS. What is to phlattothrat? Was't Marathon
Or other village-pumps you drew upon?
AESCHYLUS. My well was clean and well I cleaned my songs,
Lest I should cull the sacred meadows of the Muse
Beloved of Phrynichus. But this catchall
Dredges his up from everywhere he may,
Brothels and tavern-songs of Meletus,
Dirges and jive and Carian hep and swing!
I'll show him up forthwith. Bring me a lyre.
And yet what need of lyre for such as these?
Where is the girl that rattles on the bones?
Come, Muse and Goddess of Euripides;
These are the songs for thy true worship fit!
DIONYSUS. His Muse was not a Lesbian. No, not it!

AESCHYLUS. ye halcyons babbling o'er the crest
of welling ocean's watery waves
whose dewy distillation laves
your pinions bathed in frothy foam!
ye phalanxes of spiders blest
with eaves and corners of the home
whose practised toil of fingers sharp
spi-
i-
i-
ins the woof and warp
with all the singing shuttles' zest
where dolphin-flautists piping shrill
to dark-prowed ships flings into shape
or fanes or race courses at will!
o breathing glory of the grape!
o vine-leaf cluster dulling pain!
fondle my son these arms again!

Dost see that first foot there?
DIONYSUS. I do.
AESCHYLUS. Dost see his foot as well?
DIONYSUS. I do.
AESCHYLUS. Such are the songs thou dost compose!
And yet thou dar'st to blame my verse!
Would that Cyrene would rehearse [51]
All of her twelve tricks on thy toes!
These are thy songs then, yet would I not end
Without a test of thy soliloquies!

dark-shining blackness of night
what specter of gloom dost thou bring
precursor of hell's lightless sight
a living yet soulless thing
child of black night
dread horrible sight
in a corpse's grey covering?

blood blood is the fire in its eye
and claws are its fingernails
light a lantern ye maidens and hie
to draw water from rivers in pails

warm it that i
may wash my face dry
of this specter's deadly details!

hail spirit of the sea!
that's this! o fellow-travellers
watch this mystery!
she robbed me of my cockatrice
and fled, my dear glyce!
nymphs of the mountain-earth
o madness give birth!

wretched am i for i cannot relax
making a garment of lawn
spi-
i-
i-
inning it full of flax
to sell in the market at dawn!
but he is fled is fled to the air
on the downiest tip of a wing
leaving me nought but care but care
tears to shed and tears to spare
alas poor wretched thing!

cretans born on ida fair
take your arrows and prepare
loose your limbs and circle through the halls
dictynnan artemis fair maiden too
bring thy bitches search the very walls
and hecate born of zeus a goddess who
holdst the twin celestial fiery balls
light me to glyce's retreat
that i may surprise the cheat! [52]

DIONYSUS. Stop these soliloquies!
AESCHYLUS. I've had enough!
Now would I lead him to the scales of art,[53]
For they alone will try our powers just
And weight of words will test the better man.
DIONYSUS. Come over here, where I will pair your skill,
As cheese is pared, weighing the good and ill.

CHORUS

Genius is the child of work.
See! A different new invention,
Full of strangeness! It would irk
A lesser mortal's comprehension.
Surely if a neighbor had
Told me of it without showing,
I'd have thought him raving mad
And disbelieved him, all unknowing.

DIONYSUS. Come, now and stand by the balance, both of you; see to it,
AESCHYLUS *and* EURIPIDES. There.
DIONYSUS. Cling to it fast and make ready to utter a line to the air.
Don't let it go from your hand till I say to you both: "Cuckoo!"
AESCHYLUS *and* EURIPIDES. We have it fast.
DIONYSUS. Now whisper your line on the scale; first you.
EURIPIDES. "Would Argo's boat had never winged the waves!"
AESCHYLUS. "Spercheius' stream and haunts of grazing kine!"
DIONYSUS. Cuckoo! Let go. His scales are further down,
Much further down!
EURIPIDES. And what's the reason, clown?
DIONYSUS. He introduced a stream to wet his line,
Just like a merchant weighting wool with brine!
While by a winged word you made yours weak.
EURIPIDES. Let him oppose another verse and speak.
DIONYSUS. Hold fast the scales again.
AESCHYLUS *and* EURIPIDES. We do.
DIONYSUS. Recite.
EURIPIDES. "Persuasion hath no temple but in speech!"
AESCHYLUS. "Alone of gods Death craves no sacrifice!"
DIONYSUS. Let go. Let go. His almost falls from sight!
He put in death, the heaviest of woes.
EURIPIDES. And I persuasion, noblest word that goes!
DIONYSUS. Too lightly goes! And does not carry weight!
Seek out another word, a heavyweight
In size and strength, to tip the scale for you.
EURIPIDES. Where are my champions? Where?
DIONYSUS. Look!
This will do:
"Achilles threw two aces and a four!"
The final weighing-in. Speak on once more.

EURIPIDES. "His right hand held an iron-weighted spear!"
AESCHYLUS. "Chariot on chariot fell and corpse on corpse!"
DIONYSUS. He's cheated you again.
EURIPIDES. What! Not again?
DIONYSUS. Two chariots and two corpses are a strain
That scarce a hundred slaves of Egypt could endure!
AESCHYLUS. 'Tis time, methinks, to cease this verse for verse.
Let him climb in and weigh the scales himself,
His wife, his children, his Cephisophon
And all his babbling books, while I unmoved
A single couplet of my own will stake.
DIONYSUS. My friends, I cannot judge between these two.
I would not willingly be foe to either man;
One brings me wisdom and the other joy!
PLUTO. Will you not finish what you came to do?
DIONYSUS. I must decide?
PLUTO. And take the one that you
Decide on, lest your journey be in vain.
DIONYSUS. Thank you, thank you. But let me tell you plain;
I came to fetch a poet. Why? To save
The city and restore my dances grave.
So then whoever shows the better flair
For politics, I think I'll take up there.
Come. Tell me first of Alcibiades,
The city's misbegotten child of ease.
EURIPIDES. What does the city feel for him?
DIONYSUS. No less
Than love, then hate, then longing to possess.
But tell me both: Do you regard him so?
EURIPIDES. That citizen I hate whose will is slow
To help and quick to hurt his fatherland,
Useless to it, to self a helping hand!
DIONYSUS. Well said, Poseidon! What have you to say?
AESCHYLUS. No lion's cub in city should be reared;
If reared, then tamed to suit the city's ways!
DIONYSUS. By Zeus! The savior still is hard to choose!
One has such cle-ah, one such clev-ah views!
But give us both one word of wisdom still:
What reformation have you for the city's ill?
EURIPIDES. Cleocritus Cinesias should woo [54]
And winds be wafting o'er the surging blue!
DIONYSUS. That would be funny!——Does it mean a thing?
EURIPIDES. Fight on the sea, take vinegar and fling
It in the faces of the enemy!
I know and wish to tell your remedy.
DIONYSUS. Speak on.
EURIPIDES. Put faith in present falsity
And falsity in faith!
DIONYSUS. Too hard for me!
Please speak more clearly; understand I must!
EURIPIDES. Distrust the citizens whom now we trust;
Use those we use not. Then all may be well.
It must be so, if only we repel
The present leaders of our evil days,
Install their foes and thus reverse our ways!
DIONYSUS. Good, Palamedes! This your own fine wit
Or did Cephisophon discover it?
EURIPIDES. My own alone; he found the vinegar!
Come, Aeschylus; your turn.
AESCHYLUS. Pray, tell me first
What men the city has. Are they the good?
DIONYSUS. The good! She hates them most.
AESCHYLUS. And likes the bad?
DIONYSUS. Oh, no! But she is forced beneath their rule.
AESCHYLUS. How could one save a city such as this,
Which neither rags nor riches satisfy?
DIONYSUS. That's yours to say, if you would live again.
AESCHYLUS. I'll say it there, but never here below.
DIONYSUS. Please do; you should send blessings up from here.
AESCHYLUS. They should consider that their foe's land is their own,
Their own the foe's, their navy wealth, their wealth all gone!
DIONYSUS. Good! Though the jurors have devoured it all.
PLUTO. Your judgment now!
DIONYSUS. Thus does my sentence fall:

I'll take the man for whom my heart is sore.
EURIPIDES. Remember then the gods by whom you swore
To fetch me back. Your friends do not forsake.
DIONYSUS. "My tongue hath sworn," but Aeschylus I'll take!
EURIPIDES. What have you done? You pestilential blot!
DIONYSUS. Judged Aeschylus the winner. Whyee not?
EURIPIDES. You dare to face me after such a shame?
DIONYSUS. What shame? . . . You hear? The audience finds no blame!
EURIPIDES. O hard of heart, will you thus leave me dead?
DIONYSUS. "Who knows if life is death?" Who was it said
"If breath is bread and sleep a woolly lie"? [55]
PLUTO. My friends, come. Dionysus, enter.
DIONYSUS. Why?
PLUTO. That I may entertain you ere you go.
DIONYSUS. I thank you; and have much enjoyed the show!

CHORUS

Happy the man who possesses
An intellect sharpened and fine—
(And the fortune of many expresses
The truth of this lesson of mine!)

This man has proved his excellence
And so goes home again,
To help his city's dying cause,
His friends and family, because
Of the superb intelligence
Of his poetic brain.

Graceless the man who professes
To nestle in Socrates' heart,
Abandoning music, and stresses
His scorn for the tragic art!

To talk with pompous phrase and word
Of high philosophy,
To spend a life of idleness
And hair-dissecting foolishness,
Oh! Surely this is quite absurd
And proves insanity!

PLUTO. Farewell, good Aeschylus. Depart.
Save our city's failing heart
With counsels sage and educate
The foolish ones; there's quite a spate!
Here's a gift for Cleophon; [56]
The tax-board gets this little loan,
Myrmex that, Nicomachus
And Archenomus this and thus!
Tell them all to speed their way
To visit me without delay.

For if they don't come quick,
By Apollo, I will stick
Brands and fetters on them all and bring them down!
With Leucolophus's son,
Adimantus, I will run
Every single one of them right out of town!

AESCHYLUS. That will I do. Give thou my throne
To Sophocles, to watch and own
Till my return. I deem his art
Has won for him the second part.
Remember not to let that foul
And lying, temple-robbing ghoul
Approach and sit upon my chair,
Howe'er reluctant be his air.

PLUTO. Raise the sacred torches high!
Escort our poet on his way!
Let his songs and dances fly
Before him to the light of day!

CHORUS

First, to our poet departing and journeying up to the light
Vouchsafe a well-omened starting, ye spirits of our world of night!
Bless with good will his city and grant it great good things to come!
We all would be rid of our pity, our anguish and misery dumb,
Our terrible strife and our battling! Let Cleophon fight, all the same,
And any who love saber-rattling, in fields where our sires won their fame!

NOTES TO THE *FROGS*

1. Phrynichus, Lycis, and Amipsias were contemporary comic poets, whose plays seem to have contained a large amount of the broad humor to which Aristophanes is here objecting.

2. The slaves who had served loyally as rowers in the battle of Arginusae, 406 B.C., received their freedom, an indication of Athens' serious loss of manpower.

3. That is, embarked as a marine on Clisthenes' ship at Arginusae.

4. Molon was a gigantically large actor who took the leading part in the first production of the *Andromeda* of Euripides.

5. Iophon was the playwright son of Sophocles and was suspected of having his father help him considerably in his compositions.

6. Agathon was a famous contemporary tragedian, ridiculed by Aristophanes and Plato for his effeminacy and for his dithyrambic diction.

7. Agathon had left Athens to visit the sumptuous royal court in Macedonia. Aristophanes puns on Macedonia and "Makares," the dead in the Isles of the Blest.

8. Xenocles was a poet who made up in stage tricks what he lacked in talent.

9. Nothing is known of Pythangelus.

10. The Greek words mean both a towing rope and rower's bench, and a hangman's rope and footstool, that is kicked away by the suicide.

11. Condemned criminals were given a cup of hemlock to drink.

12. The Ceramicus contained the finest cemetery in Athens.

13. Charon's ordinary fare was one obol, so that this would represent a round-trip ticket. There is here an allusion to the daily allowance of two obols, given to the poorer citizens to enable them to attend the theater during the festivals, which was increased and extended by vote-hungry demagogues. Theseus, the traditional hero-king of Athens, was credited with the institution of the popular ceremonies.

14. Morsimus was a bad tragedian.

15. Cinesias was an especially unmartial dithyrambic poet, who had written a Pyrrhic dance, a type of ballet that imitated a battle scene.

16. The usual Greek expression for "Go to Hell" was "Go to the crows." Near Sparta at Taenarum there was supposed to be an entrance into the earth leading to Hades.

17. Empusa was a spectral monster, belonging to the powers of the underworld, who could assume any shape at will for her nocturnal hauntings.

18. Hegelochus was an actor who, by an error of intonation in the performance of one of Euripides' plays, said what sounded like, "After the storm I see a cat," instead of "After the storm I see a calm."

19. The point of the joke seems to be that Diagoras was an atheist and therefore an unlikely person to be singing a religious hymn.

20. A pig was part of the sacrifice.

21. An obscure reference. Cratinus was a fairly successful comic poet of the old school, who however was frequently accused of drunkenness, which might explain his "spewing." The "bull-eater" may refer to a mystic rite connected with the killing of a bull.

22. Aegina was a center of smuggling during the Peloponnesian War. Thorycion was a customs officer, who would accordingly have plenty of scope for illegally increasing his income.

23. A roundabout and cumbersome jest. Children begin to cut their second teeth at the age of seven, and so Archedemus is accused of failing in seven years of office to get his teeth into politics sufficiently to gather a following. Also he bribed his way into office illegally and then turned round and accused the generals at Arginusae for having failed to rescue the Athenians whose ships were sunk beneath them.

24. Clisthenes, the general mentioned in note 3, returned from Arginusae to enter politics only to find himself deserted by his friend Sebinus.

25. Callias was a rich and good-for-nothing debauchee.

26. Corinth was an enemy of Athens during the war. The joke here comes from the fact that the Corinthians were so proud of their descent from Zeus that the literal phrase "Corinth of Zeus" which I have here rendered "Damn all Corinth" came to be a synonym for any "damnable iteration," such as the order to Xanthias to pick up his freight again.

27. There was a temple of Heracles in the deme Melite, in which Callias was enrolled.

28. Theramenes was an unfortunate, though not uncourageous, politician who attempted to steer a middle course between the extreme democratic and oligarchic parties.

29. Cleon and Hyperbolus were two notorious leaders of the democrats.

30. These three names were Scythian, from which country the policemen at Athens were recruited.

31. Whips of leek and shallot were used in certain religious ceremonials.

32. This feast was held in the deme of Diomea in honor of Heracles. Attati is probably to be taken as an expression of annoyance over the fact that because of the war the due festival was not being celebrated.

33. Hipponax was a bitter, satirical poet, whose lines might well be used as curses. Part of the joke lies in the

fact that this is a deliberate misquotation from another author.

34. Cleophon was another notorious democratic leader.

35. No one has made much sense of this stanza. It has been suggested that a trial was awaiting Cleophon, in which, even if the verdict were to be equally divided, Cleophon was certain of being convicted rather than receiving the benefit of the doubt as was usual in such cases; and it is possible that the trial was in some way connected with Thrace. The incongruity of the diction and the picture in which a swallow thunders and borrows the nightingale's prophecy of doom may have been suggested by the curious interjections of the preceding passage and the barbaric appearance of the Scythians.

36. This and the following blank verse passage form the parabasis; see Introduction.

37. Phrynichus was a general who took a leading part in the revolution that overthrew the democracy.

38. Cligenes is not known apart from this reference.

39. Clidemides is said to have been a leading actor in Sophocles' plays and to have become his literary executor.

40. This and many of the phrases and lines in the following scene are parodies of tragedy. Frequently, as here, where the allusion is to the fact that Euripides' mother sold vegetables, the tragic phrase is given an unexpected twist.

41. Euripides introduced into Attic tragedy an innovation taken from Cretan songs, in which the actor simultaneously sings and performs an interpretive dance.

42. The *Telephus,* not now extant, was ridiculed continually by Aristophanes.

43. This Phrynichus was Aeschylus' predecessor in tragedy.

44. Cephisophon was a slave of Euripides, and was rumored to have helped his master to write his plays.

45. Phormisius was an Athenian demagogue, described as thick-bearded and fearful-looking. Megaenetus, from either Manes, the name of a slave, or Magnes, a Magnesian, may also have contained a reference to a crooked play at dice.

46. Clitophon was an idle follower of Socrates. Theramenes: see note 28.

47. This is an obscure jest on Hermes as the trickster and Hermes as the guide to the underworld. In the latter capacity Hermes inherited his prerogative from the god of the dead and so is criticized by Dionysus for being the robber of his father's tomb. Euripides has no chance to complete his criticism.

48. The pun depends on the fact that there was in Greek a technical word for the return or "re-instatement" of an exile, so that an exile who simply came home without being also reinstated would have no legal rights.

49. Erasinides was one of the generals executed after the battle of Arginusae for dereliction of duty.

50. The bottle here is a little bottle or flask of olive oil, which the Athenian frequently carried with him. The humor of the following scene consists first in the fact that Euripides' verse was so neat and slick that the two Greek words for "lost his bottle here" could be fitted into the end of a line very frequently, and secondly because such commonplace objects as bottles, laundry-bags and blankets would not detract from its style. Point is lent to both by the use of a diminutive and slightly colloquial word for flask or bottle and by the lightness of the rhythm of the phrase.

51. Cyrene was a famous lady of love.

52. "A woman who falls asleep while spinning a skein of thread for the market has a nightmare dream that her neighbor Glyce has robbed her henroost. This homely story is decked out with invocations to Powers of night and passionate prayers to heaven and earth for help."—Merry.

53. A huge pair of scales is brought onto the stage on which the two poets will weigh their verses.

54. The point of this nonsense is that Cleocritus and Cinesias are no more likely to make friends and set out for a naval battle than the Athenians are likely to change their government.

55. Gilbert Murray's excellent translation of this line.

56. The gifts thus distributed are convenient instruments for committing suicide. Myrmex and Archenomus are unknown. Nicomachus was an embezzling civil servant. Adimantus, a friend of Alcibiades, also helped to betray Athens to Sparta.

The Constitution of Athens
BY THE "OLD OLIGARCH"

Translated by Paul MacKendrick

INTRODUCTION

JUST AS IT would not be realistic to judge American democracy as a whole by speeches about malice toward none and charity for all, so we must beware of concluding from the idealism of the Funeral Oration of Pericles that all his hearers shared his favorable view of government by the people. Among the several Athenians marked by an almost total inability either to see political life steadily or to see it whole, the anonymous author of the pamphlet *On the Constitution of Athens* bulks very large.

Whenever a controversial statement on a political issue appears, the reader is naturally curious to know when and by whom it was written. For example, if we have placed in our hands a document in which, beneath an apparent admiration for the "New Deal," is concealed a bitter criticism of President Roosevelt and all his works, it is a matter of more than academic interest to know whether it was written in 1933 or in 1945, and whether its author was a Democrat or a Republican, a professor or a politician, a professional author or a plain man moved by the passion of the hour. Unfortunately in the case of the "Old Oligarch" our curiosity must remain unsatisfied. All we know of him is what we read in his pamphlet: he may have been an Athenian; he wrote in wartime; at the time of writing, Athens' empire was intact and her navy unchallenged. These conditions obtained in Athens pretty much at any time between the years 431 and 415 B.C. But beyond this point one man's opinion is as good as another's, and therefore the possibilities of various interpretations form not the least fascination of the work.

Is it the work of an older man who would curb the youthful hotheads among the conservatives, or of an extremist who cares nothing for academic reformers and moderates and is ready to surrender not only the empire but his city's independence, if only the hated democracy can be got rid of? Is he writing with gay irony, or in bitter earnest? Is he making a strong plea to fellow-conservatives for a practical policy or writing a display piece to impress his sophistic friends? Is it addressed to Athenians, to Spartans, or to the discontented conservatives of the Athenian empire? Is the author confused or logical, literate or illiterate? On these questions there is at the time of writing no final answer, a state of affairs which should challenge each new generation of readers.

The contrast in point of view between the "Old Oligarch" and Pericles is striking. To Pericles, the fact that at Athens every man may do as he chooses is a matter for pride; to the Old Oligarch, it is used as an excuse for breaking one's word in treaties and contracts. Pericles' liberty is the Old Oligarch's licence, expressed, for example, when an Athenian slave will not stand aside and let a free man pass. The splendor of public festivals impresses Pericles; the fact that they delay the legal and legislative process annoys the Old Oligarch. The one counts as a blessing the variety of desirable things that other lands produce, all available in Athens; to the other, the variety is un-Greek and the product of a ruthless monopoly, embargo, and blockade. "All take part in public life," says Pericles, "and all discuss that which when carried out is to affect all." "Good government," rejoins the Old Oligarch, "requires the imposition of sensible legislation on vulgar cads, the prevention of madmen from making speeches; to find means of better government within the existing democratic framework is not easy." To Pericles' statement of the readiness of Athenians to sacrifice advantages in the common cause the Old Oligarch opposes a cynical self-interest which allows Attic land to be ravaged as long as the people's miserable possessions remain intact.

Everything that to Pericles and to us makes Athens great, the concept of equality before the law, freedom of speech, the procession of the Parthenon frieze, the *Agamemnon* and the *Frogs*, all this to the Old Oligarch means nothing but the satisfying of the people's "greed, greed of belly and pocket, and petty greed at that. Democracy is all right, for there are many profitable little offices to fill; Sophocles is all right, because I can make something singing and dancing; the temples and the gymnasia are all right, because I can go into them for nothing; the navy's good for I know how to handle an oar; and the empire's fine, it brings in money in lots of ways, an obol here, an obol there, it all helps." *

No other author of classical antiquity has gone so far to belittle ideas of art and music, order and freedom, which have been ever since what our Western culture has lived by. But the conservative tone set here is what in modified form moves Aristophanes' attack upon Euripides in the *Frogs*, Plato's attack upon democracy in the *Republic*, Aristotle's in the *Politics*, and Cicero's rallying cry to the *optimates* in his speech *For Sestius*. And the setting up of the conflict between conservative and working man as a struggle between sage and knave has its echoes in Isocrates and in Aeschines, and, with the roles reversed, in works as far apart in time as Sallust's *Catiline* and the *Communist Manifesto*. This consciousness of class would appear as one of the deadliest of our classical heritages, were we not also equally indebted to the Greeks for the concept that has moved liberals in every age, from Pericles to Franklin Roosevelt: the idea that there is a common ground upon which minds may meet without compromise of principle—a liberalizing of Aristotle's concept that Horace called *aurea mediocritas:* the Golden Mean.

THE translation is based upon the text and apparatus criticus of Marchant's Oxford edition of Xenophon. It has not seemed sensible to encumber the translation with notices of variants; scholars will recognize them and may check them against the vulgate; to others it will not matter, so long as they are assured that every effort has been made to give a conscientious rendering, even of the awkwardnesses of a Greek text which is, semantically and textually, extraordinarily difficult.

I

Introduction: The Athenian democracy is a good thing if you believe in democracy, which I do not.

1 As for the government of the Athenians, the form they chose I do not approve of, and for this reason, that in choosing it they chose that scoundrels should become better off than decent citizens. This, then, is the reason for my disapproval. But since this is the course that seemed satisfactory to them, I shall point out how well they preserve their form of government, and what their other practices are in which they *seem* to the rest of Greece to be in error.

The people, who fight for the state, argue that they should reap its profits without sharing its responsibilities.

2 In the first place, then, I say that it seems only right that the poor and the common people there should have more than the well born and well-to-do; for this reason, that it is the common people who row the ships and gird the city about with strength: helmsmen, coxswains, ship-captains, bow-lookouts, shipwrights—it is these who surround the city with power far more than the heavy-armed troops, the well born, and the decent citizens. This being the case, it seems just that all should share in ruling, both in election by lot and in voting by the show of hands, and that any one of the citizens who pleases should have the right to speak in the Assembly.

3 Then again, such offices as bring security to the whole state when they are well administered, but risk when they are not—these the common people want no part of. (For example, they do not think that they ought to share by lot in the responsibility of generalship or cavalry command.) The people know that there is more profit for them in not holding such offices personally, but in letting men of position hold them. But whatever offices there are which involve pay and making private profit, these are the ones which the common people seek to control.

The cornerstone of democracy is consideration for the working class.

4 Again, there are those who are surprised because in all cases they give a larger share to the rascals, the poor, and the popular party than to the decent citizens; but in this very case they are obviously safeguarding popular government. For when the poor, the common people, or the worse element are well off, and the number who become so is large, this increases the power of the democracy, whereas if the rich and the decent prosper, the popular party is then strengthening its own opposition. *5* Everywhere the best people are opposed to democracy, because among the best element there is least excess and injustice, and most self-discipline to useful ends. Among

* From A. W. Gomme, "The Old Oligarch," in *Athenian Studies*, suppl. to HSCP (Cambridge, 1940), to which this introduction is indebted throughout.

the people, on the other hand, ignorance is at its height, as well as disorder and vulgarity. For poverty, lack of education, and in some cases the ignorance which arises from lack of money lead them more to unseemly conduct.

Free speech may make for bad government, but bad government keeps the people masters.

6 Someone may say that they all ought not to be allowed to speak one after another, or to deliberate as senators, but only the shrewdest, and the aristocrats, but in this case too they take best counsel for themselves by letting the rascals speak too. For if the decent people were to do the speaking and the deliberating, for those who were like themselves it would be advantageous, but not so for the popular party. But as it is, any scoundrel who pleases can get up, say his say, and get what is good for him and his like. *7* It might well be asked, "What that is good for himself or for the state would such a man know?" But the people know that this man's ignorance, commonness, and good will profit them more than the virtue, wisdom, and disaffection of the conservative. *8* Perhaps it is not as a result of such practices that a state becomes perfect, but this is the way democracy would be best preserved. For what the people want is not that they should be enslaved in a well-ordered city, but that they should be free and that they should rule; and bad government concerns them but little. For what *you* think makes bad government makes the people strong and free. *9* But if you are looking for good government, first of all you will see to it that the shrewdest men impose the laws on the common people; next, the decent people will make the vulgar cads behave, the decent people will take counsel for the state, and they will not allow madmen to sit in the Senate, make speeches, or sit in the Assembly. But note that as a consequence of these reforms the people would very quickly be degraded to slavery.

Slaves in Athens have equal rights with free men.

10 Speaking of slavery, at Athens the effrontery of slaves and resident aliens is at its height; to strike them is not allowed there, and yet a slave will not stand out of the road and let you pass. And this is why that is the custom there: if it were lawful for a slave to be struck by a free man, or for an alien or a freedman to be beaten, you would often think an Athenian a slave and beat *him.* For in dress the people there are no better than slaves or aliens, and in appearance they are no better either. *11* And if there be any man who marvels at the further fact that they allow the privately owned slaves there to put on airs, and some of them to live downright magnificently, this too you will find they do with good reason. For wherever there is sea power, the slaves have to be *paid* for their slaving, and to be allowed to buy their freedom, in order that *we* may get our percentage of their hire. But in any city where the slaves are rich, it is no longer expedient for my slave to be afraid of you, whereas in Sparta my slave used really to respect you. But in Athens if your slave is afraid of me he will probably even pay blackmail to avoid personal risks. *12* So we have allowed even slaves free speech in their relations with free men, and resident aliens free speech in their relations with citizens, because the city needs resident aliens on account of the number of trades and on account of sea-faring. This is the reason then why we grant free speech also, reasonably enough, to resident aliens.

The people dance; the rich pay the piper.

13 The people have driven the practice of gymnastics and music out of fashion in Athens, ostensibly on moral grounds, but really because they know they have not the ability to practise these arts themselves. Moreover, in having the rich pay for choruses, direct gymnasia, and outfit triremes, the people know that they dance while the rich pay the piper, and that in directing the gymnasia and outfitting the triremes the rich have the expense, the poor the entertainment. At any rate, the people take it for granted that they should be paid for singing, running, dancing, and going sailing in the ships, so that they can have money and the rich get poorer. And in the courts they care not so much about justice as about their own advantage.

The Athenians support democratic governments in allied cities.

14 As for the allies, because the Athenians sail out seemingly to persecute and blackmail those they govern, and hate decent citizens (knowing that the ruler must be hated by the ruled, and that if the rich and the decent gain power in the allied cities short-lived indeed will be the power of the people of Athens), for this reason they disfranchise decent people, confiscate their money, exile them, and execute them, but scoundrels they exalt. The decent people of Athens, on the other hand, come to the rescue of the decent people in the allied cities, knowing that it is to their interest always to help the best element there. *15* One might say that the Athenian strength lies exactly here, in the allies' being able to pay tribute money; but to the popular party the gain seems to be greater if each of the Athenians has the allies' money, while the allies have just enough to live on, and have to work hard, so as to be unable to make plots.

The allies are forced to come to Athens to have their law-suits tried.

16 The Athenian people appear to be ill advised also in making their allies come to Athens for trials. But they argue in rebuttal how many advantages there are for the Athenian people in this procedure: (1) from the allies' deposits they get their jury pay year after year; (2) sitting at home without going to sea they govern the allied cities, and popular party members they acquit, while they ruin the opposition in the courts; whereas if each city tried cases at home, the allies would, since they hate the Athenians, ruin those among their citizens who were especially friendly to the Athenian people. *17* (3) Besides, the Athenian people profit from holding the allies' trials in Athens in the following ways also: (a) a higher entry duty accrues to the city from the Piraeus harbor; (b) a man with a room to rent does a better business; (c) a man may have a couple of nags or a slave for hire; (d) the town criers do a better business—and all because of the visits of the allies. *18* (4) Again, if the allies did not come on legal business, they would respect only the officials whom the Athenians sent out to them, generals, captains, and ambassadors; as things are, however, each one of the allies is forced to flatter the Athenian populace, in the knowledge that he must come to Athens and be involved in law-suits before none other than the people themselves, who are the law in Athens. And he is forced to make entreaties in the courtroom, and to pump the hand of whoever enters. This then is why the allies become more and more the slaves of the Athenian people.

The possession of allies gives the Athenians naval training.

19 Besides, on account of acquisitions overseas and foreign service, they come more and more to learn rowing, they and their hangers-on. For the man who spends much time at sea is bound to take an oar, both himself and his servants, and to learn nautical terms; (*20*) and they become good steersmen through experience on voyages and through practice, some in steering freighters, other in transport ships; some pass from these to naval command. But most of the hangers-on are able to row as soon as they get aboard the ships, since they have had practice during all their previous lives.

II

The Athenian army is weak, the navy strong: this strengthens the maritime empire, reduces chance of famine, enhances luxury and cosmopolitanism.

1 As for foot-soldiers, the arm in which Athens is apparently weakest, the situation is that they realize that they are weaker than enemy heavy infantry, and fewer. But even on land they are stronger than their allies who pay the tribute, and they think their heavy infantry suffices, if it is stronger than that of their allies. *2* Besides, fortune created this situation for them. For the subjects of a land power are able to consolidate small cities and fight *en masse,* but a sea power's subjects, being islanders, are not able to collect their citizens into one place. For the sea lies between, and their rulers are a sea power. And even if it is possible for islanders to meet together on one island without attracting attention, they will die of hunger. *3* All the mainland cities that are ruled by Athens are ruled, the large ones by fear, the small ones by sheer necessity. For there is no city that does not need imports and exports, which no city can have if it is not submissive to the ruler of the sea. *4* Further, sea powers can do generally what land powers can do only sometimes: lay waste a stronger power's territory. For a navy can sail along to where there are none of the enemy or only a few, and if the enemy attack, it can embark and sail away, with less embarrassment than the opposition who try to come to the rescue with infantry. *5* Again, sea powers can sail away from their own city as far as they like, while land powers cannot get many days' journey away from their own city. For journeys by road are slow and food cannot last long for foot travellers. And he who goes afoot must either go through friendly territory or fight his way through, while the sailor can go ashore where he is stronger, and, where he is not, he need not go ashore at that point of the coast, but may sail along until he comes to friendly country or men weaker than himself. *6* Again, blights, which are from God, the land power takes hard, the sea power easily; for the whole world is not blighted all at the same time, so that imports come to a sea power from a land where crops are healthy. *7* And if I may mention small matters also, through sea power in the first place they have gotten luxurious habits by commercial relations with ports all over the world. For whatever is pleasant in Sicily, Italy, Cyprus, Egypt, Lydia, Pontus, and Peloponnese or anywhere else is all collected into one place by sea-power. *8* Then they hear every dialect, and have borrowed one word from one dialect and another from another. Greeks prefer their own dialect, habits, and dress, but the Athenians prefer one that is a hodge-podge of those of all Greeks and barbarians.

The rich pay for the people's holidays and sports.

9 As for sacrifices, temples, feasts, and sacred precincts, the people, knowing that it is not possible for each of the poor to sacrifice, feast, rear temples, and make a fair great city to dwell in, have found out how they may have religious refinements: the city performs many sacrifices at the public expense, and it is the people that feasts and shares by lot in the sacrifice. *10* And as for gymnasia, baths, and dressing rooms, the rich own them privately, or some of them do, whereas the poor get built for their private use many wrestling grounds, dressing rooms, and baths. And the mob gets more enjoyment of them than the minority and the well-to-do.

Athenian sea power gives them a monopoly of raw materials for shipbuilding.

11 As for wealth, they alone among the Greeks and barbarians are able to retain it. For if a state is rich in shipbuilding timbers, where will it dispose of them if it does not persuade the ruler of the sea to buy? Or again if a city is rich in iron, copper, or sailcloth, the same question applies. However, these are the very things with which I equip my ships: wood from one, iron from another, copper from a third, sailcloth from a fourth, wax from a fifth. *12* Furthermore they will not allow our rivals to sell elsewhere than at Athens, or at any rate not by sea routes. And I without exerting myself reap all the products of the earth through power over the sea. No other city has any two of these raw materials, for wood and sailcloth do not come from the same place; where sailcloth is abundant the ground is smooth and unwooded. Nor do copper and iron come from the same city, nor any other two or three commodities, but rather each comes from a different place. *13* Besides, every mainland has a projecting cape or an island lying hard by or a narrow strait, so that the rulers of the sea, making their blockade at that point, can harass the dwellers on the mainland.

All they lack is location on an island.

14 But they lack one advantage. For if the Athenians were island dwellers as well as rulers of the sea, they would be able to do harm, if they liked, without suffering any, as long as they had control of the sea, without their own land's being ravaged or overrun by the enemy. But as it is, those of the Athenians that are farmers and well-to-do prefer to appease the enemy, whereas the people, well knowing that no farm of theirs will be burned or any olive tree cut down, live on without fear and without putting themselves within range. *15* Furthermore, if they lived on an island they would be free of a further fear, namely that a few malcontents might betray the city, open the gates, and let the enemy break in; for how could this happen to islanders? Nor would there be a revolt against the people if they lived on an island. But as it is, if there should be revolution, it would be made in the hope of bringing the enemy in by land to help the revolutionaries, but if they dwelt on an island they could dismiss this fear as well. *16* Since then in the first place they did not have the good fortune to dwell on an island, their present practice is to store up their property in the islands, putting their trust in their sea power, and to ignore the devastating of Attic soil, knowing that if they feel pity for it they will be deprived of other greater advantages.

A democracy can afford to be irresponsible about treaties and contracts.

17 Furthermore, oligarchical states have to bind themselves with alliances and oaths, and if they do not keep their convenants the name of the wrongdoer will be known on account of the small number of those who made the agreement. But whatever convenants the people makes, it can ascribe the responsibility to one man, the one who made the motion and put it to the vote, and to the other party to the treaty can deny all responsibility, saying, "I wasn't there, and I don't like it, either," even though the other party learns that the covenant was made in full popular assembly. And if the covenant does not please the people, they have found in the past a myriad excuses for not doing whatever they do not want to do. And if some harm should come from the people's deliberations, they charge that the oligarchy, working against them, destroyed them, but if good comes of it, they take the credit for themselves.

The Athenian people forbid anyone to satirize them.

18 They do not allow the people to be satirized or slandered, lest they hear ill of themselves. But in individual cases they encourage random attack, well knowing that the butt is not usually from the people or the majority, but someone rich, pedigreed, or powerful, and that few of the poor or the popular party are satirized, and not even they unless they have been busybodies, and have tried to get more than the people, so that they do not get angry when these are satirized, either.

They hate the virtuous: any such who espouse their cause are traitors to their class.

19 So I for my part maintain that the Athenian people recognizes which are the decent men among the citizens and which the scoundrels, and those who are serviceable and advantageous to them they consciously favor, even though they may be rascals, while the decent people on the other hand they tend to hate. For they think that inborn virtue exists not for their advantage but to their harm, and yet there are some who are by birth of the people, though they are not by disposition democratic. *20* Democracy for the people themselves I can understand, for to do what is best for oneself is always understandable, but when a man who does not belong to the people chooses to live in a democratic rather than an oligarchic city, it is because he is meditating some injustice and knows that his wickedness is more likely to escape notice in a democratic than in an oligarchic city.

III

Recapitulation: Granted that democracy is good, the Athenians know how to preserve it.

1 I disapprove of the turn the Athenian government has taken. But since they prefer to live in a democracy, they seem to me to be preserving the democracy very well by using the kind of government I have described.

The pressure of legislative and legal business in Athens is such that a year's delay is not uncommon.

Further, I see some criticizing the Athenians because sometimes it is impossible there for a man, though he sit idly by for a year, to do business with the Assembly or the Senate. This happens solely because crowded agenda make it impossible to send everyone away with his business settled. *2* For how could it be possible, in a city where in the first place they have to celebrate more festivals than in any other Greek city (during which time there is less opportunity to transact city business); and where besides they have to settle civil and criminal cases and audit the magistrates' accounts in numbers greater than all the rest of mankind put together, and where the Senate has to deliberate a great deal about war, revenues, new legislation, and current city business, together with matters concerning the allies, receiving the tribute, and managing the dockyards and sacred precincts? Then what wonder is it that with so much on the docket it is not possible to do business with everyone?

Even bribery would not clear the crowded docket.

3 Some say, "If a man with money comes before the Assembly or Senate he will get his business done." For my part, I agree with them that money manages much in Athens and would manage more, if more people would pay. But on the other hand I know this, that the state is inadequate to do what he asks for every petitioner, not even if a man should give as much gold and silver as you like.

Ten sample kinds of court cases

4 They have to give judgment if a man does not repair his ship, or has erected a building on state property, and besides they have to decide every year who can best afford to pay for a chorus at the Dionysia, Thargelia, Panathenaea, Prometheia, and Hephaesteia. And four hundred trierarchs are appointed every year, of whom those who wish should have their ability to pay passed on annually. And besides, qualifications for office have to be investigated and judged, and the claims of state wards looked into and prison warders appointed. *5* This has to be done every year. Then from time to time judgment has to be passed on bad strategy, and any other injustices that may suddenly come up, or extraordinary group insolence or impiety. There is still a great deal that I quite omit, but the most important matters have been mentioned except assessing the tribute, which happens usually every four years.

Large population overcrowds the docket.

6 Very well, then, ought one not to think that everything ought to be passed on? Let any man name a single matter that does not have to be passed on there. And if there is agreement on the principle that everything has to be passed on, this must necessarily happen all year long, as, even as it is, though they sit right through the year, the jurymen are not sufficient to put a stop to crime which is committed on account of the size of the population.

If you decrease the number of jurymen, you increase the chances of bribery.

7 Well, someone will say that we ought to have juries, but that they ought to be smaller. Necessarily, then, unless there are few courts, there will be few jurors in each court, so that it will be easier to get one's tricks ready when there are few jurymen, and to bribe them wholesale to judge far less justly.

Holidays interfere.

8 Besides, it must be remembered that the Athenians have to keep festivals, too, whereon they cannot try cases; and they keep twice as many festivals as other people, but I am comparing them only to the city that keeps fewest.

There can be no sweeping reform as long as the democracy remains intact.

This being the case, I hold that matters at Athens cannot be otherwise than they are, except that it is possible to take away one detail and add another, and that it is quite impossible to reform the whole without detracting in some way from democracy. *9* One can find many ways to make the state better, but to find means of better government within the existing democratic framework is not easy, except minor additions or subtractions, as I have just said.

The Athenian democracy supports its own kind abroad; when it has done otherwise, history shows that democracy has suffered.

10 The Athenians may be ill advised also in choosing to side with the worse element in cities that are having revolutions. They do this deliberately, for if they sided with the better class they would be siding with a class with opinions different from their own; for in no city is the best element well disposed to the people, but rather the worst. For birds of a feather flock together, wherefore the Athenians choose the side that is related to them. *11* Whenever they have attempted to side with the best people, it has not turned out favorably for them, but within a short time the people have been enslaved, as in Boeotia; and when they sided with the best people at Miletus, within a short time these revolted and made mincemeat of the common people; again, when they sided with the Spartans instead of the Messenians, within a short time the Spartans first overthrew the Messenians and then made war on Athens.

Men deprived of citizenship offer no threat to Athenian democracy.

12 One might suppose, then, that no one has been unjustly disfranchised in Athens. I hold that there are such, though few. But there is need of no small number to attack Athenian democracy, since as a matter of fact the men who are justly disfranchised are not angry, but only the unjustly punished. How then would anyone think that it is the many who have been unjustly disfranchised at Athens, where it is the people who holds the offices, and disfranchisement follows on unjust rule, speech, or action? When one reasons in this way, one ought not to think that there is any danger from the disfranchised citizens in Athens.

SELECTIONS FROM THUCYDIDES' *History*

Translated by Gerald F. Else

INTRODUCTION

EVERYBODY knows Macaulay's judgment that Thucydides was the greatest historian who ever lived. Not so many people know Thucydides; in fact nowadays he is probably more admired than read. Or if he is read, he is read either as history, in which case he is the business of historians, or as literature, in which case he is the business of literary men. This dilemma is inevitable, our times being what they are, but it is unfortunate for Thucydides since he was neither a professional historian—that is, a professor of history—nor a literary man. He wrote about events because he saw in them the laboratory where human nature and human action were tested, and if he had suspected that one day his work would be discussed in the same breath with Homer and Sophocles, he would have felt that he had written in vain.

He belonged to a good Athenian family, of the aristocracy. Somewhere in the background is a romantic touch. Miltiades, the victor of Marathon, who was probably his great-grandfather, had married a Thracian princess from the wild north, and Thucydides' father bore the name of her father, Olorus. Probably because of the same connection, Thucydides owned property in Thrace, including a share in the fabulous gold mines of Mt. Pangaeon. These exotic threads of barbarian blood and northern gold hardly appear in his work—he is the least romantic of historians—but they probably led indirectly to the most tragic event in his life and thus to the writing of his history. While stationed off the Thracian coast in the year 424, as commanding officer of an Athenian reserve force, he failed to relieve the key town of Amphipolis before it fell to the Spartans. The Athenians exiled him, apparently concluding that he had been thinking about his property more than his duty. It was during the twenty years of exile that he began writing his history, and he came home at the end of the war, in 403, with only one purpose: to finish it.

Thus Thucydides owed the execution, if not the idea, of his life work to fortune—or was it his own failure?—which made him a spectator instead of a man of action and forced him to watch the downfall of his country from the sidelines. With characteristic energy he decided that if he could not participate in events he would understand them and record his understanding for the use of those who would live the life that had been denied to him. His work is not literature but a testament for soldiers, diplomats, and statesmen and those who wish to understand soldiering, diplomacy, and statecraft.

It turned out that his mind, background, and training were excellent for the new task after all. The good families of Athens—not all, but many—had a fund of talent and experience in public affairs, and their sons naturally gravitated that way. (Plato was another of these young men.) Periclean Athens, as Thucydides describes it in the Funeral Oration, was an unparalleled arena for exercise in politics, war, and all the other activities that make a well-balanced man, and it was also undergoing an exciting intellectual revolution. Just as Thucydides was growing up, in the 440's (he was born around 460 or 455), the natural sciences and the social studies were impinging on Athens for the first time, and the effect on the young was like a sparkling wine. For the first time they learned that there were other ways of looking at the world besides the pious patriotism of their fathers and the heroic code of conduct they had learned in school from the poets. There was such a thing as nature, with laws of her own very different from those of men—or of gods—and much more binding; and there were ways of studying and evaluating human institutions. And in both cases the master tool was an observing, inquiring, unbiassed, rational mind.

What inflamed these young Athenians so was that they had caught a glimpse of the idea of science. Thucydides was among the aptest pupils. Here he learned, from men like Anaxagoras and Protagoras, the concept of natural as against supernatural causation; the search for evidence; the suspension of judgment until, or even after, it had been secured; the presentation of argument in a balanced antithetical style. He was influenced above all by Protagoras and by the new science of medicine. The physicians were the first scientists who became explicitly conscious of their own method and at the same time had a large well-defined body of observable facts to deal with. From them Thucydides learned or developed the concept of the nature of man, a complex of physical and psychological factors which can be observed and related to each other so that valid laws of the behavior of men in political society emerge. The lump term "history" does not do justice to this cardinal idea or the equally important fact that Thucydides' new science has very little to do with "history" as practised by Herodotus and most other ancient historians.

But he did not begin at once. Like any free-born Athenian of his time, like Plato not long after him, he thought too well of himself to become a mere scientist. He went into politics, apparently as a moderate democrat and admirer of Pericles—a moderate New Dealer, unlike his kinsman Thucydides, the leader of the aristocratic party, who had been exiled in 443; and it was through election by the popular assembly that he got the generalship he held in Thrace in 424. In the intervening years, and still more during his exile, his restless, realistic, rationalistic mind found ample material to work on, and as he collected it his view of human character and destiny began to emerge.

Like every Greek of a serious turn of mind, Thucydides has a pessimistic view of human nature. Man is an inalienably selfish animal. His basic drives are toward freedom and power; two complementary motives, for power brings freedom—for oneself; and freedom means power—over others. Hence history is a record of struggles for power. The last and most cataclysmic of these struggles is Thucydides' own subject, the Peloponnesian War; and a critical inspection of the past (our first selection, "The Ancient History of Greece") reveals a steady progress towards larger and larger accumulations of power, leading in the end to the climactic struggle between the two most powerful states in Greece. The progress is realized primarily through two things, wealth and sea power.

When Thucydides turns his analytical eye on the past, he does as many other historians have done: he finds the same basic motives at work there as in the present, but on a smaller scale and under different conditions. Men have always wanted the same things but have only gradually developed the means of securing them. This calm assumption—for it is an assumption—must have shocked his contemporaries even more than the debunking of American history shocked the early twentieth century. Instead of gods, heroes, and struggles to the death for honor's sake he finds migrations, insecurity, commerce, piracy, and navies. Perhaps his most stunning feat is the cool way in which he makes the poets, particularly Homer, testify against the romantic view of the past which they themselves had foisted on their countrymen.

The assumption of the uniformity of history is by all odds the most important assumption in Thucydides' work. But it does not exclude enormous change. And the change is more than technical. Under the benign influence of security, comfort, wealth, freedom, man himself acquires new "turns" or modes of character, becomes complex, versatile, paradoxical, a new and higher kind of human being. The theme of the Funeral Oration (our second selection) is the praise of this new kind of man, the Athenian, and of his city: that is, of the complex of wealth, power, and freedom that makes him possible. City and man are complementary: no such man without such a city to live in, no such city without such men to build and defend it.

The Funeral Oration is always quoted as the ideal picture of Athenian democracy, and so it is; Pericles himself calls it a hymn of praise. But it is a realistic hymn. The value of the new way of life exemplified by Athens lies in itself, not in some ulterior justification. The city herself, her buildings and festivals and public life, and the multifarious life of the individual Athenian, are ultimate goods, independent of religion—and even of morals? Meanwhile the ugly fact of imperialism appears as the necessary reverse of the medal: the greatest democracy is the greatest imperialist state.

The Funeral Oration is better known than its companion-piece, the Plague. The Plague is significant for Thucydides' training and interest in medicine, as a piece of scientific reporting, but its significance goes far beyond the medical facts. It follows hard on the Oration, without a break, and opens up the abyss of human weakness that was momentarily veiled by that splendid vision, realistic though it was. The Imperial city helpless in the grip of a disease, the versatile and graceful Athenians dazed with misery, not knowing what to do, fighting over the stinking corpses, living for the moment and forgetting all talk of law or honor—that is the other side of human greatness and a presentiment of what the war itself will do to Athens.

Such a relapse has to be pitied and pardoned; Thucydides does not say so, but he says that the force of the calamity was too great for human nature to bear. As the war goes on and gradually resumes after the short interlude of the Peace of Nicias (421 to 418) other phenomena begin to appear, the symptoms not of disease but of war. The Plataeans are butchered in cold blood by the Spartans; Athens comes within a hair's breadth of massacring the population of Mytilene, a revolting ally; ferociously cruel civil wars break out in the Greek states (third selection, "Revolution in the Greek Cities"). In the Melian Dialogue (fourth selection) the nature of war and the meaning of power finally come into the open, in cold explicit words. It is no accident that democratic Athens plays the Machiavellian role. Athens did not invent the rules of power, she only applied them, and being the most intellectual Greek state she was the best qualified to formulate them in theoretical language. But that does not mitigate the horror of this calm exposition of jungle law by the representatives of the "best city." Melos was Athens' Lidice. In March 415, a few months or weeks after the final massacre, Euripides produced his piercing indictment of all wars of conquest, the "Trojan Women."

The position of the Melian dialogue is as significant as that of the Plague. It stands as prologue to the climactic section of the *History*, the two books (VI and VII) on the Sicilian expedition. Here Athens' dreams of conquest verge towards the monstrous, even the pathological, under the persuasions of the dazzling Alcibiades, only to end (413) in the greatest disaster of the war. Thucydides lavished all his powers of analysis and narration on these two books. They need to be read complete; then the end (our last selection)—the last major battle, the retreat of the Athenians, and the final collapse—takes on its proper proportions as the long, crashing finale to the symphony. But it is given here as the only pure sample of Thucydides' narrative.

Thucydides' style is as direct and rapid in the narrative portions as it is elaborate and balanced in the speeches. The speeches probably reflect the sophistic, antithetical style he had learned in his youth and further refined in the years of his exile, but they also reflect the comparative complexity of men's motives and arguments as against the comparative simplicity of action. But at bottom both styles are the same style, precise, strenuous, eloquent, and resolutely prosaic. Thucydides never permits himself a poetic word or figure; he did not wish his work to be confused with mere literature. *Le style est l'homme;* in the end one's dominating impression of Thucydides' mind and style alike is controlled power.

His ultimate view of the world is not ours. Some of us are too spiritual to accept it; most of us are too flabby. He admired power, freedom, intelligence above all things —they meet in his portrait of Pericles—and recognized a fourth which it is unscientific to mention nowadays, fortune. He is narrow in his self-imposed scope; no cultural history, no stories, no biography, no "human interest" in the sense of picturesque detail about individuals. He has no humor and no change of pace. And sometimes he falls from his own standard of accuracy and objectivity. But he set up the standards; he found some intelligible order in the events of his time; and his work is still what he meant it to be, not literature but a testament and commentary on action for men who are called on to act, in our time or any other.

THE TEXT is that of W. H. S. Jones (Oxford, 1942).

Preface: The Ancient History of Greece

The magnitude of the war compared with those of the past

1 This history of the war between the Peloponnesians and Athenians was written by Thucydides of Athens. I began my work at the time when hostilities first broke out between them,[1] judging that this would be a conflict of major importance, in fact the most notable one in history; my reasons were, first, that both powers were at the peak of their resources when they went to war, and second, that I saw the rest of Greece either rushing immediately to join one side or the other or thinking of doing so. It certainly was the greatest upheaval that ever occurred in Greece and certain of the neighboring countries, and by and large involved more of mankind than any other. It was impossible for me to make out for certain the facts about the preceding period or the still more distant past, because of lapse of time; but on the basis of what trustworthy evidence I could find, going back as far as possible, I judge that they were not of much account either in war or in other respects.

2 It seems clear that the country now called Greece did not have a stable population in antiquity. In those times there were constant migrations: the various groups abandoned their territory without resistance when pressed by invaders more numerous than themselves. Commerce did not exist; there was no free, safe access from one country to another by land or sea; each people gathered a bare subsistence from its own land, without accumulating any capital or even planting trees and vines;[2] and since no one knew when an enemy might appear and carry off everything—for their towns were unwalled and defenseless—and it was taken for granted that the bare necessities of life could be found almost anywhere, they changed abodes without a second thought. Hence their towns were small and they had no great resources, in manpower or otherwise.

The best land particularly underwent this constant succession of changes of ownership: the regions that are now called Thessaly and Boeotia, most of the Peloponnese except Arcadia, and the best parts of the rest of Greece. The excellence of the soil in these areas encouraged growths of power which led in turn to devastating civil wars and also attracted the envious designs of other tribes outside the country. Attica meanwhile, thanks to the thinness of its soil, remained free of internal disturbances longest of all and so kept its population intact. A striking confirmation of this statement is the fact that Attica prospered and grew from the migrations more than any other region: the most important and influential people from other parts of Greece moved to Athens as refugees from invasion or civil war, considering it the safest spot they could find, and as they became citizens, beginning at a very early date, they swelled the population of the city until finally the Athenians decided the country was too small and sent out colonies themselves to Ionia.

3 Another proof, and I think a good one, of the weakness of Greece in ancient times is that so far as we can tell it undertook no common enterprise before the Trojan War. In fact I believe that at that time the country was not even called Greece (Hellas) as a whole. The name did not even exist before the time of Hellen, the son of Deucalion; instead the names of various races were given to the territory, and that of the Pelasgians had the widest currency. Later, after Hellen and his descendants came to power in Phthiotis [3] and were invited in to help other cities, the name "Hellenes" began to be used here and there by natural association, but it was still a long time before it became the dominant term. Our best evidence is from Homer: he lived much later, in fact long after the Trojan War, yet he nowhere calls the whole army Hellenes. He limits the name to Achilles' followers from Phthiotis, who were actually the original Hellenes, and calls the Greeks as a whole Danaans, Argives, or Achaeans. For that matter he does not use the word "barbarians" either,[4] just because, in my opinion, Greeks had not yet been marked off from non-Greeks by a single distinctive name.

As I was saying, then, no concerted effort was achieved by the Greeks—either the ones who borrowed the name from each other by random association or the larger group that acquired it later—before the Trojan War, because of their weakness and lack of intercommunication. And even that expedition was not undertaken until they had made some progress in seafaring.

Sea power and piracy

4 Minos was the first king mentioned in our tradition who built a navy. He extended his power over a very wide area of the present Aegaean sea and made himself not only the ruler of the Cyclades but also the first colonizer of most of them, by driving out the Carians [5] and establishing his own sons there as local governors; and he apparently swept piracy from the sea as far as his power extended, with an eye to diverting the revenue to himself.

5 In ancient times not only the Greeks but the neighboring peoples of the Asia Minor coast and the islands, once they took to sea-travel and communication with each other, turned to piracy.[6] Led by strong men who were out for their own profit but also looked after the maintenance of their weaker brethren, they would attack and plunder unprotected towns still dispersed in villages, and in fact made the greater part of their living in this way. At that time piracy was no disgrace but if anything a matter of pride. So much is clear from the practice along some parts of the coast even today, where they make it a point of honor to be good pirates, but even more from the fact that in the old poets [7] all seafarers, no matter where they land, are asked whether they are pirates: it is assumed that those who are asked the question will not be ashamed to admit it and those who ask are not implying any blame.

Piracy, or brigandage, was also practised on land, and life has gone on in the old way in many parts of Greece even down to our own day: [8] for example among the Ozolian Locrians, in Aetolia, Acarnania,[9] and along the western coast of the peninsula. The carrying of weapons has also persisted in those parts, as a relic of the ancient practice of brigandage. *6* All Greeks once carried arms, because their homes were unprotected and the communications with other regions were unsafe; hence that way of living became habitual among them as it has among other peoples. The survival of the custom in those parts of Greece is evidence that at one time it prevailed uniformly over the whole country.

Athens and Sparta contrasted

The Athenians were among the first to lay aside their arms and take up a more comfortable, even a luxurious, mode of life. It is not so many years since the older men in rich Athenian families stopped wearing linen tunics and tying up their hair on top of their heads in a knot fastened with gold locust-shaped pins,[10] and for a long time the fashion was common among the older men in Ionia as well, in imitation of their Athenian kinsmen.

The Spartans were the first to wear the unpretentious garb and style that is common nowadays, and in other respects too they were the first people among whom the rich took to living almost exactly like the poor. Again, they were the first to strip, that is, to undress in public and rub themselves with oil before exercise, whereas in antiquity the athletes wore loincloths when they competed in the games, even at Olympia; in fact it is not many years since the practice ceased. Even now, among those non-Greek peoples—and there are some, especially in Asia Minor—who hold contests and give prizes for boxing and wrestling, the custom is to wear loincloths. And one could show that in many other respects too the ancient Greek way of living was similar to that in the present-day non-Greek world.

Changes in ways of living after the suppression of piracy

7 The most recent Greek cities, those founded after navigation had become commoner, started with a greater surplus accumulation of wealth and were actually built on the shore, with walls for defense, or commanding an isthmus, in a place convenient for trade and for dominating their neighbors; whereas the older cities both in the islands and on the mainland, exposed as they were to the omnipresent menace of piracy, were located farther from the sea—since the pirates indiscriminately raided each other and also any people that lived near the sea but were not seafarers—and are still located there to this day.

8 The islanders were as given to piracy as anyone; that is, the Carians and Phoenicians,[11] since most of the islands were settlements of theirs. One piece of evidence is that when the Athenians undertook to purify Delos during the present war and removed the graves of all the dead on the island, over half turned out to be Carians; this was proved by the assortment of weapons that were buried with them and by the style of burial, which is still practised by the Carians. The establishment of Minos' navy, combined with his recolonization of most of the islands, drove out the criminals from those parts and encouraged the growth of communication by sea. Henceforth the dwellers along the coast began to settle down to a life of greater security and accumulation of wealth; some of them even built circuit walls from the proceeds of their new-found riches. Feeling the lure of profit themselves, the weaker sort did not mind becoming slaves to the strong, while the strong in turn used their surplus of capital to subjugate the lesser cities. Such had been the prevailing conditions in Greece for some time before it launched the expedition against Troy.

The Trojan expedition

9 In my opinion Agamemnon's success in mustering his army was due to his superior power among his contemporaries rather than to the binding power of Tyndareus' oath on the suitors for Helen's hand.

[Here Thucydides inserts a note on Agamemnon's family background and the probable origins of his wealth and power.]

Agamemnon had inherited these resources, and at the same time extended his sea power beyond that of any rival; hence, I think, the army he led was held together by fear rather than loyalty or good will. It appears clearly from Homer,[12] if he is acceptable as evidence, that Agamemnon not only brought more ships with him than anyone else but supplied some to the Arcadians besides. Furthermore, in the passage on the "descent of the scepter" Homer says that he ruled over many islands as well as the whole of Argos; yet he, a mainland prince, could never have held power over islands, except the few just offshore, if he had not had something of a navy also. And we can and should estimate the size of previous expeditions from his.

10 The fact that Mycenae was a small place, or that the other towns of that period might seem insignificant to us today, is not good enough historical evidence to justify us in doubting that the expedition was on the scale described by the poets and maintained by tradition. If the Spartans should abandon their city, leaving behind their temples and the foundations of their permanent structures, no doubt after a considerable time had elapsed posterity would be very skeptical indeed about their power. It is true that they directly own two-fifths of the Peloponnese and dominate the rest of it, besides their numerous allies abroad; and yet since they do not live in a real city and do not have any rich or beautiful shrines and public buildings, but dwell in scattered villages in the ancient Greek style, the remains would hardly be impressive. On the other hand, if the same thing happened to Athens the visible evidence would lead people to estimate the city's power at twice its true value.

Skepticism is out of place here; one should consider the real power of cities, not their appearance, and judge that the Trojan expedition was the greatest up to its time but inferior to those of the present day. Here again I assume that we can put some trust in Homer's account; for being a poet he would naturally tend to exaggerate, yet even so the expedition seems a rather modest one. According to him there were twelve hundred ships, the Boeotian vessels carrying 120 men each and those of Philoctetes fifty. These figures are meant as maximum and minimum, I think; at least the capacity of the others is not given in the Catalogue of Ships. Further, his description of Philoctetes' ships reveals that the whole complement were both rowers and fighting men, since he says that the crew were all bowmen. And in fact it is not likely that there were many supernumeraries besides the kings and high-ranking officers, especially as they had to carry military gear on the crossing and their boats were not decked over but were built in the old style, like pirate craft. If, then, we take the average of the largest and the smallest ships, the number of men does not seem large, considering that they represent a common effort by the whole of Greece.

11 The reason for these small numbers was not so much lack of men as lack of resources. The difficulty of provisioning the army made them cut its strength down to a size which they calculated could fight and live off the land. But it appears that even after they arrived and won a battle (as they clearly did; otherwise they could not have built the wall and moat around their encampment) they still did not bring their full striking force to bear, but took to raiding and farming in the Chersonese in order to remedy their deficiencies of supply.[13] This dispersion partly helps to explain the Trojans' success in holding out for ten years: they were always a match for those who were left in camp.

If the Greeks had had a reserve supply of provisions when they arrived and had been able to prosecute the war uninterruptedly and in full force, without recourse to farming or piracy, they could easily have won a decision in battle. Instead of just holding their own with the force that was on duty at any given time they could have laid regular siege to Troy and taken it in less time and without any particular difficulty. But lack of resources, which had been the prime weakness of previous undertakings, affected this one also, and though its reputation is unequalled by any before, facts show that it was inferior to the reports concerning it and the tradition that has by now been fixed in our minds by the poets.[14]

Colonization after the Trojan War

12 Even after the Trojan War Greece was still going through the process of migration and resettlement, so that there was no peace and no real progress. The long-drawn-out return of the Greeks from Troy caused political disturbances; civil wars broke out in the cities over a wide area, and men were driven into exile by them and founded new cities in turn. The present Boeotians, for example, were driven out of Arne [15] by the Thessalians sixty years after the fall of Troy and settled in the region which is now called Boeotia but was then called Cadmeis, or Cadmus's land (actually one section of them had been in the country for some time before and went to Troy from there); and the Dorians conquered the Peloponnese twenty years later, under the leadership of the descendants of Heracles. Finally, over a long period of time Greece settled down to a certain degree of peace and stability, and then, with its population no longer on the move, began to send out colonies. The Athenians colonized Ionia and most of the islands, the Peloponnesians the greater part of Italy and Sicily and some areas of Greece proper. All these settlements were made after the Trojan War.

The rise of Corinth

13 As Greece began to flourish and grow stronger, and the accumulation of wealth went beyond anything previously known, the increase in revenue gave rise to tyrannies [16] in most of the cities, whereas the traditional constitution was an inherited kingship with limited powers. The Greeks now began to fit out navies and pay more attention to the sea. It is said that the Corinthians were the first to manage their naval establishment more or less as we do now, and that Corinth was the first place in Greece where triremes were built.[17] It also appears that it was

Ameinocles, a Corinthian shipwright, who built four ships for the Samians; he went to Samos for the purpose just about three hundred years before the end of the present war [i.e., in or about 704 B.C.]. The earliest naval battle of which we have any record was fought between the Corinthians and the Corcyraeans about 260 years before the same date [i.e., about 664 B.C.].

With their location at the Isthmus, the Corinthians always had an international emporium. In ancient times, when the traffic followed land routes more than sea routes, commerce between the Peloponnese and the outside world was carried on through Corinthian territory and Corinth was a rich and powerful city; the proof is that the old poets call it "wealthy Corinth." Later on, as the Greeks took to the sea, the Corinthians built a navy, tried to suppress piracy, and offered traders a free market; as a result the profits poured in and the city consolidated its power on both land and sea.

It was much later that the Ionians began to develop sea power, during the reigns of Cyrus the first king of the Persians and his son Cambyses; for a time they even fought off Cyrus and dominated the sea near their own shores. Thanks to sea power Polycrates, the tyrant of Samos during the reign of Cambyses, subjugated a number of the islands in the Aegaean and captured Rhenia [18] and gave it as an offering to the Delian Apollo; and the Phocaeans, while engaged in founding Massilia [Marseilles], won a naval battle against the Carthaginians.

Development of naval affairs

14 These were the most powerful navies of the day. But apparently, though they came into being long after the Trojan War, they still included few triremes; most of the armament was still penteconters [19] and the old long boats of the Trojan War period. Shortly before the Persian Wars and the death of Darius, Cambyses' successor as king of the Persians, the Sicilian tyrants and the Corcyraeans began to lay down triremes in considerable numbers. These were the last important navies to be built in Greece before Xerxes' expedition; for those of Aegina, Athens, and the few other states which had any were very small and consisted mainly of penteconters. It was not until Athens was at war with Aegina and the Persian invasion was imminent that Themistocles managed to persuade the Athenians to build the navy with which they later fought the battle of Salamis. And even then the ships were not fully decked.

15 Such was the development of naval affairs in Greece in ancient and in more recent times. The states which devoted time and thought to their navies [20] acquired considerable new power in the form of increased revenues and conquest of others; they—especially those whose territory was not sufficient for their needs—were the ones who raided the islands and subjugated them. On the other hand there were no land wars that led to any considerable accession of power. Those that did take place were all local disputes between bordering states; the Greeks simply did not go on foreign expeditions far from their own territory for the sake of conquest over other peoples. This was natural, since the individual states had not begun to form groups subject to the larger cities, and when left to themselves were not inclined to joint expeditions based on equal contribution; they preferred to fight border wars against their next-door neighbors. The largest land war was the ancient one between Chalcis and Eretria,[21] which divided the rest of the Greek world into allies of the two cities.

Impediments to growth

16 Different states found hindrances to the growth of power from different quarters. The Ionians had made very notable progress when the Persian kingdom under Cyrus destroyed Croesus, invaded the whole territory between the river Halys [22] and the sea, and reduced the Greek cities of Asia Minor to slavery; later Darius, thanks to the power of his Phoenician navy, did the same to the islands.

17 As for the tyrants in the Greek cities of the mainland, they were so absorbed in their own immediate interests, that is, in their personal safety and the aggrandizement of their families, that the watchword of their policy at all times was security. Hence they did not accomplish anything really remarkable, except in some cases individually against their immediate neighbors; the Sicilian tyrants were the ones who developed the greatest power. So for a long time all the factors combined to keep Greece from pooling its resources for any conspicuous achievement, and to make the cities individually unenterprising.

18 Finally, however, the last of the Greek tyrants except those in Sicily, including the ones in Athens [23] and throughout most of the country (a good part of it had been under tyrannical governments for a long time, before Athens), were overthrown by Sparta. Sparta, after her founding by the present Dorian inhabitants, had had a longer period of internal troubles than any other state we know of, but also acquired peaceful, orderly government at a very early date and had never had a tyrant. Thus her constitution had been unchanged for a little over four hundred years, as nearly as we can tell, down to the end of the present war [i.e., since about 810 B.C.], and to that fact the Spartans owed the power that enabled them to establish new governments in other cities. Then, not many years after the overthrow and expulsion of the tyrants, came the battle between the Persians and Athenians at Marathon, and ten years later the great Persian expedition under Xerxes came to enslave Greece.

Athens and Sparta allied against the Persians

With a major peril hanging over their heads, the leadership of the combined Greek forces naturally fell to the dominant power, Sparta. The Athenians, on the other hand, through their decision to abandon the city to the advancing Persians and the critical step of packing up their belongings and taking to their ships, became a maritime people. The invader was pushed back by their common effort, and not long afterward those Greek states that had formed the wartime coalition and those that had previously revolted from the Great King fell into two factions grouped around Sparta and Athens.[24] These two were now the greatest powers in Greece, the one on land, the other at sea. The alliance between them lasted only a short time, then the two states began to fall out and finally went to war with each other, supported by their allies; and wherever quarrels broke out in other parts of Greece the parties were drawn into their orbits. Thus from the Persian wars down to the present one, sometimes at peace and sometimes at war either with each other or with their own rebellious allies, the two cities steadily perfected their armaments and grew in military experience through practice that involved actual danger.

19 Sparta's hegemony over her allies did not depend on the payment of tribute, but she took good care to see that they had oligarchical governments whose policy would be favorable to her. The Athenians on the other hand gradually took over the ship assessments of all their allies except Chios and Lesbos and imposed a money tribute on them all.[25] The result was that Athens entered the war with equipment and resources of her own superior to anything in the palmiest days when her empire was an alliance pure and simple.

Untrustworthiness of popular notions about history

20 Such, then, are my findings on ancient history. For these things one cannot trust every last piece of evidence, since human beings tend to accept and pass on all the stories they hear about the past, even the past of their own country, in the same uncritical way. Thus the Athenians think that Hipparchus was tyrant at the time when he was killed by Harmodius and Aristogiton; [26] they are not aware that Hippias was the ruling member, being the oldest of Pisistratus' sons, and that Hipparchus and Thessalus were his brothers. The facts are that on the day in question Harmodius and Aristogiton had a sudden suspicion that Hippias had received some warning from their fellow-conspirators; they therefore decided to let him go, but wanting to perform some dangerous exploit before they were arrested, and happening to run across Hipparchus as he was marshalling the Panathenaic procession near the so-called Leocorion, they killed him.

There are many false opinions prevalent among the other Greeks also, even about present-day facts which have not been obscured by the passage of time, such as that the Spartan kings have two votes apiece instead of one, and that the Spartans have a "Pitanate" battalion, which in fact never existed.[27] So lightheartedly do most men take the problem of discovering the truth: they prefer the nearest and easiest story.

21 Still, anyone who concludes on the basis of the evidence presented here that the events in question took place pretty much as I have related them, will not go far wrong. He must be on his guard against the poets' tales, exaggerated as they are in the interest of literary effect, and the accounts of previous historians,[28] which place attractiveness to the audience above the truth.

Their stories cannot be tested, and time has given most of them a decisive turn towards the fabulous and incredible. But the reader may consider my reconstruction, based on the clearest evidence available, as accurate as can be expected for ancient history. And though men always tend to regard the war of the moment as the greatest while they are engaged in it, but to relapse into admiration of the past when it is over, anyone who honestly examines the facts will see clearly that this war was the greatest in our history.[29]

The author's own methods and aims

22 As to what was said by the participants, both on the eve of their entrance into the war and afterwards, I myself, in those cases where I was present, and my informants about what happened in other places, found it difficult to recall the precise wording of the various speeches. They are given here in the form in which I thought the persons concerned would most likely have said what was called for under the circumstances, while keeping as close as possible to the general gist of what was actually said. The other part of the action of the war, the events, I did not see fit to record on the basis of questions put to casual strangers, or of my own ideas; whether I witnessed them myself or received my information from other people, in every case my account rests on the most careful research possible. It was a difficult task, since different witnesses told different stories about the same events according to the state of their memory or their leanings toward one side or the other.

The lack of picturesque stories in my narrative may well make it unattractive to the public; but it is meant for those in any period who want to study the true course of past events and therefore of the similar or analogous events that are likely to occur in the future, according to all human probability. If they judge the work useful I shall be satisfied; for it was written as a permanent possession [30] rather than a display piece to be heard once and forgotten. [I, 1–22]

[The war broke out, as major wars so often do, on the borders of the Greek world. A dispute between Corinth and Corcyra (in which Athens took the side of Corcyra) over a colony in Epirus, and another between Corinth and Athens over the town of Potidaea in northern Greece, led to the break. The Corinthians took the lead in egging the Spartans on to declare war. Hostilities began in 431 with raids and skirmishes, including a Peloponnesian raid on Attica.]

THE FUNERAL ORATION OF PERICLES AND THE PLAGUE

The setting of the speech

34 During the following winter the Athenians, in keeping with a time-honored custom, held a state funeral for those who were the first to fall in this war. The ceremonies are as follows. First the bodies of the deceased lie in state for three days in a special pavilion; during this time the relatives bring whatever offerings they wish. In the procession to the grave cypress-wood coffins are carried on wagons, one for each tribe,[31] and each containing the bodies of the dead from that tribe. One wagon carries an empty bier, fully decked, for the missing, those whose bodies could not be found for burial. Anyone who wishes, citizen or foreigner, may join in the procession, and the women of the family also attend and set up the cry of mourning at the grave.

The burial takes place at the state monument, which stands in the most beautiful suburb of the city. All the war dead of Athens have been buried there except the men of Marathon, whose valor was considered so pre-eminent that their tomb was built on the battlefield itself.[32] After the interment is finished, a man chosen by the citizens, someone of high reputation for intelligence and prominent in the community, pronounces a fitting eulogy over the dead, and the gathering disperses. Such are the state funerals; and the custom was maintained throughout the war whenever there was occasion for it. At this first observance the chosen speaker was Pericles son of Xanthippus. When the proper moment came he stepped forward from the monument onto a high platform constructed so that he could be heard by as many of the throng as possible, and spoke more or less as follows:

Difficulty of the speaker's task

35 "Most of the previous speakers on these occasions have praised the man who added this oration to the ceremonies; they considered it a fine and fitting thing that it should be delivered over our war dead. I on the contrary should think it would be sufficient for men who have shown their bravery in action to have their honors paid them in action also,[33] as in fact you see has been done in this solemn ceremony under the auspices of the state, and that the reputation of so many men should not be made to depend on the chance of a single speaker's eloquence or lack of it. It is difficult, you know, to speak fittingly on a subject in which one can hardly hope to gain credit for telling the truth. The friends of the dead, who know something about the case, may well feel that the speaker falls short of their expectation and their knowledge, while the stranger, out of jealousy at any story that goes beyond his own powers, may suspect him of exaggeration. A man can usually tolerate praise of others only up to the point where he thinks that he could have done the same; anything that exceeds his own capacity arouses his jealousy and therefore his disbelief. However, since this custom was sanctioned by past generations as a fitting one, I too must abide by the law and try to satisfy the expectations and beliefs of each of you so far as I can.

Tribute to the builders of the Athenian empire

36 "I will begin first with our forefathers. It is both right and appropriate on an occasion like this to pay them this tribute of remembrance; for they were the same stock that has dwelt in the land from the beginning, and by their valor, in unbroken succession of generations, handed it down to us a free country. They deserve our praise and admiration, but our own fathers deserve it still more; it was they who added to their inheritance the great empire we now possess and, not without toil, left it to us of this generation. Finally, those of us who are still more or less in the prime of life have given the empire its further expansion and provided our city with all the resources needed to make it completely self-sufficient in war and peace.

The way of life that has made Athens great

"The various wars and campaigns through which our conquests were made, the stout resistance that we or our fathers have offered against invasion by Greek or foreign invaders—all that you know and I do not want to dwell on it at length. Instead I will speak first of the way of life that is responsible for our achievements, the form of government and kind of character that have made Athens a great city. I am prefacing all this to my eulogy of the dead because I think it is not only suitable to the occasion but profitable for this whole gathering of citizens and foreigners to hear.

37 "Our form of government is not modelled on the constitutions of our neighbors; instead of imitating others we are actually an example to them. So far as the name goes we are called a democracy, because the power rests with the majority instead of a few. But though every citizen has equal rights under the law with respect to his private disputes, high standing and honor in the community depend on a man's merits, his achievement in some pursuit, and no one is debarred by poverty and obscurity of birth from contributing what he can to the well-being of the city. We are a free people not only in our management of public affairs but in our personal tolerance of one another's everyday conduct. We do not get angry at our neighbors for doing as they please, or try to inflict on them the petty marks of disapproval which, though harmless, are so unpleasant to experience. While this spirit of tolerance prevails in our private lives, in our public affairs it is fear more than anything else that keeps us law-abiding, obedient to the magistrates of the moment and to the laws, especially those whose purpose is to help the victims of wrongdoing and those unwritten laws which men by common consent are ashamed to transgress.

38 "Not only that, but we have provided for our enjoyment a great variety of relaxations from the day's work: games, contests, festivals lasting through the year, and beautiful private homes and furnishings. To see all this around us every day cheers us and drives away fatigue. Also, thanks to the greatness of Athens, the wares of the whole world find their way to us; we are in a position to enjoy the products of the rest of mankind as easily and naturally as we do our own crops from our own land.

39 "We also hold an advantage over our opponents in our way of preparing for war. Our city is open to everybody; there are no periodical deportations to keep foreigners from learning or observing things that might be of use to an enemy if they were not concealed.[34] We put our trust in our own inborn readiness for action rather than in armaments and military secrets. Their system of training involves the pursuit of courage through laborious discipline, beginning in their youth, while we allow ourselves some relaxation and yet are equally prepared to face any reasonable danger.

"The proof is that the Spartans have not invaded our country with their own forces alone but have brought along all their allies; we manage to attack our neighbors' territory without help and usually win, though fighting on foreign soil and against men who are defending their own homes and possessions. No enemy has ever yet encountered the full strength of our combined forces, since we have the maintenance of our navy to think about as well as the dispatch of armies by land to a number of places at once. If they do engage a small force of ours somewhere and defeat it, they boast that they have repelled us all, and when they are beaten, that they were defeated by us all. Now if we choose relaxation in the face of danger instead of endless drill, and rely on native courage rather than rules and regulations, the advantage is ours twice over: we do not wear ourselves out over future troubles, and when they do come we show as much venturesomeness as those who are forever moiling and toiling. Athens has a claim to men's admiration for all this, and for other things besides.

40 "We strive for distinction, but with economy, and for intelligence without loss of energy. Thus we use wealth to meet the needs of action, not the craving for display, and think it is no disgrace to admit poverty but a real disgrace not to act to escape it. Again, we combine the conduct of public and private affairs in the same persons and make it possible for others, though absorbed in their work,[35] to gain some insight into politics; for unlike other peoples we judge the man who takes no part in this at all a useless, not just a 'quiet,' person.[36] Hence also we arrive at sound decisions, or at least sound ideas, on policy, because we do not believe that action is spoiled by discussion, but by failure to be informed through debate before the necessary action is taken. In fact this is another point in our superiority: we are unusually daring and also unusually disposed to weigh the pros and cons of a proposed undertaking, while with others ignorance brings boldness and second thought brings hesitation. One would not go wrong in saying that the bravest men are those who foresee most clearly the dangerous as well as the pleasurable possibilities and still are not deterred from taking the risk.

"Again, so far as generosity goes we are the opposite of most men: we try to win friends not by accepting kindness but by conferring it. We know that the man who does a favor is the firmer friend: he will keep the debt alive out of good will towards the recipient, while the debtor does not feel it so keenly, knowing that a good turn will be put down as payment on his debt, not as a real favor. Our fearless way of serving others rests on the confidence of freedom rather than on calculations of profit; and in this too we are unique.

41 "To sum it all up, I say not only that our city as a whole is a model[37] for all Greece, but that in my opinion there is no other place where the individual can develop independence and self-reliance so easily, so gracefully, and in so many directions. That all this is not a matter of boastful talk for this occasion, but of plain truth, is proved by the fact of our power, which we acquired because we possessed those qualities. Athens alone, in our time, is greater than her own fame when the test comes; she alone gives the invader no excuse for annoyance at the quality of the foe who handles him so roughly, and her subjects no ground for complaint that their masters do not deserve to rule them.

"Our power is surely not unsubstantiated; we have given weighty proofs of it that will earn us the admiration of our own time and of posterity. We have no need of a Homer to sing our praises, or anyone whose poetic language will please for the moment but whose mere guesses at the facts will be wrecked by the truth. We have assured our own fame by forcing every land and every sea to become a path for our adventuring spirit and by founding memorials[38] of our enmity and favor in every part of the world. That is the kind of city for which these men died, facing battle with the high determination that she should not be taken from them; and it is only fitting that every man who is left should be willing to suffer for her.

The dead were worthy of such a city.

42 "The reason why I have expatiated on Athens at such length is that I wanted to demonstrate to you how much greater is our stake in this struggle than theirs who do not share our advantages, and also to give force to my eulogy of the dead by citing real evidence. I have almost finished; for the glories of Athens, the theme of my hymn of praise, are the garland she owes to these men and others like them. Few Greeks can show so equal a balance as they between their deeds and what we say about them. I think that their recent death, still fresh in our minds, is both the first evidence and the final confirmation of their worth as men. If some of them fell short in other things, we have every right to put their brave defense of the fatherland in time of war first in the reckoning; the good has erased the bad from our memory, the benefits of their common service outweigh any harm they did in private life. Not one of these men turned soft because he preferred the continued enjoyment of his own wealth; not one was tempted by poverty to put off the danger, hoping that he might still escape it and grow rich. Welcoming vengeance on the enemy as a prize more to be coveted than these, and considering the present danger nobler than any other, they accepted it and chose vengeance for the one part, renunciation for the other. They left to hope the unforeseeable chances of future success, but were men enough to rely on themselves in action, where the issue was already clear; convinced that to fight hard and endure is in itself a better guarantee of survival than surrender, they shrank from the reproach of men's words but stood the brunt of action with their lives, and so passed away in that brief moment in the play of fortune when their glory and not their fear was at its prime.

43 "If they were brave, then, it was a bravery characteristic of Athenians, and those who are left behind should pray that their resolution towards the enemy may be less hazardous, but determine that it shall be no less valorous, than theirs. Do not weigh the benefits merely in words—an orator could remind you at length of what you know as well as he, reciting all the manifold blessings of a firm defense against the enemy—but fix your eyes on the power of Athens as you see it in action from day to day, make yourselves her lovers, and when you find her a great city remember that men won that greatness for her by their boldness, their ability to grasp what was required of them, and the sense of honor with which they carried it out. Even when one of their ventures failed they would not stoop to injure the city by denying her the best of their manhood, but showered it upon her as their finest offering.

"Through this common gift of their lives they won for themselves individually unfading glory and the most conspicuous of all monuments: not the one in which they lie here but the one in which their fame survives them, to be remembered afresh as each new occasion arises for speech or action. For the real tomb of famous men is the whole earth; they are marked out not merely by the inscription over a grave in their own country but in other lands also by an unwritten memory, recording their spirit more than their actions, which lives on in the minds of men. Emulate them, then, in your own lives; learn from them that the key to happiness is freedom, the key to freedom a stout heart, and do not set a false value on the dangers of war. It is not the unfortunate, those with no hope of anything better, who have most reason to sacrifice their lives freely, but those who face the danger of a change for the worse if they go on living and, if they come to disaster in any undertaking, risk the greatest loss. To a man of any spirit the suffering and humiliation that go with cowardice are more painful to endure than a quick death, coming unnoticed in the full flush of strength and common hopes.

Exhortation to the bereaved relatives

44 "And for the same reason I offer good courage instead of mourning to the parents of these dead, those of them who are present. You know that your lives have seen all kinds of fortune, good and bad, and that the luckiest are those who have been vouchsafed the most glorious end, like these—or grief, like you—whose lives were so measured that their allotment of happiness and of death came to an even balance. I know this will be hard for you to believe; you will be reminded of them again and again when you see others with the happiness that you once enjoyed yourselves. And it is true, we do not grieve at being deprived of blessings we have never tasted, but at losing what we had grown accustomed to.

"But you should bear up in the hope of having more children, those of you who are still of an age to do so. Not only will the new ones help many of you individually to forget those who are gone, but the city will profit doubly, by not being depopulated, and in her security; for a citizen cannot possibly weigh the issue fairly and impartially if he has no children to contribute and so does not share the danger equally.

"As for those of you who are past the prime, set down the longer and happier part of your lives as profit, remember that the rest will be short, and let your sons' glory lighten the burden. Only the craving for honor is ageless, and in a man's declining years it is not profit, as some say, but the sense of being honored that brings real joy.

45 "Again, for those of you who are sons or brothers of these men I see a great contest in the making; for people always tend to praise those who are gone, and you will find that it takes a supreme effort to be rated, not even equal, but nearly equal to them. Men envy the living because they are competitors; what does not stand in their way they honor freely, with a good will untouched by rivalry.

"Finally, if I must say something about womanly virtue, for those of you who will be widows henceforth, I will sum it all up in one brief exhortation. Great is your good name when you do not fall below the standards of your sex, and when you give men the least occasion to talk about you, whether it be by way of praise or blame.

46 "Thus, so far as words go, I too have complied with the law and said what I had to say. As for acts, part of the funeral honors have already been paid the dead, and the rest will be paid by the city in public maintenance of their children until they come of age. That is the garland, worth while to the survivors as well as the dead, which she awards for this kind of contest: for the best men serve that state where the best prizes for merit are offered. And now make your lamentations, each for your own relatives, and then depart."

Outbreak of the plague (early summer, 430 B.C.)

47 Such was the state funeral that was held in Athens that winter; and with the passing of the winter the first year of the war ended. Promptly at the beginning of summer a two-thirds levy of the Peloponnesian and allied forces descended on Attica as they had the year before, under the command of the Spartan king Archidamus son of Zeuxidamus, settled down, and began to lay waste the countryside. They had only been in Attica a few days when the plague first broke out in Athens. It is said that it had already appeared in a great many different places, on the island of Lemnos and elsewhere, but there is no record of an epidemic of such proportions, or with such a high mortality rate, anywhere else. The doctors tried at first to treat it without any prognosis, and failed; in fact they suffered the highest mortality because they came in the closest contact with it. No other human art was of any avail either, and the supplications that were offered up at the various temples and oracles and such places were so futile that people finally gave them up of their own accord, in utter despair.

48 The disease originally began, it is said, in Ethiopia to the south of Egypt, then spread to Egypt itself and Libya, and over the greater part of the Persian empire. It struck Athens very suddenly, attacking the Piraeus first, which led to a rumor among the inhabitants that the Peloponnesians had poisoned the cisterns (at that time the Piraeus did not have public fountains); then it made its way up to the city proper and the death rate immediately rose sharply. I leave it to anybody who wishes, physician or layman, to state his own opinion as to the probable origin of the disease and what contributing factors can have exerted a force sufficient to account for this great increase in severity; I will merely record how it developed and describe the symptoms, which I hope will enable an observer to diagnose it[39] if it should ever break out again—all this on the basis of my own experience as a patient and other cases which I observed personally.

49 Everyone agreed at the time that Athens had been remarkably free from disease that year, so far as other kinds of sickness were concerned; and if a person was already ill with something else it tended to turn into this. Most of the victims, however, were taken suddenly in the midst of good health, with no visible cause. The first symptoms were intense heat around the head, with reddening and a burning sensation in the eyes; the internal parts, tongue and throat, immediately turned blood-red and the breath had a peculiar unpleasant odor; this was followed by sneezing and hoarseness, and in a short time the pain worked down into the chest, accompanied by severe coughing; finally, when it settled lower it upset the stomach and induced vomiting of bile in every form that has received a medical name, all of them intensely painful. Most patients contracted a dry retching which led to violent cramps; in some cases these subsided with the retching, in others they lasted much longer.

The surface of the body was not particularly warm to the touch, and not pallid but reddish, livid, broken out in small pustules and ulcers. Internally, on the other hand, it was so burning hot that the sufferers could not stand even the lightest clothing, or fine linen sheets, or anything but complete nakedness; their strongest impulse was to throw themselves into cold water. And in fact many who were not carefully watched did plunge into cisterns, they were so tormented by unassuageable thirst (for that matter it made no difference whether one drank little or much). Also, throughout the whole course of the disease there was a persistent sleeplessness and the desperate feeling of not being able to rest.

And yet the body did not waste away while the disease was at its height; it held up surprisingly considering the amount of suffering. Hence if the patient died on the seventh or ninth day, as most of them did, from the effects of the internal inflammation, it was while he still had some strength; or if he survived, the infection passed on down into the bowels, severe ulceration took place accompanied by violent diarrhea, and in most cases he died later from that cause, out of weakness. Thus the malady which had originally centered in the head spread downward through the entire body, and if one escaped the worst it at least left its mark on the extremities: it would settle in the genitals, or the hands and feet, and some escaped with the loss of those parts, others with the loss of their eyes. Some were stricken with total amnesia immediately after their recovery and did not know either themselves or their best friends.

50 Thus the unfathomable character of the disease was shown by the power with which it attacked its victims, far beyond any normal human resistance. But the most striking indication of how utterly it differed from the ordinary was that, although there were a great many corpses unburied, the birds and animals that normally take to human carrion would not go near them, or if they tasted of the flesh they died. The evidence, so far as the birds were concerned, was that the carrion-eating kind became noticeably scarce and were not seen either around the corpses or elsewhere. It was easier to observe the effect on the dogs, because of their domestication.

51 Omitting a number of other extraordinary developments, which varied with the incidence of the disease on this or that individual, these were the general symptoms and effects of the plague. There were no attacks of any of the usual diseases during the period, or if there were they passed into this. Some of the deaths were due to neglect; but others died who had been very carefully tended. Practically speaking not a single remedy was found that could be counted on for relief: what helped one injured another; and so far as human strength and weakness went no constitution proved able to withstand the disease: it overpowered all alike, no matter what kind of treatment they received.

The most frightful thing about the whole calamity was the despondency of the victims when they realized that they were sick—they promptly gave way to hopelessness, and this mental attitude more than anything else led them to surrender without a struggle—and the further fact that they caught the infection and died like sheep from taking care of each other. In fact that was the cause of the worst mortality. If people avoided contact with others out of fear they died in isolation (many a house lost all its inhabitants for lack of nurses), but they also died if they went out, and especially those who made any claim to kindness. It was they who went to see their friends for conscience' sake, disregarding their own safety, because often the patient's own relatives were overcome by all their suffering and finally would not bother even to mourn over the dying. Oftener, however, it was those who had recovered that were moved to lamentation for the sick and the dying alike. They knew the symptoms and were past the stage of fearing for themselves; for the disease never struck the same person twice, at least not mortally. These survivors were envied and congratulated by the rest, and they themselves in the excessive joy of the moment were prone to foolish expectations about the future, that they would never die of any other disease.

General demoralization at Athens

52 The misery of the plague itself was aggravated by the crowding of the country population into the city,[40] and it was these refugees who suffered most. They had no houses but lived in crude huts, stifling with the summer heat, and among them the mortality knew no bounds. Men lay dying in heaps on top of one another or wallowed in the streets and around all the fountains, half dead with craving for water. The sanctuaries in which they had camped were full of corpses, as people died on the spot; the force of the calamity was so overpowering that men did not know where to turn and began treating profane and holy places with equal disregard. All the customary rites that had been observed at funerals in the past were thrown to the winds and everyone buried his dead any way he could. Many resorted to unseemly modes of burial simply out of lack of the proper furnishings, so many members of the family had already died. Sometimes they would rush to a pyre intended for someone else, lay their own dead on it before the owners could arrive, and light the fire; others would bring a corpse, place it on a pyre that was already burning, and go away.

53 The plague was also responsible for the beginnings of other kinds of lawlessness. People found it easier to venture what they had always wanted to do but had previously kept hidden, when they saw fortune changing sides so rapidly: the rich and prosperous dying suddenly and their property snapped up on the spot by others who had never owned anything before. They concluded that they had better take their pleasures quickly, with an eye to enjoying themselves, since life and property seemed to be equally ephemeral. Nobody was eager to add to his misery for a thing called honor when it was uncertain whether he might not die before he ever reached it; instead the pleasure of the moment, and anything that might conceivably serve it, were accounted both honorable and useful. No fear of gods or laws of man had any restraining effect. They judged that religion and irreligion were all the same, since everybody was dying alike, and as for law, nobody expected to live long enough to be brought into court and pay a penalty for his crimes; the real fact was that their case had already been decided, the sentence had been suspended, and before it was carried out no one could blame them for getting a little enjoyment out of life.

Alleged predictions of the plague

54 Such were the misery and hardship into which the Athenians had fallen, with men dying inside the city and the country being devastated outside. In their plight they naturally recalled a line of verse, which the older folk said had been uttered long ago: "Once shall a war with the Dorians come, and a plague shall come with it." Then a dispute arose over the text, some alleging that in quoting it the ancients had not used the word "plague" (loimos), but "famine" (limos). Of course the view that they had said "plague" won out for the time being: people adapted their memory to their present circumstances. But I have no doubt that if Athens gets involved in another war with the Dorians in the future, and there turns out to be a famine, the verse will be quoted the other way. Those who knew about it also recited the oracle that had been delivered to the Spartans at Delphi: when they asked Apollo whether they should go to war he answered that if they warred with all their might victory would be theirs, and added that he would take their side himself.[41] So some Athenians jumped to the conclusion that what was happening sounded like the oracle: after all the plague had started immediately after the Peloponnesians entered the country, and it had not attacked the Peloponnese to speak of but had wrought its worst havoc in Athens and then in the other cities with the largest population.

So much, then, for the history of the plague.

[II, 34–54]

Revolution in the Greek cities

[Party strife, often leading to actual civil war (the Greeks called both stages *stasis*), broke out in most of the Greek states at some time during the war. These local upheavals were connected with the main struggle, because the oligarchs everywhere ("the few") looked to Sparta for aid and comfort and the democrats ("the many" or "the people") to Athens. The first spectacular outbreak took place at Corcyra in 427, beginning with an oligarchic *coup d'état.* The Athenians negotiated a settlement between the parties, but it broke down; the democrats then armed for action and most of the oligarchs fled for safety to the sacred precinct of Hera. At this point a Peloponnesian fleet appeared, under Alcidas, made its base on the mainland opposite Corcyra, and commenced raiding operations. The democrats naturally expected a direct attack on the city.]

Corcyra in the hands of the democrats

80 Meanwhile the Corcyraean democrats, being very apprehensive of an attack by sea, held a conference with the refugees and the other oligarchs on measures of defense, and managed to persuade some of them to serve in the navy (they had already gotten thirty ships manned, in spite of everything, in anticipation of an attack). But the Peloponnesians only continued their looting until noon and sailed back again. About nightfall they got a beacon signal that sixty Athenian ships had been sighted coming from Leucas; this force, under the command of Eurymedon son of Thucles, had been dispatched by Athens when news came of the revolution and the imminent departure of Alcidas' fleet for Corcyra. At this the Peloponnesians immediately set sail for home as fast as they could go, keeping close to shore, portaged their ships across the Leucadian isthmus so as not to be seen crossing outside Leucas, and got away safely.

81 When the Corcyraeans realized that the Athenian fleet was approaching and the enemy had departed, they brought the five hundred Messenians [42] into the city—they had previously been camped outside—and ordered the ships that had received complements to sail around to the Hyllaic harbor.[43] While this movement was under way they set out to kill every oligarch who fell into their hands; then they brought ashore and executed those of them who had been induced to serve in the navy; and finally they went into the precinct of Hera, persuaded about fifty of the refugees there to stand trial, and sentenced them all to death. Most of the refugees, however, remained unpersuaded and when they saw what was going on began destroying each other right in the sanctuary: some hanged themselves from the trees, the rest got themselves dispatched any way they could. For seven days after Eurymedon's arrival, while he stood by with his sixty ships, the democrats carried on the slaughter of their alleged enemies. The general charge against them was attempted overthrow of the democracy, but some were actually killed to satisfy private grudges and others to cancel debts owed them by their captors. Death and murder appeared in all their forms, the things that normally happen at such a time all came to pass, and still worse: fathers actually killed sons, men were dragged from the sanctuaries and slain on the spot, and one group was even walled up inside the temple of Dionysus and left to die there.

Party strife and its effect on civic life

82 To such inhuman lengths did the civil war go; and it seemed even worse because this was one of the first outbreaks. Later, of course, the unrest spread over practically the whole Greek world, as differences arose in the various cities between the leaders of the popular party, who wanted to bring in the Athenians, and the oligarchs, who wanted the Spartans. In peacetime they would have had neither pretext nor desire to call in these powers; but under the pressure of the war, with each side reckoning how a foreign alliance would damage its opponents and at the same time strengthen its own position, it was easy for revolutionaries in both camps to secure intervention from abroad.

Party strife, then, brought a host of troubles upon the Greek cities, troubles which of course have recurred and will always recur as long as human nature remains the same, but which, if anything, are likely to be less severe and take different forms according to the different way in which circumstances change at one period or another. By this I mean that in times of peace and prosperity states and individuals alike have kinder dispositions, because they are not forced into want and privation; whereas war, by stripping life of its ordinary margin of comfort, keeps a hard school and generally shapes men's feelings to match their present circumstances.

Not only were the cities racked by civil war but the latecomers, hearing what had already been done before them, carried the progressive radicalization of thought to even further extremes by refining on previous methods of attack and inventing unheard-of forms of reprisal. They also reversed the customary application of words to actions as they saw fit. Harebrained recklessness now became the courage of a true party member; prudent hesitation, cowardice under a nicer name; self-restraint, an excuse for lack of manly spirit; and intelligence in any respect, supineness in all respects. Impulsiveness and vehemence were taken as the mark of a man, and an attempt at caution in laying a plot was a specious pretext for desertion. An angry man was to be trusted every time; anyone who opposed him was under suspicion. To bring off an intrigue was a sign of intelligence, to suspect one, a sign of genius, while the man who planned things so as not to need all this was a wrecker of the party and browbeaten by the opposition. In general there were two ways to win respect and approval: to anticipate someone else in a crime, or to urge him to one before he thought of it himself.

Again, party affiliation became a closer bond than family ties: party mates could be counted on to do anything, without qualm or scruple, because the purpose of these associations was not true benefit under established law but self-aggrandizement in defiance of it and their mutual confidence got its sanction not from the divine law but rather from their partnership in law-breaking. A fair offer from the other side was received skeptically, with an eye to what they might do if they got into power, not in a frank, open spirit; and revenge on an opponent was a finer thing than staying out of trouble oneself. If a settlement was somehow reached after all the binding effect of the oaths was purely temporary, since both sides took them only as a last resort, out of desperation, and the first to regain its nerve by catching the enemy off guard when a chance offered enjoyed its revenge more for the breach of faith than it would have from an open attack: not only were such tactics safe, they felt, but a victory won by cheating brought with it a further prize, for astuteness. It is easier for most men to get their rascality called cleverness than their stupidity called virtue, and they are ashamed of one epithet but proud of the other.

Ultimately all these troubles were caused by greed and ambition; it was they that bred the spirit of contentiousness and made men so passionate. The leaders of the two parties in the various cities, campaigning under high-sounding slogans like "equal political rights for the masses" and "responsible government by the best men," paid lip service to the common welfare but really treated it as party spoils; they committed frightful crimes in the all-out struggle to get the upper hand of each other, and their reprisals were even worse. Far from keeping the latter within the bounds of justice and the public interest, they fixed their sentences according to what the party wanted at the time; and in first winning power, whether it was achieved by unjust votes of condemnation or simply by force, they did not hesitate to gratify the animosities of the moment. In short, neither side paid any real heed to conscience or honor, but the one that managed to perform an odious act under cover of fine phrases was better spoken of. And meanwhile the citizens who stood between the parties were destroyed by both, either because they would not take part or simply out of jealousy that they were still alive.

83 So, thanks to the civil wars, every kind of viciousness made its appearance in the Greek world. Simplicity, the chief element in a noble character, was laughed to scorn and disappeared; instead drawn antagonisms and mutual distrust prevailed far and wide. No assurance was strong enough, no oath formidable enough, to reconcile the parties; too clever for that, they could not bring themselves to trust anybody and preferred to stake their survival on calculation, counting security as hopeless. Actually it was the less intelligent who usually won out. Conscious as they were of their opponents' cleverness and their own lack of it, fearful lest these tricky adversaries take them in with fine words and suddenly confront them with a plot before they suspected one, they proceeded ruthlessly to act; while the others, scornfully confident that they could see the blow coming and need not take by action what they could have by thought, relaxed their guard and were destroyed. [III, 80–83]

The Melian dialogue

[During the first years of the war the Peloponnesians faithfully invaded the countryside of Attica every year and destroyed the crops, but Athens itself was impregnable behind its walls and its ships. The Athenians in turn raided the coasts of the Peloponnese and its outposts regularly and gained one small but spectacular victory over the Spartans themselves at Pylos, on the southwest coast (424). Shortly afterward the

Spartan Brasidas made a series of lightning conquests in the north (Macedonia and Thrace), but they fell apart at his death in 422.

After ten years of this inconclusive sparring between land power and sea power the war was a stalemate, and Nicias very sensibly made peace (421) on the basis of the status quo. But it did not last. Egged on by the irresistible young Alcibiades, Athens gradually resumed the contest. In the year 416 she determined to clean up one of the last remaining neutral spots in the southern Aegaean, the island of Melos.]

Athenian expedition against Melos, 416 B.C.

84 The following summer Alcibiades made a raid on Argos with a fleet of twenty ships and took prisoner three hundred of the Argives who were still under suspicion of being favorable to the Spartans; the Athenians interned them on the near-by islands that were under their control. The Athenians also sent an expedition against the island of Melos; the force consisted of thirty of their own ships, six from Chios and two from Lesbos, twelve hundred Athenian infantry, three hundred archers, twenty mounted archers, and approximately fifteen hundred infantry from the allies and the islands. The Melians are a colony of the Spartans who had refused to become Athenian subjects like the other islanders; for some time they had remained neutral in the war, but now, under threat of Athenian invasion and pillage, they made ready for open hostilities. When the expedition arrived, with the complement mentioned above, the two generals, Cleomedes son of Lycomedes and Tisias son of Tisimachus, sent spokesmen to hold a conference before they proceeded to hostilities. The Melians did not present the envoys to the popular assembly but invited them to explain to a gathering of the officials and influential men what they had come for; and the Athenians then spoke more or less as follows:

Debate between Athenians and Melians

85 "Since this discussion is not being held in the assembly, for fear the citizens in general might find our arguments attractive, in fact irrefutable, at first hearing and so be led astray—for we are well aware that this is why we have been brought before this select group—you who are present can make things still safer for yourselves if you like: you may judge the case item by item, without any long speeches, interrupting whenever you think one of our points is not well taken. First, then, say whether you accept this procedure."

86 The Melian representatives replied: "We cannot quarrel with the reasonableness of a leisurely exchange of views, but the warlike preparations we see already surrounding us, not merely in prospect, have a different look. It is obvious that you have come to sit in judgment on the discussion and that in all probability, if we win the argument on the score of justice and therefore do not give in, the result of our talk will be war, and if we submit it will be slavery."

87 ATH. Well, if your purpose in this meeting is to deal in vague conjectures about the future instead of planning how to save your city on the basis of present observable facts, we may as well stop now; or, if you accept our condition, we will continue.

88 MEL. It is natural and forgivable that men in a situation like ours should try many shifts, in their speech as well as their thoughts; however, the purpose of this meeting is to discuss the preservation of our city and the discussion may proceed along the lines you suggest, if you wish.

89 ATH. Well then, we will not spin out a long, wearisome round of speeches, with fine phrases about how righteously we gained our power by destroying the Persians, or how this attack was provoked by some wrong we have suffered; and in return please do not count on convincing us with arguments about your not joining us in the war because you are colonists of the Spartans, or about your never having done us any harm. Let us deal with practical possibilities, the basis of our real intentions on both sides, since you know as well as we do that in their stated arguments and conclusions about justice men are under equal constraints, but when it comes to practice the strong do as they please and the weak acquiesce.

90 MEL. The way it looks to us (and we have no choice, since you have laid it down that we are to ignore justice and talk expediency), you would find it advantageous not to rule out the common good, but to leave open to all who may be in danger an appeal to reason and justice, and the hope of bettering their position by argument, even if they fall short of proof. Actually that is in your own interest, considering that if you fail disastrously others will treat you by your own example.

91 ATH. We are not worried about what may happen to our empire, even if it comes to an end. The real danger is not the threat of being beaten by another ruling nation like the Spartans—and after all we are not arguing with the Spartans here—but the possibility that subject states may revolt against their rulers and subjugate them. Anyhow, you can leave that risk for us to deal with. We will state frankly that we are here to further the interests of our empire and that what we are about to say is for the preservation of your city; that is, we want to subdue you with the least effort and leave you unharmed for your sake as well as ours.

92 MEL. But, granting that your power is profitable to you, how can slavery be so to us?

93 ATH. In that you have a chance here to submit before you suffer the worst consequences, while we stand to gain by not utterly destroying you.

94 MEL. Would it be acceptable to you if we took no part in the war and remained friendly to you but neutral towards both sides?

95 ATH. No, because your hostility is not as dangerous to us as your friendship would be; our subjects would take the friendship as a standing sign of weakness, and the hatred as a sign of our power.

96 MEL. Do your subjects consider it reasonable not to make any distinction between those who are no kin to you and those—mostly your own colonists—who have rebelled against you at one time or another and been reduced to subjection?

97 ATH. Why, so far as pleas of justice go they consider that both groups have a case, but that those who elude us owe it to their power, because we are afraid to attack them. That is why, aside from the enlargement of our empire, your subjugation will bring us security: the failure of you, an island and a rather weak one, to win against a sea power would be especially striking.

98 MEL. But don't you think there is any security in our proposal? Here again, since you have excluded arguments based on justice and have told us to consider only your advantage, it is incumbent on us to try to show you convincingly where our own interests lie, if it happens that yours lie in the same direction. Now those states that are neutral at present will inevitably join the fight against you when they see what has happened here and become convinced that some day you will attack them too. In short, what are you accomplishing by all this except to strengthen your existing enemies and force others, who had never thought of such a thing, to join them?

99 ATH. No, you see we are not much afraid of potential enemies on the mainland; they are so used to their freedom that they will procrastinate a long time before putting up a defense against us. Our chief threat is from the islanders, those who are independent like yourselves and also those who have been irritated by the constraints of our empire. They are the ones who are most likely to give way to folly and involve themselves and us in dangers that they might have foreseen.

100 MEL. Upon our word, if you are ready to take such extreme risks to maintain your empire, and those who are already your slaves to rid themselves of it, it would be the most contemptible cowardice for us who still have our freedom not to go to any length to avoid slavery.

101 ATH. Not if you look at the matter sensibly. What faces you here is not a free and equal contest in bravery, to sustain your honor; the issue is self-preservation, that is, not to struggle against a far superior power.

102 MEL. And yet we know that the chances of war often turn out to be more evenly balanced than the difference in numbers between the two sides would indicate; so in our case immediate surrender would mean giving up hope, but if we try to do something there is hope that we may still succeed.

103 ATH. Hope is a consolation in time of danger, and those who have plenty of other resources are not ruined by it, though they may be damaged. But those who stake everything they have on hope (which is a spendthrift by nature) only recognize it for what is is after they fail: while there is still time to see through it and put themselves on guard, it retains its full strength. Now you are a weak nation and dependent on a single turn of the scale; do not let yourselves suffer the fate of so many others. In a situation where they might be saved by their own efforts, when they have their backs to the wall and visible hopes have abandoned them, they resort to the invisible kind—divination, oracles, and other things that destroy men by feeding them on hope.

104 MEL. We think as you do, make no mistake about it, that it will be hard for us to compete with your power and fortune combined, if she turns out not to be impartial. However, so far as fortune is concerned we have faith that with divine help we shall not lose out in this contest between piety and injustice, and we rely on an alliance with the Spartans to make up the deficiency in our power; they will be forced to help us because of our kinship with them and from a sense of honor, if for no other reason. So our confidence is not quite so irrational after all.

105 ATH. Well, as for enjoying the divine favor, we do not expect to come off second best either. In our demands and in our actions we are not departing in any way from the norm of what men practise towards the gods or desire for themselves. You see we believe that divine beings, and we know for certain that human beings, by a necessity of their nature, rule wherever they have the power to rule. We did not establish this principle and were not the first to use it once it was established; we found it in force when we began, expect to leave it in force after us, and meanwhile take advantage of it, knowing that you or anybody else, if you had our power, would do the same. So we have good reasons for not fearing to lose out in the competition for divine favor.

As for your expectations from the Spartans, your faith that they will come to the rescue for honor's sake, we admire your innocence but do not envy your lack of common sense. The Spartans, in their treatment of each other and their domestic institutions, are models of virtue and honor; their conduct towards others would make a very long story, but one can sum it up by saying that of all nations known to us they are the most conspicuous for identifying honor with their own pleasure and justice with their own interests. Surely such an attitude is not conducive to your present foolish hopes of salvation.

106 MEL. But that is the very reason why we place so much trust in their seeing where their interest lies; that is, we are sure they will not choose to forfeit the confidence of the Greek states that are favorable to them, and lend aid to their enemies, by betraying their own colony, Melos.

107 ATH. Apparently you aren't aware that the pursuit of one's own interest is safe enough, but just and honorable conduct is a risky business—and the Spartans are generally the last to take that risk.

108 MEL. Yes, but we think that they would consider the risks lighter in our case and be more inclined to face them for our sake than they would for others, since in case of action we are close to the Peloponnese and thanks to our kinship they can trust our way of thinking more than that of others.

109 ATH. A potential co-belligerent does not base his confidence on the good will of his would-be allies, but on the fact of a clear predominance of power. The Spartans are especially given to this way of thinking—at least they seem to distrust their own resources and attack their neighbors only at the head of a host of allies—so it is not likely that they will venture offshore to help an island while we have command of the sea.

110 MEL. There are others they might send; besides, the Cretan sea is broad and makes the dominant power's task of search and seizure more desperate than the efforts of the hunted to escape. And if their efforts should fail they can try a diversion against Attica or the rest of your allies, those whom Brasidas never got to; [44] then you will have a hard struggle for your confederacy proper and your own territory, instead of land that does not belong to you.

111 ATH. Any of the things you mention might happen to you too, for that matter; you have had experience with them. Also you are aware that Athens has never yet abandoned a siege out of fear of anybody. But it strikes us that though you said you would discuss your own salvation here, in this whole long argument you have not said a thing that normal human beings would consider a reliable guarantee of salvation; your strongest assurances are nothing but hopes, still unrealized, and your actual resources are slim indeed to win out over those that face you. You are showing a gross lack of intelligent thinking if you do not recess this conference now, before it is too late, and come to a more sensible decision. Surely you are not going to give way to shame, the most ruinous impulse one can have when facing a really shameful and foreseeable danger. Often, that is, while men can still foresee what they are being swept into, the thing we call shame, having first overcome their resistance by the power of a seductive word, the work of a mere phrase,[45] lures them on to fall of their own accord into irreparable disaster and incur a new shame, more shameful because brought on by folly, not fortune. If you think carefully you will avoid this error; you will consider it no disgrace to be conquered by the greatest city in Greece, when she generously offers you the chance to become autonomous tribute-paying allies,[46] and will not make a poor decision out of mere stubbornness when given a choice between war and security. In general, those who stand their ground against their equals, behave well towards their superiors, and are decent towards their inferiors, will get along best. Think seriously, then, after we withdraw, and remind yourselves again and again that the issue here is your country: that you have only one, and her success or failure hangs on a single decision.

The Melian decision; the siege begins in earnest.

112 With that the Athenians withdrew from the discussion. The Melians, after conferring among themselves and finding that their sentiments had not changed from those they had expressed before, made the following reply: "To begin with, gentlemen, our views are still the same as they were, and secondly we do not propose to sacrifice in a few hours the freedom of a city that has now existed for seven hundred years. We will try to achieve our own salvation, trusting in the good fortune from heaven that has saved us up to now, and also in human sympathy and help, particularly from the Spartans. Here is our offer: we to be on friendly terms with you but remain neutral in the war, and you to withdraw from our territory after we have arranged a truce that both parties consider acceptable."

113 This was all that the Melians said in their reply. The Athenians, as they left the conference, made this statement: "Well then, it seems to us, judging from these proposals, that unlike all other human beings you consider future possibilities plainer than present facts and view uncertainties as if they were already happening, because you want them to. You have staked everything you have, placed all your reliance, on mere hopes, good luck, and the Spartans, and your failure will be correspondingly complete."

114 The Athenian representatives then returned to the army. The two generals, seeing that the Melians were not going to submit, immediately opened hostilities and walled off the city, parcelling out the work among the various allied contingents. Then, leaving a force of Athenian and allied troops to guard the place by land and sea, they withdrew the major part of the expedition; and those who were left behind settled down to conduct the siege.

115 [Later in the summer the Melians broke through the siegeworks at one point and brought in supplies.]

116 [During the following winter] the Melians captured another section of the Athenian siege wall, where the force on guard was light. Later, however, seeing what was going on, the Athenians sent out a second expedition under the command of Philocrates son of Demeas; the Melians were now under heavy siege, treason appeared in their own ranks, and they surrendered to the Athenians with the understanding that the latter would decide their fate. The Athenians executed all the adult male prisoners they captured, enslaved the women and children, and took over the site for a colony of their own; later they sent out five hundred settlers to occupy it.

[V, 84–116]

The end of the war in Sicily

[In spite of Nicias' prudent warnings Alcibiades lured the Athenians into a really grandiose scheme: the conquest of Sicily. The greatest Greek expeditionary force ever assembled set out for the west in 415 under Nicias, Alcibiades, and Lamachus, with golden dreams of power and fortune whirling in their heads. Here is Thucydides' description of the scene at their departure from Piraeus (VI, 32, 1–2)]

Departure of the expedition

Then, after the crews and complement had gone aboard and the supplies they were to take with them had all been laid in, there was a trumpet call for silence and they offered up the prayers that are customarily offered before putting to sea, not ship by ship this time but the whole fleet at once, following the herald's signal; wine was mixed in the mixing bowls throughout the entire armada, and marines and officers together poured the libations from drinking cups of gold and silver. Meanwhile the other throng on shore, made up of citizens and any others who had come down to wish them godspeed, joined in their supplications. Then, after singing the paean and completing their offerings, they stood out to sea, first issuing from the harbor in column and then racing each other as far as Aegina. They were in hot haste to reach Corcyra, where the rest of the expedition, the allied forces, were assembling.

[But the high spirits did not last. Alcibiades was summoned home on a religious charge after the fleet reached Sicily (he was too intelligent actually to go home and settled in Sparta instead), leaving Nicias to fight a war he did not believe in.

The key to Sicily was Syracuse. Athenian strategy was predicated on the hope of winning the help of the other Greek cities and the Sicels (native non-Greek population). The Sicels joined, most of the Greek cities did not, and the Athenians sat down to besiege Syracuse. Syracuse got itself a new commander-in-chief from Sparta, Gylippus, and by the end of 414 the besiegers themselves were besieged. A relief expedition came out from Athens under Eurymedon and Demosthenes (not the orator), and at the beginning of September 413 we find the combined force making a final effort to break out of containment inside the Great Harbor of Syracuse. The war is almost over. Conquest is fading; the issue now is survival. The selection begins just after Nicias' speech of encouragement to his men and Gylippus' counterspeech to the Syracusans and their allies.]

The Athenians attempt to escape.

69 Gylippus and the Syracusan generals, after these and similar speeches of encouragement to their troops, began to man their ships as soon as they saw the Athenians doing so. But Nicias was completely unnerved by the situation; realizing what kind of danger they faced and how near at hand it was (since the fleet was just on the point of sailing), and feeling, as a man will at times of great stress, that everything they needed to do was still undone and what had been said in his speech had not been said adequately, he went around once more, speaking personally to every ship commander, addressing them ceremoniously by name, father's name, and tribe; [47] exhorting everyone who had any reputation of his own not to betray it, and those who had illustrious ancestors not to let their family glory be tarnished; reminding them of their country, the freest in the world, and how there everybody had full license to live his own life, subject to no man's orders; and so on, repeating all the things that men will say at these crucial moments, not caring whether they may sound trite and old-fashioned, the appeals that are always brought forward in the same way on such occasions, in the name of wives and children and ancestral gods: worn phrases that are revived and shouted once more because they seem helpful in the face of terror and panic.

After these exhortations, which he considered necessary if not adequate to the situation, Nicias set out, leading his land forces down to the shore and deploying them over as wide a front as he could so as to give all possible encouragement to the men on board the ships. Meanwhile Demosthenes, Menander, and Euthydemus, the generals who had taken command of the Athenian fleet, put out from their own camp and sailed straight for the barrier at the mouth of the harbor and the opening that had been left in it, intending to force their way through.

70 But the Syracusans were too quick for them. They and their allies put out with as many ships as the Athenians, and sooner; they not only posted a detachment to guard the entrance but patrolled the entire harbor so as to be in position to attack the Athenians from all sides at once, and meanwhile their land forces were ready to come up in support wherever the enemy might put ashore. The Syracusan naval commanders were Sicanus and Agatharchus, each holding one wing, with Pythen and the Corinthians in the center.

When the rest of the Athenian forces reached the barrier they charged. Their first rush carried the ships that were stationed near it and they started trying to undo the fastenings, but at that moment the Syracusan and allied vessels bore down on them and the fighting became general, not only at the barrier but throughout the harbor. It was a hard-fought battle, the hardest of the entire campaign. For one thing, the rowers on both sides were on the alert and eager to pull the moment the word of command was given; for another, there was great professional jealousy and competitive spirit among the steersmen; and the marines [48] were on the *qui vive*, when ship struck ship, to see to it that the deck fighting did not fall below the standard of the other services; every man was out to distinguish himself in the duty to which he had been assigned.

With so many ships engaged in such a small space (there was a record number of vessels in a very small area, almost two hundred in the two fleets combined), there were few chances to back water or break through the enemy line, and therefore few deliberate rammings, but numerous chance collisions as one ship fell afoul of another while trying either to escape or charge at a third. While another vessel was bearing down, the men on deck facing her would keep her under heavy fire with javelins, arrows, and stones; then, after they collided, the marines on each ship would move in at close quarters and attempt to board the other. The maneuvering space was so narrow that often one ship would have rammed another and been rammed by still another, and sometimes two or even more would be inextricably entangled around a single one; steersmen found they had to defend themselves on one side and carry out offensive maneuvers on the other, not one at a time but in several directions at once; and the continual crash of dozens of ships colliding resulted not only in panic among the crews but inability to hear the boatswains' commands.

For a great shouting of orders and words of encouragement was going on among the boatswains on both sides, spurred by the rivalry of the moment as well as the demands of their work: on the Athenian side the cry was to force the passage out of the harbor and strike out boldly now, if ever, for the chance to return to their country alive; on the side of the Syracusans and their allies, how fine a thing it would be to prevent the enemy's escape and win new glory, each contingent for its own country. In addition the Athenian and Syracusan high command, when they saw a ship backing water where it was not necessary, would call out the commanding officer's name and ask him a question: the Athenians wanted to know whether their men were backing off because they thought the soil of their bitterest enemies was more their own than the sea which they had mastered by so much effort; the Syracusans would ask their men whether they couldn't see for themselves that the Athenians were trying to escape at any cost: were they going to run from men who were on the run themselves?

Suspense of the Athenians on shore

71 The two armies on shore suffered agonies of suspense and conflicting emotions as long as the fighting on the water was evenly balanced, the natives exultant and eager to add to the glory they had already won, the invaders fearful that their final state would be even worse than their present situation. Not only were the Athenians apprehensive of the outcome as never before, now that their fate depended wholly on the fleet, but their view of the battle from the shore necessarily varied with the variation in their position. That is, since the range of vision was very short and the whole army could not look at the same thing simultaneously, those who saw their compatriots winning at one point would be jubilant and fall to invoking the gods not to deny them their chance of returning home; others, with a reverse taking place before their eyes, would give way to loud wails and cries of grief and were more cast down in spirit than those in the midst of the action; still others, watching a part of the battle where the fighting was nip and tuck, and overcome by the long-drawn-out uncertainty of the struggle, would reel back and forth together in an agony of fear, bodies swaying in time with their feelings. These last were among the worst sufferers: they were always just on the verge of escaping or being cut to pieces.

So, as long as the battle was nearly even, every kind of exclamation could be heard at once in the Athenian army—wails of grief and shouts of joy, "They're winning!" "They're losing!"—all the manifold cries that would naturally be wrung from a large body of troops under stress of great danger. The men on board ship went through the same mixed emotions, until finally, after the battle had gone on for a long time, the Syracusans and their allies routed the Athenians and pursued them ashore, pressing them vigorously and cheering each other on with loud shouts of encouragement. At the same time the Athenian naval complement, those who had not been captured on the water, drove for a landing at scattered points along the shore and rushed pell-mell for camp. The feelings of the land forces ceased to be divided; they all suffered alike under the new turn of events and burst with one accord into sighs and groans; some went to lend a hand at the ships, others to help post a guard over the remainder of the wall, still others—and they were the largest number—began to think about themselves and their own salvation. The panic in the army at this point was as great as any in the whole war. They had undergone a defeat like the one they themselves had inflicted on the Spartans at Pylos, when the latter had their ships destroyed and lost the men who had crossed over to the island besides. So in this case the Athenians had no hope of getting away safely by land, unless some miracle should occur.

The Athenians refuse to try another escape by sea.

72 Thus after all the hard fighting and the loss of many ships and men the Syracusans carried the day; then, gathering up their wrecks and their dead, they sailed back to the city and erected a trophy. The Athenians on the other hand were so dazed by the magnitude of the disaster that it did not even occur to them to ask permission to retrieve the dead or the wrecked ships; their sole idea was to retreat as soon as night fell. Demosthenes, however, went to Nicias and suggested another scheme, that they man the remaining ships and force their way out through the gap in the barrier at dawn, if possible; he pointed out that they still had more ships in serviceable condition than the enemy, about sixty as against less than fifty on the other side. Nicias agreed to the plan and they tried to man the ships; but the sailors refused to go aboard, they were so utterly dejected by their defeat and convinced that they could not win again.

The ruse of Hermocrates

73 The Athenians, then, were unanimously agreed on the idea of retreating by land. But Hermocrates the Syracusan,[49] suspecting their intentions and thinking it was dangerous to have so large an army fall back by the land route, settle somewhere else in Sicily, and be in a position to make war on Syracuse again in the future, went and made representations to the authorities that the Athenians should not be allowed to leave during the night. He explained his reasons, and proposed that the whole Syracusan and allied force should go out immediately to block off the roads and seize and hold the key points commanding the narrowest passes before the Athenians could reach them. He found that the authorities thought as he did and agreed that his proposals should be carried out; however, since the men were thoroughly enjoying their first rest after the long fighting and there was also a festival going on (it happened that that was the day for one of the sacrifices to Heracles), they thought it would not be easy to get them to obey: most of them, overjoyed by their victory, had taken to drinking at the festival and were likely to listen to almost anything rather than a command to fall in once more and go out on duty.

When the officials presented all these arguments and insisted the thing could not be done, Hermocrates saw that he was not winning his point and resorted to another stratagem, for he was afraid the Athenians would get away in the night and negotiate the most difficult key points without hindrance. He sent some of his personal companions to the Athenian camp with a cavalry escort, just as it was getting dark. They rode up close enough so that a man's voice could be heard and asked for certain Athenians by name, pretending they were good friends of theirs (and in fact Nicias did have informants inside the city); then they told them to warn Nicias not to move his troops during the night, because the Syracusans were guarding the roads, but to make full preparations and retire during the daytime, when he would be undisturbed. With this they rode away; the men they had spoken to passed the message on to the Athenian generals, and they held up the retreat overnight because of the warning, not suspecting that it was a trick.

The Syracusans block the roads.

74 Then, since they had not started out immediately after all, they decided to wait over the next day as well, so as to give the men all the opportunity they could to pack up the most useful supplies; they intended to leave behind all the rest of the stores they had on hand and take along on the march only those that were needed for personal subsistence. Meanwhile the Syracusan land forces under Gylippus marched out ahead of them and barricaded the roads throughout the countryside wherever the Athenians were likely to pass; they also set guards at the stream and river crossings and posted themselves at chosen spots where they could receive the enemy and prevent their passage. The fleet sailed over also and began hauling the Athenian ships down off the beach; the Athenians had managed to burn a few according to plan, but they gathered up the rest at their leisure, without interference, from the various places where they had run aground, took them in tow, and pulled them to Syracuse.

75 Not until the third day after the battle, when Nicias and Demosthenes considered that their preparations were satisfactory, did the withdrawal of the army actually begin. It was a fearful experience in more ways than one: not only were they in retreat, with all their ships lost and the prospect of real danger ahead, instead of high hopes for themselves and their country, but even in the process of departing from camp every man was confronted by things that were painful either to behold or to think about. The bodies of their dead were still unburied, and whenever a man saw one of his own comrades lying there he was overcome with grief and fear together. But the living—the wounded and sick who were being left behind—were far more pitiable objects to the living than the dead, more utterly wretched than those who had perished. They drove them frantic with the entreaties and lamentations they set up, begging to be taken along and crying out at every friend or relative they saw anywhere along the line of march, hanging on their former tent mates as they passed by, following after them as far as they could go and at last falling behind, as their physical powers failed, with a few last pathetic groans and appeals to the mercy of the gods.

With all this the whole army was reduced to tears and so distracted that they could hardly bring themselves to leave, even though the country round them was hostile and their recent disasters as well as their apprehensions of what might happen to them in the uncertain future were too overwhelming for tears. At the same time there was a general wave of dejection and self-reproach. And in fact they looked like nothing so much as the population of a city in panic flight after losing a siege—and a large city at that, for, counting all the hangers-on, there were not less than forty thousand people in the line of march. All the others among them were dragging everything usable they could carry, and the military personnel, infantry and cavalry alike, contrary to usual practice, had their own provisions tucked in with their weapons, either for lack of servants or lack of confidence in them (the servants had started deserting long since, most of them immediately after the battle). Even so, what they carried was insufficient; for there was no more grain left in the camp. But the rest of their sufferings, this new equality in misfortune, though it was somewhat lighter for being shared with so many others, seemed especially hard to bear in their present situation, when they remembered how gloriously and boastfully they had begun and saw to what a miserable end they had now come. This was in fact the greatest reverse ever suffered by a Greek army: to have come expecting to enslave others and now to depart dreading that the same thing might happen to themselves; to set out for home again uttering imprecations—how different from the prayers and paeans with which they had sailed from home; and to be travelling by land instead of by sea, relying on the infantry instead of the fleet. And yet in spite of everything, considering the magnitude of the danger that still hung over them, all this seemed endurable.

Nicias encourages his men.

76 Nicias, seeing the army so dispirited and its morale so radically changed, went up and down the ranks trying to encourage them and cheer them up as best he could under the circumstances, raising his voice more and more in his zeal as he moved from one group to another and feeling that it might help them somehow if he shouted as loud as possible:

77 "Athenians and allies, even in this situation you must keep up your hopes—others in the past have escaped from even worse dangers than this—and not blame yourselves too much for your reverses or the undeserved misery you are suffering now. I certainly am no stronger than any of you, in fact you can see for yourselves how I am affected by my illness; [50] and though I was once considered as happy and prosperous as any man, in private life and public life too, now I am at the mercy of the same danger as the poorest of you. And yet throughout my life I have paid all due respect to the gods and treated men fairly, so that no one could hold any grudge against me.

Because of that I am still confident for the future, in spite of everything, and our misfortunes do not frighten me as they might. Perhaps they may even begin to let up; the enemy is satisfied with his present success, and if by chance one of the gods was offended at our undertaking we have amply atoned for it by now. Others before us have gone on foreign expeditions; their actions were only human and in return their sufferings were bearable. So in our case it is only reasonable to expect milder treatment from the gods in the future: as we are now we have more claim on their pity than their jealousy.

"Furthermore, look at yourselves, think what good soldiers you are and how many there are of you still in fighting order, and do not be too despondent. Count up and you will find that you make a city all by yourselves, wherever you choose to settle; no other city in Sicily could very well withstand an attack from you or drive you out again once you were established anywhere. It is your business to see to it that security and order are maintained on the march; and you can do it if every man tells himself that whatever spot he is forced to fight in will become his home and his fortress—if he wins. We will have to move fast on the road, both at night and in the daytime, because we are very short of provisions, and we cannot feel assured of being in safe country until we reach some friendly village in the territory of the Sicels; they are still loyal to us out of fear of the Syracusans. Messengers have been sent on ahead to them and they have been told to meet us and bring more provisions.

"To sum it up, soldiers, make up your minds now that there is nothing for it but to conduct yourselves like brave men. There is no strong point near by where you can find salvation if you turn cowards; whereas if you escape the enemy now, you in the allied forces will live to see what I know you are longing to see again, and the Athenians will be saved to help restore the mighty power of our city, though it has fallen so low. For a city is its men, not walls and ships without men."

Slow progress of the retreat

78 So Nicias went up and down the ranks plying his men with exhortations like these, and also reforming and tightening up the formation where he saw men straggling or dropping out of line; and Demosthenes did the same in his command, with the same kind of speeches or others like them. The army was marching in hollow rectangle formation, with the baggage-carriers and most of the main mass surrounded by the infantry. When they reached the crossing of the Anapus river they found some Syracusan and allied cavalry drawn up to meet them on the bank; they routed these units after a skirmish, gained possession of the bridgehead, and began to move forward again. But the Syracusan cavalry continued to ride on their flanks and the light-armed troops kept them under javelin fire.

On this first day the Athenians marched approximately five miles and bivouacked for the night near a low hill. The next day they set out early in the morning and after marching about two and a half miles came down into a level space where they pitched camp, intending to get something to eat from the houses (for it was an inhabited place) and some water to carry with them when they moved on, water being scarce for a number of miles ahead in the direction they were travelling.[51] But while they were halted the Syracusans went on and began walling off the pass at a point on the road ahead of them; it was at a steep hill with precipitous ravines on both sides, called the Acraean ridge.

The next day the Athenians resumed the march, with the Syracusan and allied cavalry and javelin-throwers hanging on their flanks in heavy force, impeding their advance and maintaining a steady javelin fire. The Athenians kept up the running fight for a long time, then gave way and returned to the camp they had just left. This time the shortage of supplies was more acute, since they could not leave camp to forage because of the cavalry.

Blocked, the Athenians try a new route.

79 They broke camp early and set out again, and forced their way as far as the wall that had been built from the hill across the pass. Here they found the enemy infantry drawn up in front of them behind the wall, in very deep formation because of the narrowness of the pass.[52] The Athenians charged and tried to storm the wall, but coming under heavy fire from the hill, whose steep slope brought them within easier range of the men farther up, and not being able to force the passage, they fell back again to rest. It so happened that just then a thunderstorm and some rain came up—a common occurrence at that time of year, in late autumn, but the Athenians were more dejected than ever and felt that all this too was meant for their destruction. While they were resting, the Syracusans under Gylippus sent back a detachment to build another wall behind them, on the road along which they had just come up; but this time the Athenians sent some of their own men to head them off and managed to prevent it. They then withdrew their whole force in the general direction of the plain and bivouacked for the night.

The next day they advanced again. The Syracusans now attacked them from all sides at once and wounded a large number of men. Every time the Athenians rushed them they would fall back, only to press in again the moment they gave ground; and especially they kept falling on the rear guard, hoping that perhaps by routing them a few at a time they might throw the whole army into a panic. The Athenians maintained their defense against these tactics for a long time, then finally retreated about three-quarters of a mile into the plain; whereupon the Syracusans left them and returned to their own camp.

80 By now the army was suffering badly from lack of provisions, and there were a great many men wounded from the enemy's constant cavalry attacks. During the night, therefore, Nicias and Demosthenes decided to light as many watch-fires as possible and then withdraw the army, not along the road they had planned to follow, where the Syracusans were watching for them, but in the opposite direction, towards the sea. The general direction of this new route was not towards Catane but along the other coast of Sicily, towards Camarina and Gela and the other Greek and foreign cities on that side of the island.[53] So they lit a great many fires and set out during the night.

Panic and surrender of Demosthenes' division

Then a thing happened that is common, for that matter, in all armies, and particularly in very large ones; they are all subject to sudden outbreaks of fear. So the Athenians, especially as they were travelling by night in enemy territory, and with the enemy himself not far away, fell into panic and confusion. Nicias' column, which was leading, stayed together and got a long way ahead, but Demosthenes' division—a good half and more of the whole army—began to get dispersed and out of formation. They reached the sea at dawn, however, struck into the so-called Helorine road, and continued the march, intending when they reached the Cacyparis river to cross it and follow it upstream into the interior; they were hoping that the Sicels whom they had sent for would meet them here. But when they reached the river, again they found a Syracusan patrol building a wall and palisade at the crossing. They forced their way through, crossed the river, and on the recommendation of their guides went on towards another river, the Erineus.

81 Meanwhile, when dawn came and the Syracusans and their allies realized that the Athenians were gone, the majority accused Gylippus of deliberately letting them get away. However, they set out in hot pursuit along the road which the enemy had clearly taken and caught up with them about noon. When they made contact with the rearmost troops, Demosthenes' men, who were still straggling and in ragged order from the confusion of the night before, they immediately fell upon them and began fighting; the latter, separated as they were from the rest of the army, were easily surrounded by the Syracusan cavalry and driven together into a compact mass. Nicias' column was a full six miles or more ahead of them: he was moving faster, thinking that at this point their salvation did not lie in deliberately waiting for the enemy and courting a battle but in withdrawing as fast as they could, fighting only if and when they were forced to.

Demosthenes' circumstances were different, and so were his methods. On the whole he was much more steadily exposed to trouble by being second in the line of march and so the first target for enemy attacks; and on this occasion, when the Syracusans appeared in pursuit, he spent more time drawing up a battle line than moving forward, until finally, thanks to his delay, he was encircled and both he and the men under his command were thrown into wild confusion. Crowded together in a small space surrounded by a wall, with a road on each side and containing a number of olive trees, they were under fire from all directions. The Syracusans were very sensible in employing attacks of this kind instead of fighting at close quarters:[54] at this stage it would have been more in the Athenians' interest than their own if they had taken serious risks against a body of desperate men, and at the same time victory was so clearly in sight that they felt a certain reluctance to throw away their lives prematurely. They were confident that they could wear down and capture the Athenians by the tactics they were using.

82 So, after keeping the Athenians and their allies under fire from all sides the rest of the day, and seeing them by now in desperate straits with wounds and misery of all kinds, the Syracusan and allied forces under Gylippus issued a proclamation. It provided first that all islanders [55] who would come over to them would be guaranteed their freedom; and some of the island contingents went over, but not many. Later a general agreement was reached with the rest of Demosthenes' command, specifying that they were to surrender their arms and that no one was to be put to death by execution, imprisonment, or withholding of minimum subsistence. On these terms the whole body of six thousand men surrendered. They also gave up all the money they had; it was thrown into upturned shields and filled four of them. These men were immediately sent back to Syracuse under escort; and on the same day Nicias and his column arrived at the river Erineus, crossed it, and encamped on a piece of high ground.

Nicias is trapped; his surrender

83 The Syracusans overtook Nicias the next day, told him that Demosthenes and his command had surrendered, and urged him to do likewise. But Nicias was skeptical and sent back a cavalryman under truce to investigate. When the man returned and confirmed the report of the surrender, Nicias notified Gylippus and the Syracusans by herald that he was ready to offer in the name of Athens to repay all costs that Syracuse had contracted on account of the war, on condition that he and his troops be released; pending payment of the money he would post Athenian citizens as bond, one man per talent.[56] But Gylippus and the Syracusans would not accept the terms; they closed in on the column, surrounded it on all sides, and kept it under fire throughout the day. Nicias' men also were in bad condition from lack of food and supplies in general; but still they waited till the quiet part of the night and started to move on. They had just taken up their arms when the Syracusans heard them and sounded the battle warning. Seeing that they were detected the Athenians laid down their arms again, except one group of about three hundred men who fought their way through the patrols and went off in the darkness any way they could.

84 In the morning Nicias led the army on again; and the Syracusans and their allies pressed on their flanks as they had before, showering them from all sides with missiles and javelin fire. The Athenians meanwhile pushed on towards the Assinarus river. They were suffering under the constant attack of large cavalry and other forces coming at them from all directions and thought things might be a little easier if they could cross the river; at the same time they were in a bad way from exhaustion and extreme thirst. When they reached the river bank they abandoned all formation and plunged in, every man trying to be the first across; and this if nothing else, combined with the constant pressure from the enemy, made the crossing difficult.

They were so squeezed together that they could not help falling over and treading on each other; some were killed outright in the press of spears and miscellaneous baggage, others got entangled and were swept downstream. The Syracusans stood on the far bank, which was a steep one, and fired from above on the confused mass of Athenians in the shallow water, most of whom were drinking greedily, while the Peloponnesians came straight down into the river and butchered them wholesale. The water was befouled in no time, but they kept on drinking it just as it was, muddy and full of blood; in fact most of them were ready to fight for it.

85 Finally, with corpses piled high on top of each other in the river and the army destroyed, part of it lost in the carnage at the river itself and what little had got across cut down by the cavalry, Nicias surrendered personally to Gylippus because he trusted him more than the Syracusans; he told Gylippus that he and the Spartans could do whatever they pleased with himself, but he begged them to stop slaughtering the rest of the men. Gylippus then issued an order to take prisoners henceforth; and the rest, all who had not been spirited away by the Syracusans [57] (and that happened to many), were gathered up alive.

Treatment of Nicias and the other prisoners

The number of men who were thus collected as state prisoners was not very large, while those surreptitiously carried off were very numerous—later all Sicily was filled with them—because they were not covered by explicit terms of surrender like Demosthenes' men. Also, there were a considerable number killed: the slaughter at the river was enormous, as high as in any action of the war; and a good many had been killed in the constant cavalry attacks during the retreat. Still, there were also many who escaped. Some did so immediately, others ran away later after serving as slaves; and the escapees could always find refuge at Catane.

86 After the battle the Syracusan and allied forces reassembled, gathered up the booty and as many of the prisoners as they could, and returned to Syracuse. All the Athenian and allied personnel they had captured were thrown into the stone quarries, that being the safest place of confinement they could think of; but Nicias and Demosthenes were slaughtered outright, over the protests of Gylippus who thought it would be a great personal triumph, as a climax to his other achievements, if he took the generals who had been his rivals back to Sparta with him. It so happened that Demosthenes was the Athenian the Spartans hated most, on account of the Pylos-Sphacteria episode, while they were most friendly toward Nicias for the same reason; for it was he who had exerted himself, at the time when he persuaded Athens to make peace, to arrange for the release of the Spartans who had been captured on the island. Hence they had very friendly feelings towards him, and that was one of the chief reasons why he had placed himself in Gylippus' hands when he surrendered.

But some of the Syracusans, it was said, had previously been in communication with Nicias and hence were afraid that he might be put to torture because of it and make trouble for them in the midst of their success; and others, including the Corinthians particularly, were afraid he might escape by bribing certain people—for he was a rich man—and later cause them new difficulties again; so they talked their allies into executing him. Such was the cause of Nicias' death, or something very much like it; and yet of all the Greeks of my time he least deserved to come to such a miserable end, after a lifetime spent entirely in honorable, upright conduct.

87 The men in the quarries got harsh treatment during the early part of their confinement. Crowded as they were, large numbers of them, into a small pit open to the sky, they suffered at the beginning from the sun and the choking heat; then came nights that were quite the other way, with the chill of late fall, and the changes in temperature lowered their resistance to sickness still further; they had to do everything they did on one spot, and the bodies piled up alongside them, heaped on top of one another, as men died of their wounds and the change of seasons and the like, so that the stenches were unendurable; they were constantly plagued by hunger and thirst (for eight months the Syracusans gave them only one cup of water and two cups of food apiece per day); and of all the other miseries that men trapped in such a place would naturally experience, not one was lacking. After some seventy days of this kind of existence together, all the prisoners except the Athenians and some Sicilians and Italians who had taken part in the expedition were sold as slaves. The total number of men captured,[58] though hard to estimate accurately, was at least seven thousand.

As it turned out, this was the greatest and most decisive action of the war—and for that matter, I think, of recorded Greek history—the most brilliant for the conquerors and the most disastrous for those who were destroyed in it. They were utterly beaten at every point and suffered severely from every defeat they underwent, until finally, in utter ruin and destruction, as the old phrase goes, they lost their army, their ships, and everything they had, and few out of the many who set forth ever came home again.

So much, then, for the events that took place in Sicily.

[VII, 69–87]

NOTES TO SELECTIONS FROM THUCYDIDES

1. Thucydides obviously does not mean that he began writing at the outbreak of the war, but that he began observing and, probably, taking notes that early.

2. Besides the vine, Thucydides is thinking primarily of the olive tree as a sign of intensive, organized cultivation. To the Greek the olive was not and is not a mere condiment but a basic food and a prime source of fats for cooking and hygiene (in lieu of soap). The standard Greek meal has always been bread flavored with olives, onions, or cheese and washed down with wine. But to an Athenian the olive had a special significance: the olive orchards, first promoted on a large scale by Solon, were the glory of Attica and the cornerstone of her economy. They were ruined by the war. Sophocles recalls them with poignant pride and love in his last play, the *Oedipus at Colonus* (lines 694–706), written in 406.

3. Phthiotis, or Phthia, "deep-soiled Phthia," the home of Achilles, the rich district on the west shore of the gulf of Pagasae, in southern Thessaly. It was from this region also that the ship Argo sailed in search of the Golden Fleece.

4. "Barbarian" (*bárbaros*) was simply the Greek term for anybody who did not speak Greek—for example, us. It did not necessarily connote a sneer or imply a judgment on the value of non-Greek cultures. Herodotus often cites "barbarian" customs in the spirit of Sterne's "They order these things better in France." Here the meaning is perfectly objective.

5. The Carians were an Anatolian people of doubtful racial affiliations, settled in southwestern Asia Minor and many of the Aegaean islands long before the coming of the Greeks, as modern archaeological research has shown. Thucydides' statement also is based on excavation, the one performed at Delos.

6. Piracy was endemic along the southwestern coast of Asia Minor throughout antiquity and the Middle Ages. It was there that Julius Caesar was captured by pirates and later turned the tables on them (Plutarch, *Julius Caesar*, ch. 1–2). The Knights of St. John on the island of Rhodes were an outpost to guard the Crusaders' route against Anatolian pirates and other foes.

7. Piracy and commerce are first cousins in the early stages of trade by sea; compare the activities of the English freebooters in the fight against Spain for the New World. In the *Odyssey* (III, 72), Nestor hospitably entertains Telemachus and then, after dinner, asks him in the most friendly tone whether he and his company are traders or pirates. When Odysseus wants a plausible yarn to take in the suitors he spins one about how he had been a pirate, made a raid on Egypt, etc. (XVII, 415–444).

8. Not only down to Thucydides' own day, but down to ours. The rugged terrain and poverty of Greece, and the Greek passion for freedom and independence, have driven men to the mountains for 3,000 years and made life hard for every government—Roman, Turkish, or Greek. The Greek brigand is a practical character but also has his idealistic or romantic side, as Byron was aware. The *klefti* (modern Greek for "brigand," from ancient Greek *kleptes*, "robber") is the standard hero of modern Greek song and legend; some of them played a heroic role in the Greek War of Independence (1821–27); and many of the "Communist" guerrillas in the Greek mountains during the last few years were really *klefti's* at heart, though led by real Communists.

9. Ozolian Locris, a rocky, mountainous district east of Mt. Parnassus, lying across the main road from Athens north. Thermopylae is its northern gate. Guerrillas operating from here imperilled German communications during the recent war. Aetolia and Acarnania are west of Parnassus and north of the Corinthian Gulf. These areas are still among the wildest in Greece.

10. These two customs may not sound very luxurious to a modern American, whose everyday life would have seemed fantastically luxurious to Thucydides—and still does to his countrymen. On the basic discomforts of Athenian life see Alfred Zimmern, *The Greek Commonwealth* (4th ed., Oxford, 1924), pp. 214–15. There was a certain tendency towards luxury, or sensuousness, among the Athenian aristocracy in the sixth century (it is reflected in late Archaic art), and the locust-shaped brooches were a symbol of it. But the Persian wars put an end to that; the Parthenon shows us the utmost simplicity in Athenian garb, and the "Old Oligarch," an embittered aristocrat writing about 425 or before, says that at Athens you could not tell a citizen from a slave by his dress.

11. Thucydides is wrong in thinking that the Phoenicians had *settlements* of any consequence in the Aegaean. But they traded throughout the area and left their mark on it. It was from them that the Greeks learned to write.

12. *Iliad*, II, 576–77, 612, in the "Catalogue of Ships." Modern scholars, like Thucydides, use the Catalogue for evidence on the geography and ethnology of early Greece.

13. The whole trouble in the *Iliad*, over the girls Chryseis and Briseis, arises out of raids around Troy; cf. also VI, 415; XI, 625. Farming is not mentioned in our *Iliad;* it may have been in the lost *Cypria*, the poem which preceded the *Iliad* in the epic "cycle." In Thucydides' time the *Cypria* was ascribed to Homer.

14. This may seem to contradict what Thucydides said at the beginning of chapter 10. But the contrast is between two kinds of historical evidence, not merely two estimates of the size of the expedition. External evidence, the mere appearance of a place, is not enough to controvert the standing tradition; but internal evidence,

arrived at by analysis of the basic causes of power—in this case man power—is enough to do so. Homer himself yields up the evidence which, when examined, proves that he has given an exaggerated total impression.

15. A town in southern Thessaly. See *Iliad,* II, 507.

16. "Tyranny" in Greek parlance meant simply rule by a single man who owed his position to his own efforts, not to inheritance, family position, wealth, or tradition though he might possess any one or more of these qualifications. A tyrant was not necessarily "tyrannical" in our sense, but enough of them were so that the word began to take on the meaning of "irresponsible despot" even in the fifth century. Cf. the famous Dantesque portrait in Plato's *Republic,* Books VIII–IX. But most of the tyrants came to power as champions of the people, or at least the new commercial class, against the old landed aristocracy, and that was their real offense in the eyes of conservatives.

17. Trireme, a boat propelled by three banks of oars or a similar arrangement. The invention was important for two reasons, one technical and one political: (1) the great increase in speed, power, and maneuverability, and (2) the fact that at Athens the new demand for rowers was filled by the poor citizens, not slaves, so that the proletariat had a direct economic interest in the expansion of Athenian sea power and empire. Hence also the Athenian navy, unlike modern navies, was an intensely democratic service and the backbone of the democratic party. See the "Old Oligarch," ch. 2.

18. A small island adjacent to Delos.

19. Penteconter, "fifty-oared ship," a longboat with some decking fore and aft; essentially a larger version of our traditional Coast Guard rescue craft.

20. Thucydides was the first historian to grasp the importance of sea power, and he had no successors to speak of till Mahan. Note that he has in mind its economic as well as its military significance.

21. Chalcis and Eretria, rival towns on the south shore of Euboea, the long island just north of Attica. They had been leading commercial cities in the seventh century.

22. The Halys flows in a great circle clockwise from Armenia, southwest, then west, then north into the Black Sea. It roughly divides Asia Minor into eastern and western halves; Thucydides means the western half.

23. Hippias, son of Pisistratus, was driven out of Athens by the Spartans in 510 B.C. He came back with the Persians in 490, hoping to climb back into power on their shoulders; but Marathon ended the threat forever.

24. The nucleus of the Spartan hegemony was the wartime coalition of mainland states, most of whom had been dependent on Sparta for some time; the nucleus of the Athenian empire (beginning as the "Delian League"), the Ionian cities of Asia Minor and the islands which had been subject to Persia since the time of Cyrus. The revolt of these states (499–494) led to the punitive invasion of Greece proper in 490.

25. The conversion of the original assessments in kind into cash tribute, in return for which Athens supplied the requisite ships, crews, and stores, gave her a monopoly of military, especially naval, experience and her businessmen and working class a monopoly of the profits (see above, n. 17).

26. Thucydides is not merely correcting Athenian tradition here, he is debunking it. The popular story made Harmodius and Aristogiton into real tyrannicides, i.e., enders of the tyranny, thus conveniently overlooking several facts: that their motive was purely personal, that they did not kill the real ruler (Hippias), that the end of his tyranny only came four years later (510), and that it was finally brought about by the Spartans. Thucydides reminds his countrymen of these unknown or unwelcome facts at some length in Book VI, chs. 53–59.

27. The "Pitanate" battalion is mentioned by Herodotus (IX, 53). The polemical reference to him is pretty clear, but Thucydides may have others in mind also.

28. Here Thucydides is not referring merely to Herodotus, but in general to the "logographers" and genealogists who had dominated the field of general Greek history before himself. Herodotus does not systematically cover the early history of Greece proper.

29. The "archaeology," as Thucydides' survey of previous history is traditionally called, was written primarily to prove this point. In doing so Thucydides is setting his face against the major tendency of Greek thought, which was to see the past as glorious and the present as degenerate. Thucydides had learned his belief in progress from the Sophists. Compare his attitude with that in Aeschylus, *Prometheus Bound,* 436–471, and Sophocles, *Antigone,* 332–375.

30. The usual translation, "a possession forever," rouses vague suggestions of Keats's "a joy forever," or of a museum piece like the Mona Lisa: a treasured object to be placed on a shelf and admired for all time. Thucydides' meaning is quite different. He wants his work to be permanently available for use; he hopes, as we say, that it will be kept in print. In this paragraph again, in the references to picturesque stories and display pieces, it is customary to see a dig at Herodotus. It is true that the latter loved a good story and probably published his work through public recitation. But Thucydides' point is general rather than specific, and anyway Herodotus had probably been dead a quarter of a century when these lines were written.

31. The Athenian people were officially divided into ten "tribes," and civic activities in peace and war were carried on as a competition among the tribes. Our analogy is the States; but the tribes were not geographical divisions.

32. The mound still stands on the plain at Marathon.

33. The idea that what we say about the heroic dead is of little moment compared with what they did is familiar to us from the Gettysburg Address. The parallels

between the two speeches have often been pointed out, though there is no evidence that Lincoln knew Thucydides. For another striking parallel between the two men see John H. Finley, Jr., *Thucydides* (Cambridge, Mass., 1942), p. 182 n.

34. Sparta was consistently suspicious of foreigners and periodically deported them, as a matter of general policy. Cf. the behavior of the Russians toward newspaper men and others in our time.

35. Pericles seems (if the Greek text is correct) to be alluding quietly to a basic fact: even in the most extreme democracy—and fifth-century Athens was the most extreme democracy that has ever existed in a major state for more than a few months—not all the citizens take an active part in politics. He claims here that even the inactive ones manage to think, and think sensibly, about public affairs, though these are managed by others. Cf. the next to the last sentence in the speech. The regular Athenian definition of a citizen was "one who rules (i.e., holds office) and is ruled in turn."

36. The person who takes no interest at all is contrasted with both the classes just mentioned. The word translated "quiet" was the term the aristocrats liked to apply to themselves in their dignified aloofness from politics and the lower forms of money-making. They called the populace "busy, full of bustle, busybodyish." Pericles is quietly challenging their pride in being quiet.

37. The word *paídeusis* ("model" in this translation) means literally "education" and is usually so translated. But the connotations are wrong in English. Education to us is primarily an intellectual affair, whereas to a fifth-century Athenian the education of a child (beyond the three R's) was above all a direct training of his character by giving him models to admire and follow. Pericles does not mean that Athens is a "liberal education," as we say, to other Greeks—that they can increase their knowledge or broaden their minds by studying her—but that they can enrich their lives directly by imitating her.

38. The "memorials" are Athenian colonies, planted in some places as a friendly gesture, in others as a hostile base or a punishment.

39. Unfortunately for Thucydides' very practical purpose, medical men are still not agreed on the identification of the disease. Its symptoms have affinities with both pneumonic (pulmonary) and bubonic plague. In any case Thucydides' clinical description is based on the best medical practice of his time; for examples see the selections from the *Epidemics* of Hippocrates in the section, "Greek Scientists," below. There is a notable adaptation, almost a translation, of the account of the plague in Lucretius, VI, 1138–1268.

40. The Peloponnesian raids bore hard on the farmers, since Pericles' policy was to concentrate on the war at sea and not waste men guarding the borders. For the mixed feelings of the country folk see Aristophanes' *Acharnians*, produced in 425. The bulk of the refugees pitched camp in the open space between the Long Walls connecting Athens and Piraeus, and it was up this crowded human ladder that the plague passed, growing in virulence as it went (ch. 48 above).

41. The Delphic Oracle, being by nature a conservative institution and having more traditional ties with the Dorian than the Ionian part of the Greek world, sided quite openly with the Spartans. In the *Ion*, written late in the war (probably around 410), Euripides roundly impugns the good faith of the Apollo of Delphi.

42. The Messenians, from southwest Peloponnese, had long been under Sparta's heel—playing Ireland to Sparta's England—and many of them served in the Athenian armed forces. This detachment had been left as reinforcements for the Corcyraean democrats by Nicostratus, the Athenian admiral who had negotiated the truce.

43. On the west side of the island, away from the center of oligarchic strength.

44. A sarcastic dig at the Athenians. Brasidas had run wild in Macedonia and Thrace for two years (424–422) and Athens had done very little to stop him. (It was for his failure in this campaign that Thucydides was exiled: see the translator's introduction.) The Melians are hinting that the Spartans might carry on from where Brasidas left off, sweeping along the Thracian coast to the Hellespont (Dardanelles) and the Propontis (Sea of Marmora), the economic heart of the Athenian Empire.

45. "Shame" or "sense of honor," like "quietness" (see n. 36 above), was an aristocratic catch phrase, suggesting a high-born distaste for the pushing, enterprising, commercial spirit of the popular party. The roots of the concept go back to Homer, and it is strong in Pindar. In the fifth century it is comparable to that great English tradition, "it simply isn't done." For a study in the workings of this code, by a man who inwardly sympathized with it, see Sophocles' portrait of the young Neoptolemus in the *Philoctetes*, where Odysseus is a caricature of the imperialist politician.

46. The Athenian "allies" (whom Pericles frankly calls "subjects" in the Funeral Oration, ch. 41) were autonomous in internal matters, but besides paying tribute were practically required to have democratic governments (that is, by the democratic party), were part of the Athenian customs system, and had to try their commercial cases at Athens.

47. In everyday life an Athenian was identified simply by his name and his father's name, e.g., Socrates son of Sophroniscus. But in official documents and ceremonial address the name of his deme (ward or voting district) or his tribe was added.

48. Athens had developed specifically naval tactics—squadron coördination, encirclement, breakthrough—to a high level, thanks to her semi-professional navy; but naval armament as such hardly existed and the basic aim was still either to disable the enemy by ramming

him or driving him aground, or to board him. Hence the main sphere of action of the Athenian marines was boarding at sea, not landing operations. See J. F. Charles, "The Marines of Athens," *Classical Journal,* XLIV (1948–49), 181–88.

49. Hermocrates was the ablest and most important man in Syracuse, chief general before the arrival of Gylippus, and the author of a kind of Monroe Doctrine, "Sicily for the Sicilians"—that is, for the Greeks in Sicily—which was aimed chiefly at Athens. The democrats in Syracuse exiled him shortly after the end of the campaign.

50. Nicias had been suffering from "kidney disease," probably a form of malaria or induced by it, for over a year and had long since requested to be relieved of his command.

51. They were moving west, towards the interior of the island, hoping to get into Sicel territory and then turn north towards Catane (modern Catania), their first landing point and original base.

52. The terrain is roughly similar to that of the last scenes in Hemingway's *For Whom the Bell Tolls:* a road running up a narrow, deep ravine, closely overhung by steep slopes. The Syracusan wall is at the narrowest point, where the crest of the ridge runs down to the road, with light-armed troops deployed on the slope overhanging the road below the crest.

53. The new direction of march is south along the coast road south of Syracuse. The road runs to the southeastern tip of Sicily and turns west towards Gela, etc. (the south shore where our landings were made in the recent war) ; but we learn in the next paragraph that the Athenians' intention is to leave it and turn inland at the next main river. To reach the road at all they have to double back eastward to the coast, and it is during this first march that the panic takes place.

54. Nowhere is Thucydides' objectivity more spectacular than in this calm commendation of the enemy's tactics. One has to remind oneself that the poor devils trapped in the olive grove were his own countrymen.

55. I.e., from the Aegean islands. An obvious attempt to drive a wedge between the Athenians and their allies.

56. The talent was worth about $1,100 in gold dollars, vastly more in modern purchasing power.

57. That is, smuggled away by individual Syracusans to be sold as slaves, for private profit.

58. Thucydides means the total of those who had been thrown in the quarries. The Athenians were left there through the winter, and the survivors were sold or put at hard labor.

THE ATTIC ORATORS

Translated by H. Lamar Crosby

INTRODUCTION

THE GREEKS appear to have had an innate love of the spoken word. Homer's poems abound in speeches. We learn that Phoenix was commissioned to teach Achilles to be "both a speaker of words and a doer of deeds." Nestor is proclaimed as the "clear-voiced speaker from Pylos, from whose tongue there flowed speech sweeter than honey." The Trojan Antenor in his tribute to the eloquence of Odysseus testifies to the power wielded at that early date by a forceful speaker, and also to the existence of standards of platform behavior to which a public speaker was expected to conform.

The Greek city-state of post-Homeric days provided conditions peculiarly favorable to the development of the art of oratory, and none more favorable than democratic Athens. Throughout most of the fifth and fourth centuries B.C., Athens played either a dominant or at least a leading role in Greek affairs. Questions of war and peace, as well as domestic matters of absorbing interest, were debated in frequent sessions of the popular assembly, which all citizens were free to attend. Pericles in the Funeral Oration (II, 40) paints an interesting picture of conditions in his day: "An Athenian citizen does not neglect the state because he takes care of his own household; and even those of us who are engaged in business have a very fair idea of politics. We alone regard a man who takes no interest in public affairs, not as a harmless, but as a useless character; and if few of us are originators, we are all sound judges of a policy. The great impediment to action is, in our opinion, not discussion, but the want of that knowledge which is gained by discussion preparatory to action."

Such seasoned critics as his hearers, with a personal stake in the outcome of the debate, challenged the speaker to put forth his best efforts. Pericles rose to the occasion and for a whole generation controlled and guided Athenian policy, not alone by his admitted wisdom, but largely by his gift of persuasive eloquence. The comic poet Eupolis has left us a glowing tribute to the power of oratory he wielded: "He was the ablest orator of them all. Whenever he mounted the platform, like your good runners, though starting with a ten-foot handicap, he overtook and passed the field in eloquence. A rapid speaker you call him, but besides his speed, persuasion sat upon his lips. Such was the charm he exercised, and he alone among the orators left his sting in those who heard him." Cleon, who succeeded Pericles as leader of the Athenian democracy, though far different in statesmanship and character, owed no small part of his authority as a politician to his own brand of oratory. If we may place any confidence in the words of Aristophanes, it was a form of oratory that relied heavily on bluster and abuse. We have no genuine specimens of the eloquence of either Pericles or Cleon, but Thucydides incorporated in his history speeches which he undoubtedly considered characteristic of each. Indeed, he made plentiful use of speeches for the purpose of delineating the personal qualities of the chief figures in his history, of indicating the policies they each espoused, and of bringing into sharp relief the clashing interests of the rival states and parties. Later historians, both Greek and Roman, employed the same device.

But oratory served other purposes besides those of statecraft. It is safe to say that nowhere in the ancient world was there a greater volume of litigation than at Athens. Both the Council of the Five Hundred and the Assembly had frequent occasion to sit in judgment on cases involving offenses against the state. The courts themselves at times were composed of so vast a number of jurors that the speaker who addresses them uses terms appropriate to an assembly of the citizens. Under such conditions it is understandable that an appeal to emotions and prejudices would be likely to carry more weight than a straightforward presentation of the claims of justice. Athens had no District Attorney versed in the law, and the presiding officer at a trial was just an average citizen with no authority to rule on points of law, his function being rather that of attempting to preserve order in the court.

Now, custom prescribed that both parties to a suit must make their pleas in person. Since not all Athenians were equally well endowed with legal knowledge and rhetorical skill, it became the practice to resort to those who had achieved some reputation along those lines and thus to secure from them speeches to be memorized and delivered at the trial. The composing of such speeches sometimes served as a stepping stone to a career in politics, as was notably the case with Demosthenes; in other instances a man devoted his whole life to that activity, as was true of Lysias and Isaeus. Speeches concerned with questions of assault and battery and the like would not attain the high level of orations involving matters of statesmanship, but they do contain a wealth of information on many aspects of Athenian life and court procedure, and they reveal the extent to which oratory served a very useful, if lowly, purpose.

The great days of Athens came to a close when Macedon became the overlord of Greece. The stirring events, tense rivalries, and perils that had marked the preceding two centuries and had been the occasion for the best of Attic eloquence became a memory. Teachers of rhetoric maintained their schools at Athens, Rhodes, and elsewhere and competed with the philosophers for students. They collected and dissected the writings of the famous orators of the past and used them as models in the classroom. Cicero came under their influence at both Athens and Rhodes. Seven centuries after Alexander's death Libanius was imparting to St. John Chrysostom the fire and the vituperative power of Demosthenes. But when in the second century B.C. the canon [1] of Attic Orators was drawn up, only one of the ten who were included had not at least begun to be active by the time of the Macedonian conquest of Greece, and he was so far inferior to the rest that Dionysius the critic challenged his right to be numbered with the nine.

In the pages which follow will be found characteristic passages from eight of those nine; Isaeus alone is omitted, since his speeches are concerned with highly technical questions of inheritance. It should be remembered, however, that the effectiveness of oratory, like that of poetry, is largely dependent upon the sound of the words, the mental images they evoke, and the skill with which they are marshalled in the sentence. Such elements are difficult to reproduce in an alien language with its own peculiar idiom. Yet even in English dress we may hope to catch a glimpse of the fire that once inflamed the Greek listener, to gain some acquaintance with the caustic wit that made its victim squirm, to find amusement in the foibles of men so like ourselves, and to realize that many of the problems and anxieties of today were faced with courage centuries ago.

The following texts were used in making these translations: the texts of F. Blass (Leipzig: Teubner) for Antiphon (1881), Andocides (1881), Isocrates (1888), Demosthenes (1887), and Hyperides (1881), except for section 33, for which the text of E. E. Genner (Oxford, 1928) was used; the texts of Karl Scheibe (Leipzig: Teubner) for Lysias (1885) and Lycurgus (1888); and the text of F. Franke (Leipzig: Teubner, 1887) for Aeschines.

ANTIPHON

ANTIPHON was born at Athens sometime early in the fifth century B.C. and therefore is the earliest of the Attic orators belonging to the canon. His death occurred soon after the downfall of the oligarchical constitution of the Four Hundred in 411 B.C. An ardent oligarch, he had been most active in the revolution that brought that government into being, and after its brief existence had ended in the restoration of the democracy, Antiphon was tried as a traitor and executed.

We know very little regarding his family or his private life. Thucydides, who is said to have been a student in his school of rhetoric, praises his skill in framing an argument and calls the defense which Antiphon made when on trial for his life the best speech of the kind yet delivered. Unfortunately the speech has not been preserved.

Antiphon was active not only in politics and as a teacher of rhetoric but also in the composing of speeches to be delivered by his clients in court. He seems to have specialized in murder cases, to which category belong all fifteen speeches now extant. He attached great importance to the argument from probability [2] and used that device with much effectiveness. Therein he displayed a trait which is truly Greek—reliance upon reason rather than upon human testimony. In modern times there has been a tendency to feel that there is an element of unfairness in deciding a man's fate on the basis of circumstantial evidence, but of late the validity and extreme importance of such evidence appears to be gaining recognition. The overcleverness of Antiphon, as the ancient critics termed it, perhaps deserves our praise. The mere swearing of an oath was not then and is not now a guarantee of the veracity of the witness.

Oration V

On the Murder of Herodes

This is a speech which was actually delivered in court, probably about the year 416 B.C. Helos, the defendant, for whom the speech was written, was a citizen of Mytilene, on the island of Lesbos. He became involved in the case on his way to visit his father in Thrace. In the course of that voyage, according to the prosecution, he had murdered an Athenian named Herodes and had thrown his body into the sea.

Although the alleged crime had been committed at Methymna, another Lesbian community, the case had to be tried in Athens. The accusers were kinsmen of Herodes. The defendant makes much of the fact that, though they charged him with murder, they had brought his case to the attention of the police commissioners, had kept him in prison pending the trial, and were now prosecuting him as a "malefactor" instead of as a murderer, and in an ordinary court of law instead of before the Court of the Areopagus, where trials for murder were regularly held. Some scholars think the whole charge was invented to discredit the defendant's father, who had political enemies in Mytilene. We are not informed as to the outcome of the trial, but the argument of the defendant seems fairly convincing. In fact, his very plea of inexperience is written in balanced periods which only an expert could achieve.

Proem: Request for a fair hearing

1 I wish, gentlemen, that my ability as a speaker and my acquaintance with practical affairs matched my misfortune and the evils I have encountered. As it is, I have tasted the one more fully than I deserve, and I lack the other more than is good for me. *2* When I was confronted with bodily injury on a charge that was not rightfully mine, experience lent me no aid at all, and now that my salvation depends upon a truthful statement of what took place, my deficiencies as a speaker are a detriment to me. *3* In the past, persons who lacked the gift of eloquence were often disbelieved and ruined by the very truths they uttered, merely because they could not present them clearly. On the other hand, able speakers have often won credence by lying and have been saved because they were effective liars. So when a man lacks experience in court procedure, his fate depends more upon the words of the accusers than upon the facts themselves and the truthfulness with which those facts are stated.

4 Now, gentlemen, what I am going to ask of you is not what most defendants ask—an attentive hearing. To do so shows they lack confidence in themselves and have decided against your honesty and fairness in advance. It is to be expected that men of honor will listen to the defendants without being asked to do so, just as they listen to the prosecutors without any such appeal. *5* What I am asking is that, in case I make some slip of the tongue, you may overlook it and attribute the error to my inexperience rather than to criminal intent; and that, if I put some point successfully, you may ascribe it to truthfulness rather than to cleverness. It is not fair that the perpetrator of a criminal act should find salvation by means of words, nor that one whose deeds have been upright should suffer death because of words. The word is the error of the tongue, the deed of the will. *6* When a man's life is in jeopardy, he will inevitably make a slip somewhere. He has to bear in mind not merely what he is saying but also what the outcome is to be. Whatever is still enveloped in uncertainty depends upon chance more than upon foresight. All this necessarily is most disturbing to one whose life is at stake. *7* Personally, I find that even persons very familiar with court procedure speak much less effectively than usual when faced with some peril. In matters involving no risk they are more effective. My request, then, is both legal and righteous, and it accords with your concept of justice no less than with my own. Now I shall proceed to defend myself touching the charges against me one by one.

[The defendant begins his case by complaining of the treatment he has received at the hands of his accusers. He has been brought to trial as a "malefactor," rather than on a charge of murder, so that the plaintiffs have not had to take the solemn oath required in murder cases. He has been kept in prison illegally. The case has been so framed that, even if he is acquitted, he can later be brought to trial for murder. Finally, he has not been allowed the privilege of having bondsmen post bail for his appearance in court.]

18 You see, it was to the interest of my accusers, first of all, that I be caught as poorly prepared as possible, not being able to give personal attention to my affairs because I was in prison; secondly, that I should undergo physical suffering and thus find my own friends more eager to testify falsely for the prosecution than to tell the truth for me. Then too, they have placed upon me and my kinsmen a stigma of disgrace which we shall carry to the grave.

19 Thus here I stand on trial, having received the worst of it in many aspects of your laws and of justice. Yet even so, I shall try to prove my innocence. It is a difficult undertaking to refute forthwith lies and plots framed long ago. It is not possible even to guard against things one never expected.

The background of the murder charge

20 I set sail from Mytilene, gentlemen of the jury, a passenger in the same ship that carried this Herodes whom they claim I murdered. We were bound for Aenus, I to visit my father, who happened to be there at the time, and Herodes to negotiate with certain Thracians for the ransom of some slaves. The slaves that he was to release were sailing with us, as also the Thracians who were to effect their ransom. . . .[3] *21* These are the reasons why each of us made the voyage. But we had the misfortune to encounter a storm. We were forced to put in at a place in the district of Methymna, where there was anchored this vessel to which Herodes transferred and where he is alleged to have met his death.

Now first of all observe that these incidents occurred, not because I had planned them, but by bare chance. Nowhere is there anything to prove that I persuaded the man to sail with me. He made the voyage independently, of his own volition, and for his own private interest. *22* Moreover, it is manifest that I had good and sufficient reason for sailing to Aenus. Our touching at the place referred to was not the result of scheming on my part, but because we were forced to land there. Again, when we had anchored, the transfer to the other vessel did not take place because of any plot or deception, but once more we acted through necessity. The ship on which we had been sailing was not decked over, whereas the one to which we transferred was. What we did was occasioned by the rain. . . .

23 After transferring to the other ship we fell to drinking. There is no doubt that Herodes left the ship and did not come aboard again, but I did not leave the boat at all that night. Next day when the man was nowhere to be seen, I sought to find him as zealously as the rest of us. If anyone felt that the business was terrible, I felt so quite as much. It was I who was responsible for sending a messenger to Mytilene, and it was on my motion that one was sent. *24* When no one else, either from the ship's company or from Herodes' party, would make the trip, I offered to send my own attendant. And yet surely I would not wittingly send a person who could turn informer against me. When, in spite of our search, there was no sign of Herodes, either in Mytilene or anywhere else at all, when the weather cleared the boats all put to sea and I continued with my voyage. . . .

My story proves my innocence a priori.

25 There you have my story of what happened. What conclusions may reasonably be drawn from it? In the first place, when I set sail once more for Aenus, Herodes already having disappeared, not a single person brought any charge against me, although by that time my accusers had learned the news; otherwise I should never have continued with my voyage. For the moment, the truth of what had happened was too strong to permit them to accuse me. Besides, I was still at Methymna. But when I had resumed my voyage, when these fellows had treacherously concocted this story and plot against me, that was the time they chose for making their accusation.

The prosecution's story combatted

26 Their story is that Herodes died ashore, and that I hit him on the head with a stone, I who did not leave the boat at all! They know this perfectly well; but they cannot offer any likely explanation to account for the man's disappearance. Evidently the thing must have happened somewhere near the harbor, for he was drunk and it was night when he went ashore. Very likely he could not control his own movements, and whoever tried to abduct him could find no plausible excuse for taking him on a long excursion at night. *27* The search continued for two days, both at the harbor and at some distance from it, but no eye-witness was discovered, nor any blood, nor any clue at all.

Well now, I accept this tale of theirs, though producing witnesses to prove I did not leave the ship. But even if I had left the ship as often as you please, it is most unlikely that I could have made away with Herodes without detection, since he certainly did not go very far from the water.

28 But, they say, his body was thrown into the sea. From what boat? Evidently the boat must have been one of those in the harbor itself. Why, then, could it not be found? Surely one might expect some clue to be found in the boat if a dead man had been put on board and thrown out at night. But now they claim to have discovered clues in the boat where he had been drinking and from which he went ashore, the boat in which they admit he did not meet his death. But as for the boat from which he was thrown into the sea, they have not found the boat itself or any trace of it at all. . . .

29 After I had gone off on my voyage to Aenus and the boat on which Herodes and I had been drinking arrived at Mytilene, for the first time they went on board and made a search. When they found the blood, they said the man had been murdered there. But when this turned out to be impossible, since it proved to be sheep's blood, they abandoned this story, arrested the crew, and put them to torture.

The prosecution attempts to secure evidence by torturing two slaves.

30 Now the one whom they examined right away on the spot said nothing to incriminate me; but the man whom they tortured many days later, having in the meantime been kept in their custody, is the one who was induced by them to lie about me. . . .

31 That the examination took place so much later is in the testimony you have received. But, gentlemen of the jury, observe what kind of examination it proves to have been. The fellow was a slave, and doubtless my accusers had promised him his freedom. Moreover, it was for them to say when his torture should cease. Possibly both considerations induced him to tell lies about me—the hope of obtaining his freedom and the desire to be released from his torture at the moment. *32* You doubtless know that those who are most intimately connected with the torture have it in their power to cause their victims to say what is likely to gratify them. By so doing the poor devils can gain relief, especially if it happens that the victims of their lies are not present. If I could order the man to be put to the torture on the ground that he was not telling the truth, perhaps that in itself would persuade him not to lie about me. However, the same persons both administered the torture and were the judges of what served their purpose.

Evidence secured under torture recanted

33 Now so long as he felt that the lies he told against me afforded him good hope of reward, he persisted in this tale of his; but when he began to think he was going to be killed, at last he told the truth and said that he had been persuaded by my accusers to lie about me. *34* But though he had made a determined effort to tell what was false and had later told the truth, neither course did him any good. No, they took him away and slew him, slew this informer on whose testimony they rely for my prosecution! Such behavior goes counter to the regular practice. People regularly reward their informers with money, if free men, with freedom, if they are slaves. But the reward in this instance was death, though my friends tried to forbid it and secure his reprieve until I could get there. *35* Evidently it was not his body that they needed, but only his words! If he had lived, he would have been submitted to the same ordeal at my hands and would have denounced their plot against me; now that he is dead, he robs me of the chance to put truth to the test by the mere fact of his having died, and I am threatened with destruction because of that man's words, false as they were, as if they were true!

[The defendant goes on to point out in more detail how unfair it is to use against him the words of a man who has been slain before his testimony could be put to the proof. Besides, he had later disavowed the testimony which is now being used against the defendant. There follows an argument based on probability, in the course of which the speaker disputes the authenticity of a letter said to have been found aboard ship, in which it is claimed that he promised a certain Lycinus to murder Herodes.]

A murderer should have a motive.

57 Now, why should I have killed Herodes? We had no quarrel. They have the audacity to say I killed him as a favor to Lycinus. Whoever did such a deed as a favor to someone else? No, I imagine there must be great enmity between persons if a man aims to commit murder, and it must be manifest that he reached that decision and laid his plans long beforehand. But Herodes and I had no quarrel at all.

58 Very well, did I do it through fear that I myself might be killed by him? A person might be driven to do such a thing for that reason. But I had no such suspicion regarding him. Well then, was I going to profit financially from the murder? Herodes had no money. *59* I might, sir, with greater propriety and truthfulness ascribe to you this motive—that you seek my death in the hope of gain. My relatives could more justly convict you of murder if you bring about my death than you and Herodes' relatives could convict me. I can prove your manifest intent with regard to me, but you are trying to cause my death by using a dubious story. . . .

[In the omitted sections the defendant seeks to discredit the charge that he had been the tool of Lycinus, who had no reason to desire the death of Herodes and, if he had, could not have secured the aid of the defendant. The latter was not on intimate terms with him and could not have looked to him for financial reward. In the absence of proof of his guilt, it is unjust to demand that he account for the disappearance of Herodes.]

Innocence of the defendant proved by absence of divine anger.

81 Whatever proof is to be found in human evidence and testimony has now been presented. But in casting your vote in such a case as the present one you ought also to attach great weight to the signs provided by the gods. It is by paying strict heed to these signs that you administer successfully your public business, both in matters fraught with danger and in such as are devoid of danger.

82 But you should consider these tokens as most important and reliable also in private matters. You must know that often in the past men with unclean hands or with some other form of pollution have gone aboard a vessel carrying other persons and have involved those shipmates in their own destruction, men whose hands were pure in the sight of heaven. In other instances, though actual death may not have resulted, men have been placed in extreme peril through contact with such criminals. Again, when attending a sacrifice, men have been discovered to be impure, when by their presence they prevented the performance of the customary rites. *83* In all these relations my experience has been just the opposite. All with whom I have sailed have had most prosperous voyages, and the sacrifices I have attended always proved most propitious. These facts I claim are weighty evidence to prove that my accusers are making a false charge against me. . . .

[The speaker concludes by stressing the legal point that, while he has been charged with being a "malefactor," the court is being asked to convict him of murder, a crime in which it has no jurisdiction. First acquit him of being a malefactor, and then let his accusers institute fresh proceedings on the charge of murder in the court established for such hearings. This plea is not an attempt to evade justice: if the defendant had had a guilty conscience, he would have stayed away from Athens.]

ANDOCIDES

Andocides belonged to an aristocratic Athenian family, for generations distinguished in war and politics. Born about the year 440 B.C., he spent his early years amid the excitement and political maneuvering attendant upon the Peloponnesian War. We hear nothing about his schooling, but he should have had the best educational advantages then available. Family tradition may well have inspired him with the ambition to play his part in public life, and we learn from his own lips that he belonged to a political club in his twenties.

His was a life of adventure. Arrested in 415 B.C. on suspicion of complicity in the mutilation of the Hermae,[4] those quaint representations of the god which stood before private dwellings and temples and in various public spots in and around Athens, he secured his release from prison by turning state's evidence and implicating himself and others. A decree passed at that time debarred him from entering the market place or the temples, and he therefore quitted Athens and spent the next few years in trade and travel up and down the Mediterranean, in the course of which he acquired a very comfortable fortune. After two abortive efforts to secure restoration to full citizenship, he finally was reinstated in consequence of the general amnesty of the year 403 B.C. His return to Athens marked the beginning of an active and successful career in politics. The Athenians may have attributed his imprisonment in 415 to partisan politics, for he was promptly chosen to fill several important posts in succession and in 391 he was sent to negotiate with Sparta regarding peace with Athens. The only serious threat to his career after his return was his trial in 399 [5] on the charge of impiety, a charge against which he successfully defended himself in his speech *On the Mysteries.*

As an orator, Andocides does not rank alongside the other members of the canon. He was a practical businessman and politician with no desire to make oratory a profession. Of the four speeches which have come down to us bearing his name, only two are universally recognized as genuine, and they concern his own personal affairs. He probably laid no claim to special merit as a public speaker, but some prowess in that department was essential to success in public life in Athens. His was the rough and ready style (but imaginative and evocative, especially in the peroration, sec. 148 ff.) that doubtless any Athenian of the time who had good social background and political ambitions might have displayed. As examples of that style, as well as for the interest inherent in the topics treated, the two admittedly genuine speeches, *On the Mysteries* and *On the Return*, are worth reading.

Oration I

On the Mysteries

This is the speech which won acquittal for Andocides in his trial on the charge of impiety in 399 B.C. The principal count in the indictment, as is suggested by the title, is that Andocides had attended the Eleusinian Mysteries and had entered the Eleusinian shrine at Athens. The Mysteries were a secret cult of great solemnity and widespread importance throughout the ancient world. To participate, a person must have been duly initiated. Andocides was an initiate, but it was claimed that he was still under the ban created by the decree of 415 B.C. In order to prove the charge of impiety, it was necessary to show that the defendant was subject to that decree. Accordingly the prosecution introduced also the whole affair of the Hermae. The notoriety of that affair lends additional interest to the speech of Andocides, in the course of which he supplies many intimate details and gives a vivid picture of the panic created at Athens by the sacrilege and by the suspicions of an intended revolution.

The setting of the trial was highly impressive. It was held at Eleusis itself during the progress of the sacred festival, and the judges were all members of the cult. Both parties to the suit were supported by prominent politicians, so that it is plain that the case was no ordinary one.

1 The scheming and the eagerness of my enemies to harm me in any and every way ever since I first returned to Athens is well known to virtually all of you, my judges, and there is no need of my making a long harangue upon that subject. Justice is what I mean to ask of you, a justice both easy for you to grant and highly important for me to win.

The defendant is in court of his own volition:

2 In the first place, I would have you remember that I am here under no compulsion to remain. I have not furnished bail, nor am I a prisoner forced to appear in court. Rather, it is because I relied first of all upon the justice of my case, and also upon you, believing that you would render a just verdict and not suffer me to be unjustly ruined by my enemies, but that you would much rather save me justly as the laws prescribe and the oaths which you have sworn, which bind you in the decision you are to render.

3 You might reasonably hold the same opinion about men who voluntarily place themselves in legal jeopardy as they hold about themselves. In the case of all who refused to stand trial, by so doing they have convicted themselves of injustice, and you are right to form the same opinion about them that they have formed themselves. So also when men have awaited trial, trusting to their complete innocence, it is right that you, too, should entertain the same opinion about them that they did about themselves and not convict them in advance.

[Andocides points out that his accusers expected him to leave Athens; but he is so confident of his case and so eager to remain in the city that he has refused to do this. He warns the court against being swayed by false accusations and explains why he turned state's evidence. He then passes to an account of the proceedings in the Assembly after the affair of the Hermae and before the sailing of the fleet for Syracuse. One Pythonicus had arisen and offered to produce a witness, a servant of one of the accused, to prove that the Mysteries had been violated. To the evidence of the servant was added that of the metic Teucrus; of an Athenian woman, Agariste; and of a slave who accused the father of Andocides. Andocides had persuaded his father to remain and stand trial; he was acquitted by a large majority—but Andocides is now being accused of having violated the Mysteries himself and then of accusing his own father to obtain immunity!

After summing up to his satisfaction his proof of innocence regarding the profanation of the Mysteries, Andocides reminds the jurors of the solemnity of their oath and then takes up the affair of the Hermae, recalling that Teucrus had implicated eighteen men in that crime, some of whom made their escape from Athens, while others had been arrested and put to death.]

Dismay in Athens over mutilation of the Hermae

36 When these events had taken place, Pisander and Charicles, who were on the board of inquiry and had the reputation of being most friendly toward the democracy at that time, said that the affair was the work of no few men, that it was aimed at the overthrow of the democracy, and that consequently the investigation must be pressed and not be dropped. Athens was in such a state that whenever the Herald gave the order for the Council to proceed to the Council Chamber and lowered the flag, at the same signal that brought the Council to its hall the people in the market place would flee, each fearing for his own arrest.

Dioclides volunteers information.

37 Now Dioclides was so disturbed by the distress in Athens that he made an announcement to the Council, claiming that he knew who had mutilated the Hermae and that they were as many as three hundred, and he proceeded to tell how he came to witness and to stumble on the business. I beg you to pay close attention to what I shall say and to recall it later, if I speak the truth, and so inform each other. Dioclides told his story in your presence and you are my witnesses regarding what follows.

38 He said he had a slave working in the mines at Laurium and he had to go and collect his hire. So he got up early in the morning, having been deceived as to the hour, and started on his way. It was full moon. When he was near the entrance to the sanctuary of Dionysus, he saw a crowd of men on their way down from the Odeum into the orchestra of the theater. He took fright and went and sat down in the dark between the column and the pedestal which bears the bronze statue of the general. He could see men to the number of three hundred. They were standing in a circle in groups of fifteen or twenty. He saw and recognized the faces of most of them by the light of the moon.

39 This was the prologue to his story, gentlemen, a shocking performance in my opinion. He wanted to be able to claim that any Athenian who suited his purpose was one of these men and to say that anyone he chose was not.

After witnessing this scene, he continued, he went on to Laurium. Next day he heard that the Hermae had been mutilated. So right off he knew it had been the work of these men.

40 On reaching Athens he found that investigators had already been chosen and a reward of one hundred minas had been proclaimed for the giving of information.

Seeing Euphemus, the brother of Callias son of Telecles, sitting in a blacksmith shop, he took him up to the shrine of Hephaestus and told him what I have told you. He said he had seen us that night, but he had no desire to get money from the state rather than from us, hoping to have our friendship. Euphemus, he stated, said he was glad he had told him, and he urged him to do him the favor of going to the house of Leogoras, my father, "in order that you, in conjunction with me, may there confer with Andocides and others whom you must meet."

41 Next day, Dioclides said, he went there and was actually knocking at the door when my father by chance came out and said to him, "Are you the one these men are expecting? Friends like you must certainly not be refused admission." With that my father went off. In this way Dioclides was trying to ruin my father, showing him to be in the plot.

He went on to say that we told him we had decided to offer him two talents of silver in place of the hundred minas offered by the state. Moreover, if we got control of what we were after, he could be one of us, and we were to exchange pledges to bind the agreement. *42* His answer was that he would take these proposals under advisement. We then urged him to come to the house of Callias the son of Telecles, so that Callias also might be present. Thus he was working to destroy my kinsman. He said he went to Callias' and agreed to give us his pledge on the Acropolis. We on our part contracted to pay him his money the following month. But we played him false, he said, and did not produce the money. Consequently he had come to reveal what had taken place.

Effect of Dioclides' story

43 Such was the nature of his report, gentlemen, and he listed the names of those he claimed to have recognized, forty-two in number, first of all Mantitheus and Apsephion, who were members of the Council and were seated in the Council Chamber at the time, and after them the others also.

Pisander arose in the meeting and said the decree that had been passed in the archonship of Scamandrius [6] should be rescinded and the men on the list should be put on the rack, in order that before nightfall it might be learned who were involved. The Council gave a shout of approval, (*44*) on hearing which Mantitheus and Apsephion seated themselves at the sacred hearth, begging not to be put to the torture but to be permitted to furnish bail and be given a judicial trial. With much difficulty they obtained their request, but after they had furnished sureties, they straddled their horses and disappeared from Athens, deserting to the enemy, and thus abandoning their bondsmen, who necessarily were subject to the same penalties as the men for whom they had gone bail.

The citizens of Athens alerted

45 The Council, after it had retired and conferred in private, arrested us and put us in the stocks. Then it summoned the generals and ordered them to issue a proclamation that the city dwellers should go to the market place under arms, those in the suburbs to the Theseum, and those in the Piraeus to the market place of Hippodamus. And furthermore, before nightfall the trumpeter was to give a signal for the Knights to go to the Anaceum, the Council to the Acropolis, and the Prytanes to the Tholos,[7] and sleep there. The Boeotians, after they had learned what was going on, had taken the field and were at the frontier of Attica. Dioclides, who had been the cause of all this, was conveyed in a carriage to the Prytaneum as the savior of Athens, was given a crown, and was entertained there at dinner!

[Andocides proceeds to narrate, first, how he was prevailed upon by relatives in prison to save them and himself by telling what he knew, and then how it happened that, although he had knowledge of the plot, he had no part in it. By his confession he proved Dioclides to have given false testimony.]

The condemnation and execution of Dioclides

65 The Council and the board of investigation looked into the matter, and when they found the facts to be as I had stated and to be so agreed on all sides, they summoned Dioclides. There was no need of a long examination of the man, for he at once admitted that he had been lying, and he begged to be set free if he told who had induced him to make this statement, naming Alcibiades of Phegus [8] and Amiantus of Aegina as the guilty ones.

66 Those two men took fright and fled the country. As for Dioclides, after hearing his statement you turned him over to the court and had him executed. Those who had been put in prison and were facing death you set free because of me—my own kinsmen—and you allowed those in exile to return to Athens. You yourselves took your arms and went home, released from many hardships and perils.

Andocides appeals for sympathetic understanding of his conduct.

67 In all this, gentlemen, I might well be pitied by everybody for the evil fortune that fell to my lot, but for what I did I might reasonably be accounted an excellent citizen. When Euphiletus proposed the most incredible pledge imaginable, I took the other side and spoke against it and reviled him as he deserved; and when the culprits had committed their crime, I helped them to conceal their part in it. When Teucrus denounced them, some were put to death and others fled before Dioclides caused our imprisonment and doomed us to destruction. Then it was that I informed against four men: Panaetius, Diacritus, Lysistratus, and Chaeredemus. *68* These four fled on my account, I admit, but my father was saved, as were also my brother-in-law, three cousins, and seven other relatives, all of whom were in peril of suffering an unjust death. Because of me they now behold the light of the sun, as they themselves admit. Besides, the man who had thrown all Athens into confusion and exposed it to the very worst perils was through my efforts convicted, and you were freed from awful terrors and your suspicions of one another.

[There follows a detailed discussion of the

legislation passed after the restoration of the democracy, whose purpose had been to wipe the slate clean and create concord in the state. Andocides proves that on the basis of that legislation he is not subject to punishment on the charges lodged against him.]

Athens' record for clemency and justice

106 In order that you may know that the measures you adopted to restore concord are not ill-advised but that you did what was fitting and for your own advantage, I wish to discuss briefly the following matters.

When great misfortune had befallen Athens, at the time when the tyrants controlled the city and the democrats were in exile, your forefathers defeated the tyrants at Pallenium [9] under the leadership of Leogoras, my great grandfather, and Charias, whose daughter was Leogoras' wife and my grandfather's mother. On their return to the fatherland, the democrats slew some, condemned others to exile, and disfranchised others, though allowing them to remain in Athens.

107 Afterwards, when the Great King [10] made war on Hellas, recognizing the seriousness of the dangers confronting them and the preparations of the King, they decided to welcome the exiles home again, to restore citizenship to the disfranchised, and to make safety and danger the same for all alike. This done, they exchanged pledges and solemn oaths and saw fit to make themselves the champions and defenders of all the Greeks, meeting the barbarians in battle at Marathon. They believed their own valor was sufficient with which to meet the horde of the foe in pitched battle. So they won the day, freed Hellas, and saved their country.

108 But after that glorious deed of daring they did not think it right to bear a grudge against anyone for what had been done in the past. Therefore, though they found Athens in ruins, its temples burnt to the ground, and their walls and dwellings torn down, though they had nothing with which to start life anew, because they were at peace with one another in Athens they became the leaders of the Greek nation and left to you your city in all its grandeur and power.

109 At a later time you yourselves encountered evils no less great than theirs, and being noble offspring of noble sires, you displayed the virtue you had inherited. You, too, saw fit to welcome home again the exiles and to restore citizenship to the disfranchised. Then what feature of their goodness remains for you still to display? To bear no grudge, knowing that Athens in days gone by, starting with resources far inferior to those we have today, grew great and prosperous. It can become so now, provided that we its citizens prove ready to live at peace with one another.

[There follows a long account of intrigue against Andocides, involving rival claims to an "heiress" and jealousy on the part of men whom he claims to have prevented from defrauding the state.]

The loyal patriotism of Andocides' ancestors deserves recognition.

141 Therefore I beg you all to hold the same opinion about me as you do about my ancestors, so that I too may have the opportunity to emulate them. Remember that they have proved the equals of those who won for Athens very many rich blessings. They behaved as they did for many reasons, but particularly out of loyalty to you, and also in order that, if ever any danger or disaster should befall them or any of their descendants, you might grant them pardon and salvation.

142 It is reasonable that you should remember them, for the virtues of your own ancestors have proved of utmost value to Athens as a whole. When the fleet had been destroyed,[11] many wished to involve our city in utter ruin, but the Spartans, though then our enemies, determined to preserve Athens because of the virtues of those men of old who took the lead in freeing the entire nation. *143* Therefore, since Athens owes its salvation as a state to the virtues of your own ancestors, I claim the right to find salvation through mine as well. My ancestors contributed in no small measure to the very deeds whereby Athens was preserved, and so it is right that you should give me too a portion of the salvation you yourselves received from the Greeks.

Andocides has learned by bitter experience the great value of his citizenship, and his wide acquaintance can prove useful to Athens.

144 Consider also what kind of citizen you will have in me if you spare my life. At first I had great wealth, the extent of which you know, and then through no fault of mine but because of the misfortunes of our city I was plunged into the depths of poverty and distress. Thereupon I made a new living in honest ways by perseverance and the labor of my own two hands. Besides, I am one who knows what it is like to be a citizen of so fine a state (*145*) and what it is like to be an alien living in the country of our neighbors. I know what it is like to be discreet and well advised. I know what it is like to encounter hardship for mistakes committed. I have met many men and put very many to the test, securing the hospitality and friendship of many—kings and cities and private individuals besides. If you spare me you will be able to share their friendship and to make use of them in any matter that will serve your interest.

Renewed appeal for favor because of merits and distinction of house of the speaker

146 As for yourselves, gentlemen, this is the situation. If you destroy me now, not a single member of our house will be left to you, but it disappears, root and branch. Is not the residence of Andocides and Leogoras a reproach to you by its very presence? Nay, it was much more a reproach in the days when I was an exile and it was occupied by Cleophon the lyre manufacturer. Not one of you who passed our house could recall any injury he had suffered, either privately or publicly, at the hands of its former occupants. *147* Very often they had filled the office of general, and many are the victories on both land and sea which they brought home to you. They held many other offices, they handled your finances; but they never were convicted in a single suit. We never did you any harm, nor did you harm us. Our house is the most ancient in Athens, and its hospitality is always extended most freely to those in need. Moreover, on no occasion has any member of my family in a law suit asked any favor of you in payment for all that they have done.

148 They themselves are dead, yet do not forget the services they have performed. Recall their deeds. Imagine you behold their forms beseeching you to save me. Whom, pray, shall I call to the stand to plead in my behalf? My father? Dead. My brothers? No longer living. My children? I have none yet. *149* You, then, be father, brothers, children to me. To you I flee for refuge. You I implore and beseech. Ask your own selves for my salvation. Do not decide to give citizenship to Thessalians and men of Andros for lack of Athenians and then put to death those who are admittedly citizens, those whose heritage it is to be honest men, and who will have the desire and the ability to be that. This, too, I beg of you: since I benefit you, let me be honored by you. If you heed my entreaty you will not deprive yourselves of the benefits which I may be able to bestow upon you, but if you listen to my enemies, even if you later repent, repentance will do you no good. *150* Then do not deprive yourselves of what you may hope for from me or deprive me of what I hope to bestow upon you.

I think it is fitting that these men here [with a gesture toward his friends], who have already given you proof of their distinguished service to your democracy, should come forward and advise you concerning their views about me. This way, Anytus and Cephalus, yes, and Thrasyllus and the other members of my tribe who have been chosen to support my cause.

LYSIAS

LYSIAS WAS the son of Cephalus, a prosperous shield manufacturer from Syracuse, who came to Athens on the invitation of Pericles and lived there thirty years. Foreign residents, or metics as they were called, did not enjoy the rights of citizenship at Athens, but Cephalus had the friendship of intellectual Athenians, as Plato indicates by selecting his home as the scene of the *Republic.*

It was in that atmosphere that Lysias spent his early years. Later he resided for a time at Thurii, an Athenian colony in southern Italy, where he is said to have studied under the famous Sicilian rhetorician Tisias, but toward the close of the Peloponnesian War he returned to Athens. When in 404 B.C. the Thirty Tyrants for a brief period ruled that city, Lysias was selected as one of their intended victims. They confiscated his property and slew his brother, but he managed to escape with his life, as is narrated in the passages, from his speech *Against Eratosthenes,* which have been chosen for translation.

After the overthrow of the Thirty, Lysias returned to Athens. A resolution was passed in the Assembly awarding him citizenship because of his services to the democrats in their struggle with the Thirty, but this was subsequently annulled, and he remained a metic down to his death in 380 B.C.

His speech *Against Eratosthenes,* delivered by him in person (Autumn, 403 B.C.) with a view to avenging the murder of his brother and the destruction of the family fortune, seems to have established the reputation of Lysias as a skillful pleader at the bar. Henceforth his life was devoted to the writing of speeches for others, many of which are still extant. He was notably successful in suiting those speeches to the personality of the men for whom they were written. He ranks high among the orators of Athens as a master of simple, accurate prose. Plato (*Phaedrus,* 228a) called him "the cleverest writer of our time."

Oration XII

Against Eratosthenes

4 My father Cephalus came to this country by invitation of Pericles. He lived here thirty years, and neither he nor my brother and I ever were in court as plaintiff or defendant. Our life under the democracy was so upright that we did not wrong our neighbors and were not wronged by them.

5 But when the Thirty came to power, evil extortioners as they were, they said the city must be purged of its criminals and the rest of the citizens be led into the paths of virtue and justice. Such were their words, but they did not have the grace to act accordingly, as I shall try to remind you by reciting what happened to me and to you as well.

The Thirty plot against the metics.

6 In a meeting of the Thirty, Theognis and Pison stated that some metics were hostile to the administration and that therefore there was an excellent pretext for ostensibly inflicting punishment but actually enriching themselves. Certainly the state was impoverished and the administration needed money. *7* They had no difficulty in persuading their hearers, who thought nothing of putting men to death but a great deal of getting money. So they decided to seize ten men. Two were to be poor men, so that with reference to the others they might be able to claim that they had acted not for gain but for the best interest of the state, just as if they had performed some honorable deed.

Lysias arrested and his property confiscated; he plans to escape.

8 Well, they took separate houses as their assignment and set off. They found me entertaining some guests at dinner. They drove out my guests and gave me into Pison's keeping. The rest of the party went into our factory and confiscated the slaves. I asked Pison if he would consent to save my life for a sum of money. *9* He said yes, if the sum was big enough. I told him I was prepared to pay him a talent of silver, whereupon he agreed to do the job.

I understood of course that he thought nothing of gods or men, but still my situation made it appear most essential to get a pledge from him. *10* So when he had sworn an oath—in which he called down utter destruction upon himself and his children in case of nonfulfillment—that if he got the talent he would save me, I entered my bedroom and opened up the chest. Perceiving what I was doing, Pison came into the room and at sight of the contents of the chest he called two of his attendants and ordered them to take everything there was in it. *11* Inasmuch as he now had not merely what I had agreed upon, gentlemen of the jury, but three talents of silver, four hundred Cyzicene staters, a hundred gold darics, and four silver bowls, I begged him to give me money for my journey. His reply was that I could count myself lucky if I got off with my life.

12 As he and I were leaving the house Melobius and Mnesithides met us on their way from the factory. They encountered us right at my front door and asked where we were going. Pison told them we were on our way to my brother's to inspect the contents of that house. So they told him to proceed but said I must accompany them to the house of Damnippus. *13* Pison came close and urged me to keep quiet and not worry, for he was coming to Damnippus' himself. On our arrival we found Theognis there guarding some other prisoners; so they turned me over to him and went away.

In such dire straits I decided to take a chance, for death confronted me anyway. *14* I called Damnippus and said to him: "You are a good friend of mine. Here I am in your house. I have done no wrong but am being put out of the way for the sake of my money. Seeing that I am the victim of such foul treatment, do what you can to save me." He said he would. But he thought it best to speak a word to Theognis, for he believed he would do anything for money.

15 While he was parleying with Theognis—for I happened to be acquainted with the house and knew it had two entrances—I decided to try to save my life in that way. I figured that if I escaped detection I should be safe, but in case I were caught, provided Theognis had been persuaded by Damnippus to accept a bribe, I should nonetheless be set at liberty. Otherwise my life was forfeit anyway.

Escape effected

16 Having reached this decision I began my flight, my captors meanwhile standing guard at the main entrance. There were three doors which I had to pass, but all were open, as luck would have it. On reaching the house of Archeneus the ship captain, I sent him to Athens to ask about my brother. On his return he reported that Eratosthenes had caught my brother on the street and had taken him to prison. *17* At this distressing news I sailed across to Megara the ensuing night.

Fate of the brother of Lysias

My brother Polemarchus received from the Thirty their usual order, to drink the hemlock, before ever being told the charge on which he was to die—so far was he from being given a trial and the opportunity to plead his case! *18* Besides, when his dead body was being carried from the jail, though we owned three houses, they would not allow a single one to be used for the funeral. Instead, they rented a shanty in which they laid him out. We owned many cloaks, too, but despite requests they gave none for the funeral. It was my brother's friends who supplied the necessary things, one a cloak, another a pillow, and others whatever it might be. *19* The Thirty had seven hundred shields of ours, a great quantity of silver and gold, bronze and ornaments and furniture and women's apparel in such abundance as they never thought to acquire, to say nothing of one hundred and twenty slaves, of whom they took the best for themselves and turned the rest over to the Treasury. Yet they became so insatiate in their greed, so shameless in their thirst for gain, made such a display of their character, that the gold earrings which the wife of Polemarchus happened to be wearing when Melobius first entered the house he tore out of her ears! *20* Not in the smallest portion of our estate did we receive from them any mercy.

The record of Lysias and his family contrasted with that of the Thirty

No, they mistreated us because of our wealth as no others would treat persons against whom they were angry for great injuries. We did not deserve such treatment from Athens. We had performed all the liturgies, contributed generously to the war chest, always behaved in a law-abiding fashion, done everything we were told to do, earned no man's enmity, but had ransomed many Athenians from the enemy. Yet that was the way the Thirty thought fit to treat us, though our behavior as metics was better than theirs as citizens. *21* They drove many citizens into the camp of the enemy, they slew many unjustly and then deprived them of burial, they disfranchised many who had enjoyed full citizenship, many times they prevented the marriage of girls who were on the eve of marriage.

22 What is more, they have grown so bold that they have come here to make their defense, and they claim they have done nothing wrong or disgraceful. I wish that were the truth, for in that case my share in that blessing would be no small one. *23* However, they can make no such claim with reference either to Athens or to me. Eratosthenes, as I told you earlier, slew my brother, not because he had a private grudge against him or because he saw him wronging Athens, but just because he was bent on indulging his own spirit of lawlessness. . . .

[There follows a brief cross-questioning of the defendant, who claims to have acted under constraint. This is shown to be unlikely: the past record of Eratosthenes is bad. Moreover, it will do him no good to stress his friendship with Theramenes, who was active in the revolutions of both 411 and 404, for he betrayed the democracy and he paid for his crime by his death.]

What penalty would be adequate payment for the crimes committed?

81 Such are the charges lodged against Eratosthenes and against the friends on whom he will rest his defense and in whose company he has committed these crimes. But justice is not the same for Athens as for Eratosthenes. He was himself both prosecutor and judge of the men he condemned to death, whereas we now are assigned the role of prosecutor and defendant. *82* These men slew without trial men guiltless of any wrong, but you think it right to try according to the law men who destroyed the state, men whom you could not punish as befits their crimes against the state, even if you wished to violate the law. What punishment would be a fitting penalty for their deeds?

83 Would their death and the death of their children be sufficient satisfaction for us whose fathers, sons, and brothers they murdered without a trial? Would the confiscation of their property satisfy either the state, which they robbed wholesale, or the private citizens, whose homes they pillaged? *84* Since, then, no matter what you do you could not exact full justice from them, is it not disgraceful for you to omit any penalty at all that any one may wish to impose upon them?

This is a test case of much importance.

In my opinion, a man would dare any and every thing, who in a court composed of the victims of his lawlessness has come here to plead his cause before the very witnesses of his villainy. Such is the extent of either his scorn for you or else his reliance upon others. *85* You should take both these points into consideration. Reflect that he and his band could not have committed these crimes without assistance, nor would they have undertaken to come here now unless they counted upon the same accomplices to save them. However, those men are here not to lend aid, but rather in the belief that they will enjoy not only full immunity for past crimes but also licence to do whatever they wish in the future, provided that after laying hands upon men guilty of the greatest crimes, you let them go.

86 Moreover, one might well wonder whether those who are to second them in their defense will ask you to favor them on the score of being good and honorable citizens. Will they try to prove that their own merits outweigh the villainy of the accused? I wish they were as eager to preserve the state as the Thirty were to destroy it. Or will they rely upon sophistic rhetoric and try to show that the deeds of these men were most estimable? Not one of them ever attempted to say even what is just in your behalf.

87 The witnesses, too, deserve your notice. In testifying for the defendants they are accusing themselves. They must think you are very forgetful and simple-minded if they imagine that, thanks to this court, they will have nothing to fear in saving the Thirty, when, thanks to Eratosthenes and his associates in crime, men feared even to attend the funeral of their victims. *88* If the Thirty are spared, they might again destroy the state, whereas the men they murdered, once dead, have no more chance of exacting vengeance on their murderers. Is it not shocking, then, that even the friends of those unjustly slain perished with them, while many, I fancy, will come to the funeral of the very ones who destroyed the state—since so many are preparing to come to their rescue.

89 I think it far easier to speak against the Thirty about the wrongs you have suffered than to speak for them about the wrongs they have done. They claim that Eratosthenes has done the least wrong of all the Thirty, and therefore they think he deserves acquittal; but they do not think he deserves death for having sinned against you more than any other Greeks.

90 You must show how you feel about his conduct. If you condemn Eratosthenes, it will be evident that you are angry over what has been done; but if you acquit him, it will be seen that you would like to do the same things they did. Besides, you will not be able to claim you did what the Thirty ordered, (*91*) for now no one is compelling you to vote acquittal contrary to your judgment. Therefore I advise you not to acquit these men and thus condemn yourselves. Do not imagine you are casting a secret ballot. All Athens will know how you voted.

[Lysias concludes his speech with a brief but forceful review of what the members of the jury have suffered at the hands of the Thirty and paints in lurid colors the fate that would have been theirs if they had failed to overthrow them. His final words are justly famous, more terse than any translation can make them: "You have heard; you have seen; you have suffered; you have them in your grasp. Judge."]

ISOCRATES

ISOCRATES (436–338 B.C.) was the son of a prosperous Athenian flute-maker. He received an excellent education, in the course of which he came under the influence of Prodicus and Gorgias and possibly other sophists, to whom in no small measure he was indebted for his literary style. As a youth he had some contact with Socrates and his circle, but when it came to the choice of a career, he selected oratory rather than philosophy, apparently to the disgust of Plato.

At the close of the Peloponnesian War Isocrates, in his early thirties, found it necessary to earn a living. For some time he seems to have supported himself by composing speeches for litigants in the courts. Six such speeches have survived. But his training and temperament led him to abandon that calling, and about the year 390 B.C. he founded a school of oratory in his native city and carried it on to the end of his life. It is safe to say that no school of ancient times attracted a more distinguished clientele, drawn from all parts of the Greek world. His lectures were attended by future generals and statesmen, kings, historians, tragedians, and orators, the last named including four of the canon of Attic Orators: Aeschines, Hyperides, Isaeus, and Lycurgus. Aristotle enrolled with Isocrates at first, but after a brief stay transferred to Plato's Academy. There was much rivalry between the two schools.

A weak voice and a natural diffidence prevented Isocrates from appearing as a speaker on public occasions, but he composed speeches on weighty matters of both local and national interest and used them as models for his students. In those speeches he expounded his views on public policy, a favorite thesis being that the states of Greece should unite under the banner of Philip of Macedon against the barbarian East and thus achieve internal concord and prosperity. Such a Pan-Hellenic dream was not to be made a reality. The patriotic realism of Demosthenes triumphed over the doctrinaire idealism of the professor, and Isocrates did not long survive the national disaster at Chaeronea, dying at the ripe old age of ninety-eight.

If he was a failure as a statesman, his long career as a teacher of oratory enabled him to place his stamp upon the literary style of many men of varied interests, and his influence was felt for generations. His was a highly artificial style of composition, one in which seemingly more attention was paid to elaborately constructed, lengthy sentences, to nicely balanced clauses, to the scrupulous avoidance of everything unpleasing to the ear, and to the cultivation of certain rhythmic cadences than to the profundity of the thought. Wilmer Cave Wright has well said: "But though sentences as long as his have seldom been written, long sentences have at least never been more lucid." [12] On many grounds, not least those of style, it is with him and not with Demosthenes that Cicero should be compared.

Oration VII

THE AREOPAGITICUS

This oration may have been composed as early as 357 B.C. It is a plea for a return to the good old days, symbolized by the Areopagus, that ancient Athenian court which originally was made up of members of the nobility but which had been stripped of its prerogatives and authority, first by Solon and later by Pericles, until its jurisdiction now covered only cases of murder or sacrilege. The evils against which Isocrates inveighs were real enough, but it is doubtful that he hoped that the Areopagus of olden days could actually be revived to cope with them. One must remember that the speech was not really delivered and was not intended to be: it is a political pamphlet in the form of an imaginary speech.

The present power of Athens may lead to disaster.

1 Many of you, I fancy, are wondering what on earth was my purpose in addressing you on the subject of public safety, as if Athens were in danger or its affairs in a shaky condition. On the contrary, it has more than two hundred triremes, it is enjoying peace on land, and it is supreme at sea. *2* Furthermore, we have many allies who will aid us willingly in case of need, and many more who pay us tribute and take our orders. In these circumstances one might say that it is reasonable for us to feel confident, convinced that dangers are remote, and for our enemies to stand in fear and deliberate on the subject of their own safety.

3 If you use this line of reasoning, you feel scornful, I am sure, of what I have come here to tell you, and you expect to dominate all Hellas by this power of yours. On the contrary, these are the very reasons, as it happens, that make me fearful, for in my experience the cities which think they are in the best condition make the worst plans, those which are the most confident find themselves faced with the greatest multitude of perils. *4* The cause of this is that neither good nor evil comes to men distinct and unalloyed.

Closely allied and concomitant with wealth and princely power is folly, and along with folly comes licentiousness; but with poverty and humility there are joined sobriety and temperance, (*5*) so that it is hard to decide which of the two portions one would consent to leave as heritage for his own children. From that which is held to be more commonplace we may observe that conditions generally tend in the direction of improvement, while from that which on the surface appears preferable they habitually alter for the worse.

6 I can supply very many illustrations of this truth from private dealings, for these are subject to very frequent vicissitudes, but more significant and better known to my listeners are the things which have befallen us and the Lacedaemonians. When Athens had been ravaged by the barbarians, because of our anxiety and our close attention to affairs we rose to a position of leadership in Greece, but when we came to believe our might to be invincible, we narrowly escaped becoming slaves. *7* As for the Lacedaemonians, though they started out in insignificant, humble settlements in olden times, because of their sane, martial mode of living they gained control over the Peloponnese; but afterwards they grew more arrogant than they should, and after gaining dominion on both land and sea, they had to face the same dangers as ourselves.

Athens is in far worse condition than in former days.

8 Therefore anyone who knows that so many changes of fortune have taken place and that such mighty powers have been destroyed, and yet trusts to our present status, is very foolish, especially since Athens is in far worse condition now than in those days, and since the Greeks have revived their mutual hatred and their enmity toward the King, to which we owed our downfall in the fighting of that time.

9 I know not whether to assume you care nothing for the common weal or to think that you do care but have grown so callous as not to notice how chaotic affairs in Athens are. That seems to be your attitude. We have lost all the cities in Thrace, we have spent to no purpose more than a thousand talents on mercenary troops, (*10*) we have been maligned to the Greeks and brought into a state of warfare with the barbarian, and, what is more, we have been compelled to try to save our Theban friends but have lost our own allies. And yet in such a sorry state of affairs we have already twice made a thank offering for good news, and in the meetings of the Assembly we deal with these conditions more casually than people do who are in the best possible status.

11 Such behavior and such experiences are what might be expected, for nothing can turn out as it should for men who have not deliberated rightly about the administration as a whole. If they do succeed in some undertakings, either because of the kindness of fortune or through the valor of a man, after a brief respite they are back again in the same straits as before.

The trouble with Athens is that its constitution is not what it should be.

This may be illustrated from our own experience. *12* When all Hellas had fallen under the sway of Athens after Conon's seafight and the campaigns of Timotheus [394 B.C.], we were able to enjoy our successes no time at all, but speedily obscured and did away with them. We do not have a constitution which can deal properly with our affairs, and we do not search for one as we should. *13* Yet we all know that successes are vouchsafed and endure, not because men have encircled themselves with the finest, greatest walls or because they have gathered in the same place with the greatest number of human beings, but rather because they administer their own state most ably and most prudently.

14 The fact is, a city's soul is nothing other than its constitution. It serves the same purpose as the mind in a human body. A constitution is that which deliberates about everything, preserving the good things and avoiding the bad. Laws and statesmen and private citizens necessarily conform to it, and in every instance their fate conforms with their constitution. *15* Now that our constitution has become corrupt, we are not at all concerned, nor do we seek means of improving it. As we sit in our workshops we attack the administration and declare that we were never worse governed under democratic rule, but in our actions and our aims we regard that democracy with more affection than the one left to us by our ancestors. It is in behalf of that democracy that I mean to speak and have composed my address.

We must restore the Solonian constitution.

16 I find that we can ward off the dangers of the future and rid ourselves of our present evils only if we are willing to restore the democracy which Solon, the greatest friend the people ever had, established by his laws and which Clisthenes, after he had expelled the tyrants and had brought the people back to power, re-established. *17* No more democratic constitution than that could be found, nor one more beneficial to the state. Here is the strongest proof. Those who employed that constitution, after accomplishing many noble deeds and winning the acclaim of all mankind, received the leadership by free grant of the nation; but those who became enamored of the one we have today, hated by one and all and the victims of many awful trials, narrowly escaped being involved in the very worst disasters. *18* How should one laud or cherish this form of constitution, which has brought us so many evils in the past and is now getting worse each year? How can one help being fearful that, when our course is steadily getting worse, we may finally run aground upon more jagged rocks of difficulty than the ones encountered in days gone by? *19* In order that your choice and decision regarding these matters may be based, not upon a summary statement, but upon accurate knowledge of details, it is your duty to pay close heed to what I am about to say. I shall try to give you as concise an account of both forms of constitution as I can.

Merits of the Solonian constitution

20 Those who lived in Athens in the days of which I speak [13] established for themselves a constitution which was not merely nominally most democratic and kindly but actually found to be otherwise by those who had experience of it, nor yet one which trained the citizens to believe that intemperance means democracy, lawlessness, liberty, freedom of speech political equality, and licence to indulge in such practices true happiness. No, that constitution hated and punished such persons and thus made all the citizens better and more temperate.

21 What contributed most to the good management of Athens is that, though there were held to be two forms of equality,[14] the one distributing alike to all, the other only what was appropriate for each, the people did not fail to understand which is the more useful. Equality which holds that good and bad are worthy of the same rights was rejected as unjust, (*22*) but equality which honors each citizen according to his worth was adopted and used in the administering of the state. Athens did not choose officials by lot from among all the people, but picked out the best and the most efficient for each function. She hoped that the rest of the citizens would be like the men who were in charge of the administration.

23 Besides, this system was thought to be more democratic than election by lot. In election by lot luck would act as umpire, and often the oligarchic party would obtain the offices, but by giving preference to the most capable the people would have the authority to select the men who had the greatest affection for the established constitution.

24 The reason why the majority were satisfied with this system and did not fight over the offices is that they had learned to work and save and not to neglect their own property and conspire against that of others, not to use public funds for private ends but, in case of need, to support the general welfare out of what each possessed, and not to have more precise knowledge of the income to be derived from the magistracies than of the income from their private business.

25 They held aloof from public affairs to such an extent that in those days it was harder to find men willing to accept office than it is today to find men who do not beg to do so. They believed that attending to public business was not a merchandising activity but a public service. They did not on their first day in office go and look to see if their predecessors had left them any profits. What they wanted to find out was whether any business that urgently called for completion had been neglected. *26* In a word, they saw clearly that the people must set up its officials in the manner of a tyrant and punish the wrongdoers and pass judgment regarding matters in dispute. They saw, too, that men in a position to live at ease, men with sufficient livelihood, must look after the public interests as servants of the state, and if they proved honest they should be praised and rest content with that reward, (*27*) but if they had been bad stewards they must obtain no pardon but be punished most severely. How could one find a democracy more secure and just than this, which placed in charge of its affairs the most competent, but gave the people authority over these very ones?

28 This was the form of constitution those men had, and so it is easy to understand that they consistently managed their daily business correctly and in conformity with tradition. Inevitably those who adopted honorable principles concerning the administration as a whole would behave in like manner respecting their individual share in it.

[In every way the government of Athens was at its best when the Areopagus was supreme. Religious rites were duly and soberly observed; humanity and honesty governed commercial relations, and the citizens, whose character was under the surveillance of the Council, were virtuous and honorable. The education of the young men was regulated with an eye to the position they would later fill. As a result, manners were purer, and in her relations to the rest of the world Athens was more secure. The prosperity of the city was judged, not by the ostentation of the public spectacles, but by the sane administration of the state, by the daily life of the citizens, and by everyone's having what was needful. Isocrates disclaims any desire to bring about a revolution; his whole purpose is to reform the democracy. He contrasts the moderation and righteousness of the restored democracy with the excesses and wickedness of the oligarchy of the Thirty.]

76 Let no one imagine that this eulogy of mine has to do with the men who now run our government. Quite the contrary. Such words are in commendation of men who show themselves worthy of their valiant ancestors, but in denunciation of those who by their indifference and baseness dishonor their noble lineage. That is precisely what we are doing—for the truth must be spoken. Endowed as we are with so fine a nature, we have failed to safeguard it, but have fallen into folly and confusion and a passion for wicked ventures. *77* However, if I follow up what is open to censure and denunciation in our present conduct, I fear I shall wander too far from my theme. I have spoken of these things before and I shall speak of them again, unless I persuade you to cease making such mistakes. When I have discussed briefly the matters on which I based my address in the first instance, I am stepping aside for those who wish to counsel you further about these things.

78 If we continue to manage the state as we are doing now, inevitably we shall plan and fight and live and, in virtually all respects, act and be acted upon precisely as at present and in the years that have preceded. But if we change our constitution, by the same reckoning clearly our situation will be just like that of our forefathers, for from the same policies there must always result the same or similar outcomes. *79* We must place the most important of them side by side and then consider which are the ones for us to choose.

Let us return to the good old days when Athens was prosperous at home and respected abroad.

First of all, let us consider the Greeks and the barbarians, to see how they felt toward that early form of government, and how they feel toward us today. You see, those peoples contribute no small share to our prosperity when they feel toward us as they should. *80* Now then, the Greeks felt such confidence in our government in former times that most of them voluntarily entrusted Athens with their lives and fortune. The barbarians were so far from meddling in Greek affairs that they did not sail with war ships this side of Phaselis, and they did not move their armies this side of the Halys river but kept very quiet. *81* But now our affairs have experienced such a change that the Greeks hate Athens and the barbarians despise us. How the Greeks hate us you have heard from our generals themselves; how the Great King feels toward us he has made plain through the letters he has sent.

82 Besides, in addition to all this, under the good conditions of former days our citizens were so reared in the direction of moral excellence that they did not harm one another and yet conquered in battle all who tried to invade their land. Today it is the reverse. We do not let a day go by without making trouble for one another, but we have so neglected military matters that we do not have the grace to attend reviews unless we are paid for it. *83* But here comes the most important point of all. In former times no citizen lacked the necessaries of life, and none disgraced his city by begging from those who met him; now the needy are more numerous than the prosperous, and they deserve much forbearance if they take no thought at all for the common welfare but consider only how to exist from day to day.

84 Now then, it is in the belief that if we imitate our ancestors we shall get rid of these evils and save both Athens and the whole Greek world that I have prepared this address and spoken these words. It is for you, after due consideration of all these things, to vote as you decide will be for the best interest of our state.

AESCHINES

AESCHINES was the son of an Athenian who had suffered exile at the hands of the Thirty and who, after serving as soldier of fortune in Asia Minor, established himself as schoolmaster in his native city. We need not accept at face value all that Demosthenes said about Aeschines in later years, yet it is plain that he was a self-made man. In early manhood he for a time played minor tragic roles in provincial theaters, but either tiring of that life or meeting with indifferent success as an actor, he deserted the stage to take a job as clerk of the Assembly. He seems never to have pursued formal instruction in rhetoric, but both stage and Assembly were well suited to develop such gifts for public speaking as nature had granted him. He is said to have had a good presence, a fine voice, and a notable ability to speak without previous preparation.

Aeschines entered politics at the age of thirty-two, but we hear little of his activities in that field until Philip of Macedon began to claim his attention. After denouncing Philip in connection with the seizure of Olynthus in 348 B.C., two years later as an envoy of Athens at the Macedonian court he appears to have experienced a sudden change of heart. Whether because he believed it to be for the best interest of Athens or because, as Demosthenes never tired of charging, he had succumbed to Philip's blandishments and bribery, from then on he was an active member of the pro-Macedonian party and a remorseless foe of Demosthenes. Their feud accounts for most of the fame that Aeschines has today.

In the year 336 Ctesiphon, who had introduced a motion to award Demosthenes a golden crown for his services to Athens, was indicted by Aeschines on the charge of including illegal proposals in that motion. He was the ostensible object of attack, but in reality Aeschines was challenging Demosthenes, who took up the gauntlet in his famous oration *On the Crown*. When the matter came before the jury in 330 B.C., though from a legal point of view the case of Ctesiphon appears to have been weak, Aeschines had made the mistake of stressing the career of Demosthenes, and the speech *On the Crown* was so powerful a defense of that career that the plaintiff failed to secure the prescribed number of votes, was fined a thousand drachmas, and withdrew from Athens to spend his remaining days as a teacher of rhetoric at Rhodes.

The speech *Against Ctesiphon* has always suffered by comparison with the reply of Demosthenes. It is vigorous and lively, it displays a power of invective which clearly stung the speaker's more polished antagonist, but one's sympathies go rather to Demosthenes, whom one instinctively admires as the champion of Greek liberty against foreign aggression, and whose patriotic utterances sound more genuine.

Oration III

AGAINST CTESIPHON

[By way of preamble, Aeschines charges that political scheming has long threatened the welfare of the democracy. Unconstitutional proposals are being put to a vote in the Assembly in contravention of justice and traditional procedure. If a member of the Council whose duty it is to preside at such a meeting announces the vote correctly, he is threatened with impeachment. Neither laws nor Prytanes nor presiding officers have been able to protect the democracy, and therefore recourse must be had to indictments for unconstitutionality. If it is proved that Ctesiphon has proposed a measure which is unconstitutional, fallacious, and harmful to the state, the vote approving it must be rescinded and the politicians must be punished who act contrary to the laws, the state, and the interests of the people.]

9 What I have said by way of preface regarding my accusation as a whole is, I trust, sufficient; but I wish to speak briefly regarding the laws themselves which deal with persons subject to audit, laws which Ctesiphon, as it happens, has violated in his resolution.

It is against the law to award a crown to a man who has not yet passed his audit.

In days gone by certain persons who held highest office and administered state revenues, and accepted bribes in each of these capacities, won over in advance the speakers in Council and

Assembly, and thus by eulogies and proclamations tried to frustrate the auditing of their accounts. Consequently in examining officials the accusers, but even more the judges, encountered the greatest difficulty. *10* Very many who were subject to investigation, though notorious embezzlers of public funds, when tried in court escaped conviction, as was to be expected. The jurors, I imagine, felt ashamed to have it become known that the same man in the same city, and possibly in the same year, had been heralded as the recipient of a golden crown from the people as a reward of virtue and honesty but after a brief interval, had left the courtroom convicted of embezzlement. Thus they were forced to cast their ballots, not with reference to the crime they were to judge, but rather in support of the people's honor.

11 In view of this situation a certain lawgiver established a law, and a very good one too, expressly forbidding the award of a crown to men who had not yet passed their audit. But despite these precautions of the lawgiver, arguments have been invented which will deceive you unawares unless someone forewarns you.

Ctesiphon has not even taken refuge in a formula sometimes employed in such cases.

Some who propose to crown men subject to audit are respectable persons, if indeed anyone is respectable who proposes what is illegal. However that may be, these men cloak their shame in a measure by including in their proposals in such cases the clause, "when he shall have given an accounting of his office." *12* Yet the state is the victim of the same wrong-doing, for the audit is prejudiced by eulogies and crowns. The mover of the resolution makes it plain to his hearers that he has proposed what is illegal and is ashamed of his crime. But Ctesiphon, men of Athens, overstepping the law which deals with men still subject to audit, not resorting to the subterfuge of which I have just told you, has proposed to crown Demosthenes before he has presented a statement, before he has submitted to an audit, in the very midst of his term of office!

Aeschines examines minutely the argument that Demosthenes is not an official but merely a commissioner, and hence not subject to the law.

13 But they will offer a further argument, one quite different from the one just mentioned, to the effect that any duties a person performs in consequence of election by decree do not constitute an office but rather a commission, a service. They will claim that officials are men whom the Thesmothetae choose by lot in the Theseum, together with those whom the Assembly is accustomed to select by show of hands—generals, cavalry commanders, and members of their staff—but that these other activities are appointments in consequence of a decree.

14 To combat these arguments I shall present a law of yours which you passed in the belief that it would do away with such pretexts. In this law it is expressly written, "the officials chosen by show of hands"—the lawgiver including under the single term "officials" all whom the Assembly chooses by show of hands—"and also the supervisors of the public works"—Demosthenes is a commissioner of fortifications, a supervisor of the most important work of all—"and all who conduct any municipal undertaking for a period of more than thirty days, as well as all who receive jurisdiction over courts of law." Supervisors of public works all exercise jurisdiction over a court. What does the law bid them do? Not render a service, (*15*) but hold office, after first securing court approval. Even officials chosen by lot are not exempt from securing such approval; they cannot hold office until they are approved. Furthermore, they are ordered to file a statement and an account with the clerk and the board of auditors, just like all other officials. In proof of what I say, the clerk will read you the laws themselves.

[After dealing with the purely legal aspects of the prosecution, Aeschines begins what must have been for him the core of his attack, an arraignment of the whole career of Demosthenes. One forgets that Ctesiphon is the nominal defendant in the suit.]

Ctesiphon's praise of Demosthenes is false.

There remains for me a part of my accusation in which I am particularly interested, namely, the pretext on account of which Ctesiphon thinks Demosthenes worthy of a crown. This is what he says in his resolution: "and let the Herald proclaim in the theater before the assembled Greeks that the people of Athens are crowning him as a reward of virtue and good citizenship," and most serious of all, "because he always says and does what is best for the democracy."

50 What I have to say next is thus made quite simple for me and quite easy for you to pass upon when you have heard it. My duty as accuser is to show you that this praise of Demosthenes is false, that he did not begin to say what is best and that he does not now continually do what is to the interest of the people. If I show this, Ctesiphon will richly deserve conviction, for all the laws prescribe that no one shall include false statements in public decrees. The defendant must show the opposite of this. You will be the judges of what we say.

Alleged scandals cited in the career of Demosthenes

[Aeschines refers briefly but pointedly to several incidents in the life of Demosthenes which he treats as scandalous and in contradiction to the laudatory statements made by Ctesiphon.]

53 These items and others of similar nature I think I shall pass over, not because I am betraying your interests or compromising my suit, but because I fear I may find that, though you may credit the truth of what I say, you may deem it ancient history and too well recognized. And yet, Ctesiphon, when the most shameful conduct is so credible, so well known to the hearers, that the accuser gives the impression of telling not what is false but what is stale and thoroughly admitted in advance, ought the perpetrator of such crimes be rewarded with a golden crown or be censured? Ought you, who have the effrontery to write what is false and illegal, be permitted to flout the courts or be punished by the state?

The public career of Demosthenes bitterly attacked

54 I am going to speak more bluntly regarding the public misdeeds of Demosthenes, for I learn that when the defense gets its chance to present its case, he intends to recount to you that the state has already faced four crises [15] in which he was active in public affairs. One of these, the first on his list as I hear, is the period when we were at war with Philip over Amphipolis. This he delimits by the treaty of peace and alliance which Philocrates of Hagnus drew up, together with Demosthenes himself, as I shall show. *55* His second period is that during which we were observing the peace, that is to say, down to that fateful day when this same orator broke the peace which Athens then enjoyed and introduced a resolution which brought about the war. The third is our war period down to the unfortunate affair of Chaeronea. Fourth, our present situation. He will list these, as I hear, and then call upon me and ask which of these four periods of his I denounce and at what time I claim he did not sponsor the best policies for the state. He says that if I am unwilling to reply but hide my face and try to evade him, he will come and unmask me and lead me to the stand and force me to answer.

56 Now then, in order that he may not resort to force, and that you may know in advance, and that I may make reply, in the presence of your judges, Demosthenes, and of all the other citizens who stand outside about the courthouse, in the presence also of all the Greeks who have made it their business to listen to this trial—and I see no few are present, but a throng such as no one can remember ever having attended a public trial—I answer that I denounce all four of your periods, Demosthenes. *57* If the gods are willing and the judges gives me an impartial hearing and I can recall to mind what I know about you, I am quite confident that I shall show the court that it was the gods who saved Athens, along with those who handled the city's affairs in a spirit of benevolence and moderation, and that Demosthenes has been to blame for all its misfortunes.

[Aeschines proceeds to take up one by one the periods which he says Demosthenes plans to use in support of his claim to honor. He accuses him of servile behavior toward Philip, of accepting his bribes, of treasonable conduct in negotiating the peace of Philocrates, of double dealing with the states of Greece, and finally of falsehood in claiming that Aeschines had brought Philip into the war over Amphissa.]

130 Nay, did not the gods foretell it, did they not warn us to be on our guard, all but assuming human speech? I have never seen a state which the gods did more to save, and certain orators to destroy. Was not what was witnessed at the Mysteries sufficient warning to be on our guard—the death of the initiates? [16] Did not Aminiades warn us to be careful in this connection and to send to Delphi to inquire of the god what should be done? But Demosthenes opposed him and said the priestess was a partisan of Philip, boorish creature that he was, who took undue advantage of the licence you allowed him! *131* When finally the sacrifices proved not acceptable or propitious, did he not send forth the soldiers to encounter manifest peril? Yet only recently he had the presumption to declare that the reason why Philip did not invade Attica is that the omens were not favorable for him. What punishment do you deserve to suffer, you accursed plague to Greece? If the conqueror did not enter the country of the conquered because the omens were not favorable, but you sent forth the soldiers before receiving favorable omens, ought you be crowned for the misfortunes of Athens or ought you instead be driven beyond its borders?

132 What unexpected, what unlooked-for happening has not taken place in our time? Our life has not been the life of human beings. Nay, we are fated to be a source of wonder for future generations to prate about. Is it not true that the King of Persia, who dug a canal across Athos, who bridged the Hellespont, who demanded from the Greeks earth and water, who dared in his letters to write that he was lord of all mankind from the rising of the sun to the setting thereof, is it not true that he is now fighting, not to be lord of others, but to save his own person? And do we see the same people who actually liberated the sanctuary at Delphi deemed worthy of that distinction and of leadership against the Persian? *133* Nay, Thebes, Thebes, our neighbor, in a single day has been destroyed from the midst of Hellas! Their fate may have been deserved for having been ill-advised regarding our national interest, yet their infatuation, their madness, arose from no human agency but by the will of heaven. Again, the wretched Lacedaemonians, because they only took a hand at the start in these operations connected with the seizure of the shrine at Delphi,[17] the Lacedaemonians who once claimed the right to lead the Greeks, now are doomed to be sent to Alexander as his hostages and to provide a spectacle of their misfortune, both they and their country destined to suffer whatever suits his pleasure. They will be judged with the moderation of the conqueror, of the man whom they had previously injured!

134 And our own city, the common refuge of the Greek nation, the city to which in former times came the embassies of all Hellas, each city severally seeking to secure from us its salvation, now no longer is contending for the leadership of the Greeks but actually for the very soil of the fatherland! These misfortunes of ours date from the time when Demosthenes entered public life.

[In his peroration Aeschines taunts Ctesiphon with being the tool of Demosthenes and asks why he feels it necessary to have Demosthenes speak in his defense. Demosthenes is a bribe-taker, a coward, a deserter, a bad influence in the state. To acquit Ctesiphon will mean to crown Demosthenes, and the jurors will thus suffer in the eyes of their children and their fellow citizens, and Athens will be thought as base as the man whom it has crowned.]

255 Then do not deliberate as if in behalf of an alien city but as for your very own. Do not hand out your honors indiscriminately, but on the basis of sound judgment. Reserve your awards for better persons, more noteworthy men. Trust not alone to your ears, but scrutinize yourselves carefully with your eyes and then consider who among you are the ones who will rescue Demosthenes. Will it be those with whom he used to hunt or with whom he practised athletics in his prime? Nay, by Zeus of Olympus, he has passed his life not hunting wild boars or attending to his physical well-being but practising tricks on men of substance. *256* Have an eye for his bombast when he claims that it was his services as envoy which snatched Byzantium from Philip's clutches, stirred Acarnania to revolt,[18] and amazed the Thebans by his claptrap. He imagines you are such simpletons as to swallow even these statements, as if, indeed, you were nurturing in Athens Mistress Persuasion herself and not a blackmailer!

Solon, Aristides, and Themistocles are invoked as witnesses against the court in case it decides in favor of the defendant.

257 When at last he reaches the conclusion of his speech and calls upon his associates in corruption to second it, imagine that you behold upon the platform where I now stand and speak those who of old did well by Athens. There they stand, holding their ground against the licentious scoundrels. Behold there Solon, who adorned the democracy with most beautiful laws, a philosopher and noble lawgiver, beseeching you soberly, as would become him, never to rate the eloquence of Demosthenes higher than your oaths and laws. *258* There, too, behold Aristides, who established for the Greeks what taxes they should pay, Aristides whose daughter the state gave in marriage at his death. He utters indignant protests at the disgraceful abuse of justice and asks if you are not ashamed that Arthmius of Zelea, who brought to Greece the Persian gold, Arthmius who had visited Athens and was an official representative of our democracy, your fathers very nearly stoned to death and banished from Athens and from every land over which Athens has control, (*259*) whereas Demosthenes, who did not bring the Persian gold but accepted bribes and has them still today, is about to be honored with a golden crown. As for Themistocles and the heroes who died at Marathon and Plataea, think you not that they will groan aloud if the man who admits that he sided with the barbarians and worked against the Greeks is to receive a crown?

260 Well then, O Earth and Sun and Virtue and Intelligence and Education, by whose aid we distinguish between the honorable and the disgraceful, I have lent my help, I have spoken. If I have made my accusation well and in a manner befitting the crime, I have spoken as I wished to speak, but if less ably, then as best I could. But do you judges, on the basis both of what has been said and of what is left unsaid, in behalf of our city, vote that which is just and for its welfare.

DEMOSTHENES

Demosthenes was the son of a wealthy Athenian maker of armor. Born in 384 B.C., he witnessed the overthrow of Spartan power at Leuctra, then a brief period of Theban leadership under Epaminondas, and finally the subjugation of all Greece to Macedon. Stouthearted and tireless foe of Philip's aggression, he was fated to behold the collapse of all his hopes to preserve Greek liberty and Athenian honor, and rather than endure an ignominious death at the hands of the Macedonian overlord, he took his own life in 322 B.C.

His early youth gave no hint of the brilliant career as orator and statesman that was to be his. Nature had given him a frail body, an impediment in his speech, and the timidity that might well accompany such handicaps. His father died when Demosthenes was not yet eight years old, leaving his estate to be administered by three kinsmen. Their mismanagement of the trust inspired the lad with the determination to secure redress through the courts. The iron will that was so characteristic a trait during his whole life enabled him to master his physical handicaps; he is said to have acquired the fundamentals of public speaking from a famous actor, and some knowledge of legal procedure from Isaeus, a specialist in the law of inheritance; and at the age of twenty, when at last permitted by law to plead his own case in court, he filed suit against Aphobus and, despite the obstacles thrown in his way by that wily guardian, eventually, by the vehemence and technical skill of his oratory, secured a favorable verdict.

He seems to have recovered very little of the inheritance that should have been his, but his training in preparation for the trial and the experience and fame gained from it were to prove more valuable than any wealth he may have hoped to salvage. His services as a writer of speeches for others were in great demand, and his success in that field ultimately led him to take a prominent part in state affairs. Ten years after the trial of Aphobus he began to appear in person in public causes, and from then until his death he exerted a powerful influence in law court and Assembly. He was the ablest leader of the anti-Macedonian party, and his fame today rests chiefly on the speeches he delivered in the cause of Greek liberty. The term Philippic owes its origin and connotation to a group of such speeches, and his speech *On the Crown,* in which he successfully defended his whole career against the violent attack of his political adversary Aeschines, is universally acclaimed as a masterpiece of Attic eloquence.

The qualities which distinguish his work at its best are earnestness, patriotic fervor, lofty idealism, bitter invective, biting sarcasm. Less capable of portrayal in translation is his unrivalled mastery of word and phrase, but Dionysius the literary critic, writing three centuries after the death of Demosthenes, has this to say of the effect he experienced in merely reading the speeches: "When I take up any speech of Demosthenes I am entranced. I am borne this way and that, experiencing one emotion after another—disbelief, anxiety, fear, scorn, hatred, compassion, benevolence, anger, envy, all the emotions that sway the mind of man. . . . And I have been moved to wonder what must have been the experience of men of his day as they heard him speak these words, if we who are so far removed in point of time and have had no connection with the doings with which he deals are so enthralled and overpowered and carried along wherever the speech leads us. . . ."

Oration IX

The Third Philippic

Philip of Macedon year by year had been extending his empire in the north and by intrigue and corruption had obtained a foothold in many parts of Greece. There had been no formal declaration of war, but Demosthenes foresaw that war must come and tried repeatedly to rouse his countrymen to a sense of reality. But Philip's partisans in Athens, notably Aeschines, had made his task difficult. At last in 341 B.C., three years before the disastrous battle of Chaeronea, Demosthenes delivered his *Third Philippic* in the Assembly and won both a personal triumph and a victory for the policies of the patriotic party. Some have regarded that speech as his masterpiece.

1 Men of Athens, many speeches are delivered in almost every session of the Assembly regarding the crimes Philip has been committing ever since he made the peace, not merely against you but against the others as well. All, I am sure, even if they refrain from doing so, might well say that our words and acts should aim to compel him to abandon his wanton insolence and make amends. Yet, I observe, our undertakings are so misdirected and neglected that, even if it be blasphemy to say so, I fear it is true that, were all who address you eager to propose, and you to adopt, measures bound to result in the most deplorable conditions, we could not be worse off than we are today.

Individual selfishness is crippling Athens.

2 Many factors, no doubt, are responsible for this state of things. Our fortunes have not reached this pass through any one or two. But if you examine our situation aright, you will find it is due chiefly to those who aim to please their hearers rather than to tell them what is best for them to hear. Some of these, studying to preserve the foundations of their own popularity and power, have no regard for the future and therefore think you need have none, either. Others accuse and slander men in public life and devote their efforts to making Athens punish Athens and be absorbed in that activity, so that Philip may be free to undertake and accomplish his desires.

Candor versus flattery

3 Such policies are familiar to you, but they are the source of your troubles. Therefore, men of Athens, if I speak to you with some candor, pray do not be angry with me on that account. You see, you hold that in other matters free speech is an essential privilege of all in Athens. You have even allowed foreigners and slaves to share in that privilege, and servants may often be seen saying what they please with greater licence than citizens in some other states; yet you have banished it completely when it is a question of offering you advice. *4* Accordingly in meetings of the Assembly you are spoiled and flattered, every word spoken being aimed to please you, though in your enterprises and experiences you are already in extreme peril. If you are of that frame of mind today as well, I know not what to say; but if you will consent to listen to what is for your welfare, devoid of flattery, I am ready to speak.

Athenian inertia responsible for present conditions

If our affairs are in very bad shape and many interests have been sacrificed, still if you will do your duty all this may yet be rectified. *5* What I am about to say may surprise you, but still it is true. The worst feature of your past dealings turns out to be the best augury for the future. And what is this? It is that your sorry plight results from your doing nothing, either great or small, that you should have done. If things were in this state despite your doing your whole duty, there would not be even a hope of their improvement. As it is, Philip has vanquished your inertia, your indifference, not Athens. You have not been beaten; you have not even budged. . . .

[Demosthenes protests that he is not a warmonger, but those who still believe Greece is enjoying peace are deluded. Philip has carefully avoided a declaration of war, but ever since the peace treaty was signed he has been busy throughout Greece waging actual war and gradually making himself master of the Greek people. They, Athens included, have allowed him to do in thirteen years what neither Athens nor Sparta nor Thebes had attempted during their much longer hegemony. His arrogant conduct knows no bounds, and yet each Greek state treats his aggression as if it were a hailstorm, which they severally pray may not strike them. Yet none is so far off as to escape his onslaught.]

Ancient Athens intolerant of corruption

36 What is the cause of these events? Not without reason and just cause were the Greeks of old so ready to defend their freedom but now so resolved on servitude. Men of Athens, there was then something in the spirit of the people which is not there now, something which overcame even Persian gold and kept Hellas free, something which admitted defeat on neither land nor sea. Now the loss of that has ruined everything and made chaos of our affairs. *37* What was that thing? Nothing involved or tricky. It was just that one and all hated those who accepted bribes from men who aimed to rule or ruin Hellas. To be convicted of taking bribes was a most grievous crime; yes, they punished the guilty one with the utmost severity, and there was no room for intercession or pardon. *38* Therefore the right moment for achieving each enterprise, the opportunity Fortune often extends even to the indifferent at the expense of the vigilant, could not be bought from statesman or from general, any more than could our mutual good will, our distrust of tyrants and foreigners, or any such thing at all. *39* But now these possessions have been sold off like market wares, and in exchange there have been imported things which have brought ruin and disease to Hellas.

And what are these things? Envy, if a man has received a bribe; laughter, if he admits it; indulgence for a man proved guilty; hatred for his critic; and all the other things that come from bribery. *40* As for warships, troops, abundance of funds and equipment, and all else that may be held to form the strength of our cities, in every instance they are present in greater abundance and extent than in days gone by. But all this is being made useless, unavailing, unprofitable because of those who traffic in them. . . .

[After calling attention to the misfortunes of certain Greek states which had already fallen into Philip's clutches through listening to his agents and hoping to fare better through being subservient, Demosthenes continues.]

Athenian complacency and self-seeking disastrous.

67 It is folly and cowardice to indulge in such hopes and, though ill-advised and unwilling to do anything you should, but lending an ear to those who speak in favor of the enemy, to believe that you dwell in a city of such size that, come what may, you will suffer nothing dreadful. *68* It is disgraceful to say after the event: "Who could have imagined this would happen? By Zeus, we should have done thus and so, and have avoided that." The Olynthians could mention many things today the knowledge of which at the time would have prevented their ruin. So could the people of Oreus; so could the Phocians; so could each of the peoples which have been ruined.

69 But what is the good of all this? So long as the ship is safe, be it large or small, that is the time when sailor, pilot, every man in turn, must be alert and look to see that no one, wittingly or unwittingly, capsize it. When the sea has broken over it, efforts are fruitless. *70* We too, then, men of Athens, while we are safe, while we still have a mighty city, abundant resources, fairest reputation—what shall we do? Perhaps some one seated in this assembly has been longing to put that question. I will tell you, by heavens. I will even offer a resolution, and you may adopt it if you will.

Definite proposals for defense of Athens

First, let us ourselves take steps for our defense, let us equip ourselves—I mean with ships and funds and troops—for though all others consent to be slaves, we at least must fight for our freedom. *71* When we have provided ourselves with all these things and have made them matters of public knowledge, then let us issue a call to the others and send envoys everywhere to spread the news—to the Peloponnese, to Rhodes, to Chios, yes, to the Persian King, for it is not wholly unconnected with his interests that Philip be prevented from becoming master of the world. Thus if you persuade those people, you will have partners to share expenses and perils in case of need; otherwise you will at least gain time for your operations. *72* Since the war is against an individual and not against the might of a consolidated state, even that has its advantage. Last year's missions to the Peloponnese were not fruitless, nor the accusations with which I and our noble Polyeuctus yonder and Hegesippus and the other envoys made the rounds of the country. We made Philip hold back and neither attack Ambracia nor set out for the Peloponnese.

Athens must exert herself.

73 However, I do not bid you summon the others if you yourselves are unwilling to do anything needful in your own behalf. It is folly to neglect your own interests and then profess concern for the interests of others, to try to frighten others about the future while quite indifferent as to the present. No, that is not my proposal. What I say is that we must send funds to the forces in the Chersonese and do everything else they think fitting; we must ourselves make preparations; we must assemble the rest of the Greeks, get them together, instruct and admonish them. These are the measures appropriate for a state which has the high repute of Athens.

74 If you imagine Chalcidians or Megarians are going to save Hellas while you evade the issue, you are mistaken, for we can be very thankful if they each save their own necks. No, this task is for you to perform. Your forefathers gained and bequeathed this right to you at the cost of many mighty perils. *75* If each one of you is going to sit with folded hands, seeking to satisfy his own desires and not planning to do anything himself, in the first place he will never find the persons who will do the work, and secondly, we may find it necessary, I fear, to do all at once everything we do not wish.

76 This is my proposal, this is my resolution. I believe that even now if these steps are taken our situation may be rectified. If anyone has anything better to suggest, let him speak and give us his advice. Whatever you decide, God grant it turn out to your salvation.

Oration XVIII

On the Crown

In the year following Philip's victory at Chaeronea in 338 B.C., Athens decided to strengthen her fortifications. Demosthenes, the proposer of the measure, was chosen by his tribe as one of the commissioners to execute the work. In 336 Ctesiphon introduced before the Council the proposal to award Demosthenes a golden crown in the theater at the performance of new tragedies "because he always says and does what is for the best interest of Athens."

Aeschines, who had become a bitter political foe of Demosthenes, was quick to object that the proposal was contrary to the law on three counts: first, a man must not be honored by the state until he had presented an audit of his conduct in office; second, the award of a crown must not take place in the theater; and third, it was untrue that Demosthenes always spoke and acted for the best interest of Athens. Therefore he indicted Ctesiphon for unconstitutional behavior. The first two counts in the indictment seem to have been legally valid, but it was the third count upon which Aeschines laid the greatest stress, arguing that it was forbidden to introduce into a public document an untrue statement. It was plain that he was aiming at Demosthenes and not really at Ctesiphon in the suit that he was bringing.

Although Attic law required both parties to a suit to address the court in person, it permitted friends to second the speeches of the litigants, and it was as a friend of Ctesiphon that Demosthenes delivered his speech *On the Crown.* In that speech Demosthenes, seeing clearly that the purpose of Aeschines was to discredit him, pays slight attention to the legal aspects of the case but devotes most of his attention to reviewing his public and private life and to contrasting it with that of his enemy. The verdict of the court was so decisive in favor of the defendant that Aeschines withdrew from Athens.

1 Men of Athens, I pray to all the gods and goddesses, first of all, that the good will which I have always cherished for the state and for you all I may in like measure receive at your hands for this trial; and secondly, that they may implant in your breasts that which most concerns you and your reputation for piety, the determination not to let my adversary dictate to you how you must hear me—for that would be outrageous—(2) but rather to be guided by the laws and by the oath you have sworn. In that oath, in addition to the other points of justice, is the promise to hear both sides alike. That means not merely never prejudging a case, not merely granting an equal measure of good will to both, but also allowing each to arrange his arguments and make his defense as he has determined and elected in advance.

The handicaps under which Demosthenes labors in the present trial

3 There are many points in which Aeschines has the advantage of me in this suit, but two are of great importance. In the first place, I have more at stake. It is more serious for me to fail to win your favor today than for him to fail to win his case. I—but I do not wish to say anything unpropitious in beginning my speech—whereas he has me at a disadvantage in making his accusation. My second handicap is that all men naturally enjoy listening to abusive language and accusations but are irked by self-laudation. *4* Of these two styles of argument, the one which tends to please the listener falls to the lot of Aeschines, while the one which disgusts virtually everybody is left for me. If in my effort to avoid displeasing I refrain from speaking of my achievements and policies, you will infer that I cannot refute his charges or show why I think I deserve to be honored. But if I discuss my achievements and policies, I shall often be compelled to speak about myself. I shall try to do so with the utmost moderation; but Aeschines, who instituted such a law suit, deserves the blame for whatever the situation itself makes necessary.

5 I believe, men of Athens, you all would agree that this trial concerns Ctesiphon and me in common. It merits as serious attention on my part as on his. To be deprived of anything is distressing and painful, especially at the hands of an enemy, but it is most distressing to be deprived of your good will and benevolence, just as it is of extreme importance to obtain them.

6 These are the issues involved in the present trial, and so I ask and entreat you all alike, as I defend myself against his charges, to give me a fair hearing as the laws prescribe. Solon, who instituted those laws in the first instance, being well disposed to you and a champion of the democracy, believed they should be binding not merely because he had framed them but also because the jurors have sworn to uphold them. Not, I believe, that he distrusted you, (*7*) but he saw that the charges and the slanders on which the plaintiff relies as being the first to address the court cannot be overcome unless each of you judges, preserving the sanctity of his oath, gives a kindly reception also to the points of justice urged by the second speaker and bases his verdict regarding the case as a whole upon a fair and impartial hearing of both sides.

8 And now that apparently I am to give today an account of both my whole private life and also my public policies, I wish once more to invoke the gods and in your presence pray, first, that in this trial I may receive the same measure of good will that I have always had for the state and for you all, and secondly, that the gods may inspire you to make such a decision regarding this trial as is destined to contribute to your good name as a people and to your respect for religion as individuals.

[Aeschines had introduced in his speech malicious slanders having nothing to do with the case against Ctesiphon. These must be disposed of first. Therefore Demosthenes recalls the events leading up to the Peace of Philocrates and Philip's behavior with reference to that peace, charging Aeschines with having been Philip's tool in lulling Athens into a false sense of security.]

42 But I have embarked upon topics which perhaps are more appropriate for later presentation. Accordingly I shall return to my proofs that these men have been responsible for the troubles that we face today.

Aeschines accused of selling out to Philip

When you had been deceived by Philip through the agency of these men, who when serving as your envoys hired themselves out to him and brought back here utterly false reports, and when the poor Phocians had been tricked and their cities destroyed, what happened? *43* The disgusting Thessalians and thick-witted Thebans regarded Philip as friend, benefactor, savior. He was all in all in their eyes. They would not listen to a word if you wished to say anything different.

Philip, though nominally at peace, prepares for war.

But you Athenians, though suspicious and resentful of these transactions, still kept the peace, for there was nothing you could do. The other Greeks, too, though swindled like yourselves and cheated of their hopes, kept the peace. Yet for a long time they had, in a certain sense, been the victim of hostilities. *44* Philip had been moving about, subduing Illyrians and Triballians, and even some Greeks. He had been getting control of many large forces. Certain individuals from the Greek states, and among them Aeschines, had been trudging north with the freedom that the peace conferred and accepting Philip's bribes. Already, therefore, those against whom he had been making these preparations were involved in war.

Bribe-taking and local selfishness ruinous

That they were not aware of this is another story and does not concern me. *45* I was continually warning and protesting both in Athens and everywhere I was sent. But the Greek states were in a bad way. Politicians and statesmen were taking bribes and succumbing to the lure of gold, while the private citizens, the masses, either lacked foresight, or else were ensnared by the comfort and freedom of their daily existence. Moreover, everybody was under the delusion that the danger which was on its way would not reach himself, but that by sacrificing the rest of Greece he would be able to protect his own interest at will. *46* Therefore it turns out that the masses have bought their untimely carefree life at the expense of their liberty, and their leaders, who imagined they were selling everything but themselves, have come to realize that they sold themselves first of all. Instead of "friends" and "associates," which is what they were called while they were receiving their bribes, they now are called toadies and reprobates and every other term they so richly deserve.

Those who accept bribes are self-deceived.

47 No one, men of Athens, is seeking the traitor's interest when he pays him money, and once the master of what he purchases from him, he no longer employs his services as advisor. If that were not the case nothing would be more enviable than the role of traitor. But it is not the case; of course not; far from it. When the man who seeks to rule obtains control of his affairs he is also master of those who sold it to him. Then, yes, then, knowing their villainy, he hates, distrusts, insults them.

48 Let me illustrate. For if the time for action is gone by, the time for knowing such matters is always at hand for men of discernment. Lasthenes was called friend, until he betrayed Olynthus. So was Timolaus, until he destroyed Thebes. So were Eudicus and Simus of Larisa, until they placed Thessaly under Philip's sway. Thus the whole world is now full of men harried, insulted, subjected to every imaginable evil. What of Aristratus of Sicyon? What of Perilaus in Megara? Have they not been cast aside? *49* It is very plain to see that he who is most vigilant in guarding his own country, most vocal in opposing these miscreants, that man, Aeschines, preserves for you traitors and hirelings the wherewithal for getting bribes. Moreover, it is because of the majority of the members of this court and those who obstruct your plots that you and your gang are safe today and drawing pay from Philip, for your own actions would have brought you to ruin long ago.

Aeschines is a hireling of Philip and Alexander

50 I still have much I might say about the transactions of those days, but I fancy even what has been said is more than enough. However, you can blame Aeschines, for he doused me, as it were, with the stale dregs of his own villainy and crimes, and I had to rid myself of the mess, keeping in mind those among you who were not living at the time. Perhaps I have bored those who knew of his venality before ever I said a word. *51* He terms it friendship and intimacy; and only now somewhere in his harangue he used the phrase "the man who flings in my teeth my intimacy with Alexander." I reproach you with Alexander's intimacy! Where did you get it? How did you come to be thought worthy of it? I would not call you an intimate of Philip or a friend of Alexander—I am not that daft—unless harvesters and all the other hired laborers should be dubbed friends and intimates of those who hired them. It is not so. How could it be? Far from it. Hireling is my name for you, first Philip's and now Alexander's. That is the name you bear with all these members of the court. If you do not believe me, ask them; or rather I will do that for you. Men of Athens, in your opinion is Aeschines Alexander's hireling or his close friend? You hear what they reply.

[Aeschines has denied the truth of Ctesiphon's tribute to my statesmanship. Therefore I must touch upon my policies and achievements, showing why I deserve the honor of the crown.]

66 But to return to my theme. What was it proper for Athens to do when it beheld Philip preparing to rule and tyrannize over the Greeks? What was the counsellor to say or propose—I mean the counsellor at Athens, for that is the crucial point? I was conscious that from the very beginning down to the very day when I myself mounted the platform Athens had ever contended for the prize of leadership and honor and glory and had spent more in wealth and human lives to secure distinction and the welfare of all Greece than the other Greeks have spent for their own interests severally. *67* I saw that Philip himself, against whom we were contending, to gain empire and dominion had had his eye knocked out, his collar bone crushed, his arm and his leg maimed. Yes, any part of his body that fate desired to take away Philip would sacrifice, provided only that with what remained he might live a life of honor and glory. *68* Yet no one would dare to say that it was fitting that the man reared at Pella, a place inglorious and insignificant in those days, should have had implanted in him such lordly ambition as to crave dominion over the Greeks and to make that his settled purpose, and on the other hand that you, Athenians as you are, who day by day in everything you hear and see find reminders of the valor of your ancestors, should be so base that of your own free will you would voluntarily resign your liberty to Philip. No one could say that.

69 The only course left to us, the inevitable course, was to resist with justice every unjust move of Philip's. This you did from the beginning, as was to be expected and as was natural; but I, too, was engaged in offering resolutions and advice throughout my political career. I admit it. What was I to do? Tell me now, Aeschines. Dismiss all else—Amphipolis, Pydna, Potidaea, Halonnesus.[19] I mention none of these. *70* As for Serrhium, Doriscus, the sacking of Peparethus, and all the other wrongs that Athens suffered, I ignore them. Yet you were saying that my harping on those affairs had embroiled these gentlemen here with Philip. The decrees dealing with those matters were the work of Eubulus, Aristophon, and Diopithes,[20] not mine, you reckless liar! I shall not speak of them now, either. *71* But when Philip undertook to annex Euboea and to make it a stronghold from which to threaten Attica, when he was attacking Megara, seizing Oreus, destroying Porthmus, establishing Philistides as tyrant in Oreus and Clitarchus in Eretria, bringing the Hellespont under his control, besieging Byzantium, destroying some Greek cities and bringing home to others the men they had exiled—in all these operations was he guilty of wrongdoing, of violating the truce, of breaking the peace, or was he not? Was it the duty of some Greek to offer himself as an obstacle to such operations, or was it not? *72* If not, if it was right for Greece to prove as easy prey as the proverbial Mysians,[21] while Athenians still lived and breathed, then I have been too officious in speaking about those things, and Athens has been too officious in listening to me, and all that has been done must be reckoned my crimes and my mistakes. But if it was right for some one to put a stop to Philip's activities, who but the people of Athens was better fitted for that role? This was the aim of my policy. As I beheld Philip striving to enslave all mankind, I stood firm against him, and I constantly warned and instructed you not to yield.

[Evidence is produced to prove the truth of Demosthenes' claim that he has deserved well of Athens. He had been crowned previously and on the basis of a decree like that of Ctesiphon, but Aeschines had made no objection.]

Demosthenes defends his policy with regard to interstate affairs.

95 Moreover, the defamatory statements Aeschines made against the Euboeans and the Byzantines, recalling anything unpleasant they had done to you, I shall prove to be malicious slanders. Not merely shall I show them to be false—I think you know that already—but were they ever so true, it was to your interest that the negotiations should be handled as I have handled them. To prove my point, I want to relate one or two of the glorious deeds performed by Athens in your day, and that briefly. You know, the individual in his private life and the state in its public policy should always strive to act in the light of the noblest precedents available.

Athens had been farsighted and magnanimous in the past.

96 Well then, men of Athens, when[22] the Spartans were in control on land and sea, when with governors and garrisons they held in subjection the districts round about Attica—Euboea, Tanagra, all Boeotia, Megara, Aegina, Ceos and the other islands—for Athens at that time had neither ships nor walls—you marched forth to Haliartus, and not many days later to Corinth. At that moment Athens might have cherished many a grudge against Corinth and Thebes for their conduct in the Decelean war, but they did not do so, far from it.

97 Both these exploits, Aeschines, they undertook for the sake of men who were not their benefactors, and they were well aware that they were risky ventures. Still they did not on that account abandon those who had sought their protection, but in the cause of glory and honor they were willing to expose themselves to the perils of war—an upright and noble resolve. Death is the end we all must face, even if we shut ourselves up in a closet and stand guard; but the brave must always set their hands to every noble deed and make good hope their buckler of defense, bearing nobly whatever heaven may send.

98 This was the course pursued by your forefathers, this was the course of the older ones among you. The Spartans were neither friends nor benefactors, but when the Thebans, victorious at Leuctra, set to work to destroy them, you put a stop to it, not fearing the strength or fame of the Thebans at that time nor stopping to consider the past conduct of those for whom you were going to risk your lives. *99* No, your actions made it plain to all the Greeks that, no matter what wrong men may have done you, though you cherish anger for it in connection with everything else, if their freedom or safety is at stake you will neither bear a grudge nor take into account past injuries.

Not only in the case of Sparta did you take that stand, but when later on the Thebans aimed to grab Euboea you were not indifferent,[23] nor did you recall the injuries Themison and Theodorus had done you regarding Oropus.[24] Instead, you rushed to the aid of these men, too. It was the first time that Athens had used volunteers to equip her fleet, and I was one of them. *100* But I am getting ahead of my story.

You acted nobly, too, in merely saving Euboea, but much more nobly still when, after becoming masters of their persons and their cities, you made just restitution to the very ones who had done you wrong, taking into account none of the injuries you had suffered. Countless other actions that I might mention I am omitting, expeditions and engagements on land and sea, campaigns both ancient and modern, all of which Athens conducted for the freedom and salvation of the rest of Greece.

101 Therefore, having observed that in so many and so momentous crises our city was willing to fight for the best interests of our fellow countrymen, what was I to bid or counsel it to do at a time when, in a certain sense, her deliberations concerned her own welfare? Harbor a grudge, I presume, toward those who wanted us to save them, and seek excuses for abandoning everything! Who would not have had a perfect right to put me to death if I had undertaken by word alone to bring disgrace upon any of the noble deeds our state can boast of? Of course I know you would not have acted upon such a word, for had you so desired, what was to hinder? Was the thing impossible? Were not Aeschines and his accomplices on hand to bid you do it?

[It is charged that Aeschines had been responsible for getting Philip elected leader of the Amphictyonic Council and for stirring up hatred between Thebes and Athens.]

The seizure of Elatea alarms Athens.

168 When through the machinations of these men Philip had created such a feeling of hatred and suspicion between Thebes and Athens, elated by these decrees and the responses to them, he came with his forces and seized Elatea,[25] believing that, no matter what might take place, Athens and Thebes would never again achieve unity. The confusion that then arose in Athens is familiar to you all, but still listen to a few details, just the most essential.

169 It was evening, and a man came to the Prytanes with the word, "Elatea is taken." At that some instantly arose in the midst of dinner, drove the tradesmen from their booths in the market, and made a bonfire of their stalls; others summoned the generals and called the trumpeter. The city was full of uproar. Next day at dawn the Prytanes called the Council to the Council Chamber, you made your way to the Assembly, and before the Council could deliberate and pass a resolution, the entire populace was seated on the Pnyx.

170 When the Council arrived and the Prytanes reported the news they had received and introduced the messenger and he had spoken, the Herald put the question, "Who wishes to address the meeting?" Not a man came forward. He put the question again and again, but still no one rose to his feet, though there were present all the generals and all the orators and the common voice of our country was calling for some one to speak in behalf of safety—for the voice of the Herald speaking in accordance with the laws may rightly be regarded as the common voice of Athens. *171* Yet if it had been the duty of those who wanted Athens to be saved to come forward, you and all other Athenians would have arisen and proceeded to the platform, for you all, I am sure, wanted Athens to be saved. If it had been the duty of the wealthiest, the Three Hundred would have arisen. If it had been the duty of those who were both patriotic and wealthy, then those who later made the large donations would have come forward, for they did so through patriotism as well as affluence.

Demosthenes rose to the occasion in defense of Athens

172 But apparently the crisis of that day called for a man who was not merely patriotic and wealthy but who also had followed closely the course of events from the beginning and had calculated correctly the reason why Philip was taking these steps and with what end in view. Anyone who did not know these things, who had not examined them carefully far in advance, for all his patriotism or his wealth, would be no more likely on that account to know what should be done or any better able to advise you. *173* Well, on that great day I was found to be the man I have described. I came before you and said things which I want you to listen to with close attention for two reasons. First, I want you to know that I was the only orator who did not desert his duty as a patriot in the hour of peril; instead, I proved in both speech and resolution to offer what was needed for your safety in the very extremity of danger. Secondly, by the expenditure of a brief moment you will be much better acquainted with your whole policy for the future.

[There follows a digest of his speech, in which he urged a calm analysis of the situation, a display of Athenian military power for the purpose of restoring confidence among Athenian partisans in Thebes, and the appointment of envoys to form an alliance with that state.]

Alliance with Thebes the work of Demosthenes

188 This was the first beginning of a settlement of our relations with Thebes. Previously our two states had been brought by these men into a condition of mutual enmity and hatred and distrust. This resolution of mine caused the peril that then encompassed Athens to pass away like a cloud. Then was the time for the upright citizen to show to all if he had anything better to propose. Today it is too late to be finding fault. *189* Statesman and demagogue, though alike in nothing, are most unlike in that the statesman sets forth his opinion before the events and makes himself accountable to his followers, to fortune, to opportunity, to anyone at all, while the demagogue, after having kept silent when he should have spoken, if anything unpleasant takes place, casts upon it the eye of malice.

Demosthenes challenges Aeschines to prove the Theban alliance a mistake.

190 That, as I have said, was the moment for the man who had regard for his city and for words of justice. But I go so far as to say that even now if anyone can point out something better, or if anything at all was possible except the course I chose, I admit that I did wrong. If there is anything which anyone now sees that would have been helpful if adopted then, I admit it should not have escaped my notice. But if there neither is nor was any such policy and no one to this very day could name it, what was the statesman to do? Was he not to choose the best measures visible and practicable? *191* That, Aeschines, is what I did when the Herald cried, "Who wishes to address the meeting?" not "Who wishes to bring charges concerning the past?" or "Who wishes to guarantee the future?" Yes, when you were mute, though seated in the Assembly on those occasions, I came forward and spoke. But since you said nothing then, at least tell us now. What word, pray, should I have spoken or what opportunity to the interest of the state did I neglect? What alliance, what enterprise was there to which I ought preferably to have led these gentlemen?

192 Ah well, bygones are bygones always with everybody, and no one anywhere presents a plan concerning the past. The future or the present is what demands the role of counsellor. At that juncture some of our perils, it was thought, were in the future, but some were already present. Examine my choice of policy amid those perils; do not carp at the results. The outcome of every enterprise is as heaven wills, but the statesman's choice of policy itself reveals his purpose. *193* Do not enter it to my discredit that Philip chanced to win the battle. That outcome was in God's keeping, not in mine. Nay, if I failed to adopt all measures that human calculation could consider feasible, if I did not administer affairs with justice, with scrupulous attention, and with labors beyond my strength, or if I did not institute projects which were honorable and worthy of our city, yes, and necessary, show that, I bid you, and then and not before accuse me.

194 If the tornado which struck us has proved too violent not only for Athens but for the rest of Greece as well, what is to be done? If a ship-captain, after taking all measures with a view to safety and equipping his ship with what he supposed would assure that safety, then encountered a storm and had his tackle damaged or even absolutely ruined, would you blame him for the shipwreck? "I was not piloting the ship," he would object—neither was I in command of the troops—"and I did not control fâte, but fate controlled everything."

[If the future had been plain to all Athens and Aeschines had given warning, still the course adopted was the only one consistent with honor and tradition. Athenians had always been bold and independent. Though Themistocles, over a century before, urged the citizens to abandon Athens and take to the ships, they made him general; they stoned Cyrsilus for proposing that Athens bow to Xerxes.]

205 The Athenians of that day were not looking for an orator who would lead them into slavery. They did not even ask to live, unless they could live as freemen. Each man among them felt that he had been created not merely for his father and his mother but for his country, too. What is the difference? He who thinks he has been created only for his parents awaits his destined, natural end, but he who acknowledges also the claim of fatherland will willingly lay down his life rather than behold that fatherland in slavery. He will regard the insults and the indignities which slavery brings upon a city as more terrible than death itself.

The good name of Athens is involved in the decision to be taken by the court.

206 If I sought to claim the credit for inducing you to cherish principles worthy of your ancestors, anyone at all might justly censure me. No, those principles are your own, and I am showing that Athens had this spirit before ever I was born; yet I do claim that in the administering of individual projects I, too, have had a share. *207* When Aeschines denounces all this and bids you feel bitterly toward me as having caused the city's terrors and perils, he is eager to rob me of my honor for the moment, but he is thereby robbing you of your praises for all time to come. If you condemn Ctesiphon on the ground that my policies were not the best, men will think that you made a mistake in adopting them, not that the misfortunes you have suffered were occasioned by an unkind fate.

208 Nay, men of Athens, it cannot be, it cannot, that you were wrong in taking upon yourselves the danger involved in defending the freedom and safety of all Greece. Nay, by our forefathers who bore the brunt of battle at Marathon, who stood shoulder to shoulder at Plataea, who manned the fleet at Salamis and Artemisium! Nay, by all those other heroes who for their valor lie in public sepulchres! That burial, Aeschines, Athens accorded them all alike, deeming them all worthy of the same honor, and not just the successful or victorious.

[After recalling that he had previously been crowned without any protest on the part of Aeschines and that the mover of the resolution, which contained the same phrases as that of Ctesiphon, had successfully defended himself in court, Demosthenes refers with pride to the achievements of his policy of friendship toward Thebes.]

Demosthenes contrasts his situation with that of Philip.

232 Nor shall I hesitate to assert that whoever wishes to examine the orator with justice and not with malice would not make such charges as you did just now, Aeschines, inventing illustrations and mimicking expressions and gestures. The course of Greek affairs, you see, depended wholly upon my using this word and not that or upon my moving my hand in this direction and not in that! *233* No, he would examine me in the light of my achievements themselves, noting what resources and forces Athens had when I entered into public affairs, and what resources and forces I amassed for it thereafter when I took control, and how things stood with our opponents. If I had made our forces less, he would point out that the wrong lay at my door, but if I had increased them greatly, he would not subject me to malicious falsehood. Since you have shunned this type of inquiry, Aeschines, I will undertake it myself. Let the judges consider whether my account is just.

234 Under the head of forces, Athens then had the islanders—not all, but the weakest, for neither Chios nor Rhodes nor Corcyra were on our side. The financial contributions came to forty-five talents,[26] and that was collected in advance. As for infantry or cavalry, apart from our own home forces, not a man. Most terrible of all, and most helpful to our foes, Aeschines and his confederates had made all our neighbors—Megarians, Thebans, Euboeans—more nearly enemies than friends of ours. This was the status of Athenian resources, and no one could in any way alter my statement. *235* As for Philip, with whom we had to contend, consider what his situation was. First of all, he ruled his followers with an independent authority vested in himself, a factor of highest importance in military matters. Secondly, his troops had their weapons in their hands at all times. Besides, he had ample funds. Then, too, he regularly did what suited his own pleasure, giving no warning through public announcements, never deliberating in the open, not having to defend himself against charges of unconstitutional action, accountable to no one at all, but in his own person being lord, leader, master of all.

[Demosthenes should not be compared with famous men of old. The living always suffer more or less from envy. Let Aeschines compare him with himself or with any man then living.]

The unswerving loyalty of Demosthenes contrasted with the treasonable conduct of Aeschines.

321 Two things, men of Athens, should characterize the citizen of average natural endowment—for to use that expression in speaking of myself is least invidious. When in authority he should consistently uphold his city's honor and preeminence; and in every crisis, every enterprise, he should maintain his loyalty. Loyalty is determined by his nature, but ability and power by other factors. Loyalty you will find to have been my abiding quality absolutely.

322 They demanded that I be handed over, they instigated law suits before the Amphictyons, they threatened impeachment, they set these accursed scoundrels to attack me like wild beasts, yet never did I prove false to my loyalty toward you. From the very start I took as my policy the path of uprightness and justice. I aimed to foster the honor, the power, the good name of my country, to exalt them, to identify myself with them. *323* I do not walk about in the marketplace with cheerful countenance, rejoicing over the good fortune of foreigners, extending the right hand of fellowship and telling the glad news to the ones who I imagine will take word to Philip. When Athens meets with some success I do not hear the story with a shudder and a groan and a downcast look. That is what these godless creatures do, who ridicule their city as if in doing so they were not ridiculing themselves, but who keep their attention fixed on Macedon and when the foreigner has had a stroke of luck involving disaster for the Greeks, praise that and say steps must be taken to insure for ever his achievement.

324 Nay, all ye gods, may none of you nod assent to such actions. Much rather implant even in these men a better mind and heart; but if they are past recovery, grant that they themselves and they alone may be completely, utterly destroyed on land and sea, and that we who remain may find speediest deliverance from the dangers that impend and secure salvation.

LYCURGUS

LYCURGUS (fl. 338–324 B.C.) was fortunate in his birth. His family was one of the most distinguished in Athens. It belonged to the noble line of Eteobutadae, it held priestly office by inheritance, it was wealthy, and it had a record of civic munificence of which it was justly proud. Lycurgus was a credit to his family. Its proud traditions made him jealous of his city's honor. He was deeply religious, and he did not squander the family fortune in personal gratification, but spent it with lavish hand for the beautification and aggrandizement of Athens. To him is attributed the building of the stadium, the restoration of the Lyceum, and the remodeling of the theater of Dionysus, with which his name is indissolubly linked. He also was responsible for the preparation of an official text of the plays of the three great tragic poets.

In order to exert an influence in state affairs, it was still necessary for an Athenian to employ the art of public speaking. Athens was an extreme democracy, and all matters of public interest were debated in the popular assembly. The term orator thus was synonymous with that of statesman. Lycurgus prepared himself for this practical aspect of statesmanship by enrolling in the school of Isocrates. His style reflects the influence of that schooling—formal and dignified and lofty, lacking the flexibility of a Lysias and the fire of Demosthenes, but seemingly what we might expect from a conservative aristocrat of proud traditions.

So far as we know, he wrote no speeches for others to deliver. He had no need to earn a living. In antiquity there existed fifteen speeches that bore his name, all dealing with political matters, and most of them belonging to the twelve-year period following the disastrous battle of Chaeronea. It was in that period that he held office as minister of finance and public works. He proved an able administrator. He developed the navy and he put Athenian finances on a sound basis.

As might be expected, Lycurgus belonged to the same political party as Demosthenes. Ardent patriot that he was, he showed himself intolerant of corruption or lack of loyalty toward Athens. He was born in 390 B.C. and died about the year 324, thus covering almost exactly the lifetime of Demosthenes. The latter evidently held Lycurgus in high regard, for after the death of Lycurgus he used his influence in the defense of his sons.

Against Leocrates

Of the fifteen speeches attributed to Lycurgus in antiquity, this is the sole survivor. It was delivered in the year 330 B.C. The defendant in the case seems to have been an obscure Athenian citizen who had had the bad judgment to take fright after the defeat at Chaeronea and to seek safety in flight. He remained abroad some six years, during which time he caused his household effects to be brought to him from Athens.

Upon the return of Leocrates to Athens in 331 B.C., Lycurgus arraigned him on the charge of high treason and demanded the death penalty. One may be surprised at the vindictiveness displayed in the prosecution of so insignificant a person. We know of no personal reasons to explain the bitterness Lycurgus exhibits. It must be remembered that Athens had passed through much anguish and terror in the days that followed Chaeronea. Those who had stood the test would not be likely to feel kindly toward any who had shown the white feather, and both by family tradition and temperament Lycurgus was not the one to palliate the desertion of Athens in such a crisis even by so ordinary a man as Leocrates seems to have been. The votes, luckily for the defendant, were even and he escaped with his life.

[In his opening address to the court Lycurgus claims to have no personal motive for prosecuting the defendant. He is merely doing his duty as a good citizen. The only reason that Athens has no law specifically bearing on the crime of desertion such as that with which he is accusing the defendant is that no such crime had ever been committed in the past or regarded as possible. The clerk is asked to read a decree introduced by Hyperides to cope with the situation resulting from the defeat at Chaeronea.]

37 You learn from this decree, men of Athens, that the Council of the Five Hundred were instructed to go down to the Piraeus with their arms to deliberate regarding the defense of the Piraeus and in full accoutrement to take such measures as seemed to the interest of the democracy. Yet if those who had been exempted from military service for the purpose of deliberating for the welfare of the state were spending their time as soldiers, do you believe that Athens was then in the grip of any trifling, ordinary terrors?

38 It was in such circumstances that the defendant Leocrates of his own accord went and ran away from the city, removed his possessions, sent for his sacred ancestral images, and went so far in his traitorous behavior that, so far as he was concerned, the temples were without defense, the garrisons of the forts without support, and the city and country abandoned to attack.

The pathetic state of affairs at Athens following the battle of Chaeronea (338 B.C.)

39 At that moment, men of Athens, who would not have pitied Athens—not just a citizen, but even an outsider who once had visited Athens? Who at that time was so hostile to either democracy or Athens that he could bear not to be found at his post of duty? The defeat in battle with its attendant distress for the democracy was being reported; the city was distraught over what had happened; its hopes of salvation depended on men over fifty years of age; (*40*) freeborn women were to be seen in their doorways quaking with fear and asking whether husband, father, brother was still alive, a spectacle discreditable to themselves and to their city. Men who were physically unfit, too old for active service, and by law exempted from bearing arms were that day to be seen wandering helplessly throughout the city with their mantles pinned about them double! [27]

41 But though many dreadful things were happening in the city and all the citizens were involved in the very worst disasters, one would have suffered the most anguish and have wept with grief when it became known that the people by decree had made the slaves free, the aliens Athenians, the disfranchised full citizens [28]—that people which in the past had prided itself on being sprung from the soil and freeborn! *42* Aye, so great a change had come over the people that, though once accustomed to fight for the liberty of the Greeks, it now felt happy that it could without faltering fight for its own safety. Once, the Athenians were masters of much barbarian territory; now they were facing the Macedonians in peril for their own. Then too, that people [the Athenians] whom once Lacedaemonians and Peloponnesians and Asiatic Greeks were wont to call upon for aid was now entreating men of Andros, Ceos, Troezen, and Epidaurus to rescue it!

Leocrates deserted Athens in her direst need

43 Then, gentlemen, a man who in the midst of such awful terrors and mighty perils and great disgrace deserted his city and neither bore arms in defense of his country nor submitted himself to his general's direction but fled and betrayed the safety of his people, that man, I say, what juror with any patriotic blood, any respect for his oath, could vote to acquit? Who that bears the name of orator could lend assistance to the traitor to his city, to the man who did not even have the grace to join in mourning his country's misfortunes, made no contribution toward rescuing his city and his people?

44 Yet at that critical moment there was no age group that did not dedicate itself to the salvation of the state. The very soil gave its trees, the dead their tombs, the shrines their arms! Men were busy constructing walls or trenches or palisades. Not a man in Athens was idle. But Leocrates offered his services for none of these tasks. *45* You would do well to remember these things, to remember that he who refused even to help carry the dead or to attend the funeral of those who gave their lives at Chaeronea for the liberty and security of Athens should be punished with death. So far as he is concerned, those patriots are still unburied, for he experienced no shame when he passed by their graves as he greeted their fatherland seven years later.

[Lycurgus introduces what is virtually a small funeral oration like those spoken by Pericles and by Hyperides (below), in praise of the dead at Chaeronea. Leocrates, he says, devoid of all the virtues those dead displayed, basely deserted the city. The defendant's claim that he was away on a trading voyage is false, and his insistence that he was not guilty of treason because he held no military post is worthless, since at that time the city had need of everyone; though Leocrates was only one unimportant person, the welfare of a city always depends on the support of all its citizens: "he that offends in one point is guilty of all."]

The speaker bitterly rejects the comparison of Leocrates' desertion with the abandonment of Athens by its citizens before the battle of Salamis.

68 What galls me most of all, men of Athens, is to hear one of his associates declare that it is not treason for a man to leave his city, since our forefathers once left Athens, during their war with Xerxes and crossed over to Salamis. The man is such a fool, has such utter contempt for you, that he has seen fit to compare the most heroic deed with the basest crime. *69* Is there anywhere that the valor of those heroes is not lauded to the skies? Is anyone so envious or so utterly lacking in ambition as not to pray that he might have shared in their achievements? They did not abandon Athens, they merely changed its location, taking a noble resolution in the face of the approaching danger.

70 Eteonicus the Lacedaemonian [29] and Adimantus the Corinthian and the Aeginetan naval contingent were planning to flee for safety under cover of the night; but our forefathers, when threatened with desertion by all the Greeks, by main force won freedom for all the rest as well by compelling them to fight along with them against the barbarian in the naval battle at Salamis. All by themselves they got the upper hand over both the enemy and their own allies, as was proper in both cases, proving superior to the latter in benefaction and to the former in giving battle.

Pray tell me, is that in any sense comparable to the behavior of the man who made a four-days' voyage to Rhodes as a fugitive from his country? *71* No doubt those heroes of Salamis would readily have tolerated such a deed and would not, on the contrary, have stoned to death the man who brought disgrace upon their own renown for valor! So dearly did they all love the fatherland that, because Xerxes' envoy, Alexander, formerly a friend of theirs, demanded earth and water, they nearly stoned him to death.[30] Inasmuch as they saw fit to punish him merely for what he said, they would not, I suppose, have inflicted severest penalties upon the man who by his deed betrayed Athens to domination by the foe!

72 Aye, it was such principles that caused them to hold the leadership in Greece for eighty years; to ravage Phoenicia and Cilicia; to prove victorious on land and sea at Eurymedon; to capture in fighting a hundred warships of the barbarians; to cruise about harrying all Asia. *73* The principal feature of their victorious career is that they were not content to erect their trophy at Salamis. Nay, after establishing for the barbarians such boundaries as assured the liberty of Hellas and after preventing the violation of those boundaries, they imposed an agreement providing that the barbarians should not sail with a warship between the Euxine and Phaselis and that the Greeks should be free and independent, both in Europe and in Asia, too. *74* Do you imagine that if they all had adopted the principles of Leocrates and had fled, they would have accomplished any of these noble deeds, or that you would still be dwelling in this land? Then, just as you praise and honor the good, so also must you despise and punish the base, especially Leocrates, who neither feared nor respected you. . . .

[In the second half of this speech Lycurgus dwells first of all upon instances of heroic devotion: Codrus, who sacrificed his own life that Athens might be spared; Erechtheus, who for the same purpose offered up his daughter; an anonymous Sicilian, who at the risk of his own life chose to save his aged father during an eruption of Mt. Aetna; the Athenians who fought at Marathon; the Spartans who died at Thermopylae; Apollodorus and Thrasybulus, who narrowly escaped execution for having killed a traitor. Their conduct is contrasted with the cowardice of Leocrates. The orator then passes to a discussion of cases of treason and the punishment inflicted upon traitors, the most famous instance being that of Pausanias, king of Sparta, who was condemned to death for his intrigues with Persia. In the course of his remarks on those topics Lycurgus recites a good bit of poetry: four iambic trimeters from an unidentified poet, a fifty-five-line passage from Euripides' *Erechtheus,* six lines from the *Iliad*, a thirty-two line fragment from Tyrtaeus, besides the famous epitaph in honor of the Spartans who fell at Thermopylae and one in praise of the Athenians who fought at Marathon.]

HYPERIDES

Hyperides was born in Athens about the year 389 B.C. He came of a prosperous middle-class family and doubtless received an excellent education. He may have been a pupil of Isocrates, though his extant speeches do not display much similarity to the style of that writer.

He began his career as a writer of speeches for others to deliver, but none of that work has survived. In early manhood he entered the political arena, where he played a conspicuous role as a member of the anti-Macedonian party. In that capacity he came into close contact with Demosthenes, whom he supported with notable fidelity. That he felt called upon to speak against him in the famous Harpalus affair may testify to his honesty of purpose. Though in his private life he gave occasion for the jests and gossip of the comic poets as being a man of easy morals and indulgent habits, in relation to the state his attitude was that of an ardent patriot.

He ranked high as an orator in the esteem of ancient critics. Cicero placed him by the side of Demosthenes. Dionysius has left us this appraisal of his qualities: "Hyperides is sure of aim, but seldom exalts his subject. In diction he surpasses Lysias, in subtlety of composition he surpasses all. He maintains throughout a firm grasp of the points at issue and sticks close to essential details. He has plenty of intelligence and is full of charm. He seems simple, but he is no stranger to cleverness."

When the Turks invaded Hungary in 1526, what is said to have been a complete manuscript of his works, the only one to have survived that long, was consumed by fire. But since the middle of the nineteenth century there have been retrieved from the sands of Egypt six speeches in more or less complete form, all on public themes. In general they support the testimony of Dionysius. If he rarely attained the high level of Demosthenes and is less meticulous regarding euphony, he is easier to understand.

The Epitaphius

This oration is noteworthy as being the sole surviving specimen of a memorial address that had actually been delivered. The occasion was a state funeral accorded Leosthenes and his fellow Athenians who in the winter of 323–322 B.C. lost their lives in the vain endeavor to storm Lamia, the stronghold of the Macedonian Antipater, whom Leosthenes had earlier defeated on the field of battle. Hyperides was not given to the oratory of display, but his close associations with Leosthenes and, no doubt, the tension of the times moved him to heights of eloquence which he did not commonly reach. It may have been his last public appearance, for he was executed shortly afterwards by order of Antipater.

Except for the proem, the text of this speech is either virtually intact or else capable of reconstruction with fair certainty. The following translation omits only the beginning of the proem.

4 To discuss in detail each of the previous exploits of our city affecting the whole of Hellas requires more time than is now at my disposal. Besides, this occasion is not suitable for a long address, nor is it easy for a single speaker to review and call to mind deeds so numerous and so glorious. I shall not hesitate to speak of Athens in general terms, (*5*) for just as the sun traverses the whole earth, arranging the seasons appropriately, establishing all things beautifully and, for the benefit of sensible, capable human beings, attending to the production of their food and crops and all the other things useful in their living, so also Athens is ever chastising the evil and protecting the upright, preserving equal rights for all instead of personal advantage for the few, and by its courage and self-sacrifice providing freedom from fear for all Greeks everywhere. *6* However, as I said before, I shall refrain from discussing the public affairs of our city, and I shall speak rather about Leosthenes and the other men whom we are honoring today.

But I am at a loss to know where to begin or what to mention first. Shall I speak of the family of each of them? That I conceive to be foolish. *7* If one should attempt to eulogize certain other people, men who have come together from many quarters of the world to form a single city, each having contributed to it his own family stock, it would be necessary to trace the lineage of them man by man; but in speaking of Athenians, whose common origin, sprung from the soil as they are, insures nobility of birth without a peer, I believe it is idle to eulogize individual families. *8* Shall I, then, refer to the training of these heroes and tell how as lads they were reared to practise great self-control, how they were educated in those subjects which are customary in Athenian schools? I fancy everybody knows that the purpose for which we educate our sons is that they may grow to be brave men. Those who have shown themselves in war to be men of surpassing valor manifestly as boys were nobly educated. *9* Accordingly it seems the simplest course to recount how valiant in war these men have proved and to show that they are the cause of many blessings which have been received by their fatherland and by Greeks in general.

Leosthenes eulogized

I shall speak first of their commander, for that is right. *10* Leosthenes saw that all Hellas was humbled and cowering in terror, ruined by those who accepted bribes from Philip and Alexander at the expense of their own people, and that Athens needed a man—and the nation a city—that would be competent to take the lead. Therefore he devoted himself to his fatherland, and his fatherland to the Greek people, in the cause of freedom.

Having marshalled a force of auxiliaries (*11*) and having accepted the leadership of the citizen army, he gave battle in Boeotia and vanquished those who had been the first to array themselves against Greek liberty—Boeotians, Macedonians, Euboeans, and the rest of their allies. *12* Next proceeding to Thermopylae and seizing the passes through which in days of old [31] the barbarian horde had marched against the Greeks, he prevented Antipater from advancing into Greece. Encountering the enemy in that district, he defeated him in battle, shut him up in Lamia, and subjected him to siege. *13* The Thessalians, Phocians, Aetolians, and the other inhabitants of that region Leosthenes brought into alliance with his forces, and those whom Philip and Alexander had made a great point of leading against their will, gladly accepted the leadership of Leosthenes. Thus it came to pass that he gained the mastery in the ventures he had chosen—but fate he could not overcome.

14 But Leosthenes deserves our gratitude first and foremost, not merely for what he accomplished while he lived, but also for the battle which was fought after he had died, and for all the other blessings which Greece attained in this campaign. On the foundations laid by Leosthenes the men of today are erecting the structure of their future exploits.

To praise the leader is to praise his men.

15 Let no one imagine that I am paying no heed to the other heroes of our city but praising Leosthenes alone. It so happens that to praise Leosthenes for his martial deeds is to praise the others, too. The commander is responsible for planning wisely, but those who freely risk their lives are accountable for victory in battle. Thus when I laud the victory that was won, I am lauding both the generalship of Leosthenes and the valor of his men. *16* Who would not rightly praise our countrymen who perished in this war, who gave their lives in the cause of Greek liberty, believing that the clearest token of their desire to clothe Hellas with liberty is that they died fighting for its sake?

The defeat at Chaeronea and the consequent destruction of Thebes fired the patriotic fervor of the troops of Leosthenes.

17 That earlier battle which was fought in Boeotia did much to increase their eagerness to fight for the fatherland. They saw how pitiably Thebes had vanished from the earth—its citadel garrisoned by men of Macedon, its inhabitants enslaved, its soil parcelled out among aliens. With those frightful catastrophes before their eyes, they became resolute to dare all dangers with ready hearts.

Thermopylae will ever recall their deeds of valor.

18 Nay, but the battle which was fought near Thermopylae and Lamia, as it happens, has won them no less renown than the one they fought in Boeotia, not merely because in that engagement they vanquished Antipater and his allies, but also because of the field where it was fought. Twice each year the whole Greek nation will come there to the Pylaean Congress and will in imagination become spectators of their deeds. No sooner will they gather there than they will recall the valor of these heroes. *19* No men that have ever lived contended for nobler prizes or against mightier competitors or with fewer helpers.[32] Valor they judged to be their might, manhood was their military force, not mere numbers of individual men. Freedom they have bequeathed to all alike, but the glory of their deeds they have placed about their country's brows as a crown peculiarly its own.

The awful fate from which they saved Athens

20 Now then, it is fitting that we should reckon up what we believe would have been our situation had not these men fought in keeping with their character and tradition. Would not the whole world be subject to a single master? Would not Hellas be forced to abide by what he ordains as law? In a word, the arrogance of Macedon, not the might of justice, would prevail in each man's house. No man's wife or virgin daughter or youthful son would be secure against constant violence. *21* Behold under what compulsion we exist even now. We are compelled to witness sacrifices being offered to human beings; to behold images, altars, and temples of the gods finished off with lack of care, but those of mortals with utmost pains; to honor the oppressor's slaves as if they were demigods! *22* If through the arrogance of Macedon the ordinances of heaven have been destroyed, what must one think concerning the ordinances of men? Would they not have been utterly abolished? The more dreadful the things to which, in our opinion, we should have had to look forward, so much greater the praise we must believe the dead deserve.

The hardships suffered

23 No campaign has manifested the valor of the combatants more than the one now ended. In that campaign our men had to array themselves for battle every day, to fight more battles in a single campaign than has fallen to the lot of all other men in the history of the world, and to endure with heroism such utter lack of all the many things needed in one's daily life that it is hard even to put it into words.

24 Then must not Leosthenes, who induced his fellow citizens to display such fortitude, who inspired them to stand their ground unflinchingly, and also the troops who eagerly followed such a commander as helpers in the strife, be deemed fortunate for their display of valor rather than unfortunate for having lost their lives? By the sacrifice of their mortal bodies they have gained immortal glory, by their courage as individuals they have achieved freedom for all Greeks to share.

What kind of prosperity can there be apart from freedom? *25* No threat of man, but only the voice of law, should rule where men are prosperous. To be accused should hold no terrors for free men, only conviction in a court of law. Security of the citizens must not rest with those who fawn upon princes and falsely denounce their fellows, but rather in the honesty of the law. *26* To insure all these blessings the men we are now honoring performed labor upon labor, and facing danger daily they have relieved from the fear of danger their fellow citizens and the nation for all time to come. Aye, they offered their lives a sacrifice to the end that the others might nobly live.

They are not really dead, but rather born anew into a better life.

27 Thanks to these men, fathers are in high repute; mothers are viewed with admiration by their fellow citizens; sisters have obtained, and will continue so to do, marriages which befit their station as ordained by law; sons will rather have, to help them on their way to public favor, the valiant record, let us not say of the dead, for it is not right to use that term of men who gave their lives to gain such noble ends, but rather of those who have gone to join the immortals. *28* For if death, which with other men is the most grievous of all evils, with these has come to be the chief of mighty blessings, how can we rightly view them as not fortunate, or how judge that their life has ended and not suffered a new birth to a life far nobler than the one they had before? Then in boyhood they lacked judgment; now they are become brave men. *29* Then through long years and many perils they had to prove their valor; now, with that record as their starting point, they are famous everywhere, memorable for their manly virtue. *30* When shall we ever fail to recall their courage? Where shall we fail to find them receiving highest praises? Will they not receive them when their city is prosperous, but will what they have brought to pass cause others to be praised and remembered in their stead? Will they not be praised when we as individuals are successful? Nay, it is their valor that will insure the safe enjoyment of those successes. *31* In what time of life will men not count them blessed? Will not the older citizens so deem them? Will they not believe that it is they who have made it possible for them to spend their remaining days free from fear and secure? Will not the men of their own age? *32* Will not the younger men and boys? Will these not glorify their death and be eager to imitate their life, making it their model, because they left behind a heritage of valor? *33* Must we not, then, deem them happy in such great honor? What poets and philosophers will be at a loss for words and songs to offer in memory of the exploits of these heroes? Among whom will their campaign not be eulogized more than that which overcame the Trojans? Everywhere in Greece generations yet unborn can praise their heroism in speech and song, for both are well deserved by Leosthenes and by the troops who died with him in this war.

34 If it is to afford pleasure that men recall such deeds of fortitude, what could afford more pleasure to the Greeks than praise of those who won from the Macedonians the liberty they now enjoy? If, on the other hand, such remembrance aims at practical advantage, what words would do more good to those who hear them than words in praise of heroism and heroes? Nay, but with us and with all others as well they must be held in honor, as is clear from this assemblage.

They will receive a noble welcome from the heroes of old.

35 But it is fitting to consider who will extend a hand of welcome in the lower world to their leader. May we not suppose Leosthenes will be welcomed and admired by those demigods, as they are called, who campaigned against Troyland? His exploits were akin to theirs, but with this difference: they had all Hellas to support them in taking a single city, but Leosthenes, with only Athens to lend support, humbled the power which ruled Europe and Asia.

36 Again, those men of old went to the rescue of just one woman who had suffered violence; but Leosthenes prevented violence that threatened all Greek women, and he did it with the aid of those who now are being buried with him, men born later than those heroes of the Trojan War but men who performed deeds worthy of their valor.

37 I pass now to Miltiades and Themistocles and their men and to the others who set Hellas free, brought honor to their country, and made their own lives glorious. *38* Leosthenes so far surpassed them that, though they punished the barbarian force which had invaded Greece, he went so far as to prevent invasion. Again, they witnessed the foe giving battle on their own native soil, but he overcame his enemies on their own soil.

39 I fancy, too, that those who gave to Athens with greatest constancy a demonstration of their mutual affection—I speak of Harmodius and Aristogiton—believe that none are more akin to them than Leosthenes and the men who fought beside him, none more loyal to you. Nor are there any whom they would rather meet in Hades. Of course not, for their deeds are not inferior to those of Harmodius and Aristogiton, rather—if I may be permitted to say so—even greater. *They* put an end to the tyrants of Athens, but these men have put an end to the tyrants of all Hellas.

40 How noble, how incredible, the daring they displayed; how glorious and magnificent the choice they made; how surpassing their manly valor amidst perils, the valor which they freely devoted to the common cause of freedom for the Greeks!

Consolation offered to those who survive

41 It is perhaps hard to console those who are overwhelmed by such misfortunes. Sorrow is not lulled to rest by either speech or ritual. Nay, each one's nature and affection for the departed sets the limit to his grieving. Still one must be of good courage and assuage his anguish so far as possible. Remember not only the death of the departed but also the record for courage they have left behind. *42* If what they suffered merits funeral dirges, what they have accomplished calls for highest praises. If they have not lived to share the old age which fate allots to mortals, at least they have won a fair renown that never ages and are completely happy. Such of them as died childless will have in the praises of their countrymen undying children. Those who left children behind them will find in their country's love a faithful guardian for them. *43* Moreover, if death be like never having been born, these men have been released from disease and grief and all other ills that befall our mortal life; but if instead there is consciousness in the lower world and divine providence, as we assume, we may fairly suppose that those who rushed to the rescue when the honors of the gods were in deadly peril are enjoying the divine care and providence in fullest measure.

NOTES TO THE ATTIC ORATORS

1. The scholars of the museum of Alexandria (founded about 280 B.C.) were fond of drawing up lists or "canons" of great books and great authors: five each in epic and tragedy, nine in lyric, ten in oratory, etc. Compare the modern "Five Foot Shelf" and "Hundred Great Books."

2. I.e., the idea that, in the absence of certainty, likelihood is the most reasonable criterion. This form of argument is found in the "Old Oligarch," Thucydides on revolution, and Plato, *Republic*, VIII. See J. H. Finley, Jr., *Thucydides* (Cambridge, 1942), pp. 46–48.

3. Here the defendant calls upon his witness. The MSS, as usual, do not record the testimony, merely inserting the word "Witnesses." Such notations will regularly be omitted from the translation.

4. This sacrilegious act, perpetrated on the eve of the Athenian fleet's departure on the ill-fated Sicilian expedition, filled orthodox citizens with the same horror a Catholic would feel at the desecration of the statue of a saint.

5. Socrates was tried in the same year on the same charge.

6. No such archon is listed. The MSS may be corrupt. The decree referred to at all events forbade the torturing of an Athenian citizen.

7. The Anaceum was a shrine of Castor and Pollux; the Tholos was a circular building near the southwest corner of the market place, headquarters of the Prytanes, or executive committee of the Athenian Senate, who dined there daily.

8. The phrase "of Phegus" was used to differentiate this Alcibiades from his more illustrious cousin by the same name who figures prominently in the narrative of Thucydides and in Plato's *Symposium*. Phegus was an Attic deme, with one of which each Athenian citizen was associated, no matter where he had his residence. Such demotics were regularly employed when it was desired to avoid possible confusion among men who had the same personal name.

9. Andocides here confuses a victory by Pisistratus in 549 B.C. with a defeat suffered by his son Hippias about 510. Athenians were sometimes shaky about their own history.

10. Xerxes, in the Persian War. Neither audience nor orators ever tired of this theme.

11. In the battle of Aegospotami, 405 B.C.

12. *A Short History of Greek Literature*, p. 343.

13. I.e., after the reforms of Solon and Clisthenes and before the weakening of the Areopagus by Ephialtes, about 461 B.C.

14. Compare Aristotle, *Politics* (V, I, 7).

15. In 357–346, 346–341, 341–338, and 330. Demosthenes in the oration *On the Crown* naturally refers to the events of those years, but he nowhere sets up the periods mentioned.

16. During their ritual bath they were either drowned in the sea or else seized by sharks—a bad omen for Athens.

17. See Harvey, *Oxford Companion to Classical Literature, s.v.* "Social War."

18. Philip besieged Byzantium in 340 B.C., but was compelled to withdraw through the efforts of Demosthenes, who received from Athens an official vote of thanks. The people of Acarnania, a district north of the entrance to the Gulf of Corinth, feeling threatened by Philip, sought an alliance with Athens not long after the Peace of Philocrates (346 B.C.).

19. Philip had taken these places before the Peace of Philocrates (346 B.C.); the three next mentioned fell within three or four years thereafter. All were in the region of the North Aegean.

20. On Eubulus, see Harvey. Aristophon was an Athenian statesman of the first half of the fourth century. His program was to unite Athens and Thebes against Sparta. Diopithes was the Athenian general who in 343 B.C. saved the Chersonese from Philip.

21. Notorious for their tame submission to the attacks of their neighbors.

22. After the battle of Aegospotami, 405 B.C.

23. In 357 B.C., one of two factions in Euboea called for the support of Thebes, but Athens helped restore the old regime.

24. Oropus was on the border between Attica and Boeotia. In 366 B.C. these two men from Eretria, in Euboea, took the city from the Athenians.

25. In Phocis, a few miles southeast of Thermopylae and only three days' march from Athens. Philip took and refortified it in the spring of 338 B.C. and asked Thebes to join him in an invasion of Attica, or at least to allow him free passage through its territory.

26. Roughly $48,000, about 4 per cent of the annual tax levied against the members of the Delian League at the height of the Peloponnesian War. Of course the purchasing power of that money was immensely greater than it would be today.

27. The battle was fought in August, at which time the heat in Athens was doubtless intense. The reference to the doubling of the mantle presumably was intended to emphasize the feeble health of the old men.

28. Citizenship at Athens was a prized possession, scrupulously guarded, but at great crises the bars were let down. Thus Andocides recalls (*On the Mysteries*, 107) that when Xerxes was about to invade Attica the exiles were recalled and those without the franchise were given citizenship. Before the battle of Arginusae (406 B.C.), slaves who agreed to serve as oarsmen in the navy were given their freedom.

29. More garbled history. Lycurgus means Eurybiades; futhermore, Herodotus definitely links the Aeginetans with the Athenians in urging that the battle be fought at Salamis (*Histories*, VIII, 56–74).

30. Garbled. Darius, not Xerxes, demanded earth and water; Alexander was Mardonius' envoy; and the stoning (Herodotus, IX, 5) involved Lycides, a member of the Athenians' own Council.

31. In 480 B.C. See Herodotus, VII, 215 ff.

32. Compare Winston Churchill's eloquence about how never in the history of human conflict have so many owed so much to so few.

THE GREEK SCIENTISTS

Translated by Herbert M. Howe

INTRODUCTION

BY THE TERM "science" we today usually understand the study of nature in accordance with certain well-understood principles and logical procedures. We are so used to them that we take them for granted; but their discovery was a long and slow process, and their combination into the methods of investigation to which we are accustomed did not take place until quite modern times. For many of the earlier advances in man's knowledge of nature we are indebted to the Greeks.

At the very base of scientific work is the assumption that similar causes have similar effects, and that nothing happens without a natural cause. Primitive man, on the contrary, commonly believed that the world was governed by the whims and desires of a multitude of unpredictable spirits. In the *Iliad*, the rivers of Troy leave their beds and try to flood the Greek army—not because of heavy rains upstream, but because Apollo has persuaded the river gods to come to the defense of Troy; and they are thwarted when Hephaestus, a supporter of the Greeks, sends a wave of fire to dry them up. In the sixth century B.C. we find the first attempts, by Thales and his followers, to formulate general principles for the actions of nature.

A second fundamental assumption of the scientist is that, generally speaking, the information given us by our senses is accurate and reliable. There were some ancient thinkers who were so impressed by the gulf between the world of matter, which we perceive by the senses, and that of the mind, to be grasped only by reason, that they insisted that only the second was real; matter and change they regarded as illusory, and scarcely worth the trouble of investigation. To such men, of course, there could be no experimental knowledge, for they doubted the only evidence we have about the world outside ourselves. They were extremists; but most thinkers maintained that the results of reasoning were more reliable than those of sense perception.

Even when these principles—that every happening is in accordance with natural law, and that the senses can be trusted—are accepted, methods of investigation must be worked out; we must be able to formulate general laws to explain what we have observed, and we must check the general laws, once we have formulated them, against the facts of our experience—if necessary, altering our theories to agree with the facts. The two parts, then, of scientific investigation are observation and reasoning. One of the weaknesses of ancient science was a tendency to magnify one or the other of these processes.

Let us first consider the observers, best represented by the physicians. When one of them was confronted by a suffering patient, he was concerned with the illness of the particular man affected; his problem was to cure this particular case. Later, if he wished, he might generalize about this and similar cases; for the present his attention must be fixed on the man before him. Accordingly, in some of the early medical works—by no means all—we find a distrust of facile theory and a great concern for the careful description of symptoms in each individual case. Knowledge, these physicians felt, can come only from experience; theory must follow practice, and we must not be too hasty in seeking theory out. Ancient medical observation was thus more productive than ancient medical theory.

This method of the physicians must be contrasted with that of the thinkers who devoted themselves to the study of deductive reasoning. The mathematicians, for example, reduced to a minimum their dependence on the senses; this minimum, which cannot be proved logically, they formulated as the axioms, which are universally accepted without further proof. Working from them, with no further appeal to external evidence, they built up a structure of reasoning which is still studied everywhere. Unquestionably the Greek work most widely studied today (except for the New Testament) is the *Elements* of Euclid; high school geometry is little more than a rearrangement of it with the addition of problems and applications.

Thus we have the physicians emphasizing the importance of observation and the mathematicians that of reasoning from unquestioned premises. One of the most interesting attempts to combine the two methods was that of the astronomers, who had a long series of careful and surprisingly accurate observations on which to work. Unfortunately, they started from the plausible but incorrect assumption that the earth is fixed in the center of the universe and that the heavenly bodies move round it in circles. But observation introduces difficulties; these were explained away by assuming more and more complicated subordinate motions. In spite of the complications which arose, this theory was never superseded by the relatively simple one of a system with the sun at its center. For, astronomers said, if the earth moved around the sun, the fixed stars would seem to occupy different positions when the earth was in different parts of its orbit. Men's minds were still not able to grasp the enormous distances between the stars; we acknowledge them (although we too are quite unable to visualize such a distance as a light year), for we have learned to work with very large and very small magnitudes, which have no counterparts in ordinary experience.

This is an example of the failings of ancient science, of which many could be cited; but it is more important that we should recognize some of the difficulties under which it labored. Accurate measurement was unknown in antiquity, for there were no reliable instruments for the measurement of time or of heat, and only the roughest standards of weight and length. Ancient observation was thus qualitative rather than quantitative. The ancients knew, as any child does, that friction produces heat, but they could not know that the same amount of work expended in friction always produces the same amount of heat. Whenever he can, the modern scientist tries to formulate a mathematical statement of what he observes, something very difficult for the ancients.

Even if they could have measured accurately, the ancients would have been sorely hampered by lack of mathematical technique in fields outside of geometry. Neither the Greeks nor the Romans had a system of numbers which would make possible an effective arithmetic or algebra, and a useful mathematics to describe motion was not discovered until modern times. Thus we find recourse to geometrical representation of quantities where we would use numbers or letters; see, for example, Archimedes' statement of the principle which bears his name. As long as a problem could be represented in geometrical terms, the ancients could work with it; their advances in mechanics and optics were considerably greater than those in fields like chemistry, where geometry cannot be applied.

Biologists and physicians reached a dead end partly because they lacked such instruments of close observation as the microscope. Until very late in ancient history physicians were still making great discoveries in anatomy (although they were sadly hindered by prejudice against dissection of the human body and were forced to do much of their work on animals). When they reached the limits of vision they were forced to have recourse to theory, often unprovable, which was apt to lead them astray. Thus Galen knew that the arteries carry blood and not air; but, since he could see no connections between the arteries and veins, he suggested that the blood must percolate from one side of the heart to the other through invisible pores. For centuries further investigation could neither prove nor disprove this theory; and Galen's prestige helped keep it in favor for over a thousand years.

In late antiquity the character of scientific investigation changed in some quarters and it became bound up with a sort of theology, not the old belief in a multitude of spirits but new doctrines developed from the teaching of Plato, Aristotle, and the Stoics. If we grant that the universe is created and governed by an all-wise and all-knowing divinity, we must also grant that nothing happens without an intelligent purpose. The proper understanding of this purpose then becomes an essential part of our investigation. The danger in this *teleological* view of the world is that explanation of *why* things happen may become more important than investigation of *how* they happen; an accepted theological tenet may in this way come to have more authority than the evidence of observation.

If the creator of the universe knows and plans all its actions, and if he is kindly disposed to humanity, he will, some men thought, give signs of what is to come. Just before the death of Julius Caesar a comet was observed. Instead of being treated as an interesting astronomical phenomenon, it was generally regarded as a portent of some catastrophe. Astrology, the attempt to foretell human destiny by studying the heavens, was enormously popular in late antiquity.

Astrology is, of course, "practical" science, but it is based on faulty premises. It is important to notice that the theoretical scientists of antiquity (except, of course, the physicians) had little interest in the application of their discoveries, and little material progress resulted from their work. Accordingly, ordinary men took the short cut of accepting a body of knowledge which purported to be of use to them, and, partly through wishful thinking, they did not examine too closely its foundations.

For several centuries European advance in science was slow. Yet the traditions were carried on; we have, for example, very late commentators on Aristotle who showed a keen and critical appreciation of the problems he had raised; and Galen's work was continued by the Arabs, whose studies later became known in western Europe. So it was with other scientists of antiquity, whose discoveries were preserved in one form or another. Although some of their findings have been corrected and others superseded, they started science on the road which it has followed since. Its progress has sometimes been slow, sometimes fast; but it has never had to make a completely fresh start.

THE passages translated here are based on the following texts: Hippocrates, W. H. S. Jones (London and New York, 1923); Plutarch, C. Sintenis (Leipzig, 1879); Vitruvius, F. Krohn (Leipzig, 1912); Archimedes, J. L. Heiberg (Leipzig, 1913); and Galen, J. L. Heiberg (Leipzig, 1907).

HIPPOCRATES

HIPPOCRATES, the most famous of the Greek physicians, lived and taught at the end of the fifth century B.C. on the island of Cos, near Asia Minor. In spite of the tremendous reputation he had in antiquity, we know almost nothing of his life. During the Alexandrian period, from about 300 B.C. on, a large group of works were known which bore his name; but they were certainly by many different hands, some much later than the time of Hippocrates himself, and it is impossible to prove the authenticity of any of them. Perhaps the collection, the "Hippocratic Corpus," was the library of the medical fraternity of Cos, which had been brought to Alexandria and copied there. It is repeatedly quoted by other ancient writers on medicine, several of whom wrote commentaries on its parts.

The works vary greatly in outlook, style, and excellence. The selections given below are from books which seem to be quite early and which give the most favorable view of Greek medicine. The first, from the treatise *On the Sacred Disease* (epilepsy), was written to combat those who sought a refuge from ignorance in piety. This disease, with its violent seizures, was thought to be the result of divine possession; against this notion the writer directs his fire. In like manner, the work *On Ancient Medicine* was written to combat the rising influence of abstract philosophy, which, in the writer's judgment, was undermining the foundations of medicine. The second selection is from this work; to prove his thesis, the writer includes a history of the art of medicine.

The corpus also includes several books *On Epidemics,* of which the first and third are the best and probably the oldest. They include several "constitutions," accounts of the weather and other peculiar circumstances of certain epidemics; one is included below as "A Public Health Report." There are also many accounts of individual cases, which show the careful and detailed observation of the author. The diseases described in "A Public Health Report" are mumps and tuberculosis; those of the individual cases are malaria and probably hepatitis (infection of the liver). Malaria was very wide-spread in Greece, and, in its various forms, occurs frequently in the books *On Epidemics.*

The most famous plague of antiquity, that described by Thucydides (II, 47–54), is not mentioned by Hippocrates, and does not correspond closely with any modern disease. But there can be little doubt that the historian, in his orderly and objective description of the symptoms, was influenced by the work of the physicians; indeed, their outlook on the facts they were recording is echoed all through his work.

THE "SACRED" DISEASE

The fact about the disease which people call "sacred" is this: it is no more divinely caused or more holy than any other malady, in my opinion; its cause and origin is the same as that of other diseases. Through their inability to treat it and their astonishment that it does not resemble other ills, men have always regarded it as something sent from heaven. Now this notion of the disease's divine origin is preserved because men are quite unable to understand it; but the same notion is proved false by the superficial methods of treatment people employ—such things as purifications and charms. If we ought to consider this disease sacred because it is wonderful, we must realize that there is not just one sacred disease, but a great many: I could name you many others which are no less wonderful and marvellous, which no one calls sacred, such diseases, for example, as the recurrent fevers. . . .

My own feeling is that the first people to call this disease sacred were men like the wandering faith healers of our own day, who wear a sanctimonious face and pretend to know more than anyone else. Since they had no treatment which was the slightest use, they avoided being shown up by wrapping themselves in a cloud of superstitious nonsense, and pronounced that the disease had a divine origin. . . .

But this so-called sacred disease arises from the same causes as any other—the food that enters and the excretions that leave the body, cold weather, the sun, changes of climate—and all these things are divine. There is no need to think that there is anything more sacred about this disease than any other; all are divine in origin, all can be treated by men. Each, of course, has its own peculiarities, but none is beyond human understanding, and all are capable of cure.

—*On the Sacred Disease,* 1, 2, 21

The methods and origins of medicine

Some speakers and writers on medicine begin by postulating without proof one or two principles on which their discussion is to be based—that everything is caused by hot or cold, wet or dry, or whatever else happens to please them. To this they limit the ultimate cause of human disease and death; this they regard as the origin of our ills in every case. In doing so these men are manifestly wrong. Their blunders are especially open to censure because they are made in a field where skill can arise only from experience, a craft to which all men must have recourse on the most crucial occasions, whose skilled practitioners receive the highest honors.

Now some physicians are incapable, others extremely expert. This difference would not exist unless the art of medicine possessed certain real knowledge, the fruit of investigation and discovery. Were it not for this, all physicians alike would be working by chance, with no sure information to go on, and their treatment of the sick would depend on random guesswork. But this is not the case; just as other craftsmen vary in dexterity and ingenuity of hand and brain, so also do the physicians.

For my part, I cannot see why medicine needs any unproved assumption from which to work, as does the study of such unapproachable mysteries as the heavens above and the things beneath the earth. About these a man might discover and publish the true facts, yet neither he nor his hearers could be sure that he was right, since there would be no test which could be applied to establish his correctness. But the material on which medicine works has always been right under our hands, and starting points and methods have been worked out by which, as time has progressed, many profound discoveries have been made. What is left to be discovered, moreover, will eventually be found out if the investigators are competent, if they know the work that has already been done, and if they take that work as their point of departure. If, however, they reject these methods and try to use some other pattern in their investigations, they will inevitably deceive themselves whenever they think that they have discovered something, for they will be claiming the impossible. I shall try to demonstrate why this must be so by explaining the character of the art of medicine, and thus I shall show why discoveries cannot be made in any other way.

It seems most important to me for anyone who is discussing this art to use terms understood by laymen, for all the investigations and discoveries of medicine are directed toward the layman's ills and sufferings. It is almost impossible for a person without experience in such matters to understand his own sickness, the reasons for its onset and departure, and why he gets worse or better, but this is easy enough if his symptoms are observed and explained by someone else. Then all the patient has to do is to listen and check the account with his own memory. If the physician fails to win the patient's understanding and cannot make him act thus, he cannot reach the truth. For this reason too, then, medicine has no room for the unproved postulate.

The art of medicine would never have been sought out or found in the first place if the sick had benefited from the same food, drink, and way of life as the well, and if there had been nothing better for them than such food and drink. Indeed, there would have been no need for the art. But the fact that the same things were not good for the sick as for the well forced men to discover the art of medicine. To go back further still, I do not believe that our present foods and diet would have been discovered at all if men had remained content to eat and drink the same things as the ox and the horse and other lower animals, such things as plants and fruit and leaves and grass. The animals eat them and thrive, suffering no pain and needing nothing else. Now it seems probable to me that man too first ate this sort of food, and our present ways of living have only been developed and refined over a long period of time. Men doubtless suffered terribly from such harsh and raw foods, with all their natural coarseness, and were subject to cramps and pains followed by sudden death—as we would be now if we lived in that way. Of course, the ancients were used to such a diet, and probably suffered less on that account. Most people, those with the weakest constitutions, must have perished early in life, while the stronger held out for a longer time. Even now we see people who are able to digest the coarsest of foods.

Eventually, I suppose, the ancients began to

hunt for a diet which would agree with their constitutions, and discovered the one which we still use. They learned to clean and soak and grind and sift and knead and bake; in this way they made bread from wheat, and cakes and scones from barley. They experimented with other foods, boiling, baking, and mixing; they combined the harsh and violent with the bland, and adapted everything to the human digestion. For they felt that from food too harsh and strong to be digested come sickness, pain, and death, while those that we can digest are the sources of nourishment, growth, and vigor. What better name could be given to this discovery than that of medicine? It was made for the safety and health of mankind, to replace a way of life which brought disease, suffering, and death in its train.

It is natural enough, though, that this sort of medicine should not be considered an art, for we do not use this term of a field where no one is entirely unskilled and where everyone has some knowledge based on his own needs and experience. Nevertheless, these discoveries about diet were great ones, and behind them lay much investigation and thought. Even now athletes and their trainers follow the same methods of study in the digestibility of foods, and by these methods they are constantly making new discoveries.

As the word is used in ordinary speech, "medicine" means the art which has been developed for the cure of the sick. Let us see whether this art has the same purpose as that which I have described above, and what its origin was. As I have already remarked, no one would have bothered to study medicine if the same way of life had been suitable for the sick and the healthy alike. Even now, among people who do not use the art of medicine, Greeks or barbarians, the sick try to follow the same mode of life as the well; they eat and drink what they please, and do not abstain from anything they may want. Now those who first set out to treat the sick had the same object as the men to whom I referred above, namely, diminishing the natural potency of food. The first step was to reduce the amount taken, without changing the diet. This obviously would help some patients, but not all, for some were so constituted that they could not digest even small quantities of the coarse food. Since they seemed to need something more bland, gruels were invented, mixtures of coarse food and water, compounded and boiled to reduce their strength. Some of the sick could not even handle this; they were, accordingly, reduced to carefully regulated amounts of liquid food, so compounded that nothing should be given which was either too strong or too weak.

We must keep in mind that some people are not helped even by a diet of gruel; if they take even this, their fever and pain are increased. Evidently whatever they eat produces nourishment and vigor for the disease, but wasting and weakness for the body. If anyone in this condition tries eating some dry bread or cake, no matter how little, the effect on him will be ten times as bad—and more obvious as well—as if he had followed a liquid diet, simply because the food is too rich for one in his condition. Likewise, if someone who is helped by a liquid diet rather than a solid does eat ordinary food, and eats too much, he will suffer more than if he had taken only a little, though he will suffer some pain if he eats it at all. All the causes of his trouble go back to one thing—it is the richest foods which hurt a man most, be he in good health or bad.

On the one hand, then, we have the physician (using the word in its ordinary sense), who is generally admitted to be the possessor of a certain skill and who has discovered the proper treatment and diet for the care of the sick. On the other, we have the man who in the distant past worked out for human use the diet we now follow, adapting it from a wild and savage one. What difference can be found between their purposes? It seems to me that their reasoning and their discoveries are the same. The ancient tried to eliminate things with which the digestion of a healthy man could not cope because of their harshness and crudity; the modern physician tries to eliminate things which the patient, in his temporary condition, cannot handle. What difference is there between the two, except for the superficial one that the work of the modern is more complicated and requires more detailed study, while that of the ancient came first in time and is therefore more primitive?

—*On Ancient Medicine,* 1–7

A PUBLIC HEALTH REPORT

In Thasos in the fall, from late September to early November, there were south winds with continual gentle rains. In the winter the south wind generally blew, with occasional mild northerly breezes and dry weather; this winter, on the whole, was very spring-like. When the spring came the wind blew from the south, but was raw and chilly, and brought only occasional light showers. The summer was generally cloudy, but without rain; the seasonal winds were light and irregular. As a whole, then, the weather of the year was dry, with south winds; the previous year had been just the opposite, with winds from the north.

Early in the spring a few people caught light fevers, which caused few hemorrhages [nosebleeds] and no deaths. There were a number of cases of swellings in front of the ear, on one side or both, but with most of these there was no fever and the patients did not even go to bed. A few of them had light fevers which subsided harmlessly. The swellings never infected, as those from other causes are apt to do. They may be described as big, soft, and spreading, with no inflammation or pain; they disappeared without warning. This ailment struck boys and young men, up to the prime of life, and especially those who spent much time in the wrestling school and gymnasium. Very few women were affected. Most victims had a dry cough which brought nothing up, and their voices became hoarse. A little later (occasionally after some time) a painful inflammation appeared in one or both testicles; this was sometimes accompanied by fever, sometimes not, but in most cases was very painful. Otherwise the city was free of diseases which require a physician's care.

From early in the summer on through the next winter, those who had not been feeling well for some time were forced to take to their beds with consumption, and many who had not been sure whether or not they were affected now became certain that they were. Some, too, who were constitutionally liable to consumption now first showed the signs of it. Many—or rather most—of these died, and I do not know of a single person who was already bed-ridden surviving for even a short time. Death came more suddenly than is usual in this disease; but the other sicknesses of the time were mild and not fatal, even when they persisted for a long time and were accompanied by fever. Consumption was the only one of the diseases current to kill any great number.

These were the symptoms in most cases: there were continuous sharp chills and fever, which did not cease entirely for a time and then return, but were of the sort which is milder on one day and more severe on the next, gradually increasing in violence. There was constant perspiration, but not all over the body. The hands and feet suffered severe chills, and it was hard to warm them up again. The bowels were disordered and had to be relieved frequently; their discharges were scanty, thin, and discolored, undigested, of a bilious and smarting quality. The urine was scanty, thin, and discolored, or sometimes oily, with a slight deposit; it did not settle normally, but left a raw and unfavorable precipitate. With some difficulty the patient coughed up small lumpy bits of sputum; this was especially true of the bad cases, where the sputum was hardly liquefied at all. In most cases there was a severe sore throat right from the start, with redness and inflammation. The nasal discharges were scanty, thin, and sharp. These patients lost weight and weakened quickly, and had no appetite or thirst throughout their sickness. As they approached death many became delirious. So much for this epidemic of consumption.

During the summer and fall there were many fevers, which were continuous but not severe, and, although most of the patients were sick for a long time, they were not unduly distressed. The bowels in most cases were comfortable, with no pain worth mentioning. The urine was generally clear and of a good color, but thin; as the disease approached its climax it grew thicker. There was little coughing, and that was not painful. The patients did not lose their appetite; on the contrary, it was easy to give them food. On the whole they were not very sick. They certainly did not have the chills and fever of the consumptives, and sweated only a little. The cycle of this disease varied in an unpredictable way from case to case. It reached its crisis in twenty days at the earliest, usually in about forty; but in many cases the crisis did not come for eighty days. Sometimes, indeed, the disease did not end in a well-defined crisis at all, but in a vague and uncertain way. In most such cases the fever disappeared for a little while, but then returned and started its cycle again. Such cases dragged out so that the victims were ill even during the winter.

Of the diseases mentioned in this account only

the consumption was fatal; those who suffered from the others had little discomfort, and their fevers did not kill them.

—*Epidemics*, I, 1–3

THE PHYSICIAN'S OBSERVATIONS

These are the things observed in disease from which we have learned to judge them, studying the general nature of mankind as well as the peculiarities of the individual, the disease as well as the patients, the measures taken and the physician who prescribed them. Our judgment is easier or harder in proportion to our knowledge of these matters. First of all, there is the general climate and any local peculiarities of geography and weather. Then there is the particular patient—his habits and way of life, his occupation, his age; his words, manner of speaking, talkativeness, silence; his disposition; his sleep or lack of it, the time and nature of his dreams, his gestures, his tears. Thirdly, from the onset of the disease we must consider the movements of the bowels and the urine, the spitting and vomiting; we must observe the causes of each stage in the progress of the disease, and likewise their effects, and how it finally reaches a favorable end or death. During its course we must study the patient's sweats and chills, coughs and sneezes, hiccoughs and breathing, belching and gas, and bleeding and piles. From our observation of these we must then decide what course the disease will take next.

—*Epidemics*, I, 23

REPORTS ON TWO CASES

I. Philiscus—lived near the city wall. On the first day of his illness he had a sharp fever with sweating and went to bed, but passed an uncomfortable night. On the second day he was worse, but an enema moved his bowels and he slept well. On the third day, up until noon he seemed to have gotten over his fever, but in the afternoon it returned, more severe than before, causing sweating, thirst, and a dry tongue. His urine was dark-colored. He passed a bad night, for he was unable to sleep and was, indeed, quite out of his mind. On the fourth day he was worse, and his urine was still black; this, however, turned a better color at night, when he was more comfortable. About noon on the fifth day he had a slight nosebleed of normal blood. The urine contained little round granules which would not settle out. A laxative brought a scanty movement of the bowels. He passed a painful night; sleep came only in snatches, and he kept babbling. His hands and feet were cold and would not recover their warmth. He passed some black urine, and toward morning got a little sleep. From this time on he was unable to speak. He broke into a cold sweat and his extremities turned gray. About noon on the sixth day he died. He breathed like a man who has to think about doing it, in deep breaths with long intervals between. His spleen was enlarged in a round swelling. Throughout the sickness he had cold sweats. This disease took a turn for the worse every even-numbered day from its onset.

—*Epidemics*, I, case 1

II. Apollonius of Abdera. Although this man had not felt well for a long time, he had not taken to his bed; his abdomen was swollen, and for quite a while he had felt severe pain in his liver. At this time he became jaundiced and had much gas, and his complexion turned pasty. After an injudicious dinner of beef, accompanied by much drinking, he felt hot and uncomfortable and went to bed. He then drank much milk, sheep and goat, both raw and boiled; this was a most unwise thing to do, and much harm resulted from it. His fever grew worse, and his bowels passed almost nothing of what he ate; a little thin urine was passed. He could not sleep. Later he developed a severe thirst, and presently fell into a coma. His belly was distended, with a painful swelling on the right side just below the ribs. All his extremities felt chilly. He muttered a little, but was out of his mind and could not remember what he said.

About the fourteenth day after he took to his bed he had a chill followed by fever and became delirious; he shouted and thrashed about, talking continuously. Then he began to sweat again, and his coma returned. His scanty urine was dark and thin, and his bowels were much disturbed, with bilious, crude, and undigested excreta of various sorts, either dark, thin, and purplish, or greasy, raw, and sharp; sometimes it was even of a milky consistency. About the twenty-fourth day he became more comfortable; his symptoms were much the same, but he was partly restored to his senses, although he could not remember anything that had happened since he took to his bed. But soon he went out of his mind again, and his condition deteriorated rapidly. About the thirtieth day he had a severe fever, with copious thin excrement. He became delirious and lost his voice, and his extremities grew cold. The thirty-fourth day he died. From the time I first saw the patient, his bowels were always disordered, his urine thin and dark. When not in a coma he could not sleep, and was delirious all the time. His extremities were cold for all this period.

—*Epidemics*, III, series 2, case 13

ARCHIMEDES OF SYRACUSE

ARCHIMEDES (287?–212 B.C.) studied in Alexandria as a young man, but presently returned to Syracuse in Sicily, where he lived on close terms with the king of that city. Here he continued his mathematical work, especially in solid geometry, developing various new methods of attacking problems. In his work on conic sections he even approached the discovery of integral calculus. He attempted to use the deductive method—that of basing his work on a few undoubted axioms and deriving his conclusions from them—in mechanics; in this way he made great advances, especially in the study of levers and in hydrostatics. While he did not make much use of the possibilities of experiment, he was able to realize intuitively what general laws his experiences illustrated, and to prove those laws deductively. Contrast the *inductive* proof of the "principle of Archimedes" given in a high school physics course with the *deductive* proof its inventor formulated and with the account of his discovery of the principle, an account taken from Vitruvius, an eminently practical Roman architect of the time of Augustus.

In 212 the Romans attacked Syracuse, and Archimedes was urged to help defend the town. He is said to have invented machines for hurling enormous weights at the Roman ships, great cranes which could pluck them out of the water, and burning mirrors to set them on fire. But the Romans finally took the city, and Archimedes was killed, against the orders of their commander, Marcellus. His tomb, a representation of a cylinder circumscribing a sphere, was long neglected; it was rediscovered by Cicero.

PURE AND APPLIED MATHEMATICS

Now all the siege machinery which Marcellus had brought against Syracuse was worthless against Archimedes and the devices he invented, yet Archimedes set no great store by his mechanical contrivances, and, indeed, regarded them as mere gadgets whittled out by geometry in a leisure moment. But finally King Hiero, who made much of Archimedes, persuaded him to leave his theoretical reasoning for a while and turn to everyday matters: if, said he, Archimedes would apply the abstract deductions of reason to the material things perceived by the senses, he would accomplish something of great and universal value.

It was in the schools of Archytas and Eudoxus that men first began to practise this highly prized and renowned art of mechanics, which they used to lend a certain glamor and attractiveness to geometry. Moreover, some problems which could not be solved by pure reason could, at least, be illuminated by experiment and the use of mechanical devices. So, for example, with the problem of dividing a line with two mean proportionals, a construction necessary for the solution of many problems. To this they found a mechanical solution by constructing an instrument which derived the required proportions from the ratios of sections of certain curves.

But Plato denounced these men angrily and asserted that they were apt to corrupt and destroy the valuable part of geometry, for, he said, they were seducing this science from the immaterial and spiritual to the material and bodily, things which require much menial and brutish toil. The art of mechanics was therefore separated from the science of geometry, and for a long time was looked down on by philosophers, who regarded it as a branch of the training useful to a soldier, but nothing more.

—Plutarch, *Marcellus*, 14

THE PRINCIPLE OF ARCHIMEDES

The discoveries of Archimedes were many and ingenious, in widely different fields, but of them all that which I am now going to describe seems to me best to display his unlimited cleverness.

Since the affairs of King Hiero of Syracuse had prospered and his power had been much increased, he decided to offer a golden crown in a certain temple in thanks to the immortal gods. He therefore let out a contract to a goldsmith, to whom he paid a fee for making the crown and enough beside for the exact weight of the gold that would be necessary. At the proper time the goldsmith presented a beautifully made crown to the king, having, to judge by the weight of the crown, used all the gold that had been issued to him. But a little later the king got wind of a story that the goldsmith had abstracted some of the gold and replaced it with an equal weight of silver. Hiero was furious at having been tricked, but he saw no way to prove the theft; he therefore asked Archimedes to think over his problem.

While Archimedes was considering the matter, he went one day to the city baths. There he went into a small pool [with an overflow pipe], and while in it he reflected that the submerged part of his body made its own volume of water overflow. Realization of this showed him the principle on which his whole problem hinged, and in his delight he leaped from the pool and ran home without bothering about his clothes, announcing in a loud voice that he had found what he was looking for. For as he hurried along he kept shouting in Greek, "I've got it! I've got it!" [Eureka! Eureka!]

The story goes on that after he had made this start he took a slab of silver and another of gold, each weighing the same as the crown. He then filled a large pot to the brim with water and dropped in the silver. Water equal in bulk to the silver ran over the edge of the pot; after removing the slab he measured the amount of water it took to refill the pot. Thus he found what weight of silver equalled that of a known bulk of water.

Next he dropped in his slab of gold, removed it, and measured the amount of water needed to replace the overflow; it was much less than had been the case with the silver—a difference corresponding to the smaller bulk of the gold, compared with the same weight of silver. Finally he lowered in the crown, and found that more water ran over than had done for the pure gold, although their weights were the same. From the difference in overflows of the crown and the pure gold Archimedes calculated the amount of silver alloyed with the gold in the crown, and thus proved the guilt of the goldsmith.

—Vitruvius, *On Architecture*, IX, 9–12

ARCHIMEDES' OWN STATEMENT OF HIS PRINCIPLE

Let us postulate the nature of a liquid to be such that (1) it is made up of equally distributed particles, each in contact with its neighbors; (2) particles under less pressure are driven aside by those under greater; (3) each particle would be driven straight down by the weight of the particles directly above it, were it not for the vessel which contains the liquid, or some outside force.

Propositions

I. If any surface is cut by planes which all pass through one fixed point, and the intersection of the surface and any plane forms a circle, the surface is that of a sphere whose center is the point common to all the planes. . . . [Archimedes gives a proof of all these propositions, omitted here.]

II. The surface of a liquid which is at rest is part of the surface of a sphere whose center is the same as that of the earth. . . .

III. If an object of the same weight as its own volume of a liquid is lowered into the liquid until nothing protrudes, it will move neither up nor down. . . .

IV. An object lighter than its own bulk of liquid will not be completely submerged if it is lowered into the liquid, but part will protrude above the surface. . . .

V. If an object lighter than its own bulk of a liquid is lowered into the liquid, it will sink until the liquid whose volume equals that of the submerged part of the object weighs as much as the entire object. . . .

VI. If an object lighter than its own bulk of a liquid is forced down under the liquid, it will be buoyed up by a force equal to the difference in the weights of the object and its volume of liquid. . . .

VII. If an object heavier than its own volume of liquid is lowered into the liquid, it will sink to the bottom; and it will then weigh less than it did in air by an amount equal to the weight of its own volume of liquid.

That it will sink to the bottom is apparent, for

the particles of liquid underneath the object will be pressed harder than those at the sides, since we have described the object as weighing more than its own volume of liquid [i.e., the object "presses down" harder than the liquid]. Now we shall show that the object becomes lighter as indicated.

Let the rectangle with *A* written on it represent an object heavier than its own bulk of liquid. Let the line marked *B* and *C* represent the weight of *A*, *B* being the weight of liquid equal in bulk to *A*. We want to prove that when *A* is lowered into the liquid, its weight will equal only *C*.

Let us take another object *D*, lighter than its own bulk of liquid, and whose weight equals *B*, while its volume of liquid weighs as much as *B* and *C* together.

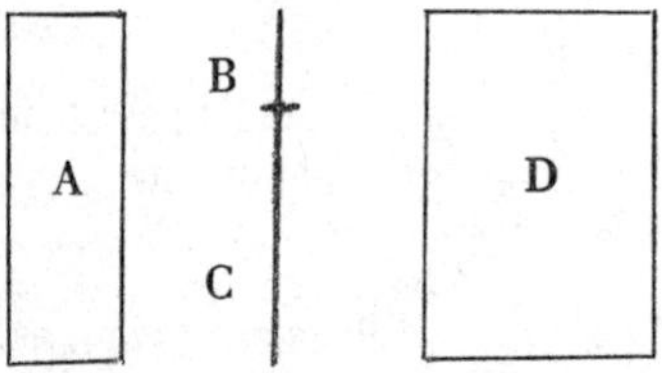

Now let *A* and *D* be fastened together. They will now weigh as much as their combined volume of liquid, for their weights together will equal the sum of their separate weights—that is, *B* and *C* added to *B;* and the weight of the liquid equal in bulk to the two joined objects will equal the sum of their weights.

Accordingly, if the joined objects are lowered into the liquid they will float in equilibrium, moving neither up nor down (Prop. III). It follows that *A*, which by itself would sink, is being drawn *up* by *D* with a force equal to its own force downward. Now since *D* is lighter than its own bulk of liquid, it will be buoyed up by a force equal to *C*, for we have shown that bodies lighter than a liquid will, if submerged, be borne up by a force equal to the difference between their own weights and that of their volumes of liquid (Prop. VI). But *D*'s volume of liquid is heavier than *D* by the weight *C*. It therefore follows that *A* is being driven down by a force equal to *C* [i.e., in water *A* apparently loses weight *B* and weighs only as much as *C*].

—*On Floating Bodies*, 318–336

TRANSLATOR'S NOTE: Archimedes rarely uses the term *force;* he thinks in terms of gain or loss in weight. The term is used here to keep the language from being too incomprehensible. Notice, too, that he does not express the notion that every substance has its own specific gravity, although it is implied.

Archimedes' proof rests on his use of substances of reciprocal specific gravities. Suppose that we use aluminum (sp. gr. 2.7) and white pine (sp. gr. .37). Let *A* be a block of aluminum 100 cubic inches in volume. It will weigh about 9.7 pounds. One hundred cubic inches of water (*B*) will weigh about 3.6 pounds; the difference between *A* and *B* will be 6.1 pounds (*C*). Now let *D* be a block of pine weighing the same as *B* (3.6 pounds). It will occupy about 270 cubic inches; this much water will weigh 9.7 pounds. If the two blocks are fastened together they will weigh 13.3 pounds; the water equal to their volume will also weigh 13.3 pounds, and they will float in equilibrium. The buoyancy of the pine, then, is equal to the apparent weight of the aluminum in water; but this in turn is equal to the weight of the aluminum in air minus the weight of its own volume of water—*Q.E.D.*

GALEN

THE MOST famous physician of later antiquity was Galen of Pergamum (A.D. 129–199). After winning great fame in his native Asia Minor, he moved to Rome and there spent most of his life, honored by the most important men in the state. He wrote over five hundred books, including many on philosophy.

In the centuries between Hippocrates and Galen a number of sects of medicine had arisen, each devoted to a theory of the sort attacked in the Hippocratic *Ancient Medicine*. Galen attacked their narrow views and tried to combine the whole of medicine into a unified system. He was a skilled observer, especially in the field of physiology, and until the Renaissance his works held the highest authority—partly, at least, because his teleological views accorded with those of the medieval church. These views are illustrated by the passage given here, from the work *On the Use of the Parts of the Human Body*. It must be remembered that this passage represents only the philosophical side of Galen's activity; space does not allow the inclusion of examples of his immense advances in the field of observation. Much of this passage was borrowed by Galen from Aristotle.

Galen was best known to the physicians of western Europe through Latin translations of Arabic versions until the thirteenth century, when he was translated directly from the Greek.

THE PURPOSE OF THE HUMAN HAND

2 All the parts of the body are subservient to the soul, for they are, as it were, the tools of which the soul makes use, and the parts of different animals vary just as do their temperaments. Some animals are fierce, some timid; some wild, others tame; some gregarious, others solitary; but in every case the beast's body is suited to its nature and character. Thus the horse has solid hoofs and is adorned with a mane, for he is a swift, proud creature. In like manner the lion, who is fierce and spirited, is endowed with sharp teeth and claws. . . . But nature has given man his hands rather than any other weapon for defense, for he is an intelligent animal, the only one in the world with the divine faculty of reason. The hand is the instrument he must use for all his arts, those of peace as well as those of war. He feels no need of a horn sprouting from his head, for whenever he needs them he can grasp with his hands the sword and spear, weapons sharper and more deadly than any horn. . . .

He is a peaceful and social animal too. With his hands he has written down laws and raised altars and statues to the gods; he has built ships and fashioned flutes and harps, knives and tongs, and all the instruments of his work, and has written down the record of what he has learned about them. Because of letters and the skill of man's hand you can converse even now with Plato, with Aristotle, with Hippocrates, with all the great men of the past.

3 Man is thus the most intelligent of animals, and his hands are organs suited to a creature of his intelligence. He is not clever because he has hands, as Anaxagoras used to preach: he has been given his hands because he is wise, as Aristotle correctly pointed out. Not his hands but his powers of reason gave man his skill. The hand is only the tool of the mind, as the harp is the tool of the musician and the tongs that of the smith. The harp did not train the one nor the tongs the other, but every man is skillful because of the talents with which he is endowed. Yet however gifted he may be, he cannot display his skill without tools. He derives his talents from within himself, but he cannot perform the work for which he was born without the necessary instruments. . . .

5 Now let us consider this part of the body, not asking idly whether or not it is useful and suitable for an intelligent being, but whether it might not be better if it were designed in some other way. The first question to be asked about a well-planned organ for grasping is whether it can easily take hold of objects of all the sizes and shapes that man is strong enough to move. Would it be more effective for it to be divided in parts or to be one solid piece? A silly question—if the hand were not divided into fingers it could seize only objects of its own size; but, broken up as it is, it can take hold of things much bigger than itself, and can also pick up tiny little objects. For the big things it can stretch out and spread the fingers, while for the small the tips of two fingers suffice; it does not need its whole extent, and, indeed, if it tried to pick small things up so, they would roll away and escape. Thus the hand is admirably made for grasping objects bigger or smaller than itself. Again, the divided form of the hand is beautifully adapted for grasping things of all shapes. It can be cupped around a curved object and thus seize it from all sides; it can also lay hold of straight and concave things. Since this is so, it can grasp everything, for all objects are bounded by plane, convex, or concave surfaces.

Since there are many objects too big to be taken in one hand, nature has given us two, each to help the other, so that the two together can seize a large object as well as one great hand could. So, too, for the sake of this sort of action the hands were made to face each other, and both arms were made the same length. This arrangement, moreover, is well suited for a pair of organs each of which must do the same things in the same way.

—*On the Use of the Parts*, I, 2–3

SELECTIONS FROM PLATO

Translated by William C. Greene

INTRODUCTION

THE DIALOGUES of Plato hold a central position in the development of philosophical thought. Before his time there had been in Greece detached moral sayings of "wise men," and speculations about the underlying unity of the physical world; there had been groups of religious men who held that the soul is immortal and can win a blessed release from the body (the members of the Orphic cult), and others who added to this conviction a remarkable success in mathematical studies and their applications to astronomy and music, and even to ethics and politics (the Pythagoreans). In the middle of the fifth century B.C., when Athens had achieved a democratic form of government, individual educators professed to train young men for public life by instruction in literature and "the art of persuasion" (the "Sophists," such as Gorgias and Protagoras). Most of them were honest; but some were interested only in the immediate success of their pupils, so that they had a profoundly unsettling effect on a society that honored tradition and the institutions of the state religion. Their contemporary Socrates (469–399 B.C.) did not share their professional claims, and charged no fee of the young men who came to talk with him; but he probed their minds and tried to find foundations for conduct more secure than tradition; and he criticized the unenlightened ways of the democracy and its leaders and their craze for money and power. Only the real welfare of the soul mattered, he urged. It was easy for the comic poet Aristophanes, in his play, *The Clouds*, to confuse the activities of the queer Socrates with those of previous speculators on nature and with those of certain Sophists; but after the defeat of Athens by Sparta in the Peloponnesian War, the Athenian democracy, when restored to power, struck at Socrates more in anger than in laughter and condemned him to death on the specious charge that he had corrupted the young.

Socrates left no writings; but his young associate, Plato (427–348 B.C.), wrote dramatic dialogues which set forth the character and the teaching of Socrates, and further dialogues that gathered various problems and ideas, partly Socratic and partly from other sources, and developed them in the direction in which Plato's own thought was moving; in the later dialogues Socrates is less prominent, till in the last of them, the *Laws*, he does not even appear. Even in the dialogues of Plato's middle period, it is often difficult to determine how far we are presented with the views of the historic Socrates and how far Plato is using his master as the mouthpiece for his own views. But there can be no question about the fundamental sympathy of Plato for the Socratic attempt to find a firm base for conduct in principles or laws that are not at the mercy of custom or individual fancy. His inquiries led him into logic and science, into mathematics and metaphysics, into religion and ethics and politics, into psychology and the theory of education, with excursions into economics and history and literary criticism. When the work of Plato in turn was continued by that of his brilliant pupil Aristotle, the direction did not greatly change. Socrates and Plato were reformers of society, with flashes of visionary insight, while Aristotle's patient observation and analysis, often critical of Plato, tended to remain on the level of objective appraisal, but they were all in a single stream of thought, which the Stoics and Cicero and many Christian writers and modern humanists have carried further. Epicureanism, and its Roman spokesman Lucretius, began from different premises, and have been continued by the researches of modern empirical science. A major task for contemporary thought is to resolve the conflicts between the humanistic and the scientific traditions. Because Plato includes in the broad sweep of his vision so much that is of perennial importance, and defines so many of the issues with such masterly skill, we are justified, then, in calling his position central in the march of thought; not without reason did one of the most original of recent philosophers declare that the course of all later philosophy consists of footnotes on Plato.

Plato was born in 427, probably in Athens, of an aristocratic family; he was trained in literature and philosophy even before his association with Socrates. He naturally looked forward to a political career; but the trend of party politics during the later years of the Peloponnesian War, and above all the political execution of Socrates, disillusioned him. He abandoned all political ambitions, and devoted the rest of his life to philosophy, in the conviction that good government could exist only when true philosophers found their way to political authority or politicians became philosophical. This explanation he gave later, in a letter which may well be genuine (Epistle VII, 324b–326b, 328a), in which he also referred to the conviction set forth in a famous passage in the *Republic* (473, below; see also *Republic* 520). Fundamental reform, then, must be through education; so Plato established at Athens, about 388 B.C., his Academy, a kind of university for graduate studies in ethics and political philosophy and mathematics. It is not unlikely that he had already visited the Pythagorean communities in southern Italy and Sicily in which similar studies were pursued. Half-way between the founding of the Academy and his death in 348, Plato was persuaded, against his better judgment, to try to translate theory into practice by going to Sicily and training the young ruler of Syracuse to become a philosopher-king. The attempt failed, as Plato expected it would, for the young man would not submit to the long educational process necessary for any real reform. He had better success in the Academy, where he launched on their studies not only Aristotle but a number of other men, many of whom became effective administrators of Greek states. But the real justification of his career is the influence that he has had, and may still have, on readers of the *Dialogues* in all ages. It is not necessary to agree with every statement or view of Plato; it is most important to understand the main direction of his thought. Nor should one overlook his honesty in drawing attention to debatable matters, as in the case of the "Third Wave" (*Republic* 473).

In this volume, as in all modern editions of Plato, passages are referred to by the page numbers of the famous edition by the French printer Stephanus, references to portions of the pages being lettered from *a* to *e*. The selections from the *Dialogues* that follow, like all excerpts taken from their settings, can convey only an imperfect idea of the complete works. Those given here are chosen in order to present the character of Socrates and his conception of his mission, and to provide some of the more significant passages from Plato's greatest work, the *Republic*. It has been necessary to omit some important passages: certain respectful portraits of the greater sophists which partly offset the hostile tone of other references; the hard thinking of the later "dialectical" dialogues which anticipate some of the criticisms of Aristotle and others; most of the theory of poetic inspiration that has won friends for "Plato the Poet" who are not wholly captivated by "Plato the Philosopher"; the sparkle of some of the earlier and more dramatic dialogues, as well as the prosiness of the later ones. What is here given has been slightly condensed, here and there, chiefly by the omission of unessential expressions of agreement on the part of interlocutors of Socrates, who really converses more than he lectures. Even so, something of the grace and charm of style, it is hoped, remains: courteous, sometimes ironical, simple in dealing with simple matters, earnest when the theme is high.

Plato is of course more than a humanist and poet, just as Epicurus is less than a scientist in the modern sense. Dialogues like the *Theaetetus, Sophist, Philebus, Timaeus,* and *Laws* show Plato advocating the study of mathematics, astronomy, and classification of animals, the search for evidence, and the examination of the logical relations of one's beliefs. These are not the preoccupations of modern humanists, who are perhaps better represented in antiquity by Isocrates than by Plato. Isocrates' school of rhetoric gave instruction in writing poetry and speeches, and reading the "great books." Plato has the style of a poet, and he tried to convey in the form of myths the conclusions he reached by reasoning. But it is as a close reasoner that he holds his central position in western philosophy; unfortunately that aspect of his genius cannot be adequately represented in an anthology of primarily literary selections for elementary students.

The modern reader of Plato who expects him to provide all the answers to contemporary problems may be at first disappointed and rebuffed. Plato has no easy answers, but rather sayings as hard and paradoxical as many of those in the New Testament. Virtue is knowledge; it is better to suffer injustice than to do injustice; only the soul is of value; the senses can not be trusted, and the only truth is in a realm that cannot be seen; learning is remembering; education is not filling the mind with facts but turning it toward the truth; philosophers must become kings: these ideas do not belong to the world of common experience and common sense, any more than do such injunctions as "love your enemies," or "whosoever will save his life shall lose it." Indeed it is necessary to weigh Plato's sayings, and those of the New Testament, with great care, and to interpret them fairly in their whole context.

Especially is this true in considering Plato's judgments on politics, lest prejudice lead to quick disagreement about details and then to a deep misunderstanding of larger matters. We are so accustomed to the democratic process, with its background in English constitutional development and the Common Law, in the French Revolution ("liberty, equality, fraternity"), and in the faith of the founding fathers in the rights of the common man, that we accept as final the verdict of orderly elections and peaceful compromises between the desires of reasonable men. But Plato had seen enough in Athens of the extremes of democracy to have a profound distrust of average human nature and its desires; if we are candid, we must admit that democracy has its weaknesses today. The tyrannies that Plato knew in Sicily and elsewhere were far worse, since they enslaved the many to the whims and cruelties of one man; we, too, have seen the like. What Plato sought, then, was the government of all, for their own good, by those best qualified by nature and training; this meant an aristocracy of high-minded experts, or conceivably a single "philosopher-king." The counterpart of such a "just" state would be the healthy individual whose desires are controlled by his reason, aided by his emotional qualities; and such is Plato's psychological analysis of human nature in the *Republic* (below, 415), further illustrated by his myth in the *Phaedrus.* Such justice, such health of mind and body, is happiness. It is even liberty, though not equality; for the state or the man that is enslaved by indiscriminate and conflicting desires is not really free.

Once the cardinal importance is established of the rational direction of society by experts, various possible misunderstandings are cleared away. The censorship of literature, for example, though not desirable in itself, at least can be justified for early education. We may well reject the communism of property and of the family that Plato contemplates for his small group of rulers (though not for society in general); but we shall note that his purpose is not to enable everyone to "share the wealth," but to liberate these rulers from private obligations in order to devote themselves wholly to their unselfish tasks. We may hesitate to believe with Plato in the possibility or the wisdom of entrusting to even the most enlightened and disinterested rulers, supposing them to have been found and trained, such absolute powers (remembering Lord Acton's dictum, that "all power corrupts, and absolute power corrupts absolutely"); for we are less pessimistic than Plato about the ignorance and incompetence and selfishness of the average man, and more ready to insist on the right of the sovereign people to make its own mistakes. We remember, too, how the German universities were exploited by a dictatorship. Even so, we are the more required by our own convictions to share Plato's belief that any true reform must spring from education, and therefore to extend education to more people and to improve its quality. We may deplore Plato's slighting remarks about the effects of manual labor (below, *Republic* 495); yet this is not snobbishness, but rather pity for those who are incapacitated by their natures, as well as by their occupations, for true freedom.

And what is freedom? Plato would agree with the saying: "Ye shall know the truth, and the truth shall make you free." But what is truth? Not the fickle evidence of the senses, or the changing opinions and votes of the many, Plato would answer. As the mathematician uses a chalk triangle on a blackboard to represent the real triangle that he is thinking about, so the philosopher is not thinking merely about the imperfect objects and activities of this world but also about the eternal realities which they only approximate; these realities are the famous "Ideas" or "Forms" which many would regard as Plato's most important and most characteristic contribution to philosophy (below, *Phaedo* 65–66; the use of quotation marks about these terms indicates that Plato attached a special meaning to them). Philosophy, therefore, and education generally, consist in turning the mind from the world of the senses to the steady contemplation of these realities, which may also become the objects not merely of intellectual apprehension but of ardent aspiration and love, and, in turn, the source of artistic inspiration and creation (in "idealistic" works). If, finally, we ask the ultimate question which man must always ask, why and how the "Ideas" exist and what their power is, Plato pauses, and points toward a still higher reality, the "Idea of Good," the source of the "ideas" and of all life and being, which he can further define only by the analogy of the sun (below, *Republic* 508–9). It is tempting to see in the "idea of good" Plato's conception of God; yet it is an impersonal conception. In the *Republic* he insists on the goodness of "the gods"; in the *Timaeus* he describes a divine creator or "Demiurge" fashioning the universe; in the *Laws* he argues against atheism. All these religious ideas are the more personal expression of the impersonal idealism of Plato's philosophy.

These few pages can give only a suggestion of the richness of Plato's thought; the reader will do well to explore as much more as he can by wider reading. But he will discover that the great value of Platonism lies not in special statements with which he may agree or disagree, or even in a massive system of thought inviting his intellectual assent. It consists rather in its power of persuading the reader to face problems honestly for himself, and to ask whether materialism, economic and political tinkering, the satisfaction of personal desires, the realistic recording in literature and art of things as they appear, will in the end be enough, or whether they must not be transformed in the light of "that good which every soul pursues as the end of all her actions, dimly divining its existence, but perplexed and unable to grasp its nature with the same clearness as in dealing with other things, and so missing whatever value those other things might have" (*Republic* 505e; compare the ideal of doing everything "to the glory of God"). It is no small gain to be compelled, like Socrates, to confess in all humility that one knows less than one has supposed. And if Plato's thought at times seems abstract and difficult, we may return with him to the person of his master Socrates. Why did he refuse to escape from prison? Not because bones and muscles would not easily have carried him away but because he thought it more just and honorable to remain (*Phaedo* 98c–99d). Here is philosophy itself, personified in compelling form.

THE FOLLOWING selections are grouped to develop two themes: the life and character of Socrates, and the development of Plato's thought. The text translated is that of John Burnet (Oxford, 1899–1905).

THE LIFE AND CHARACTER OF SOCRATES

From the SYMPOSIUM

THE SYMPOSIUM recounts a series of speeches at a banquet, in the course of which Socrates develops the theory of a realm of eternal Ideas transcending the world of the senses. The excerpts given here are chosen for the light that they throw on the impression made by Socrates on a very different kind of man, the brilliant but selfish Alcibiades.

ALCIBIADES. I will try to praise Socrates, gentlemen, by means of images. He may think that I do so in order to ridicule him; but my purpose is not ridicule but truthfulness. Now I say that he is just like the figures of Silenus that are set up in statuaries' shops, holding pipes or flutes; and when they are opened up they show that they have inside them the images of gods. And I say that he is like Marsyas the satyr. You will not yourself deny, Socrates, that in your face, at any rate, you are like a satyr; listen now while I show that you are like one in other ways, too. You are a bully, aren't you? If you won't admit it, I shall produce witnesses. And a flute-player, too? Yes, one more wonderful than Marsyas; for he charmed men with instruments, by the power of his lips . . . whereas you produce the same effect by your words alone, without any instrument.

When we hear any other speaker, however good, he has no effect on us; but whenever anyone hears you, or hears your words from the lips of even an indifferent speaker, we are amazed and spellbound, man, woman, and child alike. . . . When I heard Pericles and other great orators, I thought they spoke well, but I had no such experience as this; my soul was not disturbed or angered at the discovery of my slavish condition. But I have often been reduced by this Marsyas to such a state (*216*) that I have felt that life was unendurable for me if I lived as I do. *Touché*, Socrates? Even now I realize that if I were willing to heed him I could not hold out against him but should suffer the common lot. For he compels me to confess that I neglect my own shortcomings while I carry on the public business of the Athenians. So I stop my ears, as against the Sirens, and run away, so as not to grow old sitting at his feet. But it is only in his presence that I feel, what some might suppose I have not the grace to feel, ashamed of myself. For I realize that I cannot refute him or prove that I ought not to do what he bids; but when I take my leave of him I am undone by the flattery of the many. . . .

[The endurance of Socrates, on military service, was remarkable.] *220* Moreover, when one morning he was reflecting upon some subject and getting nowhere with it, he would not give up, but stood where he was, lost in thought. Now when it was high noon, and people took note of him, word got round among the wondering crowd that Socrates had been standing and thinking about something ever since daybreak. Finally in the evening, after supper (for it was then summer), some Ionians brought out bedding and slept outdoors, keeping an eye cocked to see whether he would stand there all night, too. Well, he did stand there till dawn and sunrise; and then, after a prayer to the sun, he took his departure.

Now, if you like, I'll tell about his behavior in battle, for it's only fair to pay him this tribute. When the fight took place after which I was awarded the prize of valor, it was no one but Socrates who saved my life, and would not leave me when I was wounded, but rescued me and my arms. And I then urged the generals, Socrates, to give the prize to you (no, no; you can't deny it); but since the generals were impressed by my rank and wanted to award the prize to me, you were more eager than the generals that I, rather than you, should receive it. . . .

221 Much else that is wonderful could one say in praise of Socrates; his ways in general one could perhaps compare with those of another man, but his complete unlikeness to any other man either of olden times or of our day is absolutely amazing. One might compare Brasidas and others with Achilles, or Nestor and Antenor with Pericles, and so forth; but for this strange creature no one could ever find a likeness, past or present, unless it were the likeness that I have mentioned, not men, but Sileni and Satyrs; and this figure represents both the man and his words. For I neglected before to say that his words are very much like the images of Silenus when they are opened. If one listens to his words, they sound quite ridiculous at first, clothed in language like the skin of the wanton satyr; for he talks of pack-asses and smiths and cobblers and tanners, and seems always to speak of the same things in the same terms, so that any ignorant novice might laugh at his speech. *222* But once the images are open, and one looks inside them, first one will find that they are the only words that have sense in them, and then that they are divine, with many an image in them of virtue, and of the widest range, or rather let me say ranging to the full scope of all that becomes any man who is to be noble. [215a–222a]

From the PHAEDRUS

A walk by the Ilissus

229 SOCRATES. Let's turn aside here and walk along the Ilissus, and then we may sit down in some quiet place, wherever we please.

PHAEDRUS. Well, I'm lucky in having come barefooted, and you never wear sandals; so we may easily wade in the brook, which will be pleasant especially since it is noon and summer.

SOCRATES. Lead on, then, and see where we may sit down.

PHAEDRUS. Do you see that tallest plane-tree?

SOCRATES. Certainly.

PHAEDRUS. There is shade, and a gentle breeze, and grass to sit on, or to lie upon, if we wish. [They discuss a local myth—a less important matter, says Socrates, than self-knowledge.]

230 SOCRATES. But is not this, my friend, the tree to which you were leading me?

PHAEDRUS. Yes, this is the tree.

SOCRATES. By Hera, it is a fair retreat. This plane-tree is tall and spreading; and the agnus castus, high and shady and in full blossom, fills the place with fragrance; and the spring that flows beneath the plane-tree is delightfully cool to the feet. To judge from the little votive images, the place must be sacred to Achelous and the Nymphs. How lovely and how sweet the breeze is! Its summer shrillness answers back to the chorus of the grasshoppers. But best of all is the grass, sloping gently like a pillow for our heads. My dear Phaedrus, you have been an excellent guide.

PHAEDRUS. You strange and absurd creature! From your talk you would seem to be absolutely in the hands of a guide, and not to be a native. I believe you never at all go outside the city wall into the country.

SOCRATES. Forgive me, my good friend. You see I am a lover of knowledge, and the country and the trees teach me nothing, whereas the men in the city do teach me. But I think you have found a charm to entice me forth; as men draw hungry beasts by dangling a bough or fruit before them, so you, by holding before me a book, may well lead me all over Attica or wherever you will.

[Thus it appears, after all, that it is not merely the beauty of the landscape but the love of discourse that leads Socrates to this rustic retreat. In the rest of the dialogue, Socrates discusses the difference between conventional rhetoric and a true rhetoric founded on knowledge of truth, on inspiration by a vision of a beauty transcending the world of the senses.] [229a–230e]

From the APOLOGY

Socrates defends himself in court.

[Socrates, after ironical compliments to the cleverness of his accusers, begs to be allowed to use his customary plain style; he will merely tell the truth, first explaining the causes of his present predicament.]

18 SOCRATES. First, then, I ought to reply to the earlier charges against me and my earlier accusers, and then to the later ones. For there have been many accusers for many years, though their charges have been false; and I am more afraid of them than of Anytus and his associates, though they, too, are formidable. But the earlier are still more formidable, since they began when most of you were children to persuade you by false accusations that there is one Socrates, a wise man, who speculates about the heavens above and investigates what is beneath the earth, and who makes the worse appear to be the better case. They who have broadcast this rumor are my really formidable accusers; for their hearers suppose that those who investigate these matters do not believe in the existence of the gods. Then, too, these accusers are many and have been at work for a long time during your most credulous years, when you were children or young men, and when there was no one to answer them. And what makes it hardest of all is that I do not know and cannot name any of them—unless perhaps it be some comic poet. All who by envy and malice persuaded you, some of them actually themselves persuaded, are most difficult to deal with; for I cannot put any of them up here for cross-examination, but must engage in shadow-fighting in my defense, and must ask questions when there is no one to answer me. . . .

Well, then, I must defend myself, and I must try (*19*) in a short time to clear away a slander that you have accepted for a long time. I hope I may succeed, if success is for your welfare as well as mine. But I think, indeed I know, it will be difficult. Yet God's will be done; and I must make my defense in obedience to the law.

Let us begin at the beginning. What is the accusation that lies behind the slander against me, relying on which Meletus has brought this charge against me? Well, what do the slanderers say? I may phrase their charge as follows: "Socrates is guilty of busying himself with inquiries about subterranean and celestial matters and of making the worse appear the better case and of teaching these matters to others." There, that's the sort of charge; and you yourselves have seen it embodied in the comedy of Aristophanes, in which "Socrates" is presented as suspended aloft and proclaiming that he is "treading on air" and talking a lot of other nonsense about which I understand nothing either great or small. Not that I disprize such knowledge on the part of any one who really knows about such matters; I hope I may not have to defend myself against Meletus on such a charge. But the fact is that I have nothing to do with such matters. I appeal to most of you as witnesses of this fact, and I beg you to speak up to one another, as many as have ever heard me discoursing; tell one another whether any of you have ever heard me talking about such matters in brief or at length. You see; and from their response to this question you will judge that the rest of the gossip about me is of the same cloth.

[And it is not true that Socrates, like the Sophists, undertakes formal instruction and charges fees.]

20 Perhaps, then, some one of you may ask: "Well, Socrates, what is this occupation of yours? How have these slanders against you arisen? Surely all this talk would not have sprung up if you had not been busying yourself with something out of the ordinary. Tell us then what it is, so that we may not judge you arbitrarily."

Fair enough; and I'll try to show you what has given me this reputation and this slander. Listen. Perhaps I shall seem to some of you to be speaking in jest; but I am going to tell you the whole truth. I got this reputation wholly because of a kind of wisdom. What sort of wisdom? Well, perhaps it is such wisdom as man can make his own; I rather think I have that kind of wisdom. The gentlemen whom I mentioned a moment ago may have a superhuman wisdom, or I don't know what to call it; I don't understand it, and any one who says I do speaks falsely in order to slander me. Now, gentlemen, don't make a disturbance even if I seem to say something extravagant; for the point that I am going to make is not mine, but I am going to refer you to a witness as to my wisdom and its nature who is deserving of your credence: the god of Delphi.

You must have known Chaerephon; he (*21*) was a boyhood friend of mine, and as your friend he shared in the recent exile of the people and returned with you. And you know what manner of man he was—very impetuous in all his undertakings. Well, he went to Delphi and had the audacity to ask the oracle—now, as I was saying, please don't make a disturbance, gentlemen—he asked the oracle if there was any one wiser than I. And the Pythian priestess answered that there was no one wiser. Since Chaerephon is dead, his brother here will vouch for this statement.

Consider now why I tell you this; I am going to explain to you the source of the slander against me. When I had heard the answer of the oracle, I said to myself: "What in the world does the god mean, and what is this riddle? For I realize that I am wise in nothing, great or small; what then does he mean by saying that I am the wisest? Surely he does not lie; that is not in keeping with his nature." For a long time I was perplexed; then I resorted to this method of inquiry. I went to one of those men who were reputed to be wise, with the idea of disproving the oracle and of showing it: "Here is one wiser than I; but you said that I was the wisest." Well, after observing and talking with him (I don't need to mention his name; but he was a politician), I had this experience: the man seemed in the opinions of many other men, and especially of himself, to be wise; but he really wasn't. And then I tried to show him that he thought he was wise, but really wasn't; so I found myself disliked by him and by many of those present. So I left him, and said to myself: "Well, I am wiser than this man. Probably neither of us knows anything noble; but he thinks he knows, whereas he doesn't, while I neither know nor think I know. So I seem to have this slight advantage over him, that I don't think I know what I don't know." Next I went to another man who was reputed to be even wiser, and in my opinion the result was the same; and I got myself disliked by him and by many others.

After that I went to other men in turn, aware of the dislike that I incurred, and regretting and fearing it; yet I felt that God's word must come first, so that I must go to all who had the reputation of knowing anything, as I inquired into the meaning of the oracle. And by the Dog! gentlemen, (*22*) for I must tell you the truth, this is what happened to me in my quest: those who were in greatest repute were just about the most lacking, while others in less repute were better off in respect to wisdom. I really must expound to you my wanderings, my Herculean labors to test the oracle. After the politicians, I went to the poets, tragic, dithyrambic, and the rest, with the expectation that there I should be caught less wise than they. So picking up those of their poems which seemed to me to be particularly elaborated, I asked them what they meant, so that at the same time I might learn something from them. Now I am ashamed to tell you the truth, but it must be spoken; almost every one present could have talked better about the poems than their authors. So presently I came to know that the poets, too, like the seers and the soothsayers, do what they do not through wisdom but through a sort of genius and inspiration; for the poets, like them, say many fine things without understanding what they are saying. And I noticed also that they supposed because of their poetry that they were wisest of men in other matters in which they were not wise. So I left them, too, believing that I had the same advantage over them that I had over the politicians.

Finally I went to the craftsmen; for I knew that I knew hardly anything, but that I should find them knowing many fine things. And I was not deceived in this; they knew things that I did not know, and in this way they were wiser than I. But even good craftsmen seemed to me to have the same failing as the poets; because of his skill in his craft each one supposed that he excelled also in other matters of the greatest importance; and this lapse obscured their wisdom. So I asked myself whether I would prefer to be as I was, without their wisdom and without their ignorance, or to have both their wisdom and their ignorance; and I answered myself and the oracle that I was better off just as I was.

From this inquiry many enmities have arisen against me, (*23*) both violent and grievous, as well as many slanders and my reputation of being "wise." For those who are present on each occasion suppose that I have the wisdom that I find wanting in others; but the truth is that only God is wise, and that by that oracle he means to show that human wisdom is worth little or nothing. And by speaking of "Socrates" he appears to use me and my name merely as an example, just as if he were to say, "Mortals, he of you is wisest who, like Socrates, knows that in truth his wisdom is worth nothing." That is why I go about even now, questioning and examining in God's name any man, citizen or stranger, whom I suppose to be wise. And whenever I find that he is not wise, then in vindication of the divine oracle I show him that he is not wise. And by reason of this preoccupation I have no leisure to accomplish any public business worth mentioning or any private business, but I am in extreme poverty because of my service to the god.

Besides this, the young men who follow me about of their own accord, well-to-do and with plenty of leisure, take delight in hearing men put to the test, and often imitate me and put others to test; and then, I believe, they find no lack of men who suppose they know something but who know little or nothing. Then the people who are quizzed by them are angry with me, not with themselves, and say, "There is one Socrates who is a rascal and who corrupts the young." And when any one asks them what this Socrates does or teaches, they don't know and have nothing to say, but so as not to seem to be at a loss they repeat the ready-made charges made against all philosophers, about things celestial and things subterranean, and not believing in gods, and making the worse appear the better case. They wouldn't like to admit the truth, I suppose, which is that they have been shown up as pretenders to knowledge that they do not possess. Now since they are ambitious and energetic and numerous, and are well marshalled and persuasive, they have filled your ears with vehement and oft-repeated slander. [18a–19d; 20c–23e]

[Turning now to the immediate charges, Socrates has no difficulty in showing their shallowness and insincerity. But he has no illusions about the deep and dangerous prejudice that lies behind them, though he will not therefore abandon his divine and philosophic mission, even to save his life. "For I go about doing nothing but persuading you all, young and old, not to care for your bodies or for money more than for the excellence of your souls, saying that virtue does not come from money, but that it is from virtue that money comes and every other good of man, both private and public."]

Socrates the gadfly

30 Now therefore, Athenians, I am far from arguing merely in self-defense, as one might suppose; I am arguing on your behalf, to prevent you from sinning against God by condemning me who am his gift to you. For if you put me to death you will not easily find another like me, one attached by God to the state, which (if I may use a rather ludicrous figure) is like a great and noble steed, but a sluggish one by reason of his bulk and in need of being roused by a gadfly. I am the gadfly, I think, which God has attached to the state; (*31*) all day and in all places I always light on you, rousing you and persuading you and reproaching each one of you. Another like me you will not easily find, and if you will take my advice you will spare me. But perhaps you may be annoyed by me, like people who are roused from slumber, and may slap at me and kill me, as Anytus advises; and then you would doze through the rest of your lives—unless God in his mercy should send you another gadfly. . . .

Socrates has been deterred by his inner voice from entering politics.

It may seem strange that I go about busying myself with private advice but do not venture to enter public life and advise the state. Well, the reason for this is what you have often and in many places heard me mention: that divine warning, or voice, which has come to me from childhood, and which Meletus ridiculed in his indictment. When it speaks, it always diverts me from something that I am going to do, but never eggs me on; and it is this that opposes my entering politics. And quite rightly, I think; for rest assured, gentlemen, that if I had tried to engage in politics I should have perished long ago without benefiting either you or myself. Now don't be angry at me for telling you the truth; for the fact is that no man who honestly opposes you or any other crowd, trying to prevent the many unjust and lawless deeds that are done in the state, will save his life. *32* He who fights effectively for what is just, if he wants to save his life for even a brief time, must remain a private citizen and not engage in public life. [30d–32a]

[After a few further arguments, and a dignified refusal to indulge in emotional appeals to the jury (or judges), Socrates rests his case. He is condemned by a narrow margin; to the accuser's proposal of death as penalty he is tempted to propose as counter-penalty that he be honored by the support of the state, but is persuaded by friends to offer instead a fine of money, which they will guarantee. By a larger margin, he is condemned to death. The rest of his speech is addressed, first to the judges who voted against him, then to those who voted to acquit him.]

A prophecy of judgment

39 And now, you who have voted to condemn me, I wish to proclaim to you a prophecy; for I am now approaching death, and it is when men are about to die that they are most given to prophecy. I tell you who have brought about my death that immediately after my death there will come upon you a punishment far more grievous, by Zeus, than the punishment that you have inflicted on me. You have voted in the belief that you would rid yourselves of the need of giving an account of your lives; I tell you that the very opposite will befall you. Your accusers will be more numerous, men whom I restrained though you were not aware of them, fiercer because younger; and you will smart the more. If you think that by killing men you are going to prevent any one from reproaching you for not living well, you are not well advised; for that riddance is neither possible nor noble. The noblest and the easiest means of relief is not to cut short the lives of others but to reform your own lives. That, then, is the prophecy that I give to those who have condemned me, before I depart.

To those who voted to acquit me I would gladly talk about what has befallen, while the magistrates are busy and I am not yet on my way to the place where I must die. Do remain, gentlemen, just these few minutes, for nothing prevents our discoursing while it is permitted. *40* For I should like to show you, friends as you are, the meaning of what has happened to me. Why, judges (you I may rightly call judges), something wonderful has befallen me. That customary divine warning of mine has frequently prevented me in time past from acting wrongly, even in trifling matters; but on this occasion, when what would generally be regarded as the worst of evils befell me, it did not oppose me when I was leaving my house in the morning, or when I was on my way hither, or at any point in my speech, though it has often checked me in the midst of other speeches. This time, it has opposed no deed or word of mine in the whole affair. What then am I to suppose to be the explanation? I will tell you: I am inclined to believe that what has happened is a good, and that they are mistaken who suppose death to be an evil. A great token of this has been given me; for my customary sign would have opposed me if I had not been going to fare well.

Let us consider another argument for there being great reason to hope that death is a good. There are two possibilities: either death is nothingness and utter lack of consciousness, or as men say it is a change and migration of the soul from this world to another place. Now if there be no consciousness, but something like a dreamless sleep, death would be a wondrous boon. For if one were to select that night during which he had thus slept without a dream, and were to compare with it all the other nights and days of his life, and were to tell us how many days and nights he has spent in the course of his life better and more pleasantly than this one, I think that any private citizen, and even the great king, would not find many such days or nights. If then death be of such a nature, I say that it is a boon; for all eternity in this case appears to be only a single night.

But if death is a journey to another place, and if, as men say, it is true that all the dead abide there, what greater good could there be than this? [Socrates pictures his arrival there and his discourse with the great men of old.] *41* Above all, it would be pleasant to spend my time examining the men there, as I have those here, and discovering who among them is wise and who thinks he is but is not. What would one not give to examine the leader of the great expedition against Troy, or Odysseus, or Sisyphus, or countless others, both men and women? It would be an indescribable delight to converse with them, and associate with them, and examine them. For surely they don't put men to death there for asking questions; those who dwell there, besides being happier than men here are in general, are immortal, if what is said is true.

So, my judges, you must be of good cheer about death and be assured of this one truth, that no evil can befall a good man, in life or in death, and his estate is not neglected by the gods; nor have my affairs been determined by chance, but it is clear to me that for me to die and to take my leave of troubles is now for the best. That is why my sign did not divert me, and why I am not really angry with those who condemned me or with my accusers. To be sure, they acted not with the intent of helping me, but thinking to hurt me; for this I have a right to find fault with them.

I have nevertheless this request to beg of them: when my sons are grown up, punish them, gentlemen, and trouble them just as I troubled you, if they seem to be more concerned about money or about anything else than virtue; and if they pretend to be something when they are really nothing, reproach them as I reproached you for wrong concerns and false pretensions. *42* If you do this, my sons and I shall have received justice from you.

But now it is time to depart, for me to die, for you to live. Which of us goes to the better state, God only knows. [39c–42a]

From the Crito

"We ought never to return evil for evil, whatever we may suffer."

[After the condemnation of Socrates, his elderly friend Crito visits him in the prison and tries to persuade him to escape to some other city. Socrates refuses to let his personal misadventure outweigh the principles that he has upheld all his life and to play truant against the laws of Athens. He imagines these laws to address him, as follows.]

50 Socrates. "Tell us, Socrates," they will say,

"what it is that you have in mind to do; is it not to destroy us, the laws, and the whole state, so far as you are able? Do you suppose that a state can exist and not be overturned whose verdicts have no force, but are made null and void by individuals? . . .

"Since you were brought into the world and reared and educated by us, can you deny in the first place that you are our child and slave, like your fathers before you? And if this is so, do you think you are on equal terms with us, and that it is right for you to do to us what we seek to do to you? It would not be right for you to retaliate against your father or your master, if you had one, (*51*) because you had been struck or reviled or otherwise injured by him; well, if we deem it right to destroy you, is it your privilege to destroy us, the laws, and your fatherland, so far as you are able? Are you going to say that you would be justified in doing so, you who are concerned with real virtue? Has your wisdom failed to understand that our fatherland is more precious and holier and more to be revered by gods and men of sense than any mother or father or ancestor, and that if it is angry it must be respected and soothed even more than a father, and either persuaded or obeyed? If it commands suffering, or blows, or bonds, or leads you into battle and wounds or death, you must suffer in silence and obey, as is right, neither yielding nor leaving the ranks; in battle or in court of law or anywhere else you must do what your fatherland commands, or you must persuade it to find a different conception of what is just. . . .

52 "There is clear proof, Socrates, that we and the city were pleasing to you; for more than all other Athenians you have remained in the city, and never travelled, as other men do. . . . Moreover in this very trial you might, if you had wished, have set the counter-penalty at exile, and have done with the city's approval what she now forbids. But you then made a show of fine sentiments, and said you would rather die than go into exile; and now you are ashamed of those sentiments, and give no heed to us the laws, but seek to destroy us. Why, you are doing just what the meanest slave might do, trying to run away from the compacts and agreements that you made as a citizen. . . .

54 "Now, Socrates, listen to us who brought you up, and do not regard children or life or anything else as having a claim prior to justice; so you may go down to the realm of Hades and make your defense before the judges there. For neither here nor there, if you do as Crito urges, will you or your kindred be happier or more just and holy. But as it is you will go forth in innocence, the victim of injustice not from us the laws but from men; whereas if you go forth after basely returning evil for evil and breaking the agreements and compacts that you made with us and wronging those whom you ought least of all to wrong—yourself, your friends, your fatherland, and us—we shall be angry with you while you live, and in the realm below our brothers, the laws that dwell in Hades, will receive you in no friendly spirit, knowing that you did all that you could to destroy us. So give heed to us, and not to Crito."

That, my dear friend Crito, is the voice that I seem to hear, like the sound of the flutes that the mystic initiates seem to hear; these words are ringing in my ears so that I can hear nothing else, and I am sure that if you speak to any other purpose you will speak in vain.

CRITO. Well, Socrates, I have nothing more to say.

SOCRATES. Then, Crito, let me follow wherever God leads me. [50a–54e]

From the PHAEDO

The last hours in the life of Socrates

THE *Phaedo* represents an account supposed to have been given, some months or years after the death of Socrates, by his follower Phaedo to a friend named Echecrates. It is distinctly stated that Plato was not among the considerable number of friends who were present; "Plato, if I am not mistaken, was ill." This may be Plato's way of showing that the account is not to be taken in detail as an actual transcript of what Socrates said, but is rather his own interpretation of the significance of his master's death. This is particularly true of the philosophic argument in defense of the immortality of the soul which comprises the central and major part of the dialogue, but which is not included here.

In his *Apology*, Socrates has pleaded formally, at least, for his right to live; in the *Crito* he has refused to run away from death; and now in the *Phaedo* he defends his readiness to die against those who deplore his death. The belief in immortality was as old as Homer, but it promised little of good cheer except for the fortunate few. The initiates into the mystical religious bodies, such as the Eleusinian, the Orphic, and the Pythagorean cults, to be sure, had hopes of personal salvation, and the *Apology* referred to immortality as one of two alternative possibilities. But here the argument is elaborate and determined. Curiously enough, Socrates and Lucretius are both concerned to prove that man should not grieve at the approach of death, but for opposite reasons: Lucretius because the soul is, as he holds, mortal, and this life is all; Socrates because the soul is immortal, and there is a blessed hereafter for the righteous. The soul that can entertain abstract and eternal ideas must itself be eternal; philosophy is indeed the gradual discovery of the real world that lies beyond what the senses reveal to us; the philosopher, by learning to rely on mind rather than on body, is always "rehearsing" that final separation of soul and body which we call death.

However much or little of this argument the modern reader may be disposed to accept, he cannot fail to be moved by the exquisite picture of Socrates and his courage and considerateness in the face of death. If the glowing account of the ideal world that Socrates has set forth over the wine cup in the *Symposium* (in a passage, 201c–212a, not included here) is a "L'Allegro," here in the *Phaedo* before drinking the hemlock cup Socrates more soberly, yet cheerfully, contemplates the same world in an "Il Penseroso." For many a reader of Plato, or of philosophy in general, and for many a student of religion, the ultimate question will be not whether to give or to withhold intellectual assent, but whether the life and the attitude toward death of a Socrates or of a Jesus command personal respect and loyalty.

58 PHAEDO. I had a strange feeling at being in his society; for no sense of pity came over me, such as I should have expected to feel when present at the death of a friend. For in words and manner, Echecrates, he died so fearlessly and so nobly that to me he seemed happy; so that he gave me cause to believe that he was not going to Hades without divine favor, but rather that he, if any man, would fare well when he arrived there. *59* That is why I did not feel the pity that would have been natural on a sorrowful occasion. But I did not take pleasure, as usual, in philosophy, which was the subject of our conversation; pleasure and pain were strangely mingled as I reflected that he was soon to die. And all of us who were present were now laughing, now weeping. . . .

On the previous days we had been accustomed to gather early in the morning at the court where the trial had taken place, for it is near the prison. There we waited, talking together, till the prison door was opened (for it was not opened very early); and when it was opened we went in and passed the day with Socrates. Now on this last day we gathered earlier than usual, since we had learned when we left the prison the previous evening that the ship had arrived from Delos [after the arrival of which Socrates was to die]; so we arranged to come as early as possible to the usual place. When we met, the jailer who usually answered our knock came out and told us to wait until he called us. "For the Eleven," said he, "are setting Socrates free from his chains and are giving orders for him to die today." Not long afterwards he returned and told us to go in. On entering, *(60)* we found Socrates just released from his chains, and Xanthippe—you know her—sitting by him with their child in her arms. When Xanthippe saw us, she gave a cry, and said, as women will, "O Socrates, this is the last time that your friends will talk with you, or you with them." And Socrates glanced at Crito, and said, "Crito, let someone take her home." And some of Crito's household led her away crying out and beating herself. [58e–60b]

Socrates now develops the main thought of the dialogue: that "the real philosopher has reason to be of good cheer when he is about to die," since he has already learned to prize the soul and its concerns rather than those of the body.

65 SOCRATES. What about the actual acquisition of knowledge? Is the body, if made a partner in the quest, a hindrance or a help? I mean, have sight and hearing any truth, or are they not, as the poets are always telling us, inaccurate and obscure? If so, when does the soul lay hold on truth, since it is clear that when she attempts to consider anything in partnership with the body she is deceived? Must it not then be by the process of thinking, if at all, that reality becomes clear? And thought is best carried on when the soul is not troubled by hearing or sight, by pain or pleasure, but when she is most by herself and takes leave of the body as far as possible and reaches forth after that which is; so the philosopher's soul dishonors the body, and runs away from it, and seeks to be by itself.

And then, too, do we not say that there is such a thing as justice, and beauty, and goodness? But we never saw any such thing with our eyes, or grasped them with any of our bodily senses; no, nor greatness, nor health, nor strength, nor in a word any of the other realities in their true natures. He comes nearest to knowing each of them who most clearly thinks about their several natures. And he attains to the purest knowledge who most proceeds to each by thinking, without employing in addition sight or any other sense, (*66*) but by the use of pure reason seeks to hunt out the pure nature of each, ridding himself as far as possible of eyes and ears and body in general, since they disturb and prevent the soul from acquiring truth and knowledge. He, if any man, attains to that which is. So genuine philosophers must be led by their reflections to say to one another something like this: "The path of our thought seems to carry us to the conclusion that so long as we are in the body and the soul is confounded with its ills we shall never satisfy our avowed craving for the truth." [65a–66b]

67 Now if this is so, there is great reason for hope that going where I go I shall attain there, if anywhere, that which has been the object of my lifelong pursuit. So that this departure now required of me is attended by good cheer, as it would be for any man who believes that his mind is ready and made pure. And this purification, as I have said before, is the separation of the soul from the body, as far as is possible, and her habit of gathering herself together and dwelling apart, as far as she can, both now and hereafter, freed as it were from the bonds of the body. This severance between soul and body is what is called death; and true philosophers, and they only, are always eager for this severance, and it is their special study. Now it would be ridiculous for a man who has in his life been preparing himself to live in a state as near as possible to death to complain when death draws near. The real philosophers are rehearsing the act of dying; so to them least of all men is death fearful. . . . *68* Many men have been willing, have been glad, to go to Hades in the hope of seeing and conversing with lost wives or sons or dear friends; well, if one is really in love with wisdom, and is firmly convinced that only in Hades can one truly be united with her, will one then complain at the moment of death, and not rather go gladly forward?

[67b–68b]

Nowhere else does Plato insist so strongly on the absolute severance of soul and body, on the absolute difference between the realm of real being and the world that the senses show us. Yet he develops the point more philosophically elsewhere: for example, in the *Meno* (see below, *Meno* 81) and in the famous doctrine of "Ideas," as in the *Republic* (see below, p. 336). The doctrine is perplexing, if not distasteful, not only to the average man who believes that thought deals with *data* provided by the senses, but also to Aristotle, who holds that "Ideas" are not separate from the world of phenomena and that "Form" and "Matter" are both aspects of a continuous reality which manifests merely various degrees of organization (see below, p. 353). In fact Plato himself reconsidered, in some of his later dialogues, this problem of the relation of "Ideas" to phenomena (for example in the *Theaetetus*, the *Parmenides*, the *Sophist*, and the *Timaeus*). He does not abandon the "Ideas," but considers their interrelationship and their penetration into the seen world; in theological language, he holds that God is transcendent and immanent—both beyond this world and operative in it.

The *Phaedo* continues with arguments, partly psychological, partly based on the criticism of earlier or opposing theories, alternative to that of Socrates, but returns to the restatement of the nature of the soul and of the eternal realm that is its natural home. An imaginative myth deals cautiously with the possible fortunes of the soul hereafter. Finally the narrative is resumed; Socrates has no concern as to what is to be done with his body: his whole argument should have made that clear.

116 When he had spoken thus, Socrates arose and went into a chamber to bathe; Crito followed him, and told us to wait. So we remained, talking about what had been said and about the greatness of our sorrow, feeling just like children who were about to lose their father and become orphans for the rest of their lives. When Socrates had bathed, his children were brought to him, two young sons and an older one; and the women of his family also came, and he talked with them in the presence of Crito, and gave them some instructions, and then said farewell to them and returned to us.

Now it was nearly sunset, for he had spent some time within. When he came out after his bath, he sat down and talked with us, but not for long; for the servant of the Eleven came and stood before him and said: "Socrates, I know you will not be angry with me, and curse me, like others when I have to bid them drink the poison in obedience to the magistrates. For during this time I have found you the noblest and gentlest and best man who ever came here; so I am sure that any hard feeling that you may have is not against me but against those who are responsible. Now you know what message I came to bring; so farewell, and try to bear as easily as you can what must be." And with those words he burst into tears and went out.

Socrates looked at him and said, "Farewell; I will do as you say." Then he said to us, "How courteous the man is! All this time he used to come and talk with me, and was the best of men; and now how generously he mourns for me! Well, Crito, let us obey him; and if the poison is prepared let some one bring it; if not, let it be prepared."

"But," said Crito, "I think the sun is still on the mountains, and has not yet set. And I know that others have taken their time about drinking the poison, when the message has been brought to them, and only after eating and drinking and making merry as they pleased. So don't hurry; there is plenty of time."

"Well," said Socrates, "it is natural for them to do so, for they suppose that they are gaining something by so doing; but I just as naturally am not going to do so, *(117)* for I think that by drinking the poison a little later I should gain nothing but ridicule for clinging to a life that is already empty. Come, now, do as I say, and don't oppose me."

When Crito heard that, he nodded to the servant who was standing near by; the servant went out and after some time returned with the man who was to administer the poison, which he carried all prepared in a cup. Socrates looked at him and said, "My good sir, you are an expert in these matters; what must I do?" "Only drink it," he replied, "and walk about until you feel a heaviness in your legs; then lie down, and the poison will act of itself." And with these words he handed the cup to Socrates, who took it quite calmly and without any fear or change of color or expression, and said with that characteristic sidelong glance at the man, "How about it? May I offer a libation out of this cup to any god?" But he answered, "Oh, Socrates, we prepare only just enough of the poison." "I understand," said he; "but at any rate I may, and I must, offer a prayer to the gods that this journey from here to another place may be a happy one. And so I pray, and so may it be." At that moment he lifted the cup and drank off the poison quite easily and cheerfully.

Now till then most of us had been able to hold back our tears fairly well; but when we saw him actually drinking the poison, and saw that it was finished, we could hold them back no longer. In spite of myself the tears flowed abundantly, so that I covered my face and wept; yet it was not for him that I mourned, but for my own misfortune in losing such a friend. And Crito even before me found himself unable to restrain his tears, and got up; and Apollodorus, who had been weeping all the time, now burst into a loud lamentation which broke down the courage of all present except Socrates. But he said, "What strange behavior, my friends! It was chiefly for this very reason that I sent away the women, so that we might not strike such a false note as this. For I have heard that one should die in peace. So do be quiet and of a good heart."

When we heard his words we were ashamed, and checked our tears. And he walked about until, as he said, his legs felt heavy, and he lay down on his back, as he had been told. Then the man who had given him the poison felt of his feet and his legs, and presently pressed his foot hard and asked whether he felt anything; and Socrates said, "No." *118* And later his legs; and so proceeding upwards he showed that he was growing cold and stiff. And Socrates felt of himself, and said that when the chill reached his heart the end would come. Now when he was feeling cold about his middle, he uncovered his face (for he had covered himself up) and said—and these were his last words, "Oh, Crito, I owe a cock to Asclepius. Mind that you pay it, and don't forget." "It shall be paid," said Crito; "have you anything else to say?" But there was no answer to this question, but after a moment there was a stirring, and the attendant uncovered him, and his eyes were set; and Crito closed his eyes and mouth.

That was the end, Echecrates, of our friend, the man who of all the men of his time whom we have known was, we may say, the best—yes, and what is more, the wisest and the most just.

[116a–118a]

THE DEVELOPMENT OF PLATO'S THOUGHT

THE PRECEDING selections have been chosen chiefly in order to give a picture of the personality and of the life and death of Socrates, though even here, especially in the *Phaedo*, something of Plato's own mature teaching was to be found. The following passages from the *Meno*, a dialogue probably written before the *Phaedo*, may serve as a transition to the fuller development of Plato's thought to be seen in the *Republic*. The *Meno*, like the *Protagoras* (a notable dialogue which is not represented here), inquires whether virtue can be taught; it therefore becomes necessary to inquire into the nature of knowledge. In the earlier part of the dialogue we have a good example of the Socratic quest for a universal definition, not a mere enumeration of special virtues (a "swarm of virtues") but a conception that shall be generally valid (as in the ideas of justice, beauty, and goodness referred to in the *Phaedo;* see above, 65–66). Later, Socrates inquires into the origin of such knowledge of universal ideas, and in the brief passage given below he attributes it to the immortal nature of the soul, which had such knowledge in a previous existence (as the *Phaedo* suggests that it will continue to have it after this life). Learning is therefore recollecting, as Wordsworth also holds in his "Intimations of Immortality from Recollections of Early Childhood"; but Plato would not agree with Wordsworth that man's life necessarily causes him to forget forever "that imperial palace whence he came," even if birth is "a sleep and a forgetting"; on the contrary, the philosopher, at least, spends his life in recapturing "the vision splendid," which we do forget (as the Myth of Er also suggests; *Republic*, 621, below). This point Plato further elaborates by having Socrates elicit from a boy who has never studied mathematics certain geometrical conclusions (the Pythagorean proposition); since he has not learned them in this life, he must be remembering, by the help of skillful prompting, what he has known in a previous life. Those readers who may be incredulous about the preexistence or the after life of the soul will nevertheless have to account for the validity of timeless ideas, mathematical or moral or aesthetic, and for the difference between them and ordinary "experience."

From the MENO

81 SOCRATES. I have heard from certain wise men and women, priests and priestesses . . . or poets, like Pindar . . . that the soul of man is immortal, and at one time has an end, which we call "dying," and at another time is born again, but is never destroyed; so a man ought always to live in perfect holiness. . . . The soul, then, being immortal, and having been born again many times, and having seen all things that exist, whether in this world or in the world below, has knowledge of them all; and it is no wonder that she should be able to call to remembrance all that she ever knew about virtue and about everything; for as all nature is akin, and the soul has learned all things, there is no difficulty in her eliciting, or as men say learning, out of a single recollection all the rest, if a man is strenuous and does not faint; for all inquiry and all learning is but recollection. [81a–d]

From the REPUBLIC

PLATO'S *Republic* is a most varied book. Beginning with the conversation of a group of friends in the home of good old Cephalus, about the nature of justice, it shows that justice cannot be defined merely as business ethics, or as helping friends and hurting enemies, or as self-seeking, or even as an outward respectability that is approved by social and religious institutions. Glaucon and Adimantus (Plato's brothers), demand that Socrates show that justice is superior to injustice because of its inward effects on the possessor. Socrates suggests that this may be better seen in the case of society, "man writ large," than in the individual; then it will be possible to return to the individual and to note the qualities that correspond to this larger justice. Accordingly he sketches the rise of a simple society which becomes more complex as it expands in size and tries to satisfy first physical and then cultural needs, and finds it an economy to practise some specialization and division of labor. Education of mind and body ("music" and "gymnastic") are on familiar Greek lines, though literature and the other arts are to be subjected to some censorship in the interest of morality; and Socrates gives an eloquent picture of the effect on the young of a healthy artistic environment. Those who are to direct this education, and the hardy life of the citizens, must be carefully selected by a series of tests, and will themselves live an austere life, from which private property and even family life is taken away (but only in the case, be it noted, of this small class of rulers); they have great powers, but are presumed to be the persons who best deserve to use them, and are not a hereditary caste.

In fact, it is in order to commend the use by society of individuals in those spheres for which their personal talents best qualify them that Socrates describes in a "noble flight of imagination" the mingling of metals, precious or base, in men's natures. The usual translation, "noble lie," does an injustice to Plato's sober though halting use of myth to express a truth which must somehow grip men's convictions. The poet Hesiod had already described successive ages of the world in terms of metals.

Where in this reformed society is justice to be found? In that very principle of the division of labor, Socrates believes, that has already been put forward; each class, laborers, guardians (soldiers, or policemen), and rulers, will exercise the functions for which it is best fitted, and will so be happiest. The wisdom of the rulers, the courage of the guardians, the application to their jobs of the laborers—these constitute their special virtues; and if they all work together harmoniously, "doing their own business" without meddling in matters beyond their competence, the state as a whole is just. Similarly in the individual: he is just if he maintains a state of inward health, subjecting his appetites to his reason, and seeing that in any case of conflict his emotions (his "spirit") side with his reason.

Can such a state be realized? Well, no ideal can be completely realized in practice, moral or artistic or political; but the best chance of such a political ideal being realized would be the union of political and philosophical power in the same natures: philosophers must become kings, or kings philosophers. It therefore becomes necessary to discuss the nature of philosophy and the vast difference that separates it from opinion or ignorance, a difference illustrated by the Parable of the Ship; by the picture of the desolate condition of philosophy, misunderstood or misused by society; by the account of the stages of higher philosophic education in the sciences and mathematics, culminating in the art of reasoning (dialectic) and the contemplation of "the Good"; and by the Parable of the Cave, in which Socrates describes the conversion of the philosopher from darkness and bondage to the free contemplation of the light and to the rescue of others.

Now that the good society and the principles necessary to effect it have been set forth, Socrates reviews the stages by which it may degenerate from perfection to imperfection, from one imperfect form to one still more imperfect, as human nature throws off restraints: the just aristocracy ("rule by the best") is replaced by the rule of wealth, by the mob rule of a democracy, and finally by tyranny, the rule of the worst. At each step the corresponding stage in the life of the individual is described. All harmony and unity of purpose have been lost; it follows that the degraded forms of society, or of personal life, have lost that healthy condition on which happiness depends. Socrates has thus met the challenge of Glaucon and Adimantus, that he show justice to be superior to injustice because of its inward effects. Nevertheless, since ideals are imperfectly realized in this world, the just man may not find justice in the environment about him; even so, he may live his own life in accordance with a better pattern.

Socrates now reviews his previous consideration of poetry and contrasts the imperfections of poetry as it is with philosophy as it would like to be. If he appears to exile poetry from an ideal state (and careless readers often remember only this satiric gesture), it is important to realize how much Plato does to do away with the "quarrel between poetry and philosophy." He always denies that truth can come from the mere photographic recording of the world of the senses, delightful though it sometimes is; but he is always ready to welcome the poetry and the art that expresses, as far as possible, the abiding realities that are imperfectly revealed in phenomena. Finally, Socrates claims that justice, now that it has been vindicated by its internal effects, is also generally the best policy in this life and is upheld by what we may reasonably believe about the world to come. The latter point is illustrated by the imaginative Myth of Er.

Thus during this night of talk the speakers, like the torch-bearers whom they were to have watched but forgot in favor of their conversation, move on from what appeared to be a small point of definition to the most fundamental questions of human life, and we are lifted out of the world of time and change till in the end we become spectators of eternal values. It surpasses the previous dialogues in its attempt to regard the realm of ideas as capable of being verified in the experience of human beings, as constituting the significance of things, as introducing order into chaos, and as being the author of moral health and of happiness.

From Book II

Why justice is better than injustice

367 ADIMANTUS. Don't prove to us merely that justice is superior to injustice, but show us what good or harm each does to its possessor, considering it simply in itself, and, as Glaucon requested, leaving out of account the reputation that it carries. For unless you leave out of account the reputation that each actually holds, and substitute for it a false one, we shall say that you are praising or denouncing merely appearances in either case, and are advising us to do wrong without getting found out, and that you agree with Thrasymachus when he said that justice is what is good for someone else, and is the interest of the stronger, and that injustice is what really pays, and what serves one's own interest at the expense of the weaker. You have agreed that justice belongs to that highest class of good things which are worth having not only for their consequences but even more for their own sakes, things like sight and hearing and knowledge and health, whose value is genuine and not dependent on opinion. So in praising justice consider only this, how it in itself benefits the man who possesses it, and how injustice harms him, and let others praise external regards and reputations. I could put up with such conduct on the part of others, letting them praise justice and condemn injustice because of their external effects; but from you I could not, unless you expressly asked me to do so, because you have spent your whole life in the study of this very question. Let me repeat, then: don't prove to us merely that justice is superior to injustice, but show us what good or harm each does to its possessor, considering it simply in itself, whether gods or men see it or not. [367b–e]

From Book III

As the twig is bent

401 SOCRATES. So it is not only the poets whom we must require to express the image of noble character in their poems, or else no longer to write poetry among us; we must supervise the other artists, too, and forbid them to set the mark of baseness, licence, meanness, lack of grace, on their paintings and sculpture, on buildings, and on the other products of their arts, or else not practise their arts among us. We will not have our guardians brought up among representations of moral deformity, as in some foul pasture where browsing day by day on many a weed, little by little, they gather without realizing it a great mass of corruption in their souls. Rather must we seek out those artists who are gifted to discover the true nature of what is beautiful and graceful; then our young men, dwelling in a healthful land, will drink in good from every quarter, from noble sights and sounds and breezes that bring health from goodly regions. So from their earliest childhood they will imperceptibly be drawn into likeness and sympathy and harmony with the beauty of reason.

GLAUCON. They could not be better brought up.

SOCRATES. That is why training in poetry and music is of sovereign importance; rhythm and harmony make their way into the recesses of the soul, and take strong hold there, imparting that grace which comes only to one who is brought up in the right way. Moreover, one who is so brought up (*402*) is quick to perceive any defect or ugliness in nature or in art; and with true taste he is offended by it; whereas all that is beautiful he approves and welcomes joyfully into his soul and is nourished by it, and so becomes noble. All this is while he is still too young to understand the reason for his tastes; but when reason comes, one who is so brought up will recognize her and greet her as a familiar friend. [401b–402a]

The Myth of the Metals

414 SOCRATES. What ingenious and convenient kind of fiction could we find, what single and noble flight of imagination, so as to persuade above all even the rulers, or at any rate the rest of the state?

GLAUCON. What kind do you mean?

SOCRATES. Nothing novel, but something on the Phoenician order [the myth of Cadmus and the dragon's teeth, whence sprang the citizens of Thebes], something that has occurred in many places in the past, as the poets tell us and have persuaded us; but I know not whether it has ever occurred in our time or ever could, and it would require no little persuasion to become credible.

GLAUCON. You seem like one who shrinks from speaking.

SOCRATES. With good reason, as you will think when I have spoken.

GLAUCON. Speak, and don't be afraid.

SOCRATES. Well, then, I will, though I hardly know how to find the audacity or the words with which to persuade first the rulers and the soldiers, and then the rest of the state, that all the nurture and education that we gave them was, as a matter of fact, something which they imagined as it were in a dream, and that really at that time they themselves were down inside the earth being moulded and reared, while their arms and the rest of their equipment were being wrought; and that, when they were wholly fashioned, their mother the earth sent them forth. So now they ought to take thought for their land, as for their mother and their nurse, and to defend her against any attack, and to regard their fellow citizens as brothers born of the same soil.

GLAUCON. Not without reason were you shy about telling your "fiction."

SOCRATES. Quite so; but just listen to the rest of the fable. "You are all brothers in this state," we shall say in our fable; "but the god who fashioned you mixed gold in the creation of those of you who are fit to rule, so that they are the most precious; and in the guardians, silver; and iron and bronze in the farmers and craftsmen. Now since you are all akin, though your children will generally be like yourselves, sometimes a golden father may have a silver son or a silver father may have a golden son, and so with the other kinds. So the first and chief command that the god lays on the rulers is that over nothing else are they to watch with such care as the mixture of metals in the souls of the children. If a child of their own is born with an alloy of bronze or iron, they shall show him no pity but shall assign to him the status proper to his nature and thrust him among the craftsmen or the farmers; likewise, if from the latter classes there is born a son with an alloy of gold or silver, they shall according to his worth promote him to become a guardian or an auxiliary. For there is an oracle, as they are to say, that the state will be ruined whensoever it shall be guarded by a man of iron or of bronze." Have you any way of getting them to believe this fable?

GLAUCON. None whatever, in the first generation; but their sons and descendants might believe it, and then finally the rest of mankind.

SOCRATES. Well, even that would have a good effect in making them care more for their state and for one another; for I think I understand what you mean. [414b–415d]

From Book IV

Justice an inward harmony of elements

443 SOCRATES. So our dream has come true; and we have verified the suspicion that we held, when we began to found our state, that by some divine guidance we had hit upon a sort of fundamental outline of justice. For it turns out that we had a helpful symbol of justice when we laid down the principle that the natural cobbler or carpenter had better stick to his craft and not do anything else. But the truth of the matter appears to be that justice, though like this principle, is not a matter of outward conduct but of one's inward self and its real concerns. The just man does not allow the several elements in his soul to usurp one another's functions, but sets his house in order and rules himself and is at peace with himself; like a musician who brings into tune the highest and the lowest and the median tones, and all the intermediate tones of the scale, so the just man only after binding together in perfect harmony the three elements in himself becomes one man instead of many [*e pluribus unum*, or "an integrated personality"]. Now he is temperate and well adjusted and ready to act, whether in matters of business or the care of the body or affairs of state. In all these activities, he calls "just" or "honorable" conduct that which contributes to the production and preservation of this condition; and "wisdom" that knowledge which presides over such conduct; while he calls "unjust" (*444*) any conduct that breaks down this condition, and "ignorance" the notions that attend such conduct. We should not seem altogether mistaken, then, if we were to claim that we had discovered the just man and the just state, and that wherein their justice consists. [443b–444a]

From Book V

Philosophers must become kings.

[Glaucon has granted, for the sake of argument, the desirability of such an ideal state as Socrates has described, and has demanded that Socrates show that it could be realized, and how.]

472 SOCRATES. Well, first let me remind you that it was in our investigation of the natures of justice and injustice that we reached this point.

GLAUCON. Yes; but what of that?

SOCRATES. Only this; if we do discover the real nature of justice, are we going to demand that a man who is just shall not fall short of this ideal in the least particular, or shall we be satisfied if he comes as near as possible to the ideal and has more of it than other men?

GLAUCON. That will suffice.

SOCRATES. When we set out to discover the real nature of justice, and of a perfectly just man, supposing him to exist, and of a perfectly unjust man, our purpose was to use them as patterns, so that we might observe their respective happiness or unhappiness, and might conclude that our own portions of happiness or unhappiness would be like that of the one whom we most resembled. But we did not set out to prove that these ideals could exist in fact.

GLAUCON. That is true.

SOCRATES. If an artist had painted an ideal portrait of a most beautiful person, with everything rendered to perfection, would you think any the worse of him if he could not show that a person as beautiful as that could really exist?

GLAUCON. Certainly not.

SOCRATES. Well, in our discourse we were creating the pattern of a good state; do you think our theory any the worse if we cannot show the possibility of founding a state just as it was described?

GLAUCON. No, of course not.

SOCRATES. That, then, is the truth; but if to gratify you I am to do my best to show under what conditions it would have the best chance of being realized, I must ask you to repeat your former admission. *473* Can theory ever be fully realized in practice, or is it not in the nature of things that practice should come less near to truth than theory? Some may not agree; but do you agree, or not?

GLAUCON. I agree.

SOCRATES. Then you must not require me to prove that our ideal construction could be realized in action in every last detail; but if we can find how the state could be ordered in the closest accord with our description, you will admit that we have found such possibility as you demand. Won't that satisfy you? I must say that I should be satisfied.

GLAUCON. And so should I.

SOCRATES. Then it would appear that we must next try to show what present defect in states causes them to fall short of perfection, and what is the least change that would transform a state into the desired kind of government: a single change, if possible, or if not, only two, and in any case as few and as slight changes as possible.

GLAUCON. By all means.

SOCRATES. Well, there is one change which, I think I can show, would effect the reform though it is not a slight or easy one, but still it is possible.

GLAUCON. What is it?

SOCRATES. Ah, now I am going to meet what I likened to the third and greatest wave. [Socrates has compared the objections of his hearers, against his plan for the education and the occupations of women and for communism of the family in the guardian class, to surf waves that he must surmount. But this third wave is the most formidable.] Yet speak I must, even though the wave break over me in laughter and drown me with incredulity.

GLAUCON. Say on.

SOCRATES. Unless either philosophers become kings in their lands or those who are now called kings and potentates are genuinely and in sufficient measure filled with the love of wisdom, and thus political power and philosophy are united, while those many natures who now have recourse to one or the other pursuit to the exclusion of the other are cut off from so doing, there can be no rest from evils, my dear Glaucon, for states nor, as I believe, for mankind; nor can this ideal commonwealth that we have described ever behold the light of day and grow to its full stature. This is what I have long shrunk from saying, seeing what a paradox it would be; for it is hard to see that in no other way can there be happiness for society or for the individual.

[472b–473e]

From Book VI

The Parable of the Ship

Socrates proceeds to elaborate the distinction between the true philosopher and the ordinary man, which turns on the doctrine of Ideas. This is Plato's own development of the general definitions which the historical Socrates had sought to discover; it has already been introduced in the *Phaedo* (see *Phaedo* 65–66), and is further discussed in the *Republic* (below, p. 335). Beyond the many changing phenomena revealed to our senses or present in action, the mind can discover unchanging realities, "Ideas" or "Forms," as the scientist discovers laws or principles. Thus particular objects may become beautiful or ugly with the passing of time, or the same object may seem beautiful to one person or generation or race, and ugly to another; but beauty and ugliness are absolutely different and mutually exclusive. The eternal unchanging "Ideas" are the proper field of intellectual or philosophic contemplation, and knowledge of them is absolute; whereas ordinary men are content to remain in the world of changing phenomena ("appearances"), about which there can be only belief or opinion, states of mind which are relative and varying and only accidentally sometimes true (as when one happens to guess correctly that it is ten o'clock). Thus the philosopher, whose constant recourse is to the real world of "Ideas," is the only person qualified to remake society.

[Adimantus, though convinced of the philosopher's fitness to rule, is troubled by the notorious fact that philosophers "generally seem queer, not to say worthless, while even the best of them are so far the worse for their pursuit as to become useless to society." He is surprised to hear Socrates agree with him. How then can he maintain that philosophers should rule? Socrates replies in the following parable.]

488 SOCRATES. Imagine this state of affairs on a ship, or on several ships. The captain [the sovereign people] is bigger and stronger than any of the crew [the politicians], but somewhat deaf and shortsighted, and his knowledge of navigation is no better than theirs. The crew are quarreling over the control of the helm; each man thinks he ought to be steering the ship, though he has never learned navigation and cannot point to any master under whom he has served his apprenticeship; what is more, they say that navigation is not an art that can be taught, and they are ready to cut to pieces any one who says it can be taught [a hint of the fate of Socrates]. They crowd about the captain, begging him and doing everything they can to persuade him to entrust the helm to them; sometimes those who do not succeed in this attempt kill or throw overboard those who have succeeded; and after stupefying the noble captain with some drink or drug they get control of the ship and make free with its stores, and as you might expect of such a crew, they turn the voyage into a feast or a drinking party. And then they salute as "Navigator" or "Master of Seamanship" or "Doctor of Naval Science" any one who is clever enough to aid and abet them in persuading or forcing the captain to let them control the ship; and any one who does not they condemn as "useless." They just don't understand that the genuine navigator, if he is to be really fit to command a ship, must study seasons and weather, sky and stars and winds and all that pertains to the art; and they have no notion that there is any way of his being able to learn, by study or by practice, along with the art of navigation, how to insure his actually exercising his authority over the helm, whether some of them like it or not. Now if that were the state of affairs on shipboard don't you suppose that the real expert in navigation (*489*) would be called by the mutinous crew a mere "star-gazer," a "babbler," a "useless fellow"?

ADIMANTUS. Indeed he would.

SOCRATES. I don't think you need to have me interpret this parable so as to show how it illustrates the attitude of society toward real philosophers.

ADIMANTUS. No, I understand it.

SOCRATES. Well, then, explain it to the person who is surprised that philosophers are without honor in their own cities, and try to persuade him that it would be more surprising if they were honored. And you may add that he is right in saying that the best philosophers are useless to the public, but that for this uselessness he should blame, not the philosophers, but those who make no use of them. For it is not natural for the navigator to beg the crew to take his orders, nor for "wise men to go about to the doors of the rich" (the author of that pretty phrase was mistaken); but the truth is that if any man, rich or poor, is sick, he must go to the door of the physician, and in general that all men who are in need of being governed should seek out the man who can govern, and not that he should beg them to accept his rule, if he is really good for anything. But you will not go wrong if you compare our present politicians to the crew of our parable, and those whom they dubbed "useless star-gazers" to the real navigators. In view of all that, it would not be easy for the noblest occupation to be held in good repute by men who practise its opposite. [488a–489c]

The desolation of true philosophy

[The true philosopher is one "born to strive toward reality, who cannot linger among the multiplicity of things which men believe to be real, but who presses passionately on to lay hold on the true nature of each thing with that part of his soul which is akin to it; then, in union with real being, he begets thought and truth" (490ab). But of the few potential philosophers, most fall by the way or are warped from their purpose by the distractions of this world, by popularity or political ambition; and the worst danger is a great nature that has gone wrong, like Alcibiades.]

495 SOCRATES. So Philosophy is left desolate by her nearest kin, deserted and unwedded; and while these potential philosophers are leading a false and unbecoming life, others make overtures to her, bereft as she is of protectors, unworthy intruders who shame her and fasten on her the very reproaches that you have mentioned, to the effect that some who associate with her are worthless and most of them deserve severe punishment. And naturally enough; for when these petty creatures, clever in their own poor trades, spy this opening which is adorned by fine names and titles, they gladly leap from their arts and crafts into philosophy, just like men who have run away from prison to a sanctuary. For in comparison with the other arts, philosophy even in her present plight still enjoys a greater prestige, which attracts many whose natures are imperfect, since their souls are battered and bruised by their mean occupations no less than their bodies are maimed by their trades. Why, they are like some little bald-headed smith who has got some money and has just got out of prison and taken a good bath and dressed up in a new coat, like a bridegroom, and is going to marry his master's daughter, who is poor and desolate. *496* Now, what sort of children do you think they will have? Won't they be mean and base-born? Of course; and when men who are unworthy of education consort unworthily with Philosophy, will not their notions and opinions be no true-born child of genuine wisdom but what we can only call "sophistry"?

Small indeed, then, Adimantus, is the remnant that is left of those who are worthy to consort with Philosophy: perhaps some noble and well-nurtured character, by exile saved from exposure to the forces that might have corrupted his natural devotion to her; or a great soul born in a petty state whose politics he despises; or again a gifted few who justly scorn some other pursuit and turn to her; and there may be some like my friend Theages, who had every inducement to abandon philosophy, but ill health, like a bridle, restrains him from entering politics. Of my own private case, and my divine sign, it is hardly worth while to speak; for I suppose it has come to few if any men before.

One who has become a member of this small company and has tasted the sweetness and blessedness of their lot, and who has seen the madness of the multitude, and realizes that there is nothing sound in their politics nor is there any ally with whom a champion of justice could go to her rescue and win salvation, but that, like a man who has fallen among wild beasts, if he will not join in their wickedness and yet could not single-handed resist them all in their fury, he would be sure to throw away his life before he could be of service to the state or to his friends, useless to himself and to others: the man, I say, who takes all this into account keeps quiet and minds his own business, like a wayfarer who takes shelter under a wall against a storm of dust and hail driven by the wind; and seeing other men full of lawlessness he is content if he can live his own life here clean-handed and free from wickedness, and take his departure hence with bright hopes, in serenity and good will.

497 ADIMANTUS. Well, he would have accomplished no mean thing.

SOCRATES. Yes, but not the greatest; not what he might have achieved if his lot had fallen in a society suited to him, for there he could reach his full stature and save the commonwealth as well as himself. [495b–497a]

From Book VII

The Good

The pessimism of the preceding passage is relieved by the ensuing discussion of the possibility of society being educated to accept the rule of those philosophic persons who, devoid of selfishness, will seek to reproduce in this world, as far as possible, the "world of unchanging and harmonious order," the ideal pattern. Such persons, or the ideal philosopher-king, would have been chosen by preliminary tests of intelligence and character and experience, and would continue their earlier education in "music" and "gymnastic" by other and more advanced studies (to be described later), all leading up to "the highest kind of knowledge" which is "the nature of the Good, from which everything that is right and good derives its value for us" (504d; 505a). This Good not only penetrates the specialized activities of human life (economic production, medicine, etc.), and the political direction of all activities by reference to moral ends (here Aristotle would agree, notably in the opening chapter of his *Nicomachean Ethics*); but it has also a broader meaning, extending to the moral and physical organization of the whole universe, which exhibits the purposes of its divine creator. (See also the quotation from the *Timaeus*, below, p. 346.) The Good thus makes the world intelligible, and is the source of life and being. (Here Aristotle will object that Plato's "Good," and his "Ideas" generally, are too abstract, are indeed superfluous. But Aristotle in his treatises on physics and biology is no less convinced than Plato that principles of goodness, fitness, form, etc., are operative in the realization of the potential natures of all things; the question is one of degree.) The definition of the word "good" is one of the most stubborn problems even in modern philosophy. When Socrates is here pressed to define the Good more precisely, he declines, but offers instead (in the passage given below) an analogy: the sun, which is "the child of the Good," and is the source of visibility and of growth. It may be added that nowhere else does Plato further define the Good, though he discusses its relation to pleasure (in the *Philebus*, as Aristotle does in the tenth book of his *Ethics*), and of course uses the term "good" constantly, as we all do, on the assumption that for practical purposes it has an accepted meaning. Gifted though he was as a writer, Plato distrusted the written word, unable to defend itself from criticism once it is committed to paper (see the curious passage in the *Phaedrus*, 274b–278b, not included here); he preferred the give and take of oral discussion, as in his Academy. And in the probably genuine seventh Epistle of Plato, dealing with the attempts of others to explain what Plato meant about "the subjects to which I devote myself," the writer says: "I certainly have composed no work in regard to them, nor shall I ever do so in the future; for there is no way of putting it in words like other studies. Acquaintance with it must come rather after a long period of attendance on instruction in the subject itself and of close companionship, when, suddenly, like a blaze kindled by a leaping spark, it is generated in the soul and at once becomes self-sustaining" (341cd; and see further "Dialectic," below, 531–534).

508 SOCRATES. This [the sun], then, is what I meant when I spoke of "the child of the Good" which the Good has brought forth in the visible world to stand in the same relation to vision and to visible things that the Good itself bears in the intelligible world to intelligence and to intelligible objects. You know that when one turns his eyes toward objects whose colors are not illuminated by the light of day but only by the moon and stars, their vision is dimmed, almost blinded; but that when the sun shines forth on these objects these same eyes see clearly. Well, consider the experience of the soul: when it fixes its gaze on an object that is illuminated by truth and reality, it has understanding and knowledge and is manifestly possessed of intelligence; but when it looks at that twilight world of things that come into being and pass away, then its vision is dimmed, and it entertains shifting opinions and seems now like a creature without intelligence.

This, then, I would have you call "the Idea of the Good"; this is what imparts to the objects of knowledge their truth, and to the knower his power of knowing. It is the cause of knowledge and truth, both precious things; yet you will do well to esteem it as something still more precious than either. For just as in our analogy we found it right to think of light (*509*) and vision as like the sun, but not as identical with it, so here it is right to think of knowledge and truth as like the Good, but not to identify either of them with it; we must find for the Good a still higher place of honor.

GLAUCON. What an extraordinary brilliance it must have if it is the source of knowledge and truth and yet surpasses them in brightness! I don't suppose you mean that it is pleasure?

SOCRATES. Heaven forbid! But consider our analogy still further. You will agree that the sun not only makes visible the things that we see but also brings them into being and gives them growth and nourishment. So for the objects of knowledge the Good provides not only the possibility of their being known but their very being and reality; yet the Good is not the same thing as being, but something even beyond being, something surpassing it in dignity and power.

[508b–509b]

The Parable of the Cave

Socrates continues to discuss the training of the future rulers and the movement of their experience from the world of appearances to the world of absolute ideas, and illustrates it by describing a line, divided into four segments, corresponding respectively to (a) shadows and reflections, (b) natural and artistic objects, (c) mathematical figures and numbers, and (d) intelligible "Ideas"; or, again, to the mental states that are related to them: (a) imagining, (b) belief, (c) thinking about unproved premises, and (d) intelligence, or knowledge in the fullest sense, also called "dialectic."

This mental progress is now further illustrated by the Parable of the Cave. The world of appearances is compared to a dark subterranean cave, the world of reality to the brilliant light outside; the unenlightened minds of ordinary people have their counterpart in the prisoners in the cave, deceived by the shadows of puppets, while the conversion of the philosopher is symbolized by the liberation of a prisoner who is compelled to make a *volte face* and emerge into the dazzling light; his social conscience, by his return to the cave (and his need of becoming accustomed again to its darkness, however awkwardly), to set others free. There is obviously some degree of correspondence between the Parable of the Cave and the figure of the Line, though it cannot be worked out in complete detail. The Line develops the relationship between its parts by showing that "the mind uses as images those actual things which themselves had images in the visible world," but that it also is capable of moving directly to the contemplation of "ideas"; this relationship is stated in the form of a proportion: a : b :: c : d; or, again, (a + b) : (c + d). Similarly, the parable proceeds to extend its meaning by showing that the objects outside the cave and the sun, though manifestly "real" in a sense in which the contents of the cave are not real, are in turn only pale approximations when compared with the "ideas" and with the supreme reality, the Good. Accordingly, for the assistance of the reader, references to the divisions of the Line are inserted in the earlier portion of the parable, but only in that portion.

For the parable Plato had certain hints in earlier Greek philosophical poetry and perhaps in the religious thought of the Orphic cult, which assumed the body to be the prison-house of the soul; and he may have seen in Attica such a cave as he describes. The modern reader will gain both amusement and enlightenment if he sees in the parable a fairly detailed description of the movies and of the Hollywood mind; indeed it will bear some application to the novel, to social life and manners, and to political conventions, as well as to education and philosophy.

514 SOCRATES. Next, consider the stages in the unenlightenment or enlightenment of our natures in the terms of the following parable. Imagine men living in a subterranean cave with a long passage extending all the way to the light. They have been here since childhood, chained by their legs and their necks, so that they cannot move, and can look only forward and cannot turn their heads. Considerably above and behind them is the light of a fire, and between the fire and the prisoners there is a raised track with a parapet along it, like the curtain at a puppet-show that conceals the people who show their puppets over it. Now imagine people behind this parapet carrying (b) various artificial objects, among them images of men (*515*) and animals made of wood or stone, which project above the parapet. As you might expect, some of these people are talking, others are silent.

GLAUCON. That's a strange parable, and those are strange prisoners.

SOCRATES. They are like ourselves. For in the first place, they see nothing of themselves or of one another except (a) the shadows thrown by the firelight on the wall of the cave opposite them.

GLAUCON. Of course, if they can never move their heads.

SOCRATES. And they would see only (a) the shadows of (b) the objects that are carried past. And if they could talk with one another, they would suppose (a) what they saw to be (b) real objects. And if their prison had an echo from the opposite wall, and (b) one of the people passing behind them spoke, they would suppose that the sound came from (a) the shadow passing before them. In all respects, then, such prisoners would suppose that the only reality was (a) the shadows of those objects.

Now consider what would happen if they were to be released from their chains and healed from their folly in this way. Suppose that one of them were set free and suddenly forced to stand up and turn his neck and walk and look toward the light; all this would be painful, and because of the dazzle he would be unable to distinguish (b) the objects of which he was hitherto accustomed to see (a) only the shadows. What do you think he would say if some one told him that (a) what he had formerly been seeing was nonsense, but that now he was nearer to (b) reality and to real objects and was getting a clearer vision? And if some one went so far as to point to (b) each of the objects that was carried by and compelled him to state what it was, would he not be at a loss, and would he not suppose (a) what he saw before to be truer than (b) what was now shown to him? And if, further, he were compelled to look at the firelight itself, would not his eyes ache, and would he not try to turn back to the things that he could distinguish, convinced that they were really clearer than the objects now shown to him?

GLAUCON. Certainly.

SOCRATES. Well, if some one were to drag him forcibly up the steep and rough ascent and not let him go until he had hauled him into the sunlight, would he not be pained and annoyed, and when he had come into the light, (*516*) would not his eyes be so dazzled by its brilliance that he could not see a single one of the things that he was now told was real? He would need some habituation, if he were going to look at the things in this world above [i.e., mathematical studies, before moral investigations and the final ascent to "the Good"]. First he would most easily make out (a) shadows, and reflections of men and things in water, and later (b) the things themselves; after that he would more easily observe (c) the heavenly bodies, and the sky itself, at night, looking on the light of the moon and stars, rather than on the sun by day and its light. Last of all, he would look on (d) the sun, not reflected in water or any alien place, but as it is in itself in its own place and in its own nature. And thereupon he would draw the conclusion that it is this, the sun, that causes the seasons and the years and controls everything in (c) the visible world and in a sense also (a and b) everything that he and his fellow-prisoners used to see.

Then if he called to mind those prisoners and their "wisdom," he would be very thankful for his change, and sorry for them. If they had prize contests and honored those among themselves who marked most clearly the passing shadows and remembered best the order of their appearances and thereby could make the shrewdest guess as to what was likely to come next, do you suppose that the escaped prisoners would covet those prizes and envy the prize-winners, or would he, like Homer's Achilles, prefer to "be the serf of a poor man" or suffer any fate whatsoever, rather than hold his former beliefs and way of life?

GLAUCON. Yes, he would rather suffer anything else than such a life.

SOCRATES. Imagine now what would happen if he were to return again and sit in his old seat; coming suddenly from the sunlight, his eyes would be blinded by the darkness. And if he had to deliver opinions in rivalry with the perpetual prisoners, while he was still confused (*517*) and before his eyes were steady (and this might take some time), they would laugh at him, and say that his ascent had ruined his eyes, and that it was not worth while to try to make the ascent. And if they could lay their hands on the man who was attempting to set them free and to lead them upwards, and kill him, they would do so.

This parable, then, my dear Glaucon, I would have you apply to our earlier discussion, comparing the prison dwelling to the realm that appears to us through the sense of sight, and the firelight inside it to the power of the sun. If you assume that the ascent and the contemplation of things above corresponds to the upward journey of the soul into the realm of the intelligible, you will not fall short of my surmise, since that is what you wish to hear. God knows whether it is true; but that, at any rate, is the way it appears to me. In the realm of the intelligible, the last thing to be beheld, and that only with difficulty, is the "Idea of Good"; but once it has been beheld, it must be concluded that this is the cause of all that is right and fair; in the realm of the visible, it is the parent of light and of the lord of light [the sun], and in the realm of the intelligible it is itself sovereign and the parent of intelligence and truth. Any one who is to accomplish anything wisely in private or in public life must have had a vision of it.

GLAUCON. I agree with you, at least so far as I can follow.

SOCRATES. Then you may agree also that there is nothing surprising in the reluctance of men who have attained to this vision to engage in human affairs, and their desire to dwell forever in that upper realm—it is natural enough, if our parable is valid. Nor is it surprising if one who comes from the contemplation of divine things to the ills of human affairs cuts a sorry figure and seems quite ridiculous when, while his eyes are still dazed and not yet accustomed to the darkness, he is compelled in a law court or elsewhere to engage in an argument about the images or the shadows of images of justice among men who have never had a vision of justice itself. But a man of sense (*518*) would remember that the eyes may be confused in two diverse ways: by a change from light to darkness, and by a change from darkness to light. The same is true of mental confusion. So when one sees a soul in distress and unable to discern anything clearly, he will not laugh thoughtlessly but will inquire whether it has come from a brighter life and is unable to see because it is unaccustomed to darkness or whether it has emerged from abysmal ignorance into a brighter realm where it is dazzled by the light; in the former case he would count it happy, and in the latter case he would count it pitiable; and if he ventured to laugh at it, he would laugh with better justification than at the soul that has come down from the light.

If that is true, education is not, as some of its professors claim, their putting of knowledge into a soul that does not possess it, like the insertion of vision into blind eyes. On the contrary, our discussion indicates that every man's soul has the power of learning and the organ by which to learn; and that just as if it were impossible for the eye to see light instead of darkness except by turning the whole body around, so the whole soul must be turned around from this world of becoming until it can bear to look upon reality and that brightest of all realities which we have called the Good. So there may well be an art of accomplishing this very thing, this turning about of the soul, in the easiest and most effective way: not of implanting vision in it (for it already has that), but of contriving that instead of being turned in the wrong direction it shall look where it should.

Now the other so-called virtues of the soul seem to be rather closely allied to those of the body, in that they can be produced by habituation and practice in a soul that did not originally have them. But wisdom seems to be the virtue, more than anything else, of something more divine; it never loses its power, but whether it is used for good or for evil depends on the direction in which it is turned. *519* Or haven't you noticed how sharply the petty souls of clever rascals penetrate with their gaze whatever their eyes are turned to? There is nothing the matter with their vision, but it has been forced into the service of evil, so that the sharper their vision the more harm they do.

GLAUCON. Quite so.

SOCRATES. But if their natures had been shorn from earliest childhood of these hindrances, arising from pleasures and gluttonies, that like leaden weights carried through this mortal life have bent their souls' vision downwards, and if, set free, they turned toward what is true, then the same faculties in these same men would see the truth as keenly as what they now see.

Is it not likely, or indeed inevitable in view of what has been said, that neither the uneducated, who have no experience of truth, nor men who are permitted to spend their whole lives in the pursuit of education, will govern a state properly? The one group have no single bull's-eye at which to aim in all their actions, private and public; while the others will not voluntarily engage in action, supposing that while still alive they are dwelling apart in the Islands of the Blessed. It is our task, then, as founders of a state, to compel the finest natures to make the ascent to that "highest kind of knowledge," as we called it, and to have a vision of the Good; but when they have made the ascent and looked upon it long enough we must not permit them, as we do now, to remain there and to refuse to come down again among those prisoners, or to refrain from taking part in their labors and their rewards, whether these are worth little or much.

GLAUCON. But shall we not be doing them an injustice in compelling them to live a life worse than they might have?

SOCRATES. Ah, but you have forgotten again, my friend, that it is not the business of our legislation to make any one class especially happy, but rather to contrive that the whole state shall be happy. By persuasion or compulsion it brings the citizens together in harmony, causing them to share (*520*) whatever benefits they can severally contribute to the common good; and in producing such men in the state its purpose was not to let each man do as he pleases but to have them as its means of binding the state together.

GLAUCON. Yes, I had forgotten.

SOCRATES. So you see, Glaucon, that we shall do no injustice to the philosophers who will grow up among us in compelling them to care for the others and to watch over them. We shall have the right to say to them: "In other states in which men like you are to be found, they may reasonably refrain from the labors of the state, since they grow up there like plants that are self-sown, in spite of their countries' institutions; they owe their nurture to no one, so they may justly feel grateful for it to no one. But you were brought forth by us for the sake of your country, as well as for yourselves, to be the leaders, the queen-bees of the hive, better and more perfectly educated than the rest, and better able to share in your double duty, private and public. You must go down, then, each in his turn, to dwell with the others and to have your eyes accustomed to the darkness. For you will then see infinitely better than they, and you will know at its true worth every image, and what it stands for, because you have seen beauty and justice and goodness in their true natures. And thus you and we shall find life in our state a reality, and no mere dream, such as it is in most states, where men spend their lives fighting about shadows and quarrelling for office, as if that were any boon. The truth of the matter is that the state is best governed and with least dissension in which those who are to rule are least eager to rule; and the converse is also true."

Well, do you think that our pupils, after hearing that, will be disobedient and will refuse to take their turns at sharing in the labors of the state, dwelling most of the time together in the realm of pure light?

GLAUCON. They cannot; it is a fair demand, and they are fair-minded. Doubtless each will serve his turn in office, as a necessity, quite unlike the rulers of the states of our day.

Socrates. Yes, my friend; you can have a well-governed state only (*521*) if you can discover for its future rulers a better life than office-holding; only in such a state will the rulers be those who are really rich, not in gold but in the wealth that brings happiness, a good and wise life. But if men who are starved for any good in their private lives go into public life in the hope of seizing their good in this quarter, then the state cannot fare well; for office-holding becomes the object of strife, and this internal conflict is the ruin of the rulers and of their country. [Cf. Aristotle, *Politics* III, 6: "In our time men seek to be always in office for the sake of the advantage to be gained from office and from the public funds."] The only life that looks down on office-holding is that of lovers of true wisdom; and lovers of political power must be debarred from office; otherwise rival lovers will start fighting. Whom else, then, can you compel to undertake the guardianship of the state than those who have the best understanding of the principles of government and, what is more, enjoy a better life than that of the politician and rewards of another kind?

Glaucon. I can make no other choice.

[514a–521b]

Dialectic

Socrates now proceeds to explain in some detail the course of higher studies that will qualify his future rulers to engage in pure thought. For this purpose the subjects that he finds best suited are the various branches of mathematics, already studied by the Pythagorean philosophers and others: arithmetic, plane geometry (to which solid geometry is here added), astronomy, and "harmonics" (the mathematical theory of musical tones). In all of them the emphasis is not to be on empirical methods or on the practical uses of these sciences; and indeed the ancient Greeks were deficient in experimental methods (Aristotle's biological observations, and the creation of modern physics and chemistry, were yet to come), though in mathematics and astronomy they had made notable progress, and Plato's own Academy was particularly devoted to these sciences. The reason why mathematics is chosen for extended study in a curriculum lasting ten years is that it is the best instrument for training the mind to think in abstract terms, to deduce principles not from the phenomena revealed to the senses, but from the realm of pure intelligible being; this is preparation for the abstract thinking about moral principles that is still to come. Nevertheless even the branches of mathematics, though self-consistent, must utilize various hypotheses or axioms which are yet to be proved or linked to an unconditional and absolute first principle; this final step will be the task of dialectic. If Plato were familiar with the empirical methods and results of modern science, he would doubtless find in them some confirmation of his own attitude, though he would insist that material drawn from the changing world of the senses can never be more than an approximation to the real world of absolute being that is disclosed to the reason. And we may well compare the disinterestedness of the laboratory scientist, who must set aside every prejudice and preconception and consideration of personal advantage, to the spirit which Plato is trying to inculcate. Plato might question whether the "social scientist," even with the best of intentions, could ever achieve an equal degree of disinterestedness in the scrutiny of human nature. And if we ask why Plato believes that rulers who have been trained so long in abstract mathematical and philosophical studies are particularly fit to deal with human nature, average people, his answer will be, first, that only such rulers will have the necessary grasp of the pattern for all conduct; and, second, that these rulers have grown up among ordinary people, have been chosen for their characters as well as their brains, and will gain practical experience on the job in administrative posts in the Cave (539e–540c). But it should be added that they will not think it their task merely to carry out the desires of ordinary people.

The final stage in the higher education, from the age of thirty to thirty-five, will be given to the gathering together of all the mathematical sciences, hitherto pursued separately and on the basis of unproved hypotheses, in a synoptic vision of reality. Now, and only now, it is time to consider moral ideas, not as expedients in the world of phenomena, but as manifestations of the Good, which manifests itself also in the order and beauty of the heavens. "Dialectic," here used by Socrates to describe the "coping stone" of education, means the method of question and answer, of cross-examination and scrutiny of notions and the establishment of sounder ideas, that the actual Socrates had used, and that is illustrated by many of the "Socratic" dialogues. But whereas he had dealt mostly with materials from ordinary experience, proceeding inductively from many cases to a common definition, "dialectic" is now conceived as the supreme example of deduction, deriving all being from the Good. As such it is an imaginative ideal for philosophy, never fully to be realized by any philosopher, and never fully described by Plato any more than the Good is fully described. Philosophy, in other words, is an unending quest, not a completed result; it is the love of wisdom, not the possession of it (*Symposium* 201–212). The following translation is somewhat condensed.

531 Socrates. The whole course of studies that we have described will be wasted and will not contribute to the desired end, unless the several sciences are so gathered together that we can view their mutual relationships. And that is only the prelude to the main hymn; we must be able to give a rational account of knowledge, or get others to do so.

532 Here we come to the hymn that "dialectic" expresses. Though it belongs to the realm of the intelligible, we have something like it [in the Parable of the Cave] in the power of vision, which we said tried to look at living creatures, and then at stars, and finally at the sun itself. So with the journey of dialectic; by it one seeks through the reason, not by any of the senses, to reach the real nature of everything, not flinching till he reaches the utmost limit of the intelligible and grasps the Good. [As the progress of the prisoner, liberated from the Cave, was from shadows to "real" objects] so the study of mathematics has the effect of lifting the noblest faculty of the soul toward the contemplation of the highest reality. . . .

GLAUCON. Yes; let us assume that this is true. But what is the nature of "dialectic," and what are its divisions and methods? I think we are near the end of our journey.

533 SOCRATES. It will be hard for you to follow, however willing I am to tell you what I think; I should be showing you not an image but truth itself as I see it. And whether I see it as it really is, I am not ready to affirm. Yet I may affirm that there is some such reality and that it is our business to see it; moreover, that it can be revealed only to one who has been trained in the studies that we have discussed, and to him only by the power of dialectic.

GLAUCON. That we may affirm.

SOCRATES. At any rate, there is no other method of inquiry into the real nature of every several thing. All the other arts are concerned with human opinions and desires, or with the production or use of things. The mathematical sciences do to some extent lay hold on reality, but only as in a dream, so long as they leave their hypotheses unexamined and can give no account of them. For if your premise is an unknown quantity, and the conclusion and the intermediate steps are also woven out of unknown quantities, they may hang together, but they can never be absolute knowledge. So dialectic is the only method that proceeds to do away with hypotheses and go straight to the first principle, so as to stand on firm ground. It finds the eye of the soul buried in the slough of barbaric ignorance, and gently frees it and guides it upwards, using as handmaids the arts that we have described, arts which through force of custom we have called forms of knowledge, though they really demand some other name implying something clearer than opinion but less clear than knowledge. "Thinking" was, I believe, the term that we adopted earlier; but in matters of such importance we need not dispute about names.

So we may accept, as before, the names we gave to the four divisions of the Line: knowledge, thinking, (*534*) belief, and imagining, of which the last two have to do with the apprehension of appearances in the realm of becoming, the first two with intelligence related to being. And as being is to becoming, so is intelligence to the apprehension of appearances; or, again, so is knowledge to belief, and thinking to imagining. Further elaboration of the proportion would require a far longer discussion; but we may sum up by saying that the dialectician deserves his name in so far as he demands an account of the real nature of each thing.

All this applies also to the Good. Only he deserves the name of dialectician who distinguishes it rationally from everything else, battling his way without faltering through every test by the standard not of appearances but of reality. Otherwise it will not be the Good or any good thing that he knows, but only some image of it that he lays hold on, not by knowledge but only by opinion; and he will dream away this life till he reaches the realm of everlasting sleep.

So if you were ever actually charged with the education of your imaginary children, you will not allow them to rule in your state as long as they have not reason in them, but will lay down the principle that they must especially master the art of asking and answering questions. So dialectic completes, like a coping stone, the structure of our studies, and there is no other study that could justly be set above it. [531c–534e]

From Book VIII

The Tyrant

Socrates now sketches the orderly curriculum of studies for his future rulers, and the ages at which each subject is to be pursued, and then sends them to their administrative tasks, in which they will increase their practical experience; later, they will divide their time between study and government. So philosophy may reform society.

But everything human is subject to flow and ebb. Accordingly Socrates is constrained to describe imaginatively, not quite historically, the gradual degeneration of society, as earlier he has described its growth and reformation; and likewise with the individuals, whose natures correspond to the successive stages. Thus aristocracy (the rule of reason, or the best) declines into timocracy (the rule of honor, military efficiency, or wealth, as in Sparta), followed by oligarchy (the rule of the wealthy but dronelike few), then by democracy (the rule of the many, the people), and finally by tyranny (the despotic rule of the one worst dictator). Aristotle's classification of constitutions, it may be added, is based on two principles: he asks where power is vested, whether in an individual, or in few, or in many; and whether it is exercised normally, for the good of the community, or is perverted to serve private interests; he therefore does not follow Plato's order (*Politics*, III, 7). Athens ran the gamut of these experiences, also in a slightly different order from Plato's: aristocracy was succeeded by the more or less benevolent tyranny of the Pisistratidae, which unconsciously helped democratic forces (that had already gained ground under Solon) to assert themselves when the last of the Pisistratidae (now really "tyrannical") was driven out, so that democracy prevailed during most of the fifth and fourth centuries, though with frequent attempts of oligarchs to check it or to seize power. The democracy of the Age of Pericles, best summed up in the "Funeral Oration" of Pericles recorded by Thucydides (II, 35–46), certainly has an ideal character, with its tolerance and versatility and the freedom that it gave the common man, though always with the conviction that the common good transcends any private claim. But Socrates condemned it for its *laissez-faire* and anarchy, for substituting for the rule of reason the indiscriminate appetites of the many; and we do not forget that the Athenian democracy condemned its critic Socrates to death.

If democracy gives equal rights to every one, it suffers its nemesis when one man, usually masquerading as the champion of the oppressed against reactionaries, seizes power unconstitutionally (that is all that the term "tyrant" originally implied) and presently by armed force (i.e., a "bodyguard") gains absolute power and enslaves the people; now he has "tasted blood," and becomes a "tyrant" in the familiar and bad sense. Plato knew of many tyrants, good and bad, in the outlying regions of the Greek world, notably in Sicily, where tyranny followed democracy. His picture of the transformation may be further documented by what we have learned about modern dictators in fascist states.

In the picture of the individual "tyrannical man," Socrates refers to the master passion that dominates him as "Eros," the familiar personification of love or desire, the child or attendant of Aphrodite. Elsewhere (notably in the *Symposium*) Eros shows a quite different character, as the craving for beauty or truth that leads to philosophy; love, in other words, may be either a curse or a blessing.

566 SOCRATES. Let us describe the "happiness" of the man, and of the state in which such a mortal appears. At first he greets every one whom he meets with a smile, and says he is no tyrant, but makes lavish promises to individuals and to the public; he cancels debts and makes distributions of land to the people and to his retainers, and puts on a gracious and mild mien toward everybody. But when he has got rid of his exiled enemies by coming to terms with some and destroying others, he is always stirring up one war after another, so that the people may stand in need of a leader, (*567*) and so that by having to pay taxes they may be reduced to poverty and be forced to earn their daily bread and be less able to plot against him. And if he suspects any of them of liberal ideas and of withholding power from him, he finds pretexts for exposing them to the enemy. So for all of these reasons a tyrant must always be stirring up wars.

GLAUCON. Yes, he must.

SOCRATES. If so, he will be more and more hated by his fellow citizens. And if any of those who have helped him to power happen to be courageous and to criticize his course of action among themselves or to his face, he must get rid of them, if he is to maintain his rule, till he has left no friend or foe of any account. He must mark sharply any one who is courageous or high-minded or wise or rich; and he is so "happy" that he must, willy-nilly, be at odds with all such and plot against them, till he has cleaned the state of them, quite unlike doctors who purge the worst elements out of bodies and leave the best. He is under the blessed compulsion of either living among men who are mostly worthless, or of not living at all. So the more he is hated by the citizens for his actions, the more numerous and the more trustworthy bodyguards he will need. These will flock to him of their own accord, if he offers pay: foreign mercenaries and nondescripts—drones, we may call them. And as for natives, well, he can rob citizens of their slaves by setting them free and enrolling them as his bodyguards, and most faithful would they be. What a blessed lot is the tyrant's, (*568*) if he has exchanged his former friends for such trusty henchmen! These are the cronies who admire him and gather round him, while decent citizens hate and shun him. . . . But how is he to maintain his fine, motley, shifting retinue?

GLAUCON. Doubtless he will spend any treasures that there may be, stored in temples, and the confiscated property of his victims, so as to lighten the burden of taxation.

SOCRATES. And when that gives out?

GLAUCON. Oh, he will support himself and his boon companions on his ancestral estate.

SOCRATES. By "ancestral" you mean, I suppose, that the common people who brought him forth will support both the tyrant and his companions.

GLAUCON. Just so.

SOCRATES. But what if they complain that it is not right for a grown-up son to be supported by his father, and that it ought to be the other way round, (*569*) since they didn't bring him forth and set him up with the idea that after he had grown great they should be slaves to their own slaves and feed him and all his rabble; but he was to be their champion and free them from the rich and the "upper classes?" And what if they order him and his companions out of the state, like a father driving a prodigal son and his fellow revellers out of the house?

GLAUCON. The people will then realize what sort of creature it has bred and fostered in its bosom; but that the child is now too strong for its feeble parent to drive out.

SOCRATES. You mean that the tyrant will dare to do violence to his father and beat him if he resists?

GLAUCON. Yes, after disarming him.

SOCRATES. Then your tyrant is a parricide, and has no pity for starving old age. This means, it would seem, unabashed tyranny; and, as they say, the people would have jumped out of the frying-pan into the fire—from the service of freemen into the tyranny of slaves, from their former and excessive freedom into the grievous and most bitter garments of slavery to their former slave. Shall we be right in saying that we have now described adequately the transition from democracy to tyranny, and the nature of an established tyranny?

GLAUCON. Quite adequately. [566d–569c]

From Book IX

571 SOCRATES. It remains then to inspect the man of tyrannical character, his transformation from the democratic character, and his manner of life, whether happy or wretched. But I must first define more fully than before the number and nature of the desires. Of pleasures and desires that are unnecessary some seem to me to be lawless.* Doubtless they are innate in every man; but when they are disciplined by law and by the higher desires with the help of reason, they can in some cases be altogether eradicated, or at least weakened, while in other cases they remain comparatively numerous and strong. I mean such desires as are awakened in sleep, when the gentler and more rational and controlling part of the soul slumbers, and the wild beast in us, sated with food or drink, casts off sleep and capers in quest of whatever will gratify its instincts. It is emancipated, you know, from all sense of shame or prudence, and at such times will dare anything—in imagination it does not shrink from intercourse with a mother or anyone else, man, god, or beast, or from violating any scruple; in a word, it goes to the furthest limit of folly and shamelessness.

GLAUCON. Quite true.

SOCRATES. Not so the man who is sound in mind and body; before he goes to sleep, he awakens the reason within him, and feasts it on fair thoughts and meditations, communing with himself. He has neither starved nor surfeited his desires, so that they are asleep and do not trouble (*572*) that better part with joy or sorrow, but leave it free to reach out in pure thought toward some new perception of what is past or present or to come. He has soothed his passions, too, so that he may fall asleep with no anger roused against any man. So, with desires and passions quieted, and that third part of him aroused in which wisdom dwells, he takes his

* These desires and pleasures were mentioned in an earlier discussion of democracy, which was criticized for not sufficiently curbing them and restricting society to the satisfaction of simple and "necessary" desires. In the following sentences the reader will find an anticipation of Freudian psychology, and even of the unfortunately misnamed Oedipus complex. It should be unnecessary to add that Plato, unlike some of Freud's less cautious followers, does not condone the "subliminal" self.

rest; the visions of his dreams are not lawless, and he is in a mood to lay hold on truth.

But I have strayed from my point, which was that in every man, even the most respectable of us, there are strange and wild and lawless desires, which reveal themselves in dreams. Now we said that the democratic man was reared in his early years by his parsimonious father, who respected only such desires as are useful in business, and who had no use for the unnecessary ones, as conducive only to amusement and conspicuous spending. But after association with more fashionable people who gave rein to unnecessary desires, he launched on every excess, like them, and despised his father's miserliness. Still he had a better nature than his corrupters; so he compromised, getting the best, as he supposed, of both ways of living: by striking a balance between the meanness of the one and the licence of the other. And that was how the democratic man was descended from an oligarchic father.

Now suppose him in turn grown older, with a young son reared in his pattern, exposed to the same environment, and drawn by his seducers into that complete lawlessness which they call "complete freedom" while his father and friends still support the policy of compromise. And when those dread wizards who would presume to set up a tyrant in him cannot get hold of him otherwise, they contrive to engender in him a passion that offers to lead all the idle desires that are seeking to divide up his substance, (*573*) such a passion as I may call a great winged drone. When all the other desires come buzzing about it, laden with incense and perfumes, garlands and wine, and all that goes with loose living, they feed it to the full, and implant in this drone the sting of unappeasable longing. Then indeed this passion, the captain of his soul, takes madness for its bodyguard and runs amok; all lingering ideas or desires with any pretence of decency or still capable of shame it drives out or kills, till it is purged of all moderation and filled with an imported madness. That is how the tyrannical man is engendered, and why Eros has long been called a tyrant; and a drunken man has a bit of the tyrannical in his spirit; yes, and the madman who thinks to rule all men and heaven, too. So when a man by nature or manner of life, or both, is drunken, lustful, and mad, you have the complete tyrant. Such, then, is his origin and character; how does he live?

GLAUCON. In the language of the game, I give up; you tell me.

SOCRATES. I will. When Eros dwells in him and is the absolute ruler of his soul, then revels and feastings and mistresses and such pleasures become his preoccupation; every day and night new and formidable desires spring up, whose incessant demands spend whatever revenues he may have, so that he next draws on capital, and goes into debt. Now he is bankrupt, but his spawning desires continue to clamor; so, goaded by his desires and above all by that passion to which they serve as bodyguard, he runs riot and looks for any man of property whom he can rob by fraud or violence. For he must get money by hook or by crook, (*574*) or else suffer aches and pains. And just as every new pleasure dispossessed some older one, so this young man will assert his right to dispossess his father and his mother, when he has run through his inheritance, and live on the family property; if they resist, he will first try to cheat them; if he fails in this attempt, he will resort to outright robbery; if they still hold out, would he have any scruple against doing all that a tyrant does?

ADIMANTUS. I should not have great hopes for the parents of such a son.

SOCRATES. But, Adimantus, will he really, for the sake of some new sweetheart or friend who has no claim on him, beat his dear old mother and his feeble old father and his earliest friends, who have every claim on him, and will he bring these new favorites under the same roof to give orders to them?

ADIMANTUS. Indeed he will.

SOCRATES. To be the parents of a tyrannical son, then, seems to be a blessed lot!

ADIMANTUS. Blessed, indeed!

SOCRATES. Well, when his parents' property gives out, and he has in him a great swarm of desires for pleasure, first he will break into a house or rob a wayfarer by night, and then he will plunder a temple of its treasures. And all the while his childhood notions about right and wrong will be overpowered by new notions, once held under control but now emancipated and serving as bodyguard to Eros. Earlier, when he was still subjected to the democratic rule of his father and the laws, they broke loose only in sleep; but now that he is under the tyrannical rule of Eros, he is in all his waking hours what he was now and then in his sleep, with no scruple against bloodshed or any forbidden deed. *575* Eros, enthroned in him as his sole master amid every kind of lawlessness, will drive him as a tyrant drives a state into any venture that may support him and that rabble which he has gathered partly from evil communications without and partly from the emancipation of like elements within himself.

If there are only a few such men in a state that is mostly sound, they will go abroad to serve as bodyguard to some other tyrant, or to serve as mercenaries if there is a war going on; if it is a time of peace and quiet, they stay at home and commit many a petty crime, as thieves, burglars, temple-robbers, and kidnappers; or, if they are clever of tongue, as blackmailers. Petty I call their crimes, so long as the criminals are few; and all their crimes added together do not amount to anything in comparison with the misery and degradation of the state under the rule of a tyrant. For when the number of such men and of their followers increases and they become aware of their numbers, then it is they who, by the aid of the people's folly, bring forth as a tyrant from their own ranks that one who has in his own soul most of the tyrant. Well, if the people submit readily, all is easy; but if not, then just as he used to discipline his father and his mother, so now he will discipline, if he can, his once beloved fatherland, and will hold it subject to the enslavement of his new companions. And that would be the consummation of such a man's desires.

In private life, before winning power, such men associate only with flatterers who are ready to do them every service, (*576*) or they actually cringe themselves in order to gain their ends; but as soon as they have gained them, they drop their pose of intimacy and appear quite distant. So all through life the tyrannical nature is without a friend; he is always either master or slave to some one else, but never enjoys the taste of true friendship or freedom. He is faithless; and if we were right in our conception of justice, he is the perfect example of the unjust man. [571–576b]

The pattern in the heavens

The contrast between the perfectly just philosopher-king and the perfectly unjust tyrant is thus complete. Moreover, as Socrates goes on to show, the one is completely happy, the other completely unhappy; for the one is free, the other is really enslaved; the one has the fullest experience of all the ranges of pleasure, but has chosen to subordinate the lower to the higher; and intellectual pleasures are positive and "pure," not conditioned by being merely the alleviation of bodily needs or cravings. Thus the demand of Glaucon and Adimantus (see above, 367) has been met: justice has been shown to be better than injustice, not for external results (though later these will be reckoned in, too) but for its effect on its possessor. If man is likened to a composite creature, partly rational and human, partly bestial, it is injustice that fosters the bestial part, and justice that subjects it to "the human, or perhaps I should say the divine, part of him" (588b–591a).

This discussion concludes, perhaps to the reader's surprise, with a disclaimer of any hope that the ideal state can be found here and now (but compare the similar thought, above; see 495–497), or that the philosopher can often be an effective politician. His commonwealth is within his soul, and is patterned on the order of the starry heavens. Not Heaven in any Christian sense, though there are suggestions of Plato in St. Paul's "we have a building of God, an house not made with hands, eternal in the heavens" (II Corinthians 5:1), as well as in St. Augustine's *Civitas Dei,* an unseen city within the visible Roman Empire.

591 SOCRATES. Under what conditions, then, and on what ground can we say that it is profitable for a man to be unjust or undisciplined or to do any base act which will make him a worse man, though he gains thereby money or power? Or how can we say that it profits him to escape detection and punishment? By escaping he merely becomes worse, whereas by being detected and punished the bestial part of him is tamed and laid to rest, and the gentler part is set free; and his whole soul is restored to its natural excellence, winning through the temperance and justice that comes from wisdom a condition more precious than the strength and beauty that health bestows on the body, insofar as the soul is more precious than the body. So the man of sense will stretch every nerve all his life toward this goal; in the first place, valuing only those studies which will have this effect on his soul; and then as to the condition and care of his body, he will be so far from abandoning it to bestial and irrational pleasures that he will not set store primarily by health or strength or beauty, but will value them only as they conduce to soundness of mind: he will always keep his body in tune for the sake of the resulting harmony in his soul.

GLAUCON. Yes, if he is to have real music in him.

SOCRATES. And in the acquisition of wealth he will observe a similar order and harmony; he will not be confused by ordinary people's ideas about what makes a man happy, and so pile up infinite riches, the source of infinite troubles. He will look rather toward the commonwealth within himself, and will take care that nothing in it be disturbed through either excess or want; and so, as far as possible, he will be guided in adding to his property or in spending it. With the same end in view, he will gladly accept positions of honor (*592*) which he thinks will make him a better man, but will avoid any, in public or in private life, that he thinks would destroy the order established within him.

GLAUCON. In that case, he will not wish to engage in politics.

SOCRATES. Indeed he will, in his own commonwealth, though not perhaps in his fatherland, unless through some providential opportunity.

GLAUCON. I understand; you mean the commonwealth that we have been founding in our discourse; for I think it exists nowhere on earth.

SOCRATES. Well, perhaps there is a pattern set up in the heavens for him who will to see, and, seeing it, to found one like it in himself. It matters not whether it exists anywhere or will ever exist; for only in this commonwealth would he ever engage in politics. [591a–592b]

From Book X

The Myth of Er

The last book of the *Republic* renews the previous consideration of poetry, which now appears, in terms of the theory of Ideas, and of the psychological effect of poetry on character, to be acceptable only under strict conditions (see above, p. 331).

The concluding pages of the work pass from the vindication of justice in this life to speculation on its value for an immortal soul that is destined to live hereafter. This question had been expressly excluded from the earlier discussion. To the convictions about immortality, cautiously mentioned in the *Apology* and argued at length in the *Phaedo* and the *Meno,* Socrates now adds a new argument: since the soul may be injured, but not destroyed, by its specific evil, injustice, it cannot be destroyed by anything else, and must be deemed immortal. Still another argument appears in the *Phaedrus* (245c–246a) and the *Laws* (894b): unlike matter, or body, which can be moved only from outside, the soul is self-moved. In the cosmology of the *Timaeus,* which makes little use of the theory of Ideas, Plato describes the creation of the universe by the divine artist or Demiurge, who is reason personified, and who creates soul both in the universe and in individual creatures such as men (*Timaeus* 28c–29b; 30b; 34c; 47e ff.). To the question "why becoming and the universe were framed by him who framed them," Plato's spokesman replies in language that reminds one of the Idea of Good, which indeed comes near to being equivalent to God: "He was good, and none that is good is ever subject to any grudgingness with regard to anything; so he desired all things to become as far as possible like himself. This one might most rightly accept from wise men as the sovereign and ultimate source of becoming and of the universe. For God desired that all things should be good, and that nothing, so far as might be possible, should be bad" (*Timaeus* 29e–30a). Here something like the Christian doctrine of the incarnation is suggested in motive, though not in manner. And in the *Laws* Plato urges that a chief obstacle to morality and political security is religious heresy, whether in the form of outright atheism, or of the belief that the gods (Plato speaks of "God" or "the gods" indifferently, but is essentially a monotheist) take no interest in men's conduct, or of the belief that the gods can be bribed (*Laws* 885b–907d).

If the universe has been created and is maintained by a good God, the question must arise how evil can exist, either in the world in general or in individual souls. For evil in the universe, Plato has various explanations: chance, necessity, matter, nature, all of which imply that (as he argued in the *Republic*) actual existence always falls short of ideal perfection, and that a perfectly good God may not be omnipotent. For evil in the souls of individual men, Plato turns to the psychological analysis already set forth in the *Republic* (but not included above), in which the desires and the passionate element may be imperfectly subjected to the reason; this conception is powerfully illustrated by the myth in the *Phaedrus* (246a–e; 253c–254e) in which the soul of man is conceived as a charioteer driving two winged but ill-matched steeds, one striving to soar, the other plunging earthwards.

Still more impressive is the Myth of Er, which concludes the *Republic.* Like the other illustrations, images, parables, and myths of Plato, it is not to be taken literally, but is an imaginative or poetic attempt to suggest, with concrete detail, the direction in which his whole argument points. Here Plato suggests that, in a universe governed by a good and just God, individuals possessed of immortal souls and charged with freedom of moral choice will hereafter, if not in this life, have the fullest justice done to them. All seeming evils in this life "will come to some good in the end, either in this life or after death; for the gods can never be regardless of one who sets his heart on being just and making himself by practice of virtue as like a god as man may" (*Republic* 613a). So the myth, using materials from Orphic religious literature and from Pythagorean astronomy, is the narrative of one who marvelously returned to life, after apparent death in battle, to report a sort of Last Judgment. It embraces Hell and Purgatory and Heaven, as it follows the fortunes of souls, born and reborn, passing before a judgment seat and receiving their just deserts. The landscape is vague and cosmic; the language is full of tense feeling that appeals to the moral feeling of the human race. Echoes of the myth appear in Cicero's *Somnium Scipionis* and in the sixth book of Virgil's *Aeneid,* as well as in Dante and Milton. The chief point is the solemn yet hopeful conviction that man's happiness or misery throughout eternity depends on his justice or injustice in this life, or in the series of lives that awaits him (for it is assumed here, as in the *Meno,* that the soul may live several successive lives in the body before it wins a final release from earthly existence).

With the picture of human destinies is connected a picture of the cosmic order in astronomical as well as mythical terms; this emphasizes the element of encompassing necessity or determinism within which human freedom may operate. On the knees of Necessity rests the spindle which governs the movement of the heavenly bodies; her daughters are the Fates, who spin and sing, with the Sirens, the music of the spheres. At the throne of Necessity, mortals gather to choose their future lives. The order of choosing is determined by lot; for not only did the constitution of Athens make some use of the lot, but all human life includes a considerable element of luck. Nevertheless the mortals of the myth are free to choose the lives that they are to live: "the responsibility is his who chooses; God is without responsibility." It is a solemn choice; and some choose wisely, others foolishly. The several choices however, once made, become irrevocable. With the hope of blessedness for those who have chosen well, the Myth, and the *Republic,* come to an end.

614 Socrates. Er, the son of Armenius, a Pamphylian by birth, was killed in battle. Ten days later, when the dead were taken up for burial, his body was found undecayed and was carried home. On the twelfth day, as he lay on the funeral pyre, he came to life again, and told what he had seen in the other world.

He said that when his soul left his body he journeyed with many others until they came to a wonderful place, where there were two openings side by side in the earth, and two others in the sky just above them. Judges sat between them, and pronounced judgment; they bade the just to proceed on the right upwards through the sky, wearing in front tokens of their judgment, and the unjust to proceed to the left and downwards, wearing on their backs tokens of all their deeds. But when Er drew near, he was told that he must bring to men tidings of the other world, and must give heed and observe all that happened in that place.

So he saw the souls that had been judged departing on either side, upwards or downwards; and through the other two openings other souls arriving up from the earth, laden with dust, or down from the sky, clean and pure. These travellers, constantly arriving as if from a long journey, seemed glad to turn aside into the meadow, where they camped as at a festival, and greeted their acquaintances and asked one another about what had befallen them above or below. Some wept as they recounted their sufferings (*615*) and the sights they had seen during their journey of a thousand years under the earth; others told of the joys of heaven and of sights of inconceivable beauty. Now it would take too long, Glaucon, to repeat his tale in full, but the chief point was this: every sinner repaid tenfold every wrong that he had done, once in each hundred years (that being the utmost span of human life); murders, or betrayals or enslavements of country or of comrades in arms, or any other crimes, all were requited tenfold. Likewise every kind deed, every just or holy life, was rewarded in the same proportion. He had something to say about infants who died at birth or shortly after, but I think it hardly worth mentioning.

Reverence toward gods and parents, or the lack of it, or murder of parents, he said, had even greater wages. He was present when the question was asked, "Where is Ardiaeus the Great?" (Now this Ardiaeus had been a tyrant in a city of Pamphylia a thousand years before, and, among many other crimes, had killed his aged father and his elder brother.) The answer came: "He has not come here, nor will he ever come." This was one of the dreadful sights that we saw. When we drew near, after all our experiences, to the mouth of the opening, ready to come up, suddenly we spied him and other men, mostly tyrants, though some were private citizens who had committed great crimes. They thought they were about to come up, but the jaws of the opening, instead of admitting them, gave a roar whenever one of them tried to ascend whose sin was incurable or who had not sufficiently paid the penalty. Then some fierce and fiery-looking men who were at hand and who understood the meaning of the roar, seized some of them and carried them away; but Ardiaeus and others they bound hand and foot (*616*) and threw them down and flayed them. They dragged them along at the side of the road, carding them on thorns, telling the passers-by why they did so, and that they were going to cast them into Tartarus. Great though the other terrors were, and of every kind, this was the worst, the fear that each man felt lest when he sought to go up he should hear that roar; so, if it was not heard, they went up in great joy. Such, then, were the judgments, and the penalties or rewards corresponding to them.

Now when they had all spent seven days in the meadow, on the eighth day they had to pass on, and four days later they arrived at a place where they could see a straight shaft of light, like a pillar, that stretched from above through heaven and earth, resembling a rainbow, but brighter and purer. This they reached after another day's journey; and there they beheld, at the middle of the light the ends of the chains of heaven; for this light binds the heavens, holding together its whole revolving firmament, like the undergirths of a ship. And from the ends of the chains stretched the spindle of Necessity, on which revolve the orbits of all the heavenly bodies.*

617 The spindle turned on the knees of Necessity. On each of its circles, and riding round with it, was a Siren who uttered a single note, so that from their eight concordant tones came the full scale; [the music of the spheres, familiar to readers of Chaucer, Shakespeare, and Milton]; and round about, at equal intervals, sat on their thrones the three daughters of Necessity, the Fates, clad in white and wearing garlands, and singing to the Sirens' music: Lachesis of the past, Clotho of the present, Atropos of things to come. And Clotho [Spinner] from time to time with her right hand helped the motion of the outer rim of the spindle [i.e., the fixed stars], as Atropos with her left hand helped the inner circles [i.e., the planets], while Lachesis with either hand helped the outer and the inner circles alternately.

When the souls arrived, they had to go immediately before Lachesis [whose name is associated with the drawing of lots]. Then a prophet first arranged them in order, and proceeded to take from the lap of Lachesis a number of lots and samples of lives, and mounted a high platform and said: "The word of Lachesis, maiden daughter of Necessity. Souls of a day, here beginneth a new round of mortal life, to end in death. No divine guardian shall draw lots for you, but you shall choose your own guardian and destiny. Let him who draws the first lot choose first the life that shall of necessity be his. Virtue is without a master; every man, as he honors or dishonors her, shall have more of her, or less. The responsibility is his who chooses; God is without responsibility." With these words the prophet scattered the lots before them all, and each took up the one that fell near him (*618*) and that showed the order of his choice; only Er was forbidden to take one. Then the prophet spread on the ground before them the samples of lives, many more than there were persons present.

The lives were of every kind: of every sort of living creature, and of course of every human type. There were lives of tyrants, some that ran their full course and others cut short or ending in poverty or exile; there were lives of men famous for beauty or strength or success in games, or for distinction of birth; also lives of obscure men, and of women likewise. They mingled traits of wealth or poverty, sickness or health, or intermediate conditions; but the character of the soul was not indicated, since it must necessarily alter its character as it chooses this or that life.

Just here, I think, my dear Glaucon, a man's everything is at stake. And that is why he must study how to disregard all else and seek only how to learn for himself, or to discover a teacher who

* Whether the band is supposed to be the axis of the spherical universe, or whether it is a circular strip, like the Milky Way, has been disputed; undergirths were ropes used to strengthen ancient ships (as, temporarily, in Acts 27:17), but again whether longitudinally or round the hull is a matter of dispute. The picture of astronomy here and in what follows is in any case merely a verbal substitute for a working model of the concentric planets and the fixed stars as they appear to rotate in fixed orbits about the earth; the "spindle" is their common axis. Some of the details must be omitted here.

can show him, the power of discerning good and evil, and of always and everywhere choosing the best within his reach. He must consider all that we have said, in their several or in their connected bearings on goodness of life, and understand the effect for good or for evil of beauty combined with wealth or with poverty and with this or that condition of the soul, and of birth high or low, of station public or private, of strength or weakness of body or mind, and of all the other qualities of soul, natural or acquired, in all their mutual relationships. So at last, with all these considerations in mind, and with a view to the nature of the soul, he can choose between the better and the worse life, calling that one better which will make his soul more just, and the one that will make it less just, the worse. All else he will disregard; for, as we have seen, this is the supreme choice for a man, both in his lifetime and after death. *619* So when he goes to the House of Hades, he must hold this faith like adamant, lest there too he be dazzled by wealth and such evils, or meeting with tyrannies and such affairs he work harm that cannot be undone and suffer still worse evils himself, but rather that he may know how to choose a middle path and avoid both extremes, both in this life, so far as possible, and in every life hereafter. For therein lies man's greatest happiness.

Well, Er in his story reported that the prophet said: "Even the last comer, if he chooses wisely and lives earnestly, can find a satisfactory life, by no means a bad one. Let not the first to choose be careless, nor the last despair." Thereupon he who had drawn the first lot at once stepped up and chose the most complete tyranny, not noticing in his greed and folly that in it, among other evils, he was doomed to devour his own children. When he looked into it at his leisure, he beat his breast and bewailed his choice, forgetting the warning of the prophet; for he did not blame himself for his ills, but fortune, and the gods, and everything except himself. Now he was one of those who had come down from heaven, and who in his previous life had lived in a well-ordered state, and had been virtuous not through the pursuit of wisdom but only as a matter of habit. And indeed that was true of most of those who were caught in this way: they had come from heaven, and were not disciplined by suffering, whereas most of those who came from earth, since they had suffered and had seen others suffer, did not make careless choices. For this reason, and also because of the chances of the lot, most of the souls now underwent an exchange of good to evil, or evil to good. But from what Er reported, it appears that whenever a man returned to a life on earth and sought wisdom mightily, and his lot did not condemn him to one of the very last choices, he was apt to fare well both here and in his journey hence, a journey not rough and underground but smooth and heavenwards.

For it was a sight indeed worth seeing, said Er, how the several souls chose their lives; (*620*) pitiful to see, and laughable, and strange. For they chose mostly in accordance with the habits of their former lives. [The examples that follow are from Greek mythology: Orpheus, preferring to become a swan; Ajax, a lion; Thersites, a monkey; Agamemnon, an eagle; Atalanta, an athlete; similarly, certain songbirds chose human lives.] It chanced that the lot gave the last choice of all to the soul of Odysseus; disenchanted of ambition by the memory of his former toils, he went about for a long time looking for a life of quiet obscurity. And when at length he found it lying somewhere, neglected by every one else, he gladly chose it, remarking that he would have done the same if he had had the first choice. Other souls in the same way passed from beasts into men, or into one another, the unjust into wild beasts and the just into the tame, in all kinds of combinations.

When the souls had chosen their lives, they went before Lachesis in the order of their lots; she sent along with each the guardian of his destiny whom he had chosen, to protect him and fulfill the choice. And he first led the soul to Clotho, beneath her hand and the turning of the spindle, thus ratifying the portion that was his by lot and choice; then, after touching her, he led the soul to the spinning of Atropos [she who does not turn back], thus making the threads of his destiny irreversible; and finally, without turning back, (*621*) he went beneath the throne of Necessity. And when he and all the rest had passed beyond it, they all journeyed to the Plain of Lethe [Forgetfulness], through the terrible choking heat; for it is bare of trees and other growing things. They camped there, now that evening was coming, by the River of Unmindfulness, whose water no vessel can hold. Every one had to drink a certain amount of the water, but some had not the saving sense not to drink more; and each, as he drank, forgot everything. At midnight, when they were asleep, there was thunder and an earthquake, and they were all suddenly carried up from here and there, like shooting stars, to their birth. Er himself was not permitted to drink the water. But how he returned to the body, he knew not; but at dawn he suddenly opened his eyes and found himself lying on the funeral pyre.

And so, Glaucon, the tale was not lost, but was saved, and may save us, too, if we heed it, and we shall pass safely the River of Lethe and not defile our souls. If you will heed me, and believe that the soul is immortal and able to bear all things both good and evil, we shall hold always to the upward path and practise in all ways justice with the help of wisdom. So we shall be on good terms with ourselves, as well as with the gods, both while we linger here and later when we gather the prizes of justice like athletic victors, and both here and in that journey of a thousand years of which I have told, we shall fare well. [614b–621d]

SELECTIONS FROM ARISTOTLE

Translated by Edwin L. Minar, Jr.

INTRODUCTION

Aristotle (384–322 b.c.) was a native of Stagira, in Macedonia, where his father was a friend and court physician to King Amyntas II. In 367, at the age of seventeen, he traveled to Athens to study under Plato, and he remained a member of the Academy for the next twenty years—until the death of Plato in 347.

Plato's school was an institution dedicated to training, and to working out the principles for training, a new kind of political leader, but the ideal was a ruler who should be first of all a philosopher, and the Academy was deeply engaged with technical problems of philosophy. Plato and his associates were working out the implications of the theory of Ideas—discussing, criticizing, testing. They studied mathematics, theoretical astronomy, the nature of knowledge, pleasure and pain; and Plato was preparing also his latest works on political philosophy, which culminated in the *Laws*. Thus Aristotle learned in the Academy that philosophy has an all-important political bearing, and that the Good at which it aims is one which involves the whole of society. He also learned that the approach to philosophy is through mathematics and dialectic rather than observation and experiment, that truth is arrived at through the reason rather than the senses, and that only the eternal Ideas are fully real. Later he was to rebel against this point of view, complaining that the Platonists turned philosophy into mathematics; but, as we shall see, he could not really abandon it.

In 347, after Plato died and his nephew Speusippus became head of the school, Aristotle and Xenocrates went to Asia Minor to join two former pupils of Plato named Erastus and Coriscus. These men were friends of the tyrant Hermias, ruler of the cities of Atarneus and Assus, near Troy; they advised him on political matters, and in the Platonic tradition sought to make him a philosopher. While living in Assus, Aristotle formed an intimate friendship with Hermias; he is said to have assisted him in negotiating an understanding with Macedonia, and his first wife was Hermias' niece Pythias. Upon Hermias' fall and death in 345, the two philosophers went to Mytilene in Lesbos. This was the home of their associate Theophrastus, who was to be Aristotle's successor as head of his own school. In 343, Aristotle received the famous invitation to come to the court of King Philip II of Macedonia as tutor to the young Alexander. It is not known just how long this relationship lasted; but Alexander was involved at a very early age in political and military affairs. Aristotle, however, probably stayed on in Macedonia till the death of Philip in 335, when he returned to Athens.

Even during the lifetime of Plato, Aristotle had published a number of works on philosophy, mostly in dialogue form, all of which have perished. During the period of absence from Athens (347–335), he continued and extended his studies, completing some of his most important works in logic and physics, and the older parts of his books on metaphysics, politics, and ethics. Some of his biological research was done at Assus and Mytilene.

In Athens again, he founded a school of his own, the Lyceum, in a gymnasium attached to the temple of Apollo Lyceus, near Athens. The grounds included a covered court or portico (*peripatos*), from which the school received its name (Peripatetic). Aristotle's activities were mainly of two kinds: lecturing on philosophy and organizing and supervising a great program of research. The members of the school collected data and wrote reports and studies in many different fields—botany, zoology, music, the history of philosophy, and so forth—even records of winners in the athletic and dramatic competitions. One important and famous project was a collection of monographs on the "constitutions" of 158 different cities and nations. One of these, the *Constitution of Athens*, was discovered in an Egyptian papyrus in 1890. A great library was assembled, with a large number of book-rolls, maps, and also specimens and objects to aid in the study of natural history. Alexander is said to have contributed a sum of eight hundred talents toward the formation of this collection, and to have ordered his generals to cooperate in the assembling of materials. During this last period of his life, Aristotle published most of his special studies in physics and biology, and completed his works in psychology, metaphysics, politics, and ethics, as well as the *Rhetoric* and *Poetics*.

Aristotle was regarded in Athens as a partisan of the Macedonians, and when, after the death of Alexander in 323, an outburst of anti-Macedonian feeling occurred in the city, he was indicted on a charge of impiety. He chose to leave the city peacefully, and moved to Chalcis in Euboea, where he died in the following year, at the age of sixty-two.

Aristotle is one of the universal geniuses. His interests were encyclopedic; they extended literally into every branch of human learning. He was a great collector and classifier; perhaps his greatest contribution to thought is not in any original discoveries but in his systematization of the whole field of thought. His aim was to make one great unified structure of all knowledge. One result of this is that in order to understand fully any part of his system one must have at least some acquaintance with the total scheme; but the reverse is also true, that each part reflects the characteristics of the whole. This must serve as partial justification for the fact that nearly all the selections given below are from the *Nicomachean Ethics* and the *Politics*. It would be impossible in any case, though, to represent all phases of his work in a few pages; and furthermore, it seems that ideas taken from the field of politics and ethics more often lie at the base of metaphysical, physical, and biological theories than vice versa. Let us begin our brief discussion of Aristotle's philosophy, then, with a glance at some of his views on man and society, and also attempt to see whether they have any relation, as we might expect, to the political tendencies of Greece during his lifetime.

The fourth century B.C. was a time of political turmoil, both in practice and in theory. There was a struggle among the leading cities for leadership, and social unrest within each. Political theorists offered various Utopian ideas, and an ideal of Pan-Hellenic unity also emerged. In 367, the very year of Aristotle's arrival in Athens, Plato made his second journey to Sicily and his unsuccessful attempt to educate the young tyrant of Syracuse, Dionysius II, as a philosopher-king.

The most striking and important political event of the period was the phenomenal growth of the kingdom of Macedonia, and this must have made a deep impression on Aristotle. Despite his close connexion with Alexander, however, his attitude to this development is hard to characterize accurately. There is very little real information as to what he taught Alexander, in spite of the ingenuity that has been spent on conjecture. They may merely have read Homer and the dramatists together, or they may have discussed science, politics, and philosophy. Aristotle is said to have written for his pupil a book on kingship and one on colonies. There is a report that the two eventually quarrelled; and it is certain that Alexander had Aristotle's nephew Callisthenes executed for alleged complicity in a plot against the king. Aristotle seems, however, to have been on excellent terms with Antipater, by whom Alexander's affairs in Greece were managed during his tour of conquest in Asia.

It seems quite likely that in important matters neither master nor pupil exerted any very deep influence on the other. There are some fragments of letters, in one of which Aristotle advises the king "to deal with the Greeks as a leader, with the barbarians as a master, caring for the former as friends and relatives, and bearing himself toward the latter as toward animals or plants." [1] This shows that he was not at one with Alexander in the latter's ideal of world brotherhood, retaining the rather provincial ideal of the city-state and the traditional superiority of Greeks to barbarians. The philosopher certainly failed to grasp fully the vast historical importance of his pupil's career; there is scarcely a mention of Macedonia in the *Politics*, and none of Alexander, though he has a good deal to say about monarchy.

The ideal of Alexander and his father was not the destruction of the traditional city-state democracy, but maintenance of the status quo in the internal affairs of Greek cities, with Macedonian direction of foreign affairs. Thus during Aristotle's later years Athens remained a democracy, but under the leadership of the Macedonians, acting through the League of Corinth, which also operated to stabilize the domestic arrangements of the Greek cities. It has been suggested [2] that this rather ambiguous situation is reflected in Aristotle's political thought.

Aristotle does not offer any single solution to the problems of politics. He rejects any Utopian approach, and it is impossible to find one form of government, of all those he discusses in the *Politics*, which he always thinks best. There are six main forms of constitution, three "true" forms (kingship, aristocracy, and "polity") and three perversions (democracy, oligarchy, and tyranny). Kingship is best and the others represent a progressive deterioration; but there is also present in the book another view, according to which each of the three good forms may, in certain conditions, be best. He finds many good things to say about democracy, and is most favorable toward the "polity," a kind of moderate or modified democracy, which is intermediate between democracy and oligarchy but closer to the former. Thus in theory as well as in the practice of his time, monarchy and a more popular government exist side by side. The ideal monarchy of which he speaks is of course much like the ideal state of Plato, and it is buttressed by speculations about the "rule of the one best man," but it may owe something to Alexander. And the "polity" obviously has many of its characteristics from the political experience of the Athenian democracy. It has sometimes been thought that Aristotle was blind to the emergence of federal leagues, and other larger political units, or unaware of the propaganda for some sort of Pan-Hellenic union. According to Kelsen's view this is not correct. He simply rejected these solutions for Greek political problems. His ideal was a moderate, safe, property-based government (the "polity"), and along with this the leadership of the Macedonian monarchy in world affairs.

But the mere analysis of forms of government does not exhaust the subject matter of politics. We must look more carefully into some of the basic assumptions of Aristotle's political thought. The chief end, he thought, is a good life, both for the individual and for the community as a whole. Politics is thus very closely related to ethics (which is the study of the good life in the individual), but it is higher than or prior to ethics, because it is only in society that man is complete, or can achieve perfection. "Man is by nature a 'political' animal" (*Politics* I, i, 9). It might be misleading, however, to assert that for Aristotle the ideal of the good life of the community meant the good of all. Life is activity, and some activities are higher and better than others. The highest good would then be the exercise of the highest activity, which turns out to be contemplation; and this is only possible for God and godlike men. The rest of mankind finds its good in supporting this activity. In plainer terms, social organization makes life complete for the only person capable of a complete life, the free Greek citizen, by providing him an army of slaves and workers who will supply him with the physical basis for a life of refined leisure and contemplation.

Of course Aristotle derived this assumption from the characteristics of the society in which he lived. It may well seem to many modern students that what the Greek world needed most in the fourth century B.C was not new political systems, i.e., new ways of managing men, but new techniques—ways of controlling nature—which would raise the living standards of the whole population. Nevertheless, not only aristocratic thinkers like Plato and Aristotle, but democratic leaders as well failed to see this, and the key to their failure lies in the institution of slavery. This institution, by inhibiting the development of industrial techniques, kept all Greek society on a very low level of technological advance. The free artisan was affected as well as the rich landlord. His wages were kept low by slave competition and his morale sapped by the growing idea that physical work is degrading. Manual labor, commerce, agriculture are all essentially servile occupations which minister to the physical needs of the free citizen. It follows that the practitioners of these arts would ideally be all slaves, and that the free laborer is in this sense less perfect than the slave. Aristotle was right when he said that the free laborer was subject to a "limited servitude," and that "the slave belongs to the class of those who are naturally what they are; but no shoemaker, or any other artisan, belongs to that class." [3] There is much in the thought of Aristotle, as in that of Plato, which is basically antidemocratic; but his ideal was not one of cruel exploitation. He was in favor of virtue; he wanted personal morality and political justice to be based on the value and dignity of man. But since he could not envisage a society without an army of menial toilers to support the few "freemen," he had to develop a system of philosophy which denied the very possibility of true human dignity to the majority of mankind.

Readers with a different point of view from that expressed here may argue that other ancient philosophers—for example, Epicurus—who also lived in a slave society and did not foresee modern technology, developed very different philosophical systems, so that an explanation of philosophical views in terms of social conditions will seem to such objectors inadequate and even irrelevant. For the main issue seems to them to be whether the results of philosophic thought are or are not rationally and empirically warranted. The writer is not in sympathy with this point of view, but states it in the interest of fairness, inviting the reader to read Aristotle and make up his own mind.

Having fully accepted the basic assumption of a fixed hierarchical order throughout society, and by extension throughout all of nature, Aristotle's precise, system-loving mind develops its implications in all fields of thought. It would be impossible here even to summarize adequately his complicated system of logic, metaphysics, and natural science, but we may indicate a few of his leading ideas.

Aristotle's formal logic is perhaps his most important contribution to human thought. For him, logic is the same as scientific method. It is a tool for the analysis of terms and concepts, to demonstrate their interconnections and to show that each truth follows from a simpler truth till we come to the basic principles, which are not susceptible of proof. This attitude differs radically from any view which attempts to make practical verification or experiment its court of last resort; Aristotle's announced goal in science is a set of *necessary* propositions; by "necessary" propositions he means, he says, "those whose contradictories are self-contradictory." Aristotle's logical system has been all-important in defining and fostering rational discourse; but it is a system which makes very little allowance for evolutionary change or for the treatment of borderline states. There is a system or hierarchy of fixed and immutable types, and the task of science and philosophy is simply to recognize and catalogue these.

In his analysis of knowledge and being Aristotle naturally took his departure from the work of his predecessors and especially of Plato. He thought of himself as introducing a fundamental correction of Platonism. Whereas Plato had emphasized the separation of idea (form) and thing, Aristotle rejected this separation completely. He retained the forms, but thought of them as inseparable from matter; the individual, concrete thing is a union of the two, and the form can only be studied in the thing.

In studying a thing or event, Aristotle thinks the most

important statements to be made about it are expressed in terms of cause. He recognizes four causes and regards previous philosophical systems, which had sometimes seen one and sometimes, dimly, two of them, as fumbling and immature attempts to achieve the perfection of his own doctrine. The *material* cause, the matter of which a thing is constituted, had always been recognized. Some had struggled to express the idea of the *efficient* cause, the source of movement, the agent which starts the process, and the *formal* cause, or form, the pattern or formula of the thing. The *final* cause, the end, is the purpose for which the thing is made or done. The *efficient* cause imposes a certain *form* on *matter*, for a certain *end*. It is clear that formal, final, and efficient causes are closely related. In a process of manufacture, for example, the completed tool and its use (final cause) are present in the mind of the smith (the efficient cause) in the guise of the form or pattern according to which he works. Thus the fundamental opposition is between two main factors, form and matter.

The relation between these two is further illuminated by the doctrine of potentiality and actuality. The acorn is potentially an oak, the block of stone potentially a statue, the child potentially a man. The development toward the perfection of the "end" is the progressive imposition of form on matter. It must be noted, however, that this is not a principle of continuous, endless development. A thing does not become something else—it simply reaches its own perfection or maturity and there its growth stops.

The leading idea throughout is the imposition of the will or intention of Nature upon matter. The latter is refractory and recalcitrant like an unruly slave; and from this source come imperfections. This element of intent gives Aristotle's philosophy its strong teleological character and strongly influences the direction of his scientific thought.

It may be said, with some simplification, that there are two main trends or traditions in Greek scientific thought before Aristotle. One is closely related to the development of techniques in handicraft and the manipulation of natural forces in man's behalf. It is materialistic, inclined to test theory in practice and experiment. This is the tradition of the Ionian philosophers, the Hippocratic physicians, and the atomists. The other tendency, that of the Pythagoreans, Eleatics, and Platonists, is to put the testimony of reason above that of the senses, to reject observation and experiment, and to construct scientific theory on the basis of a priori assumptions, sometimes by analogy with ideas in the realm of society and politics.

What has been said in the preceding paragraphs is enough to show that Aristotle was deeply influenced by the Platonic trend. This is clearest in his speculations in the field of physics and astronomy. Here we find, for example, that the heavens are not only eternal but unchangeable and divine; that the motion of the heavenly bodies is circular, because this is the only kind of motion which has no beginning or end and is therefore eternal; that the universe is spherical because the sphere is a perfect figure, and so on.

It would be unjust to Aristotle, however, to emphasize only this side of his thought. He is also an eminent representative of the inductive, empirical school. It is generally agreed that his most successful scientific work was in the minute study and classification of biological types. He made discoveries, for example, about unusual reproductive systems in certain kinds of fish, and about care of the young by fish, which were only verified about a century ago. He made records or reports on about 540 species of animals, and personally dissected many of them. Moreover, though he was engaged in scientific studies even during the Assus-Mytilene period, the works of his latest period, as he drew progressively further from the influence of Plato and embarked on his great program of research, show the greatest devotion to observation and the evidence of the senses. It is to this bent that we owe the broad historical basis and the copious use of example in the *Ethics* and *Politics*.

Nevertheless, even in his technical scientific work he is, as Taylor says, "a Platonist *malgré lui*." This is because "his final conclusions on all points of importance are hardly distinguishable from those of Plato except by the fact that, as they are so much at variance with the naturalistic side of his philosophy, they have the appearance of being sudden lapses into an alogical mysticism." [4] Aristotle's philosophy is two-sided: he goes by the light of reason and the light of facts, but there can be no question that for him the former is stronger and more valid. He has a theory, and hopes to be able to find it exemplified in the facts. If he does not, he still sets down the facts, but in some way they must suffer. This is the meaning of the frequent discrepancy between what "nature intends" and what actually occurs.

It is typical that his political theory is prior, even chronologically, to the historical research issuing in the 158 *Constitutions*. Many arguments are *supported* by examples, but more important principles are always derived with the help of teleological presuppositions. For example, the statement of what happens to tyrannies (*Politics* V, VIII) is based on theory—on what would happen to a form which is a compound of democracy and oligarchy; but examples are added to back up this analysis.

In an important matter, the theoretical, rational, a priori method will always win out; but the experiential, pragmatic tendency is very strong and colors his whole exposition. The contradiction is never fully resolved.

Nearly all the writings of Aristotle which have been preserved for us belong to one class. They are related to his lectures in the Lyceum, though it is difficult to decide just how. They seem rather elaborate to be the lecturer's notes; it has been suggested that they are expansions by pupils of their class notes, or even a set of Aristotle's own notes, expanded by him and deposited in the library for students to consult. In any case, one must not expect any of the elegance of style for which Cicero and other ancient writers praised Aristotle. That judgment was based on more popularly written works which were actually published. In these lecture notes he is dry, compact, often repetitive, allusive, and even cryptic. He always has more in mind than is actually expressed. The present translation aims to transmit his thought as faithfully as possible, in readable English; his severe economy cannot be reproduced, but an effort has been made not to introduce expansions which would alter the sense of his argument.

THE TEXTS USED are as follows: for the *Ethics,* Bywater (Oxford Classical Texts); for the *Politics,* Susemihl-Immisch (Teubner, 1909 and 1928); for the *Parts of Animals,* Langkavel (Teubner, 1868), checked against Peck's Loeb edition. These texts have been repunctuated freely, especially the *Politics.*

NICOMACHEAN ETHICS

Book I

I. THE END, OR THE GOOD, IN PRACTICAL ACTIVITIES

Every activity aims at some end.

1 Every art and every inquiry, and in the same way every action and choice, seem to aim at some good; so that people have well defined the good as that at which all things aim. *2* But there appears to be a certain difference among ends; some are activities, and others certain products distinct from these; and in cases where there are ends aside from the actions, the products are better than the activities. *3* Since there are many actions and arts and sciences, there are also many ends: of medicine, health; of ship-building, a ship; of military science, victory; of household management, wealth. *4* But as many of these as come under some one faculty, as the art of bridle-making and the others concerned with the trappings of a horse come under horsemanship, and the latter as well as every other action concerned with war under military science, and other arts under different faculties in the same way—in all of them the ends of all the leading arts are more choiceworthy than those beneath them, for the latter are pursued for the sake of the former. *5* And it makes no difference whether the activities themselves are the ends of action or something else aside from them, as in the sciences mentioned.

II. THE HIGHEST GOOD, THAT OF POLITICS

The highest good, or end, is one chosen for its own sake. Its knowledge is of great practical value.

1 If then there is some end of action which we desire for its own sake, and other things for its sake, and if we do not choose everything for the sake of something else (for this would lead us into an infinite series, so that all desire would be ineffectual and vain), it is clear that this would be the good, and indeed the highest good. *2* Now does the knowledge of this not have a great influence in the conduct of life, and if we knew it would we not, like archers who have a mark to shoot at, be more likely to attain what is required?

It belongs to the leading art of politics.

3 If so, we must try to define in rough outline what it is and to which of the sciences or faculties it belongs. *4* It would seem to belong to that which is most authoritative, most eminently a leading art, *(5)* and this seems to be that of politics. *6* This art determines which of the sciences is to exist in each city and which each person is to learn, and to what extent. We perceive, too, that the most honored of the arts come under politics, such as military science, household management, and rhetoric. *7* Since it uses the rest of the sciences and decrees what one must do and refrain from doing, its end would include those of the others, so that it would be the good for man. *8* Even though the end be the same for an individual and a city, that of the city seems to be greater and more perfect, both to achieve and to preserve. It is worth while even for a single individual, but fairer and more divine for a people or a city. This is what our inquiry aims at, being political in nature.

III. Method in politics and ethics

The study of politics and ethics is not an exact science.

1 Our account will be adequate if it is worked out clearly as far as the subject matter at hand allows. The same degree of accuracy is not to be expected in every philosophical discussion, any more than in every product of handicraft. *2* There is much difference and fluctuation of opinion about what is noble and what is just, which are the subject matter of politics, so that some believe they are so only by custom and not by nature. *3* The same sort of fluctuation exists in the case of what is good, because harm has come to many persons through good things—some have been destroyed by wealth, others by courage. *4* Now for us, since we are speaking on matters of this sort and with principles of this sort, it will be satisfactory to indicate the truth roughly and in outline, and since we are speaking about things which are generally true, it will suffice for our conclusions to be of the same nature. What we say should of course be received in the same spirit, for it is the part of an educated person to seek accuracy in each kind of subject matter to the extent which its nature admits. It seems equally absurd to accept probable arguments from a mathematician and to demand demonstration of an orator. *5* Each man judges capably the things which he knows, and of them he is a good judge—in each particular field, the man who is educated in it, and in general, the man who is generally educated.

Since it depends on experience and on a disposition to follow reason, it is not a suitable study for the young.

This is why a young person is not a proper student of political science, for he is without experience in the activities of life, and theories are derived from these and concerned with them. *6* Furthermore, since he is inclined to follow emotion, it will be vain and unprofitable for him to listen to instruction, because the end is not knowledge but action. *7* It makes no difference whether one is young in age or merely youthful in character, for the defect lies not in age but in the fact of living and pursuing one's desires according to emotion. For such people knowledge is of no benefit, any more than for the incontinent. For those whose desires and actions are governed by reason, however, knowledge of these matters would be very useful.

8 Let this be our prologue on the student, on how the discussion is to be understood, and on what we propose to discuss.

IV. Happiness, the end of politics

All agree that the end which politics pursues is happiness, but what does this mean? There are several different ideas current.

1 Now resuming our argument, since every investigation and choice aims at some good, let us say what it is that we affirm politics aims at and what is the highest of all the goods of action. *2* As far as the name is concerned there is almost universal agreement, for both the many and the refined call it happiness, and consider living well and doing well to be the same thing as being happy. But they disagree about the definition of happiness, and the many do not account for it in the same way as the wise. *3* Some regard happiness as something manifest and obvious, like pleasure or wealth or honor, others as something different—and frequently the same person will contradict himself, in sickness calling it health, in poverty wealth. Realizing their own ignorance, people admire those who say something grand and above their comprehension. Again, some used to suppose that alongside these many good things there is something else independent which is the cause of their being good. *4* It would doubtless be unprofitable to examine every opinion; it will be enough to consider those which are most prevalent or which seem to have some reason in them.

We must begin with the known facts and proceed from them to generalizations.

5 Let us not forget that there is a difference between arguments *from* first principles and those *to* first principles. Plato did well in raising this difficulty and inquiring whether the path is from or toward the first principles, as in a race track it may be from the judges to the goal or the reverse. We must begin with the known, but this has two senses: to us, and absolutely. We at least must begin, it seems, with what is known to us. *6* Therefore one who is to be a competent student of the noble and just, and of politics generally, must be trained in good habits. *7* This is so because the starting point is in the facts, and if these are sufficiently established there will be no difficulty about the cause. A person like this either possesses already or can easily grasp the principles. Let him to whom neither of these applies hear the words of Hesiod: "Best of all is he who knows all things, good also he who obeys good counsel. But he who neither knows nor, listening to another, takes his words to heart—he is a worthless man."

[Chapter V discusses popular views of the good, as pleasure, honor, wealth. Chapter VI is a critique of Plato's "Idea of the Good."]

VII. THE NATURE OF HAPPINESS

The highest good of action is an activity chosen always for its own sake.

1 Now let us return to the good we are seeking, and its nature. It seems to be different in different actions and arts; it is one thing in medicine, another in military science, and so on for the rest. Now what is the good of each art? That for whose sake everything else is done? In medicine this is health; in military science, victory; in household management, the household—in each art something different; but in every action and every exercise of choice it is the end, for it is on account of the end that people do everything. Thus, if some one thing is the end of all actions, it would be the good of action, or if there is more than one, they would be.

2 By a gradual advance our argument has come round again to the same conclusion; [1] but we must try to clarify this still further. *3* Since ends are plural, and we choose some of them for the sake of something else, like wealth and flutes and instruments generally, it is clear that all of them are not perfect. But the highest good is obviously something perfect, so that if there is some one thing which alone is perfect, this would be what we are seeking, and if there is more than one, the most perfect of these. *4* We call that which is sought for its own sake more perfect than what is sought for the sake of something else, and that which is never chosen for the sake of something else more perfect than things chosen both for its sake and for their own, and we call absolutely perfect that which is always chosen for its own sake and never because of anything else.

Happiness fits this definition; it is completely self-sufficient.

5 Happiness certainly seems to be something of this nature, for we always choose it for itself and never for something else, whereas we choose honor and pleasure and intelligence both for their own sake (even if nothing further resulted from them we should choose them) and also for the sake of happiness, in the belief that through them we are going to live happily. But happiness no one chooses for the sake of these things, nor generally for the sake of anything but itself.

6 The same result seems to follow also from consideration of its self-sufficiency. (The perfect good surely is something self-sufficient.) By self-sufficient we mean not only what suffices for a person himself, leading a solitary life, but also for his parents and children and wife and generally his friends and fellow citizens, since man is by nature a political being.[2] *7* But there must be some end to this list, for if we extend it to the ancestors and descendants and friends' friends we could go on to infinity. This matter may be taken up again later; at present we shall consider self-sufficient that which taken by itself alone makes a life desirable and lacking in nothing; and this is the sort of thing we commonly judge happiness to be. *8* Moreover, it is the most choiceworthy of all good things, not as though it were counted as one of them, for it is clear that if it were counted as one of them it would become more choiceworthy with the addition of even the least of good things; for what is added is the measure of superiority among goods, and the greater good is always the more choiceworthy. Happiness, then, is perfect and self-sufficient, the end of action.

The nature of happiness is connected with the function of man. Its definition

9 No doubt, however, to say that happiness is the greatest good seems merely obvious, and what is wanted is a still clearer statement of what it is. *10* It may be possible to achieve this by considering the function of man. As with a flute player or sculptor or any artisan, or generally those who have a function and an activity, the good and good performance seem to lie in the performance of function, so it would appear to be with a man, if there is any function of man. *11* Are there actions and a function peculiar to a carpenter and a shoemaker, but not to man? Is he functionless? Or as there appears to be a function of the eye and the foot and generally of every part of him, could one also posit some function of man aside from all these? *12* What would this be? Life he shares even with plants, so that we must leave out the life of nourishment and growth. The next in order would be a kind of sentient life, but this seems to be shared by horse and cow and all the animals. *13* There remains an active life of a being with reason. This can be understood in two senses: as pertaining to obedience to reason and as pertaining to the possession of reason and the use of intelligence; and since the latter as well is spoken of in two senses,[3] we must take the one which has to do with action, for this seems to be regarded as higher.

14 If the function of man is an activity of the soul according to reason or not without reason, and we say that the function of a thing and of a good thing are generically the same, as of a lyre-player and a good lyre-player, and the same way with all other cases, the superiority of virtue being attributed to the function—that of a lyre-player being to play, that of a good one being to play well—(*15*) if this is so, the good for man becomes an activity of the soul in accordance with virtue, and if there are more virtues than one, in accordance with the best and most perfect. *16* And further, in a complete life; for one swallow does not make it spring, nor one day, and so a single day or a short time does not make a man blessed and happy.

Ethics is not an exact science.

17 Let this be our account of the good. It seems desirable to make a sketch first, and then later to fill it in. It would be easy for anyone to develop and work out in detail that which is well outlined, and time would be a discoverer and co-worker in such matters. This is the way the arts, too, make progress; for it is easy for anyone to add what is missing.

18 We must remember also what was said before, and not seek for the same precision in everything, but only that which is proper to the material at hand and to an extent suitable to the type of investigation. *19* Both a carpenter and a geometer aspire towards a straight line, but in different ways—the one to the extent to which it is useful in his work, the other endeavoring to discover what it is or what sort of thing, being an investigator of the truth. One should do the same in other fields as well, that subsidiary tasks may not crowd out the main ones. *20* Not even the cause is to be asked for in the same sense in all investigations, but in some it is good enough for the fact to be demonstrated, as with first principles: facts and first principles are primary. *21* Of principles some are apprehended by induction, some by sense perception, some by a certain habituation, and others in other ways. *22* But we must try to investigate each in accordance with its nature and be zealous that each be defined well; (*23*) they give a great impetus towards discovery of the rest. For the principle—the beginning—seems to be more than half of the whole, and many objects of inquiry become obvious as soon as it is discovered. . . .

[Chapters VIII–XII discuss happiness further: current beliefs about it, its origin, whether no man should be called happy until he is dead, whether the fortunes of the living affect the dead. The conclusion is that virtue is praiseworthy, but happiness is above praise. Chapter XIII divides virtue into intellectual and moral, of which the latter is the subject of the next four books.]

Book II

I. Moral virtue and habit

Moral virtue is fostered by habit; we do not have it by nature, but we have the capacity for it.

1 Virtue is of two kinds, intellectual and moral. The intellectual has both its origin and its growth mainly from instruction, so that it requires experience and time; the moral arises out of habit, and has even taken its name from that word, with only a slight change.[4]

2 Hence it is also apparent that none of the moral virtues is implanted in us by nature, for in other fields nothing which is "by nature" is changed by habit. For example, a stone, which naturally falls downward, would not be habituated to fall upward, though one should "train" it by throwing it up ten thousand times, nor fire to burn downward—nor could anything which is one way by nature be habituated to be another way. *3* Therefore the virtues do not arise in us naturally, nor yet contrary to nature, but we are naturally capable of receiving them, and perfected by habit. *4* Furthermore, of things that are natural in us, we acquire first the capacity and later the actuality. (This is clear from the senses: we do not get the faculty of sense perception from seeing or hearing many times, but the reverse. We use the faculties we have rather than acquiring them through use.)

In the virtues, as all other practical activities, we learn by doing.

The virtues, on the other hand, we acquire by first putting them to effect, as is also true in the other arts. Things that we must do after learning, we learn by doing, as men become house-builders by building houses and lyre-players by playing the lyre. In this way too, then, by doing just deeds we become just, by acting temperately, temperate, and bravely, brave. *5* Additional evidence comes from what happens in cities: lawmakers, by habituating the citizens, make them good, and this is the intention of every lawmaker, but those who do not do it well make errors, and this is how a good constitution differs from a bad one. *6* Further, every virtue is both fostered and destroyed by the same causes, as is every art: it is by playing the lyre that people become either good or bad lyre-players. The case of house-builders and all the rest is analogous; from building well they will become good builders, from building badly, bad ones. *7* If this were not the case, there would be no need of any teacher, but everyone would be born either good or bad. This is also the case with the virtues; by our activities in our relationships with others, some of us become just and some unjust, by acting in fear-inspiring situations and being habituated to be afraid or be brave, some become courageous and some cowardly. It is the same with desires and anger; some become prudent and even-tempered, others incontinent and irascible, from behaving one way or the other in relation to them. In a word, then, similar dispositions come from similar activities. Therefore it is necessary to give one's activities a certain quality; for from differences in these follow different dispositions. It makes no small difference to be habituated in one direction or another, even from childhood, but a very great one—or rather, all the difference.

II. Moral virtues and the mean

This is a practical study and must depend on judgment of facts.

1 Now since our present study is not theoretical like the other branches of philosophy (we are not conducting the investigation that we may know what virtue is, but that we may become good, since otherwise there would be no benefit in it), we must examine actions, and how they should be performed, for these are criteria also, as we said, of the quality of dispositions. *2* "To act according to right rule" is a criterion commonly agreed upon, and let it be accepted as basis of our discussion. We will speak about it later [VI, XIII], and what the right rule is, and how it is related to the other virtues. *3* Let it be understood in advance, however, that any argument concerning practical matters should be made in outline and not in detail, according to the principle we advanced before, that the type of argument to be expected is governed by the subject matter. Matters of practice and questions of what is beneficial have nothing fixed, any more than questions pertaining to health. *4* If this is the nature of the general theory, the application to particulars will have even less precision. It falls under no art or set of precepts, but those who act must constantly be considering the existing circumstances, as also in medicine and navigation.

Moral qualities are destroyed by excess and defect in the actions associated with them.

5 However, in spite of the tentative character of the present discussion, we must try to make some contribution. *6* In the first place, we must consider that the sort of things we are speaking of tend to be spoiled by defect and excess (in matters that are unclear we must use what is clear as example). We see this in the matter of strength and health; an excess or defect of exercise destroys health, and in the same way drink and food in too great or too small amounts destroy health, whereas the proper amount both creates and increases and preserves it. *7* The situation is the same with temperance and courage and the other virtues. He who fears and flees everything and stands up to nothing becomes a coward; he who fears nothing at all but advances to meet every danger is rash. In the same way he who enjoys every pleasure and abstains from none is incontinent; he who avoids every pleasure, like a rustic, is an insensible person. Thus temperance and courage are destroyed by the excess and the defect, but are preserved by the mean.

8 Yet not only origins and increase and destructions come from the same causes and the same circumstances, but the activities as well are manifested in the same material. This is also true in other more obvious examples, as with strength: it arises from taking much nourishment and undergoing much labor, and the strong man would be best able to do this. The same is true with the virtues: (*9*) by abstaining from pleasures we become temperate, and having become so we are best able to abstain from them. The same way with courage: by being habituated to despise fearful things and stand up to them, we become courageous, and having become so we are best able to stand up to fearful things.

[In Chapters III and IV, Aristotle discusses the relation of pleasure and pain to virtue and vice, and the meaning of the statement that we become virtuous by acting virtuously, passing in Chapter V to the definition of virtue.]

V. Virtue: its genus

Virtue would be a quality of the soul—either an emotion, a capacity, or a disposition.

1 Next we are to consider what virtue is. Now since there are three qualities in the soul, emotions, capacities, and dispositions, virtue would be one of these. *2* By emotions I mean anger, fear, courage, jealousy, joy, friendship, hatred, longing, envy, pity—in general feelings involving pleasure or pain. Capacities are qualities by virtue of which one feels these emotions, for example those by virtue of which we are able to be angered or pained or to feel pity. Dispositions are qualities by virtue of which we are well or ill disposed toward the emotions; for example, with relation to being angered, if we are either violent or lax we are ill disposed, if we are moderate, well disposed, and so on with the rest.

Being neither emotion nor capacity, virtue must be a disposition.

3 Now neither virtues nor vices are emotions, because we are not called good or bad according to our emotions, but according to our virtues and vices, and because we are neither praised nor blamed according to our emotions (neither a frightened man nor an angry man is praised, and one is blamed not simply as being angry but as being angry in a certain way), but we are praised or blamed according to our virtues and vices. *4* Furthermore, we are angered and afraid without the exercise of choice, whereas the virtues are choices of a sort, or not without choice. In addition, according to the emotions we are said to be moved, but according to the virtues and vices to be disposed in a certain way. *5* For this reason the virtues and vices are not capacities either; for we are not called good simply for being able to experience emotion, nor bad either, and we are neither praised nor blamed for this. Again, it is by nature that we have capacities, but we are not by nature good or bad. (This matter we spoke of previously [II, I, 2].)

6 If the virtues, then, are neither emotions nor capacities, they must be dispositions. Thus what the genus of virtue is has been determined.

VI. Virtue: the complete definition

Virtue involves the good performance of function.

1 But we must not only say in this manner that it is a disposition, but also what kind of disposition. *2* We may state that every virtue both puts into a good state that of which it is a virtue and causes the function of that thing to be well performed; for example, the virtue of the eye makes good both the eye and its function, for it is through the virtue of the eye that we see well. In the same way the virtue of a horse both makes the horse good and makes him good at running and carrying a rider and awaiting the enemy. *3* If this is so in every case, the virtue of a man, too, would be the disposition as a result of which he becomes a good man and as a result of which he performs his function well.

Definition of excess, defect, and mean, in relation both to the thing and to the individual

4 How this is to come about we have stated already, but we can make it clear in this way too, by considering what sort of thing virtue is and what its nature. Now in anything continuous and divisible one can take either a greater, a lesser, or an equal quantity, and each of these in relation either to the thing itself or to us. By equal I mean something intermediate between excess and defect.

5 By the mean in relation to the thing I mean what is equidistant from both the extremes, which is one and the same for everyone. And by that in relation to us, I mean what is neither too much nor too little; this is not single, nor the same for everyone. *6* For example, if ten is many and two is few, one takes six as the mean in relation to the thing, for it exceeds and is exceeded by an equal amount. *7* This is the mean according to arithmetical proportion.[5] The mean in relation to us, however, is not to be taken in this way. If ten pounds are much for someone to eat and two are little, the trainer will not necessarily prescribe six; this too is perhaps much or little for him who is to take it—for Milo [6] little, for a beginner in athletic training, much. The same with running and wrestling. *8* Thus every expert avoids the excess and the defect, seeks the mean and chooses it, and not the mean in relation to the thing but that in relation to us.

Like the arts and sciences, virtue aims at the mean.

9 Now if every science accomplishes its work well in this way, by keeping its eye on the mean and directing its work towards this (whence people often say of tasks well done that nothing could be added or subtracted, with the idea that excess and defect destroy excellence, while the mean preserves it, and good workmen, as we said, work with this principle in mind), and if virtue is something more precise and better than any art, as nature is, it is something which aims at the mean.

10 I am speaking of moral virtue, for this is concerned with emotions and actions, and in these are found excess and defect and the mean. For example, it is possible to fear or be bold or desire or be angry or have pity or generally to feel pleasure or pain, either too much or too little, and both extremes are bad, (*11*) but the "when one ought," and the "in what conditions," "toward whom," "for what reason," and "as one ought"—this is the mean and the best, which belongs to virtue. *12* In the same way there is an excess, a defect, and a mean in actions. Virtue is related to emotions and actions, in which excess and defect miss the mark, but the mean succeeds and is praised; and both of these are qualities of virtue. *13* Therefore virtue is a kind of intermediate position, since it aims at the mean. *14* Furthermore, it is possible to err in many ways (evil belongs in the category of the unlimited, as the Pythagoreans guessed, and good in that of the limited), but there is only one way to be right. (This is why one is easy and the other hard—easy to miss the mark, hard to hit it.) For these reasons, then, excess and defect pertain to vice, the mean to virtue. "For the good are good with single simpleness, the bad are bad in every way." [7]

Final statement of the definition.

15 Therefore virtue is a disposition, connected with choice, lying in a mean—the mean in relation to us, defined by right rule, that by which the wise man would define it. The mean is that between two vices, one of excess and one of defect. *16* And further. it is a mean in that some vices fall short and some go beyond what is required, in emotional and practical matters, whereas virtue finds and chooses the mean. *17* Therefore according to its essence and the definition which tells what a thing really is, virtue is a mean, but with relation to what is best and to excellence in performance,[8] an extreme.

Not every action or emotion has a mean.

18 Not every action or emotion, however, admits a mean. Some are named directly from their being involved with badness, as malice (joy at another's misfortune), shamelessness, and jealousy, and for their actions adultery, theft, homicide. All of these have their names from being bad in themselves, but not their excesses or defects. It is never possible to be correct in their exercise, but always wrong. In matters of this sort good performance does not lie in committing adultery with the right woman, at the right time, and in the right manner, but the simple commission of any of these acts is wrong.

The vices, of excess and defect, do not themselves have mean, excess, and defect; nor is there excess and defect of the mean.

19 A similar error is to believe that in committing injustice and acting cowardly and being incontinent there is a mean, an excess, and a defect; for in this way there would be mean of excess and defect, and excess of excess, and defect of defect. *20* But just as there is no excess and defect of temperance and courage, since the mean is in a sense an extreme, so there is no mean or excess and defect of those things we mentioned, but however they are done they are wrong. In general, there is neither a mean of excess and defect nor excess and defect of the mean.

VII. THE TABLE OF THE VIRTUES AND THE CORRESPONDING VICES

1 We must, however, not only make these assertions in a general way but also harmonize them with particulars; for in arguments on matters of practice, the general are broader in application but the particular more accurate. Actions are related to particulars, and it is there that they must fit.

Our comments on this topic may be based upon our table.[9]

2 In matters of fear and bravery, courage is the mean; of the excesses, that signifying lack of fear has no name (many of these are nameless), and one with an excess of bravery is rash. One showing an excess in fearing and a defect in bravery is cowardly. *3* In pleasures and pains—not all of them; this is less true, and in a different way, of pains—the mean is temperance, the excess incontinence. There are scarcely any who are deficient in the matter of pleasure, so that such persons have not received any name; but let us call them "insensible." *4* In the giving and taking of property the mean is liberality, the excess and defect are extravagance and illiberality. In these, people show excess and defect in opposite ways: the extravagant exceeds in putting out and falls short in taking, whereas the illiberal exceeds in taking and falls short in putting out.

5 At present we are speaking in outline, and merely by headings, but for that very reason satisfactorily to our purpose; later we shall make these distinctions more accurately.

6 There are other dispositions, too, related to property, the mean of magnificence (the magnificent man differs from the liberal, in that one is dealing with large amounts, the other with small), the excess of tastelessness and vulgarity, and the defect of meanness. These are different from the dispositions centering about liberality, but the manner of their difference will be explained later. *7* In the matter of honor and dishonor the mean is high-mindedness, the excess a sort of vanity, the defect small-mindedness. *8* There is also something which has the same relation to high-mindedness as we said liberality (which differs by being concerned with smaller sums) has to magnificence. High-mindedness is related to great honor, this other to small; for it is possible to desire honor as one ought, or more than one ought, or less, and he who is excessive in his desires is called ambitious, he who falls short, unambitious, but the one in the mean has no name. The dispositions too are nameless, except that that of the ambitious is called ambitiousness. Hence the extremes lay claim to the place of the mean; and we too sometimes call the man in the mean position ambitious, and sometimes we praise the ambitious, sometimes the unambitious. *9* Why we do this will be explained later on; now let us discuss the rest according to the method which has hitherto guided us.

10 There are also excess, defect, and mean in the matter of anger. They are nameless, practically, but let us call the man in the intermediate position even-tempered, and the mean even-temperedness. Of the extremes let him who shows an excess be "irascible," and his vice "irascibility"; one who shows a defect is "nonirascible," his vice "nonirascibility."

11 There are also three other mean states, different from each other but with a certain similarity. All are related to the sharing of words and deeds, but differ in that one is related to the truth in them, the others to the pleasure; of the latter, one is in amusement, the other in all the concerns of life. We should discuss these also, that we may see more clearly that in everything the mean is to be praised and that the extremes are neither praiseworthy nor right, but worthy of blame. Most of these, like the others, are nameless, but we must try, as in the other cases, to give them names, for the sake of clarity and consistency. *12* In the matter of truth let the man in the intermediate position be called truthful and the mean, truthfulness; and pretension—let that toward the greater be called boastfulness and he who has it boastful, and that towards the smaller mock-modesty, and he who has it mock-modest.

13 In the one of the two states related to pleasure which is concerned with amusement, the man in the intermediate position is ready-witted, and his disposition ready-wittedness; the excess is buffoonery, he who has it a buffoon; he who shows a defect is a boor, and his disposition boorishness. In the other subdivision related to pleasure, which deals with the whole of life, he who is disposed as he ought to be is pleasant and is called a friend, and the mean is called friendship. He who shows an excess, if it is for a purpose, is obsequious; if it is for his own interest, he is a flatterer; and he who shows a defect and is unpleasant in all circumstances is a quarrelsome and troublesome person.

14 In matters of feeling, there are also means related to the emotions. Respect is not a virtue, but the respectful man is praised; in these matters too one is said to be in the intermediate position, another to show an excess—the bashful man, who is in awe of everyone. He who shows a defect, or respects nothing at all, is shameless, the one in the midposition respectful.

15 Righteous indignation is a mean between envy and malice, and these are related to pleasure and pain at that which happens to one's neighbors. The righteously indignant man is pained by those who prosper undeservedly; the envious man, exceeding him, is pained by all who prosper; and the malicious is so deficient in being pained that he even rejoices. . . .[10]

[Chapter VIII shows how the extremes are opposed to each other and to the mean.]

IX. PRACTICAL HINTS TOWARD THE ATTAINMENT OF VIRTUE

Virtue is hard to achieve.

1 Enough has been said, now, to show that moral virtue is a mean, and in what sense, and that it is a mean between two vices, one of excess and one of defect, and that it is of such a nature because it aims at the mean in emotions and in actions.

2 Thus it is a hard task to be good. In every field it is hard to hit the mean, just as not everyone, but only he who knows how, can find the center of a circle. In the same way, getting angry is easy, and possible for anyone, as is giving away or spending money; but the "to whom" and "how much" and "when" and "for what purpose" and "how"—these are by no means easy, nor even possible for everyone. Therefore good performance is rare and praiseworthy and noble.

One should avoid the more dangerous of the two extremes.

3 Thus he who is aiming at the mean must, in the first place, avoid the extreme which is most opposed to it, as Calypso advised: "Steer your boat away from this mist and wave." [11] For of the extremes one is more conducive to error, the other less. *4* Since it is hard to strike the mean exactly, one must take the second-best way, as they say, and choose the least of the evils; and the best way to attain this is to follow the method we are speaking of. We must consider the sort of thing toward which we are prone, for different people are naturally disposed in different ways. We can recognize this tendency of ours by the pleasure and pain we feel. *5* Then we should drag ourselves in the opposite direction, for by drawing ourselves vigorously away from error we shall arrive at the mean, as men do when straightening a warped piece of board.

The danger of pleasure

6 In every field the thing to watch out for is the pleasant and pleasure, because we do not judge it impartially. As the elders of the people felt about Helen,[12] we ought to feel about pleasure, and on every occasion repeat their comment; sending it away in this manner, we shall fall less often into error.

One cannot always hit the mean exactly.

7 By acting in this way, to put it briefly, we shall be best able to hit the mean. But this is doubtless hard, and especially in particulars. It is not easy to define how one should be angry, and at whom, and on what conditions, and how long. Sometimes, too, we praise those who fall short and call them even-tempered, and sometimes those who are violent, calling them manly.

8 One who deviates a little from the good is not blamed, whether it is on the side of excess or defect; but one who deviates further is blamed, for he cannot escape our notice. It is not easy to define in words to what extent and degree one is to be blamed—nor anything else that depends on feeling. Judgments of this sort depend on particulars, and the judgment rests upon feeling.

This much discussion makes it clear that the disposition lying in the mean is praiseworthy, in all fields, but that it is sometimes necessary to deviate toward the excess, sometimes toward the defect, for in this way we can most easily hit the mean and the good.

[In the first chapters of the next book, Aristotle defines the conditions of moral responsibility. Then, having achieved a definition of virtue or goodness in the first two books, he proceeds to discuss the various virtues in detail—both the moral virtues like courage, temperance, and justice (Books III–V) and the intellectual virtues (Book VI). He then deals with continence and incontinence, with pleasure, briefly (Book VII), and with friendship (Books VIII–IX). In Book X, after returning to the discussion of pleasure and deciding that it is not evil in itself but a natural concomitant of virtuous activity, Aristotle turns in conclusion to happiness, whose relation to the Good for man was left rather vague in Book I.]

Book X

VI. Happiness and the Life of Pleasure

Happiness is not a state but an activity, and is self-sufficient.

1 The virtues and friendship and pleasure having been discussed, it remains to us to speak briefly of happiness, since we maintain that this is the end of human activity. By proceeding on the basis of the results already attained we may make our account more concise.

2 We said that happiness is not a state; for if it were it might belong even to someone who slept through his lifetime, living the life of a plant, or to someone who suffered great misfortunes. Now if this is not satisfactory, but happiness must be classified as some sort of activity, as we said before, and of activities some are necessary and chosen for the sake of something else, others chosen for their own sake, then it is clear that happiness should be classified as one of the activities chosen for their own sake rather than for the sake of something else; happiness needs nothing, but is self-sufficient. *3* Activities chosen for their own sake are those from which nothing is sought apart from the activity. Such are, it seems, actions according to virtue, for to do noble and good actions is something to choose for its own sake.

The same thing is true of play and of physical pleasures, but happiness does not reside in these. It lies in virtuous activity, which is what the good man prefers.

The same is true of the pleasures of play; for one does not choose them for the sake of something else. People are harmed rather than benefited by them, neglecting their physical well-being and their business. Most seekers for happiness flock to such activities, so that persons who are versatile in such occupations are popular in the courts of tyrants; they ingratiate themselves with the very kind of pursuits the tyrants wish for, and this is the kind of person the latter require.[13] These pursuits seem related to happiness because dynasts follow them, (*4*) but perhaps such persons are no proper criterion; it is not in the exercise of dynastic power that virtue and intelligence reside, from which good actions come; and if these persons, having no experience of pure and liberal pleasure, flock to bodily pleasures, one must not suppose on this account that the latter are more worthy of choice. Children, too, think that the things they value are best. Surely it is logical that as different things appear valuable to children and to adults, the same thing would be true of the mean and the eminent. *5* Now as we have often said, both valuable and pleasant things are those which are such to the good man: to each the activity in conformity with his character is most choiceworthy, and to the good man this is activity according to virtue.

6 Therefore happiness does not reside in play; it would be strange for the end to be play—that one should work and suffer his life long for the sake of playing. We choose everything on account of something else, except happiness; for this is the end. But to work seriously for the sake of play seems empty and very childish.[14] "Play for work's sake," as Anacharsis has it, seems the right motto; play is like relaxation, and it is because of inability to work continuously that one relaxes. Surely relaxation is not the end, for it takes place for the sake of activity. The happy life seems to be that according to virtue. This is serious and not a matter of play. *7* We call serious things better than ridiculous and playful things, and in every case the activity of the better—a better part or a better man—more serious; and that of the better is a priori better and more closely related to happiness. *8* And anyone might enjoy physical pleasure, a slave not less than the best of men; but no one attributes a share of happiness to a slave, any more than a life of his own. Happiness lies not in pursuits of this kind, but in activities in accordance with virtue, as has been said before.

VII. CONTEMPLATION

The activity which is happiness would be in accord with the highest virtue, or that of the highest faculty. This is reason, and its highest activity is contemplation.

1 If happiness is an activity in accord with virtue, it is reasonable that this be the highest virtue; and this would be that of the best. Now whether this is reason or something else, which seems naturally to rule and lead and take thought about noble and divine matters, whether it is something divine itself or the most divine element in us, its activity, according to its proper virtue, would be perfect happiness. It has been pointed out that this activity is contemplative.

Contemplation is the highest activity, the most continuous, the most pleasant, and the most self-sufficient. It is admired for its own sake, and is a function of a life of leisure.

2 This would seem consonant both with our earlier discussion and with the truth. This is the highest activity; and of our faculties reason is highest; and of objects of knowledge, the objects of reason are highest. Furthermore, it is the most continuous: we can contemplate more continuously than we can perform any kind of action. *3* And we think that there should be an admixture of pleasure in happiness, and among activities according to virtue, that according to wisdom is by common consent the most pleasant. Certainly philosophy seems to afford pleasures remarkable for purity and stability, and it is reasonable that the life of those who know should be more pleasant than that of those who seek. *4* Also, the self-sufficiency we spoke of would pertain especially to contemplative activity. The wise man, the just man, and all the rest require the necessities of life, but of persons adequately supplied with such things, the just man needs people toward whom and with whom he may act justly, and the same is true of the temperate, the brave, and each of the others; but the wise man can engage in contemplation even by himself, and the wiser he is, the more he can do so. Doubtless he can live better with associates, but all the same he is the most self-sufficient of all men. *5* Again, this activity alone seems to be admired for its own sake, for nothing comes from it besides contemplation, whereas in the case of practical activities there is always something aside from the action which concerns us to a greater or lesser degree. *6* Happiness seems to be a function of a life of leisure, for we engage in business that we may have leisure, as we fight that we may have peace. Now the activity of the practical virtues is in politics or war, and the actions pertaining to them are the negation of leisure, in the case of warfare absolutely so (for no one chooses to fight or prepares war for war's sake; he would seem an utterly bloodthirsty person who would make enemies of his friends that battles and slaughter might take place). But the activity of the statesman too is a negation of leisure, and aside from political activity is concerned with power and honor, or even happiness for himself and his fellow citizens, a happiness distinct from political activity, which it is also clear we must keep distinct in our investigation.

7 Now if of actions according to the various virtues the political and military excel in beauty and magnitude, and they are a negation of leisure and strive toward some end, not being chosen for their own sakes, whereas the activity of reason, which is contemplative, seems to excel in seriousness, to strive for no end aside from itself, and to have a pleasure of its own, which itself increases the activity, then self-sufficiency too, and leisure and freedom from fatigue (such as a man may have), and whatever else is attributed to a blessed man, all seem to belong to this activity. This would surely be perfect happiness for a man, with the addition of a complete span of life (since nothing pertaining to happiness is imperfect).

The life of contemplation, of pure happiness, is better than human, for man is a composite being. There is something divine in it, and man must strive for this divinity and immortality.

8 But such a life would be better than human: one would not live thus as man but as a being with something divine in him. As such a being excels man, who is a composite being, so his activity excels that of the other virtues. If reason is an element of divinity in man, then the life of reason too is divine in comparison to merely human life. One ought not, following the proverbial advice,[15] to think human thoughts being human, nor to think mortal thoughts being mortal, but to aspire to immortality, insofar as it is possible, and to do everything with a view to living according to the highest that is in him. For even though it is small in bulk, it far surpasses all else in power and honor. *9* In fact this would seem to be our real self, being the dominant and superior part of us. It would be strange if one should choose not his own life but someone else's. And what we said before applies here: what is proper to each person by nature is best and pleasantest for him—for man, the life according to reason, if this is most characteristically human. Therefore this life is also the happiest.

VIII. The contemplative life

The other virtues are merely human.

1 In second place comes life according to the other virtues, for the activities connected with them are merely human. Just and brave acts, and others in conformity with the virtues, we perform towards each other by assigning each man his due in contracts and business dealings and in all sorts of situations involving actions and emotions; and all of this seems characteristically human. *2* In some respects moral virtue even seems dependent on the state of the body, and in many respects to be connected with the emotions. *3* Prudence is connected with moral virtue, and vice versa, if it is true that the principles of prudence are in accord with the moral virtues and rightness in moral matters is in accord with prudence. These, being closely joined to each other and to the emotions, would belong to the composite part of man; the virtues of the composite part are human, and so, therefore, is life and happiness in accordance with them. But that of the reason is separate—let us say just this much about it, for to discuss this matter in more detail would be too great a task for our present purpose.

The contemplative man needs less external wealth than others, but he does need some.

4 The life of reason would seem to need external means very little, or less than the moral life. Let us even suppose that the necessary requirements were equal, even if the statesman is more concerned with the body, and so on—that would make little difference—still there will be a great difference in their activities. The liberal man will need wealth to perform acts of liberality, and the just man for his repayments. (Intentions are no clear criterion; even the unjust pretend to wish to act justly.) The brave man needs power if he is to accomplish any acts in accordance with this virtue, and the temperate man needs opportunity; how else will he or any of the others be revealed? *5* There is a question whether choice or act is more important to virtue, since it involves both, but surely it is clear that perfection requires both. It needs many things for actions, and the greater and more noble they are, the more it needs. *6* The contemplative has no need of such things for his activity; they are even hindrances to contemplation, so to speak. But inasmuch as he is a man and lives with others, he chooses to perform actions, in accord with virtue; therefore he will need such things for his human life.

Contemplation must be the virtuous activity in which the gods engage.

7 That perfect happiness is a kind of contemplative activity would appear from the following consideration as well. We conceive the gods to be superlatively blessed and happy; what kind of actions should we attribute to them? Acts of justice? Will they not appear ridiculous making contracts and returning deposits and the like? Or acts of courage? Braving fearful situations and undergoing dangers because it is noble to do so?

Or acts of liberality? To whom will they give? It will be strange if they even have money or anything of the sort. And what would their acts of temperance be? Is it not a vulgar praise to say that they do not have base desires? If we went through the whole list, the conditions involved in the various actions would appear petty and unworthy of gods. Nevertheless, everyone believes them to live and therefore to be in activity—for surely they do not sleep like Endymion. What then is left for a living being, if action is eliminated (to say nothing of production), except contemplation? Thus the activity of God, excelling in blessedness, would be contemplative. Among mortals, then, the activity most closely related to this would be closest to happiness.

Another proof that happiness and contemplation are the same: lower animals do not share in either one.

8 Another indication is the fact that the other animals do not partake of happiness, being completely deprived of such activity. For the gods the whole of life is blessed, for men, insofar as there is some approximation to this kind of activity; but none of the other animals is happy, since they do not share at all in contemplation.

As far as contemplation extends, then, so does happiness, and those who have more contemplation also have more happiness, not by coincidence but because of the contemplation; for it is honored for its own sake. Thus happiness would be a kind of contemplation.

Again, the happy man will need a certain measure of external prosperity.

9 But the happy man, being a man, will also need external prosperity. For nature is not self-sufficient for contemplation, but needs also health and nourishment and the other forms of bodily care. One must not suppose, however, if it is impossible to be blessed without external goods, that the candidate for happiness will need many or great things, for his self-sufficiency and his action do not depend on excess, (*10*) and it is possible for one who does not rule on land and sea to perform noble acts. Even with moderate means one could act according to virtue. (This is plain to see: private citizens seem to do excellent deeds not less, but more, than dynasts.) But this is all that is necessary, and the life of him who acts according to virtue will be happy. *11* Solon, it seems, gave a good definition of the happy in saying they are those moderately provided with external goods, doing the noblest deeds (according to his ideas), and living wisely; for it is possible for those with moderate possessions to do what they ought.[16] Anaxagoras, too, does not seem to think of the happy man as rich or as a ruler, when he says that he would not admire the man who seems remarkable to the multitude. They judge by external goods, since that is all they can see.

Our theory must be tested in practice. The wise man is dearest to the gods.

12 The opinions of the wise, then, seem to agree with our reasoning. Now such considerations bring some assurance, but truth is judged in practice, from deeds and life; in them lies the criterion. Thus we must examine what has been said, comparing it to the deeds and life of men, and if it agrees with deeds it should be accepted, but if it differs it should be considered mere words. The man who acts according to reason and serves it seems to be best disposed and also dearest to the gods. If the gods have any concern for mortal affairs, as they seem to, it would also be reasonable for them to rejoice in what is best and most closely related to them (that is, reason), and to reward those who cherish this most, on the grounds that such persons care for the things dear to the gods and act rightly and nobly. It is not unclear that all this applies most to the wise man. Therefore he is dearest to the gods, and it is likely that the same man is also happiest, so that by this argument too the wise man would be the most happy.

IX. PRACTICAL APPLICATION OF THEORY; TRANSITION TO POLITICS

Theory is not enough; it will persuade the noble, but the mass of mankind live by emotion and are only amenable to force and long habituation.

1 Now if enough has been said, in outline, about these matters and about the virtues, and also about friendship and pleasure, shall we consider our investigation complete? Or is it not true that, as they say, in practical matters the end is not to contemplate and know, but rather to act, (*2*) so that in regard to virtue knowing is not enough but one must also try to have it and use it (or however else we become good)? *3* If arguments were sufficient in themselves to make us good, "they would have earned many and great rewards," as Theognis says,[17] and our task would be to supply them. But as it is, theories seem capable of encouraging and exhorting free-born young men, and of rendering a well-born and truly honor-loving character susceptible to the inspiration of virtue, but they seem unable to turn the mass of men to nobility. *4* The latter, because of their nature, are ruled not by a feeling of reverence, but by fear, nor do they abstain from wickedness because of its shamefulness, but because of its penalties. Living by emotion, they pursue the pleasures proper to them and the means of attaining these, and avoid the pains on the opposite side, and have no notion of the noble and the truly pleasant, being without experience of it. *5* What argument could reform such people? It is impossible or at least not easy to change by argument things fixed in the character through a long period of time; it is remarkable, no doubt, if even a person endowed with all the things whereby one becomes good can attain to virtue. *6* Some think one becomes good by nature, some by habituation, some by teaching. Clearly, what depends on nature is not in our power, but belongs by some divine causes to those who are truly fortunate. And argument and instruction are not equally strong in all cases, but one must work up in advance, by good habits, the soul of the pupil, to love and hate nobly, as one works up land which is to nourish seed. *7* A person who lives by emotion would not hear nor comprehend a dissuading argument, and how is it possible to convert a person in this state? In general emotion seems to yield not to argument but to force.

Thus a system of law and custom is necessary, to regulate the training and way of life of both young and old.

8 It is necessary then that in some way the character suitable to virtue be present in advance, loving the noble and despising the shameful. But it is difficult for one not raised under institutions of this sort to find the right path from his youth. To live prudently and steadfastly is not pleasant to the many, especially when young. Therefore nurture and occupations ought to be regulated by law; they will not be painful when they become customary. *9* But it is not enough, it seems, for the young to receive the proper nurture and care; even when grown up they must follow these practices and be accustomed to them, and we would need laws about these matters, and generally about the whole of life; for the many are ruled rather by necessity than by reason, rather by penalties than by nobility.

[Sections 10–21, omitted here, reinforce the argument that laws are necessary to maintain moral standards.]

Transition to the Politics

22 Now since our predecessors have passed over the subject of legislation, it will be well to study the subject, and that of government generally, that our philosophy of man may be brought to completion.

23 In the first place, if anything good has been said, even in a part of the subject, by our predecessors, let us attempt to discuss it, then from our collection of *Constitutions* consider what sort of thing preserves or destroys cities and what sort each of the constitutions, and why some cities are well ruled and others the opposite. On the basis of such considerations we could perhaps see better both what kind of constitution is best, and how each is organized, and what laws and customs each uses.

Let us then begin.

POLITICS

Book I

I. Kinds and nature of human associations

The political association is highest of all, and aims at the highest good. It is basically different from other forms.

1 Since we observe that every city-state is a kind of association, and that every association is formed for the sake of some good (for everyone does what he does for the sake of that which seems good), it is clear not only that every association aims at some good, but that the highest association of all, which comprehends all the others, does so most of all. This is the so-called city-state or political association.[1]

2 Now those who think that the statesman, the monarch, the manager of a household, and the master of slaves are the same, are mistaken.[2] They suppose that the difference is in the size and not in the form of each of these kinds of rule. For example, they think that if one rules over a few he is a master, over more, a householder, over still more a statesman or monarch, so that there is no difference between a large household and a small city, and as between statesman and monarch, when one rules by himself he is a monarch, but when he rules and is ruled in turn according to the principles of the science of politics he is a statesman. But this is not so.

To back up this view we will analyze these associations into their smallest parts, and study their growth.

3 This will be clear if we study the matter according to our usual plan of investigation. For as in other fields it is necessary to analyze the composite into its elements (that is, the smallest parts of the whole), so if we study the elements of which a city-state is composed, we shall see best in what respect they differ from one another and whether it is possible to form any systematic opinion about them. If one were to watch things grow from their first beginnings he would be best able to form a theory about them, in this field as in others.

It is natural for ruling and ruled elements to be associated.

4 In the first place, things which cannot exist without each other must combine, as for example male and female do for the sake of generation (this is not from choice, but as with other animals and plants it is natural to wish to leave behind another like oneself), and the natural ruler and natural subject for the sake of safety. For that which is capable of planning ahead by means of thought is by nature a ruling and mastering element, whereas that which is capable of executing these plans by labor is by nature a ruled and servile element, so that master and slave have the same interest.

Woman and slave are both ruled, but differently. But all barbarians are natural slaves.

5 Now the female is by nature distinct from the servile. (Nature makes nothing in a niggardly spirit, as smiths do the Delphic knife,[3] but one thing for each purpose; in this way each tool is most perfect, not serving many purposes but only one.) Among the barbarians, however, the female and the servile have the same rank, for the reason that the barbarians do not possess among them the naturally ruling element, and marriage among them is between a female and a male slave. Thus the poets say, "It is reasonable for Greeks to rule barbarians,"[4] since by nature barbarian and slave are the same thing.

Growth of different forms of association: household, village, city-state. The city-state is their end, the highest natural form of human association.

6 Now from these two forms of association comes the basic household, and Hesiod was right in saying "first house and wife and plow-ox"[5] (for among the poor, ox takes the place of slave). The association which is naturally formed for the satisfaction of daily needs is the household—those whom Charondas calls "flour-bin–mates" and Epimenides the Cretan "manger-mates." *7* The primary association of several households, on a basis other than everyday needs, is the village. According to nature the village seems most like an offshoot of the household—those whom they call "sucklings of the same milk" or "children and children's children." This is why Greek cities were originally ruled by kings, as barbarian nations still are: they were formed by the union of monarchically-ruled elements, for every household is monarchically ruled by the eldest, so that the offshoots are too, because of the relationship. This is what Homer means when he says "each one governs his children and wives," [6] for they were scattered, and this is the way people lived in ancient times. For this reason everyone says that the gods are monarchically ruled, because people themselves, some to this day and some in former times, were ruled in this way; men make the gods like themselves in shape, and they do so also in way of life.

8 The association formed from several villages is a complete city-state, which we may say has already attained the goal of complete self-sufficiency, since it comes into existence for the sake of living but continues in existence for the sake of *good* living. Therefore every city is natural, if the primary associations are natural, because it is their end, and the "nature" of a thing is its end. (The way each thing is when its growth is complete we call its nature, as that of a man or horse or household.) Further, the cause and the end are best and self-sufficiency is both end and best. *9* From these considerations it is clear that the city is among things which are according to nature, and that man is by nature a "political" animal,[7] and the cityless man is, because of his nature and not through chance, either base or better than man; he is like the man who is reproached by Homer as "clanless, lawless, hearthless." [8] For the man who is such by nature is also an enthusiast for war, being isolated like a piece in a game of chess.

Association in cities is peculiar to man; he alone uses language.

10 It is obvious why man is an animal more suited to association in a city than any bee or other gregarious animal. Nature, as we believe, does nothing in vain, and man alone of the animals uses language. The mere utterance of voice is a sign of pain and pleasure, so that it belongs to the other animals as well (their nature has come this far, to have perception of pain and pleasure and to be able to indicate it to each other), but language is for explaining the beneficial and the harmful, and also the just and unjust. *11* This is peculiar to man, in comparison with the other animals, that he alone has perception of good and evil, just and unjust, and so on. Association in these things makes a household and a city.

City is prior to family and individual, as whole to part.

In nature, moreover, the city is prior to the household and to each of us.[9] The whole must be prior to the part; for when the whole is destroyed there no longer exists a foot or hand, for example, except in an ambiguous sense, as when one calls a stone hand a hand. For a hand, when destroyed, will be like a stone hand in this respect. But everything is defined according to its function and capacity, so that when something no longer has the same function and capacity it should not be called the same but merely homonymous.

Thus the city is a natural institution, but still gratitude is due to its originator.

12 It is clear now that the city is both natural and prior to the individual; for if the individual when isolated is not self-sufficient, he will have the same relation to the whole as the other parts; but he who cannot take part in an association, or who needs nothing by reason of his self-sufficiency, is no part of a city, and is either beast or god. There is then an impulse to such association naturally present in everyone, but the man who first organized one was the author of very great benefits. For just as man is in his perfected state the best of the animals, so when separated from law and justice he is worst of all. Injustice, armed, is the most savage of all things; and man is armed with the weapons of moral wisdom and virtue,[10] which can very easily be turned to opposite uses. Therefore without virtue he is very impious and wild, and worse than all others in lust and gluttony. But living justly is a function of the city-state, since judgment, which means the determination of what is just, is an ordering of the political association.[11]

II. The Household—Slavery

Elements of the household: master and slave, husband and wife, father and child; the art of acquisition.

1 Since it is now clear what the parts are

from which a city is constituted, our first task is to speak about household management, for every city is composed of households. The parts of household management correspond to the parts from which the household is itself constituted; and the complete household consists of slaves and freemen. Now since every subject must be studied first of all in its simplest elements, and the primary and simplest elements of a household are master and slave, husband and wife, and father and children, it would be desirable to consider, with regard to these three relationships, what each is and of what nature it ought to be. *2* These are the master-slave relationship, the marital relationship (for the association of wife and husband has no proper name) and thirdly the parental (this too is not called by a distinctive name).[12] Let us so call the three relationships we spoke of. But there is another part which some think is the whole of household management, some its greatest part; we must investigate the matter. I am speaking of what is called the art of acquisition.

Slavery: the problems

First let us speak of master and slave, in an effort both to obtain the answers to practical problems and to discover something better than the current conceptions by way of theoretical knowledge of them. *3* There are some to whom the master-slave relationship seems to be a kind of science, and household management, master-slave relationship, statesmanship, and monarchy seem to be the same thing, as we said in the beginning. To others the ownership of slaves seems contrary to nature; for it is by law that one man is slave and another free, but in nature there is no difference, so that it is not just, being based on force.

A slave is a living tool, used in action rather than production, and belongs wholly to his master.

Now the ownership of property is part of the household, and the art of acquiring possessions is part of household-management (for without the necessities it is impossible to live, to say nothing of living well). *4* And just as it is necessary for each particular art that its appropriate tools be at hand if its functions are to be accomplished, and of tools some are lifeless and some living (as for the pilot the tiller is lifeless but the lookout man living; for in the arts the underling[13] has the nature of a tool), so for the household manager a piece of property is a tool used in the business of living, and ownership of possessions means a quantity of tools, and the slave is a kind of living possession. In fact, every underling is like a tool which is prior to other tools. *5* If it were possible for every tool at a word of command or by intuitive perception of need to perform its function, as they say the inventions of Daedalus did, or the tripods of Hephaestus which the poet says "entered by themselves the divine conclave"[14]—if in this way shuttles could weave of themselves and plectra play harps, builders would not need underlings nor would masters need slaves. Now the tools we spoke of are tools for making something (production), but a piece of property is used in doing something (action). From the shuttle comes something else besides the use of it, but from a garment or a bed only the use. *6* Furthermore, since production and action are different in kind, and since both require tools, the latter too must show the same difference. But life is action, not production, so that a slave is an underling in matters of action.

"A possession" is used in the same sense as "a part." For a part is not only a part of something else, but belongs entirely to something else; and the same is true of a possession. Therefore the master of a slave is master only, but does not belong to him, whereas the slave is not only slave of his master but belongs wholly to him.

7 What the nature of a slave is and what his capacity, is clear from these remarks. One who by nature, though a human being, belongs not to himself but to another, is by nature a slave; a man belongs to another when though human he is a possession; a possession is a tool, separable from its owner, having to do with action.

Is slavery according to nature? In everything there is a ruling element and a ruled element. Soul rules body, mankind rules domestic animals, male rules female; so master rules slave.

Whether there is anyone who by nature fits this definition or not, and whether it is better for anyone to be a slave or whether, on the contrary, any slavery is against nature, may be considered next. *8* It is not difficult both to judge the matter theoretically by the use of reason, and to discern the truth from the facts. Ruling and being ruled belong to the class of things not only necessary but beneficial, and from their very origin some things divide themselves into ruled and ruling elements. There are many kinds of ruled and ruling elements, and that rule is always better which is over better ruled elements, as rule over man than rule over beast; for what is accomplished by better agents is a higher function. (Where one rules and another is ruled the two together discharge a function.)

9 Everything that is composed of a plurality of parts and becomes a common whole of some sort, whether the parts are continuous or discrete—in everything of this sort there is revealed a ruling element and a ruled element. This property belongs to living beings as a result of the law of all nature, for there is also present a kind of rule in things which do not participate in life, as for example in a harmony. But perhaps such a question belongs in a more popular discussion. *10* The living being is the first in the scale of nature to be composed of soul and body, of which one is by nature the ruling element and the other the ruled. We must study that which is natural in things which are according to nature rather than in those which are corrupted. Therefore we must consider the man who is best both in body and in soul; he will fulfill our requirement. But in those who are basically evil or temporarily in an evil state, the body would seem often to rule over the soul, because of their bad and unnatural condition. *11* Now, as we believe, it is first in the living being that one can see both the master-slave and the political types of rule. The soul rules the body in a master-slave relationship, and reason rules desire in a political and royal relationship. From this it is clear that it is natural and beneficial for the body to be ruled by the soul and for the emotional part of the soul to be ruled by the reason and the rational part, and that for them to be equal or for the situation to be reversed is harmful to them all. *12* The same sort of thing is true between men and the other animals; the domestic are naturally better than the wild, but it is better for all of these to be ruled by man, since in this way they are assured of safety. Further, in the relationship between male and female, one is naturally better and the other inferior, one dominant and the other subject. And the same sort of thing must be true among mankind generally. *13* To conclude, then, all who are as different from others as soul is from body or man from beast (persons are in this condition when their function is the use of the body, and this is where their special excellence lies)—these are by nature slaves, and it is better for them to be ruled, by a rule of this kind, if this is so in the other examples given.

The slave belongs to his master, but differs from a domestic animal in the use of reason (enough to follow instructions).

A man is a slave by nature who is capable of belonging to another (and this is why he does in fact belong to another), and who partakes of reason to the extent necessary to apprehend it but not to have it. The other animals follow promptings apprehended not by reason, but by instinct. *14* The manner of their use, however, differs very little, for assistance in matters of necessities of the body comes from both, slaves and domestic animals.

Nature intends to make freemen and slave easily distinguishable, physically and mentally, but often fails.

Now it is the intention of nature to make the bodies of freemen and slaves different too, those of the latter strong for necessary service, the others upright and useless for such tasks, but useful in the life of a citizen (which is divided into the services of war and those of peace). But it often happens, in just the opposite way, that some have the bodies of freemen, and others the soul; (*15*) since it is clear, that if one group excelled another only as much as the statues of the gods excel men, everyone would agree that their inferiors ought to be their slaves. And if this is true for the body, it is much more just that such a distinction be made for the soul; but it is not as easy to see the beauty of the soul as that of the body.

It is clear, therefore, that there are some who are by nature free or slaves, and that for the latter their servitude is both advantageous and just.

Some would distinguish natural slavery from slavery by law or convention, which is the result of force (capture in war).

16 It is not difficult to see, however, that those who assert the opposite, too, are to some extent correct. The words "slavery" and "slave" are used in two senses. There is also a class who are slaves by law or convention. (Law is a sort of agreement, and by it people assert that things captured in war belong to the captors.) Now many legal experts bring against this right an "indictment of illegality" (as one does against a speaker), on the ground that it is wrong for what is overcome by force to be the slave of and be ruled by that which is capable of compelling it and superior in power. Even among the wise opinions differ on this matter.

But the issue is complicated; virtue and justice are in some way associated with preponderant power. The true criterion is the possession of superior virtue. Nature intends to correlate this with birth, but sometimes fails.

17 But the cause of this disagreement and what confuses the argument is that in some way virtue itself when it has the resources is able to exercise very great force, and the controlling power always lies in superiority in some sort of good. Thus the opinion arises that force does not exist without virtue; and the disagreement is exclusively about the justice of the matter. Because of this[15] one group thinks that justice is good will, while others think justice lies in the very fact that the stronger rules. Though these arguments are in opposition to one another, neither provides any firm or persuasive proof that that which is better, in accordance with virtue, ought not to rule and be master. *18* But some persons, clinging as they suppose to some universal principle of justice (for law is a kind of justice) believe slavery as a result of war just. At the same time, however, they contradict this; for it is possible that the origin of a war may not be just, and one would never say that he who is unworthy to be a slave is really a slave. If this is not correct it will sometimes happen that those who seem best born will be slaves and descendants of slaves, if they happen to be captured and sold. Therefore they do not mean to say that these are slaves, if captured, but that the barbarians are. And yet when they say this, what they are looking for is nothing else than the naturally servile, which we were speaking about from the first; for they are forced to admit that some are slaves anywhere they are, others nowhere. *19* The same thing is true about high birth; these people consider themselves well born not only among themselves but anywhere they may be, but the barbarians only in their native lands, on the ground that there is something that is absolutely well born and free and something else that is so but not absolutely. (Compare Helen's question in the play of Theodectes: "Who would dare call me a servant, the offspring of two divine progenitors?") But when they say this they are not distinguishing slave from free and well born from base born by any other criterion than virtue and vice. They are claiming that just as man springs from man and beast from beast, so good springs from good. Nature, however, often intends to bring about this result but is unable.

Natural slavery is advantageous to both master and slave.

It is thus clear that there is some reason for this disagreement, and that some actual slaves are not naturally slaves, while some actual freemen are not naturally free. *20* It is also clear, though, that there are some among whom a distinction of this kind can be made, and that it is both beneficial and just for one group to be slaves and for the other to be masters, and that one element ought to be ruled and the other to rule, with the kind of rule they are born to exercise, even so as to be masters of others. Bad rule, however, is disadvantageous to both parties, for the same thing is to the advantage of the part and of the whole, both in soul and in body, and the slave is in a sense a part of his master, a part which is alive but separate from the body. *21* Therefore in a sense even mutual friendship is advantageous for slave and master, among those assigned to this rank by nature; but among those who do not fall into this pattern, where slavery is a result of convention and force, the opposite is true.

It is clear even from this much discussion that the master-slave relationship is not the same as a political relationship, and that all forms of rule are not alike, as some say. One is of freemen and another of slaves, and household management is a monarchy (since every household is governed by a single ruler), while statesmanship, on the other hand, is the government of free and equal citizens.

The science of being a slave, that of being a master, and that of acquiring slaves

22 Now a master is not called such because of any knowledge, but because he is such by birth, and the same is true of slave and of freeman. But there would also be a kind of science appropriate to master and to slave. That of the slave would be of the sort that the man in Syracuse taught; there used to be someone there who taught slaves their everyday duties for pay. The study of these matters might go even further—the science of cookery, and other such types of service—for some forms of work are more honored, though others are more necessary, and as the proverb says, "slave before slave, master before master." *23* All such sciences are appropriate to slaves; the science appropriate to a master is that of using slaves. This science involves nothing very great or awesome—simply that what the slave must know how to do, the master has to know how to command. This is why a steward takes over this office for those who are in a position not to have to suffer personal inconvenience, and they themselves spend their time on politics or philosophy. The science of *acquiring* slaves is different from both of these, being—when justly practised—a part of the science of war or of hunting.

Let this be the conclusion of our definition of master and slave.

[The rest of Book I treats some other aspects of household management. Book II contains a discussion of ideal states proposed by Plato and others. In Book III Aristotle discusses the various forms of government from a theoretical point of view.]

Book III

V. Forms of government; conceptions of political justice

The forms of constitution, three good and three bad

1 Since "constitution" and "civic body" mean the same thing, and the civic body is the ruling power in the city, and it is necessary that the ruling power be either one or a few or the many—since these things are so, when one man or a few or the many rule for the sake of the common good, the constitutions so formed must be right constitutions, and constitutions involving rule for the private benefit of one or a few or the many must be perversions. Either one must deny the name of citizen to those who share in a government, or they must have a part in its benefits. *2* Of the governments directed toward the common good, we ordinarily call that which is monarchical, "kingship"; that which belongs to a few but more than one, "aristocracy" (i.e., "best-rule," either because the best rule or because they rule for the best interests of the city and those who have a share in it); and when the multitude rules for the common good, it is called by the name which is common to all the constitutions, "polity." *3* (This is reasonable; for one man or a few may excel in virtue, but it is difficult for a large number to be perfected in every virtue. They can excel most in the art of warfare, for this depends on numbers—which is why, in a constitution of this sort, the group which defends the country is dominant, and those who possess arms share in it.) *4* The perversions of these forms are tyranny from kingship, oligarchy from aristocracy, and democracy from "polity." Tyranny is monarchy exercised in the interest of the monarch, oligarchy is rule in the interest of the wealthy, and democracy in the interest of the poor—and none of these aims at what is advantageous for the community.

In distinguishing between oligarchy and democracy, the economic status of the rulers is a better criterion than their numbers.

We must discuss at somewhat greater length the nature of each of these constitutions; for there are some difficulties in the matter, and it is the business of one who is pursuing an investigation in a philosophical manner, and not merely considering the needs of practice, not to overlook or neglect any point, but to make clear the truth about each.

5 Tyranny is a monarchy exercising despotic power over the political association, an oligarchy exists when those who possess wealth are dominant in the government, and democracy on the other hand when those are dominant who do not have a great deal of wealth, but are poor. Now our first difficulty is in the distinction of one from another: if the majority should be wealthy and dominant over the city, and democracy exists where the majority is dominant, and in the same way if it should even happen somewhere that the poor were fewer in number than the wealthy but more powerful and dominant over the constitution, whereas an oligarchy is said to exist where a small number is dominant, in both cases the definitions of the types of constitution would seem not to have been well made. *6* But still, even if one should combine wealth with fewness and poverty with multitude and should name the constitutions in this way, calling the one oligarchy in which the rich, being few in numbers, control the offices, and the one democracy in which the poor, being many in number, control the offices, a new difficulty would be introduced. What shall we call the constitutions we just spoke of, in which the rich are a majority or the poor a minority and these are in each case dominant over the government—if there is no other form of constitution beside those mentioned? *7* The argument thus seems to make clear two things. First, the fact of few or many being dominant is merely accidental to oligarchies or democracies, a coincidence arising because the rich are everywhere few and the poor many. Thus the causes mentioned [difference in numbers] are not the true criterion of difference. Second, the principle of difference between democracy and oligarchy is poverty and wealth. Wherever the rulers hold power through wealth, whether they be a minority or a majority, this must be an oligarchy, and wherever the poor rule, a democracy. But it does happen coincidentally, as we said, that in one case the rulers are few and in the other many. A few are rich, but all partake of freedom; and these are the grounds on which the two groups contend for political power.

Partisan conceptions of justice: democrats would extend equality in citizenship to equality in everything; oligarchs would extend superiority in wealth to superiority in everything.

8 We must first consider the customary definitions of oligarchy and democracy, and the nature of oligarchic and democratic justice. Both sides lay hold of some idea of justice, but they only go part of the way, and do not express the whole of absolute justice. For example, some think justice is equality, and so it is—not for all, but for the equal; some think justice is inequality, and indeed it is—not for all, but for the unequal.[16] These people are omitting to consider the "to whom" and the result is a faulty judgment.[17] The reason is that they are judging in their own cases, and practically everyone is a bad judge about his own personal affairs. *9* Thus while justice is relative to persons, and a just distribution distinguishes in the same way the value of the things to be distributed and the persons to receive them (as has been said before in the *Ethics* [II, VI, 4 ff.; V, III]), these disputants agree on what equality is in things but disagree on that of persons. This is mainly for the reason just mentioned, that people judge badly in matters concerning themselves. But in addition, because what each side says has a certain amount of justice, they think what they say is absolute justice. Those who are unequal [superior] in some respect, such as money, think they are generally unequal [superior]; and those who are equal in some respect, like freedom, think they are generally equal.

But rights should be proportionate to contribution to the goal of the state. This is living well, not merely living, nor mutual protection, nor commerce.

10 But they omit the most important consideration: if it is for the sake of money that they have formed their association and joined together, they have as much share in the city as they have possessions, so that the argument of the oligarchs would seem to prevail. (It would not seem just for the contributor of one mina to have an equal share of a hundred-mina partnership with one who had contributed all the rest—either in the case of the original contributors or of their successors.) But if a human association is formed for the sake of living well and not merely for the sake of living (for in the latter case there might even be a city of slaves or of animals, but this is not possible because they do not partake of happiness nor of a life in accordance with rational choice, nor for the sake of an alliance to prevent the members' being wronged by anyone, nor to promote commerce and business with one another——[18]

Digression: proof that the end of political association is a good life

If this were so the Tyrrhenians and Carthaginians, and all who have mutual treaties, would be like citizens of a single state. *11* To be sure, they have agreements about imports and treaties to prevent injustice and compacts of alliance. They do not, however, have common offices for the administration of these matters, but different ones in each country, and those on either side are not concerned with what kind of persons the others are, nor that none of those under the treaty is unjust or that none of them is tainted with evil, but only that they do not injure each other. But persons studying the problem of achieving a good system of law always devote attention to goodness and badness in the city's life. Thus it is obvious that attention must be paid to virtue in any city which is truly a city and not just called such for the sake of argument. Otherwise a political association becomes an alliance differing merely in a physical way from alliances in which the members live apart. Law, too, becomes a mere compact, and as the sophist Lycophron called it, a pledge of just treatment, but not of such a kind as to make the citizens good and just. *12* It is easy to show that our argument is correct. Even if one should produce a physical unification, so as to include the cities of Megara and Corinth within walls, still this would not make a single city—not even if they practised intermarriage, though this is one of the peculiar marks of association in a city. In the same way, if a number of people lived separately but not so far apart as not to associate with one another, and they had laws to prevent their wronging each other in trade transactions—if one were a carpenter, another a farmer, another a shoemaker, another something else of this sort, and there were ten thousand of them in all—yet if they had nothing more in common than this sort of thing, commerce and military alliance, they would still not constitute a city. *13* Now why is this so? Not because of the lack of proximity in their association. For even if they should move close together, living in an association of this kind, but each one treated his own household as a city, and they merely helped each other, as in a military alliance, against injury—even so, if their manner of association was the same whether together or apart, this would not seem to make a city, to one who examined the matter carefully. Therefore it is clear that a city is not the sharing of a common locality and the prevention of injury and the facilitating of commerce. It is necessary that all these be present if there is to be a city, yet still it is not their presence that constitutes a city, but the sharing of a good life among households and clans, for the sake of a perfect and self-sufficient existence. *14* This is not possible, however, unless the citizens dwell in the same single locality and practise intermarriage. This is why kinship groups and phratries have arisen, along with religious festivals and other public pastimes. This sort of thing is the function of friendship; for friendship means choosing to live in association.

The final end of the city, then, is the good life, and these other things are sought for the sake of the final end. A city is the sharing of clans and villages in a common and self-sufficient life, and this, we say, is a happy and noble life. We must suppose therefore that the political association exists for the sake of noble actions, not merely for the sake of living together.

Thus the most political power rightly belongs to those who contribute most; i.e., those who excel in virtue.

15 Therefore those who contribute most to such an association have more of a share in the city than those who may be equal or even greater in freedom and birth but are unequal in political virtue, or those who are superior in wealth but are inferior in virtue.

It is clear, now, that each party to the dispute over constitutions has some right on its side.

VI. The Sovereign Body

What group shall rule? Any group, ruling in its own interest, will be unjust to other groups. To say that law should rule, rather than man, will not help.

1 There is another problem, as to what should be the dominant element in the city—the multitude, the rich, the well-born, the one man who is best of all, or a tyrant. Each of these answers seems to involve some difficulty. For consider this: if the poor, because they are a majority, are to distribute the goods of the rich, is this not unjust? "No, by Zeus," someone might reply, "for it was a decree justly [19] made by the dominant power." Well, what should we say injustice is, ultimately? Going back to the beginning and considering everything, if the majority distributes the property of the minority, they are destroying the city. But surely virtue does not destroy that which possesses it, nor is justice destructive of a city; so it is clear that this law cannot be just, either. *2* Furthermore, all the acts of a tyrant must be, in a sense, just; for being superior he exercises force, as the multitude does against the rich. But is it just, then, for the minority to rule, or the rich? If they too act in the same way, and seize and carry off the possessions of the multitude, is this just? If so, the other is also just.

It is thus clear that all these actions are bad and unjust; (*3*) but should the well born rule and be dominant over all others? If so all the rest must be dishonored, deprived of civic rights,[20] not being privileged to hold political office; for we consider the offices as honors, and when the same group rules continuously the rest must be dishonored [deprived of privilege]. Is it better, then, for the one best man of all to rule? Even this is too oligarchical; for the majority will be dishonored. Perhaps someone might object that it is always bad for the dominant power to be man and not law, considering the qualities of mind and emotion that man has. Still, if the law is oligarchic or democratic, what difference will there be in our argument? What we said before will still apply.

The democrats' case has some justification, since the multitude taken as a group may be better than any individual.

4 The other problems will be discussed in another place; but the argument that the multitude ought to be dominant rather than the few best might seem to be explicable, and to have some justification—perhaps even some truth. It is possible that the many, though each one of them is not a good man, may still, when they come together, be better than the others, not as individuals but as a group, just as dinners composed of a variety of courses are better than those procured by a single purchase. When there are many, each may have a portion of virtue and wisdom, and as when they congregate they resemble a single man with many feet and hands and many senses, so the same thing may be true of character and intellect. This is why the multitude is a better judge of musical and poetical compositions; one is a better judge of one part, another of another, and the entire group of the whole. *5* The better sort of men excel each individual commoner—as they say the beautiful excel the unbeautiful and a skilful painting excels ordinary reality—in the fact that scattered elements are gathered into a unity, since when the parts are considered separately one person's eye, or some other part of another may be more beautiful than the corresponding part of the painting. Whether this superiority of the multitude to the few good can exist in every democracy or every multitude is not clear. "By Zeus, though," someone might say, "it must be impossible sometimes; for otherwise the same argument could even be extended to a comparison between men and beasts. Still, how are some multitudes—if I may so express myself—better than beasts?" Despite this objection, however, there is nothing to prevent our argument from being true of *some* multitude.

The multitude can safely be entrusted with the election and examination of magistrates.

6 In this way we might resolve the difficulty mentioned, and also the next one, namely what authority the freemen and the mass of citizens ought to have. These are the ones who are neither rich nor have any claim on the basis of merit. It is not safe for them to share the greatest offices, for through injustice and folly they would commit injuries and errors. But not to allow them anything—for them to have no share in the government—is dangerous, for when there is a great number of the poor without privileges, a city must necessarily be full of enemies. The remaining alternative is for them to share in deliberative and judicial functions. *7* This is why Solon and certain other lawgivers assign them the election and examination of magistrates, but do not allow them to hold offices individually. When they assemble, the whole group apprehends things well enough, and when mingled with their betters they are of benefit to their cities, just as impure food when mixed with pure makes the whole more beneficial than if there were only a small amount of the pure; but taken separately each commoner is imperfectly fitted for making decisions.

Two difficulties: (*a*) *Here as elsewhere, the specialist must be the final judge.* (*Answer: the multitude, as a group, may be wiser than any individual; and besides, the specialist is not the only judge.*)

8 This arrangement of the constitution offers two difficulties: In the first place, it would seem to be the function of the same person [namely, a physician] both to judge who has performed correctly a physician's tasks and to perform these tasks and render healthy someone suffering from a particular ailment. An analogous situation prevails in other crafts and arts. As the physician must test other physicians, so must the professionals in similar professions. But "physician" means three things: the general practitioner, the skilled specialist, and one who has an educated person's knowledge about the art. There are persons with this last kind of knowledge of nearly all the arts, and we attribute the power of judging no less to the generally educated than to those with special knowledge. *9* Next, the same sort of thing would seem to be true about choice, for to choose well is also the function of those who know—the geometer in geometrical matters and the pilot in nautical; even if some laymen participate in certain tasks and arts, certainly they are not more closely involved than the specialists. So, according to this argument, the multitude ought not to be given authority over either the choice or the examination of magistrates. *10* This whole argument, however, seems invalid—unless the multitude is very slavish—for two reasons. First, because of our previous contention, that though each individual is a worse judge than the specialist, the whole group acting together will be either better or not worse. Secondly, in certain fields the maker is not the only judge, or even the best one, fields in which even persons without skill are acquainted with the products. For example, to know about a house is not only the function of the builder, but the user of it (the householder) will judge it even better; and a pilot will judge a rudder better than a shipwright will; and a banqueter judges a feast, not the cook. This would seem to be an adequate solution of this difficulty, but there is another on its heels.

(*b*) *How can the lowly judge or choose among the noble?* (*Answer: they do not do so as individuals but as a group.*)

11 It seems strange for the mean to have charge of more important matters than the well-born, and the examination and choice of magistrates is a very important matter. In some constitutions, as was said [section 7], these duties are entrusted to the people, and the assembly has control of all such matters. Yet people participate in assemblies and councils and law courts on the basis of small property assessment and at any age, whereas there are high property qualifications for treasurerships and generalships and the most important magistrates. *12* Well, we might solve this difficulty in a similar way to the other, for this situation too is doubtless quite proper. It is not the juryman or council member or assemblyman that is the ruler, but the court, the council, and the people. Each individual (councilman, assemblyman, juryman) is a part of one of these bodies. Thus it is just for the multitude to have charge of more important matters; people and council and jury are composed of many members. What is more, the property valuation of these (as a group) is greater than that of any individual or of any small group who hold important offices.

Good laws are supremely important; but law is relative to the whole constitutional structure.

13 In this way we may settle these difficulties. But the first difficulty we discussed makes one thing clear above all others: that the laws—good laws—must be sovereign, and that the ruler, whether there be one or many, must have authority in matters about which the laws cannot specify exactly, because of the difficulty of making general rules to cover all particular cases. Of what nature, however, good laws must be, is not yet clear, but our old difficulty still remains. At the same time and in the same way as the constitutions to which they belong, laws will be either bad or good and either just or unjust. This at least is clear, though, that the laws are relative to the constitution, and if so it is clear that laws in accordance with a correct constitution will be just, and those in accord with a perverted form, unjust.

VII. What Group Should Rule?

The end of politics is justice, which means distribution of equal amounts to equals and unequal amounts to unequals. But what do these terms mean?

1 In every science and art the end is some good, but this is most eminently true and the good is greatest in the highest of them all, which is the subject of politics. The good of politics is justice, and that is what is advantageous to all. People in general suppose that justice is some kind of equality, and to a certain extent this is in agreement with our philosophical discussions which deal with the definition of ethical concepts. They believe that justice involves both things and people and that those who are equal ought to receive equal treatment; but one must not forget the problem, to what sort of things and people the terms equal and unequal are to apply. This presents a difficulty and leads us into the philosophical study of politics.

Not just any kind of superiority should bring political advantage. The most reasonable criteria are the things basic to the existence, and good life, of a state: high birth, freedom, wealth, justice, and military excellence—but especially culture and virtue.

2 The argument might be advanced that offices should be distributed unequally according to superiority in the possession of any good thing whatsoever, if in all other respects certain persons happen not to differ at all but to be alike—the theory being that when persons differ, their justice and their merit are different. If this is true, however, with every difference of complexion or stature or any other good thing, the superior will have some political advantage. Is there not an obvious fallacy here? That there is can be clearly seen from other arts and sciences. Of flute-players who are equal in skill, for example, an advantage in quality of flutes ought not to be given to the better-born. They will not play any better because of their birth; he who is superior in the art should receive the advantage in instruments as well. *3* If this point is not yet clear, it will be so when we carry it a bit further. Suppose someone is superior in flute-playing but much inferior in birth and beauty. Though each of these (birth and beauty) is a greater good than flute-playing, and they are proportionately more superior to flute-playing than this person is to other flute-players, still he should be given the best flutes. If the opposite were true, the superiority in wealth and that in birth ought to contribute to the performance of the function, but they do not.

4 Furthermore, according to the argument we are refuting, any good would be commensurate with any other. If a certain height is better than another, then generally height is equally important with wealth and freedom; so that if one person excels in height more than another does in virtue (even if virtue generally is superior to height), all things would be commensurable. If a certain amount of something is better than a certain amount of something else, it is clear that there is a certain amount of the former which would be equal to a certain amount of the latter. *5* Since this is impossible it is clearly reasonable that in politics too people do not contest offices on the basis of just any kind of inequality. If some are slow and some swift this is no reason the one group should have more or the other less; it is in gymnastic contests that differences in these respects receive their due honor. The contest must be set on the basis of the things which make a city; hence there is reason in the claim to power of the well-born, the free, and the rich. There must be some who are free and some who have property (for a city could not consist entirely of the needy, any more than of slaves). *6* In addition, however, if these are required, clearly justice and military excellence are also required. A city cannot be run without these, either. The distinction is that without the first two a city cannot exist at all, whereas without the latter two it cannot be well managed. All these criteria, or some of them at least, would seem to have rightful claims, with respect to the mere existence of a city; but for a good life, culture and virtue have the best claims, as was said before.[21]

Each criterion has some justification.

7 Since it is not right for those who are equal in some one respect to have an equal share in everything, nor for those who are superior [unequal] in one respect to have a superior [unequal] share in everything, all constitutions based on such claims must be perverted forms. It has been stated above [v, 8] that all the parties have some justice in their contentions, although none of them is absolutely justified. The rich are justified in that they have a larger share of land, and land is a matter of public interest; they are also, for the most part, more reliable in the fulfillment of contracts. The criteria of freedom and high birth are closely connected with each other. Their justification is in the fact that the better-born are more truly citizens than the lowly, and in every people high birth is honored; and furthermore it is likely that the descendants of better parents will themselves be better, since good birth is excellence of breed. *8* In the same way we shall say that virtue too has a just claim, for we say that justice is virtue as it pertains to association, to which all other virtues must be secondary. But the majority too has a claim, as against the minority, because they are stronger and richer and better, considering the majority as an aggregate and comparing it with the minority.

But each is also open to objection.

Now if all these groups were present in one city—I mean for example the good, the rich and the well-born, and also some other large group of a political nature—would there be a contest as to who ought to rule, or not? *9* In each of the constitutions we have described there is no question who ought to rule, for they differ from each other in the composition of the dominant element—in one it is the rich, in another the men of quality, and so on for the rest. Our question, however, is how to decide the issue when all these elements are present at the same time.

10 If the possessors of virtue should be very few in number, how shall we choose? Should we consider the fact that they are few in relation to the task—whether they are capable of managing the city or are sufficient in number to make up a city? [22]

There is a difficulty which confronts all who claim political power. Those who demand to rule because of their wealth would seem to have no just claim, and the same is true of those who allege their high birth; if there is someone who is richer than all of them, clearly, according to this same principle, this man ought to rule all the rest; and in the same way the one who excels in high birth ought to rule over those whose claim is based on freedom. *11* The same difficulty will doubtless apply to aristocracies as well, where the criterion is virtue. If there should be one man better than the other good men in the civic body, he ought, according to the same principle, to be sovereign. Furthermore, even if the multitude ought to be sovereign because they are stronger than the few, then if one or a group (more than one but fewer than the multitude) is stronger than the rest, these ought to be sovereign rather than the multitude.

12 All these considerations seem to make it clear that none of these criteria is correct, according to which people think it right for themselves to rule and for all others to be subject to them. And to be sure the multitude would have an argument with some justice even against those who claim the right to control the government because of their virtue or wealth; for there is no reason why the multitude should not be better and richer than the few, not individually but as a group.

Legislation should be in the interest of the whole community, rather than any group.

13 We may also meet in this way, when the situation described occurs, the objection which some put forward and inquire into: some question whether a lawgiver, wishing to establish the most correct laws, should legislate in the interest of the better or of the majority. The concept "right" should be understood in connection with equality, and the "equally right" in regard to the advantage of the whole city and the community of the citizens. A citizen is generally one who has a share in the business of ruling and being ruled; and this means different persons in each constitution; but in the best constitution he is one who is able and willing to be ruled and to rule, with a view to the attainment of a life according to virtue.

VIII. Outstanding individuals

Greatly superior persons cannot be considered merely as parts of a citizen body; they are above the law.

1 If there is any one individual (or any group of more than one but not enough to provide the complement of a city) who so stands out from the rest by superiority in virtue that the virtue and political capacity of all the rest put together is not comparable to theirs (if it is a group; if it is an individual, his)—such persons should no longer be reckoned as members of a city. They will be suffering an injustice in being judged worthy only of equal treatment, when they are superior in virtue and political capacity; such a person must be like a god among men. *2* Hence it is clear, too, that legislation pertains to those who are equal both in birth and capacity, but that law is not directed toward such persons as we are speaking of; they are a law unto themselves. Anyone who tried to legislate for them would be ridiculous; they might well say what the lions said (according to Antisthenes) when the hares made speeches demanding that everyone be equal.[23]

Historically, such persons have often been ostracized or banished.

It is for reasons of this sort that cities democratically ruled set up the institution of ostracism. They appear to aim most of all at universal equality, so that they used to ostracize and remove from the city for a certain period those who seemed to excel in capacity through wealth or number of friends or any other source of political strength. *3* Mythology tells that the Argonauts left Heracles behind for a similar reason. The Argo did not wish to take him along with the rest, because he so far excelled all the other passengers. Therefore we cannot say without qualification that people are right in criticizing tyranny and the advice of Periander to Thrasybulus. (They say that Periander spoke not a word to the messenger sent to ask his advice, but by cutting off the ears of grain which rose above the rest, evened off the field. The messenger did not recognize the purport of this, but when he reported to Thrasybulus what had happened, the latter perceived that what he must do was to get rid of any outstanding men.) *4* This is not only advantageous to tyrants, and it is not only tyrants who do it, but the same thing applies to oligarchies and democracies. Ostracism has the same effect, in a way, as abasing or banishing the eminent. Those who are in power adopt the same method in dealing with cities and nations as the Athenians did with the Samians and Chians and Lesbians. As soon as they were firmly in control, they humbled them, in violation of their treaties. The King of Persia, too, frequently pruned down the Medes and Babylonians and any others who became presumptuous because they had once been strong.

Such methods of dealing with exceptional individuals even exist in good governments, and they have some justification.

5 This difficulty exists quite generally in all forms of government, even correct ones. The perverted forms act in this way out of regard for their own peculiar interest, and yet the situation is not different with those that look toward the common good. This is also clearly so in other arts and sciences. A painter would not allow an animal to have a foot which was too large for the symmetry of his picture, even if it were more beautiful than the other parts; nor would a shipwright allow the stern or any other part to destroy the symmetry of the ship; nor would the trainer of a chorus allow a person who sang louder and better than anyone else in the chorus to be a member of the group. *6* So nothing in this levelling process prevents a monarch who employs it from being in harmony with the cities under him, if his rule is otherwise beneficial to the cities.

Thus in regard to the recognized kinds of eminence the argument for ostracism possesses a kind of political justification. To be sure, it would be better for the legislator to organize the constitution from the very beginning in such a way that this kind of remedy would not be required; but the second-best way, if the situation arises, is to correct it with this sort of measure. This is not what has taken place, historically, in the various cities; they have had no regard for what was advantageous to their particular form of constitution, but have used ostracism as an instrument of factional strife.

But in the ideal state, a man pre-eminent in virtue would be made perpetual king.

Now in the perverted forms of constitution it is clear that this process is advantageous and just for the particular form, though it is doubtless also clear that it is not absolutely just. *7* But in the case of the best constitution a considerable difficulty arises—regarding an eminence not in other good qualities, like strength or wealth or number of friends, but—what is to be done if someone arises who excels in virtue? Surely people would not say that such a man ought to be banished or removed, but neither is it possible to rule over such a person. It would be like demanding to rule over Zeus himself, dividing up offices with him. The remaining possibility—which seems to be what nature intended—is that all should willingly obey such a person, and that such men should be perpetual kings in their cities.

[Chapters IX–XI contain a general discussion of kingship, which is "one of the right constitutions." Aristotle begins by distinguishing the various types of royal rule that are to be seen in history: (1) the Spartan type, in which the king is little more than a general; (2) the hereditary despotisms of non-Greek peoples, much like tyrannies but legitimate; (3) "elective tyrannies" (analogous to the Roman dictatorship) found in archaic Greece; (4) the hereditary, legitimate, constitutional, but limited kingships of the Heroic Age (Homer); and (5) an absolute kingship, whose power is the same as that of the community governing itself. After canvassing briefly certain objections to absolute kingship, which center mainly on the question whether law should be sovereign or a man or group of men, and which therefore really apply to any form of absolute rule, Aristotle passes to his final judgment on kingship.]

XI. VARIETIES OF GOVERNMENT: MONARCHY

Different governments are suited to different kinds of populace. When a people can produce a man or family pre-eminent in virtue, it should be a monarchy.

10 These considerations might, however, be valid in some circumstances and not in others. For there exist by nature groups which are best ruled in a master-slave relationship, groups which are best ruled by kings, and groups which are best ruled by constitutional government, along with justice and considerations of expediency. (Tyranny is not according to nature, nor any of the other constitutions that are perversions; they all come into being contrary to nature.) But from what has been said it is clear that among those who are alike and equal it is neither expedient nor just that one should have sovereignty over all, either without laws (being a law unto himself) or with laws, or a good man ruling the good or a bad man ruling the bad—not even if he is superior in virtue, except perhaps in one sense. What that sense is we must say, though in a way it has already been defined [Chapter VIII].

11 In the first place a distinction must be made among groups suited to royal, aristocratic, and constitutional rule. A populace suited to royal rule is one of such a nature as to bring forth a family pre-eminent in the virtue conducive to political leadership. A populace suited to aristocratic rule is one able to be ruled in a manner proper to free men, at the hands of those who are pre-eminent in the virtue conducive to political rule. A populace suited to constitutional rule is one of such a nature as to have in it a people with military ability capable of being ruled and ruling in a system of law which distributes offices to the wealthy according to merit.

12 Now whenever there happens to arise a whole family or even one individual who excels all the rest in virtue, to such an extent that his virtue surpasses that of all the others together, then it is just that this family should be a royal family and exercise sovereignty, or that this one individual should be king. As we said before, it is just not only with the kind of justice which persons allege who found constitutions—whether they be aristocracies, oligarchies, or democracies. They always make their claims on the basis of a superiority—not always the same kind of superiority, however, but in the way we previously described [VIII, 7]. *13* It is not right, either, to kill or banish or certainly not to ostracize such a man, nor to demand that he be ruled in his turn. It is not natural that the part should be superior to the whole, and a man with such a pre-eminence is in this relationship to the rest.[24]

The only alternative is to obey such a man, and for him to be sovereign not merely according to a certain share, but absolutely.

This, then, may be the end of our discussion of kingship, how it differs from other forms, and whether it is advantageous to cities or not, and to which ones, and in what way. . . .

[The final chapter of Book III is a recapitulation.]

Book IV

[In Book IV Aristotle discusses the various types of actually existing constitutional forms. The principal ones are oligarchy, democracy, and the form called "polity" (*politeia:* a word which sometimes means simply "constitution"; see note 1, on *polis* and its derivatives). The latter is described, politically, as a mixture of oligarchy and democracy. The following chapter discusses it further, with emphasis on its social structure. The chapter also illustrates one aspect of Aristotle's attitude to the problem of the "ideal state."]

IX. THE "POLITY"

What is the best form of government generally attainable?

1 What will be the best form of government and the best way of life for the majority of cities and the majority of men, if we judge not according to a standard of virtue beyond the capacity of ordinary people, or an education which requires high natural ability and material good fortune, or a form of government which would be an answer to prayer, but if we look for a way of life which the greatest number can follow and a government in which most cities can share? *2* The "aristocracies" we have just been speaking of fall in some respects beyond the reach of most cities, and in other respects are very nearly like the so-called "polity," so that we may speak of the two forms as one.

The doctrine of the mean applies in politics as well as ethics.

Our decision in all matters of this kind is based on the same principles. If we were right in saying in the *Ethics* [I, x, 14; II, vi, 15] that the happy life is an unhindered life in accordance with virtue, and that virtue lies in a mean, then the best life must be one which consists in a mean—a mean which everyone can attain. *3* This same definition must apply to the virtue and vice not only of a city but of a form of government, for a form of government is in a sense the way of life of a city.

It is generally better for the middle class to be dominant than the very rich or the very poor.

Now in every city there are three parts, the very rich, the very poor, and a third class intermediate between these. Since it is agreed that the moderate and the mean is best, it is clear that a moderate amount of good fortune is also best. *4* The moderate will be most amenable to reason, whereas the overhandsome or overstrong or overhealthy or overwealthy, or the opposites of these, the overpoor or overweak or those utterly without distinction, will only with difficulty follow reason.

It will avoid the arrogance of the rich and the mean-spiritedness of the poor; being more homogeneous, the city will be more peaceful.

One group becomes arrogant and wicked in great things, the other vicious and wicked in small things; and of injustices some are committed through arrogance and others through viciousness. Further, the middle class is less apt to avoid or to seek office, and both of these extremes are harmful to cities. *5* In addition, those with an excess of good fortune—power, wealth, friends, and the like—are neither willing nor able to be ruled. This begins right at home when they are children; because of the luxury of their lives they are not even accustomed to taking orders in school. On the other hand, those with an excessive lack of these things are too mean-spirited. The result is that the latter know, not how to rule, but how to be ruled, like slaves; and the former know, not how to accept any direction, but how to rule like masters. *6* Thus there comes into existence a city not of free men but of slaves and masters, one group filled with hatred and the other with scorn. This is far removed from the friendship and community proper to a city. Community is related to friendship; people do not even wish to share a journey with an enemy. A city wants to be composed, as far as possible, of people who are equal or similar, and this is most true of the middle class. Thus this middle-class city must be best governed, from the very principles which we affirm to lie at the basis of a city.

The middle class is the most stable economically.

7 These citizens are also the most stable class in a city, for they do not desire the possessions of others, like the poor, nor do others desire theirs, as the poor desire the possessions of the rich; neither plotting nor being plotted against, they live a life free of danger. Thus Phocylides' prayer is a good one: "Many things are best for the middling; may I be a middling citizen."

Therefore the middle-class state is best, for its avoidance of extremes and of factional strife.

8 It is plain, therefore, both that a political association dominated by the middle class is best, and that cities can be well governed in which the middle class is numerous and is stronger than both of the others, or at least than either one (by the addition of its power, it swings the balance and prevents either extreme from winning). Consequently it is great good fortune for the members of the citizen body to have a moderate but sufficient amount of property, because where some have a great deal and others have nothing, there arises either an extreme democracy or an untempered oligarchy or a tyranny, through either kind of excess. For tyranny arises both from the most headstrong democracy and from oligarchy, but much less often from the intermediate types of constitution, or those closest to them. The cause of this phenomenon we will explain later in our discussion of revolutions [V, VII, 4].

9 It is clear that the middle-class constitution is best, for it alone is free of factional strife; wherever the intermediate element is numerous, there is least disagreement and factional struggle among the citizens. For this reason large cities are freer of faction, because the middle class is large, whereas in small cities it is easy to divide the whole citizen body into two parties, so as to leave no middle group, and practically everyone is either wealthy or poor. Democracies, too, are more stable than oligarchies, and last longer, because of the middle class. (They are more numerous and have more share in public offices in democracies than in oligarchies.) Whenever without the middle class the poor form a majority, mischief begins and the city is quickly brought to ruin.

10 There is also evidence for our view in the fact that the best lawgivers belong to the middle class. Solon belonged to this group (he makes this clear in his poetry), and Lycurgus (he was not a king), and Charondas [cf. I, I, 6], and most of the rest.

But the "polity" is rare in actual occurrence; usually one or other extreme prevails.

It is also clear from these considerations why most constitutions are democratic or oligarchical: since the middle class is often small, whichever gains the upper hand, either the men of property or the populace. persons who are at a distance from the mean administer the government in their own way, so that it becomes either a democracy or an oligarchy. *11* In addition, since strife and mutual conflict arise between the populace and the wealthy, whichever happens to defeat the other does not establish a constitution based on community and equality, but takes as the prize of victory dominance in the government, so that one party makes it a democracy or the other an oligarchy. Furthermore, the cities which have held the hegemony in Greece, each looking toward its own form of government, have set up democracies and oligarchies, considering their own interest rather than that of the various cities.

12 For these reasons, middle-class constitutions have been formed either never or only a few times and in a few places. Of our predecessors only one has agreed to the establishment of this kind of arrangement; [25] and the cities have long had the habit of not even wishing for what is fair and equal, but either seeking to rule or remaining in subjection.

Other forms will be rated by comparison with the "polity." But there may be exceptions.

Now from what we have said it is clear what is the best form of government, and why. *13* And of other forms (since, as we said, more are democracies and oligarchies) it is not hard to see, now that the best form has been defined, which is to be placed first and second, and for the reason that one is better and the other worse. The one closer to the best must always be better, and the one further from the mean must be worse, unless one is judging in relation to particular circumstances. I speak of judging "in particular circumstances" because frequently, though one form of government would be preferable for certain people, there is nothing to prevent another form from being beneficial to them.

[The rest of Book IV discusses the adaptation of the form of government to various types of people, and some details of political organization.]

Book V

I. General causes of revolution

1 We have dealt with about all the topics we previously proposed; our next task, after what has been said, is to consider what are the causes of revolution in constitutions, and how many they are and of what nature, and what kinds are likely to change into what other kinds, and further, what are the means of preserving them (both the means common to all and those peculiar to each single type), and also what are the particular means by which each of them is most likely to be preserved.

Recapitulation: strife arises because people wish to extend equality or inequality in one field to all others.

2 First we must take as our starting point that there have come into existence many forms of government in spite of the fact that everyone agrees on the nature of justice (that is, proportionate equality), because they understand its meaning wrongly, as we said before. Democracy rose from the assumption that those who were equal in any respect were absolutely equal: since all alike are free they believe that all are equal absolutely. But oligarchy rose from the supposition that persons unequal [i.e., superior] in some one respect were generally unequal [superior]: being unequal in property they suppose they are absolutely unequal. *3* Then the one group think that, being equal, they should share equally in everything, and the others, since they are unequal, seek a greater share, since superiority means inequality. Each constitution has an element of justice, but each is, from an absolute point of view, faulty. And it is for this reason, when they do not have shares in the constitution corresponding to the beliefs which each group happens to hold, that they engage in party strife. The ones who would be most justified of all in entering the struggle, but who do it least, are those who excel in virtue. In their case alone is it reasonable to consider them absolutely unequal [superior]. There are some who, being superior in birth, think of themselves as worth more than equality because of this inequality, for they believe that to be well born is to have the wealth and virtue of one's ancestors. *4* These are the beginnings and as it were the fountainheads of party strife.

Revolutions usually aim either to change the form of government or to transfer power from one group to another, within the same form.

Thus it is that revolutions are of two kinds: one kind is against the constitution, that they may set up another in place of the existing one, as an oligarchy instead of a democracy or a democracy instead of an oligarchy or a "polity" or aristocracy in place of either of these, or vice versa. Sometimes a revolution is not against the constitution, when people want the same constitutional arrangement but want it in their power, for example in an oligarchy or monarchy.

They may also aim at a general tightening or loosening of the existing type, or at partial revision of some kind.

5 Or a revolution may be concerned with the more or less, for example that an existing oligarchy may be more or less oligarchical, or that an existing democracy may be more or less democratic, and the same way with the other constitutions, that they may be either tightened or loosened. Again, it may be intended to change a certain part of the constitution, for example, to establish or remove a certain office, as some say Lysander tried to destroy the monarchy in Lacedaemon and King Pausanias the ephorate. *6* In Epidamnus, too, the constitution suffered a partial change, for they set up a council in place of the conclave of tribe leaders, and of the citizens it is still compulsory for the magistrates alone to attend the meeting of the assembly when some office is being voted on; and another oligarchical feature is the election of a single archon.

People confuse arithmetical and proportionate equality.

Everywhere party strife is due to inequality, where the unequal are not treated according to proportion (a perpetual monarchy is unequal, if it exists among equals). Generally party conflict is a struggle for equality. *7* Equality is of two kinds, the arithmetical and that according to merit. By arithmetical I mean that which is the same or equal in number or size, by "according to merit" that which is proportionate. For example, 3 exceeds 2 and 2 exceeds 1 by an equal amount, arithmetically, but according to proportion 4 exceeds 2 as 2 exceeds 1, since 2 is the same part of 4 as 1 is of 2, namely half.[26] But while they agree that the absolutely just is in accordance with worth, people develop differences, as was said before, some because, if they are equal in one respect, they think they are generally equal, and others because if they are unequal in one respect they think themselves worthy of inequality [superiority] in everything.

Democracy and oligarchy are the most common forms of government, because there are always rich and poor.

8 This is the reason why there are two principal forms of government, democracy and oligarchy; good birth and virtue are restricted to a few, but the qualifications of these governments exist in a larger number. Nowhere are there as many as a hundred well born and virtuous, but there are many rich and poor everywhere. It is wrong, though, for the government to be organized simply and in all respects according to either idea of equality. This is clear from the consequences, for no government of this kind is stable. The cause of this is that it is impossible, starting from an original error in principle, to avoid some evil in the outcome. Some matters, therefore, must be handled according to arithmetical equality and some according to the equality based on merit.

Democracy is more stable than oligarchy, and is closer to the "polity."

9 All the same, however, democracy is safer and freer from party strife than oligarchy. In oligarchies there are two kinds of strife, that among members of the ruling class and that against the people, whereas in democracies there is only that against the oligarchs, and factional strife of the people against itself does not occur often enough to mention. Further, the "polity," based on the middle classes, comes closer to the people than to the few, and is the safest constitution of this type.

[In Chapters II–IV, Aristotle studies in a general and somewhat schematic way the causes of change "in all constitutions." He lists the psychological *motives* (desire to achieve the "equal" or fair treatment one is entitled to); the *objects* sought (profit and honor); and the *occasions* of revolutions (insolence, fear, election intrigues, contempt, disproportionate growth of power, pettiness, etc.). A good many specific examples are given, but in the following chapters the author treats in more detail the nature of revolutions in various forms, beginning with democracy.]

IV. CAUSES OF REVOLUTION IN DEMOCRACIES

The main cause is the reckless wickedness of popular leaders. This can be seen from many examples.

1 We must now consider what happens in each form of government, taking them one by one.

Democracies are overthrown mainly through the wanton licence of popular leaders. Sometimes they cause the men of property to unite by their private persecutions (a common fear brings even the bitterest enemies together), and sometimes by publicly leading the populace against them. In many instances one can see that things have turned out in this way. *2* For example, in Cos the democracy was overthrown when unscrupulous popular leaders arose and the nobles united against them; and in Rhodes, when the popular leaders introduced payment [27] and prevented the trierarchs from being paid what was owing them, so that the latter were compelled, when suits were brought against them, to dissolve the democracy. The democracy in Heraclea was also dissolved, immediately after the foundation of the colony, because of the popular leaders; the nobles, being unjustly treated by them, went into exile, and then the exiles, joining together and coming back, destroyed the democracy. *3* The democracy in Megara, too, was overthrown in a similar manner; the popular leaders, in order to have property to confiscate, banished many of the nobles, until they produced a large body of exiles, who returned, defeated the populace in battle, and established an oligarchy. The same thing also happened in Cyme to the democracy which Thrasymachus destroyed. And in practically every other case, if one looks closely, he can see that the revolution has had this cause. For sometimes in a quest for popular favor, popular leaders have driven the nobles to unite by treating them unjustly, either dividing up their property or crippling their revenues by the imposition of public burdens; sometimes they have done this by slandering them, in order to be able to confiscate the property of the rich.

Formerly democracies often changed into tyrannies, because the popular leaders were military men.

4 In ancient times, when the same man used to be popular leader and general, they would change from democracy to tyranny, for most of the ancient tyrants developed out of popular leaders. The reason that this happened then but does not do so now, is that at that time popular leaders were chosen from the military leaders (people were not yet clever at public speaking). Now, on the other hand, since the art of oratory has burgeoned, those who are good at speaking become popular leaders, but because of their inexperience have no aspirations toward military leadership, though there may be some exceptions to this.

5 Another reason why tyrannies were more common formerly than now is in the important offices which fell to some individuals, like that which developed out of the prytany in Miletus, where the prytany had charge of many important matters. Furthermore, since the cities were not then large, and the populace, living in the country, was busy with its work, the leaders of the populace, when they had military experience, had the opportunity to establish tyrannies. They all did this on the basis of popular confidence, and this confidence lay in hatred for the rich. In Athens, for example, Pisistratus became tyrant by leading a party struggle against the "party of the plain"; and Theagenes in Megara by slaughtering the herds of the wealthy when he found them grazing along the river; and Dionysius, having brought accusations against Daphnaeus and the wealthy, was thought worthy to be tyrant, establishing confidence, by his hatred, in his democratic sentiments.

Sometimes there is simply a change within the democratic form.

6 Changes also take place from "ancestral" democracies to the latest type; for wherever the offices are elective, but not on the basis of a property qualification, and the populace does the electing, those who are eager for office, using the arts of demagoguery, bring things to a point where the populace even has power over the laws. A remedy which will do away with this defect, or at least render it less severe, is for the tribes to provide the magistrates, and not the whole populace.[28]

These are the causes of practically all revolutions in democracies.

[The next chapters deal in much the same way with revolutions in oligarchies and aristocracies, and then with the means of preventing revolution and maintaining stability in these three forms (including democracy). Aristotle then passes to a consideration of monarchies, including both kingships and tyrannies.]

VIII. CHARACTERISTICS OF MONARCHY

Two types of monarchy distinguished: kingship (closer to aristocracy) and tyranny (closer to democracy).

1 It remains to consider monarchy, and the causes by which it is naturally destroyed and preserved. What has been said about other constitutional forms is practically the same as what happens with kingships and tyrannies; for kingship is like aristocracy, and tyranny is a compound of extreme oligarchy and democracy—this is why it is the most harmful to the subjects, being compounded of two bad forms and having the deviations and flaws of both these forms.

2 The origins of the two monarchical forms are from directly opposite causes. Kingship arose to assist the better classes against the populace, and a king is established by the upper classes because of pre-eminence in virtue or the deeds which arise from virtue, or the pre-eminence of a family of this sort. The tyrant, on the other hand, is set up by the people and the multitude against the nobles, that the populace may not suffer injustice at their hands.

Origins of tyranny

3 The majority of tyrants have developed out of popular leaders, so to speak, gaining credit by slander of the nobles. Some tyrannies came about in this way after the cities were already well grown; and others, earlier, from kings who violated ancestral customs and strove for a more absolute rule; a third group from those elected to authoritative positions (in former times democracies used to give officers and magistrates a long tenure); and still others from oligarchies when they chose one man with authority over the highest magistracies. *4* In these ways it was easy for them to accomplish their purpose, if only they had the will, because they had power in advance—some that of the position of king, others that of other high office. Thus Pheidon of Argos and others became tyrants under a kingship, Phalaris and those of Ionia from other offices, while Panaetius of Leontini, Cypselus of Corinth, Pisistratus of Athens, Dionysius of Syracuse, and others, came to power in the same way after being popular leaders.

Origins of kingship

5 Now as we said, kingship is classified with aristocracy, since it is based on worth, either the virtue of an individual or a family, or benefactions, or these along with ability. All who have attained this office have done so by conferring benefits, or being able to do so, upon cities or nations—some, by war, saving them from slavery, like Codrus, others setting them free, like Cyrus, or settling or acquiring territory, like the kings of the Lacedaemonians, Macedonians, and Molossians.

6 It is the intention of a king to be a guardian, that those who have acquired property may suffer no injustice, and that the populace may suffer no violence; tyranny, however, as has been said many times, does not regard the public interest unless for the sake of private advantage. The criterion of goodness for a tyrant is the pleasant, for a king, the noble. Thus, too, of the kinds of greed, that for money is characteristic of a tyrant, that for honor of a king; and the guard of a king will be composed of citizens, that of a tyrant of foreigners.

Tyranny has the bad points of both democracy and oligarchy.

7 It is clear that tyranny has the evils of both democracy and oligarchy. From oligarchy comes the fact that its end is wealth (for it is by this alone that the tyrant's guard and his luxury can be maintained), and the fact that it does not allow trust in the multitude. This is why tyrants take away the people's arms; and oligarchy and tyranny are alike in oppressing the common people, driving them from the city into the country, and dispersing them. From democracy it gets its habit of warring against the nobles, destroying them secretly and openly, and banishing them for being rivals and hindrances to its power. This is the cause of conspiracies, too, since some want to hold power themselves, others not to be slaves. And from this came the advice of Periander to Thrasybulus, to cut off the ears of grain which project above the rest—meaning always to remove the outstanding citizens.[29]

[The rest of this chapter deals with the causes of revolutions in monarchies; as Aristotle says, "The causes of revolution must be considered to be the same in monarchies as in other forms of constitution" (VIII, 8). Book VI deals with details of oligarchies and democracies, and VII and VIII with education in an ideal state.]

PARTS OF ANIMALS

Book I

I. THE METHOD OF NATURAL SCIENCE

Two kinds of scientific knowledge: that of the specialist and that of the cultured man

1 In every investigation and discussion, the lofty and the lowly alike, there appear to be two possible kinds of relationship between the student and the subject. One we may well call scientific knowledge of the subject matter, and the other a sort of "cultural" knowledge. It is the part of a cultured person to be capable of judging accurately what is good and bad in a speaker's words. This is the sort of person we expect a generally educated man to be, and to have been educated means to be able to do this. However, we consider this sort of man, though only a single individual, a competent judge in every subject, but the other only in some restricted field; and there might be a third kind who had the sort of competence we spoke of in a part only of the field.

Points of method: (a) Should we take up the species one by one, or study group characteristics first?

2 Thus it is clear that even in investigations in natural science there must be some criteria of this nature, with reference to which one may judge the method of the exposition, aside from whether the truth is such or such. I mean, for example, whether we ought to take a single species and analyze it in itself, like the nature of man or lion or cow or something else, taking them up one after another, or whether we should set down the attributes which they share in common, in a discussion of the whole group. For many kinds of creatures, though differing among themselves, have many of the same attributes, like sleep, respiration, growth, decay, death, and other such affections and states. (It would destroy the clarity and precision of our argument to mention them all now.)

3 It is clear, however, that if we speak of each severally we shall say the same thing many times, about many species; each of the attributes mentioned belongs to horses and dogs and men, so that if we speak of each attribute in relation to each species, we shall be compelled to speak many times about the same things, those which belong to animals of different species but have no difference in themselves. There are doubtless other attributes which happen to belong to the same category, but are different in different species, like the locomotion of animals. This is not uniform; flying, swimming, walking, and crawling are all different. *4* Thus the question may not be omitted, how the subject matter is to be treated. Shall we consider first what the whole group has in common and then the individual peculiarities, or take up the individual species right from the start? As yet this has not been decided.[1]

(b) Should we consider the phenomena first and then their causes?

Neither has the following question, whether the student of natural science, like the mathematician in his astronomical demonstrations, should first consider the animals and the parts of each, and then discuss the reasons why they are as they are—their causes—or follow some other method.

(c) Which is primary, final cause or efficient cause? Answer: the final, as is also true in the arts.

In addition, since we see that there are several causes involved in the origin of natural objects, like the purpose (final cause) and the source of motion (efficient cause), we must decide about these two—which is first and which second. *5* The first seems to be what we call the purpose; for this is the rational ground [*logos*], and the rational ground is the starting point both in the products of art and in those of nature. A physician or carpenter, whether he measures his product—health or house—by thought or by sense impression, can give the rational ground and the cause of each thing he does, and tell why it must be done as it is. But the final cause, and beauty, are even more important in the works of nature than in those of art.

(d) Necessity, another explanatory principle. Absolute necessity operates in the theoretical sciences, conditional necessity in the natural sciences.

The element of necessity does not appear in the same guise in all the works of nature. Practically everyone seeks to base his account on necessity, not distinguishing the various senses in which the word is used. *6* "Absolute" necessity applies to eternal things, and "conditional" necessity to all naturally developing things, as well as in the products of the arts, like houses and other things of the same sort. It is necessary that a certain kind of material be present, if there is to be a house or any other end-product; and it is necessary that this development and motion take place first, then this other, and so on until the end is reached and that for whose sake each preceding step develops and exists. It is the same with things which develop by natural processes. The method of proof, however, and the nature of the necessity, are not the same in natural science as in the theoretical sciences. We have dealt with these matters elsewhere.[2]

7 The first principle of the theoretical sciences is "that which is"; of the natural sciences, "that which is going to be." Since health, or a man, is of such-and-such a character, it is necessary that something else be or happen; we cannot say that since this other thing is or happens, the former necessarily is or will be. Nor can the necessity of successive steps in this sort of demonstration be linked together indefinitely, so as to say, "since this first step takes place, then this last step takes place." We have discussed these matters too in another place, and to what kind of things the kinds of necessity apply, and what propositions about necessity are convertible, and why.[3]

(e) Should we discuss first the process of development of each creature, or its completed state?

8 We must not neglect the further question, whether we should follow the method used by previous investigators, and tell the manner in which each creature has developed rather than what it is like now. There is no small difference between these two methods.

Answer to (e): The completed thing, the final cause, is first; then comes the manner of its development. The process exists for the sake of the product, rather than the product being merely a result of the process.

It seems, though, that we should begin our study in accordance with the previously stated principle, to take first the actual phenomena in each kind, and then speak about their causes, and their development. This is the way with the building of a house, too; since the form of a house—or the house itself—is of such-and-such a character, it develops as it does. *9* The development exists for the sake of the thing, not the thing for the sake of the development. This is why Empedocles is wrong in saying that many of the characteristics of animals are due to their happening to develop in a certain way—for example that the spine is as it is because it happened that it was broken when the foetus was twisted. He failed to recognize, first, that there must be a seed which produces the animal, having this specific potentiality; and second, that the efficient cause is prior not only logically but chronologically. A man begets a man, so that because the father is of such-and-such a nature, the development of the child takes such-and-such a course. *10* The same thing is true of things which seem to happen spontaneously, and also in the products of the arts. Some things (like health) which come about spontaneously are the same as things produced by art. The latter, though, have a pre-existing efficient cause of a similar character to the product—for example in the art of sculpture; and the development is not spontaneous. An art is the rational plan [*logos*] of the product, without the matter. The products of chance, too, come about in the same way as the products of art. Thus, the best statement would be that since this is what it means to be a human being, this is why any individual has these parts; he could not be a human being without these parts. If we cannot say this, we must say the nearest thing, either, generally, that he cannot be a human being in any other way, or that it is good that it should be this way.

Our results will be as follows: Since man is of such-and-such a nature, his development is thus-and-so, and it is necessary that it be as it is. This is why one of his parts comes first and another second. And the process is the same in all things that are constructed by nature.

[In Chapters II and III, Aristotle criticizes at length the method of classification by "division" (employed by Plato in the *Sophist* and the *Statesman*). Chapter IV concludes that animals can best be classified and studied by "groups," such as Birds or Fishes.]

V. The study of animals

Two kinds of subjects for scientific study: the eternal and immutable, and the mortal and changeable

1 Of the substances that exist in nature, some are uncreated and imperishable for all time, and others take part in a process of coming to be and passing away. It happens that the former, though they are honored and divine, are not often the subject of investigation among us; for there is very little that is perceptible to our senses, either of the evidence from which one might study them, or even of the things we would like to know about. With perishable things, however—plants and animals—we have a wealth of opportunity to know them because we live with them. *2* Anyone who is willing to take enough trouble can learn many things about every species there is. Both kinds of study are pleasant. Though our comprehension of the former is but slight, still the knowledge of them, because of their worth, is more pleasant than that of all the things close to us, just as it is more pleasant to catch a random glance of a small part of something we love than to see many other great things very clearly. The others, because we know them better and know more of them, take the greater part of our scientific attention—and also, the fact that they are closer to us and more nearly related to our nature provides some compensation for the advantage of the branches of philosophy that deal with divine objects.

In natural science, not even the minutest details are unworthy of study.

3 Since we have already gone through theoretical philosophy, and stated our views, it remains to us to speak about the nature of living beings, omitting nothing, so far as is possible, either humble or lofty. Even in the aspects of the subject which are not pleasant to the senses, nature in her craftsmanship provides tremendous pleasures for those who are naturally philosophers and who can recognize the causes of things. It would be a strange and paradoxical thing were we to take pleasure in looking at images of these objects (paintings or sculpture) because we perceive at the same time the artistry which produced them, and fail to admire even more the sight of the products of nature themselves, at least if we can perceive their causes. *4* Wherefore, one ought not to be disgusted, in a childish way, at the study of the lower animals. In all that is natural there is something wonderful. And as Heraclitus, according to the story, said to the guests who wished to meet him, when they found him warming himself at the oven and stood there hesitating (he said, "Come in; here too are gods.")—in the same spirit one ought to approach the study of every animal, without making a face, realizing that in each of them there is the work of nature, and beauty. Occurrence not according to chance but for a purpose is present to the highest degree in the works of nature; and the purpose or end for which a thing has been constructed or has developed belongs to the realm of beauty. *5* If anyone thinks the study of the other animals is unworthy, he should have the same opinion of himself; for it is not possible without considerable disgust to look upon the component parts of the human body—blood, flesh, bones, veins, and so on. Likewise, one must regard what is said about any of the parts or structures as being said not about the material, nor for its sake, but about the whole form, as one would discuss a house, and not the bricks, mortar and lumber of which it is composed. A discussion in natural science is about the whole composite being, not about elements which never occur separate from it.

Our method: to study first the attributes common to groups of animals, then their causes

6 Our first task is to distinguish the attributes in each group, those which belong to all animals, and then attempt to determine their causes. We have already remarked that there are many attributes common to many species of animals. Sometimes they are just the same, like feet, feathers, and scales, and also certain affections, and sometimes analogous. By this I mean that, for example, some have lungs, while others do not, but another organ which does the same thing for them. Some have blood, and others something analogous, with the same power that blood has for the former. *7* To speak separately of each individual attribute, as we said before, would involve saying the same thing many times, if we were to discuss every one that exists; many species have the same attributes. So much on this problem.

NOTES TO SELECTIONS FROM ARISTOTLE

Introduction

1. Frag. 658 Rose.
2. H. Kelsen, "The Philosophy of Aristotle and the Hellenic-Macedonian Policy," *Ethics*, XLVII (1937–38), 1–64.
3. *Politics*, I, v, 10 (1260a 39ff.).
4. A. E. Taylor, *Aristotle* (London, n.d.), p. 27.

Nicomachean Ethics

1. See Chapter II, section 1.
2. See *Politics*, I, I, 1 and 9, and notes.
3. The state of having reason and the activity of using it.
4. The Greek word is *êthikê*, "moral," from *ĕthos*, "habit."
5. 2 : 6 :: 6 : 10; to "prove" an arithmetical proportion one adds the extreme terms and the middle terms $(2 + 10 = 6 + 6)$, rather than multiplying them as in a geometrical proportion (2 : 6 :: 6 : 18; $2 \times 18 = 6 \times 6$). In the former, the terms on each side differ by the same amount, in the latter by the same proportion. Cf. *Politics*, III, v, 8; V, I, 2ff.; and especially V, I, 7 and the note there. Aristotle discusses "distributive" and "corrective" justice in *Nicomachean Ethics*, Book V.
6. A famous boxer.
7. An unidentified line of verse.
8. On the Greek word *aretê*, "virtue," which includes the idea of efficiency, of being "good at" something, cf. *Politics*, note 10, below.
9. At this point Aristotle doubtless displayed some sort of "blackboard" which showed in tabular form the type of emotion or action, the excess, the mean, and the defect, for each virtue. The individual virtues are described more fully in Book IV, and he here frequently anticipates that discussion (sections 5, 6, 9, 16). It is noteworthy that so many states must remain nameless; the scheme seems to break down in practice.
10. Aristotle's scheme seems somewhat faulty here, unless a clause has fallen out of the text. There is not a proper antithesis between "malice," which means rejoicing at another's ill fortune, and "envy," which means pain at another's good fortune, particularly when it is deserved.
11. Aristotle is obviously quoting from memory. These are words of Odysseus to his pilot (*Odyssey*, XII, 219), based on the advice of Circe, not Calypso.
12. *Iliad*, III, 156 ff.: "No wonder the Trojans and well-greaved Achaeans suffer hardships for many years, over such a woman; she is terribly like the immortal goddesses in appearance. Yet even so, beautiful as she is, let her go home in the ships, and not leave behind trouble for us and our children."
13. Compare Theophrastus' Character of the "versa-

tile" man, who is the precursor of the "parasites" of the New Comedy.

14. On the idea that pleasure is an unworthy motive for a statesman, cf. Cicero, *On the Chief End of Man*, II, 112.

15. Cf. Pindar, *Isthmian Odes*, V.

16. See Herodotus, I, 30.

17. Line 434.

Politics

1. The word *polis*, sometimes left untranslated, is in these selections given either as "city-state" or "city." It refers to the normal political unit of Greece, an independent city with the surrounding territory and towns, and often is used where English would have "state." Similar qualifications must be made for the frequent derivatives of *polis: politês*, "citizen"; *politikos* as adjective, "social," "political," "constitutional"; *politikos* as noun, "statesman" (though this word really has too favorable a connotation in English, as "politician" would be too unfavorable; it simply means "he who manages public affairs in a *polis*"); *politeuma*, "civic body" (those who have full citizenship and who share in the business of ruling); *politeia*, "government," "constitution," "form of government," "polity" (the last a special form of government, described in the text); *politikê*, "statesmanship" (the art or science of politics).

2. Cf. Plato, *Politicus*, 258e ff.

3. Apparently, a knife which also served other purposes.

4. Euripides, *Iphigenia in Aulis*, line 1400.

5. Hesiod, *Works and Days*, 405. Charondas, in the sixth century B.C., drew up codes of law for various cities in Sicily and south Italy (cf. IV, IX, 10, below). Epimenides was an early (sixth century?) Cretan mystic, miracle-worker, and philosopher.

6. *Odyssey*, IX, 114 (speaking of the Cyclopes).

7. I.e., a "city-state animal," one who can achieve his highest nature only by living in such an organization as the *polis*.

8. *Iliad*, IX, 63.

9. Although individual and family are prior *chronologically* to the city.

10. Note that the word *aretê*, "virtue," connotes not only goodness but excellence, being "good at" something. In the next sentence it means positive moral virtue.

11. *Dikê*, "judgment," means the active ordering, determination, pointing out, decision; *to dikaion*, "the just," is the result of this process.

12. Aristotle apologizes for his terms *gamikê* and *patrikê*, but considers the term *despotikê* quite normal. In English the situation is reversed.

13. This word (*hyperetês*) denotes any kind of subordinate—servant, slave, helper, hireling, apprentice.

14. Homer, *Iliad*, XVIII, 376.

15. I.e., the principle, stated in the preceding sentence, that power goes with goodness. "One side interprets this to mean that power of itself implies goodness, and therefore confers a right (based on the goodness which it implies) to enslave any captive. The other side interprets it to mean that power must be accompanied by goodness —i.e. must have goodness added to it (and thereby the goodwill which goodness conciliates)—before there can be a rightful relation of master and slave which is attended, as such a relation should be, by goodwill."—Barker.

16. Here, and in other passages, "unequal" has the sense of "superior." "Justice is inequality" means that the superior person should get the larger share (of public offices, etc.).

17. "Distributive justice" involves a "what," or things to be distributed, like material goods or political offices, and a "to whom," or persons who are to receive them. Justice consists in assigning the right amount to the right person.

18. Aristotle here breaks off in the middle of his sentence, leaving the *if*-clause dangling, and is carried away into a digression. The thought of this sentence is completed at section 15.

19. "Just" is used several times in this passage in a double sense: "absolutely just," and "legal," i.e., according to the decree of the sovereign power.

20. This technical term (*atimos*), applied to a legal penalty, literally means "dishonored" or "unhonored." Its cognate *timê*, "honor," is often used for the "privileges" of citizenship or for "public office," as in the next clause. It also means "value," "price"; a citizen's *timêma* is his property valuation, which was often used as a criterion for eligibility to vote or hold office (see below, section 12).

21. The word *paideia* ("education," "culture") has not in fact been used in the preceding pages; perhaps Aristotle is referring to Chapter V, section 15, above. Here he seems to connect culture closely with virtue; in a later passage we learn that "culture and high birth are generally associated with wealth" (IV, VI, 2; 1293b 37).

22. I.e., the whole of the citizen body, those who "have a share" in the government, as distinguished from the whole population.

23. "Where are your claws and teeth?"

24. I.e., he is really the whole of the state himself, the entire citizen body.

25. It is not certain to whom Aristotle refers here—possibly Solon (Athenian statesman, archon in 594), or Theramenes (Athenian leader of the moderates in 411 B.C.), or Antipater (who managed Alexander's affairs in Greece while the latter was in Asia).

26. Arithmetical ratio: 3 : 2 :: 2 : 1; proportionate or geometrical ratio: 4 : 2 :: 2 : 1. See *Nicomachean Ethics*, II, VI, 4–7, and the footnote there; *Politics*, III, V, 8 and note.

27. For attendance at assembly and courts.

28. Aristotle has in mind a system in which the voting population is split into several smaller groups, each of which will be more subject than the entire populace would be to its aristocratic members. This is reminiscent of the Roman system (cf. Cicero, *On the Laws,* Vol. II of this anthology).

29. Cf. III, VIII, 3.

Parts of Animals

1. For Aristotle's answer see Chapter V, section 6, below.

2. The theoretical sciences are theology or metaphysics, mathematics, and physics (See *Metaphysics,* VI, I, 4). They are pursued only for their own sakes, or for the sake of contemplation (*theoria*). At the other extreme are sciences whose aim is the production of something (carpentry, poetics) or the regulation of activity (ethics, politics)—the "practical" sciences. But the most significant classification is that according to the degree of "formality." The closer the subject matter of a science approaches to "pure form" (as in metaphysics or theology) the nobler it is; the closer it approaches to "pure matter," or the less complicated the organization of the matter it deals with, the more lowly it is.

3. *De generatione et corruptione,* II, XI, 6.

SELECTIONS FROM EPICURUS

Translated by Herbert M. Howe

INTRODUCTION

Epicurus, the most important of the ancient atomists, was born on the island of Samos in 341. After studying the philosophies of several schools, including the atomism of Democritus, he set up his own in Athens soon after 307, and taught there until his death in 270. His school, called the Garden, continued throughout antiquity, reaching the peak of its popularity in the late Roman republic, when it numbered among its followers many of the most important men of the time. Like the other pagan schools of philosophy, it faded as Christianity came to power, but was still a chief enemy among the philosophies attacked by the Fathers of the Church.

The fundamental doctrine of Epicureanism was that nothing immaterial exists: everything consists of matter and empty space. Matter is made up of innumerable tiny particles, so small that they cannot be divided any further, called atoms; these are always falling through space in a sort of rain. As they fall they occasionally swerve aside from a straight line and come into collision with other atoms; since this swerve is uncaused and unpredictable, the universe is not simply the automatic working of a machine.

The human mind is made up of very fine atoms, whose motion is altered by the impact of films which arise from external objects; they strike the sense organs, and transmit their motion to the atoms of the mind. When we have seen an object several times, we form, as it were, a permanent image, a concept, in our mind; these concepts, by their combination, constitute our thought.

Since the mind as well as the body is material, its atoms are dispersed at death; there is no immortality, and our life is limited to this world. It is here that we must win our happiness, and this is to be attained through the harmonious and untroubled motion of the atoms of body and mind—that is, through pleasure. Pleasure is of two sorts: the positive sort, that we feel when we taste good food or hear good music, and the negative, the absence of pain. The first of these passes quickly, and may be followed by pain; it is at the second that we should aim. Activities like war and politics which lead to turmoil and confusion should be avoided. Rather we should try to live a quiet and retired life, removed from the turmoil of the multitude and concerned only with the cultivation of our own peace.

The gods exist, but by definition they are supremely happy, and are therefore removed from all disturbance and trouble—a state they cannot find in this world, so they are located in the vast spaces between the stars. They have no concern with human affairs, which could only confuse and bother them, and they are therefore not to be swayed by our prayers. Above all, they do not interfere with the order of the universe: comets and eclipses do not come from them as warnings of the future.

By insisting on the purely physical nature of the universe, Epicurus came astonishingly close to many of the discoveries of modern science. For example, his atomic theory, his assertion of the principle of the conservation of matter, his notion of the plurality of worlds, and his descriptions of the origins of species and of human society do not differ greatly from modern ideas on these subjects. But he was not an experimental scientist; all this was speculation deduced from his one fundamental principle, that only matter and void have a real existence. He was not interested in knowledge of physics *per se*, but only as means of removing fear of the unknown.

The enemies of the philosophy pointed out that it emphasized individualism at the expense of public duty, and that it reduced all virtue to the level of convenience. They also maintained that a world governed neither by intelligent gods nor unchanging destiny deprived life of all meaning. Throughout the Middle Ages, when thought was dominated by theology, the philosophy almost disappeared, but interest in it revived in modern times with the rise of materialistic science and humanism.

The selections here are from two letters of Epicurus and a collection of extracts from his writings, the *Golden Maxims,* found in Book X of the *Lives of Eminent Philosophers* of Diogenes Laertius. The text is that of R. D. Hicks in the Loeb Classical Library (London and New York, 1931). Most of the works of Epicurus are preserved only in fragments, and much of what we know of his teaching comes from the writings of his disciples, like the Roman poet Lucretius.

I. Physics

37 The first thing we must fix in our minds in the study of physics, Herodotus, is the reference of the terms used, so that we may have a sure standard of judgment in our investigations, and so that an unproved assumption may not spawn meaningless phrases forever. *38* For every word we utter we must be able to call up a clear mental picture, which needs no further definition, to which we can refer our problems. In the second place, it is axiomatic that we must refer constantly to our sensations, to the judgments of our mind or any other standard we accept, as well as the reports of our senses. Thus only can we confirm the obscure and uncertain.

When these two points are well understood, we can begin to study things which are not obvious. First of all, nothing can come into being where nothing was before, for if it could, anything could arise from any origin, since it would have no need of its own proper source. *39* And nothing can disappear into nothingness; if a thing which disappears to the sight were really annihilated, everything in the world would long since have perished without a trace. The sum of the matter in the world has always been just what it now is and what it always will be. There is nothing outside matter into which matter can change, nor is there anything nonmaterial which could enter in and cause such a transformation.

The whole universe is made up only of matter and empty space. Our own senses bear witness that matter exists, and it is on our senses that the reason must base its advances into the unknown. *40* Now if there were no empty space—call it "void" or "room to move in" or "the intangible" or what you will—there would be no place in which bodies could exist or move about, as we see them doing. Aside from these two, matter and void, there is nothing of which we can form a mental picture, nothing of which we can conceive on the analogy of anything else. . . .

[Epicurus then demonstrates that space is infinite]. *45* There is an unlimited number of worlds, some like this one, some not. For the atoms, which are infinite in number, are always spreading out further and further; and the particles from which a world could be formed could not all have been used up in making this one world, or any limited number. There is, then, nothing to prevent there being an infinite number of worlds. . . .

II. Psychology

63 Our next principle—and here we must examine our perceptions and sensations with care, so that our reliance on this principle may be as sure as possible—is that the "soul" itself is a tenuous sort of matter, dispersed through our whole body. It resembles a mixture of air and fire, being something like each of these substances. But there is also a third part of it, far lighter than air or fire, and because of its lightness it penetrates the whole body. That all this is true is shown by the activity of the mind—its sensitivity, its nimbleness, its power of thought—all things whose loss means death. . . .

*49** We should realize that we see things and think about them when something material passes into us from them. For it is unlikely that external objects should register their shape and color on our minds by pressing the air between them and us, or by rays or currents passing from us to them; it is more reasonable that films of atoms enter us, of the same shape and color as the objects from which they arise. Once in, these films stimulate the sense organs or the mind, depending on the size of their atoms. These films move at enormous speed, (*50*) which is why they present us with a single continuous image. Their atoms keep the same relative position that was impressed on them by the atoms in the depths of the object. Whenever we have an image of something's shape or other property, in our eyes or in our minds, it is that of the object and not of something else; it is produced because the atoms of the film cling together, or, at least, part of them do. Falsehood and error arise, not from our perceptions, but from the conclusions to which we jump about things which have not yet been established as true; in such cases further investigation may not confirm our first opinions, and may even disprove them. . . .

64 Most of our capacity to perceive resides in the soul, but this could not be so unless the soul

* In the letter of Epicurus this paragraph is part of the discussion of the properties of matter (omitted here). Since, however, it contains a good account of the Epicurean theory of perception and thought, the translator has introduced it at this point.

were contained in the body and permeated its every part. The body, by providing the necessary framework, shares with the soul the responsibility for perception, but does not possess all the soul's powers. When the atoms of the soul are scattered in death the body loses its ability to perceive. This power it does not possess of itself, but only as a loan from the soul, which is born with the body. The soul is potentially able to feel; when its atoms are set in motion the potentiality becomes real. It then imparts this power it has gained to the body by its penetration and intimate connection. . . .

III. Anthropology

[The fifth book of Lucretius gives an account of the origins of society which came from Epicurus, but the original is not preserved. In one of the letters, however, Epicurus speaks thus of the origin of language.] *75* The names of things were not originally given them by general agreement among men. People of different tribes perceived and experienced different things. Each man, moved by his perceptions and experiences, shaped the air which he breathed in his own way, a way which was affected by the climate in which his tribe dwelt. *76* Later on the men of each tribe agreed on a common usage, so that their ideas would be less obscure to each other and their communication would be more concise. . . .

IV. The Fear of the Gods and of Death

81 The greatest anxiety suffered by the human mind arises from the belief that the heavenly bodies are divine and imperishable, but still are able to desire and act and cause things. Moreover, men cringe in dread as if they were doomed to some unending evil, probably because of the fairy stories they have heard, and await in terror the unfeeling nothingness of death—as if, forsooth, that affected us at all! They do not suffer thus because they have thought things out, but through a quite unreasoning panic. Indeed, those who set no limit to their frightened pondering are perturbed as much as or more than men who make only random and careless conjectures on these matters. *82* Real peace of mind means freeing one's self from all these bugbears and constantly remembering the real and supreme truths.

Let us, then, confine ourselves to the evidence of sense and feeling, our own and that common to all men, and pay attention only to what can be clearly judged by reliable standards. If we study this evidence, we will understand and eliminate the causes of our fears and anxieties, and will be able to observe with tranquillity the happenings in the sky, and other portents which cause the most extreme terror in the rest of mankind. . . .

123 First believe that God is alive, immortal, and blessed, as the consensus of mankind indicates, but do not attach to him anything inconsistent with his immortality and blessed state; rather believe what supports them. For assuredly the gods exist, and knowledge of them is certain; but they are not like those in whom most men believe, for the multitude is not consistent in the conception it forms of the gods. . . .

124 Accustom yourself to the realization that death concerns us not at all. For good and bad exist only by being perceived, and death deprives us of perception. Once we understand this truth, that death does not concern us, even our mortality becomes a source of pleasure: we give up our attempts to add eternity to our span of life here, and can abandon our vain longing for immortality. Life holds no terrors for him who realizes that there are none in death. This worst of horrors, the fear of death, affects us not at all; for while we are, death is not, and when death is, we are not.

V. Ethics

127 We must remember that of our desires some are natural, others purposeless; of the natural ones, some are necessary, others not. Of the necessary desires, some are essential to life, others to bodily comfort, others to happiness.

128 The man who understands this will govern his choices and his rejections by considering the health of his body and the tranquillity of his soul; this is the purpose of a happy life. To this end of feeling no pain or insecurity we direct all our actions; when once we have gained this, the storms that trouble the soul are calmed, and we no longer need to go in search of what we lack or hunt for anything good to fulfill the needs of body or soul. When we suffer from a lack of pleasure, then only do we feel its need; when we are not in pain, we need no more. *129* Pleasure, then, we call the beginning and end of a happy life. We know that it is our first and inborn good; for its sake we choose or avoid things; we use our feelings as the standard for measuring every good.

Pleasure is our greatest good, and desire for it is born in us; yet we do not clutch at every pleasure that offers itself but sometimes pass over delights from which a greater pain may result. Pain itself, indeed, often seems preferable to pleasure, if greater pleasure will follow our enduring it. Everything pleasant is good, for it is naturally fitted to us, but it does not follow that we should choose it. In like manner every pain is an evil, but not all painful things must be avoided. *130* By a sort of calculus, by examining and comparing the good or evil in things, we must decide our course. Sometimes we will regard pleasure as an evil and pain as a good.

Independence of external things, too, we regard as a great good, not in order that we may always want to live frugally, but that we may be content to do so if we should have to. For we are convinced that those who need luxury least enjoy it most. Natural pleasures are easily gained; it is the useless ones which are costly. Simple food brings as much delight as rare and choice dishes, even when the edge of appetite is dulled, (*131*) and bread and water bring the highest pleasure to one in real need of food. . . .

When we assert that pleasure is the chief motive of life, we are not speaking of dissipation and intemperance, as some ignorant, prejudiced, or malicious people think. No; we mean the absence of discomfort in the body and disturbance in the soul. *132* Wild revels and orgies, gorges of rich food, cannot produce a happy life; the soul can best free itself from anxiety and tumult which haunt it by sober thought and searching out the reasons for its choices and rejections. Common sense is the beginning of this, and is the most valuable thing a man can have. It is more precious even than philosophy, for all the other virtues arise from it. It shows that we cannot live happily unless we live with intelligence, honor, and justice, and that we cannot live intelligently, honorably, and justly without being happy. All the virtues merge in the happy life, which cannot be separated from them.

133 Can you think of anyone who is better off than a man who leads this life? His ideas about the gods are reverent. He has no terror at the thought of death, which he views as the end established for us by nature. He knows how easily his natural desires can be fulfilled, and that any evils which he suffers are either short-lived or not severe. Destiny, which some [the Stoics] bring in as the ruler of all things, he laughs at: some things, he says are predestined, some happen by chance, and some come about through our own activity; if destiny ruled, man would have no responsibility, and if chance, she is a fickle tyrant. No; our choice is free, and on the choices we make depends the praise or blame we deserve. . . .

VI. Selection from the Golden Maxims

1. *139* A blessed and immortal being feels no trouble in himself and makes none for others. He is, therefore, subject neither to anger nor to affection, things which only accompany weakness. . . .

2. Death is nothing to us; for when the body has been destroyed it feels nothing, and a state of feeling nothing is no concern to us.

3. The limit of the intensity of pleasure is the removal of all pain. As long as we feel pleasure, there can be no pain or sorrow in the body or the mind.

4. *140* Severe pain of the flesh does not last long. Extreme anguish is very short-lived, and even pain which barely outweighs pleasure remains only for a few days. Diseases which do last a long time may even allow the sufferer to feel more pleasure than pain. . . .

11. *142* If the phenomena of the heavens had never terrified us, if we had never felt ourselves somehow concerned with death, and if we had never failed to recognize the limits of pain and desire, we would never have had any need to study the workings of nature. . . .

14. *143* First of all we seek a reasonable degree of security from other men. After that our desire seeks something else, the security of a quiet life, withdrawn from the crowd. This depends on our having a comfortable prosperity and wealth enough to support us. . . .

18. *144* Pleasure cannot be increased in the flesh once the pain caused by want has been removed; from then on it can only be varied. . . .

31. *150* Natural justice is a short term for the expediency found in not harming others on condition that they shall not harm us. . . .

33. There never was such a thing as abstract or absolute justice, but men made contracts in various times and places not to harm others or be harmed themselves. . . .

37. *152* If the letter of any law is admitted to be appropriate to the conditions of men's relations that exist, by that very fact the law acquires the character of justice, whether or not it be the same for all. But if someone writes a law which turns out not to be useful in men's relations, it no longer shares the spirit of justice. If conditions of usefulness change, so that they fit the terms expressed in the law only for a little while, the law is just for that little while and no more—if, that is, we look at the facts and do not bother our heads with mere empty verbiage.

PLUTARCH'S *Life of Tiberius Gracchus*

Translated by Herbert M. Howe

INTRODUCTION

THE PRACTICE of writing accounts of the lives of famous men goes back at least as far as Xenophon's biographies of Socrates and Agesilaus in the early part of the fourth century B.C., and there are many later examples of the form; but the most famous ancient biographies are surely the *Parallel Lives* of Plutarch. Their author was born in Chaeronea in Central Greece about A.D. 46; he studied in Athens, and later spent some time in Italy on political business. During his stay there he lectured on philosophy. Returning to Chaeronea, he remained there teaching and writing for most of the rest of his life. He was active in the politics of his town, and may have been made consul at Rome; the Emperor Hadrian appointed him procurator of Achaea (Greece). He seems to have died about 127.

The language used by Plutarch is Greek, and his work is an excellent example of the Greek culture which continued to flourish long after the decline of the great cities of Greece—a culture which borrowed heavily, first from Asia and then from Rome, but which still used the old language. Even after the political supremacy of Rome had been established for centuries, there was hardly an author born in the East who wrote in Latin; even those who wrote on Roman history preferred Greek.

Plutarch's works fall into two groups: the *Lives* and a long series of miscellaneous works on such diverse topics as philosophy, archaeology, and politics, the *Moralia*. The forty-four *Lives* are almost all arranged in pairs, one of a famous Greek being coupled with one of a Roman whose life was similar. Most of the pairs are followed by a comparison of their subjects. The emphasis is on the characters of the men described rather than on the history of their times, for Plutarch was a moralist who was convinced that history is made by the characters of its actors rather than by their social or economic surroundings.

The life of Tiberius Gracchus is taken from the only set of four biographies—those of Agis and Cleomenes, Spartan kings of the third century B.C., who tried to revive the decaying institutions of their city, and those of Tiberius Gracchus and his brother Gaius, who tried to cope with the decay of rural Italy. The devastation of the peninsula in the war with Hannibal and the many foreign wars of Rome, which drew farmers into the army for long periods, had made small-scale farming by free citizens impracticable; and the situation was made worse by the practice of importing cheap foreign grain. Many farmers migrated to the city to live a life of poverty; their land was taken over by men with enough capital to embark on the more profitable production of olives, wine, and livestock. This trend the Gracchi tried to reverse, but with only partial success; the main result of their endeavors was the drawing of the line for political conflicts of the next hundred years.

Plutarch's *Lives* have always been among the most widely read works of antiquity, and mention should be made of two examples of their influence. An English translation by Sir Thomas North appeared in 1579 (made not from the Greek but from an earlier French version); this translation was the source used by Shakespeare for *Coriolanus, Julius Caesar,* and *Antony and Cleopatra.* Two hundred years later the founders of the American and French republics took many of their ideas on government from antiquity, and their notions of Athens and Rome came largely from the *Lives.*

THE GREEK text translated is that of C. Sintenis (Leipzig, 1889).

---

1 Now that we have told the story of Agis and Cleomenes, we shall compare with them a pair of Romans, Tiberius and Gaius Gracchus, whose lives were no less tragic. They were the sons of Tiberius Gracchus, who was censor and twice consul of the Romans, and who celebrated two triumphs. Yet his reputation for virtue was even greater than the fame of his achievements, and on this account he was considered a suitable husband for Cornelia, the daughter of Scipio, the conqueror of Hannibal, after her father's death. This was true even though Gracchus had by no means been a friend of Scipio, but had, indeed, been at odds with him.

The story is told that Gracchus once caught a pair of snakes in his bed, and consulted the soothsayers about this portent. They replied that he should neither kill both nor let both go, but should decide which one he would destroy: if the male were killed, it would bring death to Gracchus, while the female's death would mean the end of Cornelia. Now Gracchus was very fond of his wife; and he felt that it was better for him to die than her, since he was the elder and she was still quite young. Accordingly, he killed the male snake and let the female go. A little later, the story continues, he died, leaving Cornelia with the twelve children she had borne him.

Cornelia took over the children and the estate, and displayed such modesty, affection, and greatness of spirit that her husband may well be thought to have chosen wisely when he died for such a woman. When Ptolemy, the king of Egypt, wanted to marry her and offered to share his crown, she refused him. During her widowhood she lost all her children but one daughter, who married the younger Scipio, and two sons, Tiberius and Gaius, about whom I am now writing. She brought them up with such care that, although they were unquestionably the most talented of all the Romans, it was agreed that their education contributed more to their ability than did their natural character.

[Plutarch here inserts a comparison of the brothers: Tiberius quiet and restrained, Gaius fiery and outspoken; both brave and completely honest. He then describes the marriage of Tiberius to the daughter of Appius Claudius.]

4 The young Tiberius served in the army in Africa under his brother-in-law Scipio. As he shared the same tent with the general, he learned much from Scipio's character which offered many incitements to virtue and examples of actions to imitate. Tiberius, accordingly, soon outstripped all his fellows both in discipline and in courage. At a certain siege he was the first to scale the walls, according to the historian Fannius, who claims to have gone up with him and to have shared his glorious action. As long as Tiberius was with the army he won universal good feeling, and when he left he was much regretted.

5 After this expedition he was elected quaestor, and was appointed to the staff of the consul Gaius Mancinus in the war against Numantia [in Spain]. This Mancinus was a man of good character, but was certainly the most unfortunate of all the Roman generals. In the midst of unexpected reverses and disasters the intelligence and courage of Tiberius were the more apparent; and, what is more remarkable, he still showed the greatest respect and reverence for his commander, whose misfortunes had almost made him forget that he was the general. For after Mancinus had been beaten in several major battles, he tried to abandon camp and withdraw by night. When the Numantines realized this, they promptly seized the camp; then, falling upon the Romans as they retreated, they massacred the rear guard. They then surrounded the whole army and forced it into an indefensible position, from which no escape was possible.

Mancinus now despaired of fighting his way out, and sent a messenger to ask for an armistice and terms of peace. The Numantines replied that they trusted no one but Tiberius, and demanded that he be sent to them. This they did both because of the young man's own reputation, which stood very high in the army, and because they still remembered his father. He had once fought in Spain and had subdued many tribes, but had made a treaty with the Numantines, to which he had held the Roman people with justice and fidelity. So Tiberius was sent; in the parley he made some concessions but gained such others from the Numantines that he was able to sign a peace by which he undoubtedly saved the lives of twenty thousand Roman citizens, beside those of the slaves and camp followers. . . .

[In the sack of the Roman camp, the Numantines seized the official account books of Tiberius. To get them back, he personally approached the city and asked that they be returned to him, so that he might not be accused of financial mismanagement. The Numantines not only gave back the books, but urged him to take all his own property; this offer, however, he declined.]

7 When Tiberius returned to Rome, he found that the whole affair was regarded as a disgrace and dishonor to the city. The friends and neighbors of the soldiers, who formed a sizeable part of the citizens, came to his support and agreed that it was through his efforts that these men had been saved; the blame for the failure of the expedition they laid entirely upon the general. In their anger at the fiasco, they urged that the example of their ancestors be followed. For when their generals had thought themselves lucky to have escaped from the Samnites on similar terms, the Romans had turned them over unarmed to the enemy; they had likewise given up the military tribunes and quaestors who had shared in making the treaty, and had made them responsible for the perjury involved in breaking it. [This had happened in 321; the Roman Senate refused to ratify the treaty and continued the war.] On the present occasion the people showed their regard for Tiberius in an extraordinary way: they decreed that Mancinus should be delivered to the Numantines, unarmed and in chains, but that all the rest of the officers should be spared for the sake of Tiberius. Scipio seems to have helped bring this about; he was then the most influential and powerful man in Rome. Yet even he was blamed for not saving Mancinus, and for not working to see that the treaty with the Numantines was kept, a treaty which had been arranged by his friend and cousin Tiberius. It seems to me that the differences between these two arose chiefly from the ambition of Tiberius, and were encouraged by the intellectuals who were egging him on. Indeed, I do not think that Tiberius would have met his ruin at all if Scipio had been with him when he introduced his reforms. But Scipio was out fighting the Numantines when Tiberius began his political activity.

The circumstances were these. *8* The Romans had long made a practice, when they conquered their neighbors in war, of dividing up their land. Part they sold and part they added to the public domain; this latter they distributed, for a nominal rent paid into the public treasury, to the poor and landless citizens. But presently the rich began to offer a larger rent and to drive out the small men who could not pay, and a law had to be passed [in 367] that no one man might hold over five hundred acres. For a while this law held in check the avarice of the rich and defended the poor, who could still stay on the land that they had rented in the past. Later, however, their rich neighbors again managed to take over the land of the poor, by using false names; and finally they controlled most of the public domain quite openly. The poor who were thus driven out no longer registered for military service, nor did they bother about the rearing of children. Thus the whole of Italy began to feel the lack of free laborers, and the country was filled with barbarian slaves, by whom the rich farmed the land from which they had driven the freeholders. Gaius Laelius, the friend of the younger Scipio, tried to mend matters, but was frightened by the resistance of the powerful interests and gave up the attempt; as a result he was given the surname of "the Wise" or "the Prudent" (for the word "Sapiens" might mean either of these).

As soon as Tiberius was elected tribune [for 133], he embarked on the same venture, at the instigation, as most people say, of Diophanes, the teacher of rhetoric, and Blossius the philosopher. The first of these was an exile from Mitylene, and the other came from Cumae in Italy. Blossius had been a close friend to Antipater of Tarsus [a celebrated Stoic] during his residence in Rome, and had been honored in the dedications of some of his philosophical works. Some people say that Cornelia was partly responsible, for she often reproached her sons by remarking that the Romans called her "the mother-in-law of Scipio" rather than "the mother of the Gracchi." Others claim that one Spurius Postumius was to blame. He was a man of the same age as Tiberius, and his rival in public speaking. When Tiberius returned from the army, he found that Postumius had won a reputation and influence far greater than his, and was generally admired; Tiberius then determined to outdo him by embarking on a political measure of great daring, which would arouse the highest expectations. But his brother Gaius wrote in one of his pamphlets that when Tiberius was on his way to Numantia he had to pass through Etruria [the modern Tuscany, north of Rome]. Here he noticed that the country was almost deserted, and that the few farmers and shepherds who did live there were barbarian slaves. It was then that he began to think about his reforms, which were to bring such troubles in their train. But actually the people themselves did most to fire his energy and ambition. For on all the porticoes, walls, and statues in public places they scribbled appeals to him to restore the public lands to the poor.

9 He did not draft his proposals entirely by himself, but made use of the virtue and reputation of the first men in the state; among them he consulted Crassus the Pontifex Maximus, Mucius Scaevola the jurist, who was then consul, and Appius Claudius, his own father-in-law. Surely no milder and more moderate law was ever drawn up to check such greed and injustice. For the men who certainly ought to have been forced to give up the land they held illegally, and who should have been fined as well—these men were bidden only to give up their illicitly held property in return for compensation, and to allow such citizens as needed help to settle on it. Although the proposals for reform were so moderate, the people were satisfied, and were quite ready to forget the past, if only they could prevent a recurrence of the abuse.

The rich, however, hated the law because of their greed, and its maker because of their envy; they accordingly tried to turn the people against Tiberius, claiming that he was trying to overthrow the government by his law, and was plotting all sorts of subversive activity. In this attempt they failed completely. For when Tiberius turned his eloquence, which would have made a far poorer cause seem plausible, to a matter as just and honorable as this, he was quite irresistible. Whenever the people crowded around the rostra to listen to him, he would plead for the poor in such terms as these: "The wild beasts that dwell throughout Italy have each his own lair in which to sleep, but the men who fight and die for her have a share in her air and sunlight and nothing more; they must wander, homeless and unsettled, along her roads with their wives and children. When the generals in the army exhort their men to keep the enemy from the graves and shrines of their ancestors, it is a mockery; hardly a man of all those citizens still owns the altar of his fathers, or the spot where their ashes rest. No; they must fight for the wealth and luxury of others, for these they must die; and though they are the lords of all the earth, they possess not a clod of their homeland to call their own."

10 None of the opponents of Tiberius could counter such eloquence, delivered by a man of his spirit and passionate devotion to his cause, before a people roused to enthusiastic sympathy. They therefore made no attempt to reply, but turned to Marcus Octavius, one of the tribunes, a modest and talented young man and a close friend of Tiberius. At first he declined his task out of respect for his friend, but finally, under the pressure of the great and influential men of the state, he stood up against Tiberius and forbade the bringing of the law to a vote. This right of veto is the source of a tribune's power, for if one of them objects, the others together can accomplish nothing. Angered by this resistance, Tiberius withdrew his mild proposals and introduced others more drastic to the offenders and therefore more pleasing to the people, which peremptorily ordered the occupiers to vacate the land they held contrary to former laws.

Now there were daily debates on the rostra between Tiberius and Octavius; yet in them, although the men were contesting with all their fervor, it is said that neither uttered a single word of angry abuse of his opponent; for honorable character and discipline can control the spirit, not only when it is raised by drunkenness, but at any moments of strife and anger. When Tiberius saw that Octavius himself would be liable to the law (for he held a good deal of public land), he begged him to refrain from his opposition, and offered to pay the price of the land out of his own pocket, although he was not rich. Octavius refused this offer; Tiberius then used his veto to keep the rest of the magistrates from carrying out their work until his measure should be voted on. He set his own seal on the temple of Saturn [the public treasury], so that the quaestors could neither deposit nor withdraw money, and he ordered that fines should be laid on any praetor who resisted his orders. These orders so alarmed the magistrates that they all gave up the performance of their duties. At this the wealthy put on mourning and went about the Forum as if in the deepest sorrow and misery. But at the same time they were secretly plotting against the life of Tiberius and hiring assassins to kill him; for his part, he began, with everyone's knowledge, to wear a bandit's knife for defense.

11 On the day set for the vote, when Tiberius called the people together, the party of the rich carried off the ballot boxes, a proceeding which threw everything into confusion. The followers of Tiberius, however, were numerous enough to carry things by force, and were actually preparing to do so, when Manlius and Fulvius, two men of consular rank, fell on their knees before him and begged him to show restraint. He realized how serious the consequences of his actions would be, and out of respect for the consulars he asked them what he should do. They replied that they were not capable of advising him on so grave a matter, and recommended that he refer the question to the Senate. He agreed; but the influence of the rich in the Senate was so great that his proposals got nowhere.

Tiberius then resorted to a step which was neither just nor honorable, the deposition of Octavius from his tribunate, for he saw no other way to bring the measure to a vote. First of all he asked him publicly, in the most kindly but earnest tones, to defer to the people, who were only asking for what was right, and who would receive a small enough return for the trouble and danger they had endured. Octavius rejected this advance; Tiberius then declared that it was impossible for both of them to hold offices of equal power, differing as they did on such important matters, for such a situation could only lead to open war. The only solution he could see, said he, was for one of them to give up his office. He therefore first bade Octavius take the vote of the people on whether he, Tiberius, should continue in office; he promised, if the people so decided, to descend from the rostra, a private citizen. When Octavius refused to do this, Tiberius announced his intention of taking a vote on the tribunate of his opponent, unless Octavius thought the matter over and changed his mind.

12 On these terms he dissolved the assembly. The next day the people gathered again; Tiberius once more mounted the rostra and tried to persuade Octavius. But Octavius remained immoveable, so Tiberius introduced a motion to strip him of his tribunate, and he ordered the people to give their voice at once. There were thirty-five tribes; when seventeen had voted and only one more was needed to reduce Octavius to a private citizen, Tiberius bade the people wait. He embraced Octavius, and in full sight of the assembly once more urged him, in the most affectionate way, not to submit himself to the shame of deposition, nor to force him to endure the reproach of having taken so serious and violent a measure. They say that Octavius was much moved by this request; for a long time he stood in silence, with tears in his eyes. But when he saw the rich and powerful standing by, he was ashamed of himself; and, fearing a bad reputation with them, he put off his fear and bade Tiberius to do as he pleased. The motion was passed, and Tiberius ordered one of his own freedmen, whom he used as lictors, to remove Octavius from the rostra, a deed which made the plight of Octavius seem all the sadder. The people at once fell on him, and though the rich came to his defense and warded off the blows, they had difficulty in protecting him from the angry crowd. Indeed, one of his faithful slaves stepped forward to defend him, and in doing so had his eyes torn out. All this happened against the will of Tiberius; as soon as he realized what was happening he ran up eagerly to stop the violence.

13 The agrarian law was then passed, and three men were chosen to survey and distribute the land: Tiberius himself, his father-in-law Appius Claudius, and his brother Gaius, who was not in Rome but was serving with Scipio against Numantia. These appointments Tiberius arranged without difficulty, and he had a new tribune chosen—not one of the prominent people, but a client of his, one Mucius. The powerful group resented all this, and they dreaded the rise of Tiberius to power. In the Senate he was continually insulted. For example, when he asked for a tent at public expense, to use in distributing the land—a perfectly ordinary request—he was refused, although men on far less important business had often been granted more. Again, on the motion of Publius Nasica, the Senate allowed him nine sesterces [about forty cents] a day for expenses. Nasica had surrendered entirely to his hatred of Tiberius, for he held a great deal of public land and resented having to give it up.

But at the same time the anger of the people was rising more and more. One of the friends of Tiberius died suddenly, with certain mysterious marks on his body. At this everyone shouted that he had been poisoned; the people stopped the funeral, carried away the corpse, and watched it while it was burnt. Their suspicions of poisoning were confirmed, for the body burst open and so much corrupt liquid flowed out that the fire was extinguished. More fire was brought and the pyre was moved, but whatever they did, they could scarcely burn the body. After this incident Tiberius aroused them still more by going into mourning. He brought his children to the rostra and begged the people to look after them and their mother, for he despaired of his own survival.

14 About this time Attalus Philometor [the last king of Pergamum, in Asia Minor] died, and Eudemus of Pergamum brought forth his will. In this the Roman people were named as his heirs. To consolidate the favor of the people, Tiberius introduced a bill which proposed that the money of the king should be given to the citizens who were being assigned land, so that they would have enough to buy tools and start cultivation. He also maintained that the Senate had no right to decide what was to be done with the cities of the kingdom of Attalus; this matter he would refer to the judgment of the people. This proposal, of course, infuriated the Senate. One Pompeius arose and announced that he lived near Tiberius, and therefore knew for a fact that Eudemus the Pergamene had given the royal crown and purple robe to Tiberius, since he intended to be king of Rome. [Here several other attacks on Tiberius are described.]

15 Tiberius soon began to realize that his action against Octavius had alarmed not only the powerful, but the multitude as well, for they felt that the dignity of the tribunes, which had been carefully guarded up to that time, had been weakened and insulted. He therefore made another speech before the people, part of the argument of which it would be proper to quote, so that the reader may understand the man's persuasiveness and force. He admitted that the person of a tribune was inviolable, because he was dedicated to the people and was the people's leader. "But if he changes his character and does the people harm, by checking their power and preventing the exercise of their right to vote," he continued, "he has deprived himself of his immunity by not observing the conditions on which he was elected. If this were not so, we would have to leave him untouched, even though he demolished the capitol or set fire to the navy yard. By such acts as these he would show that he was a bad tribune; but if he attacks the people's rights he is no tribune at all. A tribune, the leader of the people, can imprison a consul; would it not be a terrible thing if the people, who gave the tribune his power, could not take it away when it is used against them? For tribunes and consuls alike are elected by the people. Again, royalty embraces all power in itself, and the king is crowned with the most solemn religious ceremonies, before the very eyes of the gods. Yet the city expelled Tarquin [the last of the kings, driven out in 510] for his misdeeds; because of the arrogance of one man, the ancestral form of government under which Rome had been founded was destroyed. In all Rome who are as venerable and sacred as the Vestal Virgins, who tend the undying fire? Yet if one of them violates her oath, she is buried alive; if she transgresses the laws of the gods, she forfeits the immunity granted her on the gods' account. Surely it is no more just that a tribune who injures the people should keep the immunity that the people have granted, for he subverts the very power which upholds him. And if it is right for him to hold office because a majority of the tribes have elected him, is it not right that he should lose it if the unanimous vote of the tribes so decides? Again, there is nothing as sacred and inviolable as the offerings to the gods; yet no one has hindered the people from removing or altering these as it has seen fit. It is, then, certainly proper to shift the tribunate from one man to another, since it, too, is something consecrated. And it is evident that this office is not one from which no man may be removed, for its holders have often sworn that they were not qualified, and have voluntarily asked to be deposed." *16* These were the points that Tiberius made in his defense.

When his friends considered the threats to which he was subject and the conspiracy being formed against him, they felt that it was essential that he be reelected tribune for another term of a year. To win reelection, he sought popular support by introducing more new laws: one shortened the term of compulsory military service, another granted the right of appeal from the decision of the judges to that of the people, and a third added to the existing judges, who were all senators, an equal number of knights. Indeed, he tried in every way to break the senatorial power, rather because of his anger against the Senate than from any consideration of justice or expediency.

On the day for voting on these measures, the friends of Tiberius saw that his opponents' party was the stronger, for all the people were not present at the assembly. For a while they deliberately wasted time in dispute with other officials, and finally adjourned the meeting until the next day. Tiberius himself went down into the forum, and with tears in his eyes he humbly entreated the citizens, and then declared that he was afraid that his enemies would break into his house that night and kill him. By these words he so aroused the citizens that many of them spent that night in the open outside his house to serve as a guard.

[The next morning several evil omens appeared, but in spite of them Tiberius determined to attend the assembly.] *17* When he had gone a little way from his house, he saw two ravens fighting on the roof of a house on his left; one of them dropped a stone which fell right at the feet of Tiberius, as he advanced with a great crowd of followers—an omen which shook the bravest of them. But Blossius of Cumae, who was among them, remarked, "Truly, it would be a shameful thing if Tiberius, the son of Gracchus, the grandson of Scipio Africanus, the champion of the Roman people, should not listen to the appeals of his fellow citizens because he was afraid of a raven! How your enemies would laugh; how they would accuse you of acting already like a fickle tyrant!"

At this moment several messengers approached Tiberius from his friends in the Capitol, urging him to hurry, since everything was ready. And indeed, everything did seem to favor him at first, for as soon as he appeared the people welcomed him with cheers, greeted him with delight as he approached, and arranged themselves so that none of his foes could get at him. *18* But as soon as Mucius began to call the roll of the tribes he found that he could do nothing in proper form, because of the uproar on the edges of the crowd, where the two factions were milling and jostling each other as they forced their way in. Just then a senator, Fulvius Flaccus, climbed up on something and signalled with his hand (since he could not make himself heard) that he had something to say privately to Tiberius. Tiberius asked the people to make way; with some difficulty Flaccus approached and informed him that a group of the rich had been unable to win over the consul at a meeting of the Senate; they had therefore decided to kill Tiberius themselves, and had armed many of their clients and slaves for this purpose.

19 Tiberius reported this to the men around him. They promptly tucked up their togas and seized the fasces with which the lictors controlled the crowd. These they broke up, to defend themselves with the pieces. The people at a distance were surprised at this and asked what Tiberius was doing; he touched his head to indicate that he was in danger, since they could not have heard him speak. Those of his enemies who saw this ran off at once to the Senate House and told the story that Tiberius was seeking a crown; the proof was that he had held his hands up to his head. All the senators roared their rage; and Nasica demanded that the consul come to the aid of the state and destroy the tyrant. The consul replied quietly that he would not take any violent measures, nor would he condemn any citizen without a trial; but if the people, urged or forced on by Tiberius, voted to do anything illegal, he would see to it that their acts were annulled. At this Nasica jumped to his feet. "The man at the head of the state has betrayed it!" he cried. "All you who want to defend the laws, follow me!" With these words he pulled the edge of his toga up over his head [for protection] and ran out to the Capitol. Each of his followers twisted his toga about his arm and forced his way through the crowd, where, because of their dignity, no one resisted them; rather, the people thrust each other aside and fled. The slaves of the senators had brought clubs and bludgeons from home, and they seized the pieces and legs of the benches broken by the fleeing crowd. With these they advanced on Tiberius, striking aside those who tried to defend him, who either fled or were massacred. One of the senators caught hold of the toga of Tiberius as he turned to flee. He dropped the garment, but as he ran off without it he tripped and fell over some of the bodies of those fallen in front of him. As he leaped up, everyone saw Publius Satureius, one of his fellow tribunes, hit him on the head with the leg of a bench. One Lucius Rufus struck the second blow, and afterward gloried in it as a noble deed. Over three hundred men were killed with stones and clubs, but not a single one with the sword.

20 This is said to have been the first civil dispute in Rome to be settled by bloodshed and the murder of citizens since the expulsion of the kings; all others—some of them considerable, and over important matters—were ended when the Senate gave way out of fear of the people, or the people out of reverence for the Senate. And it is probable that if Tiberius had been treated with respect he would have compromised without making trouble, and he would certainly have given way if his opponents had not come spreading blood and injury, since he did not have more than three thousand followers. It is probable that the rising of the nobles came more from anger and hatred than from the reasons they alleged; of this a strong proof is to be seen in their barbarous and inhuman treatment of his corpse. This they did not allow his brother to carry off by night for burial, as he wished, but they threw it, along with those of the others, into the river. Furthermore, they banished some of his friends without trial, and arrested and killed others. [Here follow details of the treatment of the friends of Tiberius. Diophanes was killed, one Gaius Villius was shut up in a cask with poisonous snakes. Blossius maintained that he had done everything at the bidding of Tiberius, and stoutly insisted that Tiberius would never have given a harmful order; but he admitted that if Tiberius had done so, he would have obeyed. Blossius was acquitted, and soon afterward died in a revolt in Asia.]

21 The Senate now wished to quiet the resentment of the people at its acts, and raised no more opposition to the division of the land, and even proposed the election of another commissioner in place of Tiberius. [The number enrolled in the census, we know from other sources, increased by almost one fourth in the next five years.]

The people, however, were obviously angered by the death of Tiberius, and it was clear that they were only waiting for an opportunity for vengeance; they even made some attempts to bring Nasica to trial. The Senate, in its fear for his safety, voted to send him on a mission to Asia, although he was not needed for anything there. For the people were not hiding their resentment when they met him, but were threatening him on every occasion, calling him an accursed tyrant who had polluted the holiest of the city's temples with sacred and inviolable blood. So Nasica left Italy, in spite of the obligations of his ritual duties, for he was Pontifex Maximus. For some time he wandered about abroad, held in general contempt, and died a little later at Pergamum. We should not be surprised that the people so hated Nasica, for even Scipio Africanus (than whom none of the Romans seemed more honorable or more respected) nearly lost the favor of the people. For when he was at Numantia and learned of the death of Tiberius, he quoted the line of Homer, "So perish all who do such evil things." . . .

SELECTIONS FROM EPICTETUS

Translated by Walter R. Agard

INTRODUCTION

WHEN AUTOCRATIC rule put an end to the political initiative and responsibility which the individual citizen had enjoyed in both democratic Greece and Republican Rome, one philosophy served more adequately than any other to offer consolation: Stoicism, with its doctrine that man could still control all that essentially matters, his own moral will; and that he shares in the Universal Reason which governs the world unerringly.

Epictetus, accepting these traditional principles of the Stoics, became their greatest exemplar and teacher. Born about A.D. 50, of a slave mother in Phrygia, he lived in Rome as a slave of the Emperor Nero's administrative secretary, was permitted by his master to study philosophy, and after being freed taught in the marketplace at Rome. After his banishment by the Emperor Domitian, he established a school of philosophy in Epirus which attracted many students. He wrote nothing for publication; but one of his pupils, Flavius Arrian, took down in shorthand his comments on Stoic texts and published these *Discourses*, as well as the *Manual*, a summary of Stoic doctrine. In the *Discourses* we see Epictetus as a teacher discussing problems informally with his pupils, intent on winning them to the acceptance of his way of life.

Perhaps because of his experience as a slave, Epictetus always emphasized the idea of freedom; and because of his Oriental background his feeling toward Providence was more intimate and fervent than one ordinarily finds in philosophers. These were his most original contributions to Stoic doctrine. But his chief contribution was not in doctrine but in example; he was recognized in his own time, as he was later by Christian theologians, professional philosophers, and many others concerned with the problems of human conduct, as an outstanding ethical guide.

Like his fellow Stoics, he may be charged with neglecting the need of positive action against injustice and oppression (endurance and renunciation are not enough) and with too high a regard for the capacity of reason. But the lessons he taught and practised of human dignity, social duty, courage, and faith have continued ever since to set sparks to men's spirits.

THE TEXT on which this translation is based is that of W. A. Oldfather (London and New York, 1926). In this interpretation and the following translation special indebtedness to Mr. Oldfather is gratefully acknowledged.

I. HUMAN FREEDOM

The man is free who lives without hindrance, dealing with things readily as he wishes. But the man who can be hindered or compelled or thwarted or driven into anything against his will is a slave. And who lives without hindrance? He who aims at nothing that is not his own. And what things are not our own? Whatever we are powerless to have or not to have, or to have of a certain quality or under certain conditions. The body, then, is not our own, its parts are not our own, property is not our own. If you crave one of these things as if it were your own, you will pay the price merited by the man who desires what is not his own. The road leading to freedom, the only release from slavery, is to be able to say whole-heartedly:

> Lead me on, O Zeus and Destiny,
> Where I was once assigned by Thy decree.

—*Discourses*, IV, 1

Of all existing things some are under our control and some are not. Under our control are conception, impulse, desire, and aversion: in a word, everything which is our own doing. Things not under our control include the body, property, reputation, office, and, in a word, everything which is not our own doing. Things under our control are by nature free, unhindered, untrammelled; things not under our control are weak, servile, subject to hindrance, dependent on others. Remember, then, that if you think that which is naturally slavish is free, and that which is another's is your own, you will be hampered, you will mourn, you will be put to confusion, you will blame both gods and men; but if you think that only your own belongs to you and that what is another's is actually another's, no one will ever compel or hinder you, you will blame no one, you will accuse no one, you will do nothing against your will, you will have no enemy, no one will harm you, for you can suffer no harm.

—*Manual,* 1

Where, then, is progress? If any one of you, withdrawing from external things, has devoted himself to his own moral purpose, working and laboring on it so as to make it harmonious with nature, lofty-spirited, free, unhindered, unhampered, faithful, and honorable; and if he has learned that the man who desires or tries to escape from the things not under his control cannot be either faithful or free, but changing and fluctuating with them, must submit himself to other people who can secure or prevent them . . . this man is truly making progress, this man has not strayed off his course.

—*Discourses,* I, 4

It is impossible for that which is free by nature to be thrown into confusion or thwarted by anything except itself. But a man's own judgments confuse him. For when the tyrant says to someone, "I shall chain your leg," the man who values his leg says, "Don't do it. Pity me"; but the man who values his moral purpose says, "If it seems more profitable to you, chain it."

"Don't you mind it?"

"No, I don't mind it."

"I'll show you that I am your master."

"How can you be? Zeus has liberated me. Or do you think he would allow his own son to be a slave? Only of my dead body are you master. Take it."

—*Discourses,* I, 19

What then is the fruit of these doctrines? That which must be most beautiful and suitable for those who are truly being educated—serenity, fearlessness, freedom. For it is not the multitude whom we should believe in such matters when they say, "Only the free can be educated," but rather wise men, who say, "Only the educated are free."

"How is that?"

"Thus: Is freedom in our time anything except the ability to live as we wish?"

"Nothing else."

"Tell me then, men, do you wish to live in error?"

"No."

"No one who lives in error is free. Do you wish to live in fear, in grief, in confusion?"

"Certainly not."

"No one who is afraid or grieving or confused is free. But the man who has rid himself of sorrows and fears and confusion, this man by the same route is also rid of slavery."

—*Discourses,* II, 1

II. Man and God

Man has been brought into the world to be a spectator of God and his works, and not only a spectator but also an interpreter. For this reason it is shameful for man to begin and end where irrational animals do; rather he should begin like them but end where nature has ended concerning us; and nature ended with contemplation and understanding and a way of life harmonious with her. See to it, therefore, that you do not die before witnessing these things. You take a journey to Olympia in order to see the statue by Phidias, and each of you thinks it a misfortune to die before seeing such sights; but when there is no need of journeying, when God is already present in his works, will you not desire to see these works and get to know them? Will you not perceive who you are, for what you were born, and what this purpose is for which you have received your sight?

"But there are unpleasant and difficult things in life."

Aren't there also in Olympia? Don't you suffer from the heat? Aren't you crammed into crowded seats? Don't you have trouble in getting a bath? Aren't you drenched when it rains? Don't you have the dubious advantage of tumult and shouting and other discomforts? But I imagine you endure and put up with all these things, so unimportant are they compared with the glory of the spectacle. Come now, haven't you received faculties which enable you to endure every happening? Haven't you received courage? And what concern of mine is anything that happens if I am magnanimous? What shall upset me or confound me or seem to me painful? Instead of grieving and moaning over what happens, shall I not use my faculty to its intended purpose?

—*Discourses,* I, 6

As was fitting, only the best of all faculties and the one which controls conduct have the gods placed in our power, that is, the ability to make the right use of external impressions; the rest they have not placed in our power. Was it because they did not wish to? For my part I think that they would have entrusted those things to us also if they had been able, but they were utterly unable to do so. For since we are on earth and hampered by an earthly body and earthly associates, how was it possible that we should not be encumbered by external things?

But what does Zeus say? "Epictetus, if it had been possible I would have made both your insignificant body and property free and untrammeled. But now never forget that this body is not yours, it is merely clay cleverly mixed. And since I was not able to make it free, I have given you a certain part of our divinity, the faculty of choice and refusal, of desire and aversion, of making the right use of external impressions; if you take care of it and entrust everything you have to it you shall never be hampered, shall never groan, shall never criticize, shall never flatter any man. Does this seem unimportant to you?"

"May it never seem so."

"Are you then satisfied with it?"

"I pray the gods I may be."

But now although we are able to care for only one thing and devote ourselves to it, we wish to care for many things and to be bound to them: the body, property, brother, friend, child, slave. So, bound by many things, we are weighted and dragged down by them. "What wind is blowing?" we ask. The North Wind. "What use have we for that wind? When will the West Wind blow?" Whenever it pleases, my dear fellow, or when Aeolus, King of the Winds, pleases. For God has made Aeolus, not you, steward of the winds. "What then?" We must do the best we can with what is in our control, and use the rest in accordance with its nature. "What is its nature?" As God wills.

—*Discourses,* I. 1

You are the most important of living things, you are a fragment of God, you have within yourself an actual part of Him. Why then are you unaware of your kinship? Why do you not know whence you have come? Do you not wish to remember when you eat who you are that is eating and whom you are feeding? When you must live intimately with people, who you are in doing so? When you mingle with a crowd? When you exercise, when you converse, do you not know that you are nourishing God, exercising God? You bear God about with you, wretched man, and do not realize it. Do you think am speaking of some external God of silver or gold? No, it is within yourself that you bear Him, and do not see that you are defiling Him with unclean thoughts and filthy deeds. If an image of God were present you would not dare to do any of the things you are now doing; but when God himself is present within you, seeing and hearing everything, are you not ashamed of thinking and doing these things, unaware of your own nature? If God had entrusted some orphan to your care, would you neglect him so? Yet he has entrusted your own self to you, saying, "I had no one more trustworthy than you; keep this man for me as nature endowed him, modest, faithful, high-minded, undismayed, free from passion and confusion." After that will you fail to keep him so?

—*Discourses,* II, 8

Are you not willing by this time, like children, to be weaned and take more solid food and stop crying for mammies and nurses, cries for old women to hear?

"But if I leave them I shall distress those friends of mine."

You will distress them? No, what distresses them and you is bad judgment. What can you do, then? Get rid of that judgment; and they, if they do well, will get rid of theirs; otherwise, they will be sorry and have only themselves to thank. Man, now act desperately, as the saying goes, on behalf of serenity, freedom, and magnanimity. Raise your neck as if released from slavery, and boldly look to God and say, "Use me henceforth as Thou wilt; I am in accord with Thee, I am Thine, I ask nothing apart from what seems best to Thee."

—*Discourses,* II, 16

Remember this—you are an actor in a play, and the Playwright chooses of what sort the play shall be; if he wants it to be short, it is short; if long, it is long. Your business is to act well the part assigned you; the choice of the cast is Another's.

—*Manual,* 17

What language is adequate to praise all the works of Providence in us or to give them their proper place? If we were intelligent ought we do anything else but publicly and in private to hymn and magnify God and tell of His grace to us? Ought we not while digging and ploughing and eating to sing this hymn to God? "Great is God, who has given us these instruments wherewith we shall work the earth. Great is God, who has given us hands, the ability to swallow food, a belly, the power to grow without conscious effort and to breathe while sleeping." This we ought to sing in every situation, and in addition the greatest and most divine hymn: that God has given us the faculty to understand these things and follow the road of Reason. What then? Since most of you have become blind, should not someone fulfil this duty for you, singing on behalf of all this hymn to God? What else can I, a lame old man, do but sing God's praise? If I were a nightingale I would sing as a nightingale; if I were a swan, I would sing as a swan. But, being a rational man, I must sing God's praise. This is my task; I do it, I shall not desert this post as long as it is assigned to me, and I exhort you to sing with me this same song.

—*Discourses,* I, 16

III. Man and Society

Ask me, if you think it advisable, if he [the Cynic philosopher] is to engage in political activity.

Foolish man, do you look for a more important sort of politics than that in which he is now engaged? Would you have someone come forward and address an Athenian assembly on incomes and revenues, when he ought to be discoursing to all mankind, Athenians, Corinthians, and Romans alike, not about revenues or incomes or peace or war, but about happiness and unhappiness, success and failure, slavery and freedom? When a man is engaged in politics of such importance, do you ask me if he should engage in political activity?

—*Discourses,* III, 22

Anyone who has carefully studied the administration of the universe and has learned that "the greatest and most powerful and most comprehensive of all governments is this one which is composed of men and God, and that from God have come the seeds of existence, not only to my father and grandfather, but to all things begotten and growing on the earth, and most of all to rational creatures, since they alone by nature share in the society of God, woven together with Him through the faculty of reason"—why will not such a man call himself a citizen of the universe, a son of God, and why shall he fear anything that happens among men?

—*Discourses,* I, 9

Man, if you must be affected contrary to nature by the unworthy actions of another, pity rather than hate him; put aside this inclination of yours toward taking offense and hating; do not say with the censorious multitude, "These accursed and vile fools!"

—*Discourses,* I, 18

IV. Man and Misfortune

We act as though we were on a voyage. What is in my power? To select the pilot, the sailors, the day, the suitable time. Then a storm comes on. What further concern have I? I have done all I can, now it is the pilot's business. The ship sinks. What have I to do then? I do the only thing I can: I drown without fear, without shrieking or assailing God, knowing that what came into being must also perish. For I am not eternal, but a man, a part of the whole as an hour is of the day. Like the hour I must come on and like an hour pass by. What difference does it make, then, how I pass by?

—*Discourses,* II, 5

What troubles men is not events, but their judgments about events. For instance, death is nothing dreadful, or else Socrates would have thought it so. No, men's judgment that it is dreadful is the only dreadful thing about it.

—*Manual,* 5

As for me, I would wish death to overtake me concerned with nothing but my own moral purpose, trying to make it serene, unhindered, unconstrained, free. I would be so engaged when death finds me that I may be able to say to God, "Did I transgress Thy commands? Did I misuse the faculties Thou gavest me? Did I use my senses or my primary concepts to no purpose? Did I ever accuse Thee? Did I ever find fault with Thy governance? I fell sick, when it was Thy will: so did others, but I willingly. I became poor when Thou didst will it, but I rejoiced in my poverty. I held no office, because Thou didst not will it; I never craved office. Didst Thou ever see me down-hearted because of that? Did I ever come before Thee except with a cheerful face, ready for any assignment or orders from Thee? Now it is Thy will for me to leave the festival. I depart, giving all thanks to Thee that Thou didst consider me worthy to take part in the festival with Thee, to see Thy works, and to understand Thy governance."

—*Discourses,* III, 5

When the Emperor Vespasian sent word to Priscus Helvidius that he was not to attend a meeting of the Senate, Priscus replied: "You can prevent my being a Senator, but as long as I am one I must attend the meetings."

"Well, then, come but do not speak."

"If you do not ask for my opinion I shall be silent."

"But I have to ask for your opinion."

"And I have to say what seems to me right."

"If you do I shall have you put to death."

"Did I ever tell you that I was immortal? You will be doing your part, and I mine. It is yours to kill, mine to die unflinching; yours to banish, mine to depart without grief."

What good did Priscus do, one man against the Emperor? What good does the red border do to the mantle? What else than to be distinguished as color, and provide a beautiful example to the rest?

—*Discourses,* I, 2

SELECTIONS FROM LUCIAN

Translated by Frank W. Jones

INTRODUCTION

LUCIAN, a Syrian, was born in Samosata (now Samsat), a small town on the upper Euphrates, about A.D. 120, and died toward the end of that century. In youth, tiring of provincial life, he perfected his Greek and became a professional rhetorician. As such he made a living for a number of years, somewhat in the manner of a modern traveling lecturer, except that Lucian, as the audiences of his day demanded, concentrated on style rather than on substance. He was at various times a lawyer, a teacher, and a government official.

The knowledge he acquired from these experiences went into writings—about seventy dialogues, narratives and scenes—in which he expressed attitudes and opinions that are characteristic of Hellenism in the Roman Empire. He delights, often by way of parody and ridicule, in the poetry, myths and ideals of early and classic Greece, and views the culture of his time with a skeptical detachment that moves from tolerance to contempt. Many of his works attack various forms of intellectual and religious enthusiasm, old and new, which offended his practical, rationalistic mind. A good deal of the scene called *Ways of Life for Sale* is in this vein. The dialogue, *Charon,* is more general in scope and shows the pathos that underlies his wit.

Lucian's importance in literary history is due to his mastery of the satiric dialogue. In form, this favorite vehicle of his goes back to Plato; in function, to Aristophanes. It has many notable descendants, such as Erasmus' *The Praise of Folly,* Fénelon's *Dialogues des Morts,* and the conversational novels of Peacock.

THE PRESENT version follows the text of Jacobitz (Leipzig: Teubner, 1851), with but one deviation: the word "funerals," in the last sentence of *Charon,* translates Allinson's emendation of "hecatombs," the word which appears at that point in Jacobitz' text.

CHARON, OR THE OBSERVERS*

HERMES. What are you laughing at, Charon? And why have you left your ferry and come up to this part of the world? It's hardly your habit to concern yourself with matters above.

CHARON. Well, Hermes, I thought I'd like to see what sort of things life contains, and what men do in it: what they miss that makes them all groan so when they come my way. You know, not one of them has made the crossing without tears. So I asked Hades for a day's shore leave, like young Protesilaus of Thessaly, and here I am, up in the light. Meeting you this way was just what I needed. You'll show me around, I'm sure, and be my guide to everything, for you know all about it.

HERMES. I haven't time, ferryman. You see, I'm on an errand of human business for Zeus above, and he has a quick temper, and I fear that if I'm slow about it he'll make me yours entirely, handing me over to the nether gloom! or maybe, as he once did to Hephaestus, he'll grab me by the foot and throw me down from the threshold of heaven; and then I too will be a source of fun as I pour the gods' wine with a limp.

CHARON. So you're going to let me wander aimlessly above the ground—you, my comrade, my shipmate, my fellow conductor! Child of Maia,

* Time: the sixth century B.C. Much of Lucian's material in this dialogue is drawn from Herodotus' accounts of life in Greece and Asia Minor during that period. See especially Herodotus, Book I, on Croesus, Solon, and Cyrus.

it would be a good idea at this point for you to remember a few things. Never once have I ordered you to bale out the boat or be a rower: no, you stretch out on the deck and snore—such strong shoulders as you have, too—or if you run into some chatty corpse you visit with him the whole way over, while I, old man that I am, pull two oars alone. Oh, Hermie dear, in your father's name, don't desert me! Please show me all the sights in life, so that I'll get a good look at it before I go back home. Why, if you refuse me, I'll be no better off than blind men. They slip and fall in the dark, and I can't see in the light. Come on, Cyllenian, do me a favor; I'll always remember you for it.

HERMES. This business means blows for me; knuckles, I distinctly feel, will pay me for being your guide. Ah, well, you must be helped. What is man to do, when a friend insists? But look, ferryman, there's no way for you to see everything individually, in detail. That would take years. Zeus would have to send out word that I was a runaway, and you would be prevented from working for Death; you'd put Pluto's government in the red by ferrying no corpses all that time, and Aeacus, the tax collector, would feel bitter about not earning a single penny. But let's consider how you can get to see the main events.

CHARON. You do as you think best, Hermes. I'm a foreigner, and know nothing of what is above the ground.

HERMES. Really, Charon, we need a high place from which you could look down on it all. We'd have no trouble if it were possible for you to go up into the sky; then you could get a vivid bird's-eye view of everything. But as it's forbidden for one who constantly associates with ghosts to set foot in the kingdom of Zeus, we will have to look around for some high mountain.

CHARON. Hermes, do you know what I always tell you when we are making a trip? When we're short-hauled and a squall rises and slaps that sail and the waves mount high, then you passengers ask me, in your ignorance, to take in sail, or ease off the sheet a bit, or run with the wind; but I urge you to keep quiet, saying that I know better. So you go ahead now, just as I do then, and do whatever you think right. You're the pilot now, and I will sit in silence, as passengers should, and obey all your orders.

HERMES. Right you are. I'll figure out what to do, and find a suitable vantage point. Would the Caucasus be all right, or Parnassus, which is higher, or Olympus over there, which is higher than either? Say! As I looked at Olympus just now I had a pretty good idea. But it would take some doing, and I'd need your help.

CHARON. Say the word: I'll give what help I can.

HERMES. The poet Homer says that once upon a time, when the sons of Aloeus were still boys—there were two of them, too—they tried to pull Mount Ossa from its base and set it on top of Olympus, and then Mount Pelion on top of both, with the idea of making a ladder long enough to climb to heaven on. Well, that pair paid the penalty, lads that they were; but we aren't making this plan to harm the gods, so why not do some building like that ourselves, and roll mountains over onto one another, so as to have a more comprehensive view from a greater height?

CHARON. Hermes! Would the two of us be strong enough to lift and shift Pelion or Ossa?

HERMES. Why not, Charon? Do you think we're weaker than that couple of babies—we, who are gods?

CHARON. No, but we'll have a terrific job on our hands, or so it seems to me.

HERMES. Naturally, Charon: you're a layman, and nothing of a poet; but noble Homer brought the sky within our reach in two short lines, putting peaks together just like that. Why, I'm surprised that you think this so formidable, when you surely know about Atlas, who actually holds the sky up! He supports us all, and there's only one of him. Also, you've doubtless heard about my brother Heracles, who once took over from that very Atlas, and relieved him of his load for a while by sliding under the weight.

CHARON. Yes, I've heard those stories. Whether they're true, Hermes, you and the poets would know.

HERMES. True as true can be, Charon. Why should wise men lie? Let's go! First we'll drag up Ossa, as the epic and the engineer instruct us:

> . . . and then up Ossa
> Pelion, trembling-leaved.

See how it goes? We've done the job both easily and poetically. Now to go up and see if we'll need to build on top of that. Oh, dear, we're still away down among the foothills of the sky! To the east you can barely see Ionia and Lydia, to the west no more than Italy and Sicily, to the north merely as far as the Danube, and in that direction Crete, not too plainly. I guess we'll have to move Mount Oeta too, ferryman, and then put Parnassus on top of the lot.

CHARON. Let's do that. But look out that we don't make the structure flimsy, by stretching it out beyond the bounds of reason, and then crash down along with it. It would be a bitter trial of Homeric engineering if we ended up with our skulls crushed.

HERMES. Excelsior! It will all hold. Move Oeta over; let Parnassus be rolled upon it. Behold, I mount again. All's well, I can see everything! Now you come up too.

CHARON. Hold out your hand, Hermes. This is no trifling gadget you're making me climb.

HERMES. Ah, Charon, you said you wanted to see it all, and safety and sight-seeing don't mix. Hold onto my right hand, and be careful not to step where it's slippery. There, now you're up too! Since Parnassus is double-peaked, let's each take a summit and sit down on it. Now sweep the horizon with your eye and observe it all.

CHARON. I see much earth, and a sort of big lagoon encircling it, and mountains, and rivers wider than Cocytus or Pyriphlegethon, and tiny little men, and their holes or something.

HERMES. The things you take for holes are cities.

CHARON. Do you know, Hermes, we've got nowhere. It was no use to shift Parnassus, Castalia and all, and Oeta and the rest of the mountains.

HERMES. Because why?

CHARON. I can't see anything clearly from this height. I didn't want to see cities and mountains the way they look in pictures, but men as they are, and what they do, and the kind of things they say. For instance, when you noticed me laughing as you met me, and asked what I was laughing at, I had just heard something that amused me no end.

HERMES. What was it?

CHARON. A man was invited by a friend to dinner, I think it was, for the next day. "I'll be delighted to come," said he, and just as he spoke, a tile that someone or something had moved fell off a roof and killed him. So I laughed because the man didn't keep his promise. Well, I think I'll go down now, so that I can see and hear better.

HERMES. Take it easy. I'll fix that for you too, and render you highly sharp-sighted in a moment. I'll use a spell from Homer for this also. When I speak the verses, remember not to be dim-sighted any longer, but to see everything distinctly.

CHARON. Just speak them!

HERMES.

I have taken the mist from your eyes that once
  was upon them,
That mortal and deity both you may clearly
  perceive.

How is it? Can you see now?

CHARON. Oh, admirably! Lynceus was blind, compared to me. Now you shall instruct me and answer my questions. Would you like me to put them Homerically, thus convincing you that I'm not unfamiliar with Homer's works either?

HERMES. Come now, where would you get that knowledge? You spend all your time sailing and rowing.

CHARON. There you go, libeling my craft. While I was ferrying Homer across after he died, I heard him recite a good deal, and I still remember some of the things he said, although we ran into quite a storm on that trip. He started singing a ballad that was hardly the thing for the passengers, all about how Poseidon gathered the clouds and roused the sea, whirling his trident in it like a ladle, and spurred on the gales—and so forth at length, stirring up an ocean with his verses. Well, all of a sudden a black squall rushed at us, and nearly sank the boat; and the poet was seasick, and threw up most of his rhapsodies, Scylla, Charybdis, Cyclops and all. So it was no trouble to save a thing or two out of all that vomit. Tell me, then:

Who is that thickset man, both tall and courageous,
Outstanding 'mid mortals in height and the
  breadth of his shoulders?

HERMES. That is Milo, the athlete from Croton. The Greeks are clapping him for lifting that bull and carrying it down the middle of the stadium field.

CHARON. How much more justly, Hermes, they would applaud me! I shall take hold of that Milo in a little while, and put him into my little boat, when he comes down my way after losing a wrestling match to Death, the undefeated champion. He won't even know what tripped him. And then won't we hear him groan as he recalls these wreaths of victory and this ovation! But now he's all puffed up by the people's wonder at his carrying the bull. Would anyone think he ever expects to die?

HERMES. Why should he think of death at the height of his vigor?

CHARON. Never mind him. We'll have the laugh on him before long, when he crosses the water. He won't even be able to lift a mosquito, let alone a bull. Now tell me this:

Who is that other, that dignified man?

No Greek, to judge by his clothes.

HERMES. That is Cyrus, Charon—the son of Cambyses. He has made an empire for the Persians out of what once belonged to the Medes. He recently conquered the Assyrians, too, and took over Babylon, and now he seems about to march on Lydia to capture Croesus and be master of all.

CHARON. And where is this Croesus, do you suppose?

HERMES. Look yonder, at the big citadel with the triple wall. That's Sardis. Now you can make out Croesus himself, seated on a golden throne and conversing with Solon the Athenian. Shall we listen to what they are saying?

CHARON. Oh, yes.

CROESUS. Athenian guest: you have seen my wealth, my treasures, the vast amount of bullion in my vaults, and the rest of my luxury. Tell me who, in your opinion, is the happiest of all human beings.

CHARON. What will Solon say to that?

SOLON. Croesus, there aren't many happy people. Among those I know of, I would say that Cleobis and Biton, the sons of the priestess at Argos, were the happiest.

CHARON. Why, he's talking about the fellows who died young together, after yoking themselves to the wagon and pulling their mother all the way to the temple on it!

CROESUS. All right, let them have the first prize for happiness. Who is next, would you say?

SOLON. Tellus the Athenian, who lived a good life and died for his country.

CROESUS. And me, you scum? Don't you think I'm happy?

SOLON. I don't know yet, Croesus, since you haven't reached the end of your life. Proof positive in such affairs is death, and having lived life through happily to its conclusion.

CHARON. Excellent, Solon! You haven't forgotten me; you realize that this sort of question is decided at the ferry. But who are those men Croesus is despatching, and what are they carrying on their shoulders?

HERMES. He's sending gold bricks to Apollo at Delphi, as payment for oracles by which he will be destroyed a little later on. That man is wild about forecasts.

CHARON. So that is gold!—shiny stuff that glitters, yellowish matter with red in it. I'm always hearing about it, but this is the first time I've seen it.

HERMES. Yes, Charon, that is the name men sing about and fight for.

CHARON. You know, I can't see what's good about it, except perhaps one thing, that those who carry it are weighed down.

HERMES. Don't you know how many wars and plots and robberies and perjuries and murders and jailings and argosies and buyings and sellings and enslavements are due to it?

CHARON. To that, Hermes? A thing not much different from bronze? I know bronze, as you're aware: I collect a copper from every voyager below.

HERMES. To be sure; but there's a lot of bronze, so people don't care much about it. But this stuff is scarce, and miners dig far down to get it. It comes out of the earth, like lead and those things.

CHARON. You make men out to be frightfully silly—getting so passionate about a heavy yellow substance.

HERMES. But Solon down there doesn't seem to love it, Charon. You see, he's laughing at Croesus and his uncivilized boastfulness. I think he's going to ask him a question. Let's listen in.

SOLON. Tell me, Croesus, do you think Apollo has any need for those bricks?

CROESUS. Lord, yes. He has no votive offering in that class at Delphi.

SOLON. So you think you make the god happy in adding gold bricks to his possessions?

CROESUS. I certainly do.

SOLON. In that case, Croesus, there must be dire

poverty in heaven, if the gods have to send to Lydia when they want any gold.

CROESUS. Where else could they get as much gold as we have?

SOLON. Tell me, is there iron in Lydia?

CROESUS. Not much.

SOLON. Then you're badly off in a better metal.

CROESUS. How can iron be better than gold?

SOLON. If you don't get angry when you answer my questions, you'll find out.

CROESUS. Ask away, Solon.

SOLON. Which are better, those who save people or those who are saved by people?

CROESUS. The savers, obviously.

SOLON. Well, if Cyrus marches on Lydia, as rumor says he will, do you propose to have your army's swords made of gold, or will iron be required for that?

CROESUS. Iron, evidently.

SOLON. And, should you fail to provide it, your gold would be off to Persia, a prisoner of war.

CROESUS. Don't say such things, man!

SOLON. Oh, I hope it won't turn out that way. But you clearly admit that iron is better than gold.

CROESUS. Do you want me to offer the god bricks of iron, and call the gold back?

SOLON. The god won't need iron either; but offer him iron or offer him gold, your gifts will be a fine source of profit for others—Phocians, Boeotians, the Delphians themselves, or some tyrant or pirate. The god cares little for your goldsmiths.

CROESUS. You're constantly attacking my wealth! You resent my having it!

HERMES. You see, Charon, the Lydian can't abide that frank and forthright way of talking. It seems odd to him that a poor man should not cringe but say freely what comes to mind. He'll remember Solon a little later on, when his time comes to be captured and put to the flames by Cyrus. I know this from hearing Clotho read off everybody's destiny the other day. In it was written that Croesus was to be taken by Cyrus, and Cyrus killed by that Massagetan female over there. Do you see the Scythian woman, the one riding on that white horse?

CHARON. Do I, though!

HERMES. That's Tomyris. She will cut off Cyrus' head and toss it into a blood-filled bag. And do you see his young son? That's Cambyses. He'll be king after his father, and after colossal reverses in Libya and Ethiopia he will finally go mad and die after killing Apis.

CHARON. What a laugh. And now they act so superior you'd hardly dare look them in the face. Who would think that in a little while one will be a captive, and another will have his head in a bag of blood? But, Hermes, who's that man over there, wrapped in the purple robe, with the crown on, being given the ring by the cook who has just cut up the fish

> On a wave-circled isle? He claims to be royal
> of race.

HERMES. You're a fine parodist, Charon. The man you see is Polycrates, tyrant of Samos. He thinks he is supremely happy. But his slave, Maeandrius, standing beside him now, will betray him to the satrap Oroetes, and he'll be crucified, poor fellow; thus his happiness will topple in a twinkling. I overheard Clotho reading this, too.

CHARON. Noble Clotho, you're a marvel! Cut off their heads, dear lady, fix them on crosses—that's the way to teach them they are human. In the meantime, let them be exalted, so as to fall from a greater height: that will hurt more. And then I'll laugh when I recognize them one by one, naked in the little boat, without a purple robe or diadem or golden throne to their names.

HERMES. So much for these men's fortunes. But do you see the masses, Charon—the men taking voyages, fighting wars, conducting trials, running farms, lending money, begging alms?

CHARON. I see a patchwork of activity, a life full of confusion. To me their cities look like hives, in which every man has a sting of his own, and stings his neighbor with it, while a few, like wasps, prey on the lower classes. But what is that crowd of shapes flitting around them unseen?

HERMES. Hopes, Charon, and fears and follies and pleasures and greeds and rages and hates and all that. Folly pervades man's life at bottom, and is his fellow citizen, as are hate, anger, envy, ignorance, perplexity and greed; but fear and hopes fly in the air above him. Fear swoops down on people and shocks them, and occasionally makes them cringe, while hopes hover over their heads, and whenever a man is sure one of them is within his reach it flies up and away, leaving him gaping, just as you see Tantalus treated by the water down below. If you look closely you'll catch sight of the Fates up there, unwinding for each person the spindle from which, like all men, he hangs by a slender thread. Do you see those things like cobwebs coming down to everyone from the spindles?

CHARON. I notice that each man's thread is very thin, and most of them are entangled—this one with that one, that with another.

HERMES. Naturally, ferryman; for it is ordained that this one be murdered by that one, and he by another, and that this one be heir of that one, whose thread is shorter, and that other be his heir in turn. This is the sort of thing that's meant by the entanglement. Do you notice what a thin thread they all hang from?—Well, this man over here has been raised high up, and when he falls, as he soon will when his thread breaks under the strain of his weight, he'll make a big noise. But the one over there is only a little way above the ground, and if he comes down his fall will be light, and his neighbors will hardly hear it.

CHARON. It's all immensely comical, Hermes.

HERMES. Yes, Charon, no words can do justice to the absurdity of it, especially their extreme seriousness and the way they depart in the midst of their hopes, snatched off by our good friend Death. He has very many envoys and assistants, as you see: chills, fevers, wasting diseases, lung inflammations, swords, robberies, poisons, judges and dictators. But not one of these makes any impression on people when they're well off, although the moans and groans come thick and fast when they run into trouble. If they realized from the start that they are mortal, and that after this brief stay in life they will go out of it like a dream, letting go their grasp of everything above the ground, they would lead more sensible lives and be less wretched after death. But as it is, they hope to enjoy their present state for ever, and so they protest violently when Death's servant comes to call, and leads them off in the toils of fever or consumption; for they never anticipate being torn away from their pursuits like that. What do you suppose the man over there wouldn't do—the one who's building his house in such a hurry, and driving the workmen on—if he knew that he'll see it finished only to depart as soon as he gets the roof on, and leave the enjoyment of it to his heir, without even having had dinner in it, poor fellow? And the one over there, so glad that his wife has borne him a son, and entertaining his friends to celebrate the event, and naming the child after its grandfather—do you think he'd be so delighted by its birth if he knew that the boy will die when he's seven? The reason is that he sees a man who is fortunate in his son, the father of the athlete who has won in the Olympic games, but doesn't see that other neighbor burying his child, or know the length of the thread his own son hangs from. And you observe how many people are quarreling about boundary lines, and piling up money, only to be summoned, before enjoying it, by the envoys and assistants I have mentioned.

CHARON. Yes, I'm observing it all, and trying to think what pleasure they can find in life, and what it is that they resent being deprived of. Look at their kings, who are thought to be extremely happy. To say nothing of the uncertainty and ambiguity of fate as you present it, you'll find that they have more pains than pleasures, what with frights, disorders, hates, plots, tempers, and flatteries; for they all live in these conditions, on top of the griefs, diseases, and sufferings to which they are subject like everyone else. And if their lives are miserable, think what those of ordinary men must be! Hermes, I'll tell you what I think men and their existence are like. Have you ever looked at the bubbles that rise in water when it's stirred up by a spring? I mean the bubbles that gather into froth. Some of them are small, and break and vanish in a moment, some last longer, and when others join them they swell up to a big bulk, but even these are bound to burst eventually: it can't happen any other way, you see. This is the life of man. All human beings are swollen with wind, some to a larger size, some to a smaller. Some remain swollen for a short and fleeting time, others end their existence as soon as it begins; but they must all be shattered.

HERMES. Charon, your simile is not a bit inferior to Homer's. He compared the human race to leaves.

CHARON. Yes, Hermes; and even though that is their nature, you see how they act—how hard they try to get ahead, fighting for places of authority, and honors, and possessions, even though they'll have to leave it all behind when they come my way with a penny in their hands.

Seeing we're up aloft, would you like me to raise a tremendous shout, urging them to desist from their foolish strivings and live with death constantly before their eyes? "Fools," I'd say, "why take all this so seriously? Stop trying so hard! You won't live forever! Not one of the things you get so solemn about down there is everlasting, and you can't take it with you when you die: man must be naked when he goes, and house and land and gold must always fall to others and change their masters!"—If I roared that message at them from a commanding spot, don't you think their life would benefit considerably, and they would become far more sensible?

HERMES. Bless you, you have no idea how completely they've been conditioned by ignorance and folly. You couldn't open their ears with a drill, they've stuffed them with so much wax—just as Odysseus did to his comrades, for fear they might listen to the Sirens. How could they possibly hear you, even if you shouted till you burst? What Lethe can do in your country is here achieved by ignorance. There are a few of them, though, that haven't let the wax get into their ears, because they incline towards truth, look keenly at the world and thoroughly comprehend its nature.

CHARON. Shall we shout at them, then?

HERMES. That wouldn't be any use either—telling them what they know. Do you notice how they detach themselves from the crowd, laugh at what goes on, and completely refuse to acquiesce in it? They're evidently planning their escape from life to you already—which is natural, since people hate them for showing up human stupidity.

CHARON. Well done, my fine fellows!—But there are so few of them, Hermes.

HERMES. They're enough. Let's go down now.

CHARON. Just one more thing I wanted to know, Hermes: when you've shown it to me you'll have made a perfect guide. I'd like to see the diggings where they put away the bodies.

HERMES. Barrows, tombs, and graves are their names for that, Charon. Do you see those mounds, stone slabs and pyramids outside the cities? Those are all corpse-receptacles and body-containers.

CHARON. Why are those people wreathing the stones, and greasing them with perfume? And the others, raising pyres in front of the mounds and digging holes or something—why are they burning up expensive dinners there, and pouring wine and what looks like mead into the holes?

HERMES. I don't know what good this does anybody in Hades, ferryman. They do believe, though, that souls are sent up from below and make a flying meal, as it were, on the cooking odors and the smoke, and drink the mead from the holes.

CHARON. Eating and drinking, indeed, with those dried-up skulls of theirs! But I'm silly to say that to you, since you escort them down every day. You know well whether they could climb up here again once they've gone underground. You'd be in a laughable state, Hermes, if your worries weren't over when you'd taken them down, but you also had to bring them up again for a drink! Oh, the fools! What simplicity, not knowing what kind of borders there are that divide the world of the dead from the land of the living, or what things are like in my part of the world, not knowing that

> Death is the same for buried and unburied men:
> Irus and great Agamemnon in equal honor,
> Thersites a match for the son of golden-haired Thetis,
> All are alike as strengthless heads of the dead,
> Naked and dry roaming the asphodel meadow.

HERMES. Heracles! What a flood of Homer you're pouring over me! Since you bring it to mind, I'll show you the tomb of Achilles. Do you see it there, beside the sea? That's Sigeum, in the Troad. Ajax is buried across from there, in Rhoeteum.

CHARON. The tombs aren't big, Hermes. Now show me the famous cities we hear about below—Nineveh, Sardanapalus' town, and Babylon, and Mycenae, and Cleonae, and Troy herself. Many's the body I recall ferrying from there. For ten whole years there wasn't a moment to dock my boat or dry it out!

HERMES. Well, ferryman, Nineveh has perished, leaving not a trace. Nobody even knows where it was. Babylon is the city over there, the one with the fine towers and the big wall; but it won't be long before people start to search for it like Nineveh. Mycenae and Cleonae I'm ashamed to show you, and Troy even more so. When you got back below you'd strangle Homer, I know, for the tallness of his tales. Of course, the places were prosperous long ago, but now they too are dead. Cities die just like men, ferryman—and even, strangest of all, whole rivers. Not so much as a ditch remains of the Inachus at Argos.

CHARON. Alas for your praises, Homer, and those epithets: "holy" Troy of the "broad ways," and "nobly-built" Cleonae! But, while we are talking, who are those people fighting a war, and what are they killing each other for?

HERMES. Those are the men of Argos, Charon, and of Sparta; and that half-dead general is Othryadas writing his claim of victory on the trophy with his own blood.

CHARON. What is their war about, Hermes?

HERMES. About the plain they are fighting on.

CHARON. What folly! They don't know that even if one side got hold of the whole Peloponnese it couldn't take a foot of ground from Aeacus. And the plain will be farmed by one generation after another, and they'll keep turning up that trophy with their ploughs!

HERMES. That's the way it will be. Now let's get down, put the mountains back where they belong, and go our ways—I on my mission, you to your ferry. I'll see you again before long, with my next batch of bodies.

CHARON. You've done a fine job, Hermes: you'll be in my good books for ever. You helped me get some value out of my vacation. What a life those wretched mortals lead! Kings, gold bricks, funerals, battles, and never a thought for Charon.

WAYS OF LIFE FOR SALE

IN THIS scene, Lucian caricatures seven philosophies of varying degrees of influence in his day, paying particular attention to Cynicism and Stoicism. He also pokes fun at Pythagoras, Democritus, and Heraclitus, three pioneers of Greek thought. The contrast between these groups—venerable mystics and argumentative moderns—is enhanced by the fact that the three sages speak in their native dialect, Ionic Greek, which differs from the standard (Attic) Greek of the other speakers chiefly in having more and longer vowel sounds. An attempt has been made to reflect that speech contrast in this translation.

The fact that the philosophies (simply "lives" in the original) are sold by Zeus and Hermes is typical of Lucian's double-edged satire. His gods are nervous creatures, troubled by human irreverence as well as their own quarrels; and this sale gives them a chance to profit by the credulity which people accord to the latest fashion in the "good life" rather than to them. So Lucian mocks both old-time religion and new-fangled ideas.

If the mina is worth $6.00 (a possible equivalent in noninflated U.S. currency), then Lucian's philosophers fetch the following prices: Socrates, $720; the Peripatetic, $120; Chrysippus the Stoic, $72; Pythagoras, $60; the Epicurean, $60; Pyrrho the Sceptic, $6; and Diogenes the Cynic, two cents.

ZEUS. You there; set up the benches and get the place ready for the customers. You: bring out the lives and put them in line. Fix them up first, so that they'll look pretty and draw a crowd. Hermes, you'll be the crier, and invite the buyers to come to market under the auspices of fortune. We're going to run a sale of philosophic ways of life, of every variety and all kinds of creeds. Anybody who can't put down ready cash may provide security and pay next year.

HERMES. There are lots of people coming, so we'd better not stall around or hold them up.

ZEUS. All right, the sale is on.

HERMES. Which one would you like brought on first?

ZEUS. That long-haired one, the Ionian. He has such an impressive appearance.

HERMES. Hey, Pythagorean! Come down and let this group of people look you over.

ZEUS. Cry him up!

HERMES. I have the finest life for sale, the most majestic life. Who'll buy? Who'd like to be a superman? Who'd like to know the Harmony of the All, and how to come to life again?

CUSTOMER. His looks aren't bad. What does he know best?

HERMES. Arithmetic, astronomy, magic, geometry, music and trickery. You're looking at a first-class seer.

CUSTOMER. Is it all right to ask him questions?

HERMES. Ask, and good luck to you.

CUSTOMER. Where are you from?

PYTHAGORAS. Samos.

CUSTOMER. Where were you educated?

PYTHAGORAS. In Egypt, ba the sages theyah.

CUSTOMER. Tell me: if I buy you, what will you teach me?

PYTHAGORAS. Ah won't teach you, Ah'll remahnd you.[1]

CUSTOMER. How will you remind me?

PYTHAGORAS. Fuhst off, ba renderin' your soul puah, and washin' away the duht that is upon it.

CUSTOMER. All right: let's suppose I've been purified. How do you do the reminding?

PYTHAGORAS. Fuhst, a long sahlence. A voicelessness. No talkin' at all, for five full yeahs.

CUSTOMER. My good man, you should tutor Croesus' son.[2] I want to be a talker, not a statue. Well, anyhow, what comes after the five-year hush?

PYTHAGORAS. You'll get trainin' in ballad-singin' and jawmetry.

CUSTOMER. Delightful! First I learn guitar, then I become wise.

PYTHAGORAS. Next thing is caountin'.

CUSTOMER. I know how to count.

PYTHAGORAS. Haow do you caount?

CUSTOMER. One, two, three, four——

PYTHAGORAS. See? What you take fo' foh is really ten,[3] a puhfect trahangle and aour oath.

CUSTOMER. Not really! By four, the biggest oath of all, I never heard holier or diviner words.

PYTHAGORAS. Next, stranger, you'll luhn abaout uhth, ayah, wawda and fyah—their rotation, the nature of their fohm, and the manner of their motion.

CUSTOMER. So fire, air, and water have form?

PYTHAGORAS. Whah yes, an evident fohm. They couldn't move in fohmlessness and schemelessness, naow, could they? Next thing you'll luhn is that God is number, mahnd, and hahmony.

CUSTOMER. What wonderful things you say!

PYTHAGORAS. Besahds all this Ah've mentioned, you'll luhn somethin' about yourself. You *think* you're one puhson, but you *ah* one in appearance and another in reality.

CUSTOMER. What? I'm somebody else, not the man that's now talking to you?

PYTHAGORAS. You're you naow, but in past tahm you appeahed in a different body and under another name. In future tahm you'll transfer to still another.[4]

CUSTOMER. You mean I'll be immortal, shifting from shape to shape?—But enough of this. What's your position on diet?

PYTHAGORAS. Ah won't eat a thing that has the breath of lahf, but Ah'll eat anythin' else, except beans.

CUSTOMER. Why is that? Do you have a loathing for them?

PYTHAGORAS. No; it's because they're sacred, and their nature is miraculous. In the fuhst place, they're generation through and through: if you string a bean while it's still green, you'll notice it's built mighty lak the male ohgans. Then, if you boil one and throw it at the moon for a suhtn number of nights, you'll make blood. What's moh, the Athenians vote ba beans at their elections.[5]

CUSTOMER. You've expressed all this in a fine, priestlike way. Now take off your clothes: I want to see you naked. Heavens! He has a golden thigh![6] This seems to be no mere mortal, but a god. I'll definitely buy him. How much are you asking for him?

HERMES. Ten minas.

CUSTOMER. He's mine at that price.

ZEUS (*to* HERMES). Write down the buyer's name and residence.

HERMES. I think the man's from Italy, Zeus—one of the people who live in Croton, Tarentum and the Greek settlements in that area. This one isn't going to a single buyer, but a pool of about three hundred.[7]

ZEUS. Have them take him away, and bring on another.

HERMES. How about that filthy fellow from the Black Sea?[8]

ZEUS. By all means.

HERMES. You with the knapsack and the sleeveless shirt, come over here and walk around the room. A manly life for sale! A life of distinction! A free life! Any takers?

CUSTOMER. What's that, crier? You're selling a man who's free?

HERMES. You bet.

CUSTOMER. Aren't you afraid he'll sue you for kidnapping, and have you summoned to the Areopagus?

HERMES. He doesn't mind being sold; he thinks he's free whatever happens.

CUSTOMER. But what use could he be—all dirty, and looking like a bum? Still and all, he might pass as a ditch-digger or a water boy.

HERMES. Yes, and another thing, if you make him a janitor you'll find him far more reliable than a dog. His name is Dog, for that matter.[9]

CUSTOMER. Where is he from, and what doctrine does he preach?

HERMES. Why not ask him? That's the best way.

CUSTOMER. I'm afraid of his sullen, gloomy

expression. He might bark at me if I approached him, or maybe even bite, by God! Don't you see the way he lifts his club and knits his brows and puts on a nasty, threatening scowl?

HERMES. Have no fear. He's tame.

CUSTOMER (*to* DIOGENES). To begin with, my good man, where do you come from?

DIOGENES. Everywhere.

CUSTOMER. I beg your pardon?

DIOGENES. In me you see a citizen of the world.

CUSTOMER. What model do you follow?

DIOGENES. Heracles.

CUSTOMER. Then why don't you wear a lion-skin? You carry a club, like him.

DIOGENES. This short cloak is my lion-skin. I take the field against pleasures, as he did—not a conscript, but a volunteer. My purpose is to clean life up.

CUSTOMER. A good intention. But what may a man say you know best? What craft do you practise?

DIOGENES. I'm a liberator of mankind, and a healer of its ills. In general, I claim to be a champion of honest frankness.

CUSTOMER. All right, champ: if I buy you, what training will you give me?

DIOGENES. First I'll take you in hand and strip away your softness, plunge you into poverty and clothe you in a cloak. Then I'll sentence you to hard labor—sleeping on the ground, drinking water and filling your gut with whatever you can find. If you have money, you'll obey my orders and throw it in the sea. No marriage, children, or native land for you—that's all bunk, as far as you're concerned. You'll leave home and live in a grave, or an abandoned tower, or maybe a jar.[10] Your knapsack will be full of lupine seed and books written on both sides.[11] In this condition you'll be happier than the King of Persia. If you get lashed or tortured, you won't think any of it painful.

CUSTOMER. What a notion! How can a person be painlessly lashed? My body isn't covered like a turtle or a lobster!

DIOGENES. You'll follow the line of Euripides, with a slight variation.

CUSTOMER. What line?

DIOGENES. "Your mind will hurt, but your tongue will be unhurt."[12] Now I'll describe the qualities you'll need most. You must be brazen and impudent and abusive to everybody, king and commoner alike. This will make people respect you, and consider you a brave man. Your accent must be barbarous, your tone of voice harsh and frankly doglike, your expression strained, and your walk suited to your expression; in fact, your whole behavior must be wild and beastly. Shame, propriety, and moderation have got to go, and the blush must be rubbed completely off your face. Frequent the most thickly populated places and act as though you were alone and separate in them—greeting neither friend nor guest, for that way lies the ruin of the regimen. Have no qualms about doing in the public view what isn't even done in private; take up the funnier forms of sex activity; and in the end, if you like, die of eating raw octopus or squid.[13] This is the happiness we are agents for.

CUSTOMER. Ugh! What a foul, inhuman way of life!

DIOGENES. Easiest in the world, man; no need for a degree, or a doctrine, or any bunk at all. The road I've described is your short cut to fame. Even if you're a plain man—tanner, fishmonger, carpenter, money-changer—nothing can stop you from being a sensation, as long as you hold on to shamelessness and insolence, and become a master of abuse.

CUSTOMER. That's not what I want you for, but you might do in a pinch as a boatman or a gardener; however, only if the man here will take two obols for you. That's the most I'll pay.

HERMES. He's all yours! We're glad to be rid of him, nuisance that he is—yelling, and insulting everybody, and calling them bad names.

ZEUS. Call another one: —that Cyrenaic, the one in the purple robe, with the wreath on.

HERMES. Attention, everybody! Here's a piece of costly merchandise, asking for a wealthy buyer. Here's a sweet life, a life that is blest three times over. Who wants refinement? Who'll buy the height of daintiness?

CUSTOMER. Come and tell me what your knowledge consists of. I'll buy you if you're any use to me.

HERMES. Don't bother him, my dear fellow, or ask him any questions. He's drunk, you see, so he couldn't answer you: his tongue keeps sliding around in his mouth.

CUSTOMER. Well! Who in his senses would buy such a spoiled and naughty slave? How he stinks of scent! How he lurches and staggers! Hermes,

I guess you'll have to tell me what he's like and describe his pursuits.

HERMES. In general, he's clever at the social life, a good drinking companion, and just the man to help a lewd and vicious master pass a wild night with a flute-girl. Also, he's an expert confectioner, and cooks consummately. All in all, he's a professor of easy living. He was educated at Athens, spent some time as a slave of the tyrants in Sicily, and is exceedingly well thought of by those in their circle. The essence of his philosophy is to despise everything, make use of anything, and store up pleasure wherever he goes.

CUSTOMER. You'd better look around for someone else among these millionaires. I'm not interested in buying a gay life.

HERMES. It looks as though this one will stay on our hands, Zeus.

ZEUS. Remove him. Bring on another, or rather, those two—the laugher from Abdera and the weeper from Ephesus. I'd like to sell them as a pair.

HERMES. Come on down to the center here, you two. Two grand ways of life for sale, the wisest of all!

CUSTOMER. Lord, what a contrast! This one can't stop laughing, and that one seems to be in mourning for somebody. He cries constantly. What's the matter, fellow? What are you laughing at?

DEMOCRITUS. You-all are askin' me? Why, Ah think your business is all a joke, and you-all are too.

CUSTOMER. What? You laugh at us all, and snap your fingers at our business?

DEMOCRITUS. Ah suhtnly do. There's nothin' impohtant about any of it—it's all hollow, a bustle of atoms, a vast unknown.

CUSTOMER. It is not, but you're all hollow, and a vast fool, and that's a fact. Damn your insolence, will you never stop laughing? But you, my good man, why are you crying? I think I can have a much nicer talk with you.

HERACLITUS. Here's the way it is, stranger. Ah think human lahf is woeful and tearful, and nothin' in it is imperishable. And so Ah pity you and Ah lament. Ah attach little impohtance to the present, but Ah think the future's goin' to be dahnright awful. An refer, of course, to the fahnl conflagration and the unuvuhsal catastrophe. All this Ah lament, also the fact that nothin' is stable, but everythin' is bein' squashed all the time into a kind of stew, and that stew is painful pleasure, ignorant knowledge, big smallness, movin' around and up and down, change and change about, in the game of the Aeon.

CUSTOMER. And what is the Aeon?

HERACLITUS. A child at play, playin' checkers, a checker himself.

CUSTOMER. What are men?

HERACLITUS. Mohtal gods.

CUSTOMER. What are gods?

HERACLITUS. Immohtal men.

CUSTOMER. Say, are you talking riddles, or making up puzzles, or something? You're just like Apollo—you don't make anything plain.[14]

HERACLITUS. That's because Ah don't care a fig for you.

CUSTOMER. Well, then, no sane man will buy you.

HERACLITUS. What Ah say is, you can all go weep, young and old, the ones that bah and the ones that don't bah.

CUSTOMER. The fellow seems to be suffering from melancholia. As for me, I won't buy either of them.

HERMES. These are left unsold, too!

ZEUS. Put another one up.

HERMES. What about that Athenian, who keeps talking?

ZEUS. All right.

HERMES. Come here, you. A life of goodness and intelligence for sale! Who'll take the height of holiness?

CUSTOMER. Tell me, what's your specialty?

SOCRATES. I'm a boy-lover, and an expert in amorous matters.[15]

CUSTOMER. Then how can I buy you? I wanted a tutor for my son, a handsome lad.

SOCRATES. Who could be a finer comrade for a good-looking boy than I? I'm no lover of bodies, you see; the soul is what I consider beautiful. Why, even if lads lie under the same cloak with me, you won't hear of my giving them any bad moments.

CUSTOMER. You can't tell me that if you're a boy-lover you'd venture no further than the soul when you had the chance, lying under the same cloak and all.

SOCRATES. But—I swear to you by the dog and the plane-tree—that's the way it is.

CUSTOMER. Heavens, what queer gods you swear by!

SOCRATES. What are you talking about? Don't you think the dog is a god? Aren't you aware of the greatness of Anubis in Egypt? And Sirius in heaven, and Cerberus below?

CUSTOMER. Right you are, and I was off the track. Tell me this now: What's your way of living?

SOCRATES. I live in a city I've made over to suit myself, using an imported constitution and enacting my own laws.

CUSTOMER. I'd like to hear one piece of your legislation.

SOCRATES. Listen to the most important—my resolution concerning women. "No woman shall belong to one man only; anyone wishing to share his rights in her shall have that privilege."

CUSTOMER. What's the meaning of this—repeal of the laws against adultery?

SOCRATES. Certainly, and the whole mass of trivia surrounding such matters.

CUSTOMER. What's your resolution concerning boys in the bloom of youth?

SOCRATES. "They shall go to the bravest men as love-prizes for any splendidly high-spirited action."

CUSTOMER. Dear me, such generosity! And what is the sum and substance of your wisdom?

SOCRATES. Ideas, the paradigms of existing things. Whatever you see—earth, things on the earth, sky, ocean—of all these there are invisible images, which exist outside the universe.

CUSTOMER. Where do they exist?

SOCRATES. Nowhere. If they were anywhere, they wouldn't be.

CUSTOMER. I can't see these paradigms you talk about.

SOCRATES. Of course not. That's because you're blind in the soul's eye. But I see the images of all things: I see the invisible you, and the other me, and everything as double.

CUSTOMER. Well, now, you're a good buy, clever and penetrating person that you are. Let's see, how much will you charge me for him?

HERMES. Give me two talents.

CUSTOMER. He's mine, for what you ask. I'll give you the money later.

HERMES. What's your name?

CUSTOMER. Dion of Syracuse.[16]

HERMES. Take him, and good luck to you. Epicurean! You're next. Who'll buy this one? He's a pupil of the giggler and the drunk we were trying to sell a while back.[17] He knows more than they do, to the extent that he has less religion; but, for the rest, he's a nice fellow, and fond of good eating.

CUSTOMER. What's his price?

HERMES. Ten minas.

CUSTOMER. There you are. Tell me one thing, before I forget: what does he like to eat?

HERMES. He feeds on sweets and honey-cakes, and he's especially fond of figs.

CUSTOMER. No difficulty there: I'll buy him Carian fig cookies.

ZEUS. Call another one—that close-shaven, close-cropped fellow, the dismal one from the Stoa.

HERMES. A good idea. There's quite a cluster of men in public life around him.[18] Virtue herself for sale! The most impeccable way of life! Who wants to know everything alone?

CUSTOMER. What do you mean by that?

HERMES. I mean that this man alone is wise, he alone is handsome, he alone is just, brave, king, orator, millionaire, lawgiver, and everything else there is.

CUSTOMER. Amazing! And is he the only cook, the only tanner, the only carpenter, and that kind of thing?

HERMES. So it seems.

CUSTOMER. Come here, my good man, and inform me, as a buyer, what sort of man you are. First, don't you resent being sold, and living in slavery?

CHRYSIPPUS. Not at all. Those things are beyond our control, you see. Whatever is beyond our control is indifferent.

CUSTOMER. I don't quite catch your meaning.

CHRYSIPPUS. What? You don't understand that some of these things are preposited, whereas others are depreposited?

CUSTOMER. I still don't understand.

CHRYSIPPUS. Of course not: you're not used to our terms, nor do you have the apprehending imagination. But the serious student, who has mastered logical theory, knows not only this, but the meaning of casualty and countercasualty, and how very different they are from one another.

CUSTOMER. In the name of wisdom, don't begrudge me an explanation of this, at least! What is casualty, and what is countercasualty? I find myself quite carried away by the rhythm of the words.

CHRYSIPPUS. No grudge at all, if a man is lame, and unexpectedly hurts his lame foot by stubbing it on a stone, such a man has lameness as a casualty, but his injury is a countercasualty, superadded.

CUSTOMER. Goodness, how subtle! What other specialties do you claim in the way of knowledge?

CHRYSIPPUS. Tortuosities in words, by means of which I tie my listeners in knots, lead them up blind alleys, reduce them to silence, and absolutely muzzle them. The name of this power is Syllogism, a grand and glorious thing.

CUSTOMER. Heavens! That sounds like an irresistible force.

CHRYSIPPUS. See for yourself. Have you a child?

CUSTOMER. So?

CHRYSIPPUS. If a crocodile found the child wandering by a river, and grabbed him, and then promised to give him back to you if you told him correctly what he intended to do about restoring the little fellow, what would you say he had decided?

CUSTOMER. You're asking a tough question. I have no idea what I'd say first, to get the boy back. But you answer it, please, in heaven's name, and save my child! I don't want that crocodile to beat us to it and gulp him down!

CHRYSIPPUS. Trust me. I'll teach you things even more wonderful than that.

CUSTOMER. Such as?

CHRYSIPPUS. The Reaper, the Master, and above all Electra and the Veiled Man.

CUSTOMER. What Veiled Man? What Electra?

CHRYSIPPUS. The Electra is the famous one, Agamemnon's daughter. She knows and does not know the same thing at the same time. When Orestes meets her, and she hasn't recognized him yet, she knows Orestes is her brother, but doesn't know that this is Orestes. Now listen to the Veiled Man, a really wonderful argument. Answer me, please: Do you know your own father?

CUSTOMER. Yes.

CHRYSIPPUS. Well, then, if I put a veiled man in front of you, and ask you, "Do you know this man?" what will you say?

CUSTOMER. "I don't know him," obviously.

CHRYSIPPUS. But he was your father! Hence, if you don't know him, it's clear you don't know your own father.

CUSTOMER. I guess not, but I'd soon find out if I took his veil off. Well, anyway, what is the point of your wisdom, and what will you do when you reach the summit of virtue?

CHRYSIPPUS. Then I'll concentrate on what is first by nature—I mean wealth, health and that sort of thing. But much preliminary study is required—sharpening your eyesight on closely written books, collecting scholarly notes, and stuffing yourself with solecisms and paradoxes. On top of all that, it's forbidden to become wise unless you take three consecutive drinks of hellebore.[19]

CUSTOMER. These are fine procedures, and awfully brave. But what about being a Shylock and a usurer, as I understand you are? Is that a sign that a man has drunk his hellebore and is consummate in virtue.

CHRYSIPPUS. Definitely. Only the sage is the right man for money-lending. Since his specialty is making syllogisms, and since the logistics of finance are next door to syllogistics, both these operations should be entrusted only to the scholar. Moreover, he should get not merely simple interest, like other people, but also interest that differs from it—or didn't you know that besides primary interest there is secondary interest, an offshoot of the former, as it were? You see, I'm sure, how the syllogism would phrase this. "If he gets the primary interest, he will also get the secondary; but he does get the primary interest; therefore he also gets the secondary."

CUSTOMER. And shall we say the same about the payments you receive from the young for wisdom? I suppose it's plain that only the scholar will take wages for virtue.

CHRYSIPPUS. You get the idea. I don't take the money in my own interest, but for the sake of the giver. Since there are two types of people, prodigal and thrifty, I train myself to be thrifty, and my student to be prodigal.

CUSTOMER. But it ought to be the other way round: the youth should be thrifty, and you should be prodigal, being the only millionaire.

CHRYSIPPUS. Man, you're joking. Watch out, or I may shoot you down with the undemonstrable syllogism.

CUSTOMER. And what's the awful effect of that missile?

CHRYSIPPUS. Confusion, speechlessness, and a sprained intellect. My greatest power is that I can turn you to stone in a flash, if I so desire.

CUSTOMER. How, stone? You're no Perseus, my friend, as far as I can see.

CHRYSIPPUS. Here's how. Is a stone a body?

CUSTOMER. Yes.

CHRYSIPPUS. All right: isn't a living being a body?

CUSTOMER. Yes.

CHRYSIPPUS. And are you a living being?

CUSTOMER. I've been told so.

CHRYSIPPUS. Then you're a stone, since you're a living being.

CUSTOMER. Oh, no! Please, for heaven's sake, set me free and make me a man again!

CHRYSIPPUS. That's easy. Be a man once more. Now tell me: is every body a living being?

CUSTOMER. No.

CHRYSIPPUS. All right: is a stone a living being?

CUSTOMER. No.

CHRYSIPPUS. Are you a body?

CUSTOMER. Yes.

CHRYSIPPUS. Being a body, are you a living being?

CUSTOMER. Yes.

CHRYSIPPUS. Then you're not a stone, since you're a living being.

CUSTOMER. Thank goodness! My limbs were already freezing solid, like Niobe's. I'll buy you. (*Turning to* HERMES) How much will he cost me?

HERMES. Twelve minas.

CUSTOMER. Take them.

HERMES. Are you his sole buyer?

CUSTOMER. No, indeed. You see these people? They've all bought him.

HERMES. Hm, quite a crowd. Hefty fellows, too—fit to battle the Reaper!

ZEUS. Don't delay. Call another one, the Peripatetic.

HERMES. I'm calling you—the handsome, wealthy man. Come buy the brainiest one, the man who knows absolutely everything!

CUSTOMER. What's he like?

HERMES. Moderate, reasonable, well adjusted to life, and, above all, double.

CUSTOMER. How do you mean?

HERMES. He is said to be one man in outward appearance but a different man within. So, if you buy him, remember to call one of him esoteric and the other exoteric.

CUSTOMER. What does he know best?

HERMES. That good things are three: in the soul, in the body, and in externals.

CUSTOMER. He has common sense. How much is he?

HERMES. Twenty minas.

CUSTOMER. That's a lot.

HERMES. Not so, my dear fellow. He is said to have a little money himself, so you ought to snap him up. Here's the kind of thing you'll learn from him: the life span of the mosquito; the depth to which sunlight penetrates the sea; and what the soul of an oyster is like.

CUSTOMER. Heavens, what accurate observation!

HERMES. Yes, and how would you like to hear other things far more meticulous than that, about sperm, and conception, and how embryos are formed in mothers, and how man has the faculty of laughter but the donkey can't laugh, or build houses or sail boats, either?

CUSTOMER. This is most impressive knowledge you describe, and useful, too. I'll pay twenty for him.

HERMES. It's a deal.

ZEUS. Who's left?

HERMES. This Sceptic. Hey, Red! [20] Come up to the counter, and make it snappy. Most of the buyers are starting to drift away; his sale will be poorly attended. All the same, who'll buy this one?

CUSTOMER. I will. But first tell me: what do you know?

PYRRHO. Nothing.

CUSTOMER. How did you mean that?

PYRRHO. I meant that, in my opinion, absolutely nothing exists.

CUSTOMER. Aren't we anybody, then?

PYRRHO. I don't know that, either.

CUSTOMER. Or even that you're someone?

PYRRHO. That I know even less.

CUSTOMER. Dear me, what helplessness! What are those scales of yours for?

PYRRHO. I weigh arguments in them, and make them balance one another; and when they're all exactly alike and equal in weight, then, ah! then I don't know which is right.

CUSTOMER. What else might you be competent at?

PYRRHO. Anything, except catching a runaway slave.

CUSTOMER. Why couldn't you do that?

PYRRHO. Because, my good man, I can't apprehend anything.

CUSTOMER. Oh yes, of course. You do seem a bit slow and stupid. In your view, what is the end of knowledge?

PYRRHO. Ignorance, and neither hearing nor seeing.

CUSTOMER. You mean being blind and deaf?

PYRRHO. Yes, and unintelligent, and unperceiving, and all in all, no different from a worm.

CUSTOMER. That's just why I should buy you. (*To* HERMES) How much would you say he's worth?

HERMES. One Attic mina.

CUSTOMER. There you are. (*To* PYRRHO) What have you to say now? Did I buy you?

PYRRHO. That's uncertain.

CUSTOMER. It certainly isn't. I bought you, and put down my money.

PYRRHO. I suspend judgment on that point; it needs careful study.

CUSTOMER. Look, you come along with me, as my slave should.

PYRRHO. Who knows if what you say is true?

CUSTOMER. The crier, and the mina, and those present.

PYRRHO. Oh, we have company?

CUSTOMER. Say, I'll show you who's your master, and by a poor argument: I'll put you to work in the mill.

PYRRHO. Suspend your judgment on that point.

CUSTOMER. No, by God! I've already expressed it.

HERMES. You stop hanging back, and go with your buyer. Gentlemen, we invite you all to come again tomorrow. We're going to sell plair ways of life, in industry and trade.

NOTES TO SELECTIONS FROM LUCIAN

1. An allusion to the Pythagorean (and Platonic) doctrine that learning is really remembering what the soul knew before entering the body.
2. A deaf-mute.
3. Allusions to Pythagorean number theories. $10 = 1 + 2 + 3 + 4$, and the "perfect triangle" can be constructed by four horizontals, of one, two, three, and four points, in that order.
4. The Pythagoreans believed in transmigration of souls.
5. In electing by lot at Athens, beans were used for lots.
6. A traditional attribute of Pythagoras. Compare Yeats's lines in "Among School Children":

   World-famous golden-thighed Pythagoras
   Fingered upon a fiddlestick or strings
   What the stars sang and careless Muses heard.

7. The original number of the Pythagorean brotherhood, which was formed in southern Italy.
8. The Cynic, Diogenes, was born in Sinope, a Greek settlement on the Black Sea.
9. In Greek, "cynic" means "doggish."
10. Diogenes' tub was actually a wine jar.
11. Indications of economy in food and the use of papyrus.
12. "My tongue took oath; my mind has taken none," line 612 of *Hippolytus*, became famous as a sophism.
13. Diogenes is said to have died after sampling the former dish.
14. The oracles of Apollo at Delphi were notorious for their ambiguity.
15. Allusions to Plato's *Symposium* and *Republic* are frequent in this passage.
16. A wealthy pupil and patron of Plato. Hence his ability to pay the stiff price.
17. Epicurus was influenced by the physical theory of Democritus and the Cyrenaic doctrine of pleasure.
18. Stoicism was a favorite philosophy of statesmen and public officials.
19. Hellebore was considered a cure for insanity.
20. Pyrrhias, meaning Redhead, was a name often given to slaves. Here it is also a pun on the name of Pyrrho, the founder of the Skeptic school.

MAPS

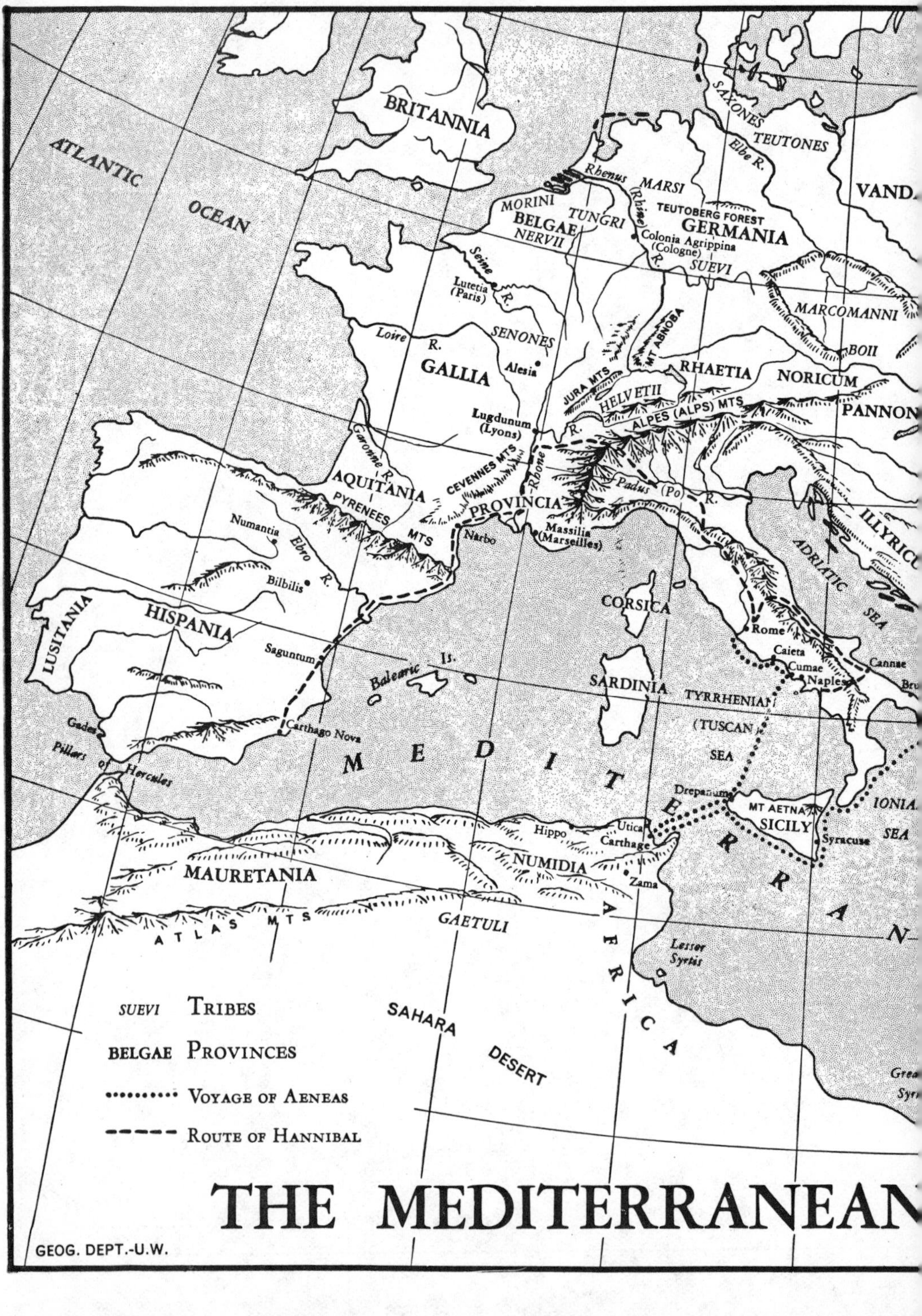
THE MEDITERRANEAN
BRITANNIA
ATLANTIC
OCEAN
SAXONES
TEUTONES
Elbe R.
VAND.
Rhenus
MARSI
(Rhine)
R.
MORINI
BELGAE
NERVII
TUNGRI
TEUTOBERG FOREST
GERMANIA
Colonia Agrippina
(Cologne)
SUEVI
Seine
R.
Lutetia
(Paris)
MARCOMANNI
Loire
R.
SENONES
MT ABNOBA
BOII
GALLIA
Alesia
JURA MTS
RHAETIA
NORICUM
HELVETII
ALPES (ALPS) MTS
PANNON
Lugdunum
(Lyons)
R.
Garonne R.
CEVENNES MTS
Rhone
AQUITANIA
Padus
(Po)
R.
PYRENEES
MTS
PROVINCIA
ILLYRIC
Numantia
Ebro
R.
Narbo
Massilia
(Marseilles)
ADRIATIC
SEA
Bilbilis
CORSICA
LUSITANIA
HISPANIA
Rome
Saguntum
Caieta
Cumae
Cannae
Balearic
Is.
SARDINIA
Naples
TYRRHENIAN
(TUSCAN)
SEA
Gades
Carthago Nova
Pillars
of
Hercules
M E D I T E R R A N
Drepanum
MT AETNA
IONIA
SICILY
SEA
Hippo
Utica
Carthage
Syracuse
MAURETANIA
NUMIDIA
Zama
ATLAS MTS
GAETULI
AFRICA
Lesser
Syrtis
SUEVI Tribes
BELGAE Provinces
Voyage of Aeneas
Route of Hannibal
SAHARA
DESERT
Grea
Syr
GEOG. DEPT.-U.W.

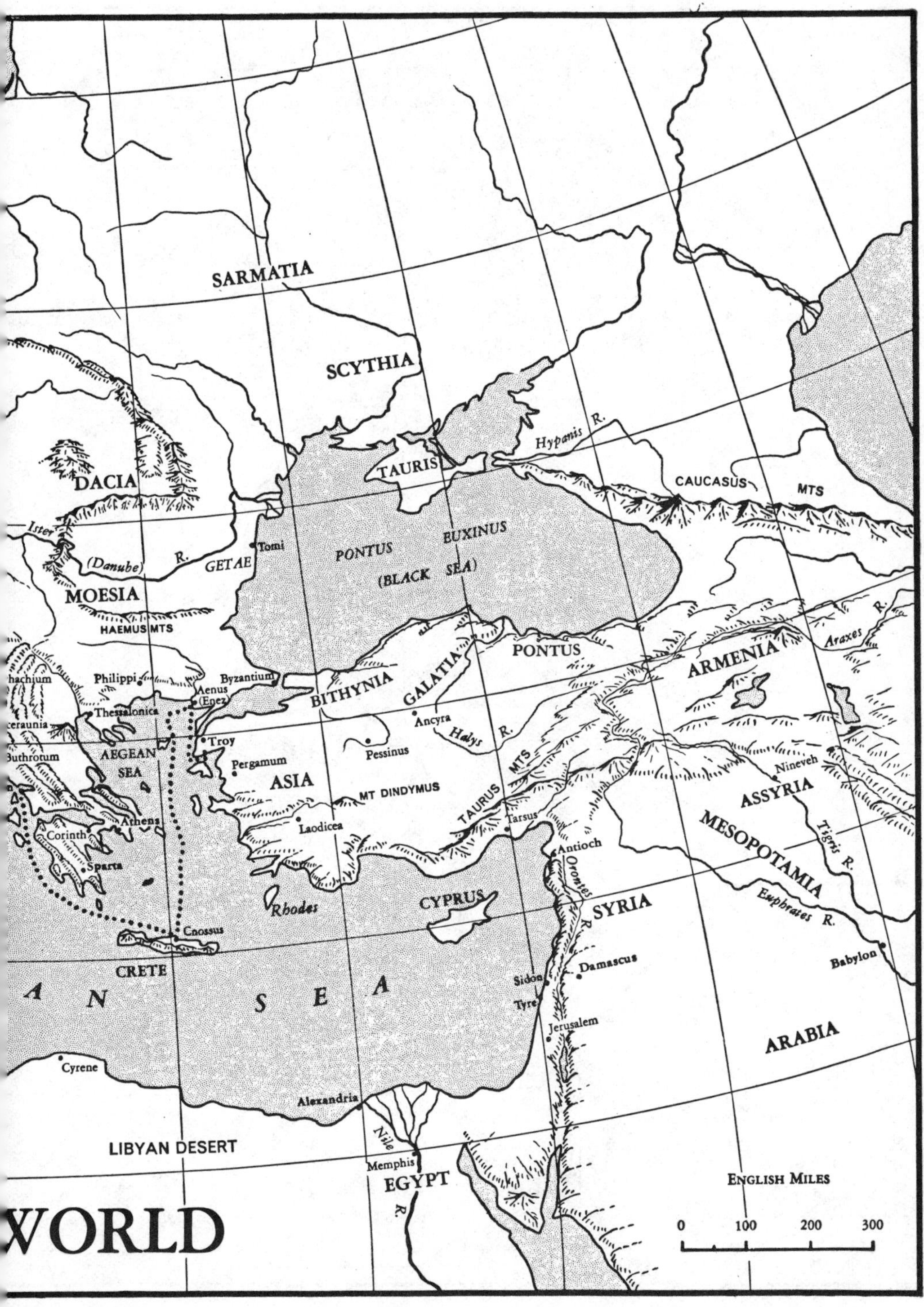

SARMATIA
SCYTHIA
TAURIS
DACIA
Hypanis R.
CAUCASUS MTS
Ister (Danube) R.
Tomi
GETAE
PONTUS EUXINUS
(BLACK SEA)
MOESIA
HAEMUS MTS
PONTUS
ARMENIA
Araxes R.
Philippi
Byzantium
Aenus (Enez)
BITHYNIA
GALATIA
Thessalonica
Ancyra
Halys R.
Troy
AEGEAN SEA
Pessinus
Pergamum
Buthrotum
ASIA
MT DINDYMUS
TAURUS MTS
Nineveh
ASSYRIA
MESOPOTAMIA
Athens
Corinth
Sparta
Laodicea
Tarsus
Antioch
Orontes R.
Tigris R.
Rhodes
CYPRUS
SYRIA
Euphrates R.
Cnossus
CRETE
Damascus
Babylon
Sidon
Tyre
Jerusalem
A N S E A
ARABIA
Cyrene
Alexandria
Nile R.
LIBYAN DESERT
Memphis
EGYPT
ENGLISH MILES
0 100 200 300
WORLD

GREECE AND THE AEGEAN
ADRIATIC SEA
Epidamnus
(Dyrrhachium)
ILLYRIA
MACEDONIA
Axius R.
Strymon R.
Philippi
Abdera
MT PANGAEUM
Amphipolis
Pella
Thasos
CHALCIDICE
Olynthus
Potidaea
MT ATHOS
Pydna
PIERIA
Haliacmon R.
MT OLYMPUS
Vale of Tempe
MT OSSA
Peneus R.
EPIRUS
Buthrotum
Corcyra
(Corfu)
Dodona
THESSALY
Larissa
Crannon
Iolcus
Pharsalus
Lemnos
AEGEAN SEA
IONIAN SEA
Ambracia
Actium
Leucas
ACARNANIA
PHTHIOTIS
Spercheius R.
Lamia
Artemisium
Oreus
MT OETA
LOCRIS
Euripus
EUBOEA
PHOCIS
Delphi
AETOLIA
Naupactus
Ithaca
Cephallenia
Gulf of Corinth
BOEOTIA
Chalcis
Eretria
Thebes
ATTICA
ACHAEA
Aegae
MT CYLLENE
MT ERYMANTHUS
Sicyon
Megara
Athens
Corinth
Zacynthus
ELIS
ARCADIA
ARGOLIS
Pisa
Olympia
Mycenae
Argos
Andros
PELOPONNESUS
Mantinea
Ceos
Alpheus R.
MT ITHOME
CYCLADES
MESSENIA
Eurotas
Messene
MT TAYGETUS
LACONIA
Pylos
Sparta
(Lacedaemon)
MYRTOAN SEA
Seriphos
Paro
Sphacteria
Gytheum
Melos
Cythera
CRETE
Cnossus
ENGLISH MILES
0 10 20 30 40 50 75 100
Thermopylae
Euripus
EUBOEA SEA
Elatea
Cephisus R.
MT PARNASSUS
Delphi
Chaeronea
Chalcis
Eretria
Aulis
Coronea
Ascra
Thespiae
Thebes
Tanagra
Delium
Oropus
MT HELICON
Leuctra
Oenophyta
Rhamnus
Plataea
Decelea
Gulf of Corinth
MT CITHAERON
Phyle
MT PENTELICUS
Pagae
Eleusis
Acharnae
Marathon
Megara
MT HYMETTUS
Sicyon
Athens
Salamis
Piraeus
Phalerum
Corinth
Cenchreae
Nemea
Mycenae
Aegina
MT LAURIUM
Argos
Tiryns
Epidaurus
CAPE SUNIUM
0 10 20
CENTRAL GREECE